The Fabulous History
of the Dismal Swamp Company

The Fabulous History of
the Dismal Swamp Company

A Story of George Washington's Times

CHARLES ROYSTER

ALFRED A. KNOPF   NEW YORK   2000

THIS IS A BORZOI BOOK
PUBLISHED BY ALFRED A. KNOPF, INC.

Copyright © 1999 by Charles Royster
Maps copyright © 1999 by David Lindroth, Inc.

www.randomhouse.com

Library of Congress Cataloging-in-Publication Data

Royster, Charles.
The fabulous history of the Dismal Swamp Company: a story of
George Washington's times / by Charles Royster. — 1st ed.
p.   cm.
Includes bibliographical references and index.
ISBN 0-679-43345-7 (alk. paper)
1. Dismal Swamp (N.C. and Va.)—History—18th century.
2. Washington, George, 1732–1799—Friends and associates.
3. Political corruption—Virginia—History—18th century. 4. Land
speculation—Dismal Swamp (N.C. and Va.)—History—18th century.
I. Title.
F232.D7R69   1999
975.5'52302—dc21   98-42773
CIP

Manufactured in the United States of America
Published October 3, 1999
Second Printing, February 2000

To
The Company of Players,
past and present,
of the Oregon Shakespeare Festival

CONTENTS

—•—

PROLOGUE

———•———

"The Lake of the Dismal Swamp"

THERE ONCE WAS A YOUNG MAN whose beloved died. He lost his mind—so people in Norfolk, Virginia, said in the autumn of 1803. In his ravings the lover denied that she was dead, insisting that she had gone to the Dismal Swamp nearby. The young man suddenly disappeared and never returned. He became a legend told to newcomers. He had gone into the Dismal Swamp in search of his beloved "and had died of hunger, or been lost in some of its dreadful morasses."

Thomas Moore, a promising Irish poet, was twenty-four years old when he heard the legend. He spent a few weeks in Norfolk as a guest of the British consul, John Hamilton, awaiting passage to Bermuda. Moore followed the reading public's fancy; tales of apparitions, ghosts, and lovers mad with grief were in fashion. Sitting in Colonel Hamilton's big brick house on Main Street, Moore wrote a forty-line ballad, "The Lake of the Dismal Swamp."

The crazed lover speaks first:

> *"They made her a grave, too cold and damp*
> *For a soul so warm and true;*
> *And she's gone to the Lake of the Dismal Swamp.*
> *Where, all night long, by a fire-fly lamp,*
> *She paddles her white canoe.*
> *And her fire-fly lamp I soon shall see,*
> *And her paddle I soon shall hear;*
> *Long and loving our life shall be,*
> *And I'll hide the maid in a cypress tree,*
> *When the footstep of death is near."*

He enters the swamp and, surrounded by dangers, seeks the lake at its heart. Reaching the spot, he calls to his beloved.

And the dim shore echoed, for many a night,
The name of the death-cold maid!

He sees on the water the reflection of a meteor and takes it to be his loved one's light; he rows a boat in the direction it had moved.

The wind was high and the clouds were dark,
And the boat return'd no more.

But oft, from the Indian hunter's camp,
This lover and maid so true
Are seen at the hour of midnight damp
To cross the Lake by a fire-fly lamp,
And paddle their white canoe!

During Moore's stay in Norfolk, he and the consul rode out to see the swamp and Lake Drummond, named for William Drummond, once a colonial official in North Carolina, later hanged in Virginia for treason and rebellion against the Crown's government there. Moore's ballad used the swamp's reputation as a weird, ghostly, and threatening morass. To him, the swamp was a "dreary wilderness." He found nature hostile in Virginia. A yellow fever epidemic had spread in the previous year. Norfolk had been hit by "a tremendous hurricane" during the previous month. Moore sailed for Bermuda without regret, taking from Virginia his ballad and a memory of dirty, odorous Norfolk, which, he said, "abounds in dogs, in negroes, and in democrats."

The poet and the consul could ride into the Dismal Swamp more easily as a result of the work of gangs of slaves, who were digging a canal to link the waters of Chesapeake Bay's tributaries with those of Albemarle Sound. Anyone could see that enterprising Virginians no longer feared the swamp. Trees were felled in ever greater numbers to provide timber for shipyards, as well as other lumber, staves, and shingles. Lake Drummond and the land around it belonged to the Dismal Swamp Company, founded forty years earlier to turn the swamp into farmland.

In those distant days, when George Washington was a young man, eminent Virginians were fascinated by land, excited by chances to acquire it. The previous fifty years had taught them that land, combined with the labor of slaves, was wealth. To a few men the Dismal Swamp seemed to beckon, inviting them to transform hundreds of square miles into inexhaustible riches.

The young Irish poet need not have come to Norfolk in 1803 to find a legend of a dead maiden, her obsessed lover, and their ghostly boat on a mysterious lake. The frightfulness of the swamp, even its gloomy name, heightened the impression of the distracted lover's desperation. Still, Moore could have set his ballad almost anywhere. The Dismal Swamp gave occasion for stories of conduct far stranger than the legend he heard, but he did not tarry in Virginia long enough to learn the remarkable history of the people possessed by a notion that they would recover what they had lost or find what they desired in the Dismal Swamp.

The Fabulous History
of the Dismal Swamp Company

I

—·—

THE LAND OF PROMISE

ELIZABETH WIRT WAS PREGNANT in the summer of 1803. Her husband feared for her life. Too many women died in childbirth; he had lost his first wife. To distract his mind, he began a series of lighthearted, faintly satirical sketches describing Virginia and Virginians. Though he came from Maryland, William Wirt tried to make himself an eminent Virginian in law, in politics, and in letters. He had joined an informal college of wit-crackers whose dean was St. George Tucker in Williamsburg. His friends wrote verse and essays. So would he.

Wirt called his pieces *The Letters of the British Spy*, pretending they had been found in a boardinghouse. Readers knew Wirt was the author. Still, a catchy title and a pose of British condescension toward provincials helped attract notice as these sketches appeared first in newspapers, then, before the end of the year, in a small book. It was published after Elizabeth Wirt gave birth to a girl.

The spy's first letter, written in Richmond, included a short account of how that city at the falls of the James River, capital of the state, had been planned long ago by the man who then owned the site. William Byrd served the spy's purpose as a striking example of unequal ownership of property in Virginia. Dead for sixty years, he was a figure of romance from past days of heroic adventure. The spy described Byrd's service in 1728 with commissioners and surveyors running a boundary line between Virginia and North Carolina. Not far west of the sea their course lay through the Great Dismal Swamp, "an immense morass" of "black, deep mire, covered with a stupendous forest." Wirt crammed his paragraph with lurid color: beasts of prey, endless labor, perpetual terror, and, wildest of all, nighttime filled with "the deafening, soul chilling yell" of unnamed hungry animals. On such a night, William Byrd received a visit from "Hope, that never failing friend of man." He planned the city of Richmond, to be erected on land he owned.

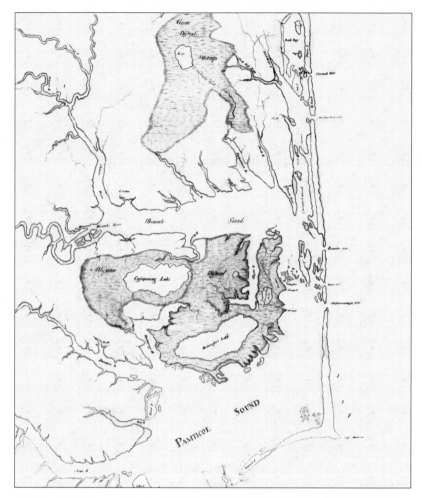

Great Dismal Swamp, Albemarle Sound, and Outer Banks. Courtesy of the William L. Clements Library. Drawn by a British Army cartographer during the Revolutionary War. The dividing line between Virginia and North Carolina runs through the Dismal Swamp.

For readers who might wonder how the spy knew all this, Wirt added a footnote citing Byrd's manuscript account, preserved by his descendants in the family home at Westover. Mary Willing Byrd, widow of William Byrd's son, still practiced, with the help of her daughter and granddaughters, the hospitality of an earlier time. A guest was welcome to read a folio volume, bound in vellum, containing the work Byrd had talked of publishing but had continued to revise and rewrite in two versions: *History of the Dividing Line betwixt Virginia and North Carolina Run in the Year of Our Lord 1728* and *The Secret History of the Line.* The volume included his accounts of two other expeditions: *A Progress to the Mines in the Year 1732* and *A Journey to the Land of*

Eden: Anno 1733. A reader could sit in the parlor on a chair covered in crimson silk damask, lifting his eyes from the page to high, wainscotted walls hung with portraits in black and gilt frames and to intricate, symmetrical rocaille plasterwork on the ceiling. Or a visitor might stay in a guest room and glance from William Byrd's writings to a painting above the fireplace, a naked Venus, lying asleep on her right side—the work of Titian, the family said. Windows opened onto terraced gardens leading down to the James River, onto the walled garden where the body of William Byrd lay buried, and onto a separate library, which once had held Byrd's thousands of volumes. In hot weather a traveler from the North lay on a sofa by the curiously carved balustrade of the big staircase in the central hall, catching any breeze that blew between the ornate stone pilasters of the north and south doorways. Reading the manuscript, he found Byrd to be "a sly joker," whose work "tickled me in some of my susceptible parts."

The family at Westover also preserved other writings by William Byrd. While in England, he had published *A Discourse Concerning the Plague*, though he had left his name off the title page, putting instead: "By a Lover of Mankind." This scholarly pamphlet drew upon his wide reading to assemble vivid descriptions of the extent and the physical effects of the plague since ancient times. How could "this dismal distemper" be avoided? He endorsed traditional measures such as temperance, repentance for sins, and abstinence from "immoderate Venery." But he concluded that those seeking the utmost security ought to surround themselves at all times with tobacco—"this powerful Alexipharmick," "this great *Antipoison*." He told them to carry tobacco in their clothes, hang bundles of it in their rooms and around their beds, burn it in their dining rooms while eating, chew it, smoke it, take it as snuff. "Tobacco being itself a poison, the effluvia flowing from it, do, by a similitude of parts, gather to them the little bodies of the pestilential taint, and intirely correct them." Virginians escaped the plague because they produced and consumed tobacco. The plague had grown rare in England as use of tobacco spread. It was, Byrd wrote, "our sovereign antidote." Thus Virginians offered a benefit to humanity, or at least to that large portion of mankind who did not get a joke.

Readers of Byrd's *History of the Dividing Line* noticed his suggestion that "a great Sum of Money" be invested to drain the Dismal Swamp and thereby make that land "very Profitable." Another, smaller manuscript in Byrd's neat, square handwriting took the form of a petition to the king. The unnamed petitioners sought a royal grant of the entire Dismal Swamp and all the unowned land within half a mile of any part of it, more than 900 square miles. To the petition Byrd added a description of the swamp and a proposal to

William Byrd, Unknown Artist. Courtesy of the Virginia Historical Society. A portrait of the elder William Byrd painted in London and brought to Virginia.

drain it and make it fertile, able to yield vast crops of hemp. Byrd made it all sound easy. Form a new company to finance the project for ten years with a capital of £4,000. Start with ten slaves to dig ditches, fell trees, make boards and shingles, render pine tar, grow rice and corn and hemp, and tend cattle. With its own food and salable commodities the undertaking would partly "carry on itself." As fast as clearing and ditching advanced, buy more slaves, thereby accelerating progress. True, the swamp's "malignant vapours" would kill some slaves, but others would "Breed" and "supply the loss." Use profits from slaves' labor to defray expenses and purchase still more slaves. There could be "no doubt in the world" that, once the original capital had been invested, the Dismal Swamp would have become as good as any soil in Virginia, with at least three hundred slaves at work and "an incredible number" of cattle grazing and multiplying. "From all which we may safely conclude," Byrd wrote, "that each share will then be worth more than Ten times the value of the original subscription, besides the unspeakable Benefit it will prove to the Publick."

More than 900 percent profit in ten years, a "Bogg" rendered productive, a region rescued from the swamp's "noisome Exhalations," a system of canals connecting North Carolina's trade to Virginia's ports, and huge crops of hemp for cordage for Britain's merchant fleets and Royal Navy—surely the Crown must make this grant and exempt the petitioners from the customary charges and quitrents. Yet "to remove all suspicion of Fraud," they would agree to pay if they did not drain the swamp in ten years. Of course, the Crown would extend their time if they met "unforeseen Difficultys." Byrd's manuscript closed with a few sentences on the sex lives and marriages of slaves, explaining the wisdom of "providing wives" who would keep men from "rambling abroad anights." At Westover, Mary Willing Byrd, then her daughter, Evelyn Byrd Harrison, at Brandon, and then her grandson, George Harrison, kept the little manuscript of William Byrd's petition for the Dismal Swamp with the folio volume of his other writings.

Some of William Wirt's friends and some of his colleagues among Virginia's lawyers were heirs or attorneys of men who had tried to carry out William Byrd's proposal long after Byrd's death. They had been among the leading men of their day; three were still living in 1803. Wirt had some tie to each of the early members of what was now called "the old Dismal Swamp Company." His best friends in Virginia—William Nelson, Jr., St. George Tucker, and John Page, the wit-crackers of Williamsburg—knew the company well. Judge William Nelson, Jr., Mary Willing Byrd's son-in-law, remained active in its affairs. His father, William Nelson, and his uncle, Thomas Nelson, had been two of the most powerful Virginians in the 1760s, when they had helped to found the company. St. George Tucker, professor of law at the College of William and Mary, gave legal advice to members of both the Farley family and the Meade family as they squabbled among themselves over estates and debts. The late Francis Farley, planter, councillor, and judge in the Leeward Island of Antigua, had been the first to try to carry out William Byrd's proposal. Farley's son moved to Virginia and became the husband of one of Byrd's granddaughters. David Meade had lived near the Dismal Swamp in the 1760s and had acquired, through his wife, the share once owned by her father, William Waters of the Eastern Shore and Williamsburg. Meade lived in Kentucky in 1803, pursuing his hobbies: landscape gardening and litigation. John Page was governor of Virginia, elected to that office in gratitude for his services during the American Revolution. Page needed its salary. Though his father, Mann Page, had given him land, slaves, a piece of the Dismal Swamp Company, and the largest, most ornate house in Virginia, he could not pay his own debts, let alone those of his father's estate.

Among William Wirt's colleagues in the law were Edmund Pendleton, Bushrod Washington, and John Wickham. Pendleton had administered the messy estate of Speaker John Robinson. The most powerful man in Virginia for many years, Robinson had a hand in money-making schemes of the 1760s; the founders of the Dismal Swamp Company prudently had made him a partner. Bushrod Washington, justice of the United States Supreme Court, was an executor of the estate of his uncle, George Washington. It still held a share in the Dismal Swamp Company, for which George Washington had done much service with high hopes long before. Young lawyers envied John Wickham, who made an ample income and lived a luxurious life. He sued Virginians in federal court on behalf of creditors in Britain at last able to collect old debts unpaid since colonial days. Most of these clients were merchants, and among them was one of the original partners of the Dismal Swamp Company, the baleful Samuel Gist in London. Nearing the age of eighty in 1803, Gist retained good health and a sharp mind. Rich and nominally retired, he still went into the City, walked on the Exchange, visited the subscribers' room at Lloyd's, and extracted money from Virginians and others.

Wirt felt fond of Francis Walker, genial, drunken son and heir of Dr. Thomas Walker. Dr. Walker had twice crossed and marked Virginia's west beyond the Allegheny Mountains. Leaders of the Cherokees, the Shawnees, and the Iroquois had known him well, to their cost. Had Virginia's land companies been a spiderweb, Dr. Walker would have been the spider. And he had shared George Washington's expectations for their Dismal Swamp Company. Wirt also knew Robert Lewis, mayor of Fredericksburg, who, with his brothers, was still pursued in court by heirs of Anthony Bacon, onetime associate of their father, Fielding Lewis. Bacon, a merchant, ironmaster, slave trader, government contractor, and member of Parliament, had been the Dismal Swamp Company's first man in London before Samuel Gist arrived. Fielding Lewis, a merchant in Fredericksburg, had represented Bacon's interests in Virginia. Lewis also had joined his brother-in-law, George Washington, in starting the Dismal Swamp Company.

In 1803, William Wirt was moving his law practice to Norfolk, where everyone knew Thomas Newton, Jr., one of the city's leading politicians and merchants. Newton promoted the digging of a canal through the Dismal Swamp, remaining loyal to the project despite its problems. He also handled the complicated affairs of the estate of his father-in-law, Robert Tucker, Norfolk merchant and founding member of the Dismal Swamp Company, whose fortunes had fallen so rapidly just before his death. Tucker was a kinsman of both Nelson brothers, William and Thomas. He was also related to Robert Burwell. Burwell had served on Virginia's colonial Council with the Nelsons, but his main interest had been horses, and his kinsmen had agreed that he was the weak link of the Dismal Swamp Company.

William Wirt had higher literary ambitions than *The Letters of the British Spy*. He had ingratiated himself with leading Virginians, including the president of the United States, Thomas Jefferson. How better to confirm his standing as a political and literary heir to eminent Virginians than by memorializing their greatest success in a book? For Wirt, a Jeffersonian, Virginia's heroic age was not the era of William Byrd or the era of Speaker Robinson and the Nelson brothers but of the American Revolution. To celebrate it, he planned a book about Patrick Henry. He would portray Henry as a hero who had freed Virginia not only from King George III and Parliament but also from the likes of the Nelsons, Speaker Robinson, and "old Colo. Byrd."

William Byrd—"Colonel" meant that he led his county's militia—planned the city of Richmond in 1733, not as he lay in the Dismal Swamp in 1728. He never saw the interior of the Dismal Swamp. Commissioners for running a boundary line in 1728 went around the swamp, leaving surveyors to hack and wade through it. Virginia's officials had sought a precise boundary for years. People had settled farther south of the James River and farther north of Albemarle Sound in greater numbers since the 1680s. Many Virginians of the "poorer sort" moved into North Carolina, where, if they bothered to seek title, they could get more land from the proprietor's office at lower cost than in Virginia. Worse, in 1706, the surveyor of North Carolina started running lines west of the Dismal Swamp on land that Virginia officials claimed as their colony's. Some in the area hoped to get title from North Carolina, as they had not from Virginia. Worst of all, this intruding surveyor began to lay out a dividing line between the colonies without consulting the government of Virginia. The Council sent someone to stop him.

Virginia officials called the oldest residents of the southernmost counties to swear under oath that no one ever had believed the boundary to run where Carolinians said it did. In the summer of 1710 the two colonies, under orders from London, appointed commissioners to establish a line jointly. These four men spent September and October gathering depositions and trying in vain to take a celestial fix with a sea quadrant to find the latitude. They had no hope of agreement: the Virginians accused the Carolinians of trying to change witnesses' testimony; Carolinians accused Virginians of cheating with the quadrant. The commissioners parted bitterly, without starting a survey. Before the delegations met, Virginians, approaching the swamp from the west, concluded that there was "no passage through the Dismall."

From a distance, the Dismal Swamp looked impassable. Ancient, immense cypress trees, massed, presented a wall of broad, bald trunks supporting feathery crowns 100 feet up, above which a few buzzards or a hawk slowly moved to and fro. In the forest were black gum trees and thick stands of white cedar. Under the right conditions, barricades of trees reverberated a shout with an echo. The great swamp had smaller tributary swamps; it sent out broad tentacles of wetland.

The Dismal Swamp's uneven surface sloped slightly downward from west to east. Almost imperceptibly, amber water flowed from it. Beaver dams deepened standing water, providing better fishing to otters and convenient frogs to great blue herons. Cypress, gum, and cedar had bases in water and roots in a deep accumulation of peat. Above the surface, the pedestals of kneelike roots of cypress and arching roots of gum trees held honeysuckle, yellow jessamine, and vines of bright hydrangea delicately climbing their trunks. Virginia creeper intertwined under branches hung with moss, locking the closely set trees together. Thick rattan stems coiled around some trees. The swamp mirrored itself where trees and their hangings were reflected in its dark water. Much of the drier, mossy ground was spongy and yielding. Where time or storms or fire had felled trees, the swamp lay choked with tumbled trunks and branches. Rich ferns grew to heights of nine or ten feet, as did reeds. These, with myriad coiled briers and hanging vines, could make any spot seem closed off from all others. Sounds did not travel far, and the swamp seemed to sit in silence, creating its own dark shade.

Yet the swamp could be noisy. On a spring or summer evening many kinds of frogs, so numerous that the earth seemed to undulate and croak, kept up a cacophony, swelling as darkness fell. In the night, frogs and bats consumed part of the vast population of insects. In summer, blood-sucking horse flies swarmed. Large mosquitoes hovered in thick clouds. Barred owls preyed on shrews and mice. At the approach of dawn, an array of birds, especially warblers and thrushes, awoke the swamp. With different cries, in autumn great numbers of grackles and crows descended.

Dense growths of tall bamboo hung in broad arches. On these, snakes sometimes sunned themselves—copperheads or a water snake exposing its bright red underside. Water snakes consumed fish and fell prey in turn to long king snakes.

On some margins of the swamp and on drier ridges and islands within it, sandy, firmer stretches supported hardwood trees—red maples and white oaks—as well as tulip poplars and forests of loblolly pine overshadowing a profuse undergrowth of cane and briers, ferns, blackberry thickets, gallberry shrubs, and rusty red and green poison oak. Blackberries, gum berries, and beehives in trees attracted black bears, the swamp's largest animals. Berries, saplings, and other ground plants were forage for flocks of white-tailed deer, some of which fell to packs of gray wolves.

Near the eastern rim of the swamp lay a broad expanse of open marsh densely covered with tall green reeds—thousands of acres of reeds swaying under the wind in waves like the surface of the sea. In its interior the swamp hid a shallow, almost circular lake ringed with old cypress trees. When its dark water lay still on a windless day outside the migrating season for swans, ducks, and geese, the swamp's silence seemed even deeper on the lake than amid the undergrowth. Around the lake the swamp's fecundity extended for hundreds of thousands of acres in every direction.

William Byrd measured his trip along the northern margin of the Dismal Swamp from the east side to the west side as 65 miles. More than any other tract in the colony, the swamp confirmed his description of Virginia. True, Virginia lacked the Garden of Eden's Tree of Life, Byrd wrote, but, apart from that, "our land produces all the fine things of Paradise, except innocence."

Visitors to the counties in southeastern Virginia and northeastern North Carolina found many residents odd. They seemed ignorant but self-satisfied, dirty but idle, poor but dishonest. They gave travelers directions that turned out to be wrong. They told learned men about strange creatures, such as the jointed snake, which broke into inch-long pieces when struck. They acted as if there were "no difference between a Gentleman and a labourer all fellows at Foot Ball." Quakers had settled in the region, hoping to be left alone; other people, with little or no religion, sought the same comfort. Poor Virginians moved into North Carolina, got 150 or 200 acres to support some corn and pigs, while the swamp fed their cattle and they tried to evade paying quitrents to the proprietor in England. Indebted Virginians crossed into North Carolina, where their creditors could not collect. "Women forsake their husbands come in here and live with other men." In the zone claimed by both colonies, some people told a Virginia official that they lived in North Carolina and a North Carolina official that they lived in Virginia. "Borderers" allowed runaway slaves to hide and farm nearby, taking a large share of their crops in return for concealment. One governor reported: "The Inhabitants of North Carolina, are not Industrious but subtle and crafty to admiration." The leaders of both colonies wished to bring more order to "the disputed bounds" near the Dismal Swamp and farther west. To do so, they needed a clearly marked line.

In the evening of February 2, 1720, the *Spotswood*, out of London, sailed between the capes and dropped anchor in Chesapeake Bay. William Byrd had returned to Virginia. He did not plan to stay long, three months at most. Yet he did not leave for England until the summer of 1721. Upon reaching London, he published his *Discourse Concerning the Plague*. A widower for almost five years, he went back to England partly to win a rich wife. After he failed with several women, he and Maria Taylor were married in May 1724. Twenty months later the couple went on board the *Williamsburg* and sailed for Virginia. William Byrd never saw England again. Back at Westover in 1726, he became one of Virginia's commissioners for running the boundary line.

By spending the year 1720 at Westover rather than in London, Byrd missed the excitement of the South Sea Bubble, an episode that would affect people's notions of companies and finance for one hundred years. He received lurid reports about the collapse of the South Sea Company's stock: "The fire of London or the plague ruin'd not the number that are now undone, all ranks of people bewailing their condition in the coffee houses & open streets." Endowed with a monopoly of Britain's trade to South America, the South Sea Company never did much trading, though its monopoly was its chief tangible asset. Instead, the directors undertook to refinance Britain's national debt, offering to retire it more quickly at a reduced rate of interest. To accomplish this, the company persuaded holders of government annuities, which made up the bulk of the debt, to exchange their annuities for stock in the South Sea Company, in expectation of much larger returns from a rising stock. The company would thus become the government's largest creditor and retire the national debt sooner at a lower cost.

As South Sea stock rose, annuities came in more easily, and investors bought more stock on the open market. In fact, its price had to rise for this scheme to work. The company helped by allowing deferred payment for stock and by lending money, accepting its own stock as security, knowing that loans would be used to buy more stock. The company bid up the price on the open exchange by buying some of its new issues. Many people made quick profits by buying and reselling in a rising market. Imitators of the South Sea Company announced new projects, promised immense profits, and invited subscriptions. They planned to use subscribers' money not for the advertised enterprise but to turn a profit in South Sea stock. During the spring and summer of 1720, avid striving for easy wealth grew more frantic. South Sea stock, selling at 116 before the annuity scheme, rose to 375 by May 19, then to 820 by August 12. On August 24, the company sold a new issue of £1,200,000 at a price of 1,000, all subscribed in a few hours. Its supposed value rested on nothing but "the opinion of mankind." Balladeers sang rhymed warnings:

> *Five hundred millions, notes and bonds*
> *Our stocks are worth in value;*
> *But neither lie in goods or lands,*
> *Or money, let me tell you.*
> *Yet though our foreign trade is lost,*
> *Of mighty wealth we vapour;*
> *When all the riches that we boast*
> *Consists in scraps of paper!*

The South Sea Company induced the government to take legal action against some of the new projects, which were "bubbles"—all stock and no substance. Calling smaller bubbles into question encouraged doubts about the South Sea Company. Its stock began to fall in September, dropping from 1,100 to 185 in six weeks. With the help of purchases by the Bank of England, the price held near 400. Speculators took heavy losses, and two-thirds of the original holders of the national debt found that they had exchanged £26,000,000 in secure annuities for £8,500,000 in South Sea Company stock. From their correspondents, Virginians heard about "the ruinous effects of the South Sea stock and other bubbles," which had thrown England on "dismall times." At Alexander Spotswood's celebration of his birthday on December 12, 1720, in the governor's new mansion in Williamsburg, the guests, including William Byrd, danced country dances and played at stockjobbing.

The collapse of the South Sea Bubble and the similar fate in Paris of the Mississippi Company and its bubble became a theme for plays, verse, tracts, and books. Thomas Mortimer began his book of advice, *Every Man His Own Broker*, with his experience: "The author has lost a genteel fortune, by being the innocent dupe of the gentlemen of 'Change-Alley.'" Plays such as *The Stock-Jobbers* and *South Sea; Or the Biters Bit* satirized such people and moralized against greed. William Hogarth created a busy, vivid print, *South Sea Scheme*, linking speculation with prostitution, theft, and depravity. After 1720, the words "South Sea" brought to mind not only stockjobbing and rash speculation but also financial disaster as punishment. After William

Byrd reached England in 1721, he carried on his search for a wife at the height of bitter reaction against bubbles. Once he and his new wife settled at Westover, Byrd wrote to his friends in England describing the merits of life in Virginia. He made his colony sound like an idyllic contrast to dangerous, smoky, corrupt London. He tried to convince his friends that he had moved to a healthier, more fruitful, more honest country. After his service along the boundary line, Byrd's descriptions of Virginia changed. Even when they professed sincerity, his celebrations of this rich land contained a broader streak of irony. The land, like the South Sea Company, was only potentially rich. And extracting wealth from it would require not only projectors but also dupes.

Running a dividing line began in March 1728. Three commissioners and two surveyors from Virginia, four commissioners from North Carolina, one of whom was also a surveyor, another Carolina surveyor, a chaplain, and more than twenty workmen, mostly Virginians with experience in cross-country travel to trade with Indians—this group assembled on the edge of an inlet separated from the ocean by a narrow spit of land. Looking out to sea, Byrd "cast a longing Eye towards England, & Sigh'd." As waves crashed on the spit, the commissioners squabbled, finally settling on a place to plant their starting post, then headed westward, along the latitude, more or less, of 36°30'.

Men cleared the underbrush with hatchets; others carried surveyors' equipment and chains; some tended horses laden with supplies, a tent, and bedding. The commissioners took notes. The surveyors blazed trees. The line passed through thickets, canebrakes, sand, mud, streams, and standing water. Before they reached the Dismal Swamp, 23 miles west of their starting post, the whole party, Byrd later wrote, could be taken for "Criminals, condemned to this dirty work for Offences against the State."

On the swamp's eastern margin, in sight of acres of reeds, the commissioners decided to push the line through the swamp. Three surveyors, with twelve workmen to carry supplies and clear the way, advanced the line, while the rest of the party took roads around the northern perimeter to the west side. The surveyors confronted a forest of cedar clogged with undergrowth and fallen trees. The swamp slowed them to a mile or two per day. Its water caused diarrhea. They had food for eight days; the swamp was fifteen miles wide. After seven days they had covered ten miles. Abandoning their survey, they pushed westward, first through dense growths of cedar, then knee-deep in water for a mile among pines. Reaching dry land, they found a farm and asked for food. After two days of rest, surveyors, chain men, and workmen waded back into the swamp and resumed the line, blazing trees for five more miles to the swamp's western margin.

Much to the surprise of Virginia's commissioners and to the delight of North Carolina's, the line came out of the Dismal Swamp farther north than anyone had expected. Acres that even North Carolina had conceded to Virginia turned out to be in North Carolina. The line mattered not only to people living near it but also to collectors of quitrents and to the Crown. Virginia's landlord was the king, but North Carolina belonged to descendants of loyal friends of the House of Stuart, who had received it as a grant from a grateful King Charles II. Even after North Carolina came under royal governance in 1729, one of those proprietors, John Carteret, Baron Carteret of Hawnes, later Earl Granville, retained the right to grant tracts and receive quitrents along its northern boundary. William Byrd, when he found time to write, heaped sarcasm on clowns who had celebrated their exclusion from Virginia.

The surveying party pushed westward, slicing across farms, passing log huts covered with cedar shingles, pausing at each road to erect a post marked "Virginia" on one side and "North Carolina" on the other. Thirty-five miles west of the Dismal Swamp, on April 5, the commissioners, worried about rattlesnakes, agreed to suspend their survey until autumn. They resumed their progress on September 21. The terrain became rolling. They forded the same winding streams several times, their wet dogs running ahead. Tree branches and bushes ripped at biscuits in deerskin bags slung across their horses, whose pack bells rang with each step. The same workmen who had carried the boundary line through the Dismal Swamp in March took it toward the mountains in the fall. Their supply of bread dwindled; hired Indian hunters killed deer, bears, and wild turkeys. The survey passed beyond the western limit of white people's settlements. North Carolina's commissioners decided to quit.

The party stood near the southern branch of the Roanoke River, 170 miles west of the ocean. The North Carolinians said they saw no purpose in continuing the line, since settlements any time soon in "so barren a place" were unlikely. Arguing against the Virginians' desire to press on, the Carolinians also thought but did not say: "we had many reasons to induce us to believe their proceeding further was not altogether for the publick." William Mayo, one of Virginia's surveyors, had just arranged to acquire from North Carolina's commissioners 2,000 acres south of the line, within five miles of where the surveyors stopped. William Byrd and his colleague, William Dandridge, thought the Carolinians' case "strange." Land along the Roanoke looked not barren but rich. They foresaw many settlements within ten years, perhaps five. But in giving this reason for a longer survey and in offering Mayo's purchase as proof, Byrd and Dandridge confirmed the Carolinians' suspicion that the survey was not carried onward solely for the public good. North Carolina's commissioners and one of Virginia's went home. Byrd, Dandridge, and Virginia's surveyors and workmen moved westward for three more weeks, marking another 72 miles of the line.

In North Carolina's delegation were the chief justice, the receiver general of revenue, and the secretary of the colony, as well as the oily Edward Moseley—councillor, surveyor general, and treasurer. They knew private interest when they saw it. Ignoring the proprietor's instructions, they granted many large tracts to themselves in payment for their six weeks of work. Before the end of the year they sold 20,000 of these acres to Byrd for £200. This oblong stretch lay just south of the dividing line, about 20 miles west of the place where the North Carolinians had abandoned the survey. On it the Irvin River flowed into the Dan, as it wound through the valley Byrd had chosen. Creeks fed it clear water. In the woods were beech, hickory, and old oak. Tall green canes lined the river banks. Bottom land was a dark, rich mold. As soon as he looked, Byrd coveted the vale, "the most beautifull stream I ever saw." After he got it, he named his purchase "the Land of Eden." Finding that the western part held hills and rocks, he envisioned mines and named one site Potosi.

Five years after his adventures in running the line, Byrd, at the age of fifty-nine, returned to the Dan. He and William Mayo surveyed tracts they had bought in 1728. Following the southern edge of his Land of Eden, Byrd saw a broad meadow of tall grass on the south bank of the Dan, where the "Saura," or Cheraw, Indians had lived before moving into South Carolina. After his party passed, moving eastward, he kept turning in the saddle to look back at the meadow. In the last year of his life he obtained a patent for those 5,490 acres from the governor of North Carolina. On the way home after their survey, Byrd and Mayo spent a night at one of their old campsites along the dividing line. They found a beech tree in the bark of which North Carolina's commissioners had carved their names. Byrd worked on the bark "to add to their Names a Sketch of their Characters."

Anyone as close to William Byrd as was his brother-in-law, John Custis, knew that Byrd's purchase of so much land in 1728 was a change. He had inherited 26,231 acres from his father in 1704; he had added about 5,500 acres in the following eight years. Then, except for land he acquired from Custis, growth of his holdings had stopped. For this Byrd and Custis blamed their late father-in-law, Daniel Parke. Parke had left Virginia for England, fought alongside the Duke of Marlborough on the Continent, carried news of the duke's victory at Blenheim to Queen Anne, gone to Antigua as governor of the Leeward Islands, and died there in 1710. After surviving an attempted assassination, he had been attacked by a mob and murdered. Some said that outraged husbands and fathers killed him in revenge for his amours. Some said that violators of laws regulating trade, who were those same husbands and fathers, killed him to stop his greedy interference.

Parke's will gave Byrd and Custis a taste of what his enemies had experienced at his hands. It treated a baby girl in Antigua—"that little bastard of Col. Parkes," Custis called her—more generously than it treated Parke's adult daughters in Virginia. The girl was to inherit his property in the Leeward Islands, worth £30,000, on condition that she took the name Parke and that her future husband did so. The will left Parke's property in England and Virginia to Frances Custis. With that legacy came liability for his debts and a bequest of £1,000 to Lucy Byrd, to be paid by her sister, Frances. Since William and Lucy Byrd were known to quarrel sometimes, ending one dispute by climbing onto the billiard table to enjoy a flourish, and since John and Frances Custis were known to quarrel constantly, though she was pregnant when she learned of her father's murder, Daniel Parke's will seemed to convey a refined malice, designed to make trouble between his adult daughters, between them and their husbands, and between the two couples and the "little bastard."

John Custis managed Parke's plantations in Virginia. To pay Parke's debts, these would have to be sold. Reluctant to see the family's holdings shrink, Byrd offered to assume the debts and bequests if Custis would give him the land: 9,760 acres in Virginia and property in England. Custis agreed, and Byrd soon found he had made a bad bargain. Instead of an obligation to pay £6,680, of which £4,000 could be obtained by selling property in England, he had acquired one closer to £10,000, while the English estate turned out to be mortgaged and involved in litigation. To his distress, Byrd remained in debt until near the end of his life. He even thought of selling Westover.

Buying land in North Carolina in 1728, buying more in Virginia in the 1730s, and getting grants in Virginia with help from his friends on the Council, Byrd hoped to turn this property into income quickly. He offered to sell the Land of Eden to a group of Swiss Protestants. He obtained a grant of 105,000 acres along the Roanoke River in southern Virginia, expecting to sell to another group of Swiss. After those immigrants went instead to South Carolina, he switched his plan for the first group, offering them his Virginia land, telling them how much better they would fare in Virginia than in

North Carolina. He already owned the Land of Eden, but the terms of his grant in Virginia required him to find settlers. In 1737, Byrd published a book in Bern: *Neu-gefundenes Eden*, ostensibly written by him, Wilhelm Vogel, but mostly drawn from earlier writers on North Carolina and Virginia.

In the summer and autumn of 1738 a vessel bearing Swiss immigrants crossed the Atlantic. Their voyage took about five months, more than twice as long as the usual passage. Upon entering Chesapeake Bay, their vessel dropped anchor near shore so that the immigrants could search for food. A winter storm stranded the vessel, drowned some immigrants, and froze others, leaving only ninety of the original three hundred alive. The following year Byrd told the Council that he could "no longer depend upon the Importation of Families to Settle on the Said Land." To keep his Virginia grant, he had to pay the customary charges. The wreck of the Swiss immigrants cost him £525. Late in 1740 he again tried to sell, this time to Germans. Knowing better, he still described a Virginia that resembled Paradise. He never closed the big sale.

Not long after Byrd returned to Virginia in 1726, Governor Hugh Drysdale died. For the following eighteen months the president of the Council, Byrd's friend, Robert Carter, acted as governor. Near the end of this time Carter, at the urging of his son-in-law, Mann Page, posed for a portrait. Artists routinely depicted large, bewigged gentlemen wearing long coats of superfine cloth and looking out from the canvas with an expression of authority, but Carter's portrait conveyed more command and self-confidence than pictures of others. It was easy to see why people called him "King" Carter. Now sixty-four, he had served on the Council since his thirties. Earlier he had been speaker of the House of Burgesses and treasurer of the colony. He owned 300,000 acres; among them were almost fifty farms and plantations. He had 750 or more slaves, worth about £10,000. An ambitious young Virginian imagining a successful career pictured himself as another King Carter.

Carter acquired much of his land by granting it to himself, his sons, and his sons-in-law during his long service as the Fairfax family's agent for their large proprietary holdings along the Potomac River. Overriding censure and resentment, he extended their claims and tripled their property. He reserved the best land, eventually amounting to 180,000 acres, for himself and his family. Grants to others brought him composition money and fees. Before he died, Carter signed thirty or more blank deeds, later used by his eldest son for new purchasers more than a year after Carter's death.

William Byrd and John Custis questioned the wisdom of Virginians' importing large numbers of slaves, but Carter welcomed ships from Africa, expertly managing some sales. In search of rent-paying tenants for his land, he encouraged Scots-Irish settlers to come to the proprietary. He invested prudently: a long annuity and stock in the Bank of England. Always in search of solid wealth, he put no faith in what he called "that plague, the South Sea Company." He fought the efforts of London tobacco brokers to make themselves indispensable middlemen. Carter called himself a man of "plain style" and "plain dealing." In 1712, Edmund Jenings, with help from friends in London, persuaded Catherine, Lady Fairfax, to dismiss Carter as agent for the proprietary and appoint Jenings. Carter and his friends in London worked against Jenings for ten years until Carter regained the agency. He then took advantage of unpaid arrears owed to the Fairfax estate to ruin Jenings financially, extracting mortgages, even one on Ripon Hall, Jenings's home. Carter finally supplanted him as president of the Council on the grounds that Jenings was senile. "We are but stewards of God's building," Carter wrote just before retaking control of the proprietary; "the more he lends us the larger accounts he expects from us." King Carter continually expanded his stewardship.

At his home, Corotoman, along the Rappahannock River, Carter was surrounded by fields of tobacco, wheat, and corn. Gristmills ground his grain. A small shipyard turned out vessels for use in the river and the bay. The plantation and its wharves formed a small village of indentured servants and slaves. Carter's large wine cellar was that of a connoisseur. He entertained "with abundant courtesy." During a three-day visit, William Byrd drank, played cards, danced minuets and country dances, and "lay in the fine room and slept very well."

Carter and his first wife had four children; he and his second wife eight more. Three of his children were married to three of William Byrd's. Carter enjoyed reading, and he took pains to educate his children, not wishing any of them to be "a dunce or a blockhead." His daughter, Judith, married to Mann Page, was, her grandson recalled, "one of the most sensible, and best informed women I ever knew." Adding Byrd's influence in England to his own, Carter helped his eldest son, John, become Virginia's secretary, an office which cost the Carters 1,500 guineas to obtain. That was how Robert "Walpool," as King Carter phonetically spelled the name of the man at the head of government, ran the empire. The secretaryship was in some ways better than the governorship; it yielded a large, steady income for life. The unsuccessful rival for the appointment was Edmund Jenings.

King Carter played favorites among his sons, daughters, sons-in-law, and grandchildren. In his later years his favorite son-in-law was Mann Page, a member of the Council at the age of twenty-three. Page and Judith Carter were married three years later, in 1717. Page called his father-in-law a "dear friend." Carter included Page in the bounty of his land grants, dividing a "great tract" with him in 1720. Nine years later Page joined Carter and two of Carter's sons in founding the Frying Pan Company, named after a run, or creek, in Stafford County where they expected to mine copper. They acquired 27,470 acres from the Fairfax proprietary, built roads, and imported Cornish miners. Despite his gout, King Carter rode to the mine to see copper extracted from ore. All to no avail—the sandstone proved less cupreous than they had hoped. Nevertheless, through inheritance and with his father-in-law's help, Mann Page accumulated more than 30,000 acres, scattered across eight counties.

Judith Carter Page found her husband affectionate and tender. To do honor to her, himself, and their children, Mann Page in 1721 began to build a new house on his plantation, Rosewell, in Gloucester County on the north bank of the York River. It replaced the wooden frame house that burned down that year. Spending the night at Rosewell in October 1720, King Carter and William Byrd were obliged to sleep in the same bed. That would hardly be necessary once Page's new house stood completed. It was the largest, most opulent home in Virginia. For sixteen years the three-story building, with its four huge chimneys, was under construction, its intricate brickwork both strong and ornamental, its roof covered with lead. Up the York River vessels bore Madeira wood, mahogany for wainscotting, pilasters and pediments of decoratively cut stone, glass for almost fifty windows, Tuscan cornices, marble mantelpieces, tiles of English Purbeck white stone and black Belgian marble for a checkerboard floor in the great hall, finely carved woodwork, and treads and risers for a staircase six feet wide. Years before it was finished, the new mansion at Rosewell had won the reputation of being "the best house in Virginia."

Mann Page spent much more money than he had. Soon his debts in England, with interest, exceeded the value of his land and slaves. He also owed money to his father-in-law. In January 1730 he suddenly fell ill. He barely had time to dictate a will, and died the same day. The executors of Page's estate were King Carter and Carter's sons until Page's sons grew to adulthood. The Carter brothers and their sister, Judith, continued work on the Rosewell mansion. They found that Mann Page's plantations did not yield enough profit to pay his creditors. King Carter obtained from the General Assembly authorization to pay Page's debts and to charge the estate for principal and interest, but Carter died a few weeks later. One of Page's chief creditors in

London, Micajah Perry, son of King Carter and William Byrd's merchant friend, grew "very angry." The brothers proposed to borrow money elsewhere to satisfy him. Though the estate operated on questionable credit, the grand house at Rosewell at last stood finished. King Carter's daughter and the grandchildren she had given him lived amid unequaled splendor.

During his lifetime and in his will, Robert Carter helped his children into large estates. Even after division of his land and slaves among his heirs, his four sons—John, Charles, George, and Landon—as well as his grandson—Robert—were among the richest of Virginians. King Carter had begun life orphaned, with 1,000 acres and £1,000. His success in amassing a fortune found no rival among young men the age of his grandson. Nevertheless, Virginians tried to emulate him. George Washington, in his thirties, explained a line of thought he had begun to form more than ten years earlier. He asked "how the greatest Estates we have in this Colony were made; Was it not by taking up & purchasing at very low rates the rich back Lands which were thought nothing of in those days, but are now the most valuable Lands we possess?" He answered: "Undoubtedly it was."

Robert Carter died in 1732, just as Virginia planters were sharply increasing the number of slaves brought from Africa and the amount of tobacco shipped to Britain. The colony held about 60,000 slaves in 1740, twice as many as in 1730. Foster Cunliffe, merchant for King Carter's son, Charles Carter of Cleve, sent his vessel *Liverpool Merchant* from Africa to Virginia in the spring of 1732 and again in the summer of 1734 to transport more than 300 slaves. In the fifteen months between those voyages, sixteen other vessels from Africa brought almost 2,700 slaves, while still others came from the West Indies. During June 1732, the *Liverpool Merchant* was one of four slave vessels anchored in the York River, with 761 slaves from Gambia, Angola, and Bonny. Buyers went on board and between decks, observing men stowed fore and women aft, naked or wearing scraps and beads. Between them boys were fore, girls aft, all naked. A visitor watched a white woman "Examine the Limbs and soundness of some she seemed to Choose." The vessels rode at anchor for weeks, until all slaves found buyers.

William Byrd feared that Virginia's blacks would follow "a man of desperate courage" able to lead them in revolt. Four slaves were hanged in 1731 on a charge of leading a conspiracy among two hundred to attack whites in Norfolk and Princess Anne counties. Maroons, Byrd said, could cause as much trouble and danger in Virginia as in Jamaica. He wished the British government would stop slave traders, who, he said, "woud freely sell their fa-

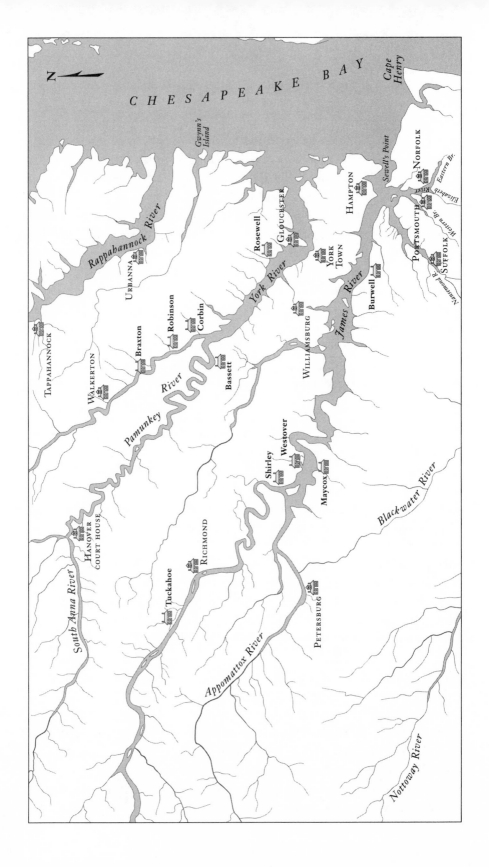

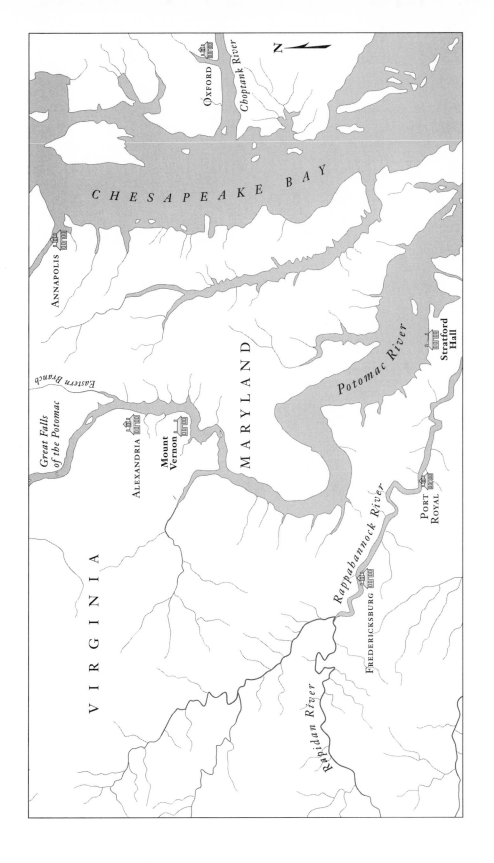

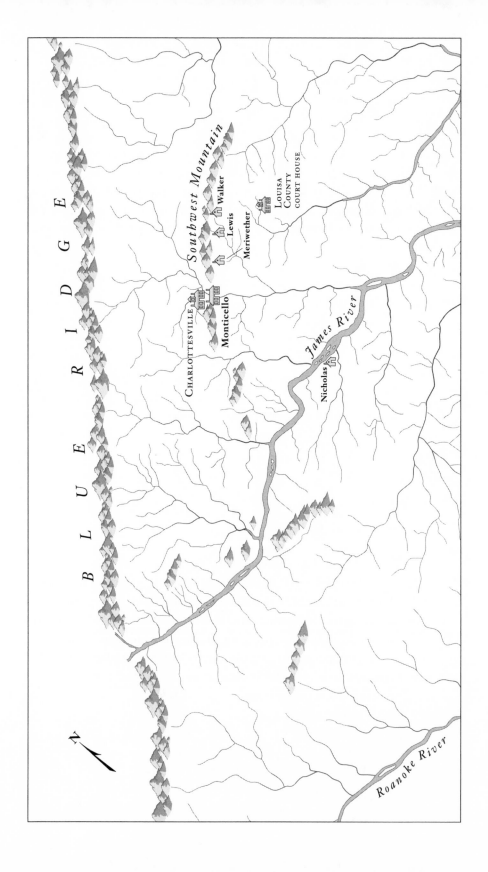

thers, their elder brothers, & even the wives of their bosomes, if they could black their faces & get any thing by them." More vessels arrived from Africa and the West Indies. By 1750, Virginia held 101,000 black people. In that year and for several more years planters' demand for slaves exceeded the supply. Better markets for tobacco, new plantations in the piedmont, new vistas for ambition—at the height of the season in 1752, vessels in the James and York rivers held 2,000 new slaves in one eight-week period. Enterprising men with capital bought dozens of slaves at a discount, then resold them one by one a few weeks later at a profit of 25–50 percent. Eager purchases "drained the Planters of Cash."

John Custis also wished the trade could be stopped. But he knew "it is so sweet to those concernd and so much concerns the trade & Navigation of great Brittain; that it will bee next to impossible to break the neck of it." By 1730, Britain had become the largest carrier of slaves in the Atlantic. The French state monopoly bought more and more Virginia tobacco. British merchants profited from this trade with the Continent; the government drew Customs revenue, especially from the domestic tobacco trade. Money or credit given to planters they soon spent, mainly to buy from merchants. The government wanted more, not fewer, vessels to cross the Atlantic. And during Byrd's and Custis's lifetimes, traffic in slaves for Virginia tasted too sweet to too many Virginians. Custis wrote to a British correspondent: "as long as wee will buy thm; you will find thm . . . it is a very melancholly thing seriously to consider it."

Few slaves brought to Chesapeake Bay came in vessels owned by Virginians. But many small sloops plied between the Chesapeake and the islands of the West Indies, routinely sailing back to Virginia with new slaves. A cargo of cured pork and boards and shingles bought a cargo of rum and slaves. David Meade, a young merchant living along the south branch of the Nansemond River, near the northern reaches of the Dismal Swamp, pursued this trade for twenty years. His father, Andrew Meade, had begun it with his sloop *Molly*, bound for Jamaica, bringing back eight or ten slaves each time. Andrew Meade had opened his large house to William Byrd and the other commissioners of the dividing line on a rainy night as they passed from the eastern to the western edge of the swamp. He also entertained Sir Richard Everard, last proprietary governor of North Carolina, though the Virginia Council suspected the governor of tricky dealing on the boundary question. In 1731, Sir Richard and his family visited Andrew Meade on their way to sail for England. David Meade, then twenty years old, had led a sheltered life. He fell in love with Sir Richard's daughter, Susannah. With his father's and Susannah's help, he won Sir Richard's permission for her to stay in Virginia.

She and David were married that year. Andrew Meade was generous to his son. Beginning the next year, David owned the sloops *Molly*, *Priscilla*, *Susannah*, and others bringing slaves to the James River from Jamaica and Barbados—sometimes one or two or four, sometimes eighteen or nineteen.

David and Susannah Meade enjoyed a happy marriage, bringing up six children and leading, one son said, "a monotonous and tranquil life." David joined his father in the counting room and warehouses near their home. He acquired larger vessels for more runs to the West Indies. With John Driver he founded the firm Meade & Driver, taking four lots in the new town of Suffolk, established along the Nansemond River in 1742. Allied with Robert Cary & Company of London, they imported merchandise. Meade sent his three oldest sons to England for education. He had portraits painted of himself, his wife, and their sons. He bought land along the Roanoke River in North Carolina. David Meade died at the age of forty-seven, leaving his partner with a stock of merchandise and a debt to Robert Cary & Company, which grew as Driver imported more goods. Meade left for his children both his share of the company's debt and his personal debt to Cary.

The pursuit of wealth through Virginia's transatlantic trade depended upon extending and receiving promises. Virginians and their commercial connections in Britain needed one another. To sustain the flow of commodities, slaves, and goods, they had to give trust and credit. Often, each side complained that it had been betrayed by the other. Yet the flow continued. In the days of William Byrd, John Custis, King Carter, and Andrew Meade, a great planter sent his tobacco to British merchants, who sold it. Merchants then expended proceeds of the sale among tradesmen, filling planters' orders for goods. The most ambitious Virginians also bought tobacco from and resold goods to their neighbors who worked on a smaller scale. At every stage of these transactions, someone charged an "advance"—a markup—or interest or a commission, or all three. Virginians often protested that merchants extracted too much money in disposing of tobacco, in handling orders for goods, in charging for freight and insuring cargoes. Merchants complained that they received too little money from and extended too much credit to those Virginians who balanced accounts late or never. Even when tobacco sales were good, Richard Corbin, Virginia's deputy receiver general of revenue for the Crown, wrote to England, "no Promises in Respect to any Payment can be depended upon."

Planters used an array of devices. They might consign their inferior tobacco to their creditors, sell their best for cash, and use the money not to pay debts but to buy slaves. They slowed suits for debt in the courts, where planters sat as judges. They consigned tobacco to another merchant, leaving their chief creditor unpaid. After a few months in the colony late in 1750, a young Englishman concluded: "there's a Vanity and Subtilty in the generality of Virginians." He attributed these qualities to "leaders of the Fashion or promoters of mean and vicious habits among the opulent, or as they are fond of styling themselves—Persons of Note." The life of a young man trying to start his fortune by commercial dealings with Virginians could be hard. Though he had a planter's word that he would get a consignment or a cargo, he learned that those hogsheads already had been loaded in a rival's vessel, bound for a different merchant. During some experiences of this kind, Edmund Wilcox started ordering his innkeeper to bring him shots of rum in the morning. Even his kinsman, Richard Corbin, did not give him a cargo Corbin had led him to expect. If a relative and friend could behave this way, Wilcox wrote to his employer, "what must you think of the generality?" Experience had made him cynical about Virginia. He concluded: "this may properly [be] called the Land of Promis without any intension of Performing."

Unhappy Virginians said their colony relied too much upon tobacco. Since the earliest days, officials had tried to force or persuade planters to grow other crops, as well. Hemp, called *Cannabis sativa* in the new Linnaean system, regularly appeared in lists of alternatives. Within a year of his final return to Westover, William Byrd foresaw that tobacco would glut the market. He became an enthusiast for hemp in 1727. It would always have a market because the Royal Navy needed it for cordage, yet relied chiefly on Russia for a supply, a dependence the British government wished to reduce.

Byrd first tried a small crop. Judging it a success, he put a "great part" of his slaves to work on hemp in 1728. The next year he shipped three tons to England. At about the same time he sent his "scheme of a project" for draining the Dismal Swamp to Martin Bladen, to the Earl of Orrery, and to Sir Charles Wager, in search of investors, he said. Once the swamp was drained, he of course proposed to grow hemp. Other Virginians were "running mine-mad," in search of iron, copper, and gold, "which proceeds from a passion to grow rich very suddenly, as the South Sea phrenzy did." Byrd bet on hemp for steady wealth. A pamphlet published in London in 1731, dedicated to Sir Robert Walpole for his understanding of the ties between "National Counsels" and "National Commerce," praised Byrd for promoting hemp: "if he succeeds he will be of more real Benefit to this Kingdom, than if he had given us 100,000 Guineas a Year for ever."

Ropemakers in London found Byrd's hemp as good as the best, but by

1732 he had lost his enthusiasm and abandoned the crop. From the beginning he knew that it cost much labor. On a visit to Bridewell Prison in London he had watched female inmates breaking hemp with mallets, in the manner William Hogarth portrayed in his fourth stage of *The Harlot's Progress*. This process for separating the long plant's bark from its fibers was tedious and grueling. After several years' trial at Westover, Byrd computed that hemp consumed too much of his slaves' time and his money. Russians produced it at one-fifth the cost in labor and shipped it at one-third the rate for freight. The Royal Navy took too long to pay, and merchants in Britain, as usual, imposed charges and commissions for handling the crop, "like the Bald Eagle, which after the Fishing Hawk has been at great pains to catch a Fish, pounces upon and takes it from him." Byrd made no profit and looked back upon the undertaking as a "wofull Experience." During his lifetime, Virginians collected bounties for only 1,000 tons of hemp. Tobacco still reigned.

Tobacco from North Carolina passed through the hands of David Meade and other merchants near the southern reaches of Chesapeake Bay. Virginia outlawed overland importation in 1726, calling Carolina tobacco inferior, but the Crown disallowed that law. By 1733, North Carolinians were driving large numbers of hogs and other livestock across the boundary and hauling into Virginia tobacco, pork, pitch, tar, deerskins, beaver pelts, and other goods worth perhaps £50,000 each year. On the Virginia side of the Dismal Swamp the produce floated in small boats down the Elizabeth River or the Nansemond River to merchants' warehouses. Carolinians made good customers. Though they devised "a thousand shifts" to avoid paying quitrents, they bought slaves and British merchandise in Virginia.

Stopping in the town of Norfolk on his way to survey the dividing line, William Byrd saw a few blocks of houses and shops along streets leading to wharves that stretched into the eastern branch of the Elizabeth River. The county held about 4,000 people. Perhaps 1,000 lived in town, drawing their livelihood from the sea. Near the mouth of the James River, only a few miles from Cape Henry, Cape Charles, and the Atlantic, Norfolk offered a convenient port to sloops, schooners, and brigantines sailing to and from the West Indies. Shipwrights and ships' chandlers, seamen, clerks, and merchants lived there. Byrd counted almost twenty vessels riding at the log wharves. New houses rose, and justices of the peace had a new brick courthouse. In other rivers the master of a vessel dropped anchor off the plantations' landings, then used boats for crates of goods and hogsheads of tobacco. At Norfolk he could find artisans able to heave down his vessel, clean her, caulk her, make repairs, and replace rigging.

Twenty years after Byrd's visit the county had almost twice as many people. Norfolk had become a borough, with its own government and a public market house. In the 1740s merchants began to build vessels, drawing timber and masts from the tall trees of the Dismal Swamp. Travelers crossing Chesapeake Bay saw more sails moving to all points of the compass. A visitor early in the 1740s found Virginians preoccupied with "Schemes of Gain," which in Norfolk took the form of the "great Number of Vessels" along the expanded wharves. In that busy port, "a Spirit of Trade reigns, far surpassing that of any other Part of *Virginia.*"

Among the first aldermen of the new borough in 1736 was a hard-working young merchant, Robert Tucker, who intended to increase his wealth with Norfolk's. The aldermen formed a closed corporation, choosing new colleagues to fill vacancies and electing a mayor each year. Tucker served as mayor three times. He had begun business with the advantage of inheritances from his father and uncle. He spent his youth in a house filled with pictures and maps, not far from his father's sloops waiting to depart for the West Indies. Two months after his father's death, his mother was married to another successful merchant, a widower, Thomas Nelson of York Town. Tucker impressed people with his tireless dedication to his work. Fellow merchants thought him the "intire Man of Business."

Importing rum, sugar, and molasses, exporting pork, corn, and wheat, Tucker widened his trade. He dispatched vessels to Madeira, the Canary Islands, and Barcelona. Only one merchant in Norfolk shipped more than he. Three years after becoming an alderman, Tucker got married to Joanna Corbin, younger sister of Richard Corbin. During the ceremony at Laneville, a plantation in King and Queen County, the Reverend William Phillips preached on the text "Marriage is honourable." The Tuckers' first child was baptized, at the age of six weeks, on their first anniversary. During the following twenty-six years, Joanna Tucker usually was pregnant. She bore eighteen children.

Robert Tucker steadily added to his holdings. He bought or built homes and warehouses, leasing them to tenants, charging rent for space on his wharf. To the sloop *Bobby* in the Barbados trade he added the sloop *Johnny*, the sloop *Salley*, the ship *Joanna*—each built in Norfolk and launched soon after the birth of a Tucker child of that name. On return voyages these vessels sometimes carried slaves, as well as rum, molasses, and sugar. In July 1750 the *Joanna* brought forty-eight "new Negroes," for whom Barbados had been only a stop on the way to Hampton Roads from Africa. Tucker's

William Nelson, after an unknown artist, Mary Burwell. Courtesy of the Library of Virginia. Merchant of York Town, colonial councillor, and acting governor of Virginia.

own slaves were artisans: sawyers, caulkers, watermen. His stores dealt in clothing, pewter, household linen, and other goods imported from Britain. He earned his reputation for "Assiduity & indefatigable Application to Business."

Among Robert Tucker's greatest objects of pride, his mills and bakeries won the admiration of all. On a point of land jutting into the Elizabeth River where it opened into a broad estuary meeting the James, he acquired 170 acres. There he erected two brick windmills, one a large double gristmill operating two sets of stones, the best French burr. From a northern colony he hired a miller at high wages. He built a brick granary 40 feet square and another holding three bolting mills. Under the same long roof he added a large bakehouse with tall chimneys and four ovens able to turn out 3,000 pounds of bread per day. The slaves working in these buildings were "very fine bakers, millers." Tucker devised a fan with paper wings to blow dust out of wheat. He expected to raise hogs on the stone floor under one granary's wheat loft, and he had a smokehouse for curing hams and bacon. One of Tucker's contractors said: "no expence was spared in the buildings or their improvement."

Tucker added two brigantines to his fleet. He acquired more land: new lots in the borough of Norfolk, as well as lots and plantations in Nansemond, Norfolk, and Princess Anne counties. He joined the rush of Virginians seeking large grants along tributaries of the Ohio River in 1749. He and his associates took 400,000 acres. He won election to the House of Burgesses, taking a seat on one of its most important committees. Elsewhere in the colony, Virginians who needed something done in Norfolk routinely said that Colonel Tucker would take care of it.

Tucker's mother, Frances Courtney Tucker Nelson, lived to the age of eighty-three, a widow for twenty years after the death of her second husband, Thomas Nelson. For forty-three years she lived in York Town, watching its commerce grow and sharing the success of her husband and her two stepsons, William Nelson and Thomas Nelson. When she moved to York Town, William and Thomas were boys, twelve and seven years old. By the time she died, they had become the most powerful men in Virginia. Her husband took advantage of York Town's position as the place vessels from Britain met tobacco from plantations along the York River's tributaries. Ships trading to other rivers also anchored in the York while their cargoes—hogsheads of tobacco weighing almost half a ton each—were restowed for an ocean voyage. In town, sailors found busy taverns, one of which belonged to Thomas Nelson. He built a wharf and a warehouse. By the 1740s only one man rivaled his dominance of the wholesale trade in imported goods. Nelson's home, with other brick houses and handsome wooden ones, "all built in the modern Taste" along rising ground overlooking the York, gave the town "a great Air of Opulence." Nelson advertised that he managed the sale of "choice young Slaves," directly off ships arriving from Angola and the Gold Coast. He prospered; he bought plantations for his sons; Frances Nelson received from her husband rings and jewels of gold and diamonds.

Her tall stepsons, William and Thomas, improved upon their father's legacy. After her husband's death in 1745, she stayed in the house that was now hers while William and Thomas built mansions nearby. Both had spent their teen-aged years being educated in England, acquiring an ideal of books and prints and elegant surroundings. Into his correspondence Thomas dropped the phrase "When I was last in England," as if he made regular visits. He bought Hogarth prints; William bought Collet landscapes. William subscribed to *The London Magazine;* a few years after his father's death he said that if he could turn the business he had inherited into liquid capital, he would "remove to England with the utmost expedition." Confined to Virginia, the brothers remained close throughout their lives. Presented with a proposal in business or politics, either man could delay or deflect it by saying that he must consult his brother. Virginians, on matters as disparate as freight rates and land surveys, appealed to the authority of the united opinion of the Nelson brothers.

Before death came to their father at the age of sixty-eight, he could take pride in leaving his sons well fixed. Like William Byrd's father, he once had worked in the Indian trade, as his sons need never do. William Nelson, at the age of thirty, played host to William Byrd, then in his late sixties. A few years later Nelson succeeded Byrd on the Council. Though Thomas Nelson had to wait several more years for his seat on the Council, he gained the biggest prize of all, the office of deputy secretary. On the last day of July 1742, Secretary John Carter died. The next day his brother, Charles, wrote to his English merchant, seeking support for an attempt to get the secretaryship. Charles Carter of Cleve offered £2,000 to buy the appointment, almost £500 more than John and their father, King Carter, had paid. But the Carters' connection in England, Robert Walpole, was no longer in power, and the Earl of Albemarle, sinecurist governor of Virginia, had an "agent," William Adair, who wanted the sinecure office of secretary of Virginia. Like his patron, he did not intend to live in the colony. The work would be done by a deputy, and Adair would, as William Byrd said, "have a snack" out of the revenues of the office. He, in turn, would share part of his income from the office with the earl, who ran through money fast. Charles Carter learned from his English merchant that the earl planned "to make the most he could of it" and had received an offer that "farr exceeded your limit." Three months after Adair became secretary, Thomas Nelson, at the age of twenty-seven, took the oath of office as his deputy. It was easy to see that Nelson's father had outbid Charles Carter.

As Secretary John Carter lay dying of dropsy, young Thomas Nelson traveled from the York River to the Rappahannock to "make his addresses" to Lucy Armistead. Most people predicted that "it will be a match," and the couple proved them right once Nelson became deputy secretary. His brother, William, already had been married for several years to a niece of

John and Charles Carter's. Elizabeth Burwell, "a very genteel, accomplished young Lady," had grown up at Rosewell, her education supervised by King Carter's bookish daughter, Judith Page. The wedding took place in the newly finished mansion at Rosewell. William Nelson took his wife and her "considerable Fortune" to York Town, where they had a son before the end of the year, soon afterward beginning a big brick house. On higher ground at the upper end of town, Thomas Nelson built an even larger house, with a tall chimney at each corner and with "European taste" inside, such as a mantelpiece of fine marble and "exquisitely sculptured" marble bas-reliefs. In front of the house a terraced formal garden led down toward the river and Nelson's storehouse at waterside. From the cupola on the roof of the mansion at Rosewell, one could see, across the expanse of the York and downriver, the two Nelson houses standing out among the buildings of York Town.

William Nelson inherited his father's stores and customers, then expanded his wholesale and retail business, selling to people as far as 100 miles west of York Town. He faulted himself for not working half as hard as Robert Tucker did, but Nelson paid close attention to his affairs, and he prospered. When the market would bear it, he charged a 100 percent markup on wholesale purchases and a 110 percent markup on retail, though the usual rate was lower. He bought and sold land, imported and sold perhaps 1,000 slaves, and performed some of the functions of a banker, lending money at interest. As payment came due, everyone knew that "Nelson insists on Sterlg. money." He owned plantations scattered from York Town to Frederick County in the Shenandoah Valley.

William Nelson was a big man; an artist painting his portrait saw a direct, clear gaze in Nelson's eyes and a firmly closed mouth with a hint of a smile—not sardonic like William Byrd's, but self-confident, with one hand in his waistcoat and one hand resting on a solid base, his hat under his arm. Nelson wore broadcloth suits befitting a businessman, not green velvet or scarlet silk, yet he showed that he was a success. His watch, chain, and seal were gold; the stock buckle at his neck was gold, and his sleeve buttons were deep red garnets set in gold. Elizabeth Nelson wore diamond rings, a gold chain, and a necklace of large, perfect pearls. William Nelson spoke and wrote with blunt directness. He carried himself with "conscious Dignity"; he made clear that "except the Governour, he is the greatest Man in this Country."

Nelson enjoyed using his power to do favors. He took an orphaned girl into his home, made her a governess and chatelaine, then gave her £200 as a wedding present. He and his brother helped an ambitious twenty-one-year-old George Washington get commissioned adjutant of the Northern Neck. But Nelson dismissed importunings and complaints. "As to the rest of your

Letter," he wrote to one of his father's debtors, "abt. the Purchase of the Land &ca., I imagine it proceeds from the Errors of your Memory, (as you have not kept Books & Minutes of those Transactions) & therefore not to be deserving of any Answer from Me at this Time." Face to face, Nelson could be abrupt and peremptory. Handing written terms of a loan to a man borrowing money, he said: "There, Sir!—Sir, if you like that!" Sarcasms and raillery strewn through his letters and conversation seemed "pleasant and entertaining" to one person but could strike another as sneers and taunts.

William Nelson sometimes spoke loudly and turned red in the face, but Thomas Nelson was cautious and noncommittal. A person hoping to manipulate him found him "prudent & sensible." Though he suffered attacks of gout, he prided himself on not having "squandered the Resources of health" in his youth. He spoke calmly, spent many hours reading, attended to his pleasure garden, and wore out the binding on his *Book of Common Prayer.* Everyone knew him as Mr. Secretary. For more than thirty years he was the one constant figure at the center of Virginia's government.

The secretary recorded, kept, and copied the colony's public and legal documents. For every official paper or sheet of vellum, he charged a fee: land patents, court writs, tavern licenses, deeds, wills, commissions, testimony, appeals—each transaction brought him a few shillings or payment in tobacco, from a few dozen pounds to a few hundred. The secretary appointed all county clerks, who remitted part of their fees to him. Thomas Nelson did not write with his own hand the documents that came from his office. He brought promising young men to Williamsburg to work without pay for five years with the understanding that he would give each a county clerkship. Fathers wanted these positions for their sons and competed "in making . . . Interest with his Honr the Secretary about procureing the Clerks place." Nelson kept the clerkships of four counties for his own sons and kinsmen. One aspirant, confronting this closed system, tried to break in by writing to Secretary William Adair in England, saying that Nelson "has Provided for all his friends." But Adair was sharing Nelson's income. In the early years they split annually about £1,000 sterling, later much more, though they left no record of the size of Adair's "snack." Much to the irritation of several governors and some ambitious young Virginians, the two men understood each other, and both lived to a hearty old age.

After the Council began, in 1745, to make large grants of western land to companies and individuals, the Board of Trade in London received complaints about "undue practices" in Secretary Nelson's office. The chief accuser was Robert Dinwiddie, resident governor. He reported that the

John Robinson, Unknown Artist. Courtesy of the Library of
Virginia. Longtime speaker of the House of Burgesses and
treasurer of the colony of Virginia.

secretary had records of almost 1,000,000 acres of grants not yet patented. A
patent brought property onto the rent roll, obliging the owner to pay an annual quitrent to the Crown. The governor and the Board of Trade concluded
that Virginians were "defrauding the crown of quitrents by delay" in patenting. Of course, Virginians well knew Secretary Nelson's "upright Character."
When the board later implied suspicion by ordering that the secretary's fees
be open to public inspection, Nelson replied that they already were open, so
"that no body may be imposed on." The Board of Trade called for a list and
abstract of all grants since the founding of the colony. Nelson brought his
chief clerk before the Council to explain why "such a perplexed and endless
work" was impracticable. Nelson told the governor that if the board wished
"to be informed of the number of Acres that ought to pay Quit rents, it will
appear with great exactness by the Rent roll." Two years later the board again
demanded a list of grants. Nelson gave a similar answer, adding a few further
difficulties to his earlier list of reasons why he could not comply. A list of
grants west of the Allegheny Mountains since 1745 and of all petitions for

western land was compiled in 1770. It was signed not by the secretary but by the clerk of the Council. A county clerk who feared Nelson's displeasure warned a friend: "it would be imprudent in you to impose upon Mr. Secretary." Neither county clerks nor the king's ministers easily imposed upon Thomas Nelson.

The president of the Council when Thomas Nelson joined it in 1749 was John Robinson, Sr., who had served for almost thirty years. He had included Nelson and John Robinson, Jr., his son, in one of the large grants of land the Council made in 1745. The Robinsons' personal attorney became Nelson's attorney. John Robinson, Sr., died in William Nelson's house in York Town. The Nelson brothers knew John Robinson, Jr., well. He was seven years older than William and twelve years older than Thomas. At the time of his father's death in August 1749, he had been speaker of the House of Burgesses for eleven years. For decades governors came and went, but the speaker and the secretary stayed.

John Robinson held two offices: speaker of the House of Burgesses and treasurer of the colony. After every election the burgesses voted him into those positions again. Beginning in 1752, he won by a unanimous vote, without opposition. As treasurer, he received taxes collected by sheriffs and duties levied on imported liquor and slaves. After the burgesses voted appropriations, he spent the money. His pay was 4 percent of the revenue—about £300 per year in peacetime, as much as £1,000 per year during war. He also collected a commission for auditing accounts of inspectors of tobacco. The Board of Trade would have preferred that the Crown choose the treasurer or, at least, that one man not hold both offices. But the government let long usage continue and heeded warnings that the burgesses' cooperation with London depended upon the Crown's accepting Robinson as speaker and treasurer.

With rare exceptions, the speaker had his way in the House of Burgesses. Before Landon Carter grew reconciled to Robinson's rule, he privately complained that in sessions of the committee of the whole, the speaker's nods and signals carried every motion: "there he sits and what he can't do himself he prompts others to do." In formal sessions, the speaker took the chair. Robed in his gown of office, sitting in state above a long table on which lay an ornate silver mace, Robinson put Carter in mind of a Turkish pasha. Robinson chose the members of standing committees, often appointing the same man to several committees at once. He expected and rewarded loyalty as well as efficiency. The Nelson brothers, during their time as burgesses, served on one of the most important committees. Members of the Randolph family consistently won committee assignments. In 1742, every standing committee had a Randolph on it. Later, Peyton Randolph seemed so close to the speaker that their wills were as one, and a loyal burgess must be "at their beck." New members soon learned how the House of Burgesses worked, and Robinson advanced some of them quickly. Describing the colonial House of Burgesses after it had ceased to exist, Edmund Randolph wrote of Robinson: "To committees he nominated the members best qualified. . . . In the limited sphere of colonial politics, he was a column."

Speaker Robinson's place among Virginians was unique. He had both power and popularity. Almost everyone who recorded an opinion admired him. Thomas Jefferson, a harsh critic of Robinson's system of politics, later described the speaker: "He was an excellent man." Amiable, generous, charitable, Robinson "had a Benevolence for all Mankind" and "a Desire to please everybody & make them happy." For these qualities he was "universally Esteemed," even "beloved," more than any other man in Virginia.

Those mentioning Speaker Robinson's "friends," however, had in mind a connection arising from more than his demeanor. His friends were his closest allies in the House of Burgesses, those able to foretell how votes would go. Upon these he lavished a "thousand little flattering attentions," and they repaid him with political as well as personal attachment. To a burgess not in favor, Robinson's "warm & private friendships" looked not admirable but ominous. Some burgesses voting to make Robinson speaker and treasurer nevertheless talked among themselves about his "undue influence." They knew of widespread suspicions that he used "indirect methods" to obtain "unnatural Influence in the House."

Rumor said that Robinson spent £5,000 improving his home and estate, called Pleasant Hill, in King and Queen County. His two-story brick house stood on an eminence commanding a long view of the Mattaponi River, just before it joined the Pamunkey River to form the York. A falling garden within brick walls led down to the water. More than 1,300 acres separated Robinson from his neighbors. George Washington, whom the speaker befriended early, called Pleasant Hill "a beautiful Situation."

For his comfort, Robinson could thank his generous father-in-law, Augustine Moore, who had amassed large holdings through the slave trade and in other ways. Robinson eventually owned about four hundred slaves, working his land in six counties. Lucy Moore Robinson died, apparently in June 1755, leaving him a widower a second time. In the summer of 1756 he went courting again to Susanna Chiswell. Her mother, Elizabeth Randolph Chiswell, belonged to the family of Robinson's chief political friends. By the time the speaker and Susanna Chiswell were married in December 1759, her father, John Chiswell, had become Robinson's business partner in a lead mine company for which Robinson furnished the capital. Chiswell had many debts and little money. The company, though unprofitable, made frequent payments to him. At the wedding in Williamsburg on Friday, December 21, as Robinson, now fifty-five, was married to his friend's daughter, "nothing appeared but youth and gaiety." The bride and bridegroom then left for Pleasant Hill.

The day after John Robinson was unanimously re-elected speaker in February 1752, he chose burgesses for the committee of propositions and grievances. Among them were Robert Tucker of Norfolk and a new member, Robert Burwell, from Isle of Wight County just west of Nansemond County and the Dismal Swamp. Tucker and Burwell were brothers-in-law; Burwell's wife, Sarah, was the daughter of the elder Thomas Nelson and Frances Tucker Nelson, Robert Tucker's mother. Although men marveled at Tucker's energy and enterprise, no one thought Burwell had either trait. A good person, he lacked "mental Qualifications." He did not read books. He preferred horse races to governmental work. He flew into temper tantrums. One acquaintance described him as "a shallow weak man."

Even so, he was "of a very good Family." His father, Nathaniel Burwell, had married one of King Carter's daughters. Nathaniel died while Robert was a baby. Robert Burwell's sister, Elizabeth, named after her mother, grew up at Rosewell, where she and William Nelson held their wedding. Robert Burwell was not as bright as the Nelsons wished, but he was family. He and his wife spent much time in York Town, where he owned houses. Their home estate overlooked the James River on its south bank. The ample brick house was graced with a rectangular garden covering more than 7,800 square yards. Across portions of the 3,500-acre estate stretched apple orchards, as well as many other fruit trees. Burwell also owned property in northern Virginia and along the Roanoke River in North Carolina, but he had too few slaves to work all his land. His debts grew. He promised to give his daughter a dowry of £1,000—the elder Thomas Nelson had given Sarah £1,500 when she was married to Robert—but did not keep his promise. As a brother-in-law, he was an embarrassment.

Burwell's daughter was married to another great-grandchild of King Carter's. The bridegroom's father was Mann Page, son of the Mann Page who had begun the mansion at Rosewell. The younger Page, twelve years old when his father died, inherited, with his two brothers, about 70,000 acres. Their uncle, Secretary John Carter, was their guardian. Mann Page came into his property upon turning twenty-one in 1740. Carter had assured Micajah Perry in London that young Page would find his estate's credit good. By the time Page reached adulthood, John Carter was dead.

On the last day of 1741, Page went to Brandon on the south bank of the James, the home of John Grymes, a member of the Council and a friend of William Byrd's. There Page was married to Grymes's eighteen-year-old daughter, Alice. Her affability and sweet temper had won his respect; her "personal Beauty" had caught his eye. (Her portrait, painted a few years later, suggests that she resembled her husband.) While she was pregnant with their first child at Rosewell, late in 1742 and early in 1743, she and her husband began to confront the difficulties of his inheritance.

During ten years of John Carter's guardianship and three years of Page's executorship, neither had made the elder Page's estate yield enough to pay his debts or bequests in his will. Fearing that creditors would bring suits, then seize and sell personal property and slaves, thereby leaving his land of little or no benefit without laborers, Page advanced "great sums" of his own money to meet some of his late father's obligations. But his father had agreed to pay interest on most debts, and accrual of interest kept him from gaining ground in repayment. To keep some of his holdings and enough slaves to work them, he must sell other land and slaves. In September 1744 he petitioned the House of Burgesses to dock the entail, removing the inherited legal restraint on sale of holdings which were supposed to remain intact for generations. The General Assembly did so in October; the Crown approved a year later. At the annual fall political and commercial gathering in Williamsburg, the first of Mann Page's auctions of land took place on October 30, 1745, to help pay for the glass, mahogany, brick, and marble of his mansion.

Mann Page lost his "Exemplary" wife before her twenty-third birthday. On January 11, 1746, Alice Page died in her third childbirth, showing "constancy & Resignation." For his second wife, Page went to Mount Airy, home of John Tayloe. Another colleague of William Byrd's on the Council, Tayloe was one of Virginia's richest men, but by 1744 he had grown "incapable of Business." He had written his will; he was waiting to die. This he did in 1747, leaving to his daughter £2,000 sterling, to be paid when she turned twenty or was married. Within months of her father's death, Ann Tayloe was married to Mann Page. In later years Page's first son recalled fondly his hours with his grandmother Judith Carter Page, but he left no mention of his stepmother.

A neighbor in Gloucester County found her "detestable." Upon the death of Judith Carter Page, Ann Tayloe Page became mistress of Rosewell.

Not long after Thomas Nelson took office as deputy secretary in 1743, he and Speaker Robinson and their friends began to lengthen their vision, casting the mind's eye farther west. William Byrd, at the age of sixty-nine, set an example by patenting 105,000 acres along the Dan River. He added the Saura Town lands in March. In the fifteen years since Byrd first had seen the Land of Eden, other Virginians had taken an interest in still more remote regions. James Patton had found "at vast Expence" tracts along a 100-mile river, now known as the Kanawha, flowing into the Ohio River. He petitioned the Council in October 1743 to grant 200,000 acres to him and his associates, including John Tayloe, Jr. Patton promised to pay all fees, to file surveys with Secretary Nelson punctually, and to settle on that land one family for each 1,000 acres. Members of the Council were friendly but skeptical, seeing little benefit to Virginia or to the Crown's revenue in moving "a handfull of Poor People" to a western river. Patton, however, feared that his plan was so good that others would imitate it as soon as they learned of it and then "Reap the benefit of my Industry." If more people followed Patton's lead, the Council would realize that Virginia could expand commerce and the Crown gain revenue by approving his petition. He won the councillors over, leaving only the question of when his grant would be made. They promised him preference, and their clerk recorded this in the Council's journal.

During the following eighteen months, the Council's president, John Robinson, Sr., his son the speaker, and Secretary Nelson resolved to get a grant for themselves and nine associates—100,000 acres along the Greenbrier River, a tributary of the Kanawha. Acting on April 26, 1745, the Council chose wording that did not oblige the Greenbrier associates to settle families there or to pay duties and fees until they filed surveys, that is, until they sold tracts of the land they had received free. Later the same day, the Council gave James Patton 100,000 acres, half of his request. His "Friend in the Governmt" assured him that he "could not miss" getting the other 100,000 as soon as he complied with his promise to find settlers. Six months later, another member of the Council, John Blair, obtained for himself and his associates a grant of 100,000 acres along the upper Potomac River. Other grants of 50,000 acres fanned out from the Greenbrier and Potomac tracts. Patton died in 1755. He had put settlers along the Kanawha, but he never received the other 100,000 acres.

Everyone concerned with grants and land titles had a close call on January 30, 1747, when the capitol building in Williamsburg caught fire. The symmetrical two-winged structure, in which Secretary Nelson kept the colony's records, was consumed. By God's mercy, the Council said, those records were "plucked out of the Devouring Flames." Finding that the fire had started in a remote upstairs room with neither a chimney nor wainscoting, yet had spread quickly, officials suspected arson. Burgesses and councillors quarreled about whether to keep the government in Williamsburg, but they quickly approved Secretary Nelson's proposal to erect a new building for his records. Loss of these would lead to "endless Strife and Confusion."

One member of the Council who had received no grants in 1745 concluded by 1747 that he and his friends ought to share the new prospects of the Ohio Valley. From the north windows of Stratford Hall, Thomas Lee could see the Potomac River. Near bluffs on its south bank, tobacco vessels dropped anchor to take on board hogsheads from his plantation. He and Lawrence Washington looked upstream, beyond Washington's home, Mount Vernon, beyond rocks and falls, to the river's upper reaches, where flatboats could float within 45 miles of a branch of the Ohio. They heard from Indian traders that lands along the Ohio and its tributaries were "vastly rich."

Lee and his associates petitioned the Council on October 20, 1747, for a grant of 200,000 acres along the Allegheny River. Secretary Nelson, still a young man not yet on the Council, joined Lee's petition; but after watching what happened in the following months, he withdrew, having learned that he could not befriend both Thomas Lee and Speaker Robinson. Virginia's resident governor, Sir William Gooch, had authority to approve grants, as he had done with those made to the Robinsons. In response to Lee's petition, however, Sir William wrote to the Board of Trade, asking for instructions from the Privy Council. An exchange of letters meant further delay. Governor Gooch wrote that he only wished to avoid conflict with the French. He predicted that "a considerable Time" would pass before Lee could people western lands because the petitioners planned to seek tenants in Europe. The governor also recommended that Thomas Nelson be appointed to the Council.

While the Board of Trade considered its report to the Privy Council, Thomas Lee asked his associate and merchant in London, John Hanbury, to use his influence on their behalf. On September 4, 1748, Thomas Lee, by seniority, became president of Virginia's Council. The following month he and his associates made plans for trade with Indians in the Ohio Valley and "for procuring Foreign Protestants to settle the Land." They called themselves the Ohio Company. Their goals were the "public good and the King's service," as well as "Justice to the Indians," Lee promised. "I have noe partial Views."

In December the Board of Trade drafted instructions for the Privy Council to send to Governor Gooch, authorizing a grant of 200,000 acres to the Ohio Company. By the time the Privy Council received this draft, they also had received from John Hanbury a petition on behalf of the company, seeking a grant of 500,000 acres. The Board of Trade interviewed Hanbury, then drew up new instructions. In them the Privy Council, on March 16, 1749, ordered Sir William to grant the Ohio Company 500,000 acres, 200,000 at once and the remainder after the company began settlements and built a fort.

Landon Carter recalled a few years later that "a Certain Person . . . had in his day drank very large drafts of Rancour and Revenge against Colo. Lee." That person, of course, was Speaker Robinson. In 1749 he drank one of those drafts. He set out to teach Thomas Lee a lesson.

Virginia's Council renewed the Greenbrier grant to the Robinsons, Thomas Nelson, and others for four years on April 14. Nelson joined the Council the following week. John Blair and the men who had received a grant of 100,000 acres along the upper Potomac in 1745 petitioned for a four-year renewal, too, but Governor Gooch said on May 5 that they must wait until the Crown's instructions arrived. Later in May, Lee heard from Hanbury that the Ohio Company's grant had won the Privy Council's approval. Within a week or two, "Mr Secretary Nelson told him . . . that he desired to be Excused and did not Intend to be one of the Ohio Company." The instructions to Governor Gooch arrived in June; he and the Council complied with them on July 12. The Nelson brothers missed that meeting.

The Council stayed in session on July 12 after making the grant to Lee, Hanbury, and their associates. It then granted 100,000 acres to Speaker Robinson's brother-in-law, Bernard Moore, and nine colleagues. It granted 50,000 acres to another group. It renewed James Patton's grant along the Kanawha for John Tayloe and others. It granted 400,000 more acres along a branch of the Kanawha called New River to eighteen men, including Speaker Robinson's closest allies, Peyton Randolph, Benjamin Waller, and Edmund Pendleton, as well as Robert Tucker, mayor of Norfolk, and his brother, John. To Councillor John Lewis and the men who formed the new Loyal Company, including Edmund Pendleton, the Council granted 800,000 acres "beginning on the Bounds between this Colony and North Carolina, and running to the Westward and to the North so as to include the said Quantity." The Nelson brothers soon joined this company. If ability to obtain land was a measure of power in Virginia, the Council's actions on July 12 held a message for Thomas Lee.

Long afterward, Edmund Pendleton gave one of the Greenbrier heirs "a circumstantial detail of the whole business" of the early land grants. His story was "voluminous." Later in 1749, Governor Gooch retired and returned to England. Thomas Lee became acting governor but died the following year. Yet Speaker Robinson kept his grudge against Lee alive, Landon Carter said, "so pleasing is Revenge that it seems as if an opportunity was wanted to exercise it on his Memory."

In 1749 the Council chose two members of the Loyal Company, Joshua Fry and Peter Jefferson, to extend the line dividing Virginia from North Carolina. It would also be the southern border of the Loyal Company's grant. With two surveyors from North Carolina, they began on Peter's Creek, a tributary of the Dan River near Byrd's Land of Eden. Working westward, they forded creeks, climbed the Blue Ridge, and descended into the valley of the New River. They stopped at a tributary of the Holston River, 88 miles west of Peter's Creek. Before winter came, Fry and Jefferson returned to Williamsburg to give the Council a report, with new maps of the line.

Members of the Loyal Company wished to know much more than where North Carolina started. Their grant contained five words not in the Ohio Company's text. These words—"in one or more Surveys"—meant that the Loyal Company's 800,000 acres need not lie in one continuous tract, combining mountains and river bottoms, but could cover scattered smaller plots of the best soil surveyors found. The partners needed to know how the land lay west of the Allegheny Mountains and north of Fry and Jefferson's line. In 1750, to find out, they sent one of their own, Dr. Thomas Walker.

Two years earlier, Walker had explored with James Patton's party farther west than Fry and Jefferson ran their line. Soon afterward, he left Patton to join the much larger Loyal Company. Dr. Walker had shown on his first trip that he had stamina. A thin, wiry man about five feet seven inches tall, he enjoyed exertion. He advised a friend: "use as much exercise as you can without fateage." He followed his own counsel and seldom showed fatigue. He had the strength of a large man with the agility of a smaller one. A connoisseur of rattlesnake meat, he dined only on the snakes he caught live. He practiced medicine, which he had studied as a young man in Williamsburg while living with his sister and her husband, Dr. George Gilmer. He was also a surveyor, a tobacco planter, and a man whose blue eyes looked across many western vistas.

Nine years before heading west on behalf of the Loyal Company, Thomas Walker got married to Mildred Thornton Meriwether, a widow who brought to the union her late husband's estate, Castle Hill—15,000 acres not far east of the Blue Ridge. By 1750, the Walkers had four children. Dr. Walker's father-in-law, Francis Thornton, was a member of the Loyal Company, as was John Thornton, Walker's brother-in-law, and John's son, Francis. Dr. George Gilmer was a partner, too. Within a few years of its founding, the Loyal Company became a web of kinsmen. The six Lewises were related to the seven Meriwethers, who were related to the Thorntons. James Maury was married to Thomas Walker's niece. Kinship and marriage created some ties almost invisible to an outsider. Elizabeth Baylor Walker, widow of Dr. Walker's older brother, took as her second husband Obadiah Marriott, an attorney who served both Secretary Nelson and Speaker Robinson. After arriving in Virginia as a newlywed, a young woman from Philadelphia wrote to her sister: "They are all Brothers, Sisters, or Cousins; so that if you use one person in the Colony ill, you affront all."

In the third week of March 1750, Thomas Walker, with five other men, eight horses, and a pack of dogs, crossed the New River along its upper reaches near the North Carolina line and headed southwestward, down the valley of the Holston River. For the Loyal Company they were "to discover the Country, and look for fit Places for Settlements." Their travels lasted four months, making a long loop westward, turning back to the east a few miles short of a point from which they could have seen Kentucky's rich, level land.

Snow fell along the Holston in the last week of March. Dr. Walker saw snow-covered mountains to the northwest. The horses climbed out of the valley, along a ridge covered with pine, then descended into the valley of the Clinch River. To cross the Clinch, the men made a raft for their baggage, letting horses and dogs swim. The next day, Ambrose Powell was bitten by a bear. Walker and his men killed and ate bears, deer, and wild turkeys, as well as a few bison and elk.

They pushed westward, carving their names into beech trees and twice using shelters left by Indians. Following an Indian route northward, they entered a pass, winding between cloud-covered mountains. Vistas of mountain ranges opened to the east and to the west. To compliment the king's son, the Duke of Cumberland, Walker called the pass Cumberland Gap. Reaching a river flowing southwestward out of the mountains, Walker named it the

Cumberland River. He saw recent tracks of seven or eight Indians, but the Virginians did not overtake them.

In May and June, Dr. Walker's party traveled northeastward, from the tributaries of the Kentucky River to the Kanawha. He took notes on the quality of the land, climbing a tree to get a better look. He named rivers after his men and a creek for Ambrose Powell's dog, Tumbler, killed by a bull elk the dogs chased. Sometimes the men hacked their way through thick vines and brush with tomahawks. During their descent into the valley of the Big Sandy River, wolves howled around them all night. In the morning Dr. Walker found that his camp had cut off the wolves from their pups. Three days later a hailstorm blew down Walker's tent and felled large trees within thirty yards of him. By the end of June, in their eastward return, they reached the Kanawha River, just below the mouth of the Greenbrier. Walker and two others stripped and waded in to find a fording place. Ten days later his party came upon houses along a tributary of the James River. The next day they visited invalids taking the waters at Hot Springs. On the 11th, they covered 30 miles to Augusta Court House. Walker reached home about noon on Monday, July 13. Within two weeks Mildred Walker was pregnant.

The Loyal Company did not begin surveys at once, but its members acted. The Meriwethers and the Lewises designed an executive committee. The partners went to court to stop Secretary Nelson from issuing patents for western land to James Patton, who felt aggrieved at being excluded from a movement he had begun. He and other critics accused the company of planning to take only the most fertile soil, using many surveys. The Loyal Company's rivals had their own designs on "that western world, that Land of promise." But its members conceived a still larger vision. Working in secret in 1753, councillors and partners planned to send men, led by Dr. Thomas Walker, beyond the Mississippi River to find the Missouri River, then follow it to discover, if possible, a connection by water with the Pacific Ocean. Walker would "make exact reports of the country." By the Council's order he drew up a list of necessary equipment and an estimate of expenses. The expedition was prevented by the start of fighting between Virginians and the French in 1754. Thus was lost, "for the present," an avenue to "the rich and costly products of the East." A member of the company wrote: "What an exhaustless fund of wealth would here be opened, superior to Potosi and all the other South American mines!"

At the expiration of the Loyal Company's first four-year grant, the Council renewed it in June 1753. Thomas Walker took the title of agent and became "the chief person in this scheme." He offered the company's land for sale at £3 per 100 acres. In February, Walker had contracted to buy Joshua Fry's share for half that price. He sent out surveyors, who soon completed ninety surveys. By the autumn of 1754 he had sold land to about two hundred families already living on the tracts before the company arrived.

William Byrd spoke in 1720 with men who had traveled partway up the Mississippi River and some of its branches. They described good soil and a fine climate. Byrd did not wish the region to fall into the hands of the French. He did not live to see Fry and Jefferson extend his dividing line or to learn about the west from Dr. Walker. Byrd wrote his will after Christmas in 1743. He attended his last Council meeting in June 1744. He died in August, at the age of seventy.

Byrd had freed himself from debts he incurred in his division of Daniel Parke's legacy with John Custis and in his purchases of land. He bequeathed the bulk of his property to his son. Maria Byrd had been pregnant when her husband left Westover to mark the dividing line on both sides of the Dismal Swamp. She had been near childbirth as he left again to continue the survey in September. The baby was named William, after his father and his grandfather. As a boy, he became "the Peculiar Care of his Father." Byrd played bowls and cards and billiards with him and raced him over frost-covered ground when the father was sixty-six and the son eleven. Byrd brought a tutor from England and heard his son recite lessons, "but was ever Stealling some good Things into Him besides the Languages."

The younger William Byrd was almost sixteen when his father died. He had to wait until he turned twenty-one to come into his inheritance, but his mother did not stint him. He spent more than a year in London, where he was admitted to the Middle Temple, though he found gambling and other entertainments more attractive than the study of law. He returned to Virginia at the age of nineteen and got married to a girl not yet seventeen: Elizabeth Carter, daughter of the late Secretary John Carter and granddaughter of King Carter.

Byrd inherited more than 179,000 acres, about 1,000 slaves, and other properties. He and his wife lived at Belvidere, a small house on high ground with a view of the falls of the James River, where it flowed through "a prodigious extent of wilderness," much of which he owned, passing the village his father had imagined as the city of Richmond.

Fire broke out at Westover on Tuesday night, January 7, 1749, consuming clothing, silver plate, liquor, furniture, and other valuables. The dead William Byrd's manuscripts and books survived in their separate building.

William Byrd, Unknown Artist. Courtesy of the Library of Virginia. The younger William Byrd surrounded himself with beautiful grounds, rooms, objects, and clothing.

Later that year the younger Byrd turned twenty-one, and Westover plantation became his, with his mother retaining use of it. Perhaps with help from the Carters, whose houses showed their familiarity with the new London fashion of Palladian architecture, Byrd began the mansion anew. For several years craftsmen, some from Britain, shaped fancy brickwork, rooms full of wainscotting, impressive fireplaces and furniture, and delicate plasterwork. Byrd bought the best billiard table in Virginia. The lost plate was replaced and enhanced with silver candlesticks, trays, castors, punch bowls, coffeepots, and an epergne for the center of an already gleaming table. Within a few years of the fire, Byrd had given his mansion the same "expensive neatness" that his symmetrical gardens and groomed meadows displayed. Long afterward an old slave told a visitor to Westover that the mansion was about fifty years old in 1803.

Byrd read in his father's will instructions to sell the Land of Eden in North Carolina, as well as lots in Richmond and other property, to pay bequests. He found a buyer named Maxwell, who gave £500 for the Land of Eden, sight unseen. The following spring, just before Maxwell's first trip to the tract, the Dan River flooded. He found more than one-third of his purchase, almost 10,000 acres, under water. Returning to Westover, he expressed "dissatisfaction." Byrd repaid him and resumed title.

Throughout Byrd's life, his civility, his polished manners, and his dignity impressed people. His round face and soft eyes resembled those of his mother, with no sign of his father's sly mask. He was appointed to the Council in May 1754, at the age of twenty-five, succeeding John Lewis, founder of the Loyal Company. Listing nominees, the colony's new resident governor, Robert Dinwiddie, gave Carter Burwell first place, then realized this was a mistake. One councillor, Philip Grymes, was the brother of Burwell's wife; another, William Nelson, was married to Burwell's sister; and the president was Burwell's brother, Lewis. Dinwiddie advised the Board of Trade not to create a Council with four members who were brothers or brothers-in-law. On the Board of Trade's recommendation, the Privy Council chose Byrd to join the body his father had left ten years earlier. In property, in society, in government, the son now held his father's place.

Many years later, looking back on the younger William Byrd's life after 1754, one could easily see that this elegant, charming man had neither inherited nor learned "the power of self-denial." He spent most of his life deeply in debt. His creditors in England heard from their agent in Virginia: "Col. Byrd has a high Sense of Honor and I believe woud not make a promise but where he thought he could perform it, but a warm Imagination supplies many things."

II

A SCHEME OF GREAT EXPECTATION

GRANTS OF LAND, large and small, flowed from Virginia's Council in 1753. One of the largest, with no fixed number of acres, gave the Virginia portion of the Dismal Swamp to four men. Three were merchants in or near Norfolk. Robert Tucker, not content with his growing trade to the West Indies and his work in the House of Burgesses, wished also to "cultivate and improve" the swamp. His friend Edward Hack Moseley owned a plantation in Princess Anne County between the Dismal Swamp and the seacoast. Francis Miller opened trade in the new town of Portsmouth, established the previous year on the south bank of the Elizabeth River, opposite Norfolk, near Tucker's mills and bakery. The fourth member of the group—his name came first in the Council's grant—was Francis Farley, a sugar planter from the island of Antigua, who was visiting friends in Virginia: among others, Robert Tucker and William Nelson.

The Council agreed that the Dismal Swamp was "at present altogether useless." Making it "beneficial" to new owners called for "great Labour and Expence"; so Farley, Moseley, Tucker, and Miller had seven years free of the usual payments to the Crown in which to survey and patent the land.

On the night of Friday, May 4, 1753, three days after the Council's action, Joanna Tucker gave birth to her tenth child, just as her oldest son, Robert, sailed for England, at the age of twelve. The baby, Elizabeth, was baptized a week later. Her godfathers were Edward Hack Moseley, godfather to most of the Tuckers' earlier children, and Francis Farley.

Farley stood at the center of society and commerce among the 3,400 white Antiguans, who lived on the labor of 31,000 slaves. A young newcomer hoping to enter trade could ask for no better help than "Introduceing me to dine at Collo Farleys with a number of Planters." Farley knew many people in the mainland colonies, eight of which he traveled in. Both Antigua and Virginia friends praised his kindness; William Nelson wrote: "He is a good man." Farley said of himself: "neither Ambition nor Avarice influence me much." Others trusted him.

His wife, Eleanor, was the daughter of James Parke, nephew of Antigua's murdered governor, Daniel Parke. The Farleys thus knew the Byrds, who owned the Virginia estates once belonging to Daniel Parke. By his marriage Francis Farley acquired the plantation his wife had inherited from James Parke: 166 acres known as the Mercers Creek estate on the northeastern coast of Antigua. In the rainy season a creek flowed along the southern edge of the plantation, below the fields of sugar cane, and emptied into a small bay, which opened into a larger bay a mile wide, separated from the sea by islands, rocks, and reefs. The northeast trade winds that gave the Leeward Islands their name raised steep swells. These rose higher, sometimes cresting, near the rocks and the coast, making heavy seas for sugar droghers or shallops bearing the plantation's produce to St. Johns. Rising from the sea, the green hills of eastern Antigua overlooked the island and its neighbors. From a summit one could see the central plain, covered with sugar cane, then a steeper range of hills in the west and, in the northwest, less than ten miles away, the capital, St. Johns. In all these sectors Francis Farley owned plantations.

In a productive year, with the work of two hundred slaves, the Mercers Creek estate yielded 140 hogsheads of sugar and 80 hogsheads of rum. Each hogshead of sugar was the product of at least ten tons of cut cane hauled from the fields. Around the plantation's stone windmill tower, where cane was crushed, stood a boiling house, a curing house, a refining house, a rum distillery, a trash house, and a cooper's shop. Skilled slaves working as coopers needed about 6,500 staves, often from Virginia, to make 140 hogsheads. The frenetic, yet precise, labor of boiling, clarifying, and curing came sixteen or eighteen months after the first and hardest work: digging holes with hoes, planting cane, and manuring the field. This work, under white overseers and black "dog-drivers," filled almost all daylight hours six days a week.

One of Francis Farley's sisters was married to Alexander Willock, Antigua's most important merchant. They lived on a plantation in the northwestern part of the island, near St. Johns. In town the wharf held hogsheads of sugar, thousands each year. The customhouse stood along the water's edge at the foot of High Street. About five hundred low houses, made of wood and covered with broad shingles, lined wide streets, leading uphill from the harbor to the heights and the army barracks. An assistant justice of the Court of Common Pleas, Francis Farley spent hours in a long ground-floor room of the new stone courthouse at the center of town. The governor, Council, and Assembly held their meetings upstairs. The courthouse had been built on a site once used as a marketplace. Slaves now held their Sunday market on the southern edge of town. Hundreds of black people offered for sale pigs, chickens, goats, yams, eddoes, plantains, and other fruits and vegetables raised on small plots they farmed for their own benefit. The St. Johns market attracted vendors and visitors from all parts of the island. Each year, vessels from the western coast of Africa, sailing windward of the shoal, under the guns of the fort overlooking St. Johns Harbor, entered with replacements for slaves who had died.

Francis Farley lived part of the time at Mercers Creek and part at his plantation called Murrays, a short ride southeast of the capital. The road out of St. Johns, cresting the heights, revealed a ridge stretching southward, parallel to the coast. Where hills were fertile, sugar cane waved in the wind. Along the eastern base of the slope, Farley owned two plantations: Hamiltons and Farleys Garden. Extending to the northwest of the island and to the south stretched an archipelago of steep-sloped green islands, many devoted to sugar.

Farley watched not only his own plantation but also those of men living in England. He was a trusted attorney, or agent, supervising young Scottish overseers. Some people thought that working for others as an attorney yielded a more reliable income than owning a plantation. But Farley said that he served without pay and lost money by neglecting his own business. Antigua's planters and merchants strove to amass fortunes from sugar. A newcomer noticed: "Every Man seems to live here with a View to some other Place to which he hopes to remove at some future Period." Farley's friend Samuel Martin, a veteran planter, kept warning that ruin awaited the sugar islands from repeated droughts, from French invasion, or from other threats. In the summer of 1751, before Farley left for Virginia, Martin advised his son to invest in "Lands in North America, as a safe retreat."

Farley had two brothers: John lived in England; Simon lived in Antigua. Francis and Simon agreed to invest jointly in Virginia land. Leaving Antigua during an epidemic of fever, Francis Farley sailed for Virginia in 1755. In Norfolk he learned that his goddaughter had died the previous summer and that Joanna Tucker was pregnant again. One of his partners in the Dismal Swamp grant, Francis Miller of Portsmouth, bought a plantation jointly with the Farley brothers. The Antiguans relied on Miller to represent their interests in their absence. The three men purchased four tracts, totaling more than 1,000 acres, thickly timbered, near the Dismal Swamp along the main road 12 miles west of Norfolk. Sixteen miles farther west lay the growing town of Suffolk, where a new courthouse for Nansemond County was almost finished.

Farley visited the Byrds at Westover. His stay came at the end of a summer of harsh drought. Travelers saw fields of withered corn stalks and parched, stunted tobacco. At Westover in October, Farley bought the Land of Eden. William Byrd could show Farley, who had not seen the 25,800 acres, his father's manuscript book of land titles. Old Colonel Byrd had called the soil "as rich as any in Egypt or on the Banks of Euphrates." Farley offered £1,000 sterling, and Byrd accepted, making a deed to Francis and Simon Farley. As Farley passed through Norfolk on his way back to Antigua, he could congratulate Robert Tucker, the new high sheriff of Norfolk County.

Simon Farley died the following year. Francis came into sole control of the Land of Eden and of the tracts near the Dismal Swamp after buying Miller's one-third share. Francis always thought of himself as holding Simon's share in trust for Simon's son and daughter, but he never conveyed title. Twenty years later, Francis Farley valued his investment "in a very growing country" at more than £3,000. He had come to believe that Britain was "a very declining almost ruined country." One was wise to hold "valuable property" in North America. Farley, Robert Tucker, Edward Hack Moseley, and Francis Miller did not survey and patent the Dismal Swamp within seven years. Their grant lapsed. Even so, Farley and Tucker still wished to own and drain the swamp.

During Farley's visit, Virginia was at war. Although the colony had only a small part in worldwide rivalry between Britain and France, Virginians began the fighting, and many people traced the war to the colony's new resident governor, Robert Dinwiddie.

Taking the oath of office in Williamsburg on November 21, 1751, Dinwiddie returned to a familiar place with new authority. Since 1738 he had been surveyor general of Customs for Pennsylvania, the southern colonies, the Bahamas, and Jamaica. He settled in Virginia in 1741. His office gave him a seat on the Council, which he took over the objections of other councillors. He won advancement from Robert Walpole and the Duke of Newcastle, exposing frauds in customs offices and collecting duties more stringently. Virginians knew Dinwiddie's cool stare, clenched jaw, and compressed lips—the face of a longtime tax collector. They knew him both as a servant of the Crown and as a man "bred up in the way of turning a penny the rite way, into his own pocket." He had done this so well that some Virginians borrowed money from him.

Dinwiddie set out to collect more taxes. He demanded that recipients of almost 1,000,000 acres in grants pay arrears of quitrents they had evaded by not taking patents. Calling them "land jobbers," he said their conduct was "a Fraud to that Revenue." He added almost 300,000 acres to the rent rolls in his first two years. This angered many burgesses and others, but they grew "too warm to be reasoned with" after he introduced a new fee, payable to him. With the Council's approval, he proposed to charge one Spanish pistole, a coin worth almost £1 sterling, to sign patents for land surveyed after April 22, 1752. Dinwiddie's critics denounced his greed, mocked his Scots accent, and tried to raise "a very general Disgust & Alarm." They pledged to defend liberty by sending to London an agent able to deprive him of support from the Board of Trade. William Stith, president of the College of William and Mary—the college licensed surveyors for a fee—said he would "break the Neck" of the governor's pistole fee. Speaker Robinson opposed Dinwiddie bluntly; the burgesses chose Robinson's ally, Peyton Randolph, to go to London. With good reason, Dinwiddie feared that "some Managem't" there would turn the Board of Trade against him. He told its members that Virginians' anger arose not so much from the "petty Fee" as from the quitrents he had pressed them to pay at last.

Dinwiddie did not oppose all land-jobbing and westward expansion. A member of the Ohio Company, two months after taking office, he wrote: "I have the Success and Prosperity of the Ohio Company much at heart." Virginia ought to gain a larger share of the trade with western Indians who dealt mainly with Pennsylvanians and with the French. Philip Ludwell Lee persuaded his colleagues in the company to appoint a factor whose father had been in partnership with Dinwiddie. Lee reported that the governor "likes this man well." The company also expected to profit by settling tenants on its grant. The Delawares, Shawnees, and Iroquois of the Ohio River watershed, pressed by both French and British, wanted no such encroachments. As the company's agent, Christopher Gist, traveled the region to map it, he kept his compass out of sight and posed as an emissary from the king. He lied to the Delawares, who nevertheless correctly "suspected he came to settle their lands." After Pennsylvania's officials decided not to build a fort, Virginians urged the leader of the Ohio Iroquois, Tanacharison, to accept both a fort and the white people's—that is, the Ohio Company's—claim to land. At the Logg's Town meeting in the first two weeks of June 1752, Virginians got what they sought and handed out wampum, liquor, butter, salt, cornmeal, beef, and tobacco. But the Indians still did not want settlers.

Dinwiddie's alliance with the Ohio Company and his push into the Ohio Valley aroused "unfavourable Surmises" in the minds of "many Gentlemen that had a share in Government." Speaker Robinson and his friends had no wish to serve the interests of the Lees or of the Ohio Company. Anyone convinced that Dinwiddie desired above all to make money could believe that he would "go to the French & provoke them." When he warned that the French were invading Virginia, he aroused suspicion that this was "a Fiction; and Scheme to promote the Interest of a private Company." In 1752, Dinwiddie called on the burgesses to counteract French designs by overtures to western Indians and by improving the militia. The General Assembly did nothing to help Dinwiddie's advance in the Ohio Valley but exempt settlers along western waters from taxes for ten years.

The French and their new governor, the Marquis Duquesne, were invading Virginia only by trying to expel British traders from the Ohio Valley and by claiming the forks of the Ohio and the land west of the Allegheny Mountains. Their presence in the upper valley disturbed the Duke of Newcastle, the ministry in London, Governor Dinwiddie, and members of the Ohio Company more than it disturbed other Virginians. Soldiers sent beyond the mountains by the French and British governments went looking for a fight. The British ministry told Dinwiddie that he could build a fort, as the Ohio Company had promised to do, sent him artillery, and said that French interference or French attempts to construct a fort were aggression. A few weeks later, Duquesne ordered French troops farther south along the Allegheny River toward the forks of the Ohio.

When news of this reached Williamsburg, with warnings that the Ohio Company's traders must flee, George Washington offered his services to Governor Dinwiddie. Washington's older half brother, Lawrence, had died in July 1752, when George was twenty years old, and George would inherit Mount Vernon. Washington aspired to distinction, preferably military. Dinwiddie tried to alarm the House of Burgesses with the French menace, but Speaker Robinson and his friends cared more about the pistole fee. Unable to make a show of force in the west, Dinwiddie and the Council nevertheless sent Washington to the upper Ohio Valley to tell the French to leave. Even with the guidance of Christopher Gist, he had a hard time finding some Frenchmen to threaten. He accomplished a long, dangerous march, but he won no support from the Iroquois and no respect from the French. Dinwiddie provided materials for the Ohio Company's fort at the forks of the Ohio.

In April 1754 the French seized that uncompleted fort and established their own, Fort Duquesne. George Washington, with 150 men, was on his way toward it when he learned that it had fallen. He moved near the French, though his force could not rival theirs. He invited combat, which ended with his surrender in the first week of July. Three weeks later, Dinwiddie asked the government to send British regiments to Virginia. In September the

Duke of Newcastle, with the help of the Duke of Cumberland, persuaded the king to do so. Newcastle thought the British could repel French aggression at the forks of the Ohio without starting a war. But Cumberland and others wished to attack the French at many points. Before the British regiments marched toward Fort Duquesne, French officials, explaining British aggression, found its excuse in the Ohio Company's claims. The Comte de Jouy wrote in February 1755: "The grants made to merchants in the Ohio territory are the work of the English government. They may even be regarded as the origin of the present dispute."

The year 1754 was hard on Robert Dinwiddie in more ways than military defeat. The burgesses voted only £10,000 for troops and arms, an insultingly small sum. In February, with the Council's assent, he offered free land in the Ohio Valley to men who would volunteer for military service. He seemed preoccupied with "rich soil" and "Millions of Acres" that might be lost to the French. The volunteers did not make an impressive force. Dinwiddie tried to get other colonies to send soldiers. All, except North Carolina, refused, though he arranged for the Board of Trade to order the governor of South Carolina to send some. A "general opinion" prevailed in Pennsylvania that Virginia land companies were trying "to embroil all colonies in a war to defend their lands." A few weeks after learning of Washington's surrender, Dinwiddie received the Board of Trade's ruling on his pistole fee. Their instructions confined his collection of a fee so narrowly that it would yield little. He grew more strident. His speech to the burgesses in August reminded them that France oppressed Britons in Asia and America. He warned that for many years the French had been planning to rule the world with a "universal Monarchy." The burgesses voted £20,000 for Virginia's forces and included in the appropriation £2,500 to repay Speaker Robinson, who had advanced money from the treasury for Peyton Randolph's trip to London to undercut Dinwiddie's pistole fee. The governor and the Council rejected this bill, thereby losing the £20,000 until October. Soldiers serving with Washington went unpaid and ill supplied. They said they had been "bubbled." Many deserted; complaints by others discouraged new enlistments. In October the burgesses authorized justices of the peace to draft unemployed men.

During the October session, Speaker Robinson tried to make the frustrated governor feel better. With his usual charm, he called on Dinwiddie and asked pardon for the burgesses' "great ill manners." Robinson could afford to be conciliatory, since the Board of Trade, beyond burying the pistole fee, had told Dinwiddie to reappoint Peyton Randolph to the post of attorney general. He found doing so "very disagreeable." Though outwardly on "a very good Footing" with Robinson, the governor expected to get even with the speaker after the next election by not allowing him to remain both speaker and treasurer. Dinwiddie complained that newspapers published "unjust and false" criticism. In November and December he became the object of satire, circulated in manuscript. He found himself portrayed in verse as a greedy, cowardly, lying warmonger. A mock-rustic letter making fun of Scots and opposing war with France was shown to him. The governor "said that the Author of that, & of the Poem too, might kiss his honrs. A-se." Speaker Robinson for his part, upon reading the satires, smiled.

Dinwiddie learned in mid-December that two British regiments were coming to Virginia to take Fort Duquesne. The government's strategy also called for the capture of Fort Niagara, of Crown Point on Lake Champlain, and of Fort Beauséjour in Acadia. British troops and Virginia recruits needed supplies. Dinwiddie appointed two commissaries: Dr. Thomas Walker and Charles Dick, a merchant in Fredericksburg and partner with Walker in the Loyal Company. Using their own credit, they must find contractors to furnish cattle, horses, wagons, and flour. Despite low pay, £200 in Virginia currency, they undertook the work, Dick mainly in Fredericksburg, Walker on the road. Walker went to Philadelphia in February 1755 to get help from "the Ingenius Franklin" and the Assembly of Pennsylvania, arranging delivery of 14,000 bushels of wheat. To assist Lewis Evans's work on a new map, Walker recalled details from his western explorations on behalf of the Loyal Company. Cynics in London said that the regiments were ordered to go by way of Virginia rather than Pennsylvania because the ministry listened to John Hanbury, who received a commission of 2½ percent for transferring money to the army in Virginia. Hanbury was a member of the Ohio Company; the army began its march at an Ohio Company post on the Potomac River and cut a road along a familiar route toward the company's lost fort. Lewis Evans disputed the cynics, showing by his map that the army followed the shortest, easiest approach.

While Walker was in Philadelphia, General Edward Braddock, commander of the expeditionary force, arrived in Williamsburg, soon followed to Virginia by troopships and the fleet commanded by Commodore Augustus Keppel. Walker joined Braddock for the march toward the French, as did George Washington, still aspiring to a military career. Washington included both Speaker Robinson and Governor Dinwiddie among those he called "*my Friends.*" Though he said he pursued no "lucrative ends," he had the general's promise of "preferment equal to my Wishes."

Braddock grew more and more angry with Dr. Walker and with Virginians as he spent several weeks along the upper Potomac, surrounded by raw logs of the new Fort Cumberland, which an Englishwoman called "the most desolate Place I ever saw." Braddock deplored his "daily Experience of the Falsehood of every person with whom I was concerned." He got stinking meat, corn instead of wheat, moldy biscuit, and too few horses and wagons. Though one of Walker's contractors for cattle failed to deliver, blaming the House of Burgesses but offering to deliver later at a further markup of 33⅓ percent, Walker and Dick said they had furnished enough provisions. By the time Braddock's army headed across the mountains, it had accumulated too many wagons, horses, and supplies. Walker recalled the "grave smiles" with which a Philadelphia Quaker had tried to shave 2,000 bushels of wheat off of Virginia's order. Yet Benjamin Franklin and Pennsylvanians won praise from the British, who damned Virginians for "Bragging and false Promises."

Thomas Walker rode in Braddock's column as it slowly climbed the Allegheny ridge, following axmen who cleared a narrow road through the forest. George Washington was eager for the army to push ahead more quickly, but "the old Soldiers" were "all uneasy for Fear of being attack'd on the long March in Defiles." With a few wagons and provisions, Walker accompanied Braddock and 1,200 men, leaving part of the force behind and advancing along the Monongahela River, within less than eight miles of Fort Duquesne. And Dr. Walker came under fire on July 9, as the enemy—250 Frenchmen and Canadians, with 640 Indian allies—sprang their ambush from the woods above the Monongahela. After three hours of intense but confused fighting, during which the British fired into one another, their retreat began. Wagon drivers and others bore the wounded Braddock in a litter. Neither Walker nor George Washington was hurt, though musket balls pierced Washington's coat. Walker lost two horses and his gear, including his spare clothes. He stayed with Braddock until the general died four days later. Then he accompanied the remnants of the column back along the new mountain road to Fort Cumberland. Braddock's successor, Colonel Thomas Dunbar, moved his force to Philadelphia, taking Dr. Walker with him.

Thomas Walker and Charles Dick had trouble obtaining reimbursement from the House of Burgesses. Speaker Robinson and the new committee supervising expenditures demanded vouchers and receipts. Walker's accounts were not settled until the following spring. Nevertheless, he and Dick continued to serve, obtaining beef and pork for the Virginia regiment. Under the command of Colonel George Washington, it was the colony's western defense.

General Braddock had hoped to be joined by Indian allies. The Delawares wished the British to expel the French; yet no Delaware men had come to Braddock after his conversation with their emissaries. The general died without knowing all the results of his words to Shingas, their leader: "No Savage Should Inherit the Land." Though Indians of the Ohio Valley sought to get rid of the French, they could see that British success would bring the Ohio Company and others into the valley more quickly. Braddock's failure made alliance with the French look advantageous and politic. During the summer after that defeat and in later months, Indian allies attacked the westernmost British colonists, killing cattle, burning crops and houses, "cutting off numbers of families." Outlying farmers fled their homes, moving toward safety "in droves of fifties." Thomas Walker fed cattle for Washington's men with corn left standing in the fields. The Loyal Company's surveyors stopped work; its settlers abandoned their tracts. Escorting ammunition for the Greenbrier Company, James Patton encountered Indians in a meadow above the headwaters of the Roanoke River. They killed him.

The burgesses moved slowly. Only after Braddock failed, Indians raided, and Charles Dick refused to provide further supplies without payment did the burgesses appropriate large sums for the war. They relied chiefly upon paper currency. The colony printed it, spent it, then drew it back into the treasury by a head tax, a land tax, and taxes on slaves. These treasury notes were redeemable with interest at specified future dates. Between May 1755 and March 1756 the burgesses authorized an emission of £115,000; the amount soon grew much larger.

Too few men enlisted in Washington's regiment, even after the colony offered a bounty of £10. The militia, which one Virginian called "a mere Farce," would not stay long in the field. Speaker Robinson told Dinwiddie: "they will all desert." Some lawyers offered to defend deserters for a small fee. In June 1756, Washington's force at Winchester was shrinking. Dinwiddie and Washington envisioned a chain of forts in the west. Washington proposed a provincial force of 2,000 regulars; rumors in eastern Virginia said that he tried to deceive the burgesses with a false alarm about the Indian threat "to cause the Assembly to levy largely both in Money & Men." The burgesses eventually authorized forts in the Shenandoah Valley and as many troops as Washington had requested, but a majority opposed "the most vigorous measures" and rejected Richard Bland's scheme to attack Fort Duquesne.

After Virginia raised a second regiment, William Byrd became its commander in the summer of 1758 at the age of twenty-nine. Early in 1756 he and Peter Randolph had gone to South Carolina to win allies for the British among the Catawbas and the Cherokees, whose men fought in Virginia and Pennsylvania. At the end of 1756, Byrd traveled to Nova Scotia to join the

Earl of Loudoun at Halifax. Loudoun took a liking to him; Byrd accompanied the regulars on their campaign. In the spring of 1758 he returned to the Cherokees. His "good Offices and Generosity" enabled him to bring more fighting men to the Shenandoah Valley.

Travel took Byrd away from his troubles in Virginia. In the summer of 1754 he said that he was "surprised and sorry" that a bill of exchange he had drawn was returned protested. Soon, his bad bills surprised no one. He borrowed money from Governor Dinwiddie. After selling the Land of Eden to Francis Farley, he drew a bill for £1,000 on a merchant, James Buchanan, getting Mann Page to endorse it, despite Page's heavy debts. Byrd's creditors grew more pressing in 1756.

At the same time, Byrd lost patience with his wife. Though Elizabeth Carter Byrd was the mother of five children, she sometimes still behaved like the sixteen-year-old Byrd had married: buying more "finery" than she could wear, lying in bed until noon, and sending peremptory letters to her mother-in-law at Westover. Maria Byrd sarcastically labeled her "the Belvidere lady." George Washington heard in August 1756 that William Byrd had repudiated his wife and that she was "in a Dilirium for his Behaviour." Byrd sent their three oldest children to his relatives in England and avoided his wife. In one of her plaintive letters to him, she described herself as "your wife, that you once honored with your love." Before leaving for Halifax, Byrd advertised in the *Virginia Gazette* to tell his creditors that his property and affairs now lay in the hands of trustees: his friends Speaker Robinson, Peyton Randolph, Peter Randolph, and Presley Thornton; his wife's brother, Charles Carter; his sister's husband, John Page; and his business manager, Charles Turnbull. His deed of trust ordered them to pay Byrd's mother £500 per year and his wife "what they think necessary."

While Byrd marched with the Earl of Loudoun and met with Attakullakulla among the Cherokees, his "many importunate Creditors" pursued his trustees, who said they might have to sell his estate. They gave bonds on his property to cover his protested bills. Late in July 1760, Elizabeth Byrd, with her two youngest children, visited her brother at Corotoman. There she died at the age of twenty-eight. The Carters said she had an accident. Her mother later convinced William and Elizabeth Byrd's oldest son that Elizabeth "had been badly used" by the Byrds. William Byrd's financial situation that fall was "Terrible"; his trustees believed that his debts almost equaled his assets. In January 1761 he was married again.

George Washington resigned his command at the end of 1758. He was succeeded by William Byrd. Washington had entered military service declaring: "I have . . . resolution to Face what any Man durst." He attracted notice and praise from the Nelson brothers, Speaker Robinson, Governor Dinwiddie, Philip Ludwell, Warner Lewis, General Braddock, and Governor William Shirley of Massachusetts. Though the burgesses remained skeptical about Dinwiddie's war, refusing to give Washington all he requested, they thought highly of him and twice voted him their thanks. Still, he often complained and spoke of resigning. His grandest ambitions went unfulfilled. He wished to be taken, with his regiment, onto the regular establishment of the British Army. British and provincial forces with their Indian allies ought to advance boldly, he said, and take Fort Duquesne in the summer of 1758. They did not; he vented his frustration to Speaker Robinson: "That appearance of Glory once in view—that hope—that laudable Ambition of Serving Our Country, and meriting its applause, is now no more!"

The fall of Fort Duquesne came almost as an anticlimax. In October, the Delawares and the Shawnees abandoned their alliance with the French. Late the following month, just before British troops arrived, the small garrison blew up their fortifications, set fire to the barracks and other buildings, then fled.

By the time Washington stood among the ruins of Fort Duquesne, his mind already had turned toward his postwar career. On a trip to Williamsburg in March he had again met Martha Dandridge Custis, a widow for the past eight months. She was being "attacked" by Charles Carter, whose hopes made him "very gay." But Martha Custis and George Washington soon agreed to be married. Four months after his betrothal, he won election to the House of Burgesses from Frederick County. At the end of the year he resigned his commission. On Saturday, January 6, 1759, he and Martha Custis were wed.

Through this union, George Washington acquired an amiable wife, a suffering epileptic stepdaughter, a spoiled stepson, a substantial fortune, and a tedious lawsuit. Martha Washington's first husband, Daniel Parke Custis, was the son of John Custis and grandson of Daniel Parke, assassinated governor of Antigua. John Custis had outlived his wife, had managed his property prudently, and had left his son a rich estate. George Washington now controlled that legacy.

The estate might have been larger had John Custis not spent so much money on litigation. The husband of Governor Daniel Parke's "little bastard" daughter in Antigua pursued Custis with a suit in Chancery, trying to make him pay debts Parke's estate had incurred in Antigua. The plaintiff's heirs continued the suit after his death. At the time of Martha Dandridge and Daniel Parke Custis's wedding in 1750, the suit had lasted for twenty-seven years. During her widowhood, her attorney complained that he had received less payment for representing the Custis cause than Secretary Nelson had received in fees for copies of papers used in the suit. Speaker Robinson became legal guardian of the two Custis children, lending his weight to their side, but the case in Chancery wore on. George Washington was still paying attorneys' fees fifty years after John Custis first had been sued under Daniel Parke's will—written, Custis said of his father-in-law, "possibly to please that adultrous strumpet, who so unfortunately intoxicated him."

Washington wished to own much more land. He planned large purchases and sought grants in the Ohio Valley promised to veterans by Dinwiddie. He and George Mercer, a partner in the Ohio Company, agreed to meet in Williamsburg in November 1759 and there "leave no Stone unturned to secure ourselves this Land." It promised so much profit that they would have to fight for it. Mercer detected "mighty Schemers" who conspired to get "all the best Land" by keeping the surveying in their own hands, excluding him. One of his rivals, Adam Stephen, slyly said: "I find the advantage of the Ohio lands despised" by the burgesses, even as he worked the capitol to make himself and his friends "absolute Proprietors." The French had withdrawn only a year past. Around its ruins, one could still trace outlines of the fosse of Fort Duquesne. Yet Virginians already wrangled over the spoils of victory.

Two harsh wartime droughts, in 1755 and 1758, left Virginia with two of its smallest crops of tobacco. In the latter year many planters grew none. Virginia's exports fell from more than 49,000 hogsheads to 24,169, of which 5,000 came from an earlier crop. In August, Dr. Thomas Walker heard an estimate that the colony's income from the year's tobacco would be £250,000 sterling less than usual. One could only guess because a shortage drove up prices. In May 1757, the "common Price" in Hanover County was 20 shillings for a hundredweight—112 pounds of tobacco. In June 1758, it had risen to 30 shillings, "all cash." In January 1759, it stood at 40 shillings, and some planters held out for 50. Even a merchant ready to pay cash was "continually riding" to find a cargo.

The colony's laws and longtime practice made taxes and fees, with a few exceptions, payable only in tobacco, as were many private debts. Crop notes and transfer notes issued by inspectors showed how much tobacco a planter had deposited in public warehouses; these circulated in lieu of transferring tobacco from hand to hand. But contracts, debts, public levies, and salaries fixed when tobacco sold for twopence per pound or less fell due in tobacco worth twice as much at the end of 1758. Amid the first drought in 1755, the House of Burgesses passed a bill by a majority of one, over Speaker Robinson's opposition, making obligations due in tobacco payable in cash at a rate of twopence per pound of tobacco. This provision expired after ten months. In 1758 the burgesses and the Council voted almost unanimously for another Twopenny Act, to last twelve months. They said the law was "founded upon the principles of Humanity and Justice intended to preserve the people from Rapine and Oppression." Planters could sell their tobacco for cash at the new, high price, then pay their creditors, usually merchants, at the law's lower rate. The larger a planter's property in land and slaves, the more money he saved by paying his taxes in cash rather than in tobacco.

Most Virginians paid their debts to merchants each year and owed less than £50. Even so, more planters were buying more goods from Britain, running up larger debts. With exaggeration, a British writer said of Virginia planters in 1757: "they live in general luxuriously, and to the full extent of their fortunes."

In the first years of his marriage, George Washington did so. He bought land and slaves; he spent more than £350 each year on china, silver, and decorative objects for Mount Vernon. Within five years he found that these things had "swallowed up before I well knew where I was, all the money I got by Marriage nay more, brought me in Debt." He owed £1,800 to his London merchant.

Virginia was growing. At the start of the war with France, the colony held 230,000 people. When war ended, there were 340,000. Counties split to form new counties. More land came into cultivation, and more slave ships arrived from Africa and the West Indies. Though many people delayed payment, Virginians were good customers. A British officer said that, while a Pennsylvania farmer would buy a durable kersey coat, a Virginia planter would buy something gaudy. Storekeepers spread throughout the colony, purchasing tobacco, selling merchandise, and, to win customers, extending easy credit. Always seeking a good investment, Dr. Thomas Walker put up one-third of the capital for a new store in Charlottesville in 1761. Three years later he had "a Great Deal of money Due to him."

Many of the new young men came from Scotland and worked for companies opening strings of retail stores. Known as factors, they strove to get the trade of "the common People . . . who make up the Bulk of the Planters."

They did so well that Virginians came to speak routinely of "Scotch stores." Scots specialized in inferior grades of tobacco, which made up most of the crop and was re-exported from Britain to France. It had one buyer: the French state monopoly, the Farmers-General. Since that market was certain and growing, Scottish companies confidently extended credit to Virginians, knowing that money spent on land and slaves would yield more tobacco. Money spent on merchandise marked up 100 percent, 150 percent, or 200 percent came back to the factor's company as profit. Long credit excused a higher markup.

To rise in the esteem of his employers and to return to Britain with a modest fortune, a factor needed ambition. As the number of merchants in Virginia grew, competition increased. Even so, in the 1750s and 1760s the Scots' share of Britain's tobacco trade steadily rose until they controlled more than half. The great Glasgow firms had found the enterprising men they needed. One of the quickest ways to get a planter's tobacco—some said the only way—was to lend money or extend credit. In 1760 a planter could "command double the Cash his Tobo was worth besides credit for what goods he had occasion for." This method of business was called "engaging of Customers."

Virginians often said that they disliked Scottish merchants as a group. Scots for their part seldom hid their opinion of colonial planters, whom they called "common buckskins." The mayor, aldermen, and Common Council of Norfolk demanded a public apology from some young Scottish merchants and others two days after the mayor took office in 1755. On election day the young men had chosen their own mayor: Richard Scott's slave, Will. They "seated him and drank to him as Mr. Mayor by way of Derision." As debts swelled in the following years, many Virginians concluded that these people who had lent them money had made fools of them, that they were "held in Derision by the Merchts . . . of the Metropolis & Factors of Glascow." They discerned a pattern: Scots took care of one another; Scots had "secrets in the Tobo Trade"; Scots were "Engrossers." With "the artful Craftiness and Cunning natural to that Nation," Scots had conspired to grow rich at the expense of Virginia. By this line of thought, victims saw themselves as "unfortunate Debtors," reduced to "Vasalage & Dependance."

Virginians remained optimistic, seeking more land and more slaves. Though they were promising to pay 5 percent interest on their debts, might their property not rise in value at an even greater rate? They needed only "prudent Management," frugality, and higher prices for tobacco. Rather than resort to slow courts, merchants often found it simpler to take a debtor's bond and hope for the best. The "maxims so generally *embraced*" in Virginia, Robert Beverley wrote in 1761, were: "being in Debt & making great Promises for the future."

Virginia had few if any debtors more stubborn than John Syme of Hanover County. He ran up a large account in the 1750s with Lidderdale, Harmer & Farell, merchants in Bristol, who shipped goods to him on credit and lent him money by accepting his bills of exchange. He consigned his tobacco to them, but its value fell far short of the advances he received.

Turning twenty-one in 1750, Syme came into possession of his late father's estate. He knew his father's face; he had the same "remarkably homely" features. The elder William Byrd noticed this when Syme was only four years old. Byrd said that, although Syme's lively, cheerful widowed mother "seem'd not to pine too much for the Death of her Husband," no one could doubt that her little son was legitimate. To celebrate his new independence Syme built a house overlooking the South Anna River, sparing no expense on a granite foundation, rose-colored brick, sandstone quoins, pedimented doorways, and rich interior woodwork. By the spring of 1753 he was "beginning housekeeping." His wife was Mildred Meriwether, daughter of Dr. Thomas Walker's wife by her first marriage. The Symes' first son was born in 1752. On the recommendation of Peter Randolph, Syme shipped 50 hogsheads to Lidderdale, Harmer & Farell, then began to "Draw largely" on them, promising to ship 100 hogsheads from his new crop. The following year he was "Oblig'd to draw largely" to buy slaves. He won a seat in the House of Burgesses in 1756 and allied with John Chiswell, father of Speaker Robinson's new sweetheart. Syme and Robinson jointly owned tobacco warehouses in Hanover County. The speaker put him on one of the most important committees. "My situation in a Publick Place," he explained to his Bristol merchants, "Obliges me to live in a Way, somewhat Expensive." In a visit to Syme's home and to other plantations, an English clergyman found Virginians hospitable but guilty of "extravagance, ostentation, and a disregard of economy."

Syme assured Lidderdale, Harmer & Farell that his influence would obtain consignments and customers for them. He did get a shipment of tobacco and an order for goods from his mother-in-law. Despite the short crop of 1755, Syme drew more large bills of exchange in 1756. This time, however, the Bristol firm returned his bills protested. He renewed them, promising not to draw more than £300 in bills each year, but he drew for much larger sums. Joseph Farell, forming a new firm, protested to Syme, saying that he and his partners had to live. Syme replied: "I am heartily for your living, & that you would let me live also." He asked for a loan of £1,000 to buy slaves. He and a partner opened a store, for which Syme ordered a stock of goods. After Farell refused to advance more, Syme got store goods from Glasgow on fifteen months' credit.

In 1763, Syme promised to "Clear off the old score," nearing £6,000 sterling, but thereafter he shipped too little tobacco to meet his current account, much less reduce his debt. To the new firm, Farell & Jones, he described a series of schemes for raising money to pay them: import a stud for his thirty or forty mares and breed horses; start a commercial gristmill; collect thousands of pounds owed to him in Virginia. Syme sought help from Farell & Jones to win the lucrative post of surveyor general of Customs in the southern district, now that its former occupant, Peter Randolph, had died. He wrote: "I always knew Colo. Randolph's Were of a *Short Liv'd Family* & I was Contented to Wait for a Vacancy." Instead of aiding him, Farell & Jones returned his bills of exchange protested, then returned them a second and a third time after he renewed them. Syme complained: "my Old Freinds, for whom I have Done so much, are Determin'd to Ruin my Credit."

Syme had many assets, amounting, Farell & Jones heard, to £15,000 or £20,000. The partners realized that Syme was "trifling" with them. Having promised that Dr. Walker would give a bond as security for the debt, Syme instead produced a letter from "his toadeater," John Hawkins, a "worthless sharping sort of a fellow," who offered to be Syme's security. The firm wanted not Hawkins's bonds but Syme's tobacco, remittances, and payment of damages for protested bills. Syme told Farell & Jones: "nothing has ever given me so much *Pain* as this affair, & your Usage to me lately." He never would have run up so large a debt, he said, but "for advantages Promis'd me, wch you now refuse." The firm ordered a suit brought against him. He began to avoid the sheriff.

Robert Dinwiddie concluded that he had made a bad bargain with the Earl of Albemarle for dividing the income of the governorship of Virginia. In the spring of 1755, Dinwiddie regretted having taken the office. Though another fifteen years of life lay before him, he felt ill. In the fall of 1756 he asked the Board of Trade to relieve him of the governorship, and late in 1757 he returned to England. The Board of Trade and the Privy Council chose as his successor Francis Fauquier, a trim, handsome man in his mid-fifties, as affable as Dinwiddie was dour.

Fauquier had an elegant demeanor and refined taste for good living. He knew William Hogarth and other artists; he also knew George Frederick Handel. He was a Fellow of the Royal Society; he had published an essay on the political economy of financing war with France. He sought the lieutenant governorship, rumor said, because he needed money. Virginians were told that Fauquier, an avid gambler, had lost so much money to Admiral George Anson, first lord of the Admiralty, that Anson felt obliged to use his influence to get the resident governorship for him. In London, Fauquier's behavior showed that "no Governor ever went abroad better disposed to make a people happy."

Robert Dinwiddie thought that some Virginians, especially Speaker Robinson and his friends, were already too happy. Dinwiddie appeared before the Board of Trade to urge that Robinson not remain both speaker and treasurer. Dinwiddie called Fauquier "a very good-natured Gentleman"; he thought the new governor needed "some directions . . . upon this point." Two days later Fauquier met with the Board of Trade, who told him what Dinwiddie had said and pressed him to end the "highly improper" practice of giving both offices to the same man. The vessel bearing Fauquier to Virginia also held letters from Dinwiddie, exulting that he had gained a victory over the speaker.

Fauquier took the oath of office in Williamsburg on June 5, 1758. Within three weeks the "principal People" had convinced him that John Robinson would be speaker and treasurer for life. Robinson had learned of Dinwiddie's appearance before the Board of Trade, and he was vexed. He dismissed it as Dinwiddie's attempt at revenge for loss of the pistole fee. The Nelson brothers, Peyton Randolph, and others scared Fauquier by saying that a mere attempt to deny Robinson one of his offices "might throw the Country into a Flame." The governor told the Board of Trade that only by winning the good opinion of the speaker's friends could he get appropriations for the colony's defense. On September 14 the burgesses unanimously re-elected Robinson speaker. He remained treasurer. A few weeks later a visitor to Williamsburg wrote: "The Govr is in general well Spoken off."

In the fall session Fauquier assented to an emission of paper money, though merchants in Britain objected vehemently. He assented to the Twopenny Act, though merchants protested and clergymen of the established Church felt cheated. They said their rightful annual salary was 16,000 pounds of tobacco no matter how short the crop or high the price. Governor Fauquier was violating his instructions. Only in this way, he wrote the Board of Trade, could he gain influence among the councillors and burgesses. He knew that he had won the esteem of the speaker and his friends. Peyton Randolph published a pamphlet in Williamsburg, defending the colony's currency. In it he addressed Fauquier: "it is the Patriot GOVERNOR alone that can represent the Patriot KING. Nor deem thou this as a Drop bubbling from the nauseous Fountain of Flattery."

The governor's house, grandly called a palace, was pleasant to visit in Fauquier's time. He played music well, joining other amateurs in weekly concerts. Champagne, white Rhine wine, Tokay, and malmsey flowed. Speaker Robinson called every so often. Fauquier thought him "the Darling of the Country, as he well deserves to be." Before long, it became clear that the quickest way to get something from the governor was to approach the speaker; "for by a proper exertion of his Interest, which is very prevailing at the Palace, any reasonable point might be carried." The Earl of Halifax, his colleagues on the Board of Trade, and others in London thought that Fauquier was too good-natured and eager to please. The governor ought not to be so accommodating to "designing People." Learning of aspersions cast on Fauquier, the speaker and the councillors came to his defense. The colony's committee of correspondence sent a letter, prepared by Peyton Randolph and others, to their agent in London, urging him to prevent any "ill impressions" arising from Fauquier's conduct. The governor, they said, had given "universal satisfaction." The House of Burgesses voted Fauquier an unusually generous present of money.

On the day Fauquier took the oath of office, Dr. Thomas Walker was working in Philadelphia, buying tents, kettles, and provisions for troops at Winchester and Fort Cumberland. Fauquier retained him as commissary for the rest of Virginia's campaigns, lasting three more years. Dr. Walker suffered censure in the autumn of 1758. Thomas Johnson, a burgess, learned that the commissary had furnished supplies for troops in Augusta County by contracting with their commander, his friend, Major Andrew Lewis, a resident of the county who wielded "great Influence amongst the Inhabitants of that Country." Walker had kept Lewis's role secret, since it obviously permitted abuses: The man furnishing rations to soldiers was also the commander attesting that the right quantity and quality had been supplied. Food bought with public funds could be falsely declared spoiled, then used elsewhere. Soldiers could be stinted in their rations while the commissary and the contractor collected the full sixpence per man per day allowed in the colony's contract. Thomas Johnson told his guests that Walker had cheated the colony out of £1,100. They asked how burgesses could be so blatantly deceived. Why did burgesses still court Walker, begging him to continue as commissary? Johnson replied: "You know little of the Plots, Schemes, and Contrivances that are carried on there; in short, one holds the Lamb while the other skins; many of the Members are in Places of Trust and Profit, and others want to get in, and they are willing to assist one another in passing their Accounts."

The House of Burgesses convened in February 1759. Johnson's remarks had been widely repeated. Dr. Walker asked for an inquiry into his conduct. Peyton Randolph and other members of the committee of privileges and elections judged the agreement with Lewis improper, but reported that soldiers had suffered no abuse and that Walker had perpetrated no fraud. Three weeks later Randolph's committee recommended that Thomas Johnson be reprimanded for his "false, scandalous, and malicious" words, as well as his criticism of the manner in which Randolph and other friends of Speaker Robinson's secured a high salary for the clerk of the House of Burgesses. Opinion was divided. After a debate, during which Johnson remained outside the chamber, the committee's resolution passed by a vote of 37 to 32. Johnson then took his place, and Speaker Robinson, from the chair above the mace, reprimanded him for his words, which "reflect highly on the Honor of the House."

Though the British had taken the forks of the Ohio and, in September 1759, France's chief American city and fortress, Québec, Virginians were still at war in 1760 and 1761 with a new enemy, their former allies the Cherokees. South Carolinians and British regulars did most of the fighting; William Byrd and his regiment went no nearer than the upper reaches of the Holston River, 200 miles from any Cherokee town. Walker said he could not supply them farther south.

Walker resumed his journeys in the spring of 1761. From Williamsburg, he went in May to Philadelphia to contract for provisions. In the last two weeks of June he traveled from Philadelphia to Fort Chiswell in the foothills of the Allegheny Mountains near the North Carolina line. He and John Chiswell served as Virginia's commissioners to the Cherokees, paying ransom in return for release of prisoners. Most Cherokees sought peace that summer, but the British did not end the war until Sir Jeffery Amherst sent a force of regulars on a punitive campaign of destruction among Cherokee towns.

William Byrd resigned his command in August. He went to Philadelphia, where his pregnant wife had remained with her parents. Mary Willing Byrd was twenty-one years old, child of a marital alliance between two prosperous merchant families, the Willings and the Shippens. She gave birth to a daughter in November. The following summer, Dr. Walker came north; and he and Byrd called on Sir Jeffery in New York to present their accounts. Amherst was both British commander in North America and successor to the Earl of Albemarle as sinecurist governor of Virginia.

Members of the Loyal Company and the Ohio Company, looking toward the return of peace, wished to make their titles secure. They sought friends. One land company made Governor Fauquier's son a partner. The Ohio Company invited Colonel Henry Bouquet, British commander in the west, to join and receive a full member's share, 25,000 acres. Fauquier and Bouquet, however, were discovering that the government in London no longer encouraged settlement west of the mountains, at least not the land grants and migration of the years before the war. The ministry preferred peace with the Indians, and the Ohio Company had disrupted peace. The new policy favored what Fauquier called "well settling and peopling a Colony." This meant controlled, orderly movement and, for a while, no movement. Bouquet told the Ohio Company: "no settlement will be permitted upon the Ohio till the Consent of the Indians can be procured." On October 13, 1761, he made this an order, prohibiting whites from living west of the Alleghenies. Later he suggested that all grants in the west be annulled and that the region have a "new government under Military Tenure."

Two years later Bouquet's policy became a royal proclamation forbidding westward migration and assigning governance of the west to the commander in chief in America. Yet many colonists thought as George Washington did: the proclamation was only "a temporary expedient to quiet the Minds of the Indians & must fall of course in a few years." Families with no grants or legal claims crossed the mountains, built homes, and began farms in "stragling Settlements" along the Ohio River and its tributaries. Men who disapproved called them "Vagabonds" and "borderers." Washington found them "very troublesome." Still, packhorses climbed through passes. Despite orders to the settlers from the governors of Virginia and Pennsylvania to return east, more and more went west. Everyone knew that soil in the Ohio Valley was "extremely fine," and, General Thomas Gage reported, "it is the passion of every man to be a landholder, and the people have a natural disposition to rove in search of good lands, however distant." Of course, the Crown could not expect payment of two shillings quitrent each year for every 100 acres occupied this way. Even holders of lawful grants living in the west refused to pay after the proclamation.

The proclamation especially displeased George Washington, Adam Stephen, the Lee brothers—four sons of Thomas Lee—and some of their friends. Just two weeks earlier, they had written to Thomas Cumming, a merchant in London, describing a new "Scheme" they had formed in June: the Mississippi Company. Their memorial to the king asked for a grant of 2,500,000 acres stretching eastward from the Mississippi River, embracing part of the watersheds of the Wabash, Ohio, and Tennessee rivers. They

Mary Willing Byrd, Matthew Pratt. Courtesy of the Library of Virginia. Second wife of the younger William Byrd, daughter and sister of Philadelphia merchants, and mistress of Westover for almost fifty years.

hoped to get this tract without paying the Crown anything for twelve years or longer. They offered to settle two hundred families on it. The company's fifty "Adventurers" would each own 50,000 acres separately, not jointly, "any thing in the said Grant to the Contrary notwithstanding," a provision they did not mention in their memorial or their letter.

The founders presented the Mississippi Company as a public-spirited undertaking. The "poorer sort" could obtain land more cheaply from the company than from the Crown because they need not hire surveyors or pay cash for patents. The region would produce commodities Britain needed: "above all things Hemp it appears peculiarly adapted to." Such a westward movement violated the government's promise to Indians to allow no settlement beyond the mountains; but, the company's founders said, Indians' attacks already had broken that agreement. To ensure the prosperity and "public utility" of the company, its memorial said, several partners had formed "a determined resolution . . . to be themselves among the first settlers."

The founders' letter to Cumming explained that they sought a patent from the Privy Council in London, rather than an order directing the governor and Council of Virginia to make a grant. In Williamsburg, measures that Speaker Robinson and his friends disliked often did not prosper: "so many persons of the first influence here, are concerned in Land Schemes; that a thousand nameless, artfull obstructions would be thrown into their way to prevent the success of their enterprize." The Crown's answer to the Mississippi Company's memorial, coming even before the memorial could reach London, was the royal proclamation forbidding migration to the west.

Dr. Walker did not let the proclamation stop his Loyal Company. On May 25, 1763, complying with instructions from London, the Council refused to confirm or renew the company's grant. The clerk recorded in the minutes that the Council had "postpond" the petition for renewal. Walker did not take this as a rejection or a ban. He believed that councillors approved of the Loyal Company's claims, a reasonable belief, since Councillors Thomas Nelson, William Nelson, and Richard Corbin were members of the company. Walker acted as if his petition had been approved. He summoned settlers who had fled their homes during the war to return; he sent surveyors to extend the company's lines; he signed contracts with hundreds of new settlers. They accepted the original terms, to take effect as soon as the company's grant was confirmed: £3 for each 100 acres, with surveyor's fees, patent fees, and composition money, on all of which 5 percent annual interest accrued until the buyer paid in full.

Within an expanse of 5,000,000 acres of mountainous watershed of the Ohio, Tennessee, and Cumberland rivers, surveyors marked more than 150,000 acres of the best land for the Loyal Company. Later, a North Carolinian, objecting to Virginians' claims, said that "secret Surveys were made in these parts by an old Land monger." But anyone interested knew what Dr. Walker was doing. People came from other colonies and settled on plots already purchased from the Loyal Company by Virginians. These squatters said that the king's proclamation annulled all western grants, throwing open the land "to the occupation of the first Adventurer," as if the proclamation had not also forbidden them to move there. Settlers taking Walker's contracts knew that recent surveys were "illegal." They, too, defied the Crown and the governor by refusing to leave. Some later petitioned to quash the Loyal Company's grant, under which they had bought their farms. They said they saw with "disappointment and regret" that Dr. Walker persisted in pressing them to comply with his terms for holding what they called "our possessions." The company, they contended, should derive no title from its "forcable or clandestine Surveys." Those who thought that "The Doctrs grant is broke" had yet to learn that they underestimated Thomas Walker.

Robert Tucker served another one-year term as mayor of Norfolk in 1759–60. Joanna Tucker conceived and gave birth to their fifteenth child, a daughter. Norfolk was growing; the county and borough held about 12,000 people at the end of Tucker's term. The borough opened its first school-house. Redrawn boundaries added new streets and residences. Tucker and other merchants acted as trustees and directors for construction of a new wharf and built more warehouses. Norfolk had become the chief port of Chesapeake Bay. While Tucker was mayor, John Sparling and William Bolden of Liverpool established their firm, Sparling & Bolden, in Norfolk. Representing Glasgow merchants, Neil Jamieson arrived in 1760, beginning a successful business. He soon owned a fine brick house with a 60-foot front and, in back, two ranges of warehouses along the east and west sides of his wharf. Thus he outstripped his fellow merchant and fellow Scot, Dr. Archibald Campbell, who had left medicine for trade and had built in Cumberland Street a house with a 50-foot front.

As George Washington and other Virginians planted more wheat, the colony became the largest exporter of grain in North America. The bulk of Chesapeake grain passed through Norfolk, bound for the West Indies in sloops and schooners often recklessly overladen. Norfolk's wharves also held bales of shingles, stacks of staves, barrels of pork, bars of iron. Proud civic verse said that a poet

> *Saw ships unnumber'd riding in thy port,*
> *And groves of masts in mazy prospect stand;*
> *Saw commerce spreading sail for distant climes,*
> *And well-earn'd profits brought in full return.*

Many of these graceful vessels, with much sail and little superstructure, had been launched from Norfolk. Slave shipwrights "were able to build a Ship amongst themselves without any assistance but of a Master Builder." Merchants exported masts cut in the Dismal Swamp. From a ropewalk's constantly turning wheels emerged strands of cable, rope, and other cordage for the rigging of new vessels and for refitting those careened for cleaning and repairs.

No one knew from day to day how many seamen were in town. There they found brothels and taverns such as John Reinsburg's, run by a former fencing master from Annapolis. Sailors who had jumped ship met crimps ready to advance money and find them a new berth. A seaman's monthly wage was £5. Masters of undermanned vessels bound for Britain, trying to complete their crews, had to pay between 10 and 16 guineas per man for the voyage. Sailors spent most of that money in the borough. Vessels not trading through the port nevertheless called at Norfolk in search of sailors.

Everyone knew that merchants were divided between "the Scotch Party" and "the Buckskin party." Though Scots took much of Norfolk's business, the Virginia buckskins controlled the borough's closed, self-perpetuating corporation. One Scot, William Aitchison, represented Norfolk in the House of Burgesses while Robert Tucker was mayor. He had come to Virginia shortly before the war, at the age of forty, and soon was married to Rebecca Ellegood, daughter of one of the borough's founders. In 1758, Aitchison joined a younger Scottish merchant, James Parker, a little man called Jamie, to establish the firm of Aitchison & Parker. Two years later, Parker was married to Margaret Ellegood, Rebecca's sister. The two sisters' cousin, Fernelia Ellegood, was married to Neil Jamieson. The Aitchisons lived in an "elegant and well furnished" house. His firm's success enabled William Aitchison to own six houses, while Parker acquired five. Their trade grew; yet they pointedly bought barrels of bread not from Robert Tucker's bakery but from Baltimore.

These Scots took an interest in North Carolina—primarily its trade, but also its land. In 1755 a seventeen-year-old boy, Thomas Macknight, arrived in Norfolk from Scotland and for three years lived with the Aitchisons. The new firm of Aitchison & Parker employed Macknight in North Carolina to open a store at Windfield on the Pasquotank River, south of the Dismal Swamp. They financed a North Carolina firm, Thomas Macknight & Company, to get a share of the colony's wheat, pork, pine tar, and lumber, as well as its retail trade. As Parker said, Macknight went to do business with the "Crackers," who "made Shoes played the Fiddle & sung Psalms for a livelyhood." He soon cut a big figure among these "¾ Checque Squires." Macknight patented and purchased property, foreseeing that better roads and easier, growing trade from North Carolina to Norfolk would raise the value of arable land. When Aitchison and Parker turned their attention to the Dismal Swamp, after noticing what the Virginia buckskins were doing, they brought in Macknight to help.

As more of North Carolina's products came into Virginia, the town of Suffolk grew to fifty or sixty houses, with a public wharf on the Nansemond River. Smaller vessels in the West Indies trade sailed up the Nansemond to take on their cargoes. Other vessels, bay craft that did not sail beyond the capes, took commodities to Norfolk. By making the last 28 miles to Norfolk a water carriage, facilities at Suffolk reduced difficulties and expense in the Carolina trade. Visitors found Suffolk "a pretty little Town," though goats and hogs roamed at large. One of its principal merchants, James Gibson, had arrived from Scotland soon after the town became important enough to erect its beautiful brick courthouse. He established connections in North Carolina; his business widened; he built more warehouses. Gibson specialized in exporting pork and importing dry goods, but he also dealt in naval stores, deerskins, and rum. If Aitchison and Parker needed a friend in Suffolk, they called on James Gibson.

Robert Tucker added another port to the destinations of his grain shipments. Already exporting to Lisbon and Madeira, he sent a cargo to Tenerife and imported hundreds of gallons of the Canary Islands' sweet wine. His brother-in-law, Richard Corbin, invested £50 in the venture. Tucker and Corbin shared their troubles. Despite ceaseless work, Tucker fell behind in some transactions and shipments he had promised to complete. Corbin held more than £2,500 in bills of exchange drawn by Speaker Robinson, which had been returned protested. And the two men had the unpleasant task of sorting out the estate of Gawin Corbin, half brother of Richard Corbin and brother of Joanna Tucker; he had died in January 1760, still owing more than £1,200 to "impatient" merchants in Britain. His widow, Hannah, sister of the Lee brothers, and Richard Corbin, with the Lees' help, put up for sale some of the estate's land and slaves, hoping to pay Gawin Corbin's debts. Thus the Corbins and the Tuckers had several reasons to travel along the Mattaponi and York rivers between Norfolk and King and Queen County.

In August 1761, Richard Corbin's eldest son returned from three years in Christ's College, Cambridge, and two years at the Middle Temple. This Gawin Corbin, namesake of his uncle and grandfather and now twenty-one years old, was open, unaffected, lovable. Before the end of 1762 he was married to his cousin, Joanna, daughter of Robert and Joanna Tucker. Sixteen months later they made the Tuckers grandparents.

· · ·

On Saturday, August 20, 1763, the ship *Two Sisters*, commanded by Captain Jeremiah Banning, sailed up Chesapeake Bay into the estuary of the Choptank River on the Eastern Shore of Maryland and dropped anchor near the warehouses and stores of Oxford. Her passage from the coast of Senegal had taken thirty-seven days. She had five slaves on board. Anthony Bacon, the merchant in London who had bought the *Two Sisters* in a public auction at Lloyd's Coffee House, would have been happy for her to take more slaves to Maryland. Three years earlier his ship *Sarah* had borne eighty from Senegal. But Captain Banning's chief duty was to take liquor and wine to British garrisons on the west coast of Africa, then return to London with tobacco from Maryland. He took slaves for his own profit, and he had difficulties doing so on this voyage.

Running southward along the Barbary Coast late in May, the *Two Sisters* was threatened by one of the Algerine cruisers that raided passing vessels. Her six artillery pieces caused the raiders to change their minds. Anchored off the sandbar that made the mouth of the Senegal River dangerously shoal, the *Two Sisters* waited while Captain Banning by barter and purchase acquired eleven slaves: six men, one woman, and four children. They were too few to pose a threat to the crew; he left them unchained. Also anchored in Senegal Roads were troop transports filled with British soldiers. A night riot among the soldiers kept Banning's crew and boats busy rowing army officers to each transport. Banning's men were tired when they returned to the *Two Sisters*.

Just before dawn, three of the African men on board saw that the seamen on watch had fallen asleep. They lowered a boat from the ship's stern and drifted seaward. Captain Banning came on deck at dawn. He found the watch asleep and a boat missing. A quick search between decks revealed that three Africans were gone. As Banning and his men looked out to sea, the moon, setting in the west, cast a long stream of light across the water. In its glow they saw their boat and the Africans. The captain ordered out a boat in pursuit. The Africans could not hope to outrun the rowing seamen. Both were followed by sharks. As the sailors' boat closed, two Africans jumped into the sea. Sharks ripped them apart. The third man hesitated; he could not bring himself to jump, and fell into the sailors' hands. Weeks later, he was one of the five slaves Captain Banning took onto the wharf at Oxford, Maryland.

After a stormy winter voyage to London, Captain Banning left Anthony Bacon's service. Bacon, in his mid-forties, was a contractor for the government. He supplied provisions for soldiers in Senegal and for sailors of the Royal Navy in the West Indies. He kept an agent in Antigua, where the navy had its main port facilities and safest anchorage in English Harbor on the island's southern coast. His roving partner on the North American mainland, Gilbert Francklyn, arranged for shipments of 100 barrels of pork at a time from Norfolk to Antigua.

Bacon had other representatives along Chesapeake Bay and its rivers, seeking cargoes for his ships *King of Prussia, Desire, Unity, Peggy,* and *Sarah.* One was Fielding Lewis of Fredericksburg, to whom Bacon gave power of attorney in 1759. At the age of thirty-four, Lewis had been a big man in Fredericksburg since his twenties. The same year he allied with Bacon, he and Dr. Walker's colleague, Charles Dick, added a private gallery for their families in the Church of St. George's Parish. Into the gallery filed Lewis's daughter by his first wife, Catherine Washington Lewis, and four sons by his second wife, the late Catherine's cousin, Betty Washington Lewis, George Washington's sister. Owning thousands of acres in the Shenandoah Valley, Fielding Lewis helped elect Colonel Washington to the House of Burgesses from Frederick County. He joined his brother-in-law as a burgess in 1760.

Fielding Lewis began his career as a merchant at the upper end of Fredericksburg's main street with help from his father, John Lewis of Gloucester County. Fielding learned from his father's first representative, John Thornton. When Fielding was thirty-two, Thornton recommended him to the governor and Council to replace the drunken, foul-mouthed John Spotswood as county lieutenant for Spotsylvania County. Thornton's sister, Mildred, was Dr. Walker's wife. Of course, Walker and John Lewis, in founding the Loyal Company, had brought in Fielding Lewis and John Thornton. They all had reason to agree with Anthony Bacon and other London merchants who congratulated William Pitt on the fall of Fort Duquesne and Britain's reconquest of "the extensive and fertile Lands of the Ohio." Fielding and Betty Lewis also owned many acres in and around Fredericksburg. Their steady sale of lots marked the town's growth. They rode past their properties in their new post chariot, drawn by six horses. Despite advantages from allying with Fielding Lewis, Bacon had cause to complain: Lewis's imports from London exceeded in value cargoes he sent to Bacon.

Among Bacon's customers in his consignment trade was George Washington, who bought materials for fancy clothes, paying in tobacco. Bacon also shipped to Charles Carroll of Annapolis in return for pig iron and to George Braxton, son of Speaker Robinson's late colleague from King and Queen County. During the war Bacon supplied arms and ammunition to Maryland, Virginia, and North Carolina. He was versatile.

Anthony Bacon went from Whitehaven to Maryland as a boy. By the end of his stay, at the age of twenty-two, he ran a store at Dover, far enough up the Choptank for fresh water to kill marine clams known as boring worms in the hulls of tobacco vessels. Months after his return to England, he became Captain Anthony Bacon, master of the *York*. In 1740 she bore 114 felons to Maryland as indentured servants, returning with a cargo of tobacco for the House of Hanbury.

After a few years, Bacon began to call himself a merchant, at an address in Threadneedle Street, between the Bank of England and the South Sea House. He still went to sea and visited Maryland, where he formed a partnership with James Dickinson at Dover. His older brother, the Reverend Thomas Bacon, had taken a parish at Dover. Thomas and the other wit-crackers of the Tuesday Club of Annapolis made Anthony their first honorary member, calling him Captain Comely Coppernose. After tobacco merchants in Whitehaven engaged him as their London agent in 1752, Bacon began to prosper. By 1757, he had moved to larger quarters on the west side of Copthall Court just off Throgmorton Street. Surrounded by merchants, bankers, and brokers, he no longer went to sea.

In his days on the Eastern Shore of Maryland, Bacon knew the Waters family of Northampton in the Virginia section of the Eastern Shore. The family owned several plantations and vessels, as well as an estate in Britain. They gave Bacon power of attorney to act for them in England. After the elder William Waters died without leaving a will, Bacon served as administrator of the estate for the benefit of William Waters, the son. Retaining property in Northampton, Halifax, and Nansemond counties, the younger Waters spent most of his time after 1754 in Williamsburg. He was a "most amiable" gentleman, living comfortably with his wife, Sarah, and young daughter, Sarah, in a house holding prints, maps, a few books, and a large stock of wine, madeira, and peach brandy.

Perhaps because William Waters lived conveniently at hand, the House of Burgesses chose him, with two other men, to oversee the printing of Virginia's new paper money in 1757. They numbered treasury notes and made sure the printer did not run off extras. Such currency alarmed and irritated Anthony Bacon and other British merchants. The burgesses made their notes legal tender; merchants feared that debts owed in sterling would be paid in paper "of a local, incertain & fluctuating value," causing creditors to lose by the exchange. Eventually, however, they saw that currency benefited their trade. Bacon studied ways to profit by the rate of exchange between currency and sterling.

Bacon joined other merchants in a petition to the Board of Trade, opposing North Carolina's legal tender paper money. Their protest showed that the colony's law treated £133 6s. 8d. in paper as equivalent to £100 sterling; yet that amount of paper bought only £70 sterling. Speaker Samuel Swann and his allies in the Assembly did not take offense. They wished to make Bacon the colony's agent in England in 1760. At the same time, their friend, Thomas Child, North Carolina's attorney general and Earl Granville's agent for the Granville proprietary, persuaded the earl to make Bacon his agent in London. Child and Bacon proposed to remit quitrents and fees from the proprietary to Granville. The system they devised would have profited them at the expense of the rent-payers, the colony, and the earl.

The quitrent was three shillings sterling per year for each 100 acres. Propertyholders paid, however, in North Carolina currency, while, at the London end, Granville wished to receive sterling. Bacon and Child intended to exploit a gap between the market rate of exchange of paper for sterling in North Carolina and the lower official rate set by a law passed by their friends in the Assembly. Thus, if part of Granville's proprietary paid the market equivalent of £578 sterling, this sum would come to the collector's hand as £1,000 in paper money at the market rate of £190 paper for £100 sterling. The colony, however, was obliged by law to redeem its currency with its sterling tax revenues at the official rate of £133⅓ paper for £100 sterling. For his £1,000 in paper money quitrent payments, Bacon would receive £752 sterling from the treasury of North Carolina. But Bacon's agreement with Lord Granville called for him to remit to the earl only the original £578 at the market rate. Bacon could hold all the money for a year before paying the earl; he would charge Granville a commission of 5 percent on money he paid; and he would collect a salary of £200 sterling per year as the colony's agent, as well as £200 per year as Granville's agent.

Members of the North Carolina Council and Governor Arthur Dobbs saw through this scheme. They refused to concur in making Bacon the colony's agent, despite Thomas Child's assurances of Bacon's "unbiased integrity." Dobbs also objected to Bacon's testimony to the Board of Trade, in which he accused the governor—falsely, Dobbs said—of misconduct. For part of 1760 and 1761 the Assembly retained Bacon as its agent. He petitioned the king on behalf of the Assembly, accusing the governor, the secretary of the colony, and the president of the Council of misapplying money appropriated for the war. After Thomas Child failed to get Bacon appointed as North Carolina's agent, Child moved to Suffolk, Virginia. There he continued to issue grants of land in the proprietary until news came that Earl Granville had died in January 1763.

With such examples before him as the growth of Norfolk, Suffolk, and Fredericksburg, Mann Page devised a scheme in 1761: a new town to rise on 100 acres of his property along the right bank of the Pamunkey River not far from Hanover Court House. A road parallel to the river passed through the site, as did an intersecting road from the courthouse to the river. Two tobacco warehouses stood on the bank. A town ought to flourish.

His mansion at Rosewell had four more children running among its many rooms. Mann Page had reason to wonder whether he would be able to give each of his sons an estate and his daughter, Judith, a marriage portion. He owed thousands of pounds to the House of Hanbury. He had endorsed a bill of exchange drawn by William Byrd for £1,000. Unlike Byrd, Page did not send his oldest son, John, to England for schooling, though he had promised his first wife that he would. Page was nearing an indebted Virginian's last resort: a mortgage on land and slaves.

Two days after the House of Burgesses convened in November 1761, Page petitioned to dock the entail on land in Hanover and King William counties so that he could sell it, entailing other land for the benefit of his heir. These sales were to include lots in a new town, Hanover-Town. Speaker Robinson liked Page. To consider the petition the speaker chose a committee, putting on it Peyton Randolph, the burgesses for King William County—Bernard Moore, Robinson's former brother-in-law, and Carter Braxton, Robinson's former ward—John Syme, burgess for Hanover County, and Benjamin Grymes, Page's partner in western land grants. The committee and the House of Burgesses acted within a week. Two days later the Council and Governor Fauquier gave their assent.

The following year, Page laid out Hanover-Town on paper. Surveyors marked and numbered 177 lots. Page announced his first sale for November 15, 1763. He and his friends had high expectations, relying on "the anxiety of numbers to become Purchasers," as one of them told Page's creditors. But bad weather ruined the day. So few of the many expected buyers appeared that Page took his friends' advice to put off a sale for three months.

Governor Fauquier and the Council met as usual on Friday, July 30, 1762. Present were John Blair, who had served on the Council for seventeen of his seventy-five years, the Nelson brothers, Richard Corbin, John Tayloe, Robert Carter of Nomini Hall, and Presley Thornton. To their surprise, they had received from London the king's warrant appointing the Nelsons' brother-in-law, Robert Burwell, to the Council. He stood before them. They must administer the oath and let him take his place.

The governor then presented a letter he proposed to send to the Board of Trade. It said that Burwell ought not to be on the Council because he was not mentally qualified for such a position and because he had "an unwarrantable Impetuosity of Temper." The councillors had "prompted" Fauquier to write and to protest against letting "private Friendships" in England determine appointments. The Council found the governor's letter "very proper and expedient to be sent immediately." Thomas Nelson proposed a further measure, a request from the Council to the king that Burwell be removed and that "some other more able and discreet person" be put in his place. The men decided to wait until they had fuller attendance before acting on Nelson's suggestion. Burwell's brothers-in-law and other councillors felt embarrassed that the British government would put him on a level with them. After hearing that the king's warrant for Burwell's appointment was coming, they convinced Governor Fauquier that theirs was "the concurrent Voice of the Colony."

Richard Henry Lee expected Burwell to be removed "on account of his extreme incapacity, to discharge the important duties of that station." Lee wished to sit on the Council, as no Lee had done since the death of his father, Thomas Lee. In a letter to Virginia's agent in London he suggested himself as a replacement, saying: "The desire I have to do my country service, is my only motive for this solicitation." The agent knew that appointments more important than the Virginia Council were "dayly done by particular Interests"; he worried that Fauquier would hurt himself in the eyes of the Board of Trade by this protest.

Robert Burwell, after hearing his kinsmen, the governor, and other leading Virginians publicly declare him unfit, wrote to his friends in London to tell them what Fauquier and the Council were doing. His friends were the heads of the House of Hanbury, Capel and Osgood Hanbury, and former Governor Robert Dinwiddie. They had persuaded Earl Granville, president of the Privy Council, to choose Burwell. Dinwiddie knew the Burwells; in the 1750s he had many chances to see what the family and its connections by marriage thought of Robert Burwell. Obviously, Dinwiddie had recommended him to insult the Virginia officials who had made his governorship so trying.

The new councillor's friends in London stood by him. The Board of Trade sent Fauquier a tart letter, telling him that they did not always need the governor's recommendation and that "many very respectable persons" supported Burwell. Fauquier's letter, for which the Board of Trade chided him, had conveyed not only the councillors' opinion of Burwell but also their resentment of Robert Dinwiddie's insatiable desire for revenge. Through Fauquier they asked: "if a private Man can obtain his Wishes to serve his Friend, will he not afterward laugh in his Sleeve and despise Consequences?"

Burwell stayed on the Council. Richard Henry Lee turned his eye to other offices. He began to suggest that John Robinson, as speaker and treasurer, held too much power. Governor Fauquier assured the Board of Trade that, among the councillors, "all is quiet." The Nelsons were willing to include Robert Burwell in their new Dismal Swamp Company.

The few people who had filed papers with the surveyor of Norfolk County to obtain land in the Dismal Swamp had sought plots of 100 acres, 300 acres, 400 acres. Robert Tucker claimed 1,000 acres in May 1762. He began a causeway through the eastern margin of the swamp. Since the expiration of his and Francis Farley's grant, ways to improve the swamp had occupied his thoughts. He was part of "a scheme" becoming public in March 1763: some men organized to drain the Dismal Swamp "at a small Expence," then profit from the "extremely Valuable" land they would hold as proprietors. A North Carolinian heard that the group consisted of "the two Nelsons Colo. Washington Colo. Fielding Lewis one Doctor Walker" and others, perhaps even Governor Fauquier. Rumor said they had "certain assurances" of a grant free of quitrents on the Virginia side of the line, and that they had made overtures to Thomas Child, Earl Granville's sometime agent living in Suffolk, for a grant on the North Carolina side.

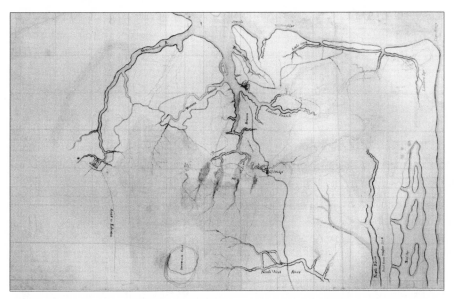

Norfolk, Suffolk, and the Dismal Swamp. Courtesy of the William L. Clements Library. Drawn during the Revolutionary War by a British Army cartographer who depicted the region surrounding the northern part of the Dismal Swamp.

The Dismal Swamp Company announced itself on Wednesday, May 25, 1763. William Nelson presented to his colleagues on the Council a petition for a grant of the swamp, signed with 151 names. The Crown lately had confined grants to 1,000 acres per person. The partners, with most of the work done by Washington, Lewis, and Walker, drew up a list of names equal to the number of thousands of acres they sought. All but a few of these signers had no interest in the project. The company would have only twelve shares and twelve members: William Nelson, Thomas Nelson, Thomas Walker, George Washington, Fielding Lewis, Robert Tucker, John Robinson, Robert Burwell, William Waters, John Syme, Anthony Bacon, and Samuel Gist. The Council postponed consideration of Nelson's petition, but his partners expressed no fear of failing.

While Nelson dealt with the Council, Washington, with his brother-in-law, Fielding Lewis, his cousin's husband, Dr. Walker, and another brother-in-law, Burwell Bassett, left Williamsburg, taking a ferry to Norfolk. They were going to ride around the Dismal Swamp. After a visit to the Norfolk ropewalk to see hemp fibers made into cordage, they crossed the Elizabeth River to Portsmouth and headed toward Suffolk and the swamp.

For two days the four men, with servants and a guide, rode southward along the road bordering the Dismal Swamp, then eastward in North Carolina, crossing the Pasquotank and Perquimans rivers, then northward back into Virginia, cutting through part of the swamp along the new road. As they began, just south of Suffolk among plantations of the large Riddick family, they reassured themselves that the swamp was passable, riding half a mile into it, their horses wading in water a few inches deep. The company would begin its work there, in the northwestern sector, among white cedars, gums, and cypresses. Most soil along the road into North Carolina was sandy and poor. Yet Washington was sure that within the swamp all was black and fertile. He tried to discern subtle contours in the almost level terrain, with an eye to channels for draining. Their shortcut while riding northward on the other side took them through the Green Sea, the vast, open tract of tall, waving reeds which had impressed William Byrd thirty-five years earlier. Though local people thought it "a low sunken Morass, not fit for any of the purposes of Agriculture," Washington felt certain that it was "excessive Rich." Passing Robert Tucker's mills and returning to Norfolk, Washington, Lewis, Walker, and Bassett spent the night at Reinsburg's Tavern, then went on board a ferry for Hampton.

In October, Washington briefly visited the Dismal Swamp again, and Robert Tucker made entries with the surveyor of Norfolk County for 2,000 more acres. At the Council's meeting on November 1, William Nelson renewed the petition "of himself and many others" for a grant of more than 150,000 acres. Since the postponement in May, the first petition had been mislaid, but the Council approved Nelson's new one. Governor Fauquier was away from Williamsburg, meeting with Indians in South Carolina and Georgia. Upon his return, the partners he called "Gentlemen of large Fortunes and great Consequence in this Colony" convinced him that their "warm Expectations" were sound.

The Dismal Swamp Company held its first meeting in Williamsburg on Thursday, November 3. In the room were William Nelson, presumably smiling, as he often did; his less voluble brother, Mr. Secretary; the restless, overworked Robert Tucker; Dr. Thomas Walker, glad to cooperate again with some of those men so understanding in the matter of the Loyal Company's surveys; George Washington, youngest man in the room and most confident of the new company's success; Fielding Lewis, a heavy, round-faced man; William Waters, living in Williamsburg, doing as little work as possible; and Robert Burwell—as everyone else in the room knew, he would rather have been at the racetrack. Dr. Walker had power to act on behalf of two absent partners, John Syme and Samuel Gist. The group already had decided to invite Speaker Robinson, but he had been too ill to do business since September. The company soon chose to gain a friend in London by making Anthony Bacon a partner.

These men agreed that they were starting a "great undertaking": "draining Improving and Saving the Land." The project needed managers to establish its claims with county surveyors, gather slaves and tools, and buy a plantation near the swamp to make the operation self-supporting, as William Byrd had recommended. To no one's surprise, Dr. Walker, George Washington, and Fielding Lewis volunteered. Byrd had written that draining could begin with ten slaves, but the partners voted to assemble fifty "able male labouring Slaves," five from each of the ten signers. The managers must report on the progress of the work. Each shareholder must contribute to defray expenses. They issued no stock. Since the days of the South Sea Bubble, incorporated joint stock companies needed a charter from the Crown. The partners foresaw that one of them or his heir might sell his share, might even sell it to "many Persons." But each share would have one vote, and the founders intended to keep as many of those twelve votes within the original circle as they could. As the meeting closed, the partners appointed the absent Samuel Gist "Clerk of the Company" and ordered him "to register all the proceedings in a Book." Dr. Walker and Colonel Washington, working together more smoothly than during the war, soon left Williamsburg to present proof of the Council's grant to the surveyors of Nansemond and Norfolk counties.

Samuel Gist once had been a clerk. He meant never to be a clerk again. He was eager to leave these provincials and return to England. No one again mentioned a book registering the company's proceedings. If Gist stayed away from the meeting because he expected to be insulted and if he read the word "Clerk" as a sneer from William Nelson and others wishing to freeze him out of the company, he saw truly. But Dr. Walker did not mind doing business with him, and if the Nelsons could bring in their shallow brother-in-law Burwell, Walker could bring Gist.

Samuel Gist was born in Bristol in January 1726. He apparently never spoke of his father, John Gist, or his mother. His uncle, Thomas Gist, was a weaver. Until his fourteenth year, Samuel was one of forty boys in a charity school, Queen Elizabeth's Hospital. He rose every morning at five o'clock to a breakfast of bread and table beer. He wore a blue uniform with a scarlet cloth breastplate bearing the initials "JC" in honor of the school's founder, John Carr. Samuel and the other boys were taught reading, writing, arithmetic, and navigation to prepare them to be useful and morally respectable artisans. When a boy was ready to leave, the school paid £8 8s. to bind him out as an apprentice.

Samuel's turn to leave came late in 1739. Among the scores of vessels moored along Bristol's curving quay, lined with houses on both sides, the *York*, the *New Kent*, and the *Virginian* were bound for Virginia. On board one of these, the small boy passed from among Bristol's old wood and plaster houses, its new brick houses, its streets crowded with women, children, sailors, burdened animals, loaded drays, and movable goods, to a country store near the right bank of the Pamunkey River in Hanover County, Virginia.

Years later, one of Francis Farley's friends in Antigua wrote: "for my amusement I am writing to Bristol for an hospital boy, of a good temper and well qualified as Reader & Writer, whom I may breed up to a Plantership." Similarly, a Bristol firm trading to Virginia sent Samuel Gist to its factor in Hanover, John Smith. At Gould Hill the boy learned storekeeping, selling the usual goods: hats, cloth, ribbon, thread, needles, salt, hoes, nails, seeds, traces, and rum. He learned well. He later said: "Store keeping requires the utmost attention." When Gist was twenty, John Smith died at the age of sixty, leaving a widow, Sarah, and two young sons. Gist took over Smith's affairs, paying doctor's bills and funeral expenses, running the store, and administering the estate of one of Sarah Smith's dead kinsmen, of which John Smith had been executor. Two years later, in May 1748, Gist and Sarah Smith were married. She was more than ten years older than he. They later had two daughters.

None of the executors named in John Smith's will oversaw any part of his estate. Gist retained control. He did not keep separate accounts for that portion of the estate bequeathed to Smith's sons, as George Washington did for the children of Daniel Parke Custis and Martha Custis. On May 7, 1752, Gist sent an advertisement to the *Virginia Gazette*, announcing his intent to move to England, but he did not leave Virginia then. In June he obtained from Hanover County Court an order making him guardian of his stepsons. Their slaves worked their land; crops and income went to Gist. He bought land, much more than John Smith had owned. To the original three houses and 440 acres in Hanover County he added 1,960 acres. From his wife's relatives he bought plantations in Goochland and Amherst counties. He became the sole Virginia representative of the English firm, Brown & Parks. Late in 1752 he imported three apprentices from Bristol. Gist's dealings in tobacco and merchandise grew to be the most extensive in Hanover County. Account books and ledgers from John Smith's store disappeared. No final accounting or settlement ever closed Smith's estate. Smith's sons remained Gist's dependents. Gist had good reason to detect one of William Nelson's satirical cuts in the Dismal Swamp Company partners' order to him to register the company's proceedings in a book.

At the age of thirty-one, Samuel Gist chartered a new ship, the *Peggy*, to transport freight to England. His tobacco could not fill her, especially since he had lost three hogsheads in warehouse fires. To turn a profit on such a voyage he needed to load her quickly and fully. He solicited freight from merchants and planters so assiduously that he agreed to ship more than the *Peggy* could hold. After she sailed, leaving hogsheads Gist had said she would take, a disappointed merchant wrote: "I had his promise, but I believe he never intended to comply with it." Gist had risen in a hard school. And he did not see these provincial planters and merchants, or even a room in Williamsburg holding the Nelsons, Dr. Walker, young George Washington, and various brothers-in-law, as the peak of his ambition. Nevertheless, if the Dismal Swamp Company expected immense profits, he could swallow an insult to get a share.

Four weeks after the company's first meeting, Samuel Gist testified in a trial in Hanover County Court. The Reverend James Maury had sued collectors of tithes in his parish for damages. While the Twopenny Act had been in force in 1759, he had received as his salary not the 16,000 pounds of tobacco prescribed for a minister of the established Church but paper money worth much less. Since the Twopenny Act had been disallowed by the Crown, Maury sought payment in full. This trial was to set the amount due him. Except for his attorney, Peter Lyons, and Lyons's friend, Gist, Maury had few supporters in the county seat. Instead of trying to impanel gentlemen, the sheriff rounded up jurors from "the vulgar herd," including several dissenters opposed to an established church and to taxes for its clergy's salaries. The justices on the bench accepted this jury. Gist was the first witness for the plaintiff. One of Hanover County's largest purchasers of tobacco, he testified that the price in May and June 1759 had been 50 shillings per hundredweight and that he had sold several hundred hogsheads. Testimony by another merchant confirmed the price of 50 shillings. With these witnesses Lyons had proven the loss Maury had sustained by being paid in currency as if tobacco had been worth twopence per pound, that is, 18s. 8d. per hundredweight.

Then a young attorney for the defendants, Patrick Henry—half brother of Gist's Dismal Swamp Company partner, John Syme—rose and spoke to the jury for an hour. Warming to his subject, he argued that the Twopenny Act had been a good law and that the king, by disallowing it, had broken the original compact between king and people, had degenerated from being a father to being a tyrant, and had forfeited all rights to his subjects' obedience. Lyons interrupted indignantly, telling the justices that Henry had spoken treason. Lyons said he was astonished that the justices could listen "without emotion, or any mark of dissatisfaction." At the same time, some gentlemen behind Maury murmured: "Treason, Treason!" Henry went on to attack the Anglican clergy for objecting to the Twopenny Act, calling them "enemies of the community." In conclusion he invited the jurors to make an example of Maury unless they wanted to rivet chains of bondage on their own necks.

The only evidence offered by the defense was a receipt showing that Maury had received £144 in Virginia currency. One of the defendants' lawyers reminded the jurors that they could set damages as low as one farthing. The jury retired for less than five minutes, then brought in a verdict for Maury, with damages of one penny. The justices rejected Lyons's motions to send the jury out again and to record the evidence given by Gist and the other witness. Nor would they find the verdict contrary to the evidence and order a new trial. After the court adjourned, Henry approached Maury and apologized for what he had said to the jury, explaining that "his sole view in engaging in the cause, and in saying what he had, was to render himself popular." Shortly after the trial, Patrick Henry was elected to the House of Burgesses. Samuel Gist renewed his plan to move back to England.

Maury's case provoked "much conversation" in Williamsburg. He and his even more outspoken colleague, the Reverend John Camm, were trying to get more money from their parishioners while the market for tobacco, as well as Virginia's trade and credit, had fallen into depression. Receiving less for their crops, planters drew fewer bills of exchange. And the rate of exchange was so high that £160 of Virginia currency bought only £100 sterling. Virginians received urgent demands from British creditors; more suits were filed. Merchants in Britain were suffering the consequences of a series of financial crises and a depression marked by a rising number of bankruptcies. The more bills of exchange that came back to Virginia protested, the less capital Virginians could command and the less planters could or would pay anyone, creditor or clergyman.

British merchants and Virginia burgesses quarreled about paper money. Merchants opposed colonial currency as a device to cheat them. Burgesses explained, and some merchants understood, that paper money made commerce possible. Demand gold and silver from every debtor, and create a colony of bankrupts. In fact, merchants were relieved to get remittances in any medium.

Seeing the need to use currency, Virginians still wondered why they had to pay so much paper to get so little sterling. Was Speaker Robinson, as treasurer, drawing in the full amount of taxes payable in currency? Was he forestalling inflation by burning retired currency as it came back into the treasury and expired? Anyone who cared to find out knew that the answer was no. Burgesses chided sheriffs for neglecting to collect and remit taxes. Burgesses devised new taxes to speed retirement of the currency. Still, much old paper money circulated because cash was convenient, and paper was Virginia's main form of cash. Speaker Robinson had much power, but he could not cause large fluctuations in the transatlantic rate of exchange. Burgesses seemed to believe that reducing the amount of currency in circulation would lower the rate of exchange. They knew that the treasury in May 1763 was holding almost £50,000 of notes "to be burnt." For those trying to lower the rate, the obvious next step was to bring more paper notes into Robinson's hands. But the timetable for destroying notes could be accelerated only by a change in the law, a change which the Board of Trade thought unlikely to win the Crown's assent. Governor Fauquier said that Robinson's "Hands are now tied up." As tax revenue came in from sheriffs, he did not burn this currency.

Some men's minds turned toward projects for easy riches. Several people noticed that wealthy Virginians were showing an interest in the Dismal Swamp. If, as rumor said, these partners had brought Governor Fauquier into their company, they must foresee large profits. If the Dismal Swamp had so much more value than anyone had guessed, why let a few rich Virginians take it all?

Joseph Jones of Suffolk parish in Nansemond County secured on July 7, 1763, a grant of two tracts in the Dismal Swamp, totaling 772 acres. James Murdaugh lived on a small plantation seven miles outside Suffolk. Only one-third of his 179 acres had been cleared for crops, but he suddenly acquired bigger dreams. In August 1763, while the Dismal Swamp Company's petition awaited the Council's action, Murdaugh entered with the surveyor of Nansemond County a claim to 2,000 acres in the sector of the swamp sought by the company. Of course, no person was supposed to receive more than 1,000 acres, but if the company could add more than 140 ghost signers to its petition, Murdaugh could try for a double portion.

James Parker and William Aitchison felt more disposed to ridicule than to emulate Robert Tucker, the Nelsons, and other Virginia buckskins of high standing. Yet, as soon as they learned of the Dismal Swamp Company early in 1763, they liked the idea of acquiring a huge tract of valuable land "convenient to Navigation" simply by draining the swamp. Parker and his North Carolina partner, Thomas Macknight, had been thinking about the swamp since 1758. In 1761, Macknight sought from the Granville proprietary 1,400 acres near the southern reaches of the Dismal Swamp. Parker, Aitchison, and Macknight heard that the Dismal Swamp Company partners had approached Thomas Child in hope of adding the North Carolina part to their Virginia grant. The three Scots formed new visions. As Parker put it: "we enlarged our plan."

Macknight went to Edenton, North Carolina, to see Samuel Johnston, nephew of a former governor, just appointed clerk of the Superior Court. Macknight told Johnston what the Dismal Swamp Company was doing and invited him to join the Scots in their rival firm, the Campania Company. They would acquire the North Carolina portion of the Dismal Swamp—as much as 120,000 acres. True, people who lived near the Dismal Swamp said: "The soil was worth nothing." Macknight knew better. "The soil of these lands was rich," needing only to be drained. The Scots and their partners intended, Macknight said, to "avail ourselves" of the Dismal Swamp Company's scheme by controlling the North Carolina acreage. The Virginians would not profit from that vast tract "unless they took us in as part of their Company." If they refused, the Scots need only wait while Virginians drained, then "reap the Benefit of their Labour." But the Scots calculated that the Dismal Swamp Company "will gladly Join us if We can only appear tolerably formidable in our first Outset."

Samuel Johnston embraced this strategy. On March 26, 1763, he made entries with the Granville proprietary's land office for 2,800 acres in the Dismal Swamp. Macknight entered for 700 acres the same day. Three weeks later, Macknight entered for another 5,600 acres. They took care to specify that they were selecting land "in the great Dismal Swamp, & joyning the so. side of the Virginia line." Whatever the Dismal Swamp Company might do, Johnston said, these holdings would "secure something to ourselves and incommode them." He thought that the Virginians "will be making a push very soon as it is a scheme of great Expectation."

Parker and Macknight also wished to include in their Campania Company James Gibson, merchant in Suffolk; another merchant in Norfolk, James Campbell; another North Carolinian, Joseph Montfort, who was clerk of the Superior Court in the Halifax district; and another brother-in-law, Alexander Elmsly. Unfortunately for them, Earl Granville had died on January 2, 1763. No grants in the proprietary after that date were valid. The land office closed in the spring of 1763. Thereafter, Parker and Macknight based their claim on a North Carolina law conferring title after seven years of possession. Alexander Elmsly later recalled that "he was one of the first concerned" in the Campania scheme. But by the time he moved to London in 1768, it was his habit "to Curse & dam all swamps & everybody Concerned in them."

In anticipation of beginning drainage, the Dismal Swamp Company partners in January 1764 rushed through the House of Burgesses and the Council a law granting them the right to dig canals or build causeways through any land adjacent to the Dismal Swamp. The company must submit to arbitration to determine compensation due to any property-holder claiming to have suffered loss. But property-holders could not sue the company because, the law read, rendering the swamp fit for cultivation "will be attended with publick utility."

The General Assembly adjourned. George Washington and Fielding Lewis left Williamsburg, took a ferry across the York River, and spent several days as Mann Page's guests at Rosewell before continuing northward to their homes. Page's son, John, about to turn twenty-one, was to be married to

Frances Burwell, daughter of Robert Burwell and Sarah Nelson Burwell. Mann Page promised to give Rosewell to his son, and Robert Burwell promised his daughter a dowry of £1,000. To further seal this alliance between the families, Burwell, early in 1764, sold to Mann Page half his share in the Dismal Swamp Company.

At the time the Dismal Swamp Company was formed, hemp enjoyed a vogue in London, in Virginia, and in other colonies. Political economists deplored Britain's dependence on Russia and the flow of large sums of cash from Britain for hemp. One estimate showed Britain paying Russians £740,000 per year for naval stores. Another set the value of hemp and flax consumed in Britain at about £300,000 per year. In 1762 the Empress Catherine cornered the Russian hemp market and ran up the price. Greater demand in wartime had shown how Britain's need could be exploited. The first lord of the Admiralty warned in April 1764 that the Royal Navy had insufficient reserves of rigging and cordage. Britain's desire for a reliable supply of hemp within its empire was common knowledge.

For some Virginians concerned about planters' heavy debts and their reliance on tobacco, even during a depression, hemp promised salvation. Charles Carter thought that people might quit smoking tobacco if fashion changed or if they learned "of the great Proportion of poysonous Quality contained in this Narcotick Plant." What would happen to Virginia then? Carter felt confident that the American colonies could fully supply Britain with hemp if they turned to that crop. Robert Beverley wondered how Virginians could escape indebtedness while tobacco prices remained low and merchants refused to honor a bill of exchange unless a planter sent enough tobacco to cover it. After careful study, he wrote: "I firmly believe the Cultivation of Hemp is the most probable Method of Discharging our Debts."

With encouragement from colonial agents, 102 London mercantile firms, including the chief firms trading to Virginia, petitioned the Board of Trade, urging Parliament to revive and increase the lapsed bounty on American hemp. Such a premium would reduce or remove the disadvantage colonists suffered in competing with Russia. Parliament enacted a twenty-one-year bounty, beginning at £8 per ton, gradually falling to £4 per ton. After accounts of this incentive reached Virginia, Governor Fauquier was happy to report good news to the Board of Trade. He told its members about the Dismal Swamp Company. The partners were "pretty sanguine in promising themselves Success." Once the swamp was drained, they assured the governor, the company would grow hemp. "I am credibly informed,"

Fauquier wrote, "that it will soon produce hemp sufficient to supply his Majestys Navy."

Anthony Bacon signed the petition supporting a bounty on hemp. By the time the House of Commons was ready to act, he had become a member of Parliament. He served on the committee to prepare a bill granting the bounty. A man holding government contracts and hoping to hold more found it useful to have a seat in the House of Commons. He provided a reliable vote and other aid to the ministry. In return, the ministry favored him with contracts, concessions, and a friendly eye when he submitted his accounts to the Treasury. While seeking a seat, Bacon, with his partners, Gilbert Francklyn and Anthony Richardson, applied for a grant of 2,000 acres on the Magdalen Islands in the Gulf of St. Lawrence. They planned "very extensive" catching and processing of cod, walruses, whales, and seals.

Bacon first stood for Parliament at a by-election in the corrupt Devonshire borough of Honiton in November 1763. Before doing so he consulted the head of the ministry, George Grenville, whom he had known for some time. Grenville told him that the election would be won by Sir George Yonge. Sir George supported the administration, and Grenville could not encourage or aid Bacon. Nevertheless, Bacon tried, and, rumor said, spent £8,000 in the borough. Sir George won. Bacon learned to listen to Grenville.

George Grenville wore a sardonic, condescending air—smooth in success, obstinate and nasty in defeat. A rival wrote: "he had a better opinion of himself than he, or perhaps anybody else, ever deserved." He took a patronizing tone toward the king. Grenville wished to help Bacon get into Parliament. An opportunity arose when the member for Aylesbury, in Buckinghamshire, John Wilkes, got himself into even more trouble than usual.

Wilkes won election to Parliament for Aylesbury in 1757 and retained his seat without a contest in 1761 by outbidding his opponents in buying votes. He despised "the vulgar," "the rabble," as he privately described voters, but he paid their price: five guineas to each of about three hundred men. Aylesbury was a poorly paved, dirty town of four hundred houses about 40 miles northwest of London. George Grenville and his brother Richard, Earl Temple, lived nearby. Though Grenville had become the king's first minister in 1763, the earl encouraged Wilkes's attacks on the ministry and on the sinister influence wielded by the loathed favorite of the king, Lord Bute. Wilkes did this through *The North Briton* late in 1762 and early in 1763. After he published Number 45 on April 23, 1763, censuring the king's speech from the throne, the Earl of Halifax ordered Wilkes arrested and charged with seditious libel. Wilkes did not remain imprisoned for long, but he gave new offense later in the year by publishing another number of *The North Briton* and by printing a few copies of an impious, obscene parody of Alexander Pope called *An Essay on Woman*. The House of Commons resolved that seditious libel was not encompassed within its members' general immunity from prosecution. Late in December, Wilkes fled to France. The House expelled him on January 19, 1764.

On January 20 a writ to elect Wilkes's successor was moved. The next day Anthony Bacon called on George Grenville. They reached an understanding. Grenville thought Bacon "a merchant of a very fair Character" and knew he was "extremely well dispos'd in all Respects"; that is, he would vote with the ministry. Grenville also knew that Bacon had enough money to satisfy the "notorious Venality" of Aylesbury's voters. Bacon left with letters of recommendation. Four days later, with the aid of the usual five guineas per voter, Bacon won the election. He took his seat in the House of Commons eight days after Wilkes's expulsion. Within two weeks the Treasury drafted a contract for Bacon to convert sterling to Spanish and Portuguese silver and gold coins and deliver these to army paymasters for garrisons in the newly occupied West Indian islands of Grenada, Tobago, Dominica, and St. Vincent. He took a commission: 2 percent of the money he handled.

Wilkes spent four years on the Continent before returning to England and more controversy. In France he had financial difficulties arising from the expense of getting elected to Parliament. By his flight he got even with some men in Aylesbury who had demanded money for their vote. Rumor said: "he is so much in debt there, that he is no great favourite." From Paris he addressed the "worthy electors" of Aylesbury in a pamphlet, thanking them for their "honourable, unanimous, and repeated marks of esteem." And he began his career as champion of "universal liberty" and martyr to a corrupt majority in Parliament, hirelings of the ministry, ready to fasten fetters on themselves and posterity. Anthony Bacon did not take offense. He collaborated with his friend, Wilkes's brother, Heaton, and Wilkes's friend, Humphrey Cotes, in seeking a contract from the Treasury to supply provisions to British soldiers in North America. Wilkes's pamphlet denounced the ministry for planning "to load their fellow subjects with the most partial taxes"; Bacon warned Grenville not to enact a general tax on American colonists. Grenville did not heed this warning. Bacon was his dependent, not an advisor. Though colonists did not convince the ministry to heed them, the Dismal Swamp Company now had a friend not only in the City but also in Parliament.

. . .

Having missed the first meeting of the Dismal Swamp Company, John Syme in the following months chose not to remain a shareholder. He left his many debts unpaid, giving as his excuse the low price of tobacco and high rate of exchange. When his share of the expenses of starting to drain the swamp fell due, his inability to command cash would become obvious to his partners. By the first meeting or soon afterward, Syme found someone to take his share: Francis Farley.

Antigua suffered hard years in 1762, 1763, and 1764, years to make a planter think of leaving. Months of drought ruined sugar cane, yet the price of sugar remained low. Farley and his family fell ill in the fall of 1762, and one of his daughters died. After some refreshing rains in May 1763, another dry summer set in. Antigua was "miserable." Empty ponds showed cracked bottoms; the water level in reservoirs and cisterns dropped; rationing parched slaves. A mysterious disease spread among livestock, killing them quickly in large numbers. Smallpox returned to the island. At Christmastime, Farley lay confined in his chamber, weak with fever. Small wonder that planters should mention the falling value of land and regret that they could not sell, except at a low price.

Farley still believed in the Dismal Swamp. He sought a share in the new company, adding to his "valuable property" in Virginia and North Carolina. He had learned that he could not rely on Virginians to take care of his interests while he lived many miles distant. He might worry less, as well as confidently venture into the Dismal Swamp Company, because members of his family were moving to Virginia: his daughter, Eleanor, and her new husband, Captain John Laforey of the Royal Navy.

Captain Laforey was one of the young naval heroes of the war with the French. In 1755, Commodore Augustus Keppel promoted him from first lieutenant to commander and gave him the sloop *Ontario*. During the next two years he commanded the sloop *Hunter* in the fleet off Cape Breton Island and the French fort at Louisburg. HMS *Namur*, Admiral Edward Boscawen's flagship, dropped anchor off Louisburg on June 2, 1758, and he soon gave Laforey an opportunity for glory.

General Sir Jeffery Amherst's army besieged Louisburg. His most advanced works were enfiladed by fire from the last two French men-of-war in the harbor, *La Prudente* and *Le Bienfaisant*. The harbor wall of the fort could be scaled if those vessels were gone. Boscawen decided to take them. He chose John Laforey and George Balfour to command the parties, giving them six hundred sailors, with boats, pinnaces, and barges from every vessel in the fleet. In the early hours of Wednesday, July 26, Sir Jeffery stood in the trenches with his men, keeping up heavy fire on the fort to distract its defenders' attention from the harbor. Concealed by night and heavy fog, Laforey, Balfour, and their two divisions of boats closed with *La Prudente* and *Le Bienfaisant*, unseen until within hailing distance. The watch challenged them. They gave no reply, and the watch opened fire. Laforey and Balfour ordered their sailors to give way alongside and board. The men began to cheer. Led by their commanders, they boarded the ships, carrying cutlasses, pistols, and muskets with fixed bayonets. French sailors rushed on deck. Fighting began, but everyone soon realized that French artillerymen ashore were firing on their own ships. The crews surrendered.

Attaching lines to *Le Bienfaisant*, Balfour and his boats began to tow her across the harbor, away from Louisburg. Laforey tried to tow *La Prudente* but found that she had stranded, with several feet of water in her hold. He and his men set fire to her, abandoned ship, and joined Balfour's boats in towing *Le Bienfaisant*. Lit by the burning man-of-war, the British boats pulled away with their prize, fired upon from an island battery at Point Rochefort, from the town, and from the fort of Louisburg. With a loss of 7 men killed and 9 wounded, they had taken one ship, destroyed another, and captured 152 prisoners. Later that day the French surrendered. Admiral Boscawen promoted John Laforey and George Balfour to the rank of post-captain. Laforey was twenty-nine years old.

In command of the *Echo* in 1759, Captain Laforey accompanied the fleet under Vice-Admiral Charles Saunders as it sailed up the St. Lawrence River with General James Wolfe's army to take Québec. In the West Indies in 1762 he served under Rear-Admiral George Brydges Rodney, cooperating with the army in the capture of the French island of Martinique in February. Laforey took command of the *Levant*. She called at St. Johns, Antigua, where he met Eleanor Farley. They were married in St. Johns on February 15, 1763. Late that year they sailed for England in the *Levant*.

Captain Laforey and Francis Farley apparently reached an agreement. Laforey suddenly possessed "a handsome fortune." He took a leave of absence from the navy to settle in Virginia. In London, Eleanor Laforey gave birth to a daughter, Julia, in March 1764. Two months later the family sailed for Virginia. In the meantime, on April 27, 1764, John Syme resigned his share in the Dismal Swamp Company to Francis Farley. Farley's daughter, son-in-law, and granddaughter moved to Maycox, a plantation on the south bank of the James, directly across from Westover. Captain Laforey received payments from Farley. William Byrd befriended him. One could find them in Mrs. Jane Vobe's tavern in Williamsburg, at a table among other gentlemen, with an active dicebox.

On the same day Syme passed his share to Farley, William Waters resigned half his share to David Meade, son of the late David Meade, merchant of Suffolk. From the age of seven to seventeen David had attended school in England. His father died during that time. Just before his seventeenth birthday, he returned to Nansemond County, and the change did not please him. Instead of pleasure gardens he saw forests and the Dismal Swamp. Instead of his schoolmates and their titled parents, he met almost as many blacks as whites. He had forgotten the faces of his mother and sisters. Four months after his return, heavy rains flooded Nansemond and Norfolk counties, sweeping away bridges, further isolating scattered farms and plantations.

Having grown "accustomed to good company" in England, Meade found living with his mother, looking out the windows at the Nansemond River, "rather monotonous." He began to visit plantations farther up the James, where he found "more congenial" society. And he could attend balls, plays, and races in Williamsburg during the public gatherings in April and October. David Douglass's traveling "Company of Comedians from London," with its repertoire of old favorites—*The Provok'd Husband, The Mourning Bride, The Gamester,* and *The London Merchant*—played in the Williamsburg theater in November 1762 and April and May 1763. George Washington saw them three weeks before his ride around the Dismal Swamp. In Williamsburg, David Meade attracted the notice of William Waters. Meade described himself as "a youth brought up to no occupation" and "a great builder of castles in the air." Waters was nearing the end of such a life, as Meade was beginning. He, too, owned land in Nansemond County but would not live there.

Meade formed ties with "many gentlemen, the most distinguished for wealth, talents and worth." None showed him so much "partiality" as did William Waters. Waters signed over to him one-half share in the Dismal Swamp Company and paid assessments for the whole share. Others saw, as Meade eventually did, that Waters wanted the young man to ask for his daughter's hand.

Though the estate of Meade's father and the firm Meade & Driver owed thousands of pounds to Robert Cary & Company in London and the elder Meade's will made all his estate liable for payment of these debts, David Meade thought of himself as "inheriting a good patrimony." He had not yet turned twenty when he began to buy land in Nansemond County. His first purchase came six weeks after he joined the Dismal Swamp Company. He acquired by inheritance and purchase about 5,000 acres and established himself as "one of the leading Men in that Country."

During the late spring and early summer of 1764, as George Washington prepared to collect slaves from members of the Dismal Swamp Company to begin work, the partners had many matters to think about. Fielding Lewis paid Washington £20 for the "Dismal Adventure." Thomas Walker's oldest son, John, was married to Elizabeth, the beautiful daughter of Bernard Moore, at the Moore home, Chelsea, in King William County. Before the wedding Dr. Walker and Bernard Moore exchanged the customary letters, stating what each would give the couple. Walker said he could not be specific about the timing of his payments because "My affairs are in an uncertain state." Moore was in even more trouble, having invested "much too greatly" in "that terrible sinking Fund Indigo." His bills of exchange came back from London protested. His letter was vaguer than Walker's. In the month of John's wedding, Thomas and Mildred Walker had their tenth child, a son they named Francis.

In Norfolk, Robert Tucker was planning a shipment of wheat and flour to Spain. Joanna Tucker got pregnant.

During a stay in Williamsburg, Secretary Thomas Nelson, suffering from gout, added to his substantial library a translation of Simon Paulli's *A Treatise on Tobacco, Tea, Coffee, and Chocolate*. Written by a former smoker, it warned him against the "narcotic Sulphur" of tobacco smoke. It urged rulers of all nations to prohibit the use of tobacco. In Paulli's list of dangers, use of tea was only slightly more tolerable "than that of *Chocolate*, and *Coffee*, which is of all others the worst."

Secretary Nelson, William Nelson, Robert Burwell, some of their colleagues on the Council, and leading men of the House of Burgesses—Speaker Robinson, Peyton Randolph, George Wythe, and Robert Carter Nicholas—were drafting a letter to the colony's agent in London. It conveyed their thanks for his help in obtaining a bounty on hemp, their assurance that the colony had resorted to paper currency only out of necessity, and their report on the Council's refusal to award damages to the Reverend John Camm for salary lost under the Twopenny Act. The letter also called "truly alarming" a proposal that Parliament enact a stamp tax. Such a tax would violate "the most vital Principle of the British Constitution" by subjecting colonists to levies made without the consent of their representatives.

In London, Anthony Bacon, with two other merchants, was petitioning the Board of Trade for a grant of land and a thirty-year lease of coal mines on Cape Breton Island. These happily had come into His Majesty's possession through heroic efforts by many men, including Captain John Laforey.

In Hanover County, Samuel Gist bought a copy of Thomas Hale's *A Compleat Body of Husbandry*. Book III of this work encouragingly described "the Improvements of Land by Inclosing and Draining." In the sixth chapter, "Of draining boggy Lands," Gist could find this advice: "he must have Resolution to go through what he has undertaken, for all will be sure Profit in the End." In May, Gist had placed an advertisement in the *Virginia Gazette*, warning his debtors to pay. Two months later he prepared for their response by purchasing twelve blank bills of exchange and twelve blank penal notes, used to demand forfeit of debtors' bonds. Gist had in mind a large new store, built with brick.

Speaker Robinson wished to get title to the lead mines he and his friend and father-in-law, John Chiswell, were developing. The land lay within the grant of the Loyal Company. The speaker paid the company's agent, Dr. Walker, £1,794 17s. 4d. in cash.

Robinson was preparing his report on the colony's paper currency: a list of past emissions and of taxes levied to retire the currency. His report said that provisions for removing treasury notes from circulation went far beyond the measures needed. He denied that the high rate of exchange, by which £100 sterling bought £160 currency, arose "altogether" from the quantity of notes in circulation. He attributed it to "the great scarcity of good Bills of Exchange owing to the poor distressed condition this Colony is at present in."

The Dismal Swamp Company's preparations attracted notice. David Campbell obtained from Governor Fauquier, on August 15, a grant of 111 acres bordering the site of the company's first work.

From Mills Riddick the company rented a plantation of 402 acres, soon known as "Dismal plantation," six miles from Suffolk on the margin of the swamp. There slaves would build houses, grow corn, and tend livestock for their own support. The managers made George Washington's young kinsman John Washington the resident overseer.

George Washington received fifty-four slaves at Dismal Plantation in July: forty-three men, nine women, a boy, and a girl. He set a value on each. By this measure of a slave's capacity to produce profit, Washington saw that his partners had contributed less than he. The five adults he furnished were valued at £365. The five Samuel Gist sent had a value of £260. For William Nelson's five, the figure was £275. Speaker Robinson sent not five but three. The ten provided by Fielding Lewis for himself and Anthony Bacon were worth £635. Owners of half-shares each sent only two slaves. Robert Burwell offered a couple in their twenties: Jack and his wife, Venus. Jack was tall and slim, Venus short and stout. They had in common a gift for fast, smooth talk. They did not look like people who would devote themselves to draining a swamp; they looked like people Burwell wished to get rid of at his partners' expense. A resident of York Town saw the company's first workforce. He thought these slaves "the worst collection that ever was made—they seemed to be the refuse of every one of the Estates from whence they were sent." Virginians knew that Nansemond and Norfolk counties, especially the Dismal Swamp, were an unhealthy place to send valuable workers.

George Washington stayed briefly at Dismal Plantation to "set the People to work." Before them lay a white marsh; beyond it stretched a sector of the swamp in which old cypress and cedar trees were fewer than large gum trees, red and white oaks, maples, and elms. Newer growths of these made the woods denser. Moving into the swamp, one waded in standing water the color of tea. Farther in, bamboo among the trees grew more thickly. Vines climbed trunks and hung from branches above huge, intricate ferns. Clouds of mosquitoes were so large as to make it hard to guess what kept all of them alive.

The slaves were to dig a ditch, beginning in sandy soil near Dismal Plantation and moving into black peat. Three feet deep, ten feet wide, and almost five miles long, running from the plantation to Lake Drummond, it was supposed to drain water from arable land into the lake. To provide some immediate income for the company the slaves felled the oldest white cedar trees and shaved tens of thousands of 18-inch shingles.

Five months after work began, the partners met in Williamsburg. They voted to assess themselves £40 more per share. Each was also to provide five more slaves; four men and one woman. Perhaps the presence of twelve more women would reduce the inclination of men at Dismal Plantation to "run about" in the night, visiting other slaves in Nansemond County. If any founders of the Dismal Swamp Company had gone to Westover to read the elder William Byrd's original proposal for draining, they had ignored his advice on this subject, and they met with the consequences he had predicted.

Days before the meeting of December 15, George Washington apparently visited Norfolk and Suffolk, perhaps accompanied by Dr. Walker. The three managers of the company—Washington, Walker, and Fielding Lewis—had agreed to buy land in Nansemond County in partnership. From several sellers they bought a little more than 1,000 acres along the road from Suffolk toward Norfolk, along the Nansemond River, and in the swamp. For one tract of 120 acres they paid almost £1 per acre. They envisioned a canal connecting the company's land to the Nansemond River, easing movement of supplies and shingles. A visit to Dismal Plantation showed anyone that work moved slowly. Faster progress required more slaves. The managers expressed confidence in the undertaking by spending their own money for the company's future benefit. One of Washington's English correspondents, who took an interest in news of the Dismal Swamp Company, congratulated him on "that truely great enterprise, not less calculated for public utility than your private Emolument."

Robert Tucker also anticipated success for "the intended good purposes" of the company. His wife was carrying their eighteenth child. The baby, if healthy, would be the ninth to survive. Tucker foresaw that, upon his death, he would leave behind him several young children. He wrote his will, bequeathing the bulk of his property to his son, Robert. If the baby not yet born turned out to be a boy, he was to inherit one-half of Tucker's share in the Dismal Swamp Company. "The other half of said Share," Tucker wrote, "I appropriate the Profits of toward the better Education and support of my unmarried Children who are under Age." If the company called on Tucker's share for more money to continue its work, that money must come from the younger children's portions of Tucker's estate. Joanna Tucker gave birth to a girl. So the young Tuckers would have all of their father's share in the Dismal Swamp Company set aside for their benefit.

Throughout 1764 and 1765, Virginia planters complained of low prices for tobacco, high prices for merchandise, scarce cash, protested bills of exchange, and lawsuits to collect debts. British merchants responded to the depression by squeezing their debtors in Virginia. Suits filled the calendars of county courts. Merchants no longer extended generous credit by accepting bills of exchange for sums far greater than tobacco or other commodities shipped to Britain would bring. William Byrd sold four hundred slaves in April 1765, a desperate act for any planter. The price of slaves had fallen almost to half the level of three or four years earlier. Samuel Gist tried to profit from tight credit by letting people know that he could get a more favorable rate of exchange than the prevailing one, meaning that their Virginia currency would buy more in his store than in others, a claim his competitor denied. With goods selling retail at a markup of 200 percent, merchants had to think fast to attract customers.

Beginning in May, drought dried Virginia through the summer. Beautiful, cloudless days became a curse. Turpentine makers in Nansemond County and in North Carolina got no yield from pines. Oaks produced too few acorns for hogs. Newly planted tobacco withered and died. People worried that grain and other crops would fall short of the colony's need for food.

Virginians learned in April that George Grenville and his supporters in Parliament, rejecting advice from Anthony Bacon and others, had enacted a stamp tax. It required that legal documents, newspapers, and pamphlets be produced on paper bearing a stamp which indicated that a tax, ranging from twopence to £10, had been paid. The law was to take effect on November 1. Grenville sought to bring more order to the government's finances and to colonists' behavior. He felt especially distressed by smuggling. Colonists were not supposed to trade directly with other nations; yet they did so, by way of islands in the West Indies and other routes. Half a million pounds sterling per year: Grenville could not get that sum out of his head—the value of North Americans' clandestine trade with Europe. Of course, they paid no taxes on it. Britain lost twice: merchants lost business; the government lost revenue. Grenville meant to tighten enforcement of Customs regulations and to tax something colonists must use and could not hide. He "fondly persuaded himself he could easily make it go down," a London printer wrote, "in any way he chose to administer it."

As enactment of the tax became certain, applicants sought the position of stamp distributor in each colony. Richard Henry Lee, having failed to win a seat on the Council, saw this newly created post as "a beneficial employment" and hastily offered himself. Peter Francklyn asked for the distributorship of Jamaica, giving as references his brother, Gilbert, and Gilbert's partner, Anthony Bacon. The government relied as usual on advice from merchants and colonial agents. Bacon and other merchants chose distributors for Québec, Barbados, and New York. The Virginia appointment went to George Mercer, who had spent the last two years in London, representing the Ohio Company.

On March 1, some of Virginia's paper currency expired. People holding notes emitted in 1757 and 1758 were supposed to exchange them for notes of later emissions. After these old notes arrived in Williamsburg during court days in April, Speaker Robinson announced that the treasury did not have enough newer notes to replace them. More recent ones ought to have been preserved as they came in through collection of taxes, but "considerable sums," he said, had instead been burned. This explanation seemed odd, since the law did not call for burning the latest emissions. Only currency due to be retired by 1765 was to be destroyed. Hardly anyone believed Robinson. In the past, he had been too slow in destroying currency, not so hasty as to burn too much. People were more willing to believe that the speaker had shown unwise leniency toward sheriffs and inspectors of tobacco who did not

Patrick Henry, Thomas Sully. Courtesy of the Virginia Historical Society. The patriot spoke eloquently about liberty, law, and land.

promptly send the proceeds of taxes and fees to the treasury. The speaker was good-natured and kindly, everyone knew. That same month he sold Henry Fitzhugh "very valuable" land for £1,160, telling Fitzhugh to take as much time as he liked before paying. A committee of burgesses later approved Robinson's accounts as treasurer, as did the House of Burgesses and the Council. At least £50,000 of expired currency remained in circulation.

Before the burgesses convened on May 22, Robinson, Peyton Randolph, and their allies devised a way to retire the colony's currency. Virginia would borrow £240,000 sterling from merchants and financiers in London at an annual interest of 5 percent. With £100,000 of this money, the treasury would redeem circulating currency and destroy it. With £140,000 in specie as a reserve, the colony could lend its own bank notes to borrowers at an interest of 5 percent. A new poll tax and tobacco tax would repay the London lenders.

Who would borrow the colony's new bank notes and pay 5 percent to do so? Planters deeply in debt, pressed by their British creditors. In the eyes of its supporters, this could "extricate our Country out of its present deplorable Circumstances." To its opponents, it was a scheme to tax those not deeply in debt in order to rescue reckless debtors and "to help the [speaker] out of the mire, in which he has plunged himself."

During court days in April, more than 5,000 people filled streets and taverns in Williamsburg. Drinking rum punch and madeira, they caroused until dawn. The stamp tax was their favorite subject of conversation. Throughout the American colonies it excited resentment and determination to prevent enforcement. Much against the wishes of Speaker Robinson and his friends, Virginia gained a reputation as a leader of defiance.

Robinson and almost all burgesses thought the tax a breach of the British Constitution and an infringement of colonists' liberty, as well as a financial blow on top of a depression. They had said as much in their remonstrances to the king, the House of Lords, and the House of Commons the past December. The speaker, Secretary Nelson, and others estimated the annual cost of the tax in Virginia. Their lowest figure was £35,000. The speaker set it at £45,000. Merchants said that the colony held only a fraction of that sum in coin. Nevertheless, Robinson and his friends disapproved of defiance of Parliament and the ministry. They had faith in less overt ways of changing the British government's conduct.

In the session of late May, most burgesses regarded their work as finished after they had passed bills, including one for the loan office, and approved Robinson's treasury accounts on May 29. The Council, including such firm opponents of all paper money as Richard Corbin and the Nelson brothers, rejected the loan office. By May 30, as two burgesses who had ridiculed the loan office, George Johnston and Patrick Henry, urged opposition to the stamp tax, only 39 of 116 members remained in the chamber. With narrow majorities they passed four resolutions asserting elected representatives' exclusive right to tax. Peyton Randolph and the speaker's friends opposed these as redundant, a repetition of the colony's earlier remonstrances. Johnston and Henry's fifth resolution said that colonists were not bound to obey any law taxing them except laws enacted in Virginia. It aroused "very strong" debate, during which Robinson accused Henry of speaking treason. The resolution passed by one vote. The next day, after Henry left Williamsburg, Peyton Randolph moved that the resolutions be stricken from the journal. He could not get a majority to expunge all of them, but he won a vote to expunge one. The printer of the *Virginia Gazette* did not publish things to which Governor Fauquier objected, but newspapers in other colonies printed not only all five resolutions, but also the draft of a sixth, declaring that anyone who asserted Parliament's right to tax colonists was an enemy. George Grenville, after reading them, said they "exceed any notions which I could entertain of that extravagance."

Much more extravagance followed throughout the continent. Colonists promised to press British merchants by refusing to buy goods and by beginning competitive American manufacture. Crowds destroyed property of officials and of friends of government. No stamped paper was safe, and all distributors must be forcibly invited to resign. George Mercer arrived in Williamsburg on October 30, about thirty-six hours before the tax was to take effect. Just outside the capitol almost all the leading planters and merchants in town for court days demanded that he resign. A crowd outside the coffeehouse seemed to menace him, but Speaker Robinson, members of the Council, and Governor Fauquier stood with him. He went home with the governor. In another part of the colony Richard Henry Lee denounced Mercer as a betrayer of Virginians' liberty by his acceptance of the distributorship, and burned him in effigy. By November 1, Mercer had decided to resign and return to England. The governor and Council unanimously adjourned the General Court because they had no stamped paper and could not lawfully act without it.

Late in 1765 and early in 1766, Virginia's courts remained closed. Suits for debt stood still. Vessels could not be cleared in or out. Trade partially resumed, risking confiscation of any vessel sailing without stamped documents. Planters in Antigua, who opposed but did not defy the tax, ran short of supplies from the mainland. They feared famine among slaves and a lack of staves for hogsheads. In Virginia, after many people stopped paying their British debts and reduced their purchases of goods, the rate of exchange fell sharply. By the end of 1765, £100 in currency bought £100 sterling.

Somewhere at sea in mid-October 1765 two vessels, probably far out of each other's sight, crossed the same line of longitude at the same time, sailing opposite courses. One bore George Mercer and stamped paper from London to Virginia. The other bore Samuel Gist from Virginia to London. Gist had visited Williamsburg during the April and May court days. He had seen the usual "vast Concourse of people" hurrying between the taverns and the capitol, thronging the street known as the Exchange just beyond the capitol. He could not avoid hearing about Speaker Robinson's embarrassing shortage of treasury notes or watching the fiasco of the loan office. Everywhere people had talked about the stamp tax. Gist had bought some blank bills of exchange.

When Gist came back to Williamsburg late in September, he stayed only briefly and never returned. He was bound for London at last. In that city he expected, as his wife wrote him, to "injoy all the health and satisfaction you often promised yr self when you got there." He placed an advertisement in the *Virginia Gazette*, naming the men who held his power of attorney and announcing his imminent departure. By October 9 he booked passage. His wife asked him to send her a good brass kettle and some magazines, apparently not expecting to follow him. She added that their daughters often had cried over his departure. Six or eight weeks after Gist reached England, George Mercer arrived back in London. He estimated his expenses as stamp distributor for Virginia at £1,113 0s. 8d.

III

———◆———

THE LAND OF CAKES

TO A FRIEND BOUND FOR LONDON from Virginia in August 1765, John Hook, a Scottish merchant in Virginia, wished a swift arrival "safe in the Land of Cakes . . . quite free from the noise and Impertinance of the Dd planters." London was the greatest metropolis in Europe. Visitors from the Continent marveled at it almost as much as did provincials from the colonies. Struck by the city's "immense Scale," a Massachusetts man wrote: "whatever I have seen in my own Country, is all Miniature, yankee, puppet-shew." Spreading out from both banks of a broad bend in the River Thames, London embraced new arrivals, making all but the most confident feel small. Shipping rode in the river, moored so thickly by the quays near the Tower and elsewhere that a forest of masts seemed to surround the sprawling old fortress. Near the west base of the Tower, customs officers waited in the long hall of their colonnaded customhouse. Farther upriver, beyond London Bridge, recently repaired, a new bridge was under construction.

For decades London had stunned newcomers, even longtime residents, with its damp, smoky darkness. The city knew windy, clear days and snowy winter days. But every place had some of those. London had stagnant fog and constant smoke rising from countless chimneys, wrapping buildings and streets in dense clouds and black grime. The city was busy and noisy. In broad thoroughfares lined with old churches and new public buildings in the Italian style, as in crooked streets and narrow lanes, coaches and wagons and carts moved quickly, threatening to run down the unwary. A Royal Navy officer walking along Thames Street behind the quays "narrowly escaped being killed by a Dray-horse." Newly laid sidewalks were crowded with busy pedestrians who jostled anyone in their hurry. The people not in a rush were maimed beggars, vagrants, peddlers, hawkers crying strange wares—old clothes, old books, old iron—"ragged and saucy Jacks and Jills." Mountebanks played hurdy-gurdies and sold quack cures. Shop windows offered a profusion of gleaming goods to buy, or tempting food to eat. A pickpocket darted away from his victim. A prostitute standing not far from St. Paul's Cathedral said to a passing gentleman from the colonies: "my Dear do you want any?" Much of London looked new. The Lord Mayor's Mansion House was only twenty years old. The rotunda of the Bank of England had just been finished. Vacant lots vanished under rows of symmetrical, connected, brick houses. Old houses were pulled down to make way for grand additions to already grand buildings. A German visitor wrote: "Everything in the streets through which we passed seemed dark even to blackness, but nevertheless magnificent."

Several years before Samuel Gist reached London, his partner in the Dismal Swamp Company, Anthony Bacon, had established an office and a residence at Number 12, Copthall Court, on the west side of a narrow lane opening into Throgmorton Street, a short walk from the Bank of England and the Royal Exchange. Bacon and his wife, Elizabeth, worshipped at the Church of St. Bartholomew, which looked across Threadneedle Street at the back of the Exchange. To the church's side, across Bartholomew Lane, stood the Bank. The Bacons' only child, Anthony Richard Bacon, turned seven in 1765. His parents felt "the tenderest affection" for him, and the boy seemed to be on the path to a rich inheritance.

Bacon had secured the interest of Sir Samuel Fludyer, member of Parliament and former lord mayor, a man said to be worth almost £1,000,000. The Duke of Newcastle thought Sir Samuel "the most considerable trader in the City of London." Bacon apparently owed his contract for shipping money for soldiers' wages in the West Indies to Sir Samuel's influence. Sir Samuel and his associate, Adam Drummond, brought Bacon into their petition to lease coal mines on Cape Breton Island. In 1764, Bacon also won other contracts: to ship provisions to the troops in the islands ceded by France; to lease ships to the government for use there; to lease to the government slaves to work for British surveying parties. Bacon often traveled along Fleet Street and the Strand, passing back and forth between Copthall Court and the offices of the Treasury in Whitehall.

Coming out of Copthall Court and turning left into Throgmorton Street, rather than toward the Bank, Bacon saw Drapers' Hall, the ornate expression of the power and prosperity of one of the worshipful companies whose leaders dominated the City. Elegant, wainscotted rooms behind columns joined by arches opened inward onto gravel walks and gardens.

Bacon, of course, more often turned right, toward the Bank and the Exchange. The Bank, built of stone ornamented funereally, enclosed a court-

A View of London and Westminster. Courtesy of the Henry E. Huntington Library

yard, the great hall, and offices. The building was safe and dark but not quiet. At midday the rotunda behind the vestibule filled with bulls and bears— noisy, rude brokers trading government securities. In the afternoon, men of business spent a few hours in the Exchange or, as they said, walked on 'Change. Behind the clock-tower and an imposing facade, a large quadrangle of upper rooms looked down on a courtyard lined with columns and oak benches. In the arcades, surrounded by advertising bills posted everywhere, men clustered with others trading to the same part of the world. Merchants concerned with Virginia walked in from Cornhill, turned left, and congregated in the southwest corner of 'Change. There they heard the latest news of sailings, prices, disasters, and opportunities. The regulars knew one another, estimated one another's credit, and closed agreements quickly. A Virginian setting out as a London merchant said: "it is inconceivable what great strokes may be made here." By walking on 'Change, retired ship captains still shared the excitement of voyages about to get under way to distant ports and of laden vessels just returned to moorings along the quays. News was the blood of the Exchange. Before entering, many men stopped at an always crowded shop. For a penny or a halfpenny one could quickly scan current newspapers. The Exchange, impressive in its proportions, presented outer walls black with grime, showing signs of decay. It needed cleaning and repair. Parliament in 1767 agreed to pay for the work.

Anthony Bacon's neighbors in Copthall Court, in Throgmorton Street, and in other courts nearby were merchants, insurance brokers and underwriters, directors of the Bank of England, and owners of stock in the East India Company. A visitor in search of a merchant in Copthall Court, not finding him in his office, of course waited for him on 'Change. The visitor might accompany the merchant, a proprietor, into the grand courtroom of East India House, not far east of the Exchange. There, surrounded by Corinthian columns, looking up at an allegorical bas-relief of Britannia seated on a globe receiving tribute from attendant female figures representing India, Asia, and Africa, the visitor observed the gathering of the proprietors—"the most riotous assembly I ever saw."

South of the Exchange, across Cornhill, stood a group of low buildings, facing one another across irregular lanes. These structures had almost as much fame as the great edifices with fronts of Portland stone. They were the coffeehouses of 'Change Alley, especially Jonathan's and Garroway's. Their crowded, dark, paneled rooms with long tables and rows of booths were the London stock exchange, as well as places to eat, drink, smoke, read the papers, and trade news. Though the food might be overpriced and bad, as it was in the Exchange Coffeehouse, no man of business could ignore these establishments, lest he go bankrupt and "waddle out of the Ally, a lame duck." Since the days of the South Sea Bubble the words "'Change Alley" had stood for high risk, sharp practice, and quick wealth or sudden ruin. A political economist wrote: "The trade of the Alley consists too much in conspiring to pick the pockets of every body not in the temporary secret." The secret might even be fiction, "a mere 'Change Alley job." But the volatile world of

The London Docks. Courtesy of the Henry E. Huntington Library

stockjobbers, usurers, and bill-kiters in the coffeehouses could not be divorced from the business under way in the long halls and colonnades nearby.

In the same year Bacon signed new contracts with the government he began to spend part of his time away from London's smoke, noise, and rush. He bought a manor, Higham Hill, about seven miles from the City. He built a country house from which he could look southwestward to London's spires or northward or eastward over broad stretches of forest or southeastward to a broad bend in the Thames. For an architect Bacon turned to William Newton, a hard-working young man who had studied in Italy and had received commissions from several gentlemen. He knew how to create a "Room for State and Entertainment in Country House for a Gent. Gay Pleasing Rich Elegant Rural."

The year after he bought Higham Hill, Bacon also built a house in Wales, across the River Taff from the village of Merthyr Tydfil, 26 miles north of Cardiff. The upper valley of the Taff lay among steep, rocky hills. But the broad vale in which Merthyr Tydfil stood was less rugged than the parish to the west, Ystradyfodwg. Across their northern horizon stretched a range of mountains. Before starting to build, Bacon had visited the valley, not for romantic landscapes but for coal and iron.

Iron had been smelted the modern way in the valley for more than ten years. The parish of Merthyr Tydfil, however, held ninety-three farms and only two or three blast furnaces. Residents of the village were mostly hedgers, ditchers, and farm laborers. Sheep wandered on the hillsides. In the summer, people met on market days at Twyn-y-waun, high above the valley. Anthony Bacon saw an opportunity to offer employment to those he called "our industrious poor."

In his enterprises Bacon almost always acted with one or more partners. For his mineral leases by the Taff he joined with a man from Whitehaven, the city of his youth, Dr. William Brownrigg, a physician and scientist who studied poisonous gases in coal mines. Brownrigg's brother, George, was the celebrated advocate of North Carolina peanut oil. His brother-in-law, Charles Wood, builder of furnaces and forges, moved to Merthyr Tydfil to serve as agent.

From Earl Talbot of Hensol and from Michael Richards, resident of Cardiff, Bacon and Brownrigg took leases of mineral rights in a tract about eight miles long and five miles wide in the parish of Merthyr Tydfil for ninety-nine years at an annual rent of £100, free of royalties. This gave them the right to extract coal and ironstone from the land occupied by the earl's tenants. The partners also leased lots at Cyfarthfa, just outside Merthyr Tydfil on the west bank of the Taff. There Wood built a blast furnace 60 feet high, and Bacon built his house nearby. He wished to see regular bursts of flame from the furnace and watch red-hot pigs of iron brought forth.

Bacon began to buy farmers' leases. Men paying the earl £3 or £4 per year for their farms received £100 from Bacon if they surrendered their land. The Cyfarthfa works quickly swallowed twenty leaseholds. Bacon offered employment at the furnace or in extracting coal carried to the furnace on horses and mules. Ironstone and coal lay near the surface and was dug by hand or scoured out by water. Where Charles Wood met resistance, he tore down a farmer's fence and pressed on with horses and carts. The arrival of Wood, as well as his master builder, his brickmaker, and others, led a Welshman to say of Merthyr Tydfil: "that place is swarm by Englishmen since the Iron work came there." Encountering rivalry from the recently established furnaces of the Plymouth Iron Works, Bacon bought out the owners and added those to his holdings. They acquired the name "Bacon's Mineral Kingdom."

He still spent most of his time in London. After George Grenville fell from power in July 1765, Bacon smoothly adapted to the new administration. During the summer he joined merchants meeting with Lord Dartmouth, new president of the Board of Trade. A long paper by Joseph Manesty, explaining the disturbances in America and analyzing colonial trade, was written for Dartmouth in Copthall Court. When Grenville heard that merchants had begun organizing to get Parliament to repeal the stamp tax, he expected Bacon to resist such "Reflections upon the late ministry" and remain loyal to his original patron. But Bacon already had abandoned him.

Bacon retained his contracts to supply cash for the army payroll and to lease slaves to the government. He still had friends on the Board of Trade. Charles O'Hara, governor of Senegambia, learned this when he stopped Bacon's agent from delivering 250 slaves to a French vessel. *Le Negrillon* was anchored in Senegal Roads to take slaves on board in violation of British law. After *Le Negrillon* sailed without these slaves, Bacon protested to the Board of Trade, declaring that British traders long had done as his agent was doing until O'Hara interfered. He said that he was losing money on his contract for the army. The board called on the governor to explain his conduct. O'Hara cited the law and estimated the loss to Britain by this trade at £200,000 per year. The board ignored his answer.

As Bacon's interests in the West Indies expanded, he thought that Anthony Bacon & Company should be represented there by one of the partners. At the beginning of August 1766 he sent Gilbert Francklyn to Antigua. From that island Francklyn could visit other islands, "superintend" the leased slaves, and represent Bacon in dealings with army officers. Francklyn stayed in the West Indies for many years. He always defended slavery. He contended that slaves were treated comparatively well in the West Indies. "No severities, there exercised," he wrote, "are equal to the cruelty of enticing poor people, by a small addition of wages, to work in lead, quick-silver, or other metals, or deleterious manufactories."

Preparing to leave Virginia, Samuel Gist made sure that his interest in the Dismal Swamp Company received attention in his absence. He gave one-fourth of his share to David Jameson, a merchant in York Town. Acting with Gist's power of attorney, Jameson would share the profits. While Gist sailed for London, Jameson paid George Washington £25, the latest assessment on each share. The following spring he paid £50 to purchase a slave for the company.

Gist provided for his stepsons by making Joseph Smith guardian of his younger brother, John. By Gist's account, Joseph owed him almost £300. Nevertheless, Gist left him with inherited property, a mill Gist had sold him, a crop of tobacco already housed, and about £363 on John Smith's account. Gist was not abandoning his interests in Virginia. He still ordered purchases of land and transfer of slaves among his plantations, and he did not mean to leave his new store in Hanover idle.

Sarah Gist stayed in Hanover for a few months after her husband's departure. In the summer of 1766 she died. Mary and Elizabeth, teen-aged "young Ladies," sailed for London to live with their father.

Gist established his home and office on the east side, Number 25, in Savage Gardens, a short street opening at its southern end onto public grounds at the base of the Tower. A few doors south of him stood the offices of the diamond merchants Joseph, Samuel, and Solomon Gompertz, of Gompertz & Heyman. A short walk took Gist to the Customhouse or the quays. He lived less than a mile from the Exchange.

On Tower Hill, he was surrounded by people who made their livings from the coming and going of vessels and goods. Lightermen, watermen, coopers, tacklehouse porters, ticket porters—these men lived near their work. Carmen hauled three hogsheads of tobacco, a ton and a half of freight, in horse carts from the wharf up to a warehouse. Many brokers and merchants also found it convenient to live on Tower Hill. John Norton had returned to London in 1764 after twenty-one years in York Town representing Flowerdewe & Norton. He ran the firm, renaming it John Norton & Son, in Gould Square, which opened into Crutched Friars near Savage Gardens. Closer to the Thames, in Black Raven Court, off Seething Lane on the other side of the Navy Office from Savage Gardens, lived John Stewart, the great Virginia and West Indies merchant. He was best known for his contract with the government to transport felons to the colonies as indentured servants. A walk along Tower Street toward the Tower, a turn left and a walk in Mark Lane, or in Seething Lane, and a turn right to walk along Crutched Friars took one past dozens of merchants' offices and warehouses.

Arriving in Savage Gardens, Gist's daughters found their father living on the edge of "a very mean neighbourhood." Immediately behind Number 25 stood fourteen almshouses in which the Drapers' Company supported aged poor men and their wives. A few yards farther east, along the course of the old city wall fronting on the Minories, were shacks, carpenters' yards, vacant lots, and dunghills. Among them moved "whores and thieves," making the almost impassable area "a terror to the neighbouring inhabitants." Anyone walking on Tower Hill met many beggars. One seaman called them "the lame, lazy and maimed." Across the Minories, in Church Street, stood a charity home for "decayed masters or pilots of ships, their wives or widows." A little farther east, in Prescot Street, a plain building devoted for the past seven years to charity had taken the name Magdalen House for the seclusion and reformation of underage "penitent prostitutes." The garrets of the Minories, like those of Grub Street, held writers trying to live by their wits.

Samuel Gist and his daughters watched their neighborhood change. The open spaces on Tower Hill still held beggars, coaches and chaises of the rich, a street preacher, and a "foreign quack doctor" offering to heal "the blind and the lame." Nearby streets and buildings were soon remade. The Corporation of London gave orders to raze hovels, tear down more of the old wall, and widen the Minories. It commissioned its architect to design symmetrical four-story brick rows in imitation of the latest triumph at Bath. Gist approved. Even the penitent prostitutes were going to move to a "very elegant edifice" on the south bank of the Thames.

Within a year of arriving in London, Gist bought his first ship, a new vessel of 120 tons, with a crew of fourteen. He named her the *Mary and Elizabeth*. She sailed for the Chesapeake, bearing the kind of merchandise Gist long had sold in Hanover. Eight months later she sailed from York Town, laden with tobacco, iron, barrel staves, and hemp. Dr. Walker consigned to Gist casks of ginseng—the rare, sovereign specific for health and vigor. Gist thought it "of indifferent Quality," bringing a lower price. He admonished Walker, who roamed where the wild root grew: "pick out the Large Spungy Roots." Gist grew angry when told that some Virginians—"vile ingratefull people," he called them—were accusing him of shipping inferior goods while also getting low prices for their tobacco. He saw malice at work: "such Stories are propogated by my enemies." He was willing to be magnanimous. He wrote, before buying another, bigger ship: "that shall not make me less ready to serve them whenever I can, as I will be so much of a Christian on this Occasion as to do them good for evil."

Sitting in his counting room next to the almshouse, Gist thought about debtors, people in Virginia who had not paid him. His attorney in Hanover, Peter Lyons, pursued in court debts as small as £1 12s. 1d. But hardly any remittances on old accounts came in, and too many current correspondents wanted too much credit. Gist grew more irritated: "a man might as well have an Estate in the moon as money in Peoples hands who will not pay it." He was already thinking about better ways to make profits. Of Virginians he said: "I can do without them."

Maintaining his consignment trade to Virginia, Gist added other interests. His trim little figure appeared not only in the Virginia Walk on 'Change but also on the other side of Exchange Alley in Lombard Street, in the crowded, smoky rooms of Lloyd's Coffee House. Another Tower Hill merchant trading to America, William Stead, was an underwriter of marine insurance there. As in all such establishments, stooped waiters served food and drink. More than others, Lloyd's filled in the afternoon with men calculating the fate of vessels at sea. The latest news of ships all over the world was posted there. Open bags awaited letters for every port. Auctions of vessels were frequent, hectic, and brief, lasting only as long as the burning of an inch of candle. Anthony Bacon had bought the *Two Sisters* for a run to Africa and Maryland in that way, paying too much, some thought. And scores of men took their usual seats in Lloyd's, offering to sign their names to policies of insurance on vessels about to sail or already at sea. Samuel Gist joined them.

Becoming an underwriter was easy. One signed the book at Lloyd's and paid a fee of two guineas per year. A man of modest means might prosper as an underwriter. When Gist reached London, John Julius Angerstein, at the age of thirty-one, had worked as a broker and underwriter for ten years and had begun a fortune. He later explained: "I am as careful as I possibly can be." Care was necessary because a man's promise to pay the portion of a policy he had subscribed, usually £100 or £200, in case of loss or damage was only as good as his own credit. To make much money, he had to sign dozens or scores of policies. A run of disasters at sea could bankrupt him. Premiums of 2 percent or 2½ percent of the insured value of vessel and cargo for a single voyage tempted some men to write their names on too many policies, hoping against the odds for calm seas and prosperous voyages in every quarter. Angerstein spoke of them as "men that I should not like to take."

Owners of vessels and cargoes could insure most securely with one of the two chartered companies, London Assurance and Royal Exchange Assurance, which had a corporate liability to pay their losses. But they charged higher premiums; they demanded security for a policyholder's or a broker's ability to pay his premium; and they asked many more questions about vessels and voyages than did private underwriters. Most of the work of circulating among underwriters at Lloyd's, quickly negotiating premiums, and securing signatures on policies fell to brokers. They knew and were known by the men in the room. Extending credit to owners of vessels and cargoes, brokers enabled them to take out more and larger policies, increasing the volume of insurance transactions.

Many underwriters were also merchants, at once insurers and insured. Samuel Gist had come to agree with one of these merchant underwriters, James Bourdieu, who later wrote: "a Man in business here, can make greater advantage of his Money than lending it at Interest in America." That was what Gist's Virginia trade seemed to have become, he said. He began to appear at Lloyd's regularly. There the first rule of success was: "an Underwriter ought always to attend and be in the way"—that is, in the way of getting policies and news. The more a man knew about vessels in the trade, captains commanding them, merchants and their business affairs, distant ports, and foreseeable risks, the better he could gauge where to insure, what to avoid, and how much to charge. He needed more information than he found in the annual *Lloyd's Register* and the semiweekly *Lloyd's List*. A cautious underwriter might stick to "regular risks"—voyages from Britain to America and back or from Britain to a Continental port and back. The more venturous subscribed to "cross risks," insuring voyages among foreign ports and voyages to several ports. Even regular risks called on an underwriter for a command of myriad discrete details, a fast calculation when offered a policy, and an ability to spot "Sea Gulls," the men who came in only when they found themselves in "stormy weather," hoping to get unusually high risks insured. Success, a veteran said, came from "long continued attention as an Underwriter." Those who made fortunes in Lloyd's Coffee House did so by collecting more and more premiums, subscribing more and more policies. It was a good place for the self-made man: "I should think that an Individual, who has nothing but his own head and his own ability and talent to forward his interest, would adhere as much to it as possible, his whole mind and time is given up to it."

Among the crowd in the Coffee House each afternoon, George Hayley was known as "a merchant of eminence, and one of the veteran 'dreadnought' Underwriters, always ready to engage in any risk at a very small premium." Like Gist, he had started as a clerk and had made a fortunate marriage—in Hayley's case to John Wilkes's sister, Mary. The widow of a

City merchant, she brought Hayley a fortune of £15,000. He rose to the head of the firm trading to America in which he had begun as a clerk. By the time Gist crossed his path, Hayley was rumored to have a capital of £100,000.

Among Gist's neighbors in Savage Gardens was Henry Chapman, son-in-law of George Hayley's "intimate & close" friend, William Neate. Another regular at Lloyd's, Neate was best known in the linen and cloth trade. He exported chiefly to Pennsylvania, New York, and Canada. "No one man in this City," he wrote, "understands the Trade better than myself or excells in so many articles." From Neate, Gist could learn that even the most able merchant might suffer for lack of remittances from customers in the colonies.

After becoming an underwriter, Gist followed the examples of Hayley, Angerstein, and James Bourdieu. Bourdieu succeeded as an underwriter, and he kept an eye out for other investments, such as East India Company stock, sugar prices in Amsterdam, and arms for the French slave trade. He bought a country estate at the age of forty-six. Gist was just starting his career at Lloyd's in his early forties.

As Gist grew acquainted with his fellow underwriters, he could survey the room and review any number of stories telling how diverse men had come to Lloyd's: Samuel Chollet, once Bourdieu's clerk, now his partner; Robert Bogle, Sr., in the Virginia trade; Joshua Mendes da Costa, who subscribed policies in the Portuguese trade and others; William Devaynes, newly returned from the Gold Coast and soon to be a director of the East India Company; John Nutt, heavily involved in the Georgia and South Carolina trade; John Shoolbred, not yet thirty, like Angerstein a rapidly rising young man, cutting an ever bigger figure in the Canada trade and the African slave trade; a merchant in Mark Lane with Shoolbred, the policy broker Thomas Bell, not to be mistaken for Captain Thomas Bell, a merchant and insurance broker in Aldermanbury near St. Paul's, who "had the Good Luck to be call'd Honest Thom Bell, in Distinction to another who frequented Loyds Coffee House." Gist had brought himself within reach of the summit. He was a player in the most important marine insurance market in Europe, a market in which a man stood as high as his reputation for skill and for capital. The Coffee House invited the shrewd and the daring, not the fastidious. Decades later, a genteel young man arrived in London with thoughts of becoming an underwriter. He met James Bourdieu, whom some people found "rather positive and peremptory," as well as many of the men at Lloyd's who had come into prominence in Bourdieu's day. To the young man they seemed rough: "the old ones here are high in mercantile Reputation, but neither their Persons or manners would strike you with much Respect."

As Gist arrived in London, many merchant underwriters at Lloyd's, with merchants elsewhere in London and in other British ports, were talking about the stamp tax and colonists' reaction to it. George Grenville's experiment, they said, had come out a disaster. It had made the depression worse. Orders from the colonies had dropped steeply and remittances had dried up. Manufacturers had discharged workers. The transatlantic trade faced "utter Ruin." George Hayley, William Neate, Robert Bogle, John Nutt—in fact, almost everyone in the American trade—wished Parliament to repeal the tax. The ministry which had replaced Grenville's also disliked it and deplored its effects. The ministry sent "Agents" to confer with merchants, who then concluded that they ought to press Parliament with petitions for repeal. The partners of the House of Hanbury "spared no endeavrs" to make themselves "instrumental" in this cause. Merchants were summoned to the bar of the House of Commons to testify about the law's consequences. Capel Hanbury and others darkly warned that Virginians might grow less tobacco and more hemp, turning their labor to manufacture of cordage in competition with Britain. Grenville and his supporters called the colonists "insolent Rebells." Nevertheless, repeal passed by a large majority on February 21, 1766. Anthony Bacon not only voted for repeal but also spoke in its favor during debate.

In the afternoon of Wednesday, April 23, Throgmorton Street was crowded with the carriages of merchants headed for Drapers' Hall. At its entrance the men stepped down, entered the courtyard, turned right, and climbed the grand staircase to enter the long, wainscotted common hall. It was set for dinner. Under full-length portraits of William III, George I, and George II, they celebrated repeal of the Stamp Act, applauding their leader, Barlow Trecothick. In Virginia, George Washington wrote to the Hanburys, thanking them for their part in winning repeal of an "Act of Oppression." William Nelson spent much of Friday, July 25, writing to various merchants in the City, congratulating them on their success in Parliament. Though Virginians and colonists throughout North America spoke of "that unconstitutional oppressive Stamp act," the men dining in Drapers' Hall had not contended that the tax was unconstitutional, only that it was inexpedient, the wrong policy. Parliament, in a Declaratory Act, stated its authority over the colonies. But after repeal of the stamp tax, George Grenville believed Parliament's authority "is now manifestly destroy'd" and "must be asserted & establish'd." Told that colonists would demonstrate universal joy and gratitude, he replied that if the merchants and the colonists' other friends would "do the same by Buckinghamshire, and double tax themselves to take off our taxes, I will engage for my countrymen here that they shall express as universal joy and more gratitude for the future."

. . .

George Washington and Fielding Lewis visited the Dismal Swamp in April before attending a meeting of their company in Williamsburg. They saw more of the perimeter than they had seen for several years by riding toward Edenton and crossing into North Carolina to call on Marmaduke Norfleet, a planter in Perquimans County. Washington and Lewis bought some of his land lying along the road seven or eight miles south of the dividing line. The tract held a good house, kitchen, and barn surrounded by a little more than 1,000 acres. Part was well timbered. Part was "exceeding rich and open meadow." All, Washington believed, was "capable of great improvement." He and Lewis offered more than £1 per acre, which Norfleet accepted.

Returning to Virginia, Washington stopped in Norfolk, where shipwrights were building a schooner for him. He spent time with Robert Tucker. If the busy merchant looked more fretful than usual, he had good reason. His many debtors would not respond to his repeated requests for payments. In vain he traveled to court days to meet them. The more cargoes he shipped in vessels of London firms, the more he risked, and he had many creditors. For the past ten weeks Tucker had drawn bills of exchange on a London house, Hasenclever, Seton & Crofts, totaling more than £1,560 sterling. He apparently did not know that this firm was not an ordinary mercantile enterprise. Founded in 1763, it provided money and credit for Peter Hasenclever's wildly ambitious projects in New Jersey and New York. Spending far more than his partners' capital, Hasenclever promised to make a fortune for them with pig iron, potash, and hemp.

Washington reached Williamsburg on Friday, May 2. The Dismal Swamp Company met on Saturday. John Washington had come up from Dismal Plantation. The members voted a further assessment of £300, or £25 per share, for the company's operations. Robert Burwell did not wish to remain a member. The company agreed to buy his one-half share. While in Williamsburg, John Washington placed an advertisement in the *Gazette*, announcing that the Dismal Swamp Company would always have shingles "ready for delivery" at the wharf in Suffolk.

The summer of 1766 did not help the draining of a swamp or growing of tobacco and wheat. Heavy rain fell in June and the first three weeks of July. Then drought hung over the region, with heat so intense that some laborers, slave and free, died in the fields. John Washington kept the company's slaves at work felling trees and cutting shingles, for which George Washington found a buyer. He traveled to Suffolk and the Dismal Swamp again in November. He and Dr. Walker and Fielding Lewis concluded that the company ought to buy Dismal Plantation from the estate of Mills Riddick. Washington negotiated the purchase of the 402 acres from Riddick's son.

The £12 10s. Mann Page paid the company to meet its latest levy was infinitesimal compared to his debts. His effort to auction lots in his new Hanover-Town had failed: he still held 146 unsold lots. He offered them through a lottery. A £30 ticket was good for one lot, to be assigned by a drawing once all tickets were sold. Month after month Page's advertisements in the *Gazette* invited people to buy. Few did. Samuel Gist suggested that a bridge be built across the Pamunkey to attract business from King William County to Hanover. He advised his correspondent: "perswade Mr. Page it will add to the value & Sale of his Lots wch. perhaps he may not otherways find out." A bridge might have helped Gist's new store. Nothing could help Page's town. Rosewell's grandeur still rested on unpaid debt.

Page's son, John, was married to Robert Burwell's daughter, Frances, early in 1765. Mann Page had promised to hand Rosewell to John and move to an estate near Fredericksburg, where a younger son lived. But Anne Tayloe Page kept putting off the day of yielding the big house to her stepson and his wife. John and Frances lived with Frances's parents for more than a year. Their first child was born in the Burwell home. One of Anne Tayloe Page's neighbors, who detested her, feared that she would hold on at Rosewell until her death. "God grant that she may reform before she dies," he wrote. Mann Page apparently did pull her away not long after his grandson, named Mann, was born.

Mann Page told his son and Robert Burwell before John and Frances were married that he would give John a plantation on the right bank of the Rappahannock River, entailed property which John would otherwise eventually inherit, with the slaves who worked there, as John's portion of his father's estate. But Mann afterward concluded that he needed to dock the entail and sell that plantation in hope of paying some debts. As a substitute legacy he conveyed to John, besides Rosewell, property in Gloucester County, Mann's portion of land on which his father and uncles and King Carter once had planned to mine copper with the Frying Pan Company, and one-half share in the Dismal Swamp Company. This was John's patrimony.

John Page loved the brick-and-glass mansion his grandfather had built, but, by the time he and Frances moved in, it was falling into disrepair. Red paint was chipping or peeling; some of the dozens of windows needed work, as did the roof. Page had happy memories of his youth there: his grandmother teaching him to read, his tutor opening his mind, and, after he had gone to the College of William and Mary, visits by his best friend, Dr. Walker's ward, Thomas Jefferson. The college had turned Page's interest toward science. He took up astronomy and acquired a large telescope. What better place for celestial observations than the roof of the tallest building in Virginia? Jefferson enjoyed the "philosophical evenings" at Rosewell with Page and said that if he lived nearby, they might "pull down the moon." Of course, the big event to which all astronomers looked forward was the transit of Venus across the Sun, coming in 1769.

Page was best suited to pursue astronomy with Jefferson or to talk about rare and curious plants with his aged neighbor, John Clayton, friend of Carl Linnaeus, as they stood in Clayton's profuse, exotic garden. Page could not make Rosewell pay. He spent more than he had expected as he and his wife set up housekeeping. Yet he could never get more than 15 hogsheads of tobacco from the plantation. And he was ill prepared to deal with his new partners in the Dismal Swamp Company. The kindly expression and customary smile on his round face suggested a trusting nature. "I have known Mr. Page from the time we were boys and classmates together and love him as a brother," Jefferson wrote, "but I have always known him the worst judge of man existing."

The months of May and June 1766 brought a stark change of fortune to Susanna Robinson, the speaker's young wife. For the rest of her life, another forty years, she could reasonably assume that her walking into a room would remind people in it of those months. Her troubles were of the kind that youngsters and strangers hear whispered warnings not to mention.

On Saturday, May 10, Speaker Robinson died at their home in King and Queen County, after much suffering from a kidney stone in his bladder. Robinson's will named his intimate friend and ally Peyton Randolph as an executor. Randolph, however, long had expected to seek the offices of speaker and treasurer as soon as Robinson retired or died. He declined to execute and sent his brother, Peter, to look into the estate. Before the speaker's death, burgesses and councillors had heard rumors of a "very considerable deficiency" in the treasury. These suspicions had come out in public comment and in "Conversation and private complaint." Once Robinson died, the deficiency ceased to be a rumor and "immediately" turned into common knowledge. Several burgesses recalled that, although they had routinely re-elected Robinson speaker without dissent, they had "often" objected to his excessive power and "arbitrary conduct." Within days Peter Randolph found that much money—certainly more than £70,000—was missing from the treasury. He told Susanna Robinson. She said she wished administration of the will to begin at once, and she called the speaker's

Peyton Randolph, John Wollaston. Courtesy of the Virginia Historical Society. John Robinson's ally and successor as speaker of the House of Burgesses, Randolph was the first president of the Continental Congress.

friend and attorney, Edmund Pendleton, to meet her in Williamsburg during June court days.

Edmund Pendleton and Peter Lyons were to be the active administrators of the speaker's estate. Pendleton had proven himself skilled at the bar, and with the proceeds of his practice he had bought an estate, Edmundsbury, in Caroline County. His sixteen-year-old nephew lived with him. Beginning soon after the speaker's death, the boy saw "a considerable concourse of company" coming and going at Edmundsbury.

Robert Carter Nicholas volunteered to become interim treasurer, and Governor Fauquier appointed him. Though Nicholas had not seen the books, he did not trust Robinson's clerk, whom Fauquier had thought of appointing. Upon taking office and learning of a deficiency in the treasury, he said four weeks later, he found "that many people were apprized of things which I was a stranger to until very lately." He first estimated that £80,000 or £90,000 was missing. He foresaw "dismal consequences to the country." Yet, despite an almost empty treasury, the colony's credit did not suffer; nor did people lose confidence in its currency. Business went on as if the missing money surprised no one.

Three weeks after her husband's death, Susanna Robinson learned that her father had murdered a man in a tavern in Cumberland County. John Chiswell and Robert Routledge had exchanged angry words. Routledge had been drunk, but Chiswell had been sober as he thrust his sword through Routledge's heart, then told his servant boy to clean the blade lest it rust. Eight witnesses had been present.

John Chiswell was so testy that he could be "affronted" even by silence. He had more reason to feel edgy in June 1766. Though he lived in Williamsburg, he had been spending much time at his and Robinson's and Byrd's lead mine, which was not yet producing lead. Payments from Robinson to the Lead Mine Company and from the company to Chiswell had become his main support. After Robinson died, Pendleton and Lyons told Chiswell and Byrd that "we could advance no money for carrying on the Lead Mine." Chiswell was insolvent when he reacted so angrily to Robert Routledge's loud claim to be "as good a fellow as John Chiswell."

After the coroner and an examining court took testimony from witnesses in Cumberland, an under-sheriff escorted Chiswell to Williamsburg to be jailed, awaiting trial. They met in the street three members of the Council: John Blair, William Byrd, and Presley Thornton. Acting as judges of the General Court, with the advice of three attorneys—George Wythe, John Randolph, and Edmund Pendleton—the councillors admitted Chiswell to bail on the spot and released him. Since Byrd and Thornton were his friends and all three attorneys had been close to his son-in-law, the speaker, this peremptory release of a man accused of capital murder struck many people as too blatant an act of "partial magistrates," doing for Chiswell that which they would not have done for anyone lacking his "connections." Chiswell left for the lead mine.

Edmund Pendleton was in Williamsburg to begin sorting Robinson's papers and putting the estate in order. The administrators published an advertisement on June 13, calling Robinson's debtors to pay immediately. In saying that the speaker had "advanced large sums of money to assist and relieve his friends, and others," they left unsaid what everybody knew: by far the largest part of these sums had come from the treasury of Virginia. Pendleton and Lyons did not yet have a list of debtors and amounts. One man who had borrowed more than £2,700 heard that Robinson had kept no correct books. Pendleton found the papers "in great confusion." Robinson had not taken security for loans, seldom had written a statement of a loan, and often had not even recorded it in the borrower's account. Pendleton reconstructed some debts from letters and "endorsements on scraps of paper." Nor had the speaker kept a record of the money he had taken from the treasury. He also had been lenient to debtors who had owed him for a long time and to sheriffs who had not remitted taxes to the treasury punctually. To sheriffs who brought tax revenues he gave receipts, but he did not enter all the payments on the treasury's books.

Was the loan office the burgesses had passed the previous year a ruse to borrow money in England and lend it to Robinson's debtors so that they could repay him, enabling him to return the money to the treasury, thereby neatly shifting the huge debt from Robinson's account to the colony's? Or had Robinson's loans gone out during the year since the Council rejected the loan office, serving as a short-term substitute?

Richard Bland decided a week after Robinson's death to seek election as speaker. Richard Henry Lee already had begun to campaign for himself, but Bland persuaded Lee to join his camp. Bland adopted Lee's view, advocating separation of the offices of speaker and treasurer, promising "to prevent any unnatural Influence in the House." Peyton Randolph hoped to succeed to both of Robinson's offices. In May, Bland wrote to Lee: "I have no suspicion that the public Funds have been converted to uses for which they were not designed." Such conversion, however, soon became the chief weapon of his candidacy as he censured Robinson for daring "to break through acts of the whole Legislature, and to controul their power by his own authority." The late speaker had used his influence "to protect him for so flagrant a breach of his publick trust." At the same time, Bland knew that many indebted Virginians remained "very importunate for a Loan office." He said that he had in mind "a Scheme of great Extent" for a loan office or a public bank.

Robert Carter Nicholas hoped to become permanent treasurer. He, too, proposed separating the offices of speaker and treasurer. He promised he would have "no Influence." He called on sheriffs to pay their arrears of taxes, warning that he would force them to comply. He said that Robinson's conduct "can admit of no excuse."

During the months between Robinson's death and the convening of the House of Burgesses in November, Williamsburg had two newspapers. Their printers, rivals for the colony's printing contract, were newly willing to publish scandal, satire, and political controversy. Supporters of Peyton Randolph accused and rebutted supporters of Richard Bland in the weekly *Gazettes*.

William Nelson thought it all "scurrilous," but he and Secretary Nelson read the papers. He had opposed paper money and had helped defeat the loan office, but he blamed Robinson's "Error, or rather let me say the Weakness" on the "set of men he was connected with," who had taken advantage of Robinson's kindness to extract loans.

The published extenuations of Robinson's conduct made a similar case. He had lent money out of charity and had done a public good by keeping more currency in circulation. With an undercurrent of passion and perhaps of private information, Edmund Pendleton and William Nelson wrote of Robinson's debtors' "application," "importunities," and "earnest Solicitation," all of which the speaker "never could resist." Critics scorned this defense. Professing to write about a hypothetical speaker-treasurer, one author called Robinson "a Man destitute of any real Goodness of Heart, and Benevolence of Disposition." He had been "shamefully bepraised." His chief offense was his "very great influence" in the House of Burgesses, enabling him to override opposition and, all could now see, to abuse his office.

The *Gazettes* also published letters debating John Chiswell's conduct and the propriety of releasing him on bail. The chief critic of Chiswell, of the councillors, and of the three attorneys was Robert Bolling, stepson of Richard Bland. With arch sarcasm, he accused the councillors of acting as if they and Chiswell were above the law. High officials should be viewed with "Distrust, the parent of security." To confirm this view he pointed to the deeds of the late speaker. Justifying Robinson, like releasing Chiswell, amounted to "subverting all ideas of virtue and morality." William Byrd could not tolerate publication of such insults. He tried to get a grand jury to indict Bolling and the printers for libel, but the jurors, headed by Mann Page, refused. Byrd's wrath only made him look more willing to violate "indifferent & impartial Justice."

In their public statements both Robinson's critics and his apologists professed surprise at the speaker's backstairs activities. The writers said that they were pained to learn that "influence" had been at work in the governing of Virginia. They had heard rumors to that effect, but only rumors. So they had not confronted the speaker with public opposition or with private friendly warnings. Indeed, they had re-elected him by acclamation. Only after his death could they see and say that he had betrayed the public's confidence in Virginia's virtue.

As he compiled a list, Edmund Pendleton did not reveal the names of Robinson's debtors. His own was among them, as were those of Benjamin Grymes and John Randolph. The largest single debt, almost £15,000, was owed by William Byrd; members of the House of Burgesses had borrowed more than £37,000. Pendleton was discreet. A graceful man, with polished manners, he "always looked to consequences." The biggest debtors asked him to allow three years to pay. He persuaded the burgesses not to take debtors to court at once, warning against "rigorous Measures," which would ruin many families. Bankrupting debtors would not secure payment. According to Benjamin Waller, who knew most of Williamsburg's political secrets, Pendleton was so smooth that, after having "exerted his every power to ward off" the burgesses' seizure and scrutiny of Robinson's estate, he nevertheless "so conducted himself throughout the enquiry, that he was finally represented as one of its authors."

Pendleton told the burgesses that the estate owed the treasury £100,761 7s. 5d. He assured them that the assets, with debts owed to Robinson, would exceed this sum. Not until years later did he reveal in private that he had felt "hopeless," foreseeing "a great deficiency of assets for satisfying the Public debt." Susanna Robinson and her three children must leave the comfortable house and beautiful gardens overlooking the Mattaponi. Everything must be sold, including Robinson's share in the Dismal Swamp Company. In the meantime, Pendleton continued to pay the company's assessments. Robinson's merchants in London, John Lidderdale and the Hanburys, quickly brought suit against the estate.

John Chiswell returned to Williamsburg on Thursday, September 11, more than two months before he was due to stand trial. If he read Purdie and Dixon's *Virginia Gazette* on Friday, he found Robert Bolling saying that in publishing letters of censure critics of Chiswell and of the councillors were not just interested in getting "the blood of Mr. Chiswell" by ensuring that he would be convicted and hanged. "We are desirous of knowing whether some Virginians may massacre other Virginians (or sojourners among them) with impunity." The following Friday, Chiswell could read John Blair, president of the Council, almost apologizing for having released him on bail. Robert Hartswell had known Chiswell and Speaker Robinson for almost thirty years. He wrote to the *Gazette* to say that he never would have suspected either man of committing such crimes. More letters appeared in October, leading up to election of a new speaker shortly before the trial. But the case of the murderer of Robert Routledge never came to trial. On Wednesday, October 15, John Chiswell was found dead in his home, amid furniture he had borrowed from Speaker Robinson.

Three weeks later the burgesses convened. By a large majority Peyton Randolph defeated Richard Bland to become speaker. By another large majority the burgesses separated the offices of speaker and treasurer. Robert Carter Nicholas remained treasurer. For several more years, Susanna Robinson and her children lived at Pleasant Hill, until Pendleton and Lyons sold the plantation at auction to a Scottish merchant. The speaker's body lay buried about 100 yards from the house. His grave never got a stone.

At the end of May 1766, a few days before John Chiswell entered the tavern at Cumberland Court House, Robert Tucker's daughter, Sarah, was married to John Taylor in Norfolk. Tucker kept busy as usual, importing hundreds of hogsheads of rum and barrels of sugar, exporting wheat. His four vessels sailed the Chesapeake and made quick runs to the West Indies. A new brigantine, to be named for his youngest daughter, was rising on the stocks. His credit was good. His bills of exchange passed in Baltimore without an endorser. His bakery under the big windmills on the point turned out a ton and a half of bread each day. Yet he spent much time writing to his debtors and confronting them, asking them to pay. He met repeated disappointments.

During the summer, Tucker heard from his London merchants, Edward and Thomas Hunt, that his bills of exchange drawn on Hasenclever, Seton & Crofts were refused by that firm. The Hunts took the bills to sustain Tucker's credit. He did not expect this news. He had loaded that firm's ships with cargo; his account with Hasenclever, Seton & Crofts showed a large balance in his favor, about £4,700. He could not relax. His interests and risks were widely extended; he did not let a shilling long lie still.

While the *Gazette* writers warred over the past and future speaker and the bailment of John Chiswell, disaster struck Robert Tucker. Interrupting the long summer drought, a thunderstorm broke over Norfolk after dark on Thursday, September 4. Lightning hit the city. A bolt fell among Tucker's six warehouses along his wharf extending into the Elizabeth River. These held dry goods, many commodities, and 6,600 gallons of rum. The buildings caught fire; nothing could prevent the flames from consuming them until the burning wharf gave way and collapsed into the river.

For two days Tucker weighed his losses. He estimated them at £2,500 of his own property and a much larger amount in that of others consigned to him. He wrote to William Nelson and to a friend in Baltimore, William Lux, saying that he would continue in business. He announced in the *Virginia Gazette* that he could fill orders for West Indies goods, bread, and flour. In adversity, Tucker showed himself to be, in Nelson's eyes, "a Man of sense & Reflection." But, reading Lux's words of consolation—"your fortune enables you to bear it without feeling it much"—Tucker knew better.

He tried without success in the autumn to get remittances or a satisfactory accounting from Robert Seton, Baltimore representative of Hasenclever, Seton & Crofts. In London, Andrew Seton went bankrupt. Edward and Thomas Hunt demanded in December that Tucker repay them for picking up his protested bills. He refused, and the Hunts went to court. In the third week of January 1767, an express messenger arrived in Norfolk, bringing word from William Lux that Hasenclever, Seton & Crofts had stopped payment in London. Robert Seton did so immediately afterward. Tucker could expect to lose almost £5,000. Trying to encourage him, Lux wrote that Tucker's "real Capital & great Integrity" would sustain his credit. At the same time, Lux promised to preserve "the greatest Secrecy" about these losses.

That winter Robert Tucker no longer worried about his credit or kept up his indefatigable work. He no longer understood what was happening around him. He had lost his reason "totally." From London word reached Norfolk of the bankruptcy of James Crisp and Francis Warren, of the firm Crisp & Warren. In their ships Tucker had loaded cargoes for the Barcelona trade. He stood to lose £1,700. No one told him. The mind once embracing many promising enterprises and directing cargoes to and from points north, east, and south of the Chesapeake capes was now dark.

William Nelson and Richard Corbin, Joanna Tucker's brother, visited her in Norfolk in May. To them Robert Tucker seemed "at the point of Death." His brother, John, promised to come from Barbados to manage the estate. With great surprise, William Nelson learned that Robert Tucker was insolvent. His accounts showed that his debts in Virginia and other colonies almost equaled his assets, other than land and buildings. Nelson roughly estimated the value of the real estate, including Tucker's share in the Dismal Swamp Company, at £5,000. Yet Tucker owed one London firm, the Hunts, almost £6,500 sterling. For more than twenty years Nelson had admired Tucker's hard work and expanding business, taking for granted "that he was very rich." He could only explain to Edward Hunt: "We are often deceived by Appearances."

As Robert Tucker lingered vacantly among his pictures and maps, his partner in the Dismal Swamp Company, William Waters, lay near death in his house in Williamsburg. Just before Christmas he had written his will, leaving almost everything to his daughter, Sarah, though his wife was to have the house and an income for the remainder of her life. Knowing that his health was declining during the early months of 1767, he made clear his affection for David Meade, the warm-hearted young dreamer he had brought into the Dismal Swamp Company.

In the evening of Saturday, May 31, William Waters died. Two weeks later his will went to probate. He owned two plantations on the Eastern

Shore and one in Halifax County along the Roanoke River. His slaves tended livestock and grew corn; most were very old or very young. His creditors went to court and won judgments against his estate, only to reveal that "there will not be near enough" to pay them. William Waters's estate was insolvent. This outcome "astonish'd every one" in Williamsburg, Robert Carter Nicholas wrote. "I always thought him so safe a Hand, that I should not have scrupled trusting him with any Part of my Property." In the months after Waters's death David Meade applied himself to business, patenting hundreds of acres in the Dismal Swamp and elsewhere in Nansemond County.

Robert Tucker died on July 1. His obituary in the *Virginia Gazette* recalled the "many years" he had "carried on a very extensive trade" in Norfolk, "with the greatest credit and honour." His executors, knowing what awaited them, held his will for ten weeks before going to probate. Dozens of creditors stood "prepared with their Bills Bonds & proved Accots.," which they took to court. William Nelson, looking back on the ways Robert Tucker had "quite mistook his own Interest," wrote his private obituary for his old friend: "a Life of so much honest Industry was hardly ever spent to so little good Purpose."

Under such heavy blows, Joanna Tucker had grown "extreamly weak." Nelson thought that liquidation of the estate, selling the contents of her house at auction, would kill her. Her brother-in-law had not yet arrived from Barbados. She and her children gained a friend in October when her daughter, Martha, was married to Thomas Newton, Jr., son of one of Norfolk's leading merchants.

A few months later David Meade, after acquiring still more land near the Dismal Swamp, declared his love for Sarah Waters in the *Virginia Gazette*. Publishing an acrostic poem encoded with the beloved's name was a favorite exercise. Meade did not use an intricate scheme of the kind John Hatley Norton devised to declare his passion for Robert Carter Nicholas's daughter. The first letter of each line of Meade's verse, read down the page, spelled "MISS WATERS." A lover of gardens, Meade used images of flowers to praise her, concluding:

> *Th'exulting florist views the various dyes*
> *E'en thus fares beauty in each lover's eyes*
> *Read o'er these lines you will see the nymph with ease*
> *She, like the rose, was made all lips to please.*

In the spring they began sixty-two years of married life together.

Executors of the Waters and Tucker estates held auctions of slaves and household goods. Sarah Meade's mother stayed in her house in Williamsburg. The Tucker auction took place fourteen months after Robert Tucker's death. The executors, Thomas Newton, Sr., and John Taylor, waited until his brother arrived from Barbados so that John Tucker could "buy the House & some other Conveniences for the Family." At the sale the executors wanted only watching, not bidding, on many items. A bystander saw Robert Tucker's skilled slaves—millers, bakers, coopers, sawyers, and watermen—bought for Joanna Tucker at one-fourth the market price. In the same manner she retained silver plate and furniture. The hammer fell on bidding for "a new, genteel, fashionable coach," with two horses, at £10. With the assent of Robert Tucker, Jr., the slave, Jenny, was sold to her husband, Talbot Thompson, a free black man, who won the Council's permission to free her. An auction of Tucker's land set aside for payment of his debts and an auction of his share in the Dismal Swamp Company apparently did not take place. Benjamin Waller, attorney for Edward and Thomas Hunt of London, objected, since the estate's land was the Hunts' only hope for payment of Tucker's debt. But the estate of the late Robert Tucker remained a partner in the Dismal Swamp Company, as did David Meade, whose marriage reunited the halves of William Waters's share.

Just before the stamp tax troubles, Dr. Thomas Walker built a new house at Castle Hill, on an elevation overlooking the gently rising and falling terrain of the piedmont. Compared to the houses of some of his partners, it was modest, a two-story clapboard building with six dormer windows projecting from its slanted roof. For eighteen months, beginning in the summer of 1767, Dr. Walker spent much time far from his new home, working for the Loyal Company, for other western land projects, and for the colony of Virginia. He treated their interests as one. He was fifty-two years old, still wiry and resilient. His energy and his appetite for travel seemed as great as in his climb through Cumberland Gap seventeen years earlier.

The Loyal Company's surveyors extended their chains in the steep valleys along the upper reaches of the Greenbrier and New rivers. Walker visited the region in the summer. He missed the wedding of his daughter, Lucy, in August, as did the rest of the family. At the age of sixteen she ran away with her lover, George Gilmer, who was twenty-four. George's mother was Dr. Walker's sister. The parents disapproved of a marriage between first cousins, but Lucy and George were "obstinate": they eloped. Early in the fall, Dr. Walker went down to the tidewater, taking casks of ginseng, which he shipped from York Town, prudently consigning only part to Samuel Gist. He did not accompany George Washington and Fielding Lewis on their excursion to Dismal Plantation in October, but he attended a meeting of several partners of the Dismal Swamp Company in Williamsburg on November 3.

At this gathering Dr. Walker saw Washington, Lewis, the Nelson brothers, Mann Page, and Edmund Pendleton, representing the late speaker's estate. And he met Francis Farley, newly arrived from Antigua, taking part in his first meeting of the company. Farley had come to Virginia, he said, "to restore my constitution by a Winter." His son, James, already lived in Williamsburg as a student at the College of William and Mary. His daughter, Eleanor, was pregnant again, and Captain Laforey had extended his shore leave for another year at Maycox. The members of the company paid Washington their portions of the last installment of the purchase price for Dismal Plantation.

Dr. Walker's trips grew longer and more urgent in the summer of 1768. Governor Fauquier died in March. In June the Council appointed Walker and his old ally, Andrew Lewis, as Virginia's commissioners to negotiations for new boundaries between whites' settlement and Indian lands. They headed northward for the upper valley of the Susquehanna River in July, accompanied by two of Walker's sons, Thomas and John. They were gone until November. In Albemarle County, during their absence, John Walker's wife, Elizabeth Moore Walker, was approached by his friend, Thomas Jefferson, who, as Jefferson later put it, "offered love to a handsome lady." After waiting at Shamokin, Pennsylvania, Dr. Walker and Andrew Lewis learned that Sir William Johnson had changed the time and place of the conference with the Six Nations of the Iroquois. The Virginians continued northward, past the Catskill Mountains, across the Mohawk River, to Johnson Hall, a mansion in the forest, where Indian guests came far more frequently than whites.

Two weeks later, Walker's party accompanied Sir William up the Mohawk to Fort Stanwix. There they watched the Indian delegations arrive in October. Hundreds from each of the Six Nations, dozens from other tribes, who had good reason to believe that the treaty would affect their interests—more than 3,000 Indians from 16 tribes gathered around Fort Stanwix. After days of speeches, bargaining, and private meetings, the treaty was signed on November 5 in a ceremony on the fort's parade ground. Twenty boatloads of stacked goods, the king's gifts formed three sides of a rectangle, within which Sir William Johnson, representatives of Pennsylvania and New Jersey, and Dr. Walker received leading men of the Six Nations, their formalities watched from the ramparts of the fort and elsewhere by hundreds of Indian men. Walker then traveled down the Mohawk and Hudson rivers, arriving in New York City in mid-November.

Returning, by way of Philadelphia, to Williamsburg, Walker prepared to head southward. John Stuart, the Crown's representative to southern Indians, had reached an agreement with the Cherokees in mid-October. As Walker had feared when he called his presence at those negotiations "an absolute necessity," Stuart had assented, in Walker's absence, to a line separating colonists from Cherokees which excluded the Loyal Company from much of its grant. Though Stuart had obeyed orders from London, Walker must go to South Carolina to show him that the Cherokees wished to cede still more land, that they even "disclaimed" land assigned to them. With Andrew Lewis, Walker left Williamsburg late in December, crossing the dividing line into North Carolina. They reached Brunswick, near Cape Fear, on January 5, 1769. Governor William Tryon promised his assistance. He had invited two Cherokee leaders to visit him, and these men accepted Walker's invitation to sail to South Carolina. In Charleston, on January 11, Walker and Lewis made their case to Stuart, adding, in a meeting two days later, testimony from the two Cherokees. Stuart was unmoved. Walker and Lewis returned to Williamsburg to make their report on February 2. On this urgent trip, Walker missed the wedding of his daughter, Mildred, and Joseph Hornsby of Williamsburg. Walker approved of young Hornsby, a rising storekeeper with solid habits.

Each of Dr. Walker's long journeys had ties to the others. The new arrangements with Indians were going to surprise and displease many people: officials in London, Indians of the Ohio Valley, Cherokees, and some colonists in Virginia and the middle colonies. Walker intended to be among those who gave surprises, not received them.

Virginians had grown more openly restive under royal prohibition of surveys and settlement beyond the crest of the Alleghenies. The House of Burgesses addressed the Board of Trade, seeking resumption of lawful settlement. George Mercer still represented the Ohio Company in London. The Mississippi Company concluded that it needed an agent, too. On December 16, 1767, the Mississippi Company made Dr. Walker a member. At the same time, some Pennsylvanians connected with Samuel Wharton, helped by friends in London, hoped to get a large grant west of the mountains, one extending into Virginia's western territory and overlapping claims of the Ohio Company. Westward migration must continue, these rivals agreed. The only question was who would get the land. Dr. Walker and Patrick Henry picked William Fleming to go to the confluence of the Ohio and the Mississippi, making note of the best soil. George Washington sent William Crawford to the Ohio Valley to choose tracts Washington could obtain from the Virginia Council as soon as the ban on surveys and settlements was lifted. People were getting ready for a land rush to begin soon after a new agreement with the Indians.

By Sir William Johnson's treaty with the Six Nations, they ceded land south of the Ohio, from the mountains to the mouth of the Tennessee. With their marks on the treaty at Fort Stanwix, leaders of the Six Nations signed away land on which they did not live, while Sir William and his colleagues treated the Shawnees, the Delawares, and the Ohio River Iroquois who lived in the valley as dependents of the Six Nations. Both parties ignored the Cherokees' long-standing claim to much of the land ceded by the Iroquois. Sir William, with his signature, accepted on behalf of the Crown a cession of land stretching farther west than his instructions from London allowed—land Wharton and his friends coveted. Dr. Walker, with his signature, gave Virginia's consent to an agreement designed to serve the interests of Wharton's associates at the expense of Virginia's claims, especially those of the Ohio Company. At the same time, the treaty gave Dr. Walker and his colleagues in the Loyal Company a boundary far to the west of the line John Stuart had drawn with the Cherokees, the Kanawha River. By next spreading gifts among Cherokees and reaching a new treaty with them, Walker and his friends might complete the Loyal Company's success, having quieted the Iroquois and the Cherokees, sold out the Ohio Valley Indians, and circumvented the British government's policy for the west. It looked worth eighteen months of strenuous travel.

Afterward, no one could prove what end Walker had sought or what he had said in private. Had he reached an understanding with Sir William Johnson during his two weeks as a guest at Johnson Hall? Had he closed an agreement with Samuel Wharton before lines were drawn on the map at Fort Stanwix? Sir William had said that Walker's presence was "Necessary," lest the absence of Virginia "appear odd to the Indians." Did his presence have a price? Dr. Walker said he had known nothing and done nothing about the substance of negotiations at Fort Stanwix. He convinced even George Mason, a leader of the Ohio Company, that Sir William had frozen him out of all conferences. He implied that he was among the last to learn what the treaty contained. John Stuart, however, had no doubt that Walker served the same purpose in visiting Charleston and in attending at Fort Stanwix. To the Earl of Hillsborough, secretary of state for the American Department, Stuart explained that Walker and Andrew Lewis had a great financial interest in the land they sought to transfer from Indians to whites: "the Rapacity of the Land Jobbers in Virginia is insatiable." During the two months between the treaty of Fort Stanwix and Walker's return from Charleston, the Virginia Council received eighteen petitions for grants of western land totaling 845,000 acres. Looking at the aftermath of the treaty, the Earl of Hills-borough said: "I . . . can only lament that a Measure of the Utility of which such great expectation was held out, and which has been adopted at so great an Expense, should have so entirely failed in it's Object, as to have produced the Very Evils to which it was proposed as a Remedy."

Three months after learning of the death of Francis Fauquier, the Earl of Hillsborough chose Norborne Berkeley, Baron de Botetourt, to be governor of Virginia. Of course, Virginia already had a governor, Sir Jeffery Amherst. But he had stayed in England, accepting £1,500 per year from Fauquier, who kept an equal share of the office's salary and fees. Hillsborough and the cab-inet ended this arrangement and ordered the new governor to live in Vir-ginia. On July 30, 1768, Lord Botetourt received the appointment from the hands of the king.

Botetourt already was a gentleman of the bedchamber, well known to King George. He was a handsome bachelor, fifty years old, who had been in Parliament for twenty-five years. He charmed people and ingratiated himself through good humor and polished affability. If he sometimes overacted, ap-pearing a little peculiar, one had to recall that Lord Botetourt "writes and speaks and thinks very much in the style of chivalry, not in the style of busi-ness." A few years earlier, while still a commoner, he had had close ties with George Grenville, who had helped him gain his peerage. John de Botetourt, the first baron, had been a fighter, following the Earl of Lancaster into re-bellion against Edward II in 1322. Edward beheaded Lancaster and par-doned Botetourt. In the following century the barony fell into abeyance; there had been no Baron de Botetourt for more than 350 years when Nor-borne Berkeley's claim won approval in 1764. The new Lord Botetourt was a courtier. His admirers saw the "politest, the most engaging manners." His detractors saw "cringing, bowing, fawning."

Of Botetourt's mission to Virginia, Horace Walpole wrote: "If his graces do not captivate them, he will enrage them to fury; for I take all his douceur to be enamelled on iron." The ministry wanted a governor who would tell Virginians what Parliament demanded, not tell the Board of Trade what Vir-ginians demanded, as Fauquier too often had done. Parliament again had levied taxes on colonists, this time on their purchases of glass, lead, paper, paint, and tea. And six weeks after Fauquier's death, Virginians again had pronounced such taxes unconstitutional, an attack on their liberties. Coun-cillors and burgesses were united, and they encouraged other colonies to op-pose taxes. The Earl of Hillsborough, the Duke of Grafton, head of the ministry, and the king sent a governor to represent the authority of Parliament and the Crown. Botetourt, since the first disputes between colonists and the government, had supported that authority in a tone of "violence & passion." His critics called him a "tool." As he sailed from Portsmouth, bound for the Chesapeake, on board a sixty-gun ship of the line, HMS *Rippon*, he knew that he was supposed to "answer the purposes of our Gracious Master." Accepting his appointment, he had told the king that he was ready to leave that night. In the following weeks he said that he would go to his post with a desire never to return.

The governorship came to Lord Botetourt opportunely. In recent months he had become insolvent, or nearly so. Long a man of comfortable wealth, he ably promoted the interests of Bristol's merchants while in Parliament. He owned coal mines, and he was a member of the Warmley Company, a large manufacturer of copper and brass. He invested heavily in expansion, apparently including new copper mines, and he borrowed to invest still more. Late in 1767 the company sought a charter from the Crown, which would permit it to raise more capital by selling stock and would free the original members and their private fortunes from liability for the company's obligations. Competitors petitioned against such a charter. Botetourt's critics charged that the costly expansion already had failed. Botetourt and his partners were trying to shield their own assets from the Warmley Company's creditors, shifting their losses to investors by selling stock in a firm they knew to be doomed. Whether from these motives or from a belief that stockholders' money might yet save the Warmley Company, Lord Botetourt showed great impatience in December 1767 and January 1768 as the Commissioners of the Privy Seal and the Earl of Chatham, Lord Privy Seal, put off final authorization of the charter after it had passed all other steps. The delay never ended; no charter came. Sailing for Virginia, Botetourt was "totally ruined." The government furnished him with the silver plate, equipage, and expense account of an ambassador, leading the wit-crackers to say that he was going as plenipotentiary to the Cherokees.

HMS *Rippon* dropped anchor in Hampton Roads on Tuesday, October 25, 1768. The next morning Lord Botetourt went ashore to an artillery salute. He arrived in Williamsburg at sunset. The houses had candles lit in all their windows. At the gate of the capitol, the councillors, Speaker Peyton Randolph, Attorney General John Randolph, Treasurer Robert Carter Nicholas, and others welcomed him and conducted him to the Council chamber. After a reading of his commission, Botetourt took the oath of office and administered an oath to the councillors. They repaired to the Raleigh Tavern for supper. At ten, the new governor retired to the palace. Botetourt was ready for a quiet life. He soon saw that Williamsburg would offer few temptations. Writing to the orgiastic Francis Dashwood, he used a slang term for copulation, "basket-making": "The trade of Basket making in a certain Stile is at a very low Ebb in Williamsburg, but agree with you that it will continue to flourish in the City of London." Botetourt said he had "completely lost every Idea of that sort."

Ten or twelve years earlier, George Washington would not have missed an event such as the governor's first day in Williamsburg. As Botetourt arrived, however, Washington and Fielding Lewis traveled to the Dismal Swamp. They spent a night at Dismal Plantation, then visited their property in North Carolina. They also ventured into the swamp, which was drier at that time of year. They reached Lake Drummond, a destination less important to Washington for his ear's detection of the stillness among the ancient trees than for his surveyor's eye on the prospects for drainage. Washington met the new governor in Williamsburg the following Monday. With the death of Francis Fauquier, the Dismal Swamp Company had lost a friend who believed in a project to meet the Royal Navy's demand for hemp. Lord Botetourt showed less interest.

From the day of his arrival, Botetourt "practised all his arts" on Virginians. They, in turn, covered him with compliments, finding in him "every Quality, that can recommend him to the good Opinion & Respect of the People." Yet neither William Nelson nor Francis Lightfoot Lee expected the burgesses and the Council to change their opposition to Parliament's new taxes. The governor was "soothing"; he knew how to make people feel happy. They still did not intend to surrender their liberty to the ministry which had sent him. On lesser matters, they accepted the generous condescension of a nobleman eager to gain influence among them. Not long after Lord Botetourt moved into the governor's palace, Dr. Thomas Walker spent time with him, explaining complex matters, especially Virginia's claims in the west and the proper boundaries between whites and Indians. Members of the Council also helped Botetourt understand. The governor became a supporter of new negotiations with the Cherokees and a new treaty to replace the one negotiated by John Stuart. As emissaries to arrange a further cession of land by the Cherokees, Lord Botetourt chose Dr. Walker and Andrew Lewis.

Francis Farley had opportunities to meet Lord Botetourt. Samuel Martin, Farley's friend in Antigua, wrote a letter of congratulations to Botetourt, to be handed to the governor by James Parke Farley. Martin commended the young man to the governor's notice. Though James looked "well made" and "stout," Antigua's steady heat made him ill. His father agreed that he should live in Virginia. A young man of "uncommon merit" ought to have an introduction to the governor.

Francis Farley's stay in Virginia lasted longer than he had intended. He at first said that he would return to Antigua in the spring of 1768, but he did not sail until the end of the year. His daughter gave him his first grandson on the last day of 1767. She and Captain Laforey named the boy Francis. Before another year passed, the Laforeys were getting ready to return to England. At auction, James Parke Farley and William Byrd bought some of their household goods. James's purchases included a woman's saddle and bridle, though he was a bachelor. Spending time with the Byrds at Westover or at Maycox or in Williamsburg, his eye fell upon William Byrd's daughter, Elizabeth, and hers upon him. She was only fourteen when he bought the saddle, but before she turned seventeen they were married.

Francis Farley enjoyed good health in Virginia, but he saw that Captain Laforey had sometimes neglected his properties. He had "to stay to put things in order." He traveled to the banks of the Dan River in North Carolina to see the Land of Eden for the first time. Before leaving Virginia, he chose an agent to look after his holdings: Robert Munford, a young planter and burgess of Mecklenburg County. Munford's grandfather had known the elder William Byrd well, and his uncle had accompanied Byrd on the trip to the Land of Eden. Munford had served under the younger William Byrd during the war with the French. He agreed to act with Byrd and with James Parke Farley as Francis Farley's representatives in Virginia and North Carolina. At last, Francis Farley sailed for Antigua.

William Anderson grew up in Louisa County in the 1750s. The family knew Samuel Gist as a storekeeper and tobacco merchant. Anderson went to sea. By the time Gist moved to London, Captain Anderson was master of the *Rachel and Mary*, a 300-ton ship with a crew of eighteen, sailing between London and the York River. Chartered by the firms John Norton & Son and James Buchanan & Company, she dropped anchor in the York early in May 1766. After taking on a cargo of tobacco, she sailed for London in August.

Captain Anderson, who was twenty-four, spent the autumn and early winter in London before making a return voyage. He approached Samuel Gist and asked for permission to court Gist's older daughter, Mary, not yet eighteen. Gist rejected him. As one would expect of a young man already master of a ship, Anderson had "a great deale of Pride." But Gist was a merchant and underwriter of "Considerable Fortune." His daughters, he boasted, had "never yet known want." His vision of their future did not include marriage to the likes of the Andersons of Louisa County. He wrote that the captain's "behaviour makes me sick of the Family." He mentioned to Mary that the captain wished to court her and that he had refused this request.

Early in April 1767, Captain Anderson and the *Rachel and Mary* sailed for Virginia, arriving in the York in the second week of June. It was a difficult year for tobacco merchants in the consignment trade. Many planters sold their tobacco in Virginia. No merchant could load a ship without buying. Gist did not like to be forced to pay cash for a cargo. Virginians complained that a conspiracy in London to restrict purchases drove down prices. People in Hanover County believed that Gist directed the plot. This notion was "ridiculous," he wrote; "threaten anybody wth. a Suit who mentions such a thing."

The *Rachel and Mary* was loaded by October. Anchored near her in the York, Gist's ship *Mary and Elizabeth* took on board tobacco, barrel staves, iron, and other commodities. That month both ships sailed for London.

Samuel Gist waxed prosperous as a tobacco merchant and an underwriter at Lloyd's. He was a discriminating judge of ginseng, indigo, and hemp. One who watched him at work wrote: "The sale of Tobacco requires great attention; and besides is one of those things in which persons may be said to be lucky & unlucky. I esteem Mr Gist the best & most thorough Tobacco Merchant of my acquaintance." After the *Rachel and Mary* and the *Mary and Elizabeth* arrived in the Thames, he had another 443 hogsheads to manage, in addition to his daily appearance at Lloyd's and on 'Change. He did not know that on several occasions, while he walked on 'Change, hearing news and closing deals, his daughter, Mary, admitted Captain William Anderson to Number 25, Savage Gardens. When her father came home, her face and voice revealed nothing to him. She had given money to the servants, and they kept her secret.

Mary's younger sister, Elizabeth, attended a boarding school. After Christmas holidays, Gist left Savage Gardens to take Betsey back to school. On Thursday, January 21, while Gist was away, Captain Anderson came to Number 25. As he and Mary had arranged, she was ready to go. Leaving word that they were fleeing to France, they headed for Scotland.

Gist returned and found only the servants. From them he learned what had happened. For months his daughter had duped him. He felt sick. She had, he thought, "treated me with black ingratitude." He resolved to strike her out of his life: "she sh[a]ll be to me a stranger for ever nor shall she ev[er] inherit the least part of my Fortune."

Mary Gist and William Anderson were married in Scotland. They returned to London in mid-February, preparing to go to Virginia. "I have not seen her," her father wrote, "& sincerely hope I never shall." John Norton had employed Anderson in the Virginia trade; he wished the young couple well. He could, however, do nothing with Gist. He could only hope to give Anderson some employment: "poor Man! I heartily wish he had to do with a less obdurate Father in Law, and one who wou'd have been more sensible of his Merit."

Gist took some satisfaction from the likelihood that the couple would soon be poor: "they have a dismal Prospect before them." Nevertheless, Mary was his daughter. After she began to "live miserably," he said, he would "supply her wth. such common necessarys as are befitting the Condtn. she has so shamefully chosen." For months his mind dwelt on the subject. He concluded that Captain Anderson was "a Villain," who could "seduce a Girl from her Duty & ruin her." And yet he could not forget his daughter's skill with "every deceitful Art in Practice upon me." Where could she have learned such duplicity?

Gist did not neglect business in the midst of his distress. He acquired another ship, of 150 tons. Registering her on March 8, he gave her the name *Elizabeth*, after his remaining daughter. She sailed for the York River, bearing a cargo of merchandise with instructions to his representative in Virginia. He gave his debtors a choice: consign their tobacco to him in the *Elizabeth*, or pay their balances at once or face a suit for debt.

Early in April, William and Mary Anderson took passage on board the *Brilliant*, bound for Virginia. She dropped anchor in the York on June 23. William found Mary "most amiable," as did everyone else, except her father. In Louisa County he began to build a store. John Norton, from his offices on Tower Hill, kept working on Gist for a reconciliation, without success.

During the summer the Andersons fell out of Gist's correspondence. He had other concerns. Many underwriters at Lloyd's wished to open a new coffeehouse with a more specialized emphasis on marine insurance and with more careful scrutiny of men offering to subscribe policies. He agreed. Gist offered to help young John Tabb, of the Virginia firm, Thomas Tabb & Son, who was in London with almost 1,000 hogsheads of tobacco consigned to DeBerdt, Burkitt & Sayre, a firm near bankruptcy, unable to accept the large bills of exchange the Tabbs had drawn. Unlike Dennys DeBerdt and Stephen Sayre, Gist kept his attention on business, not allowing himself to be distracted by colonial objections to Parliament's taxes or by troops stationed in Boston. Gist said that out of "friendship and compassion" he would handle the sale of Tabb's tobacco for a commission of ten shillings per hogshead. Indeed, he would buy much of it. But for one cargo Tabb found another buyer, who offered £400 more than Gist did, and Tabb sold that part of the tobacco himself. Gist protested at being deprived of his profit and silently raised his commission on the tobacco he sold for Tabb.

On August 10, 1768, London merchants trading to Virginia gave "an elegant entertainment" to honor Lord Botetourt at the George and Vulture Tavern in Cornhill. The new governor left for Portsmouth and Virginia with their good will fresh in his mind. Gist had recovered from the shock of his daughter's betrayal, which, he said, "allmost kill'd me." On December 3 one of the hardest workers among the Virginia merchants, Capel Hanbury, suffered a stroke which severely impaired his speech. Gist saw an opportunity. Everyone knew that Capel Hanbury had managed the firm's business. Gist also had heard that friends of the late Speaker Robinson resented the House of Hanbury's unseemly haste in suing the speaker's estate for payment. Gist might reasonably expect to draw away some of the firm's business. He waited until Capel Hanbury died, then offered his "best Services" to Virginia correspondents of the House of Hanbury, promising: "you Shall be dealt with by the Strictest Rules of Justice & Honor."

From his first days in London, Samuel Gist awoke Virginians' suspicions in his dealings as a merchant. He soon fell under political suspicion, too. Colonists followed with concern the fortunes of John Wilkes as he flamboyantly defied the government. Though "grave ones" in Virginia thought him "a wicked abandoned Bankrupt," the cry of "Wilkes and Liberty" held broad appeal among opponents of Parliament's new taxes, though Wilkes earlier had ridiculed Americans' position. In colonial leaders' stylized, theatrical way of talking, he was a hero. Burgesses who passed resolutions against taxation and in favor of a boycott of British goods would have accepted the label put on them with contempt by a visiting member of the Fairfax family: "a set of Wilkes's."

In the summer of 1767, Wilkes plotted his return to the House of Commons, this time relying on electors in London. Though he must pay for "some eating & drinking," the cost would be far less than in Aylesbury. After his victory in Middlesex on March 28, 1768, some of his followers celebrated by breaking windows. His reimprisonment under a writ of outlawry brought crowds into the streets for weeks. Riots broke out in several parts of London as Parliament came into session in May. Soldiers killed a number of people in St. George's Fields, outside King's Bench Prison.

Wilkes again brought himself before the eyes of the political world by publishing his accusation that the ministry had planned the killings in St.

George's Fields. The government expelled him from the House of Commons. During February and March 1769—Wilkes in prison all the while—he was expelled, re-elected, disqualified, re-elected, annulled, and re-elected. Bets on his fate kept brokers in Exchange Alley as busy as if he were "another regular stock." Wilkes always appeared to enjoy the ferment he stimulated. "He was an incomparable comedian in all he said or did," Sir Nathaniel William Wraxall later wrote, "and he seemed to consider human life itself as a mere comedy."

Many merchants and other men of business in London signed an address to the king to show that much of the City, substantial men, opposed Wilkes. This address appeared, ready for signatures, at the King's Arms Tavern in Cornhill, leading critics to suspect that its authors were not merchants but members of the government. It expressed the signers' "abhorrence of every attempt to spread sedition, to inflame the minds, and alienate the affection of a free and loyal people from the best of kings, and his government." After a raucous meeting at the King's Arms, promoters of the address moved it to the Merchant Seamen's Office on the upper story of the Royal Exchange, where it awaited signatures. More than six hundred men signed, Samuel Gist among them. Others were merchants in overseas trade, marine insurance underwriters, brokers, bankers, and directors of the South Sea Company, the East India Company, and the Bank of England—men who wielded great influence in the City's commerce and finance but little in its political life. Other Chesapeake merchants signed: John Norton, William Molleson, Lionel Lyde, John Buchanan.

A procession of merchants' carriages set out for St. James's Palace on March 22 to deliver the address to the king. Along the way, crowds shouting *"Wilkes and liberty," "Wilkes, and no king"* pelted them with dirt and stones, breaking the carriages' windows and blinds, dirtying coachmen, footmen, and merchants. The Horse Guards rode out of the palace grounds with sabers drawn, cleared the streets nearby, and patrolled through the afternoon and evening. Retreating into Nando's Coffee House, the merchants' chairman, Edmund Boehm, lost the address and its signatures for a while but eventually recovered it, and with a few other men, presented it to the king several hours late. After this episode, David Hume, who thought Wilkes a cunning quack, concluded that the drama had moved into its ridiculous phase. Thinking about a historian later writing on these times, he said: "I am delighted to see the daily and hourly Progress of Madness and Folly and Wickedness in England. The Consummation of these Qualities are the true Ingredients for making a fine Narrative in History."

Among merchants not signing the address, some tried to organize a demand for repeal of the new taxes on colonists. They found this difficult. The taxes might be "absurd," as Anthony Bacon called them—what sensible manufacturing nation taxed its own exports?—but they lacked the pervasive effect of the Stamp Act, and they did not arouse so strong or united a resistance. Opponents in the colonies had shown that they would dispute all claims of Parliament's right to tax, a view merchants in London did not share. Many colonists nevertheless conflated their cause and Wilkes's, drawing a sharp distinction between merchants who supported the government against Wilkes and merchants who did not, though neither group agreed with the colonists' constitutional position.

A letter from London, apparently written by Arthur Lee, was published in the *Virginia Gazette*. It said that by signing the address to the king, Gist and his fellow Virginia merchants had applauded "Ministerial conduct against America," the massacre of Wilkes's supporters, and abrogation of constitutional liberties. The letter suggested a boycott of the signers. One of Gist's correspondents told him: "They are in a ferment." He and other signers were deemed "inimical to America." Gist replied that he had opposed disturbers of government, without reference to American affairs. He thought Arthur Lee "meant to make himself appear a Patriot in the Eyes of the Ra[bb]le." No one could suppose that Gist wished to hurt America, since he was "so largely concern'd" there in his trade and investments. Three weeks after the merchants' loyal address, Middlesex electors gave a large majority of their votes to John Wilkes for the fifth time. The House of Commons declared his opponent, who was supported by the ministry, to be elected.

The day merchants took their address to the king was the second day of business for New Lloyd's Coffee House. Gist and other signers of the address well known at Lloyd's moved their insuring to this establishment. More and more underwriters, merchants, and brokers thought that the original Lloyd's in Lombard Street attracted too many newcomers who were not serious businessmen. Established insurers saw strangers of unknown credit offering to write a line of £100 or £200 on policies circulating in the room. These intruders had heard the usual stories about Lloyd's, underwriters making huge, instant profits: "A Jew last War made 40,000£ by Underwriting at one Time from a Letter, Wrote by his Correspondent in Jamaica, containing only these words, 'We are all well.' " Veterans knew that the presence of more men competing to subscribe policies drove premiums down in peacetime. And anyone could see that "every Man at the Coffee House writes policies now a days." People seeking insurance on a large scale could not always avoid unknown, unsafe insurers.

Gist and his colleagues also had tired of interference with marine insurance by hectic promoters of short-term policies which were, in effect, bets on public contingencies. Would Parliament be dissolved and a new election called in the coming year? Would East India Company stock fall to £175 per share in the next three months? Would the Bank of England's notes be discounted during the coming month? Would John Wilkes be elected member for Middlesex? Would Britain go to war with France or Spain within the next year? Was King George's mother dead or not dead? Would the Stuart pretender to the English throne soon be made king of Poland? One paid a premium, ranging from £5 to £50, and received £100 if the contingency in question occurred. During the twenty-four hours after the king's mother died, "many thousand pounds" of such policies were done on the question of her death.

Early in 1769, with encouragement from the principal brokers and underwriters of marine insurance, Thomas Fielding, a waiter at Lloyd's, leased Number 5, Pope's Head Alley, a house in a short street running between the Post Office in Lombard Street and the Royal Exchange. He had the building "genteelly fitted up" with tables and booths for underwriters. On March 21, New Lloyd's Coffee House opened. A brief period of "Confusion" about the true headquarters of marine insurance ensued, but New Lloyd's soon prevailed. Underwriters found themselves in more cramped rooms, with new neighbors in the alley: attorneys, stockbrokers, notaries, the Annuity Office, the famous Pope's Head Tavern, and John Barnes and William Golightly's State Lottery Office, crowded with people buying tickets under a lantern sign which read: "*Tickets insured.*"

New-Lloyd's List came out on Tuesdays and Fridays with shipping news and stock quotations. Any owner of an outbound vessel seeking a cargo could "put her up for freight at New Lloyd's Coffee House." Vessels for sale were "put up" there, as were reports of vessels' arrivals, departures, and mishaps. People promoting causes, such as breaking the butchers' monopoly on meat or paying a bounty to turbot fishermen, left subscription books open. The arrangement was convenient: "at Lloyd's Coffee-house the Broker can go from one Underwriter to another, who are conversant with different trades, and know how things are . . . he knows where to find each of those men, and he can form a pretty good judgment by the time he has been round, what he can do his risk for." Every summer, at the start of hurricane and storm season, premiums rose. The same underwriters wrangled with the same brokers in "a constant scene of disputes" to see who would first pay higher premiums and lead the way for all policyholders. Everyone understood the game. Samuel Gist was one of the men in New Lloyd's who "know how things are." He mastered underwriting as he had mastered tobacco-selling. To make money, he had to class his risks and spread his resources. To get safer, surer policies, he had to write some for enterprises that looked shaky. "At Lloyd's Coffee House," a broker said, "we give and we take, the good and the bad together; and . . . by having one good and another bad we are able to get on."

Gist was quick to charge policyholders with fraud. Anyone presenting a claim in which Gist found a flaw could expect many meetings with the underwriters and little chance of recovery without going to court. Gist stiffened the resolve of his fellow underwriters. His confident accusations and his refusal to pay a claim left one merchant at a loss for words to express his anger: "what more can I say of the determination of those ———." Underwriters encountered many ruses: a ship insured after she had sunk, a cargo of trash insured as if it were valuable merchandise, then mysteriously lost at sea, a vessel scuttled by her captain. One underwriter amused himself throughout his career by compiling a list of frauds attempted by policyholders. Gist saw no humor in the dishonesty he detected all around him.

The sponsors of New Lloyd's Coffee House regarded the rooms in Pope's Head Alley as a temporary home. The space was small and inconvenient; too many men too close together made the smoky air "extremely inauspicious to health." After more than two and a half years in these rooms, Gist and seventy-eight other merchants, underwriters, and brokers met on December 13, 1771, to begin a fund and a committee for "Building A New Lloyd's Coffee House." Each subscriber paid £100. They could not lawfully offer policies jointly, as a corporation, but they could jointly control the place where policies were written.

A few weeks later, the subscribers met again to choose a committee to carry out their intent. Martin Kuyck van Mierop served as chairman. Gist had seen all the committee members at Lloyd's for years: the successful James Bourdieu; John Whitmore, an underwriter and merchant trading to Portugal; Joshua Readshaw, an underwriter since 1757; John Wilkinson, a broker who had joined Gist in signing the loyal address to the king; John Townson, a merchant and underwriter with an interest in the slave trade; John Ewer, an underwriter since 1757, who uttered the talismanic words: "If I know a ship to be leaky, I should not underwrite"; and Brook Watson, who as a youth had lost a leg to a shark in Havana Harbor and now, with a peg leg, walked on 'Change, prospering as a merchant in the Canada trade. An acquaintance later described him as "a contractor, and creature of Government." Watson's sloop *Pitt* plied the Québec route, and his firm, Watson & Rashleigh, almost monopolized exports from London to Halifax. Today Watson might offer Gist a line when insuring the *Pitt* to Québec; tomorrow Gist might offer Watson a line when insuring the *Elizabeth* to York Town.

Not all men succeeded at Lloyd's as these two did. Gist watched as one of the seventy-nine founding subscribers to New Lloyd's, Timothy Bevan, Jr., brother of a well-known banker, "broke all to pieces," defaulted on his policies, and died leaving no effects. After six years in the City, Gist had mastered his part of it. Henceforth, he would be one of the regulars at Lloyd's, where newcomers from America learned the hard way that "there are so many wheels within wheels in the Trade of this Country."

Governor Botetourt opened the spring session of the General Assembly on Monday afternoon, May 8, 1769. He had brought with him in HMS *Rippon* a gilt chariot upholstered in crimson flowered velvet and decorated with the arms of Virginia. Drawn by six white horses, he rode in it the short distance from his residence to the capitol. Richly dressed in a light red coat shot with gold thread, he gave the councillors and burgesses a long, slow, solemn speech. If, however, this display of the magnificence of Britain and the British government was supposed to stun Virginians into happily paying new taxes, it failed. They marveled at Lord Botetourt's politesse; he dazzled them as a peer of the realm—but not as an official. John Page had noticed in the previous few weeks that "some People suspend their Judgement of him till after the Meeting of the Assembly." They knew that the governor would not approve of what the burgesses were going to do. The test of Botetourt would be how he reacted.

Much had changed since the days when Governor Fauquier told the public printer what not to publish. With no subtlety, the burgesses' printer, William Rind, brought out a volume of John Dickinson's "Farmer" letters and Arthur Lee's "Monitor" letters summarizing colonists' rejection of taxation by Parliament. In "Monitor" Number VII, Lee wrote that the Townshend duties, as the new taxes were called, had only one purpose: "*we are no longer to be free.*" William Nelson, George Washington, and others had been writing privately in the same vein. Eight days after Botetourt's address, the burgesses unanimously passed four resolutions claiming the sole right to tax Virginians and objecting to removal of any person for trial outside the colony, as Parliament's legislation authorized. Rind printed these resolutions in a convenient broadside. Botetourt summoned the burgesses to the Council chamber and dissolved the General Assembly.

Thus ended the political career of David Meade, at the age of twenty-four. It had lasted nine days. He had won election as a burgess from Nansemond County, looking forward to "the most splendid general assembly . . . that ever convened in the British Colonies." But on the first day, as Lord

Botetourt made his appearance *endimanché*, Meade suffered from a fever, and he felt stage fright at the prospect of rising to speak in the House of Burgesses. The governor's dissolution of the General Assembly came as a relief. Meade went home "completely cured of his ambition."

Before leaving Williamsburg, he took part in one more political exercise. After Botetourt left the capitol, Meade accompanied the other burgesses down the street to the Raleigh Tavern. There they formed "a regular Association" under which Virginians promised to restrict their purchases of British manufactured goods. They met again the next day. George Washington presented a text prepared by George Mason, which he had brought to Williamsburg before the burgesses convened. In it the associators pledged not to purchase any of a long list of goods. In this manner they would defy the ministry's effort to reduce them "from a free and happy People to a wretched and miserable State of Slavery." Meade signed; Dr. Walker signed; George Washington signed; William Nelson's son, Thomas, signed; and ninety others signed. Then they drank toasts to the king, to the governor, to friends of constitutional liberty. They drank the last toast to "The Farmer and Monitor." The following day, Richard Henry Lee assured his brother, author of the "Monitor" letters, that the Association "will undoubtedly be assented to by the whole Colony." Lord Botetourt wrote privately that his ability to accomplish the king's purposes "seems at present to be at an end."

The Association emphasized the "very great" debt many Virginians owed for imported goods. It deplored "Luxury and Extravagance," encouraging "Industry and Frugality." These sentiments were familiar, even trite. A satirist in the *Virginia Gazette* in 1766 pretended to complain about those who appealed to truth and reason "in every *trifling* debate, about the depravity of our morals, our extravagances, and our debts." Such people did not understand Virginia. "It was the boast of Sparta, Mr. Printer, that all its inhabitants were warriors. But pray what was their glory to ours? We are, I do assure you, a whole colony of Gentlemen. . . . As Gentlemen, then, what have we to do with truth and reason? Is it not evident that our gentility ought to be the only rule of our actions? Or rather, does it not entitle us to act in any manner we please?" Neither ridicule nor reason could arrest Virginians' desire for imported goods.

Merchants in Virginia, especially factors, ignored the Association. While other colonies imported less, the Chesapeake colonies imported more in 1769 than in 1768—still more in 1770. A cynic said Virginians led in opposing taxes only "when they meet in assembly." A few weeks after learning of the Association, people also heard that the ministry intended to repeal the taxes at the next session of Parliament. As that day approached, everyone knew that Virginians had not been, as William Lee delicately put it, "universally steady."

Lord Botetourt had no bitter exchanges with the colony's leaders. He and they vied with one another in expressions of esteem. During the burgesses' fall session he announced the ministry's intent to repeal taxes on glass, paper, and paint; he endorsed Dr. Walker's effort to get more land from the Cherokees. He believed he had regained his ability "to do some good in this distracted age."

London merchants trading to America wished to remove all impediments to selling more goods. Total American imports declined in 1769, but Londoners eager to reverse this trend by repealing taxes still did not defend colonists' rejection of the power of Parliament. At the London merchants' general meeting on February 1, 1770, William Neate, Samuel Gist's colleague at Lloyd's, opposed raising "the principle of the issue." They should seek results: removal of the taxes. He clung to this position even after hearing that the government retained a tax on tea. The others agreed, saying that "as merchts. they had nothing to do but to ship goods agreeable to their orders." Ten days before the House of Commons acted on repeal, the late Thomas Tabb's 150-ton ship *Nancy*, loaded with merchandise by Samuel Gist, stood out of the Downs into the Strait of Dover, bound for Virginia.

William Nelson assured Francis Farley that Virginia would soon regain her happiness after the coming repeal. If manufactured goods could restore happiness, he was right. He heard from John Norton in London that orders were larger than in the past. As William Neate had foreseen, "large quantities of Goods have been daily shipped, and are now daily shipping for Virginia, Maryland, Rhode Island, Boston, and Montreal." Such "merchants on the ministerial side" as Anthony Bacon and his partner John Durand sent cargoes. Writing for the newspapers under a pseudonym, Arthur Lee told the British that continuing the tax on tea left Americans still groaning under oppression. The colonists, he predicted, would persevere in refusing to buy goods "till their grievances are *really* redressed." But vessels in the Thames, bound for America, took on freight and dropped down with the tide to Gravesend, sailing out to the Downs.

Some merchandise wound up at Westover after passing through Thomas Hornsby's store in Williamsburg. The bills of exchange William Byrd gave in payment came back from England, protested. Thomas Hornsby's nephew, Joseph, lived in Williamsburg after he and Mildred Walker were married. Joseph acted more often on his uncle's behalf in business matters, as they pursued debts owed to the store by Byrd, by Speaker Robinson's estate, and by others.

After coming to Williamsburg from Lincolnshire in his younger years, Thomas Hornsby succeeded as a merchant. He dealt in fine cloth, among other goods, and a competitor wishing to belittle him called him "Hornsby, the Taylor." By the time his nephew began a family, Thomas Hornsby had "acquired a large Fortune in Trade." He owned a plantation in James City County, outside Williamsburg. At the age of sixty-seven, he was ready to give Joseph more responsibility. In the last week of February 1770, Thomas's wife, Margaret, died.

Joseph Hornsby came to live with his uncle and aunt at the age of seventeen. He attended the College of William and Mary the following year. He showed himself to be a steady young man, a devout communicant of the Church of England. After he made more money, he indulged one extravagance: thoroughbred horses; one stallion was descended from the Godolphin Arabian. In the years just before his marriage he gained, through living with his uncle, a close view of the consequences of extravagance: his uncle's friend, William Waters, dwelling in comfort in Williamsburg, was found after his death to owe more than he was worth. Thomas Hornsby also lost by his dealings with the late Speaker Robinson, who had promised to pay not only his own debt to the store but also that of one of his relatives by marriage. His estate lay in disarray, and the only hope for collecting the latter debt was a suit in Chancery. Thomas Hornsby took from the speaker's assets two tickets in the lottery for land held by William Byrd in 1768. Byrd tried to raise £40,000 or £50,000 by offering chances to win tracts at the falls of the James River. But even with a ticket known to have won a prize, Thomas and Joseph only received from Byrd one of his bonds. The worth of his paper was not a secret. At the start of his career, Joseph emulated his uncle, not Robinson or Waters or Byrd.

After Governor Fauquier died, members of the Dismal Swamp Company no longer spoke of hemp as their future cash crop. The latest book about North America, published in 1767, scoffed at the hemp craze. The Council acknowledged to the Earl of Hillsborough that the bounty "produced but little." William Nelson said he had learned by experience that the soil of the low country would not yield much hemp. The burgesses and the Council did not give up on it, offering a bounty in 1769. The company, however, did not try to fulfill the elder William Byrd's vision of tens of thousands of acres of hemp stalks. George Washington nevertheless had "sanguine hopes" for the Dismal Swamp Company. He received encouragement from an old acquaintance, who wrote that the company's success "would produce the most desirable end of encreasing that Fortune which you so highly deserve & at the same time shew the Colonists what enterprise & perseverance can effect."

Under John Washington's eye the company's slaves dug a ditch to Lake Drummond, grew food crops, and cut shingles. His only revenue came from sales of shingles. Members of the company relied on their "inexhaustible" supply of lumber. Cutting a road through the northern part of the swamp to the south branch of the Elizabeth River would make transportation easier. Indeed, why not dig a canal through the heart of the swamp, connecting Lake Drummond with the Elizabeth River?

At Dismal Plantation, such designs looked remote. In the years after work began, though more slaves were brought to the swamp, their numbers were "considerably lessened by deaths." Some survivors left the plantation. After Robert Burwell withdrew from the company, his slaves, Venus and Jack, now known as Jack Dismal, were moved to his plantation of orchards in Isle of Wight County, where his son lived. They continued their "very cunning and artful" career, regularly escaping from various members of the Burwell family while wearing and carrying "several different kinds of Apparel." They did not return to the swamp. A slave furnished to the company by Samuel Gist—a man called Tom, newly brought from Africa—soon showed why George Washington had set a lower value on him as a worker. He left Dismal Plantation in April 1767 and spent years "lying out," always within a few miles of the company's work, receiving help from one of Nansemond County's troublesome Quakers. Samuel Gist, listening to invitations to invest in the African slave trade, realized that the Dismal Swamp Company's efforts had been inadequate. The enterprise needed an infusion of new slaves.

Trouble befell not only the company but also its founders and their heirs. Francis Farley returned to Antigua early in 1769 to confront a short sugar harvest and a dearth of cash on the island. These compounded the difficulties of his service as representative of many absent owners. On Thursday, August 17, fire swept through the capital, St. Johns. It began when a slave threw staves from a pitch barrel into a heating oven. Flames burst through the roof and set fire to shingles. Roofs throughout the city, as well as some exterior walls, were made of shingles from Virginia. Despite the efforts of many people, steady trade winds scattered burning debris, spreading fire down to the harbor, destroying every warehouse on the wharf and almost three hundred other buildings. In autumn and winter, sickness struck the island, killing Farley's younger son.

Tobacco planters in Virginia grew a smaller crop than they had hoped. John Page was losing ground in his account with John Norton & Son. He and his wife received a bequest from Robert Tucker's mother, Frances Nelson, who died on June 9, 1766. He spent most of it buying food and drink for the voters of Gloucester County in what he called "the ridiculous Extravagance of Burgess making," helping Lewis Burwell get elected. One extravagance more or less hardly made a difference. With many other planters, Page felt sure he had hired "one of the worst Overseers in the World." Unlike others, Page lived in a huge mansion in need of costly repairs. Even "the most strict Oconomy at Rosewell" consumed far more than the value of the tobacco he produced. To distract himself, Page took advantage of two astronomical events in 1769: the transit of Venus across the Sun on June 3 and the transit of Mercury on November 9. His observations were not precise enough for scientific purposes, but he enjoyed making them, and he wrote long articles for the *Virginia Gazette*.

John Norton remained patient with Page, but other merchants stopped waiting for their debtors. Farell & Jones brought suit against John Syme. Edward and Thomas Hunt joined the crowd of creditors suing the estate of Robert Tucker. The executors admitted every claim to be just, then pleaded that, after their auctions, the estate held no liquid assets. Fielding Lewis feared the same fate for his son, Fielding Junior. A spendthrift as a boy, he was still one after he got married at the age of eighteen. Ignoring his father's advice, he ran through his wife's dowry so rapidly that her father asked Fielding Senior to take what was left away from Fielding Junior and spend it wisely on the young couple's behalf. Adding to his embarrassment, Fielding Senior ended the year owing almost £1,900 to Anthony Bacon, as well as a separate sum of more than £2,500 on what they called the "slave account." Dr. Walker spent his summer trying to make money from a grant on the Holston River, a tributary of the Tennessee. He apparently crossed the mountains to visit William Inglis on the New River, a tributary of the Kanawha. He made Inglis's home the "Office" for his project: selling land in the Wolfhills at £11 per 100 acres. Not many people then lived along the Holston. Within a few years "great Numbers" did. They sent a petition to Williamsburg, asking that "the Grant so well known by the name of Walkers Grant may be buried in Oblivion."

Who was trustworthy? At the time Lord Botetourt arrived swathed in rich colors, Williamsburg employed a visiting portrait painter. He specialized in miniatures, and planters kept him busy for months. A rich Englishman, Howell Briggs, once an intimate of the Prince of Wales, commissioned a portrait of his wife. The painter's connections enabled him to persuade a planter from Middlesex County to sign with him as security for his bond.

Soon afterward the painter left Williamsburg, sending back no message to his patron and leaving behind his oeuvres—mediocre portraits—and his worthless bond, all signed "Cosmo Medici." Who could be surprised when he later turned up in North Carolina? In the minds of Virginians since Byrd's dividing line days, that was where dishonest people fled to escape their debts.

The Scottish merchants calling themselves the Campania Company pursued their scheme to compete with the Dismal Swamp Company or force their way into a share of its immense future profits. They moved in the summer of 1769. James Parker ventured through the swamp before the worst of the heat. He returned in August with Thomas Macknight and fourteen slaves. Starting from an upper branch of the Pasquotank River, they cut their way northward through the swamp almost seven miles to Lake Drummond. In some stretches, bamboo stood so thick among the crowded cypress and cedar trees that the sweating slaves advanced only 1,300 yards by a day's labor. Parker took surveying equipment. His celestial fix at Lake Drummond showed that the southern rim lay half a mile north of the North Carolina line. Clearly, the Dismal Swamp Company, with its drainage, lumber roads, and canal, would not be able to ignore the presence, just across the line, of its insistent Scottish neighbors.

Members of the Campania Company, Parker said, need invest little, waiting as Virginians paid for the expensive work. The Scots' only concern was their title to 32,000 or 34,000 acres—or "perhaps dbl. the quantity"—in the swamp. The inconvenient death of the proprietor, Earl Granville, and the erratic conduct of his agents had clouded the transactions of 1763. But the seventh anniversary of the Scots' first claims would come in 1770. They were assured by those learned in North Carolina law, especially their partner, Samuel Johnston, that they could then "pass deeds to each Other," defining the scope of their holdings and fixing their title, based upon seven years of possession.

The Dismal Swamp Company's grant rested upon the partners' undertaking in November 1763 to return surveys to Secretary Thomas Nelson's office within seven years. In November 1769, a year before that deadline, William Nelson petitioned his colleagues on the Council for an extension. He said of the company: "they have prosecuted that great and useful work, with the utmost vigor and attention, in which they have already expended several thousand pounds, and have at present a large number of hands employ'd therein." The councillors said they were impressed by this "arduous and expensive" project to drain a swamp that was "a nuisance," making it "productive of general utility." They allowed the company another seven years "to perfect their work." The following August the partners of the Dismal Swamp Company entered claims with the surveyor of Norfolk County for all ungranted swamp east of their holdings on the Norfolk County side.

The burgesses' disagreement with Lord Botetourt over Parliament's power to tax, in which George Washington took the lead, did not prevent Washington from mentioning to the governor in May that veterans of 1754 still hoped to get 200,000 acres along the Ohio River, as Robert Dinwiddie had promised. In December 1769, Washington reminded Botetourt of their conversation in the spring. And he submitted a petition for the grant, specifying alternate sites and requesting permission to use a special surveyor, not the county surveyor, to save time and money. The Council approved his petition. This was the first step of what he called "a scheme I have in view." He wished to buy, at the cheapest possible rate, the claims of other veterans under the grant. But he did not wish them to know who was making the purchase or why. He imagined that he could accomplish his design, using his brother, Charles, to ask "in a joking way" what officers thought their share of the land was worth and then, "in earnest," buy as much as he could for £5 or £6 or £7 per 1,000 acres.

Harmony glowed in candlelight through the windows of the capitol building on Monday, June 4, 1770. The councillors honored the governor with "a grand ball and entertainment" on the king's birthday. Speaker Peyton Randolph, the burgesses, the magistrates, and the principal inhabitants of Williamsburg attended. Before leaving town three weeks later, Washington saw performances of John Gay's *The Beggar's Opera* and published in the *Virginia Gazette* an invitation to officers claiming land under Dinwiddie's proclamation to meet in Fredericksburg on August 1. "A meeting at this time," he wrote, "may be essential to their interests."

Amid the festivities of spring court days, Councillor Robert Burwell remained unhappy. His wife, after suffering a stroke, had died on March 6. Sarah Burwell, half sister of the Nelson brothers and of Robert Tucker, had been widely admired, but her death fell especially hard upon her husband. People noticed that "he seems to have nothing to be able to pass away his lonely hours with." He decided to sell his orchards in Isle of Wight County, his house in York Town, and his land along the Roanoke River. He owed about £2,800 to three British firms. He tried to borrow £4,000 from a fourth in order to consolidate his debts and pay for moving to the Shenandoah Valley to live near one of his sons and some of his grandchildren. But his demeanor made clear that he was not "able to think of anything but a wife." At forty-nine, Burwell was, Landon Carter thought, "too young to continue single; and too old for any Lady but the aged to associate with." He faced the prospect of looking "odd and foolish." During the summer of 1770, in York Town, he courted a rich widow, Mildred Lightfoot, who was forty-seven. He asked for her hand in marriage. She refused him. This had "a bad effect upon his Spirits," and he was confined to his home with a nervous fever.

The English partners in the Dismal Swamp Company, expanding their business, could not look upon their homes with satisfaction. Samuel Gist intermittently brooded about the "robbery" that Captain William Anderson had committed by taking his daughter. Gist meant to ensure that his property and his trade furnished no assistance to Anderson in Virginia.

In 1768, Anthony Bacon's architect, William Newton, created in brick and stone on Higham Hill above the River Lea a smaller, two-story version of a grand country house in the Palladian manner. The main rooms, decorated with fashionable stucco work, had tall windows overlooking Middlesex and Hertfordshire, with vistas of forest, park, or river. There Bacon could escape the rush of Throgmorton Street and Cornhill, as well as the blast furnace at Cyfarthfa. But he could not keep his only child alive. Anthony Richard Bacon was very dear to Anthony and Elizabeth Bacon. They almost had lost him to scarlet fever when he was three. After he suffered six weeks of "great trouble," God had spared him, "a comfort to us." But when young Anthony fell ill in Copthall Court in the spring of 1770, at the age of twelve, he could not be saved by prayers, by "every effort of the tenderest affection," or by "all the powers of well-adapted medicine." He died on Saturday, May 26, and his body was buried in the Church of St. Bartholomew, next to the Bank of England and the Royal Exchange. Bacon put a memorial tablet on one pillar in the church, with an inscription and a bas-relief of Time mowing down a flower.

Bacon's private life soon changed. Within a year of his son's death, a woman named Mary Bushby was pregnant with Bacon's child. At the age of fifty-three he had begun a new family. He and Elizabeth Bacon remained married, and he provided for her. He and Mary Bushby later had other children. The first child was a boy, named Anthony.

Samuel Gist moved quickly to break out and discharge the cargo of the *Nancy* after she was moored in the Thames in mid-January 1770. As usual, he thought the tobacco inferior, but he was in a hurry. He wished her to sail for the James early in February, while other merchants held their cargoes until Parliament repealed colonial taxes. Tradesmen delivering merchandise for his cargo delayed him more than a week, but he beat the rush. Gist did not give every vessel he loaded so brief a ride in the Thames. Even so, he spent much time in the years before and after this voyage of the *Nancy* sending goods to Virginia. He often said that he had better uses for his money than shipping merchandise to Virginians on credit. Yet he invested large sums in that trade.

Gist set up his younger stepson, John Smith, in the brick store in Hanover. Smith lived in the house his father had built, which now belonged to Gist, and worked for Gist as a retailer on commission. Gist preferred quick returns in commodities and cash, not higher profits based upon extending long credit. Within a year he had shipped £3,000 in goods to Smith. Six months later he put the sum at £5,000. He urged in July 1767: "be as expeditious as Possible to push all you can home." Smith tried to reach a similar arrangement with John Norton, who declined but later shipped merchandise on credit. Smith lacked his stepfather's aptitude for business. He bought tobacco at high prices and, much to Gist's annoyance, paid in cash. Gist concluded that the young man needed help. David Anderson, Captain William Anderson's father, would have done well, Gist thought, but he was out of the question after the elopement. Smith did not get enough help in good time.

Gist's older stepson, Joseph Smith, believed that Gist had cheated him out of his patrimony. He tried to keep as many as possible of the slaves formerly his father's, slaves whom Gist claimed to own. Gist sent a warning: "he will find it difficult to get shut of the scrape he will bring himself into." Joseph Smith was married to the widow of Thomas Read Rootes. The Rootes family also thought that Gist had engrossed his stepsons' property. Gist said: "I am determined to defend my Title." Yet he offered Smith credit in an amount equal to half the value of the disputed slaves, in return for Smith's conceding that they belonged to Gist. Smith's lawyer, Patrick Henry, thought this proposed compromise "a little singular" and warned his client not to accept.

Gist's ship *Elizabeth*, with a cargo of "Sundry European Goods," dropped anchor in the York on May 16, 1768. She returned to London late that summer. In February 1769, Gist sent her on a winter voyage to Virginia, under the command of Captain Howard Esten. She still rode in the York early in September, as a hurricane swept up from Cape Hatteras over Albemarle Sound and across the Dismal Swamp, then hit Chesapeake Bay in the middle of the night. Violent winds blew for fourteen hours. Heavy rain came down for half that time. Uprooted trees fell over one another. Corn crops were flattened. Gristmills washed away in flash floods. Drying sheds for tobacco collapsed and flew apart. Many old houses were blown down. Every standing house sprang leaks.

The hurricane's winds damaged almost every vessel in the rivers and the bay. In the Elizabeth River at Norfolk, in Hampton Roads, and in the York, all small craft stranded. All the larger vessels at Norfolk ran aground; many were dismasted. The *Fitzhugh*, out of Baltimore, stranded near the capes, her hold full of barrel staves, tobacco hogsheads, and salt water. In the York only the ship *Experiment* rode out the storm, after Captain William Hamlin ordered her foremast and mizzenmast cut away. The ship *Betsy* stranded and soon had 11 feet of water in her hold. A light sloop ran on Gloucester Point, stove to pieces. Gist's *Elizabeth* stranded with the others. It was the worst hurricane in living memory. Reading the first brief report in *Lloyd's List* in November, Gist could learn nothing about the *Elizabeth*. He also took an interest in the fate of the *Fitzhugh*, on which he was an underwriter.

The *Elizabeth* was soon afloat, having suffered little damage. With her help a stranded brigantine was returned to the water. Less fortunate vessels were declared a total loss. Many were sold for small sums. The owners of the *Fitzhugh*, Samuel Galloway and Stephen Steward, seeing her stranded on the sand, waves breaking over her hull, thought she looked as bad as any of the condemned vessels. Yet they did not wish to lose her, stained though she was with the dregs of sodden tobacco. To get her afloat at high tide, they threw hogsheads overboard. She righted herself. Her leaky seams stuffed with tobacco and her two pumps working constantly, she sailed back up Chesapeake Bay to her home port.

To his stepson in the Hanover store, Samuel Gist wrote as if he were sacrificing his own interests by shipping merchandise. Nevertheless, in 1770 his Virginia trade expanded. After the *Elizabeth* returned to London, he sent her back with a cargo arriving before news of Parliament's action on taxes. The *Elizabeth* sailed up the York, the *Nancy* sailed up the James and the Appomattox, bearing Gist's goods. The late Thomas Tabb, owner of the *Nancy*, had joined with Theophilus Feild and other merchants in Petersburg to start companies retailing merchandise furnished by Gist. In the spring, Feild & Company sent their ship *Two Sisters* to London. Gist also supplied the new Norfolk firm, Phripp, Taylor & Company.

Samuel Galloway and Stephen Steward submitted to their underwriters at Lloyd's a claim for insurance on 84 hogsheads of tobacco jettisoned from the *Fitzhugh*. They thought their claim modest, since they had salvaged the vessel and part of her cargo. They made no claim for damages to the ship. There could hardly have been a clearer case of what underwriters called jettison and loss overboard. To the owners' surprise, the insurers refused to pay them £692 for lost tobacco, saying that this cargo could have been landed rather than thrown into the bay. The owners protested that the tobacco, after twelve days under salt water in the *Fitzhugh*'s hold, was worthless. But Samuel Gist, they were told, "has the Assurance to preposess the rest of the Underwriters with a notion that all your proceedings are base & Dishonest." Gist and his colleagues prevailed when the claim went to arbitration. Samuel Galloway blustered about suing in Chancery, but he could only conclude: "I have learnt a Lesson not to expect even Justice from underwriters."

Fighting policyholders and extending credit to storekeepers, Gist saw his younger colleague at Lloyd's, John Shoolbred, making money in the slave trade and taking his business to Gist's region, the Chesapeake. On June 22, 1770, the captain of a vessel out of Dominica, bound for Bristol, spoke the *Providence*, one of Shoolbred's vessels, below the Tropic of Cancer. The *Providence* brought slaves from Gambia. After a stay in the Windward Islands, she was bound for Chesapeake Bay. Captain Thomas Davis said that he had "162 negroes on board, all well." Early in July she dropped anchor at Port Tobacco, Maryland. Shoolbred's representatives held a series of convenient auctions to sell men, women, and children "for Sterling Cash, or good Bills of Exchange, payable in London."

Despite low remittances, Gist in 1771 loaded the *Elizabeth*, the *Nancy*, and the *Two Sisters* again. After Phripp, Taylor & Company received three cargoes from him, the partners grew unhappy. Their competitors sold narrow thread lace for the same amount in Virginia currency that the partners were paying Gist in sterling as their wholesale price. On one batch they noticed that markings of the regular price in England, 1s. 3d. per yard, had not been fully erased before the price charged them, 2s. 6d., was written in. They blamed the cloth dealers. Somehow, they could never make enough money to clear themselves of debts owed to Gist.

On August 17, 1771, Gist's ship *Elizabeth* sailed from the York, bound for London, laden with lumber, iron, and 482,000 pounds of tobacco. Two months later, as she entered the Channel, she stranded near Cherbourg, a total loss. *La Mademoiselle* out of Cherbourg saved the crew. Gist took the first opportunity, by a vessel bound for New York, to send word to planters with tobacco in the *Elizabeth*: all of it was safely insured at £10 per hogshead.

After New Year's Day 1772, Gist reviewed his books, kept by his clerk, Aiskew Birkett. They showed that he was "in Advance" for his Virginia trade by £40,000, the gap between invoices he had sent and remittances he had received. That was far too much, he said. He decided to restrict his shipments of goods, serving only those who paid punctually. His stepson owed him £1,787. Gist cut him off. John Smith had formed his own firm, Smith & Clarke. His autumn order for goods in 1772 went unfilled. Without comment, Gist sent it around the corner to John Norton, charging Norton transatlantic postage. In July 1772, Smith closed the Hanover Store and deeded away some of the land in Goochland County he had inherited from his father. In October he made his last entry in his ledger.

The partners expanded the Dismal Swamp Company's land claims. Their entry in August 1770 for all the ungranted sector of the Dismal Swamp in Norfolk County cooperated with Anthony Bacon's arrangements in London. In February 1770 he had spoken of his intent to get the North Carolina portion of the swamp for them. He did not seem to care whether James Parker and men of the Campania Company in Norfolk learned of his moves. If Bacon hoped to scare the Scots, he succeeded. Within weeks they heard of "advances" made by the Dismal Swamp Company to the estate of the late Earl Granville. The proposed purchase was huge: all ungranted acreage in the four counties of North Carolina covering the Dismal Swamp south of the dividing line. Bacon might reasonably suppose that the Granville proprietary existed to yield cash, as in the days when he had dealt with the old earl. Parker and William Aitchison wrote to their friend in London, Charles Steuart, urging him to talk, "as it were accidentally," to people who knew what the Dismal Swamp Company was doing about North Carolina. Surely, after so many legal precautions and so much effort cutting their way into the swamp, they could not be "tossed out" now.

Steuart's inquiries revealed that Bacon was dealing not with the new earl, whom the old Lord Granville "never would see," but with those who hoped to succeed to the proprietary. The earl was childless and likely to remain so. His wife had worked as "superintendent of a bagnio" but had retired upon becoming Countess Granville. The earl long had been eccentric. "He drinks hard, and has a swelld leg, and looks heated"—signs that the Dismal Swamp Company might not have to wait long. Steuart had "no doubt" that Bacon would try to obtain the North Carolina sector of the swamp; Bacon could be "a very friendly man." The Campania partners ought to empower someone in London to counteract him. Two months later, in August, George Mercer said that the Dismal Swamp Company had secured a grant of all the swamp south of the dividing line. Steuart talked to the company's London partners. Samuel Gist said that Mercer was wrong, "but Mr. Bacon said he had got a promise of it."

Parker and Macknight had done nothing in the swamp since their expedition in 1769. A local man called the "road" to Lake Drummond cut by the slaves "a species of Road such as Squirrels use." The partners had made no other marks of possession, though they hoped to profit from cutting shingles while waiting to merge with the Dismal Swamp Company. Bacon's backstairs arrangement in London threatened to leave them with nothing to show for their ingenious plan to force the Virginians to make them rich.

Some of the Virginia partners feared threats in London to their claims in the west. In October and November 1770, George Washington traveled with some companions through the upper Ohio Valley. They went down the Ohio more than 200 miles, to the mouth of the Kanawha, then up the lower reaches of that river. Washington took notes on the land and chose some tracts for himself. He already had taken an interest in improving the Potomac River. If waterborne commerce could pass the falls by a canal or other means, the Potomac and the Ohio could become parts of a single system. He imagined a "Channel of conveyance of the extensive & valuable Trade of a rising Empire." Visitors bathing at the Hot Springs in Augusta County during the summer of 1770 saw families daily passing westward to live along the Ohio and its tributaries. No orders from London could stop them. Such migration foretold a rising empire and gave Washington another reason to act quickly.

Virginians knew in the early months of 1770 that Samuel Wharton of Pennsylvania, his London ally, Thomas Walpole, and a group of Pennsylvanians, with help from English partners, sought a vast tract: 20,000,000 acres of western Virginia. They envisioned a new colony, with its own government "a necessity." They contrasted their own "public Spirit" with Virginians' attempt "to monopolise on narrow and sinister Principles the Country to the Westward of the Allegheny Mountains." Wharton, Walpole, and their partners offered to pay the Crown for its grant by assuming the expense incurred in the treaty of Fort Stanwix.

George Washington said that such a grant would "give a fatal blow" to Virginia's interest. The prospect was "alarming" to Dr. Walker and to the Loyal Company. After a brief attempt to fight Wharton and Walpole, George Mercer joined them. He united the claims of the Ohio Company with the petition of Wharton and Walpole in return for a $\frac{1}{36}$ share of the new scheme, to be divided among the twenty members of the Ohio Company. He took a $\frac{1}{72}$ share for himself, hoping to win appointment as governor of the new colony. Though the Lee brothers were members of the Ohio Company, Arthur Lee, representing the Mississippi Company in London, opposed Wharton and Walpole. He wrote: "there are not a sett of greater knaves under the sun." Wharton, in moving to London, left behind large debts in Pennsylvania. His sometime partner, George Morgan, called him "faithless & dishonourable." Wharton feared arrest in London for unpaid tradesmen's bills. Only success with his new company might save him. He could not afford scruples. He thought of naming his colony Pittsylvania but changed his mind: "in Compliment to the Queen, it will be called Vandalia; as her majesty is descended from the Vandals." One of his former partners wrote in November: "The worst wish I pray may happen to this Generous gratefull, Polite Partner of ours is Abundant Success in all his honest undertakings."

Wharton mocked the Virginians. He sarcastically asked whether Washington thought the Mississippi Company's "very extraordinary petition" for 2,500,000 acres gave a fatal blow to Virginia's interests. Washington's "patriotic sentiment" in that instance went no further than desire for free land. Though Wharton could alarm and disparage rival speculators, he could not easily get around them. The Earl of Hillsborough, secretary of state for America, did not trust land speculators and did not approve of promoters eager to buy from Indians and sell to new settlers. Hillsborough used Virginians' claims as grounds for prolonging consideration of Wharton's proposal. Uncontrolled migration westward, though Hillsborough deplored it, went on, but neither Wharton's associates nor their rivals profited from it.

Virginia's opponents of Parliament's taxes tried to revive "the Spirit of Association" in the summer of 1770. They drew up another list of goods and promised not to import these items of "luxury and extravagance." Lord Botetourt and the Earl of Hillsborough agreed that promptings from England began this effort. The colonists may have hoped that their signatures would help their allies in London win repeal of the tax on tea. In June and July the Association attracted many signers. Scottish merchants and Samuel Gist's stepson, John Smith, signed. David Meade served on the committee of enforcement in Nansemond County. Yet the effort did not last out the year. Neither merchants in other colonies nor signers in Virginia sustained the cause. A meeting called for December 14 brought so few associators to Williamsburg that those present immediately adjourned.

Lord Botetourt did not live to see the final collapse of the spirit of Association. He contracted a fever on September 23. His condition turned sharply worse on Friday, October 12—he suffered three severe convulsions. After the third he expected to die. He faced this prospect with composure and resignation, but before dawn he said: "'tis a little unluckie, had I Stayd a little longer the people in America would have been Convinced, that I had their good at heart." These were almost his last words. Less than forty-eight hours later he died.

Members of the Council praised Botetourt, calling his administration "Golden days." They covered his casket with superfine black cloth fastened by double rows of large gilt tacks; they held services for him in Bruton Parish Church and buried his remains in the chapel of the College of William and

Mary. In the sale of the estate's effects, William Nelson bought the six white horses and the post coach. The ornate state coach was retained for future governors. John Blair, president of the Council, was eighty-three years old. He slept through Botetourt's administration, waking only to eat. The Council announced after the governor's death that Blair made "a free & voluntary Resignation." William Nelson became president of the Council and acting governor. Although Lord Botetourt died "universally lamented," no one surpassed Nelson in commending him for bringing to Virginians "the compleatest Happiness We ever experienced."

Robert Munford, burgess for Mecklenburg County, a friend of Francis Farley's and William Byrd's, had stood with Patrick Henry in opposing the stamp tax and had signed the Association of 1770. Political life in Virginia disillusioned him as much as it disappointed David Meade. Unlike Meade, Munford stayed in office. In private, however, he wrote satirical verse and plays. He began *The Candidates*, his portrait of ambitious politicians and loutish freeholders, with his version of Virginians' reaction to their governor's death. A burgess named "Wou'dbe" enters with a newspaper in his hand and begins a soliloquy: "I am very sorry our good old governor Botetourt has left us. He well deserved our friendship, when alive, and that we should for years to come, with gratitude, remember his mild and affable deportment. Well, our little world will soon be up, and very busy towards our next election."

IV

·—·

THE LAST VOYAGE
OF THE SLAVE SHIP *HOPE*

PART 1: *The Voyagers*

SHE WAS A SNOW, NOT A SHIP. She had two masts, not three, and her rigging, though baffling to anyone but a sailor, was less elaborate than rigging of ships of her burden, 150 tons. By her name in the Admiralty's register, a clerk wrote: "French made free." Such vessels had been built in France for the smuggling trade. They bore thousands of gallons of wine and brandy to British waters, where smugglers' boats came out to meet them. Some were unlucky: revenue cruisers took them, and customs officers seized them for the Crown. Thus they were "made free"; they could be purchased from the Crown and turned to new service. The *Hope* became a slaving vessel, owned by Samuel Gist and others. She was to sail to the Gold Coast, and from there, take hundreds of slaves to Virginia. But she did not reach Chesapeake Bay. As a slave ship, she brought misfortune, loss, or death to almost everyone connected with her. This is her story.

In the autumn of 1770, Gist began to write to his Virginia correspondents about his "African Scheme," a voyage to buy slaves on the Gold Coast and take them to Virginia. If all went well, he could pay £16 or £20 in Africa for a slave to be sold for £45 in Virginia. He wrote to his partners in the Dismal Swamp Company, urging them to "add largely" to the force working in the swamp. Such expansion made all the more sense in light of the company's effort to acquire more of the swamp in Norfolk County and all of it in North Carolina. Gist offered to lend the company any amount its members chose to spend on new slaves, charging 5 percent interest, the maximum allowed by law. If, as he obviously expected, his partners bought from him, he would profit from the sale and the loan. He shipped clothing, tools, and other supplies for the company's slaves on credit.

Gist mentioned his plan to Virginia storekeepers. Neither John Tabb nor Roger Atkinson wished to sell slaves—"it is a Business I was never fond of," Atkinson told him—but they and others believed that slaves would find buyers. In a letter written to a planter that fall, a friend in London congratulated him on his return to "what you call your *Land of Promise*" to enjoy the colony's ideal life: "a comfortable Habitation, an extensive and fruitful Estate, amply stocked with what constitutes the principal Riches of your Province, viz. a large Number of healthful robust Negroes." The 187,000 slaves in Virginia made up 40 percent of its population. Gist felt sure that planters would buy as long as they had money or credit. He envisioned an annual ship from Africa. Some slaves were imported into Virginia from the West Indies, but most new slaves came from Africa. Planters preferred those from the Gold Coast. Why should Gist not send them what they wanted by a direct route, to their mutual advantage? With proper effort by his representatives in Virginia, his vessel, like most slave ships sailing back to Britain, would return laden with tobacco.

By paying £2, Gist became a member of the Company of Merchants Trading to Africa, joining Anthony Bacon and many underwriters and merchants he saw every day on 'Change and in Lloyd's. The law did not allow corporate ventures by the Company of Merchants, and few men in Gist's position wished to bear alone the whole expense and risk of a slaving voyage. He needed other investors and an ally who specialized in the trade to help finance and guide his African scheme. He turned to his acquaintance at Lloyd's, John Shoolbred.

A Cutter Off Shore, Samuel Atkins. Courtesy of the Henry E. Huntington Art Gallery. A cutter sails toward a vessel similar to the *Hope*.

In January 1771, Shoolbred's small ship *Providence*, which had taken slaves to Port Tobacco, Maryland, the previous year, sailed for the African coast, then took 170 slaves to Georgia. At the age of thirty-one, Shoolbred was a rising man in the Company of Merchants. One of his associates described him in August: "a merchant in the City, an Underwriter or Assurer, who transacts a vast deal of Business & is chiefly concerned in the African Trade." He was also a member of the Laudable Society for the Benefit of Widows. Though he complained about control of the trade by the dominant influence of Gilbert Ross and James Mill, of the firm Ross & Mill, he was taking steps toward changing the firm to Shoolbred, Ross & Mill. The ship *Peggy* in the Gold Coast trade changed her registered owner from Ross & Mill to John Shoolbred, making him an employer of Captain Hercules Mill, brother of James Mill. Shoolbred was a pitiless competitor. An investor in the *Hawke*, which he dispatched to Africa in the fall of 1771, said after the skewed division of profits: "I have indeed been monstrously abused by Shoolbred." Samuel Gist saw that Shoolbred would become the most important man in the slave trade. Shoolbred later wrote: "the Effects of this Trade to Great Britain are beneficial to an infinite Extent . . . there is hardly any Branch of Commerce in which this Nation is concerned that does not derive some Advantage from it." He added more vessels to his Africa fleet and sought new investors, such as Gist. Large profits might flow from a single voyage, especially one bringing to England a cargo of commodities from the port where slaves landed. Not all voyages succeeded; some barely broke even; some vessels and their crews never returned. Investors bought a cargo

Eddystone Lighthouse, John Cleveley. Courtesy of the Henry E. Huntington Art Gallery. A view of the English Channel south of Plymouth. The lighthouse was completed in 1759.

of manufactured goods on credit, and they bought insurance at a premium of 7 percent or 8 percent. In the course of many voyages, they could expect a profit of as much as 14 percent.

With help from the government, the Company of Merchants maintained a chain of forts along the Gold Coast. The men appointed to governorships by the company made the work of a ship's captain seeking a cargo of slaves easier or more difficult. Any shipowner was supposed to rest assured that all vessels on the Gold Coast were treated alike. The happiest owners, however, had a friend in command of the fort where their ships dropped anchor. The senior officer in the company's service on the Gold Coast was the governor of Cape Coast Castle, a position newly filled by David Mill, brother of Captain Hercules Mill and James Mill. The second-ranking man commanded the fort at Annamaboe, ten miles to the east. Charles Bell, according to his harshest critic, was "a man of the most rapacious, avaricious, mean disposition of any in the service." Yet, during the voyage of the *Hope*, Gist and Shoolbred always found him eager to help.

In the years 1768 to 1772, English vessels annually took about 38,000 slaves from Africa to the western hemisphere. Of these, on average, almost 6,000 came from the Gold Coast. In 1771, Samuel Gist invested in the *Meredith*, a 120-ton ship, part of the fleet of slaving vessels sailing from Liverpool for Miles Barber & Company. Liverpool's Africa trade far surpassed that of London and Bristol combined. Few ships had been designed and built to carry slaves; "any vessel was thought good enough for it." Mariners spoke of a vessel that looked unseaworthy as "not better than a Guineaman." Departing on September 30, the *Meredith* made a successful voyage to the Windward Coast of Africa and the Leeward Islands. By the usual standard, she would have been fully laden with 264 slaves on board. She took 280 to St. Kitts. During her voyage, Gist wrote: "The high Prices Negroes have sold for all over the West Indies Carolina & Georga. will I hope Prevent many Comg. to Virga." He was unhappy that Barber had offered planters twelve months of credit without interest if the *Meredith* sold slaves in the Chesapeake. "This Mr Barber has certainly dreamt, for I never Promisd it." Gist got his wish. The *Meredith* did not have to sail to Virginia to dispose of her cargo.

As the *Meredith* began her long voyage, ship's carpenters, joiners, painters, and caulkers, as well as tradesmen, prepared the *Hope* for hers. No matter how much work they did, she would still be a French-built ship, "liable to all the accidents, to which ships of that construction are peculiarly subject." She had to be converted from a smuggler to a slaver, leaving more space between the main deck and the lower deck, less in the hold. As she disposed of her cargo of goods on the Gold Coast, she would fill with Africans confined between decks most of each day. At 150 tons, she was about average for a slaving vessel. She needed manacles, fetters, and chains for three hundred men, women, and children. Slave ships took gallons of vinegar to be poured over the lower deck for cleaning. The best trading cargo included colorful patterned cotton cloth from India, silk taffeta, chintz, linen from Europe, woolen goods from England, felt hats, brass pans, gunpowder, gunflints, tobacco pipes, bottled beer, and malt liquor.

The owners and the captain hired a crew of thirty-eight for the *Hope*. Ten or twelve able seamen sailed a snow; the rest of a slaver's complement were a chief mate, a second mate, a surgeon, a carpenter, a cook, a tailor, a number of ordinary seamen making their second or third voyage, and tradesmen whom the sailors called "Landsmen." Captains met at Lloyd's and agreed upon a uniform wage. Seamen's pay ranged from £1 10s. to £2 per month. They received two months' pay in advance and half their pay when vessel and slaves reached port in the West Indies or North America.

Gist found that buying the *Hope*, manning her, fitting her out, and furnishing a cargo of goods came to "a great deale of money." The brig *Unanimity*, of the same tonnage as the *Hope*, was purchased at about the same time for £680 and prepared in London for the Africa trade at a cost of £4,658 15s. 1d. Gist paid a "Considerable" portion of his share of the *Hope*'s costs before she sailed. The remainder typically fell due six, nine, and twelve months later. By extending credit, manufacturers and storekeepers supplying goods for the Africa trade enabled men such as Miles Barber and John Shoolbred to send more vessels, to attract more investors, and to take bonds, not just cash, from purchasers of slaves. Eventually, Miles Barber & Company expanded its ventures to a total of more than £100,000, "never having a capital of a tithe of the money their own property." Their "great push" ended in bankruptcy. Shoolbred and Gist were more prudent.

For master of the *Hope*, the owners turned to a man with experience in the slave trade, James Dougall. He had commanded vessels sailing from Bristol for the firm Thomas Jones & Company. He had just returned from a sixteen-month voyage to Annamaboe, St. Thomas, and Grenada. Four months after mooring at Bristol, he was getting ready to take the *Hope* from London to Annamaboe. Masters of slave vessels received a salary of £5 per month; a "coast commission" of £4 for every £104 worth of slaves bought in Africa; and the right to buy, transport, and sell five slaves on a private account. A chief mate took three slaves, a second mate two, and a surgeon three.

Compared to other routes, Africa voyages attracted seamen who were "more disorderly and irregular," a retired captain said. Many had "a turbulent, refractory Disposition." For their part, sailors told stories of especially cruel captains in slave ships—tales of short rations, little water, kickings and beatings with handspikes, musket butts, and rope ends. Captain George Colley, who took slaves to Fredericksburg in the snow *Hare* in 1761, was an "inhuman monster," who caused the deaths of some seamen. Captain Samuel Pemberton, master of the ship *Matty* on the African coast with the *Hope*, treated his men in "a very barbarous manner." Accounts of his brutality still made the rounds seventeen years later. With more violence or with less, or with threats of it, ships' masters ruled their crews.

These captains had reason to stay wary not only of slaves between decks but also of crewmen. Sailors often wound up in the trade because their fortunes were desperate. Captain Joseph Spencer departed for the coast of Africa a few months after the *Hope* did and returned safely to Liverpool. But on his next slaving voyage he died at the hands of his men. The boatswain and part of the crew of his brig *Will* plotted to seize her and become pirates. About 200 miles east of Madeira, during the night, the men of the watch killed Spencer, his chief mate, and the carpenter, then threw the bodies overboard. The boatswain proclaimed himself commander. To reduce the size of the crew, he ordered men out in the longboat, intending to leave them at sea. One sailor, fearing the boatswain's enmity, killed him with a hammer. The second mate regained command. Another seaman was killed and four put in irons. A few days later, the *Will* arrived at Madeira, bearing a story that spread quickly. Owners and masters ran risks in sending out large crews in small vessels, but they needed these seamen and officers because the African trade "requires experienced men on the coast as much as the Greenland trade requires experienced Harpooneers." Captain Dougall had shown that he could control a crew, as well as buy and sell a cargo of slaves.

Sailors in the slave trade who did not mutiny still had more than the usual excuse for "Debauchery and Intoxication" when they reached port. One of their chanteys ran:

> *Beware and take care of the Bight of Benin*
> *There's one comes out for forty goes in.*

Anchored along the coast of Africa or sailing across the Atlantic with a cargo of people in chains, mostly young men, who outnumbered them eight to one, they faced both the customary perils of the sea and special risks. While James Dougall made a safe voyage from Bristol in 1770 and 1771, other vessels did not. The *Duke of Bridgewater* out of Liverpool was boarded by Africans and set on fire. On the coast of Sierra Leone the *African Queen* was boarded and run aground, with Captain North and nine of his crew killed. Every man in the *George* except Captain Bare was killed by an African boarding party off the Windward Coast, taking Africans whom Bare had bought. Seriously wounded, Bare sailed for Liverpool with a new crew, but the *George* foundered at the entrance to Liverpool Harbor. After a successful voyage to Africa and Barbados, the *Sam*, bound for Liverpool, foundered off the coast of Ireland. Her crew was picked up by a passing vessel. The *Loyalty*, bound for Georgia from Gambia, foundered during a gale in the Atlantic. All the slaves went down, as did all but two of the crew.

Few words at sea troubled a sailor's ear as much as the word "founder"— to fill with water and sink. On January 16, 1770, the sloop *Expedition*, two days out of Senegal with 110 slaves on board, began to take on water. Captain Edward Williamson hailed a passing sloop, the *James*. Her master agreed to take on board the crew of the *Expedition*. The *James* then sailed on, leaving behind chained Africans in a leaking sloop. Three weeks later the *James* arrived at Barbados. Captain Williamson filed a report, enabling Edward Grace, owner of the *Expedition*, to recover £3,200 insurance on the sloop and her cargo. He thought this sum "full as much as they could have produced if they had arrived at a market."

But the *Expedition* had not foundered. The leak was not so bad as her captain reported. With no one at the helm, she drove before the wind until her tattered sails had blown from her yards. Below deck Africans died, their corpses still chained to the living. When sailors of the ship *Gregson* sighted her, she looked like a ghost vessel, adrift with neither canvas nor crew. By admiralty law, she belonged to anyone who took her. Of the 110 Africans from Senegal, 60 still lived. The *Gregson*, out of Liverpool, also pursued the slave trade. Captain Richard Hanly took the *Expedition*'s survivors on board his vessel, adding them to his cargo of slaves. Since the *Expedition* could not make way without sails, he scuttled her. She went to the bottom at last, and the *Gregson* sailed on to the West Indies.

The members of the Dismal Swamp Company in Virginia took Samuel Gist's advice to buy more slaves. They accepted his offer to lend money for this purpose. They wrote to John Tucker, brother of the late Robert Tucker, in Barbados with an order for twenty slaves and instructions to draw a bill of exchange on Gist to pay for the purchase. This was not what Gist had expected. The *Hope* was going to deliver slaves to Virginia. How could his partners suppose that he would advance £800 or more to buy slaves in Barbados? Gist wrote to Tucker "to desire he will not make the Purchase." He let William Nelson and others know that he would not honor Tucker's bill. Nelson had to scramble to make sure that some other merchant in London would take up any bill Tucker drew. To one firm he vented his anger at Gist: "He is (S.G.) a dirty Fellow, and I was sorry he was admitted a Partner."

Gist sent instructions to John Tabb for selling slaves. The *Hope*, he said, would bring more than three hundred Gold Coast slaves but would not arrive early in the selling season of May to August. "These Slaves are rather too good for Virga.—that is ordinary slaves sell for near as much money." He remembered thirty years past, during rapid expansion of slavery in Virginia— William King & Company sold a Gold Coast slave for £5 more than one from elsewhere. Now he had to rely on Tabb to make the best of the *Hope*'s cargo. A few days after Gist wrote, John Shoolbred approached him with an offer. Would Gist take a share in another Shoolbred slave ship, perhaps the *Mentor*? Gist declined, later telling Tabb he had done so because "you do not chuse to go deeper in that Article."

On Wednesday, December 11, 1771, Captain James Dougall obtained a pass for the *Hope* from the Admiralty. The following week she dropped down the Thames, passing miles of flat fields, to the anchorage at Gravesend. On December 20, the *Hope* weighed anchor and, with a southwest wind, sailed out of the estuary, bound for Africa.

Vessels to the Gold Coast usually followed a familiar route. Its three principal points were the Canary Islands, the Cape Verde Islands, and Cape Palmas, where the African coast turned eastward. Once past Cape Finisterre, the *Hope* could run before the northeast trade winds. Dougall guarded against the easterly current into the Straits of Gibraltar that wrecked vessels on the coast of Morocco. From the Canary Islands the route lay amid strong land winds and dangerous waterspouts between the Cape Verde Islands and Senegal, westernmost point of Africa. The *Hope* sailed through the horse latitudes and picked up the Guinea current. On this passage, early in winter, sailors encountered the harmattan, a dry wind from the northeast bearing clouds of red dust lifted off the Sahara. These darkened the sky, parched the skin, and coated decks and sails far from shore, giving vessel and crew their first taste of Africa.

A wise captain rounded Cape Palmas well out to sea, reducing the risk that southerly winds or a mistake in calculating longitude would land his vessel west of the cape. It was safer to make landfall at Drewin, 120 miles east of Cape Palmas. Sighting high ground at the mouth of the Sassandra River, experienced seamen knew that a few days' run would bring them to Annamaboe. The *Hope* dropped anchor in Annamaboe Road in February 1772, after a voyage of about eight weeks.

The *Hope* mounted two pieces of artillery. Custom and courtesy required Captain Dougall to fire a salute to the great fort at water's edge. A gun would return the salute from the fort. Sailing along the Gold Coast, the *Hope* had passed other forts belonging to the Company of Merchants Trading to Africa, as well as Dutch and Danish posts. More lay to the east. All had been built to protect the slave trade. Looking westward from his anchorage, Dougall saw, ten miles away, Cape Coast Castle atop a rocky headland jutting into the sea. There the Company of Merchants' chief officer, David Mill, had his headquarters. From his vantage point, Mill kept his eye on shipping anchored in the road.

Shipping was almost always in sight. English slavers trading as far west as Appolonia or as far east as Great Prampram and Little Prampram, beyond Accra, remained at Annamaboe. Often a dozen or more vessels rode at anchor a mile off shore. The shore's edge was rocky. Winds and breakers, though severe only during spring rains, warned any vessel to beware. Men and trade goods in canoes plying between ships and land sometimes arrived soaked. From May to August a "dreadfull Sea" often came on from the southwest, forcing canoes to stay on the beach, breaking them to pieces if they did not. The waves were high enough to swamp a ship's longboat. A man in the water might not live long, because the "road is full of sharks."

Above the shoreline at Annamaboe, thick woods and shrubs covered low hills and valleys, except where fields of corn grew. In the distance, 100 miles north, a chain of hills ran along the coast—the land of the Asante, as every master of a slave vessel knew. Back of the beach stood the new white fort, two stories high, 40 yards square, built of imported bricks covered with white-washed plaster. The southwest and southeast bastions pointed out to sea, the northwest and northeast overlooked the town. In its parapets, embrasures opened for artillery and slits for small arms. Within, its buildings were stone. Inside the northeast bastion stood holding cells for slaves, a row of narrow vaults with stone floors and high, dark walls. The fort held forty-seven cannons but only one gunner. It was authorized a garrison of thirteen soldiers but had only nine. It was a post for trade. Around it lay a town with two districts: the English called them Fishing Town and Fantee Town. Both contained substantial dwellings holding several thousand people. Another large brick building near the northwest bastion loomed over the town. Its owner, Richard Brew, called it "Castle Brew." A former employee of the Company of Merchants, he was a private trader in slaves. Within his home he strove for the effect of an English country residence. His guests were masters of vessels anchored in the road.

To acquire a cargo of slaves, Captain Dougall had to negotiate with the slave dealers of Annamaboe. They were Fante, and the principal man—or *omanhene*—at Annamaboe, Amonu Kuma, was friendly to the trade. The most important British posts lay within the territory of the Fante states, stretching along the coast from the Pra River, 90 miles eastward, almost to Accra. The Fante took pains to deny their neighbors, especially the Asante, direct access to the sea and to white men who came to buy slaves. The British on the coast believed that dealing with local leaders within a Fante confederation served their interests better than if the trade were controlled by the Asante. Still, Dougall knew from past months at anchor in Annamaboe Road, and other British captains complained steadily, that Fante businessmen were shrewd bargainers. A former governor of Cape Coast Castle had called them "the most rapacious set of People on earth." Yet the British were glad to deal with these men whose greed they reproached. Governor David Mill believed that, without the Fante, "our trade would be totally ruined."

Since Captain Dougall had been away from Annamaboe only a year, he could expect to welcome on board the *Hope* the same Fante gold-taker who had worked with him before. In some vessels he dined at the captain's table. One or more of the gold-taker's men lived on board as long as the *Hope* remained at Annamaboe. He and his men ensured the quality of gold used in transactions and arbitrated any dispute between Dougall and slave dealers. By old custom they received salaries, and the gold-taker a commission equivalent to 4s. 6d. or 5s. on each slave.

All captains knew the principal slave dealers in Annamaboe. These included Amonu Kuma himself and a man claiming to be his son, Kwasi Tuh. The chief elders of Fishing Town and Fantee Town, known to the British as Yellow Joe and Little Adu, as well as Sham, who lived in Fishing Town, were discriminating judges of merchandise in a slave ship's trading cargo. Kwasi Kuah was a great trader; a variety of other men operated on a smaller scale: the bush trader Amuru, the military man Kwasi Nkomah, the corn merchant Kobea, and the linguist known as Old Tooth John. Annamaboe had more than sixty slave dealers, and many people in the towns sold a few slaves to make extra money. A young Fante man, Philip Quaque, who had returned to the Gold Coast after his ordination in the Church of England, deplored "the vicious practice of purchasing flesh and blood like oxen in market places." He wished to evangelize, and he blamed the "gentlemen of the fort" for opposing anyone who might obstruct the "cursed slave trade."

Enslavement had a long history in West Africa. Most people sold on the Gold Coast in the decades before the voyage of the *Hope* had been prisoners or spoils of war, as the Asante expanded their rule. Opportunities for profit made war more lucrative, and Europeans brought to the coast weapons making combat more effective. During his previous stay at Annamaboe, Captain Dougall had disposed of lead, gunflints, and gunpowder. The Fante prohibited sale of these to the Asante, but demand among the Asante was "fully, tho' secretly, supplied, by those very Fantees."

Slaves bought on the Gold Coast might be Asante, Fante, or Koromanti. People could be enslaved for unpaid debts, for witchcraft, and for crimes such as murder, adultery, and theft. Others had been kidnapped. Passing through the hands of several African dealers and on board Europeans' ships, slaves found few who showed interest in the story of their enslavement. One English trader said: "The Gold Coast Brokers go from 100 to 150 Miles up the Country to pursue them; from what further Distance they may be brought, it is impossible to say; but it is probable they come from a very great Distance, and from different Countries, for they talk different Languages." Bound with rope made of grass or bark, lying wet in a canoe at the feet of a Fante dealer, slaves were rowed out to the *Hope* and other vessels. Dealers sold slaves from Gabon, Lagos, and Benin, sometimes persuading a novice captain that he was buying Gold Coast Africans. On his first voyage to Annamaboe, one trader wrote of the Fante: "they think it meritorious to Cheat a White man all that lyes in their power."

Captain Dougall began buying in February. He found the trade slow and the supply unequal to the demand. His cargo of goods would not go as far as Gist had calculated. It looked as if he would have to linger at Annamaboe longer than he had stayed in the autumn of 1770. To buy an adult male slave at the latest price set by dealers, ten ounces, Dougall must pay either five ounces of gold, which was out of the question, or goods valued at ten trade ounces, slightly more than £20 retail. But he could not get a slave solely with manufactured goods. Dealers insisted on at least some gold with each transaction. Captains found gold expensive; Africans might hold out for £30 in goods as the price for five ounces of gold. Nor did dealers always accept whatever goods were offered—they expected to receive an assortment of their own choosing. Fashion changed rapidly. An official of the Company of Merchants wrote: "the Choice of Goods entirely Commands the Trade."

One commodity was always in demand on the Gold Coast: tobacco from Brazil, grown in the Portuguese colony of Bahia. A 50-pound, 300-foot roll of this dark, rank, "reject" tobacco, slathered with molasses by the Portuguese, substituted for an ounce of gold. Yet Dougall could buy it from the captain of a tobacco vessel for £3 in goods. A large Portuguese snow might be laden with 5,000 rolls. And such vessels visited or sailed by Annamaboe Road often, bound eastward to buy slaves for Bahia. Both the government in Lisbon and Dutch officers on the Gold Coast told Portuguese captains not to trade with the British, but neither orders nor punishments stopped them. John Shoolbred said that tobacco from Bahia was "essential to the African trade," and he knew from his captains and from governors of the Company's forts that the rolls were "not to be got accidentally." The Dutch disliked sales between tobacco vessels and the British because the Dutch wished to be sole suppliers, forcing the British to buy from them.

Charles Bell and David Mill usually kept a stock of tobacco in Annamaboe Fort and Cape Coast Castle, just as they kept slaves. Bell and Mill offered these for sale but at higher prices than the Portuguese or the Fante dealers charged. Since Captain Dougall was working for men in London who were close to the committee of the Company of Merchants, he could expect courtesy and assistance from Charles Bell and David Mill. The governors sold tobacco or slaves, however, not as representatives of the Company of Merchants but as private traders. Bell meant to make his fortune and retire to Rose Street in Edinburgh. He supplemented his salary and profits from slave sales by embezzling £7,000 from the Company of Merchants. No one need look to him for bargains. A captain buying slaves in the forts was a captain in a hurry to leave the Gold Coast or a captain who could get slaves nowhere else.

Shortly after the *Hope* reached her anchorage, the snow *Greenwich*, out of Bristol, sailed into Annamaboe Road, bringing with her a schooner from Jamaica and a story of the kind familiar to men in the slave trade. The *Greenwich* had been out eleven months and still did not have a full cargo of slaves. Her captain had died and been succeeded by Captain Edmund Williams. Off Grand Bassam, 190 miles west of Annamaboe, Williams sent out a longboat. An officer in it sighted the Jamaica schooner in distress. On board were only two boys. They said that along the Ivory Coast above Grand Bassam the schooner had been boarded by Africans, who killed Captain John Blow and all the crew except themselves. They got off with the vessel but could not make a voyage on their own. Captain Williams delivered the schooner to Governor David Mill, and he put her up for sale. The auction was attended by most of the captains in Annamaboe Road. The *Greenwich* did not sail for Tobago with a cargo of slaves until she had stayed on the African coast for eighteen months.

Spring brought no increase in the number of slaves for sale on the Gold Coast. It did bring more news of other captains and crews. On the coast of Sierra Leone, upriver from Yawri Bay, slaves on board a brig from London, the *Exeter*, concerted an uprising. They killed Captain Richard Savery, a veteran of the trade between Sierra Leone and South Carolina, his mate, and twelve of his crew, allowing only a boy to live. They cut the *Exeter*'s anchor cable, stranded her, and escaped.

The ship *Betty and Jenny*, commanded by Captain Alexander Thomson, sailed from London a few weeks before the *Hope* departed. She took on a cargo of slaves at Gambia. Bound for Charleston, South Carolina, she was nearing Dominica, in the Leeward Islands, when the Africans rose against Thomson and his crew. In the fighting, the sailors killed several slaves. The rest were "got under" by force. Captain Thomson, taking no more chances, sold them in Dominica.

James Dougall and the *Hope* had waited in Annamaboe Road more than a month, but trade had grown worse. He bought, on average, two slaves every three days. At that rate, he would take a year to get a full cargo. Ever since she had dropped anchor, the *Hope* had shared the road with twelve to eighteen other vessels, yet fewer than three hundred slaves had been offered for sale in the first three months of 1772. Fante dealers raised their prices to eleven trade ounces for a man and nine trade ounces for a woman. They demanded two ounces of gold with each purchase and scorned the best silk taffeta, insisting on gold. Of course, the cost of gold rose: "you must sell your goods 20 per cent under prime cost, and you may think yourself happy to get it even at that rate." Charles Bell and David Mill, by their private purchases at the forts, competed with the captains.

On Dougall's previous voyage he was one of eighteen captains buying slaves, and he took nine months to fill his vessel. Finally, his snow *Thomas* and the other Bristol vessels—the *Roebuck*, the *Maesgwin*, and the *Marlborough*—sailed to Grenada. All but two or three of the rest sold their slaves in Barbados or Jamaica. In that competitive autumn of 1770, to make their purchases of slaves easier, Dougall's fellow captains from Bristol—Thomas Gullan of the *Roebuck*, Robert Howe of the *Maesgwin*, and John Marshall of the *Marlborough*—bought rolls of tobacco from the captain of a Portuguese bark. No one knew the Gold Coast trade better than John Marshall, who made nineteen voyages before he retired. He spoke the Fante language fluently, and he spent more of his adult life on the coast of Africa, mainly the Gold Coast, than in any other one place.

The *Maesgwin*, this time commanded by Captain Windsor Brown, returned to Annamaboe Road in the spring of 1772. She spent a year there to get 270 slaves for South Carolina. James Dougall also shared the market with the *Sally* and the *Surry* from London, the *Swallow* from Liverpool, and a rum vessel from Rhode Island, the *Adventure*.

The slow trade at Annamaboe came almost to a stop in May. The borderland between the Asante and the Fante, home of the Assin, usually welcomed its neighbors to hold their markets, exchanging European goods from the coast for slaves from the interior. Surprising their victims, Assin began to plunder Fante traders, taking many goods. Fante elders assumed that the Asante ruler, Osei Kojo, had approved these attacks as a sign that the Asante would soon wage war against the Fante. War did not come; the Asante already were fighting on their eastern front, and they did not attack the coast. But, during the months of threats, the Fante and the Asante suspended their usual commerce. Few slaves were brought to the coast. After ten weeks at Annamaboe, Captain Dougall had purchased fewer than seventy slaves.

The slaves lived between decks, men forward, women aft. In slave vessels of the *Hope's* tonnage anyone confined below who was taller than about five feet four inches, could not stand erect. Iron fetters locked one man's leg to another's. Partitions of grating separated men, women, and children. Wooden platforms on each side ran the length of the vessel. On these, slaves sat or lay. Slave ships were not quiet. Despite occasional vinegar washes, they were not clean. At her widest part, the snow's beam was less than 25 feet. Slaves remained between decks for at least two-thirds of the day. Heat and cramped confinement made them cry out. When rain hit, sailors pulled tarpaulins over the deck gratings; "hideous yelling" rose from below. Where a dozen or more slave ships rode at anchor, no passerby could mistake the nature of their trade, even from a distance. In April and May rain, clouds, fog, and boisterous winds covered the Gold Coast, and the leeward current ran strong to the east.

While James Dougall waited helplessly, his previous vessel, the *Thomas*, under the command of Captain Thomas Lewis, sailed to Virginia by way of Africa and Grenada. At the end of July she dropped anchor in the James River "with two Hundred fine healthy SLAVES" on board, according to Lewis. She had departed from Bristol for Africa only three weeks before the *Hope* left the Thames. In the middle of October she was safely moored in her home port.

Four months before the *Thomas* reached Chesapeake Bay, the House of Burgesses approved an address to the king on April 1. It asked the Crown to change the governor's instructions and allow him to approve a law prohibiting importation of slaves from Africa. In saying that the traffic "greatly retards the Settlement of the Colonies with more useful Inhabitants," the burgesses meant white immigrants. In saying that its continuation "will endanger the very Existence of your Majesty's American Dominions," the burgesses hinted darkly at slave revolt. Though some people in Britain "may reap Emoluments" from sending slaves to Virginia, the burgesses added, it "hath long been considered as a Trade of great Inhumanity." In London the address began its slow movement through the Board of Trade and a committee of the Privy Council.

By the end of the first week of May, James Dougall, now grown impatient or desperate, took action—rash action. He sighted a Portuguese tobacco vessel passing Annamaboe Road on the easterly current, and decided to barter with her captain. He lowered the *Hope*'s longboat, heavily laden with trade goods. He took with him his chief mate and six seamen. All went armed. They set the longboat's sail and stood out to sea in pursuit of the Portuguese. Dougall, his men, and his boat were never seen again.

Mr. Gricewood, second mate of the *Hope*, and Charles Bell in Annamaboe Fort waited several weeks for Dougall to return. Vessels sailing to leeward down the coast sometimes could not beat their way back for weeks. But Bell finally concluded that Dougall and his men had gone down at sea, and he wondered what had happened. Had Dougall overloaded his longboat with goods and found himself in the water among sharks? Why had he armed everyone? Portuguese captains were usually friendly and eager to trade. Had he tried to force the Portuguese to trade? Had the tobacco vessel sunk the longboat with her guns? Or were Dougall and his men facing confinement in one of Brazil's prisons? Another captain found these "filled with murderers and such an inhuman race of mortals no Christian could suppose were under the denomination of Christians."

At last Charles Bell left his fort and went out to the *Hope*. Masters of other vessels anchored in the road also came on board. Together, they drew up an inventory of the remaining merchandise and confirmed Gricewood as captain of the *Hope*. He and the surgeon wished to make a success of the voyage by completing their cargo of slaves before October.

The month of June 1772 was memorable to men of business in Britain: a financial panic spread over the country. Robert Bogle wrote that "the South Sea affair was a Triffle to what has now happened." The firm Bogle & Scott stopped payment on June 20, and the family's estates were put in trust. John Shoolbred worried about two hundred slaves bound for Virginia in one of his vessels. He had consigned them to the agent of Bogle & Scott in Norfolk, John Gilchrist. He did not wish these slaves to be "disagreeably interwoven with Messrs. Bogles & Scott's property." A friend wrote for him to John Tabb, agent for Samuel Gist, and to John Tayloe, asking them to relieve Gilchrist of the consignment. The day of that letter Robert Bogle, Jr., "in a phrenzy," jumped out of a window of his home. The *London Chronicle* reported his death. Soon people learned that "he happily fell in such an attitude as only to bruise his latter end." But by the end of the year it was clear that "every Shilling of Mr Bogles Fortune & Mr Scotts is sunk in this most unfortunate Abyss." In Norfolk, the following year, John Gilchrist, "from some unknown cause," killed himself with a pistol.

In the summer and autumn Captain Gricewood and the surgeon of the

Hope worked to buy a full complement of slaves. Other vessels arrived in Annamaboe Road: the *Swallow*, the *St. John*, the *Barbara*, the *Bee*, the *Africa*, the *Ingram*, and the *Hannah* from Britain, as well as four from Rhode Island. In November, John Shoolbred sent his snow *Woortman* from London to Annamaboe. During the summer, rain swept over the ships. In squalls with onshore winds, longboats stranded and were lost. Every morning and evening fog hid ships from one another and from the fort. After the fog lifted, few canoes came out to offer slaves for sale. No one could recall a time when the trade had come so close to a dead stop. Some vessels had been anchored near the *Hope* for six months but had on board fewer than fifty slaves. Perhaps a victim of the fever that took lives in other vessels, Captain Gricewood no longer commanded the *Hope*.

After Captain Ferguson became master of the *Hope* in the autumn, he found that she had sprung a leak—a bad leak in a bad place. If she did not get repairs, she would sink in Annamaboe Road. To stop the leak she must be heaved down to let a carpenter work on her hull. But the African coast had no port and no place to careen a vessel. The nearest such facilities were on the Portuguese Ilha do Príncipe, known to the British as the Island of Princes, 650 miles southeast of Annamaboe, just north of the equator. Captain Ferguson had no choice. The *Hope* must sail there or go to the bottom.

The captain and the surgeon oversaw removal of the slaves. The Africans were put back into canoes and borne to the fort. After James Dougall disappeared, Governor Bell promised the owners of the *Hope* that he would give her all assistance in his power. He locked the slaves in his fort's dark cells, known as "the Hole." Captain Ferguson discharged the *Hope*'s remaining cargo of merchandise, which Bell stored in the fort to await her return. The surgeon remained at Annamaboe with goods and slaves.

Catching a land wind rising from the continent at dawn, the *Hope* stood out to sea and sailed for the Island of Princes. Fortunately for men working her pumps, she was not becalmed in the doldrums. Before the island came in sight, sailors knew they were close; they saw thousands of birds diving for fish. The island's high, sheer rocks rising from the sea, its mountaintops hidden in clouds, and its deep, overgrown valleys were familiar to veterans of the slave trade. Every year, more than thirty vessels called there for water and provisions. The *Hope* sailed between Captain's Point and Point of the Salt Beach, then dropped anchor in four and one-half fathoms under the guns of the fortress of Santo António da Ponta da Mina.

As soon as any vessel entered the harbor of Santo António, a customs officer came on board to collect anchorage fees in goods or gold. This officer or a soldier remained with her throughout the vessel's stay. The *Hope* had fallen under the jurisdiction of the *capitão-mor* of Príncipe and São Tomé, Vicente Gomes Ferreira. Among the Portuguese he was notorious for his "arbitrariedades e extorsões"—injustices and exactions. The Island of Princes depended upon the slave trade, charging high prices for ships' supplies. To Gomes Ferreira, every arrival offered an opportunity. In April he had confiscated a schooner out of Liverpool, the *Fancy*, worth more than £1,300. Her owners, Thomas and John Case, and the British government protested in vain that this seizure was unlawful.

Once the *Hope* was careened and closely inspected, she turned out to be "totally irrepairable" and was condemned. In accordance with custom and admiralty law, Gomes Ferreira ordered Captain Ferguson to pay the sailors their wages. About £18 was due each man. While waiting to get a berth or passage in a visiting vessel, they could spend their money in Santo António.

Several weeks after the *Hope*'s seamen were discharged, a brig sailed into the harbor of Santo António: the *Nancy*, out of Liverpool. She had sailed with a cargo of slaves from Cape Lopez, at the southern end of the Bight of Biafra, intending to call at the Island of Princes. Her master, Captain Roger Williams, died at sea, as did her other officers, leaving only the carpenter, the seamen, and the slaves. No one knew how to navigate. The Island of Princes lay only 180 miles from Cape Lopez, but the *Nancy* spent three and a half months wandering in the Gulf of Guinea. On short rations, slaves began to die. The crew buried thirty Africans at sea before finding the birds and sighting the green mountains of the island.

Leaving behind his former crew and the hulk of the *Hope*, Captain Ferguson took passage to Annamaboe in a vessel calling at Santo António. At the fort, he found that the *Hope*'s surgeon had died in December. Charles Bell and David Mill sent to the owners a report of the slaves and goods remaining. In May 1773, Ferguson was still awaiting passage home. In April the *Hope*'s obituary appeared in *Lloyd's Evening Post*, *New-Lloyd's List*, the *London Chronicle*, and the *Daily Advertiser*: "The *Hope*, Ferguson, late Dougall, is condemned on the Coast of Africa."

Learning that Captain Dougall had vanished with his men and his longboat, Samuel Gist said: the "[un]derwriters must pay." His reaction to the news that the Portuguese had condemned the *Hope* was: "the Ship is Insured." Gist knew that underwriters would not pay until slaves and trade goods from the *Hope* had been sold. Only then could they fix an exact amount of loss. The ship *Ingram* sailed from Liverpool for Annamaboe in June, and Captain James Paisley took a letter from the committee of the Company of Merchants to Governor David Mill. After reading it, Mill assured the committee: "Particular attention shall be paid to the Concern of the Sneau

Hope." At first, Gist hoped to get the slaves to market quickly, in one or more of the vessels in Annamaboe Road. But months passed, and he could only wait for word that the slaves had been transported to the West Indies and sold.

As the *Ingram* sailed from Liverpool, John Shoolbred received news from the Gambia River. His snow *New Britannia* was a total loss. Far upriver, at Yanimarew, in the hill country, Captain Stephen Dean had purchased 230 slaves, about two-thirds of the number he intended to buy. While he and Shoolbred's resident agent were getting more, some of the African boys in the *New Britannia*, who were not chained, found the ship's carpenter's tools. They took these below and gave them to adults. The Africans ripped up the deck beneath them. In the hold the trading cargo contained guns and gunpowder. Early in the morning of January 24, 1773, the Africans rose against the crew. Blacks and whites fought for more than an hour, with deaths on both sides. Realizing they could not get free of the vessel, the Africans fired the powder magazine. The explosion blew up the *New Britannia*, killing more than three hundred people, including all but ten of the slaves and about ninety other Africans. Shoolbred's agent died, as did most of the vessel's officers and one-fourth of her crew.

Notwithstanding loss of the *New Britannia*, Shoolbred's fleet of slave ships grew. In 1773 he sent at least six vessels to Africa. Others already were on the coast, at sea, or in the West Indies or Charleston Harbor or the Chesapeake. That year the slave trade flourished on the Gold Coast. In 1772, the number of slaves exported dropped to 3,725. In 1773, it rose to 6,820; and in 1774, to 8,156. Among these were the slaves once held in the *Hope*. They suffered the middle passage, probably in Shoolbred's snow *Peggy*, commanded by Captain Hercules Mill. A vessel of 200 tons, she sailed from Annamaboe to Grenada with four hundred slaves.

As the day of sale approached, slave ship surgeons tried to heal or hide damage done to Africans by months of being shackled between decks—"putrid dysenteries" and "foul ulcers, tending strongly to mortification." Advertisements told planters that newly arrived slaves were fine and healthy. In port, slave dealers or the captain usually sold the slaves on successive days, in descending order of their value for labor. In the autumn of 1773, as the *Peggy*'s slaves were taken ashore and sent to the sugar plantations of the Windward Islands, a cargo of slaves from Annamaboe arriving in Jamaica sold for £54 each, on average. Five times as many of the best slaves would have sold at the highest price. If Captain Mill had not found a good market at Grenada, he could have sailed on to Jamaica, as others did.

Writing a letter in the first week of February 1774, Samuel Gist gave signs of impatience. Insurance on the *Hope* remained unsettled. He still waited for an account of sales of slaves and for bills of exchange in remittance. Even as he wrote, the *Peggy* was sailing up the Thames to her mooring near Tower Hill. After all the papers lay before them, Gist's colleagues at Lloyd's who had taken a line on the *Hope*'s policy did not offer as much as Gist sought to recover. He sued them. Almost a year passed before the case was resolved. Gist did not recover his full claim because some of his underwriters went bankrupt. But he congratulated himself on bringing the story of the *Hope* to "a tolerable good end."

PART 2: *The Partners*

While partners of the Dismal Swamp Company tried to extend their holdings into North Carolina and Samuel Gist hoped to ship slaves from Africa to Virginia, Sir George Colebrooke set out to corner the world market in hemp. The dapper little baronet had inherited a fortune. Married to a rich heiress with plantations in Antigua, he spent lavishly and invested boldly. He was a leading director of the East India Company, a banker in Dublin and London, a builder of the new Stock Exchange, and a partner of Samuel Wharton and Thomas Walpole in their campaign for a grant of 20,000,000 acres in the Ohio Valley. His capital was estimated at £400,000. By 1771 he had contracts to buy so much hemp in Russia and elsewhere that he hoped to dictate the price for naval and commercial ropewalks.

The time had come for the fruition of the elder William Byrd's scheme to drain the Dismal Swamp and grow thousands of acres of hemp. Elizabeth Harris, mother of Britain's envoy to Berlin, wrote to her son about Sir George's contracts: "if he should be ordered to be hanged, no one will have hemp enough to find him a halter." Hemp from the swamp, as Byrd had imagined it, could now have gone either to Sir George or to rival "Combinations" soon formed among other buyers angry with his "rapacious and monopolizing Spirit," who sought hemp not under his control. But the Dismal Swamp Company did not have any to sell. The moment passed. Sir George's corner collapsed. Nothing loth, he set out to corner the world market in alum. In two years of trading commodities he lost £190,000.

Anthony Bacon, with more feasible ambitions, enlarged his enterprises, winning more contracts from the government. His sloop *Providence* plied between London and the Senegal River, laden with supplies for soldiers. By 1770 his partner, Gilbert Francklyn, had put four hundred slaves to work for commissioners, governors, and surveyors in the formerly French islands of the West Indies. Their partners, John Durand in London and Anthony Richardson in Grenada, arranged shipments of food to the islands. Some of the hired slaves were "very ill used." Those working under contract died at a greater rate than slaves on a plantation.

Francklyn left Antigua for London late in 1770. Within a few weeks of his arrival the Board of Trade put him on the Council of Tobago, but he did not return to the West Indies until 1774. He and Bacon, members of the Company of Merchants Trading to Africa, joined a protest against the special arrangements among the London committeemen, the firm Ross & Mill, and the governors of forts on the Gold Coast. Bacon and other merchants appeared before the Board of Trade to be told that no action would be taken against the committeemen. Unlike John Shoolbred, who became an insider, Bacon persisted in his objections for years. But he could not stop Shoolbred's rise to a dominant place in the Company of Merchants.

Since 1768, Anthony Bacon and John Durand had held a contract to supply masts from North America for Royal Navy vessels. They sought a privilege conceded to their predecessors: permission to sell masts to the East India Company. In other ways they departed from previous practice. Their agents felled white pines along the Kennebec River on land claimed by proprietors of the Kennebec Purchase. The proprietors expected payment for these pines, as in the past. Bacon's agent replied that such an expense "would turn out too dear to the present Contractor." Claiming that the trees grew "in the King's Woods," Bacon's men cut them down, "wholly regardless of the Damage" to soil and undergrowth. Along the way, they took many trees unsuitable for masts, converting them to lumber.

Bacon did not have everything his own way along the coast of Maine. Lumbermen and makers of shingles and clapboards felled white pines suitable for masts. They damaged hundreds of others by scoring to see whether a tree would split free. Bacon had learned in Wales, in Canada, in Africa, in the West Indies—he and his partners in the Dismal Swamp Company had seen in Virginia and North Carolina—that a promising scheme attracted rivals and enemies. He did not rest. He must find new ventures and broaden old ones.

Samuel Gist made himself more infamous among Virginians in June 1771. He led a group of London merchants in persuading the Board of Trade to advise the king to disallow a popular Virginia law. The law looked innocent and simple. It confined the jurisdiction of the Court of Hustings in Williamsburg to suits arising within the city limits. This court previously had exercised an unlimited jurisdiction over suits in equity and in common law arising anywhere in the colony. Many people disliked the court because, apart from York County Court, it was the only one in the colony willing to hear and decide cases promptly. Creditors resorted to it for judgments against tardy debtors. Not surprisingly, Gist and other merchants objected to losing the one recourse at law which did not delay suits for three years.

The merchants appeared before the Board of Trade on June 14, 1771, and persuasively argued that the Court of Hustings ought to retain its broad jurisdiction. After the Crown disallowed the law, Arthur Lee, writing as "Junius Americanus," published an open letter to the Earl of Hillsborough. He belittled opponents of the rejected law, calling Gist "a very insignificant merchant." He censured Hillsborough for overruling Virginians' "general complaint" against the court in Williamsburg. To raise revenue in America and to reduce colonists to bondage, the government was willing to poison justice. Gist's success with the Board of Trade showed, Lee warned, that "the colonies are to feel not only the hand of oppression, but the finger of indignity and insult."

The *Virginia Gazette* reprinted Lee's letter; Gist had his mind on other things. Artisans were fitting out his captured French smuggler, transforming her into the *Hope* for her voyage to the Gold Coast. A week before she sailed, Gist and his colleagues at Lloyd's set up their fund for a new home for marine insurance, entrusting it to an elected committee charged with finding or building convenient rooms.

To William Nelson the doings of Samuel Gist, "a little Gentleman, that walks the Change," meant only minor irritation. Nelson enjoyed himself as acting governor of Virginia. He used Botetourt's six white horses to run back and forth between Williamsburg and York Town. He retained Botetourt's coachman and gardener. He said that he would be guided in office by a heart disposed to do right. Asking a London merchant to report on the man as soon as a new governor was chosen, Nelson did not wish to hasten that day. But, by the time Nelson wrote in December 1770, the day had come.

The government chose John Murray, Earl of Dunmore, thirty-eight years old, a man happiest outdoors. For the previous two months he had served as governor of New York. His main qualification was being the brother-in-law of the president of the Privy Council, Earl Gower. William Lee wrote from London: "his character here is by no means a respectable one." New Yorkers already knew "Ld Dunmore's Weaknesses," which they reported to Virginians. William Nelson, never able to suppress a joke, replied to official notification of Dunmore's appointment by professing to be "conscious that his Lordship's abilities and disposition will restore the people nearer to that perfect State of happiness they experienced under his worthy predecessor, than can be expected from any thing I can do."

The news reached Dunmore in New York on February 10, 1771. He refused to believe it. He had no desire to go to Virginia, "where there is little or no society." He wrote to Nelson, saying he would try to remain governor of New York, and he wrote to the Earl of Hillsborough, asking to be allowed to do so. Nelson wished him success. As acting governor, Nelson collected a salary of £2,000 per year, with fees amounting to about £500. He welcomed a "longer Run in a pretty Good Pasture." In Norfolk, William Aitchison also thought that Dunmore's staying in New York would be wise. "I'm almost sure he will not be happy here," Aitchison wrote; "they begin already to have false reports of him."

In May court days in Williamsburg, the Dismal Swamp Company held a general meeting. Several members had failed to heed the company's call in 1765 to provide another slave. They were assessed £7 per year. All members were assessed £100 in Virginia currency. They voted to use more than half this sum to buy Speaker Robinson's share from his estate in order to increase each partner's dividends as soon as profits began.

A few days later, Susanna Robinson was married to her second husband. At the same time, William Nelson's son, Hugh, was married to Judith Page. Her grandparents were Mann Page, builder of the mansion at Rosewell, Judith Carter Page, the elder William Byrd, and Maria Byrd. William Nelson put Hugh to work in his store in York Town, watching to see whether he seemed "disposed to do Business properly."

Amid court days and weddings, Williamsburg and the tidewater enjoyed beautiful spring weather and cloudless skies. West of Richmond, however, rain was falling continuously for ten days or more. Rivers in the tidewater, especially the Rappahannock, the James, and the Roanoke, rose. By Sunday morning, May 26, the Rappahannock at Fredericksburg was higher than anyone had ever seen; it continued to rise for the next twelve hours. The James rose at the rate of 16 inches per hour until it reached a depth of 40 feet above normal. A mass of brown water swept away houses, trees, livestock, crops, topsoil, and thousands of hogsheads of tobacco, leaving behind a layer of white sand. Floating debris sank some vessels; others helplessly fell downstream or stranded. Some people, carried off in their houses, drowned. The Roanoke River disgorged into Albemarle Sound logs, lumber, fence rails, corn stalks, and pieces of houses. Along the southern margin of the Dismal Swamp, "every thing in the marshes and low grounds is lost." The water receded, revealing piles of tangled debris, within which animal carcasses rotted. Planters set the damage in Virginia at £2,000,000 sterling.

William Nelson summoned burgesses to Williamsburg to enact measures of relief. They authorized emission of £30,000 of treasury notes to compensate planters for lost tobacco stored in public warehouses. The burgesses congratulated Nelson on becoming acting governor, praising him for his "known Attachment to the true Interests of this Colony."

As burgesses gathered, William Tryon left North Carolina, sailing to New York to become governor. The day the Earl of Dunmore dreaded had come. He offered to exchange governorships and let Tryon go to Virginia. Tryon declined. On Tuesday morning, July 9, he took the oath and received the great seal of the colony. After the new governor went in procession to the town hall, Dunmore spent the rest of the day drinking. He struck Tryon's secretary, Colonel Edmund Fanning, and called Tryon "a Coward who had never seen Flanders"—that is, never served in combat. After nightfall Dunmore ran about the streets of Manhattan, assaulting people at random and saying drunkenly: "Damn Virginia—Did I ever seek it? Why is it forced upon me? I ask'd for New York—New York I took, & they have robbd me of it without my Consent." He waited more than two months before leaving for Williamsburg.

On the last day of the special session burgesses voted unanimously to commission from a sculptor in England a marble statue of Lord Botetourt. All his successors ought to have before their eyes this example of the burgesses' gratitude for a "prudent and wise Administration" and their admiration of his "public and social Virtues." The Council and Acting Governor William Nelson quickly assented.

Lord Dunmore arrived at York Town late in September. William Nelson escorted him to Williamsburg on Wednesday, the 25th. Dunmore took the oath of office in the governor's palace and spent the day with councillors and other gentlemen. In the evening the windows of Williamsburg were lit with candles.

Dunmore hoped to find one consolation in the governorship of Virginia: money, not just salary and fees but also land. He petitioned the king for a grant of 100,000 acres free of quitrents within the limits of the most recent Cherokee cession. He had no interest in restricting westward migration; he meant to profit from it. Remembering the blandishments with which Virginians had beguiled Francis Fauquier, the ministry forbade Dunmore to accept gifts from the General Assembly.

In his first months in Williamsburg, Lord Dunmore began to perceive that he was not the central figure in the workings of the colony's government. He learned the importance of clerks of county courts, many of whom sat in the House of Burgesses. They owed their clerkships to Secretary

Thomas Nelson. Though the secretary remained less conspicuous than his brother, the president of the Council, he had "more weight in the Colony" than anyone, including the governor. Dunmore found that he had no influence with county clerks; they were "indifferent" to him. He suggested to the Earl of Hillsborough that the Crown give the governor power to appoint county clerks. William Adair, sinecurist secretary by whose favor Thomas Nelson held office, was, Dunmore wrote, "a very old man." Changes in his office could soon be made easily.

Thomas Nelson had served as resident secretary since Dunmore was eleven years old. He did not owe his long tenure to good luck. He knew that others coveted his office. William Byrd, hoping to rescue himself from debt, realized that Adair was "a very old gentleman & can not possibly live a great while longer." He suggested that Sir Jeffery Amherst ask for the secretaryship, then take the deputy secretaryship from Nelson and give it to him. Rumor put Secretary Nelson's income from fees at £1,000 to £1,400 sterling per year, after paying Adair his share. Byrd offered to keep only £500. Richard Henry Lee also knew that Adair was old; Lee had "an eye to the deputy Secretarys place." He said he would give "a pretty good sum" to get the position from Adair's successor, then remit all but £700 per year.

Lord Dunmore received from the Earl of Hillsborough a swift, abrupt reply, rejecting the idea of taking clerk appointments away from Nelson. Hillsborough did not need to be told that William Adair was old. Hillsborough wanted the secretaryship for his son, who was nineteen. He reminded the head of the ministry, Lord North, that he had taken good care of the office "by not yielding to any Sollicitations for Reversions." Unfortunately for all of them—Dunmore, Byrd, Lee, and Hillsborough—William Adair was "very hearty." The Earl of Dartmouth, after succeeding Hillsborough in office, wrote more sympathetically to Dunmore but gave him the same answer. Someone had planted in Dartmouth's mind the suspicion that Dunmore, if given power to appoint county clerks, intended to sell these offices. This Dunmore denied, even as he asked the government to pay him more. Secretary Nelson kept his position, its power, and its income.

The Earl of Dunmore's bearing and conduct differed sharply from Baron de Botetourt's. The baron had met opponents unflinchingly but with smooth civility; the earl flew into a rage. Both held what Virginians called "Tory principles"; Botetourt's had remained masked behind polished courtesies, while Dunmore boasted that he had studied under Lord Bute as a companion of the prince, now King George III. Dunmore's notion of ingratiating himself with the people of Virginia was to get a large land grant, then sell parcels of it to settlers in a manner "advantageous to my family." Members of the Dismal Swamp Company thought him ready to assist their plans across the mountains. To benefit from his administration they need not share his principles or enjoy his company.

George Washington and Thomas Walker worried about surveys in the spring of 1771. Washington hoped to complete the long-awaited grant to veterans of 1754, which Dunmore later approved. Walker wished to get the Loyal Company's surveyors on the land along Virginia's southern border newly ceded by the Cherokees. He impatiently waited through the summer while John Donelson, Alexander Cameron, and a group of Cherokees ran the new boundary between Indians and whites beyond the Cumberland Mountains and along the Kentucky River. Walker was eager to travel west, but he stayed at home while surveyors' chains left some farms on the Cherokee side of the line. These unhappy settlers might start "some disturbance," whereupon he would be suspected of encouraging them in order to get still more land from the Indians. Discretion kept him at Castle Hill until August: "some man had better steal an Horse than other look over the Hedge." George Washington obtained from the college an appointment of his representative, William Crawford, as surveyor of the veterans' grant. Crawford selected land for Washington while choosing tracts for the grant.

Balancing his books at the end of 1771, Washington wrote off his investment in the Mississippi Company as a total loss. He had no wish to do the same with his land along the Ohio River. He and Dr. Walker knew that migrants moved westward all the time, "settling on the choice spots," expecting to get title by possession. Crawford expelled six men from one of Washington's tracts in March 1772, but he could not promise to protect all of Washington's property: "People Croud out in such numbers the Like was never Seen."

Dr. Walker preferred to wait before driving settlers off the Loyal Company's land. Doing so only to leave it vacant might discourage buyers. When the time came to eject squatters, their labor in creating farms would have added value to the land. After the Cherokee line was drawn, Walker got Dunmore and the Council to issue a proclamation ordering settlers "immediately to evacuate their Possessions." But the squatters held out against the sheriffs. Others ignored the new line and moved into Cherokees' land. Cherokee leaders complained that "they see the smoke of the Virginians from their doors." Lord Dunmore explained to the Board of Trade: "the established Authority of any Government in America, and the Policy of Government at home, are both insufficient to restrain the Americans . . .

wandering about seems engrafted in their nature; and it is a weakness incident to it, that they should for ever imagine the Lands further off, are still better than those upon which they are already settled."

As the *Hope* arrived in Annamaboe Road, Virginia merchants in London heard of the death of one of their colleagues. On Tuesday, February 18, 1772, John Stewart died at his house in Black Raven Court on Tower Hill. For ten years he had held the government's contract to convey felons sentenced to transportation to Virginia and Maryland from prisons in and near London. In the Chesapeake he sold convicts as servants for seven-year terms. The government paid him £5 for each felon transported; he sold them for £10. Skilled artisans went for as much as £25. By taking one hundred to two hundred felons in each vessel and returning with a cargo of tobacco, he contrived doubly profitable voyages.

Anthony Bacon moved swiftly. Less than a week after Stewart died—before his longtime partner, Duncan Campbell, submitted an application—Bacon got a contract from Lord North, though not a long-term, exclusive one. Other merchants competed afterward for each shipment of felons. Padlocked in iron collars, chained to one another in groups of six, convicts were taken from Newgate, Bridewell, and other prisons to the contractor's vessel. In the ship their chains were locked to a board in a narrow hole. There they remained most of the time until sold in the Chesapeake. More than 14 percent of those in Duncan Campbell's vessels died. So many merchants sought to take part that the government stopped paying £5 per head. Contractors bore expenses of the voyages in expectation of making their profit on sales.

Bacon did not succeed with Lord North after the death in July of John Roberts, sinecurist receiver general of quitrent revenues in Virginia. Bacon tried to get control of the choice of Roberts's successor, an appointment he could in effect sell. But Lord North had a needy kinsman, his wife's uncle, George James Williams. A wit-cracker in Horace Walpole's circle, "Gilly" Williams required an income without official duties in order to live as a man of fashion. The post of receiver general for Virginia sustained him until Lord North advanced him to receiver general of excise. North assured Bacon that another vacancy would be his. If it occurred in Virginia, John Norton stood ready to "come on Terms with him for it." Bacon promised him, "under the Rose," a first chance.

Like everyone else who walked on 'Change in the summer of 1772, Samuel Gist had more pressing concerns than the fate of the *Hope*. Long after June 22, men in the City remembered "black Monday" as the worst day of a run on the banks. Throngs of depositors and holders of banknotes and bills of exchange demanded payment in gold and silver. No one knew who would suddenly stop meeting obligations. Perhaps every banking house would fail and "universal bankruptcy" follow. A man on 'Change might at any moment learn that he was ruined. Fear swept through the City. On the evening of Black Monday a merchant returned to his house and wrote: "distress seems picture'd in each Countenance on change."

The panic had begun on the morning of June 10. All the night before, Alexander Fordyce of the banking firm Neale, James, Fordyce & Downe sat up, going through his books, juggling bills of exchange. He was getting ready to abscond. At six in the morning he left for France. Before noon a commission of bankruptcy was issued against him. Other failures followed. Merchants closed their doors and stopped payment. Rumors of suicides spread. The belief that "everything is gone" seemed to make itself come true. The Bank of England temporarily furnished hundreds of thousands of pounds to other banks to help them weather the panic. Its officers decided that they must also support Sir George Colebrooke. So much of his paper circulated on the Continent that his fall, they feared, would bring down Amsterdam. For a brief time Sir George nevertheless looked as if he might go under because the Bank of England could not issue notes fast enough to meet the run on him.

Even before Black Monday, Fordyce's exposed position had been no secret in the City. He and other bankers, especially some in Scotland, long had run big risks. They had drawn bills on other banks in amounts totaling much more than their assets. As bills fell due, bankers covered them with other bills. A large portion of such men's apparent capital consisted of these kited bills. One merchant called them "Immense quantitys of circulating paper, for which there is no real property." No wonder Scottish firms and others could extend Virginia planters so much credit and buy their tobacco at 20 or 30 shillings per hundredweight. As long as demand for tobacco increased in Europe and prices held, everyone in the chain of credit flourished.

As Sir George Colebrooke did, Fordyce speculated heavily in stock, especially that of the East India Company. Trouble in India and a threat of war with Spain over the Falkland Islands in 1770 led to fluctuations in stocks from which Fordyce never recovered. To meet his obligations in the stock market, he used depositors' money from his bank. He was only one conspicuous risk-taker in a network of overextended bankers and investors. Floating bills and East India stock were also popular on the Bourse in Amsterdam. There the House of Pieter Clifford & Sons helped Sir George make his contracts for the world's alum, totaling more than £166,000. After the Bank of

England turned more cautious in accepting bills of the most exposed banks, contraction followed. As soon as Fordyce fell and panic began, people spoke knowingly of the South Sea Bubble and "Fictitious & bad bills & notes." At the end of the week begun on Black Monday, David Hume wrote: "It is thought, that Sir George Colebrooke must soon stop; and even the Bank of England is not entirely free from Suspicion."

Anyone walking on 'Change felt himself surrounded by uncertainty. After mixing with unhappy merchants, brokers, and underwriters, Duncan Campbell wrote on Tuesday, June 23: "fear & doubts appear almost in every mans face—Brother dare hardly trust Brother." Mistrust led to refusing to accept bills of exchange. Credit must contract, at least until one could tell who was sound and who would break. Six weeks after Black Monday, Samuel Gist told his representative in Virginia that bankruptcies had not ended. Merchants and brokers "Continue still to drop off, & many more are yet to go." As did most men he knew, Gist expected to curtail credit and reduce the scope of his trade. With everyone else, he pressed for immediate remittances. He said that he would sell the *Hope* when she returned to London from Virginia. Prudently, when buying East India Company stock in April, he had confined himself to £500 face value, the minimum investment giving a stockholder a vote in the company's General Court.

The *Molly* was one of the first vessels to arrive in the James River bearing the "dismall news" from London. Bankrupt merchants, closed banks, confusion—her captain had trouble finding enough money in coin to clear her out of port. In Suffolk, David Ross foresaw the panic's consequences: "Cr[edit] will be vastly curtailed . . . the French agents will take the advantage of the peoples necessity & run down the Tobo. to a triffle." Virginians, like men in the City, knew that they had been playing a dangerous game. Ever since the Association to reduce imports had failed, merchandise from Britain had almost fallen into their laps. New firms, aggressive competition, and low prices seemed to force them to buy more goods on easy credit. The *Molly's* full cargo was a small part of more than £1,000,000 in imports to Virginia and Maryland during 1772. These strained even Virginians' capacity for consumption, overwhelming the ability of many to pay.

Before Black Monday, Scottish merchants held out in an attempt to get the highest price for huge French purchases of tobacco. After June 22, they were happy to get $2\frac{1}{3}$ pence per pound. Later the price fell as low as $2\frac{1}{8}$ pence. By the end of the year prices in Virginia had fallen to 16s. 8d. per hundredweight. The great spring flood left many planters with short crops. Plantations unaffected by the flood would not derive the customary advantages from their position because Scottish storekeepers received from their home companies urgent instructions to contract their commitments and to send every possible remittance. Samuel Gist sought to collect his debts quickly, knowing that "the Scotch Factors ... will push close for their Money & reduce their trade." Planters who had adapted easily to higher tobacco prices and lower prices for goods behaved as if stunned by demands that they pay more, pay sooner, and receive less. The brunt of the panic's effects did not fall on them, but they resented it. Debtors stayed away from merchants' meetings in Williamsburg, the customary time to pay. British merchants and Virginia planters disagreed about who had been spoiled and who had been fleeced, but both felt distressed to see paper with their signatures on it come back to them so soon.

Men on 'Change received another shock on New Year's Day, 1773. The Amsterdam mail brought news that Pieter Clifford & Sons had failed. Estimates of their obligations ranged from £700,000 to £1,000,000. The panic had spread to Europe, and many other firms went down. Two weeks later, a letter from Amsterdam, describing the collapse of credit, concluded: "It is now become a general Saying here, 'That nothing but Hope remains to Mankind.' " For three days the Royal Exchange held no gatherings of merchants. More failures in London followed. Newspapers later reported that, in the year after Black Monday, "120 considerable Merchants, Bankers, and Traders, have been absolutely ruined." In 1772, more than half of all bankruptcies in Britain occurred in London. In 1773, the number of bankruptcies rose to 623, an increase of 225 from the previous year. Rumor said that William James, second partner of Neale, James, Fordyce & Downe, frequented the office where the bank's creditors received partial payments from its assets and begged each one to let him have twopence of every pound.

Having driven up the price of alum, Sir George Colebrooke's effort to corner the world market collapsed. He never had acquired a lock on the supply. Prices fell, and he could not be kept afloat. Newspaper writers gloated that Lord North had abandoned the "little commerce-jobbing Baronet." Trustees took control of his firm; his real and personal property was sold at auction. Two days after Sir George stopped payment, Alexander Fordyce's former partner, Henry Neale, died. Obituaries gave the cause of the banker's death as "a broken Heart."

Among those overtaken by the crisis of January 1773 was James Russell, tobacco merchant in London. He stopped payment, called in his creditors, and opened his books. He owed more than £50,000, but more than £100,000 was owed to him. A few weeks later Russell wrote to a Maryland merchant: "as you justly observe there were too many goods sent to Ammerica last year." His creditors chose trustees to oversee his transactions. On Saturday morning, April 17, without saying good-bye to his friends, he sailed for the Chesapeake. At the age of sixty-five, he spent the summer calling on his debtors in Virginia and Maryland, then returned to London. The thought of such a voyage upset Samuel Gist: "tis horrid indeed that a man at his time of Life & worth near £40,000 shd. be obliged to go abroad to Collect his Debts."

Two months after Sir George Colebrooke stopped payment, Samuel Foote, actor and playwright, announced that he was preparing "a new piece for the light entertainment of the Summer." *The Bankrupt* opened at the Haymarket Theatre on July 21. Much of the villainy in it, as well as its laughs, comes from two lawyers, Resource and Pillage. They advise any nearly ruined client on ways to raise money: for example, by getting others to advance cash for a "scheme of his, to monopolize sprats and potatoes." Such a design would surely find investors: "The people of this country are always ready to bite at a bubble." Foote's hero, Sir Robert Riscounter, nobly refuses to run up even bigger debts before declaring bankruptcy, though Resource tries to persuade him to do so, saying: "consider you are a knight, and your dignity demands you should fail for a capital sum." But Sir Robert dismisses the lawyers and sententiously utters the moral of the story: "Mutual confidence is the very cement of commerce. That weaken'd, the whole structure must fall to the ground."

The structure did not fall in 1772 and 1773. Despite speculators' and risk-takers' bankruptcies, European exchanges were not seriously threatened. Confidence and credit revived in 1774. The flow of commodities from Virginia and of merchandise to Virginia continued through familiar channels. Though the days of seemingly unlimited easy credit from merchants had ended, the days of easy collection of old debts had not begun. "I think Punctuality Seems either Fled or dead," a British merchant in Norfolk wrote. "It seems hardly to be found in Virginia."

William Nelson fell ill in June 1772. A disorder in his stomach and bowels weakened him and, he wrote, "affected my Nerves." After attending a meeting of the Council on July 27 he believed that he was recovering, but he did not go to the capitol for Council sessions in August. His illness lingered, becoming "tedious and painful." It baffled his physicians. Eventually he realized that he was dying.

As Nelson began the sixth week of his suffering, a violent gale struck the Outer Banks of North Carolina, then moved over Pamlico Sound, Albemarle

Sound, the Dismal Swamp, and the James River. In the waters of North Carolina, schooners and sloops from New England, New York, Philadelphia, and Virginia stranded or sank. Several crews were lost. The storm did less damage in Virginia. Gratifyingly, the Royal Navy frigate *Glasgow* in Hampton Roads was struck by lightning, ruining her fore topgallant mast and topmast. Her officers had irritated merchants and planters by boarding many vessels in Chesapeake Bay to inspect cargoes and papers. Earlier in the year, Benjamin Harrison had complained: "there is no doing any thing in the smugling way."

The day before the storm hit the Outer Banks on September 1, a hurricane passed over Antigua. The island already had suffered other ills. For two years, unusually dry weather had reduced sugar crops and dangerously lowered reserves of water. From Dominica the island was invaded by large carnivorous ants, which killed and consumed birds and small animals. On Friday, three days before the hurricane, a heavy storm severely damaged shipping in the harbor at St. Johns. The small ship *Tom*, with 150 slaves from the Windward Coast between decks, drove from her moorings and ran aground on the shoal.

The hurricane arrived on Monday, August 31. It passed almost directly over the island, sweeping it with winds of "amazing Violence" and with rain "in Torrents" for more than twelve hours. Blacks and whites died in collapsing houses. Francis Farley's house just outside St. Johns was leveled. He was safely elsewhere. The four Royal Navy vessels in English Harbor lost their masts and drove on shore. Some trading vessels foundered at anchor; others ran aground. In the fields, sugar cane was shredded, broken, or flattened. Plantation outbuildings fell down or lost walls and were gutted. "The strength of the Winds is incredible," a planter wrote; "they seemed to contend & battle together."

When news of the Antigua hurricane reached Virginia, William Nelson "was said to be dieing." He wrote his will on October 6, with David Jameson, his neighbor in York Town and partner in the Dismal Swamp Company, as a witness. He appointed as his executors his brother, the secretary; his two oldest sons, Thomas and Hugh; and Treasurer Robert Carter Nicholas. Saying that his property was "so much above my desire," he divided his store and houses in York Town and his plantations and slaves in seven counties among his wife and sons. To his youngest sons, Nathaniel and William, students at the College of William and Mary, he bequeathed £5,000 sterling each and joint ownership of his share in "The Dismal Swamp Scheme." As long as his condition permitted, he took communion, as he had always done. John

Camm, quarrelsome rector of Nelson's parish, found him facing death with equanimity and working to ease the minds of his family. All of Nelson's best qualities, Camm said, "sat easy upon him."

The scheme in which Nathaniel and William, Jr., would become partners had progressed. Slaves cut and dug the "great Ditch" running from Dismal Plantation to Lake Drummond. It was a narrow, shallow waterway opening an almost straight line through the northwestern corner of the swamp, closely flanked by large cedar, cypress, spruce, and white oak trees, tangled with undergrowth. Drainage into it was supposed to lower the water table in nearby land. The slaves then could fell trees, clear more land, and grow more crops.

The partners had not yet acquired the North Carolina sector of the Dismal Swamp. Earl Granville paid no attention to his vast proprietary holdings and collected no quitrents. He spent much of his day strolling in the mall of St. James's Park, occasionally stopping to converse with "servant maids, street walkers, and needy adventurers." The governor of North Carolina warned that the northern part of the colony had become an asylum for "the outcasts and fugitives of the other Provinces who retire to it and sit down where they like." The "barbarous ignorance" of the people already living there proved receptive to "vices and corruption" brought by these newcomers. The governor urged the Crown to purchase the proprietary from the earl, but, after some prodding, Granville appointed an agent, reopened his land office, and collected quitrents. He made the governor his agent and limited all new grants of land to 650 acres.

Among the lessons William Nelson taught his son, Thomas, in preparing him to run the family business was a warning: Samuel Gist was "a shabby fellow." Gist's snow *Planter*, commanded by Captain James Miller, rode at anchor in the James River as Nelson lay dying in York Town. She had sailed from London in the third week of July, laden with three hundred packages of European goods. Gist had registered her five days after Black Monday and dispatched her promptly. He demanded remittances. Captain Miller spent only ten weeks in the James, then sailed for London with 256 hogsheads of tobacco, 5,000 barrel staves, and 400 pounds of sassafras, a much smaller cargo than the *Planter*'s capacity. While she remained in the James, Anthony Bacon's representative, James Mercer, announced in the *Virginia Gazette* that he would attend the merchants' meeting in Williamsburg on November 15. He called for payment of debts due to Anthony Bacon & Company. Mercer was a lawyer; he warned debtors they were "at their Peril to take Notice that I can wait no longer with them." Gist, too, expected to be paid "as speedily as possible." His books showed that his stepson, John Smith, owed him almost £1,800. Smith's bills of exchange were protested in Bristol and London. Gist also refused to accept them.

The *Virginia Gazette* published an advertisement by William Byrd, announcing an auction, to take place on November 10 in Duke of Gloucester Street in front of the Raleigh Tavern in Williamsburg. Byrd's property in Chesterfield County—2,000 acres at the falls on the south bank of the James, "the most valuable Plantation in this Colony"—would be offered for sale.

Maria Byrd—her son called her "my Deluded & superannuated Mother"—had died in August 1771, forty-seven years after her wedding and her arrival at Westover. Her will included a bequest of £500 sterling to James Parke Farley, recently wedded husband of her granddaughter, Elizabeth. James and Elizabeth lived at Maycox, across the river from Westover, replacing James's sister and Captain Laforey. William Byrd already owed immense sums, and he resented this further drain on what remained of his father's estate. Obeying, he said, "the unjust will of my insane Mother," he paid his son-in-law.

The trustees nominally managing Byrd's affairs had grown more "uneasy" about his large debts. Farell & Jones's representative threatened to foreclose on Byrd's mortgages. Byrd at last agreed to sell land and slaves in December 1771. James Parke Farley wished to buy the land in Chesterfield County, but he could do so only with help from his father, which Francis Farley refused. Francis Farley held on to his investments, turning down an offer for the Land of Eden. But he did not put more money into Virginia. At the auction late in 1771, Byrd sold about sixty slaves; no one bid on his land. So it would be offered again at the sale in front of the Raleigh Tavern. Besides land in Chesterfield County, he offered tobacco warehouses, ferries, a fishery, and several 100-acre lots.

At the sale in Duke of Gloucester Street on Tuesday, November 10, 1772, the property in Chesterfield County, "equal to any in America," was knocked down to John Mayo. He thought it worth £8,000, though he got it for much less. Even so, the purchase called for more money than he could "conveniently get," he said. He asked Samuel Gist to lend him £2,500. Gist refused. Sixteen months later, Mayo tried to sell 1,000 acres of the land he had bought at Byrd's auction.

A second auction of slaves took place upriver on December 8. The next day Byrd executed a new deed of trust securing Westover and another plantation to his wife after his death. Mary Willing Byrd relinquished her dower right in his remaining property. Byrd and his trustees were free to sell it.

George Washington worked to acquire land while William Byrd reluctantly let go of his. Upriver from York Town, in New Kent County, at Eltham, home of Burwell Bassett, Washington spent the last week of October preparing William Crawford's surveys for presentation to the governor and Council. Crawford had come with him to help. At last, after almost twenty years, the time had come to get title to most of the grant Governor Dinwiddie had promised to the officers and soldiers of 1754. Washington devised a way to apportion Crawford's surveys among them. In Williamsburg he dined with Lord Dunmore on Wednesday, November 4, with Speaker Randolph on Thursday, and with members of the Council on Friday. He tried to persuade the councillors to allow him in the remaining future surveys to substitute better tracts for the rocky, hilly parts of the originally designated area. Washington's plea invoked his wartime service: "it is the cream of the Land if one may be allowed to use the expression which stimulates men to such kind of Enterprise." The councillors rejected his request; but on Saturday, November 6, they approved patents for land Crawford had surveyed. Washington's portion, with his purchases from other veterans, was 20,147 acres, 10 percent of Dinwiddie's grant.

After a painful series of attacks and apparent remissions, William Nelson died on Thursday, November 19. His widow gave way to her "deep affliction." Her son, Thomas, worried that she grieved too much. In death William Nelson received much praise. He had stood firm for American liberty. He was the best that Virginia could produce: "The chief ornament of this Country." Nelson's body was buried in the churchyard in York Town on November 25. John Camm preached a sermon celebrating Nelson's public service, his charity, his private virtues, and his Christian devotion, calling others to "tread in his steps." Hardly any other prominent Virginian since the death of the elder William Byrd could have written to his London merchant, while suffering from a fatal illness: "I told you once before that it is as great an offense to a Virginia Planter to find fault with his Tobo as with his Mistress."

John Norton's ship *Virginia* arrived in the York River in mid-May 1773 bearing the life-size marble statue of Lord Botetourt. With one leg advanced and a slight forward inclination of the body, his figure seemed to have been caught in the middle of a graceful gesture. His relatives in England thought it "a magnificent Statue." The burgesses put it in the capitol, facing the room where the General Court sat. There Lord Dunmore could read the inscription on its pedestal: "America, behold your friend! who, leaving his native country, declined those additional honours which were there in store for him, that he might heal your wounds, and restore tranquility and happiness to this extensive continent." This description was not accurate, but monuments were supposed to edify rather than inform. Virginians liked to refashion their governors even while the men were alive.

Hoping to profit from western land, Dunmore showed favor to George Washington and other friends of expansion. He approved in December 1772 a grant to Washington of 10,990 acres on the left bank of the Kanawha River near its confluence with the Ohio. Three months later, Samuel Gist and his associates in Bristol and in Virginia asked Dunmore and the Council to renew a grant of 100,000 acres along the New River and the Holston River they had received in 1750 but had not yet surveyed and patented. The Council tabled their petition, awaiting word of the government's new policy in the west. The news was unfavorable: the king and Privy Council ordered governors to suspend all grants except to veterans. On December 1, 1773, Washington received another grant farther up the Kanawha. During the following spring, Dr. Thomas Walker traveled to the valley of the Holston River. He called settlers on the Loyal Company's property to meet him at the home of Samuel Briggs in April 1774. He took their bonds for the price of their tracts and gave them his bonds for conveyance of title as soon as they paid. Until then, he charged interest.

The Council of Virginia gave permission in 1773 for surveys beyond the mountains in tracts with settlers already on them. All other surveys, except those for grants to veterans, had been prohibited, in obedience to the Crown's orders. Nevertheless, during the ten years since the royal proclamation, Dr. Walker had surveyed and sold 1,756 tracts covering 156,164 acres. Added to his surveys before the war, these totaled one-fourth of the Loyal Company's original 800,000 acres. The Council authorized another set of grants under Dinwiddie's proclamation in November 1773. Patrick Henry warned the councillors about men awaiting the Crown's permission to patent large holdings west of the mountains. They had colluded with county surveyors and now stood poised to enter their premature surveys on the books, under false dates to make them look lawful, as soon as issuing of patents resumed. But these men did not have the right friends, as Walker and the Loyal Company did. After listening to Henry, the councillors added to their order for veterans' grants a provision invalidating all surveys made without an order of Council or not already entered on surveyors' books. To prevent tampering, the Council appointed a committee to inspect the books: John Byrd of Fincastle County, John Mayo of Botetourt County, and Dr. Thomas Walker.

Black Monday and the flight of credit and capital almost ruined the East India Company. Famine and war in India, huge debts and extravagant dividends in Britain left it unable to meet its obligations. A special session of Parliament took up the company's affairs. In exchange for rescuing it, the ministry subjected it to supervision by the government.

After lending the company £1,400,000, the government had an even greater interest in helping it to sell tea. High taxes and competition from smugglers left the company with large stockpiles of unsold tea. Lowering its price ought to encourage buyers. The company could do this if the Treasury refunded Customs duties on tea re-exported to the colonies. Tea would be even cheaper if the ministry also removed the tax payable in America, the last of the Townshend duties designed to assert Parliament's right to tax colonists. Lord North was willing to refund duties collected in Britain but not to withdraw the colonial tax, even if doing so promised greater returns to the East India Company. The Tea Act became law on May 10, 1773.

Some directors of the East India Company suspected that the ministry passed this law "to make a cat's paw of the Company and force them to establish the 3d pr. lb. American duty." Nevertheless, an opportunity to ship newly inexpensive tea to America attracted some of the most important merchants, men who cut large figures on 'Change and who underwrote policies at Lloyd's: John Nutt and William Greenwood in the South Carolina trade; Frederick Pigou, Sr., in the Philadelphia trade; William Kelly and Frederick Pigou, Jr., in the New York trade; and the irascible Brook Watson in the Boston trade. Anthony Bacon warned them that many Americans still opposed the tax and held the "Utopian" notion "that men should have no cause of complaint on any occasion whatever." Such people saw cheap, taxed tea as a threat, not a gift. Even so, in the summer of 1773 the men at Lloyd's stood ready to transport the East India Company's tea, part of it consigned to their associates in the colonies. Recommending their Boston connections as factors at a commission of 6 percent, Brook Watson and his partner wrote: "we are ready to give security to the amount of ten thousand pounds for their performance."

Anthony Bacon foresaw resistance in the colonies, but he supported the Tea Act, saying that its propriety was "obvious," blaming opposition on "a seditious spirit." Whatever his private opinions and predictions, he must follow the ministry. He was one of those members of Parliament known to their critics as "Ld North's contractors."

Bacon gave up some of his contracts and dissolved his partnership with

Anthony Richardson and Gilbert Francklyn, apparently in 1773. He remained at Number 12, Copthall Court, in the afternoon shadow of the Bank of England, but no longer as Anthony Bacon & Company. Gilbert Francklyn's ambitions went beyond Bacon & Company or the Council of Tobago. He spent time with his friends on the Board of Trade, trying to become governor of New Hampshire. Fielding Lewis, still Bacon's representative at Fredericksburg and in the Dismal Swamp Company, had not paid his debt—more than £2,300 and rising. For a while, apparently between contracts, Bacon received a pension of £600 per year from the government's secret service money, disbursed to cement political loyalty to the ministry.

Having established himself in the iron industry at Merthyr Tydfil, Anthony Bacon sought the acquaintance of other ironmasters. Among the most important was John Wilkinson of Broseley in Shropshire, 25 miles northwest of Birmingham. After becoming Bacon's agent, Wilkinson also supplied cylinders to James Watt and Matthew Boulton for their new steam engine. With Bacon, Wilkinson contracted to make cannon for the government. He was proving the superiority of artillery pieces bored out of a solid piece of iron, not molded around a core. His foundry used the best iron from coke-fired furnaces. Wilkinson knew how to make guns; Bacon knew how to reach the Board of Ordnance. Bacon offered the new cannon to the government "upon his reputation, as a man of honour and integrity, as he expects the future favour of the Board." He received his first order for experimental pieces in July 1773.

The trials succeeded. The government's master founder at Woolwich reported: "casting guns solid in the manner of Mr. Bacon is infinitely better than in the ordinary way." The Board of Ordnance gave Bacon a contract, and he sold artillery to the East India Company.

In Wilkinson's works at Broseley and in others nearby, Bacon saw what Merthyr Tydfil might become. This part of the valley of the Severn was filled with furnaces, forges, and foundries, interspersed with warehouses and large piles of coal, lime, and ore. Bellows blasted and furnaces flamed night and day. Clouds of black smoke obscured nearby hills. Almost everything seemed to be made of iron: door arches, window cases, chimney-tops, water sluices, water wheels, wheels of slitting mills. Roads for transporting coal and ore were paved with iron. There was even a design to span the Severn with a bridge of iron. In his will, John Wilkinson directed that his body be buried in an iron coffin.

Happily, the works at Merthyr Tydfil always had smelted with coke and needed no conversion from charcoal to coal. Coal mining had expanded in recent years; the turnpike along the River Taff reached Merthyr Tydfil. In

1771 and 1772, Bacon added five new leases to his landholdings. Wherever more people gathered to work in mines, furnaces, and foundries, rents rose. As soon as Anthony Bacon chose to increase his iron operations in Wales, all stood ready.

After four years in Louisa County, William and Mary Anderson almost had fulfilled Samuel Gist's wish that they live miserably. William's first venture as a tobacco merchant, in partnership with his brother, Matthew, lasted only through 1769 and 1770. They depended upon the good will and generous credit of John Norton. Norton and his wife tried to reconcile Gist to his daughter and son-in-law, but Anderson called this goal "impracticable."

William Anderson went into business as a merchant by himself in 1771, announcing his intent to "deal largely in Tobacca of the best Quality." His competitors in Louisa County, Scottish factors in nearby stores, received their merchandise from Glasgow earlier in the season, giving them "a great advantage." His store offered the usual goods: cloth, clothing, pewter dishes, utensils, pans. He promised Norton bigger consignments of tobacco than he shipped. Illness obliged Anderson to spend a month at Warm Springs in the summer of 1771. His business did not survive the panic of 1772. Norton stopped filling his orders. At this low point in their fortunes, William and Mary Anderson were rescued by an unlikely combination of events—the deaths, a few months apart, of both of Mary's half brothers, John and Joseph Smith, stepsons of Samuel Gist.

The Smith brothers had not heeded Gist's urgings to shun the Andersons as punishment for their elopement and their ingratitude. The brothers remained the Andersons' friends. Joseph quarreled with Gist over the division of property left by his father. Gist warned him against going to court: "the Law is expensive . . . the event will show who is Right." Joseph, his wife, Martha Jacquelin Rootes Smith, their son, and her young son by her first husband lived on a plantation in Hanover County with sixteen slaves. He tried to make extra money by selling lumber. Gist called him "a very improvident Man."

During the panic of 1772, John Norton and Gist provided neither money nor goods to John Smith. His last order filled by Norton was for a spinet. He was popular in Hanover County; voters sent him to the House of Burgesses. He owned land in three counties and five times as many slaves as his brother did. But John Smith failed as a merchant, partly at Gist's expense.

Joseph Smith died in the latter part of 1772. William Anderson became administrator of his estate. Edward Jacquelin Smith, Joseph's infant son, became Anderson's ward. John Smith died in January 1773, unmarried and childless. The obituary William Rind published in the *Virginia Gazette* conveyed an opinion about Gist's conduct as a stepfather by saying of John Smith: "He died without a parent to lament a son." His will appointed William Anderson as his executor and made Mary Anderson his chief heir. When Gist's wife, Sarah, died in 1766, her will left Gist only a life interest in land she held. Upon Gist's death, the land was to go to John Smith and his heirs. With the deaths of the Smith brothers, possession or reversion of thousands of acres in Virginia rested with Mary Anderson—the daughter Samuel Gist had sworn never to see again. And control of the Smith brothers' estates lay in the hands of William Anderson, whom Gist had said he would always despise as a villain and a seducer, with whom Gist had sworn "never to have any Connexion."

A little more than a week after John Smith's death, William Anderson wrote to John Norton, promising to pay his debt soon. He added: "I hope to have the Pleasure of settling myself in London . . . but this I would not willingly have mentioned until you hear more of it." In transatlantic correspondence, Samuel Gist embraced his wayward daughter and her husband. Soon William Anderson was writing to him to secure insurance at Lloyd's on 30 hogsheads of tobacco. Anderson advertised auctions of the personal property and some of the real estate of the Smith brothers. Most of the land in Goochland County offered for sale as Smith's never had belonged to John Smith, though the auction supposedly was "Pursuant to the Will." Part belonged to Gist, and part would have belonged to Mary Anderson after Gist's death. Gist had his eye on better tracts. William Anderson began to solicit consignments of tobacco for Gist and to advise him about the best port in Virginia for a voyage by his ship. Anderson sold his store in Louisa County and worked to collect debts. If John Norton could wait no longer for remittances, Anderson wrote, "I expect that Mr. Gist will pay you some money for me." The Andersons hoped to move to London in 1774. That year Gist ordered a new 300-ton ship built in Yorkshire. He named her the *Mary*.

Gist was ready to move into one of the "excellent houses" nearing completion just east of Savage Gardens on Tower Hill. In the past few years the architect for the Corporation of London, George Dance the younger, had transformed vacant lots and dunghills along the Minories into three "convenient and elegant districts": Crescent, Circus, and America Square. In his almost uniform rows of adjoining four-story brick buildings it was easy to see the influence of new buildings in Bath, as well as a resemblance to Grosvenor Square and Cavendish Square, rendered on a reduced scale. Gist took one of the best locations: Number 16, America Square, a corner house overlooking both the square and John Street, which ran from Crutched Friars to the Minories. Among his new neighbors were his fellow tobacco merchant William Molleson, on the other side of America Square, and his colleagues at Lloyd's, Thomas Wooldridge and William Kelly, in Crescent. Gist acquired more space for his office and his counting room; he lived in a manner befitting his prosperity. His success in London could now plainly be seen from the street.

As his reconciliation with his daughter and son-in-law showed, Gist had not lost interest in Virginia. He paid £24 15s. 10d. to the Dismal Swamp Company in September 1773 for hiring a slave. Rather than buy slaves from Africa or in Barbados, the members had voted to hire laborers from slave-owners. Since April, when Gist had learned of the condemnation of the *Hope* at the Island of Princes, he had turned to another enterprise: shipping indentured servants to Virginia.

More widespread, energetic recruiting of servants, combined with dislocation and economic depression after the panic of 1772, swelled the number of people willing to engage themselves for four years of servitude in return for passage to Virginia in search of better opportunities. John Hatley Norton, in York Town, urged his father and brother in London to invest on his behalf in a shipment. A large vessel full of servants might return a profit of £700. John Norton sought Samuel Gist's opinion. Gist warned him that expenses would be higher than young Norton expected and the profit small. John Norton sent only half as many servants as his son requested. At the same time, Gist wrote to some of his Virginia correspondents, asking them to help William Anderson dispose of servants Gist would dispatch to Virginia soon.

In January 1774, Gist's snow *Planter* rode at her mooring in the Thames at Ratcliffe Cross, beyond Wapping, well below the Tower. Her master, Captain David Bowers, had followed the Virginia trade since the age of fifteen. In cold rain, then heavy snow, his seamen rigged the vessel, bending sails to the yards, loading cargo and provisions. Captain Bowers spent his time writing indentures with artisans who came on board and agreed to sail with him and to work four years as servants. They had come from all parts of England, Scotland, and Ireland—weavers, bricklayers, cabinetmakers, carpenters, farmers, husbandmen, and men of other occupations. Gist said the *Planter* would take them to the Rappahannock River "unless Mr. Anderson orders to the Contrary." After Captain Bowers had signed seventy-five indentures, he was ready to sail. The *Planter* slipped her mooring and dropped down the Thames with the early morning tide on Friday, February 4. Four days later, after a heavy snowstorm, she stood out to sea in a hard, cold northwest wind.

The *Planter*'s voyage was long and difficult. The day after she passed

Lands End, she encountered such strong winds and high seas that the crew battened down the hatches. Among the servants confined between decks in the dark, there were "some sleeping, some spewing, some pishing, some shiting, some farting, some flyting, some daming, some Blasting their leggs and thighs, some their Liver, lungs, lights and eyes, And for to make the shene the odder, some curs'd Father Mother, Sister, and Brother." In the following weeks, officers, seamen, and servants were stricken with fever. Three servants died. The *Planter* made Cape Henry eleven weeks after leaving the Downs. Sailing into Chesapeake Bay, Captain Bowers dropped anchor in Hampton Roads, remaining briefly, then at Urbanna and Tappahannock on his way up the Rappahannock River to Fredericksburg. There she discharged the last of her merchandise. On Sunday, May 15, William Anderson came on board.

Ten days earlier, Anderson had advertised in the *Virginia Gazette* the arrival of the *Planter* "in the Interest of Mr. Samuel Gist." Sale of servants' indentures was to begin on Monday, the 16th. That day prospective buyers came on board, two of whom were men known as "Soul drivers," buying the indentures of groups of servants, then taking the servants around the countryside for resale, one by one. While dealing with buyers, Anderson and Bowers loaded the *Planter* with hogsheads of tobacco. She also called at Port Royal and in the James River. She suffered a mishap in the James when she drove on shore and ran a fluke of her anchor through her bottom. After her repairs and replacement of lost tobacco, Captain Bowers sailed for London in the first week of September, completing a profitable voyage. Three months later, one of the servants who had arrived in the *Planter* wrote to his wife in the Shetland Islands: "I yet Hope (please God) if I am spared, some time to make you a Virginia Lady among the woods of America."

V

———◆———

THE AGE OF PAPER

TO ANTHONY BACON, such a notion as "the natural rights of mankind" was nonsense. He contended that people "have no rights, but such as are given by the laws of that society to which they belong." Of course he rejected colonists' assertion that taxation by Parliament violated their God-given liberty. Their line of thought would break down all control over colonial trade. North Americans then would deal with Europeans in the Caribbean; the British West Indies would be ruined. The law prohibited colonists from milling iron. Without such restraint, "they would be able to manufacture iron on cheaper terms than we can; and the meanest mechanic in Birmingham, or Sheffield, must foresee what would be the consequence if the Americans should assume to themselves this article of trade." Bacon supported the ministry's intent to treat American colonists with "a little wholesome severity." At the same time, he said he knew Americans well enough to predict that, though they might be wrong, they would resist.

The East India Company's tea arrived in American ports in November and December 1773. Word of its approach went before it. Assembling in force, as in the days of the Stamp Act, colonists opposed to the tax persuaded merchants scheduled to receive consignments that the company's tea was not welcome. After Bostonians dumped 90,000 pounds of it into their harbor, destruction of tea became popular throughout the colonies. Faced with such defiance, King George, still resenting repeal of the Stamp Act, let his ministers know that he expected the government to use force. Frederick North was no sneering George Grenville, at pains to show others their inferiority. Witty, amiable, self-deprecating, North had a "naturally conciliating disposition." He did personal favors for his political opponents. He conciliated the king by doing as the king wished. North hoped, in Bacon's words, "to bring back the Americans to their duty," as North and his followers believed colonists must be brought.

In the spring of 1774 Parliament enacted a set of laws to close the port of Boston, change the government of Massachusetts, revise operations of courts, and allow army officers to quarter soldiers on property owned by civilians. Speaking in the House of Commons on behalf of the port bill, Anthony Bacon predicted that it would not hurt British merchants. "The town of Boston will be very materially hurt by this Act. [We] intend it should be." As soon as the bill passed, Lord North sent a note to the king with a list of members who had spoken in debate.

British merchants trading between London and America did not resist enactment of the new coercive measures, and they did not join in petitions to Parliament and the king to seek repeal. They had no wish to offend Lord North and the king; nor did they believe that colonists would be "totally enslaved" by North's policies. And if a violent contest began, they did not intend to fight the government. William Lee, one of the forlorn petitioners against coercive measures, found that tobacco merchants did not expect planters to achieve an effective agreement to withhold tobacco. He warned his brother in Virginia: "instead of doing you any good their whole influence will be against you, unless you force them thro' interest to take an active part in your favor which can only be done by stoping both exports & imports to G.B."

After the text of the Boston Port Act reached America, William Hoopes of North Carolina wrote: "Nothing but a total Interruption of trade with G Britain can serve the purposes of the Colonies." Americans opposed to Parliamentary taxation agreed. The North ministry's new laws persuaded more colonists that Americans faced, as Virginia's burgesses said, the threat of "Destruction to our civil Rights, and the Evils of civil War." These words appeared in a resolution designating June 1, 1774, a day of fasting, humiliation, and prayer. Learning of it, Lord Dunmore dissolved the General Assembly. The next day most burgesses signed an Association to prepare for a general congress of all colonies, with a threat "to avoid all commercial intercourse with Britain." On Tuesday, May 31, burgesses still in Williamsburg called a convention to meet two months later.

Among the delegates to the convention in Williamsburg during the first week of August were George Washington; John Syme; Dr. Thomas Walker and his son, John; the late William Nelson's eldest son, Thomas; the late Robert Tucker's son-in-law, Thomas Newton, Jr.; Samuel Gist's agent, John Tabb; and William Anderson's brother, Richard. Working quickly, delegates chose Speaker Randolph, George Washington, and five other men to represent Virginia at the general congress, then adopted an Association calling for no imports from Britain after November 1, 1774, and no exports of tobacco

George Washington, Charles Willson Peale. Courtesy of the
Virginia Historical Society

or other commodities to Britain after August 10, 1775. They said they
viewed tea "with Horrour" and would not even use the tea they had at home.
They proclaimed any merchant not signing the Association an outcast whose
goods, if imported after the deadline, could be seized and reshipped or
stored. They agreed to import no slaves. And they called for a new day in
Virginia, an era of "the greatest Industry, the strictest Economy and Frugality, and the Exertion of every publick Virtue." Two weeks later, back at
Mount Vernon, Washington wrote: "I could wish, I own, that the dispute had
been left to Posterity to determine, but the Crisis is arrivd when we must assert our Rights, or Submit to every Imposition that can be heap'd upon us;
till custom and use, will make us as tame, & abject Slaves, as the Blacks we
Rule over with such arbitrary Sway."

In Philadelphia, Washington and the other Virginia delegates stood out
at the general congress, grandly called the Continental Congress. Virginia
was the largest, most populous colony. Not surprisingly, Speaker Peyton
Randolph was elected president. The Continental Association, signed on
October 20, owed much to Virginia's example. The congress approved several declarations and addresses explaining Americans' rejection of the min-

istry's new laws and of Parliament's broad powers. No one went further than Virginians in asserting Americans' right to autonomy and self-government. During the summer, public meetings in many courthouse towns had assured delegates to colonial and continental gatherings that they must defy the North ministry's "fixed Intention" to enslave Americans.

In colonists' conduct Anthony Bacon saw selfishness and sedition. He assumed that the leaders of the resistance intended "republican usurpation." He could see why "those who have nothing to lose" would welcome "a general scramble"; but why would "men of property and honour," such as his partners in the Dismal Swamp Company, join a rush to "inevitable ruin"? Americans had no real grievances. Bacon could only conclude that his partners and others like them were "dupes" misled by the artifices of men who had neither property nor honor.

During debate in the House of Commons on one of the bills to coerce Massachusetts, Lord North replied to American petitioners' protest that Parliament was violating "the unalienable Right of the Subject." He said: "I am sorry to hear a charge thrown out, that these proceedings are to deprive persons of their natural right. Let me ask, of what natural right, whether that of smuggling, or of throwing tea overboard? Or of another natural right, which is not paying their debts?" With Lord North, Anthony Bacon deplored "unseasonable speeches, petitions, and remonstrances." Bacon scorned the colonists' appeal and proclaimed his support for North's measures.

The king decided in August that an early election would strengthen the ministry in the House of Commons. A surprise dissolution of Parliament would leave the opposition less time to prepare. And if Americans remained defiant, the spring of 1775 would not be a good time for a general election. So, in October, Anthony Bacon left his office in Copthall Court and his country house overlooking park and forest to travel to Aylesbury, the small, dirty town on a hill.

Aylesbury returned two members. Bacon's colleague was his sometime business partner, John Durand. A wise candidate gave an open supper at the Bell Inn and entertained lavishly at the time of voting. He also offered most voters the usual gift of money; only about seventy of the four hundred refused it. The rest, a local historian wrote, "cared nothing for Peace, Retrenchment, or Reform; they only required a definite answer to one question—'How much money have you got?' " In the election six years earlier, Bacon had spent £2,500 for his seat. The voters in 1774 expected a bigger gift than the £8 they had each received last time. Speaking of the practice known as "occasional conveyances," whereby a landlord could temporarily fill his burgage houses with men who would vote as they were paid to vote, Bacon said "that he once knew a Gentleman who lost his Election, though infinitely the more preferable Candidate, because that waggon, which carried the Gentleman's occasional Voters, did not arrive so soon as the waggon which contained the occasional Voters of his opponent." Bacon made sure he did not lose.

Preparing for the election, the secretary to the Treasury, Lord North's main political operative, wrote next to the names of Bacon and Durand: "They say the *same again*, but Query, A Nabob or two, and being outbid, see them." The secretary feared that a candidate with riches from the East or West Indies might throw more money into Aylesbury. No one outbid Bacon. His colleague, however, came last of four in the poll. Aylesbury's cheerfully unprincipled voters elected Bacon, a loyal supporter of Lord North, and John Aubrey, a strong critic of the ministry who opposed taxing or coercing American colonists. After polling ended throughout Britain, Lord North had about the same number of followers in the new House of Commons as during the previous Parliament.

The prospect of no exports from North America frightened Francis Farley and other Antiguans. On the recommendation of the Board of Trade, the king had appointed Farley to the colonial Council in December 1773. The welfare of Antigua concerned him officially as well as privately. If the island got no food, staves, and shingles from the mainland, ruin must follow. Planters agreed to devote one-third of their land to gardens of corn, yams, and potatoes if the American trade stopped. But such relief would come late or, if the rains failed, never. A curse seemed to have fallen on the island. The hurricane's damage still scarred it. Drought returned. Some planters emigrated to the fresh soil of the islands acquired from France. A war might be the last stroke. Antigua had 4,000 white people and more than ten times as many black people. In a famine Farley expected the slaves to rebel. He said: "we shall stand a bad chance."

Francis Farley comforted himself by getting married to a much younger woman, Elizabeth Thomas, niece of a former governor of the Leeward Islands. She owned a plantation overlooking Willoughby Bay on the southern coast of Antigua. While ill in 1770, she had trouble with overseers. Farley calmed her ruffled temper and helped manage her property. After they were married in June 1774, he found her prudent, obliging, and affectionate. She was soon pregnant.

Samuel Martin expected news of these events to alarm Eleanor Laforey. She had given Farley his only grandson. Would much or all of her father's property go to children of a second marriage? She and her husband had returned to England, but Captain Laforey had held only one command since the end of the war, and his stay in the frigate *Pallas* was brief. Political conflict ran through the navy; he allied with Vice Admiral Augustus Keppel, the favorite of the opposition to Lord North's ministry. Captain Laforey, though an excellent officer, also was "much given to talking & writing," the first lord of the Admiralty later noted with disapproval. Eleanor Laforey could draw reassurance, Samuel Martin thought, from the news early in 1775 that her father's new wife had suffered a miscarriage.

In the first six years of Elizabeth Byrd and James Parke Farley's marriage she gave birth to four daughters, Francis Farley's other grandchildren. At Maycox, James repeated on a smaller scale some of the mistakes of his father-in-law at Westover. He entered his mare in subscription purse racing, but she was beaten with ease. He handled William Byrd's interest in the enduring but dubious Chiswell lead mine, which still owed money to Speaker Robinson's estate. Francis Farley feared that his son was running up gambling debts, but James was running up many kinds of debt. He owed thousands of pounds to Dinwiddie, Crawford & Company of Glasgow; he apparently borrowed money from William Byrd. James Parke Farley's creditors went unpaid, and his obligations swelled to a sum greater than the worth of his assets.

William Byrd could not afford the generosity for which he was often praised. His debts in Britain remained large, though he at last sold his estate there for £20,000 and reduced them. He still sought "an advance" from merchants. The agent of Farell & Jones promised the Bristol office: "I shall be moderate with him." Byrd owed more than £2,000 to Patrick Coutts, a merchant in Richmond, owner of the 250-ton ship *Westover*. To help him, Byrd, working through his London merchants, tried to persuade Samuel Gist to fill Coutts's order for merchandise. Gist said that "Mr. Couts might be a good man but he had not been altogether punctual to his promises." Even so, Captain John Stevens, master of the *Westover*, predicted that Gist would fill the order. Byrd's merchants declined to do so. After the *Westover* reached Virginia in October 1774, Coutts offered her for sale or lease. Her new owner was Samuel Gist.

Francis Farley worried about the security of his holdings in North Carolina and Virginia should violence break out between colonists and the government. He thought the ministry could not conquer America, but most of his anger settled on the "vile People, at Boston, that . . . were the Author of all this mischief." Thomas Hutchinson and his like had misled the ministry, while Samuel Adams and his like had "inflamed and misled the common People." Among the results he foresaw were starving slaves in Antigua and the ruin of Francis Farley.

James Parke Farley would take no part in opposing the government unless forced to do so, his father wrote. Both of Francis Farley's other representatives in Virginia, William Byrd and Robert Munford the playwright, deplored the prospect of a civil war. Francis Farley advised his son to leave Maycox, move his family to the Land of Eden, and "remain there quietly" to "avoid the troubles."

Francis Farley held half of the tract in North Carolina for his niece, Elizabeth, and his nephew, John Simon Farley, an officer in the British Army. Believing that his late brother's share of 25,800 acres was worth more than £3,000, Francis warned the improvident Jack not to lose it. Jack's misery would be complete when he and his "poor family" were "obliged to sell their share of the land of Eden." Since Francis had not conveyed a title to his niece and nephew after their father's death, Jack could not sell what he did not hold. Nevertheless, any threat to this possession distressed Francis. Moving his son there promised the best hope of security for both his son and his title to the land.

Francis Farley had sent more than thirty slaves from Antigua to North Carolina; another forty were on the Maycox plantation. With those working for the Dismal Swamp Company and elsewhere, he had about one hundred slaves in the two colonies. James Parke Farley would have enough laborers for the land the elder William Byrd had thought so rich. For the first time, it ought to yield a profit. While Francis Farley enjoyed the early months of his second marriage, James Parke Farley, Elizabeth Byrd Farley, and their two small daughters moved to the Land of Eden.

The plantation at Maycox was sold to Francis Farley's partner in the Dismal Swamp Company, David Meade, who had just turned thirty. Thirteen years had passed since his return from England to Nansemond County. He still did not enjoy living near the Dismal Swamp, selling lumber to troublesome buyers. His wife, Sarah, who was pregnant, and his mother were ready to join him in going up the James to Prince George County. He bought 600 acres at Maycox and sold his 4,000 acres in Nansemond County to his brother, Andrew. Late in the summer of 1774, the Farleys left Maycox, and the Meades moved in.

The soil at Maycox was poor, but David Meade had little interest in agriculture. He loved "domestic tranquility," and, visitors noticed, "he rarely attends to business." He devoted himself to making the interior of his hand-some brick house "extremely well fitted up" and to his chief enthusiasm, a pleasure garden. His slaves worked not on crops but on fulfilling his design for the landscape. Across 12 acres of rolling mounds on the south bank of the James he laid out terraces rising from the water, mirroring those in sight at Westover, and, behind them, artfully juxtaposed trees and plants framing a series of vistas of the river. He especially sought a smooth turf. Viewing the house, the gardens, the river, and Westover in the distance, visitors said: "charming," "enchanting." Meade kept all in "complete order." He appar-ently modeled his effects on English gardens he had seen, striving for woods and vales and turnings and changing perspectives, gratifying the eye with the picturesque. Had he set out to surround himself with scenes bearing no like-ness to the Dismal Swamp, he could hardly have done better.

Elizabeth Farley did not share her grandfather Byrd's enthusiasm as she looked out over the broad meadow on the south bank of the Dan River and the valley where the Irvin met the Dan. Rows of tobacco plants covered part of it. On a high, dry knoll above the valley, a setting she conceded was "pretty," a house was taking shape. Her husband grandly called it "Belview." While he hunted deer, she wrote to her father: "Mr. Farley talks of making improvements, which I cant say gives me any satisfaction as it seems to con-vince me he always intends living here." She apparently did share her grand-father Byrd's view of North Carolinians. Receiving letters from Virginia and writing replies were, she said, "the two greatest pleasures this part of the world can afford me." A wagon arriving from Westover without letters from her father and friends made her feel worse.

Elizabeth called James Parke Farley her "Friend & Husband." If he stayed at the Land of Eden, so would she. But aside from the presence of her husband and daughters—she was pregnant with her third—she found it a lonely life. James spent much of his time, first, driving squatters off the land "after some difficulty," then dividing many of the 25,800 acres into farms and plantations for tenants. He kept old William Byrd's favorite tract, Saura Town, for himself, placing upon it not only tobacco but also cattle, sheep, and swine. His new purchases included pewter spoons, spirits of turpentine, nails for tobacco hogsheads, and sheep shears. True, he also bought rich bro-cade, silk garters, and chocolate. A few luxuries did not turn Elizabeth's mind from the difference between life at Westover, which a European guest called "worthy of Paris," and living near her neighbor by the ford of the Dan, "a plain back wood's planter, with a large family . . . a hospitable, but uncult-vated mind, and rude manners." For her husband's welfare and for the security of Francis Farley's property she remained at Belview, watching the east-ward road along the Dan and the northward road to Petersburg, hoping to see a wagon or a horseman carrying letters.

With Francis Farley, Samuel Gist took alarm at the "Unhappy differences" between American colonists ready to defy the British government and a min-istry determined to force them to submit. Associations, closing of ports—no doubt fighting would come next—threw business out "of its usual Channel." Gist meant to get as much tobacco as possible from Virginia to London as fast as he could. To his vessels the *Planter* and the *Elizabeth* he added the *Mary* and the *Westover.* He kept all four busy.

As the *Planter,* with her cargo of indentured servants and manufactured goods, dropped down the Thames with the tide in the first week of February 1774, the *Elizabeth* was already at sea. She arrived in the James River in the first week of March, under the command of Captain Alexander Leitch. In her were European goods for Phripp, Taylor & Company of Norfolk and "a steddy young lad" from Bristol, Samuel Sellick. Phripp, Taylor & Company had asked Gist to find an apprentice to work in their store. He sent them his kinsman, Sellick, with the usual indentures. Captain Leitch apparently had orders from Gist to return to London quickly. The *Elizabeth* moored in the Thames six months and ten days after she began her voyage to Virginia.

While the *Elizabeth* rode at anchor in the James and the *Planter* remained in the Rappahannock, Gist and his colleagues at Lloyd's moved into their new rooms in the Royal Exchange. For two years a committee of underwrit-ers had tried to find accommodations better than the cramped quarters in Pope's Head Alley. After the British Herring Fishery Society moved out of the Exchange, vacating two large, lofty upstairs rooms looking out on the Bank of England and Threadneedle Street, John Julius Angerstein, acting for the committee, leased them for twenty-one years. On the first weekend in March, underwriters, brokers, ship captains, admiralty attorneys, merchants, waiters, messenger boys, and newspaper readers moved themselves, their pa-pers, and their tea, coffee, and snacks across Cornhill and into the rooms above the East Country Walk on 'Change.

In the inner room, about 1,000 square feet under a 20-foot ceiling, each underwriter claimed his corner of a table in a four-man booth, where he sat every afternoon, awaiting policies. In the past five years the number of sub-scribers had more than doubled. On a bookstand in the wide passageway be-tween the public room and the subscribers' room lay a folio volume bound in green vellum. In it clerks wrote reports of arrival or loss of vessels in all seas.

Old Thomas Fielding and young Thomas Tayler, masters of Lloyd's, oversaw the waiters, the serving of food and drink, and admittance to the rooms. At the height of business, between three and five o'clock, the rooms were almost always full, and the busy crowd, many smoking, kept up Lloyd's reputation for "pestiferous Air," "much worse" than the smoke hanging over London.

Moving to the Royal Exchange, underwriters acquired new neighbors. One was an organization they helped by large contributions. The Marine Society, which was eighteen years old but newly chartered in 1772, prided itself on rescuing boys who were "vagabonds," "distressed orphans," or "untoward servants," and turning them into seamen. The kingdom held too many boys "hardened in iniquity," "too volatile" and "too bold." Founders of the Marine Society said: "The more abandoned the common people become, the more attention should be shewn to *salutary police*," by which they meant good policy. In the three years before the society won its charter it had indentured more than 1,100 boys to merchant vessels and the Royal Navy. Since its beginning it had sent almost 12,000 to sea, "chiefly of the overflowing of these vast cities." Beyond the joint contribution of the men at Lloyd's, underwriters served as governors and members of the committee of the Marine Society. Anthony Bacon was a committeeman and a governor. The society received contributions from Lord Clive, conqueror of large parts of India, from the Company of Merchants Trading to Africa, and from many other merchants. Thus it continued its effort to rescue the indigent and redeem the vicious, teaching "the rising generation to defend their Country, and promote her Commerce" by going to sea.

In Lloyd's new rooms a conspicuous sign in large gilt letters stated a unanimous resolution of the subscribers: "as the common Method of insuring Lives upon Speculation, and without any particular Interest, was contrary to the Laws of Humanity, and subversive of the Rules of Society, such Practices should be ever held in the utmost Abhorrence by the subscribers." The sign was not effective. In October an underwriter sitting not far from it subscribed a line of £200 on a policy insuring the life of Frederick the Great for one year, charging a premium of £16. Such scenes happened often, though business at Lloyd's overwhelmingly dealt with marine insurance. Compiling *A Complete Digest of the Theory, Laws, and Practice of Insurance* a few years later, John Weskett found Lloyd's messy. The air was bad; frequent "mutually hurtful Altercations" broke out. Tradesmen, shopkeepers, all sorts of inexperienced and credulous people wandered in from the street to get rich as underwriters, only to be duped out of their money. Underwriters otherwise reputable wrote "GAMING POLICIES." If Weskett had posted a sign in the public room of Lloyd's, he said, it would have warned of "the great and constant Danger of DECEPTION." Brokers and merchants obtaining policies often used "Insinuation, Plausibility, and *artful* Diversification" in describing their vessels and voyages to underwriters. Some underwriters drafted "loose, hasty" policies, while others wrote in a "crafty Manner." Weskett was appalled to find almost every day "no less than 4 or 5 *Attornies* at LLOYD's Coffee-House! What a *Degradation*"—merchants and underwriters ought not to sue one another so often.

The disorder and duplicity came with the openness to all and the volatile scale of transactions making Lloyd's the leading insurer of risks at sea. A merchant underwriter later explained: "the facility given at Lloyd's Coffeehouse, in effecting Insurances on risks of an inferior description, brings to it the Insurances of a better description." A broker said: "As long as I can find good names and facility in the Room I think it is more pleasing to all parties to stay there." By four o'clock, noise in the rooms rose to a busy hum of many voices. A person unable to overhear a conversation still could watch the "calculating features" of the brokers and underwriters as they agreed on policies. Samuel Gist, about to turn fifty, was one of the underwriters known as "the old standards," men who "always remain in their places, and whenever they can get their Premium they will write." He prospered.

Captain Leitch moored Gist's ship *Elizabeth* in the Thames during the last week of June. Gist was irritated that John Mayo had shipped him 128 barrels of flour. He wrote: "had you Ship'd Tobacco this Year it would have answered very well for you." He discharged the *Elizabeth*'s cargo and loaded her with goods in less than four weeks. As the volume of his tobacco and other freight in London grew, Gist concluded that carmen working at waterside charged too much: 1s. 2d., for carting a half-ton hogshead a half mile up Tower Hill to a warehouse. Most carts held three hogsheads. Gist thought that one shilling per hogshead was "ample and sufficient." He and a few other merchants persuaded the Corporation of London to reduce the rate. In the *Elizabeth*, Gist sent more indentured servants: shoemakers, tailors, ropemakers, curriers, a housemaid, and a schoolmaster. Returning to Virginia, the *Elizabeth* bore Gist's orders to Mayo: "I hope it will suit you to give Capt. Leitch good assistance this voyage & as he will be late in the Season I should not like to have him detain'd." The pilot went ashore at Deal on August 2, and Leitch sailed for Virginia. In September, the *Elizabeth*, bound for the James River, and the *Planter*, bound for London, were both at sea.

The servants on board the *Elizabeth* made an easier crossing than those who went to Virginia in the *Planter*. The *Elizabeth* dropped anchor in Hampton Roads seven weeks after she sailed out of the Downs. Captain Leitch was in a hurry to sell the servants' indentures and obtain tobacco. Four weeks after he reached Virginia, he got married. Two weeks later, before he had unloaded his ship, he was dead.

Acting for Gist in Petersburg, John Tabb chose a new master for the *Elizabeth*, James Barron, brother of the captain of Tabb's ship *Nancy*. Barron was a thirty-four-year-old Virginian who had gone to sea as a boy; he had commanded ships for more than ten years. From December until mid-February he and Gist's representatives tried to get tobacco. Virginians had made this more difficult by closing their courts as part of their defiance of Britain. The planters had grown "so saucy now they'll have their price or not pay their debts since they can't be compelled to do it." Even so, he managed to load the *Elizabeth* with 494 hogsheads and to sell all the servants' indentures. The rest of her hold he filled with barrel staves. He was cleared out of port for London on February 15, 1775. He did not yet know that Gist, having just dispatched his new ship *Mary* to Virginia, wished Barron and the *Elizabeth* to return to Chesapeake Bay for one more cargo before exportation stopped on August 10.

High on the wall at the end of Lloyd's public room were two large dials. One was a clock; the other showed the direction from which the wind blew. Day after day in February the needle of the latter stood somewhere between southwest and south-southwest as a storm swept over the Channel and southern England, followed by weeks of hard wind. Even if newspapers had not told him, Gist would have known from the vane that the *Mary*, with many other vessels, remained in the Downs. Twice Captain James Miller set sail and, with the *Mary* close-hauled, tried beating into the Strait of Dover. Both times he and vessels with him put back into the Downs. The *Mary* did not sail for Virginia until four weeks after her departure from London. Gist could do nothing about the hogsheads she would miss. His only consolation was that eight or ten other vessels, owned by men with the same thought of a profitable voyage to Virginia, could not sail.

Captain Barron moored the *Elizabeth* in the Thames at the end of March. He learned that in a few weeks Gist was dispatching him to Virginia with unusual orders to John Tabb. For ten years Gist had warned his representatives not to buy tobacco for cash, except as a last resort. Now, as a result of Americans' nonimportation Association, he could not ship goods. He told Tabb to buy as much tobacco as possible. Gist also used another 300-ton ship, the *Liberty*, belonging to Thomas Bennett, one of the governors of the Marine Society. Under the command of Captain William Outram, who had orders to return with tobacco, she had sailed from the Downs in ballast two weeks before Barron and the *Elizabeth* arrived. Captain John Stevens with the *Westover* also could bring a cargo from Virginia. All these captains—Miller, Barron, Outram, Stevens—must make haste. Soldiers were boarding troop transports bound for America. The navy was stationing more men-of-war in American waters. Anthony Bacon had contracts to furnish coal and provisions to the army in North America. Gist wrote: "if these Unnatural differences were once propperly settled I should hope Tobacco would again fetch a very good Price." If they were not settled, tobacco would bring an even higher price. No Virginian need hesitate to sell tobacco to Gist. He explained that he obeyed the nonimportation Association which took effect on November 1, 1774. His vessels arriving in Virginia after that date did not bring British merchandise. He complied so strictly, he said, that he had not even sent clothes and boots for the slaves on his Virginia plantations. He wished only to collect debts and buy tobacco. In the last week of April 1775, Captain Barron and the *Elizabeth* sailed for Virginia.

Late in 1774, Dr. Thomas Walker's son-in-law, Joseph Hornsby, hoped to do as Samuel Gist had done nine years earlier: move back to England. In the past five years Joseph and his wife, Mildred, had made Dr. Walker a grandfather of two girls, Hannah and Mildred. Joseph planned to take Dr. Walker's daughter and granddaughters far from Castle Hill and Williamsburg. Joseph's brother, William, already was in England.

Joseph Hornsby prospered. His uncle had died in May 1772, leaving the bulk of a "large Fortune" to him. He inherited houses, lots, and a well-stocked store in Williamsburg, with slaves and livestock. He had become a justice of the peace and a vestryman of Bruton Parish. He was thirty-four years old. For two years he had worked to collect debts owed to his uncle's estate. William Byrd owed him more than £4,000; Speaker Robinson's estate still owed more than £850. But Byrd and many other debtors remained unmoved by requests or by threats "to commence Suits without Respect to Persons." The European goods in Hornsby's store at the time he announced his imminent departure were worth, he said, £1,200 sterling. He offered to sell them and his land in the country "very cheap," expecting to leave in the middle of February 1775.

Joseph Hornsby did not go to England. Nor did he sell his store or his plantation. In the spring his brother returned from London. On June 17, Dr. Walker gave Joseph one-half of a share in the Dismal Swamp Company.

. . .

Lord Dunmore was "a jolly, hearty companion, hospitable & polite at his own table." But after spending a few days with him a young British officer concluded that, as a governor, Dunmore was "the most unfit, the most trifling and the most uncalculated person living." Dunmore thought about himself so much that he often failed to notice what others were doing. In 1774 he looked forward to a long, lucrative stay in Virginia.

From the start he showed no interest in enforcing the Crown's proclamation against settlement in the west. He sought friends among Dr. Walker's friends: William Preston, William Christian, George Washington, men who owned tens of thousands of acres beyond the mountains and coveted more. Dunmore shared their alarm at the prospect of a large grant to the Pennsylvanians and Londoners led by Samuel Wharton and Thomas Walpole, trying to found a new colony, Vandalia, between the mountains and the Ohio River. Early in the spring he transmitted to the Earl of Dartmouth a remonstrance against creating Vandalia, signed by more than 150 residents of the west. Dunmore was eager to make grants, which brought him fees, and he did not wish land to be removed from his jurisdiction.

Dunmore encouraged settlers near the forks of the Ohio River to assert Virginia's claim to the region. They defied Pennsylvania, re-establishing a fort from which the army had withdrawn and calling it Fort Dunmore. In the spring, with the governor's approval, William Preston's surveyors worked on both sides of the Kentucky River. They went down the Ohio more than 50 miles beyond the mouth of the Kentucky. At the same time, William Byrd, Patrick Henry, William Christian, and others collaborated in a plan to buy land from the Cherokees along the Clinch, Holston, and Powell rivers, west of the latest Cherokee line, drawn in 1771. In Philadelphia, Henry told a backer of Vandalia: "Ld Dunmore is your greatest friend, what he is doing will forever hereafter, secure the peace of your colony, by driving the Indians to an amazing distance from you."

During the summer and early autumn Dunmore waged war on Shawnees in the Ohio Valley. Murders of Indians by western whites had provoked reprisals. George Washington warned of "a confederacy of the Western, & Southern Indians," saying: "a general war is inevitable." Others, however, believed that "the Indians have been the most barbarously treated, & that his Lordship ought to have had justice done them for some late murders committed upon them under a cloak of friendship." Though some Shawnees tried to form an alliance among tribes, Cherokees, Ohio Valley Iroquois, and most Shawnees, as well as others, wanted peace. Dunmore and his men in the west sought war to drive the Shawnees north of the Ohio and to assert their own claims and Virginia's right to the western lands. As Dunmore left Williamsburg to lead this campaign, the Earl of Dartmouth, in his office in Whitehall, was writing to him: "while these Compacts with the Indians remain in full force and The King's Sacred Word stands pledged for the observance of them, every attempt on the part of the King's Subjects to acquire title to and take possession of Lands beyond the Line fixed by His Majesty's authority & every encouragement given to such an attempt, can be considered in no other light than that of a gross Indignity and Dishonour to the Crown, and of an Act of equal Inhumanity and Injustice to the Indians." After the governor reached Fort Dunmore and tried to awe emissaries from the Delawares, the Wyandots, and the Iroquois, a Delaware man, seeing him, asked: "What old litle man is that yonder playing like a boy?"

Dunmore's October campaign was brief; his western volunteers suffered few casualties. They behaved, he conceded, with "Shocking inhumanity," and they "impressed an Idea of the power of the White People, upon the minds of the Indians." Shawnee leaders got peace—most had been trying to keep peace all year—by agreeing to withdraw from the region south of the Ohio. Returning to Williamsburg, Dunmore found the Earl of Dartmouth's reprimand awaiting him. He was pained. He wrote a report of his campaign, assuring Dartmouth that he had not "acted only in conjunction with a parcel of Land Jobbers." His real motive, he said, was "Duty to His Majesty, and Zeal for his Service and interest."

Richard Henderson of North Carolina and his associates threatened Virginians' designs on the west from another flank with a scheme to buy 20,000,000 acres from the Cherokees—all the land west of the Kentucky River, south of the Ohio River, and north of the Cumberland River, with a broad stretch of land south of the Cumberland. They called it Transylvania. Its eastern boundary was the western boundary of the land Wharton and Walpole called Vandalia. Henderson invited Patrick Henry to become a partner in Transylvania, but Virginia speculators said that Vandalia and most of Transylvania had always been Virginia and must remain so. Dunmore had his eye not only on land North Carolinians were trying to acquire but also on rich tracts along the Mississippi River. He issued a proclamation calling Henderson's purchase a "Pretence," ordering that anyone acting on it be "immediately fined and imprisoned." Henderson ignored him.

Dunmore's letter to the Earl of Dartmouth justifying his campaign against the Shawnees also condemned Virginians. He said that royal government had broken down in the colony. Local officials enforced resistance, not loyalty. He recommended that the Royal Navy blockade Chesapeake Bay. Earlier in December, Virginians learned that the ministry had ordered an end to private shipments of arms and ammunition to the colonies. Throughout America people already had begun to arm themselves. Newspapers published instructions for producing ingredients of gunpowder at home. In Fredericksburg, George Washington's brother-in-law and partner, Fielding Lewis, commanded the Spotsylvania County militia. He was unanimously elected chairman of the Spotsylvania County Committee in December. With some of his colleagues, he visited his fellow merchants to make sure of their compliance with the nonimportation Association and he led a committee for purchasing gunpowder, lead, and gun flints. He owned an 80-ton vessel, the *Fanny*, and a 90-ton vessel, the *Fredericksburg*; many such vessels sailed from the mainland colonies to the West Indies for munitions.

A few weeks after he became chairman, Lewis wrote to Anthony Bacon, manufacturer of artillery for the British government, acknowledging that he owed a large sum. Bacon put it at £2,448 7s. Lewis promised to pay, though his debts, he said, exceeded £5,000. As a beginning, he would ship flour. Upon receiving this letter, Bacon gave power of attorney to a man about to leave London for Virginia, authorizing him to collect from Lewis.

One source of these large debts was Lewis's new house. He was fifty years old, and his wife was forty-one. The youngest of their many children was three. They left the house on Princess Anne Street, overlooking the Rappahannock River near his brick warehouse, and moved to a hilltop plantation east of town, called Millbrook. There he had built an imposing two-story brick house with four chimneys. Spare and almost unadorned on the outside, it was rich and ornate within. Its drawing room, looking out on Fredericksburg through recessed windows, stood comparison with rooms at Westover or Rosewell: a rectangle covering 500 square feet, with ceiling and mantelpiece displaying the best stucco-duro decorative plasterwork in Virginia, more of which appeared elsewhere in the house. The painter and plasterer were still at work in the spring of 1775, so the Lewises had not yet moved their mahogany bedstead and table or their Windsor chairs into their new home.

On the second day of spring, three months after Fielding Lewis had begun collecting munitions, the Virginia Convention in Richmond resolved that the colony should be "immediately put into a posture of Defence." The delegates appointed a committee to arm and train a sufficient number of men. Four weeks later, Lord Dunmore, obeying instructions from the Earl of Dartmouth, removed gunpowder from the colonial government's magazine in Williamsburg and put it on board a Royal Navy vessel in the James River. When news of this reached Fredericksburg, Lewis wrote to George Washington: "it seems we must submit or dispute the matter Sword in hand, every person I think that has any regard for Liberty must prefer the latter." Lewis expected Washington to help him get more gunpowder for Fredericksburg when Washington went to Philadelphia to attend the meeting of the Continental Congress. In many parts of Virginia word of Dunmore's action led people to assemble and talk of marching on Williamsburg.

A week after Dunmore seized the gunpowder, an express rider passed through Fredericksburg from the north with news that fighting had begun after British soldiers marched out of Boston to confiscate arms and ammunition. The next day, Saturday, April 29, about six hundred armed men gathered in Fredericksburg, ready to go to Williamsburg and force Dunmore to surrender the gunpowder. Speaker Randolph wished to forestall violence. His message from Williamsburg reached Fredericksburg on Saturday and persuaded the armed men to go home and wait. Other militiamen were marching around in other parts of Virginia. Lord Dunmore threatened to arm slaves and wreak devastation.

During the first week of June the General Assembly remained in session. Virginians' military display appeared among the burgesses and in the capitol. Men wearing fringed hunting shirts, the uniform of liberty, passed the marble statue of the ever graceful Lord Botetourt. The burgesses said they often had heard Botetourt declare "that the business of a Governor of Virginia was much easier than he could have conceived, as he found that the government almost executed itself." Dunmore, Dartmouth, Lord North, and the king had not learned that happy lesson.

For a week the burgesses, Dunmore, and people in the streets of Williamsburg vied for control of the powder magazine. John Pinkney, setting type for Thursday's edition of his *Virginia Gazette*, due to appear on June 8, added a newly acquired excerpt from the letter Dunmore had written to Dartmouth the past December—the passage in which Dunmore called for a naval blockade. At two o'clock Thursday morning Dunmore left the governor's palace with his family and his aide. They went on board a Royal Navy schooner, then transferred to HMS *Fowey* in the York River. Six days later, in Philadelphia, Congress voted to begin raising a Continental Army. The next day delegates unanimously chose George Washington as its commander in chief. A report to the British on Virginians who might remain loyal to the Crown said of Fielding Lewis: "has abilities & Influence, but I suppose will follow the Fortunes of his Brother in law."

As Washington headed for the outskirts of Boston, his partners in the

Dismal Swamp Company took advantage of the gathering in Williamsburg to hold a meeting. After ten years, the company had Dismal Plantation, a drainage ditch to Lake Drummond, and about fifty slaves. Forty of these were "good working hands," able to grow corn, tend livestock, cut shingles, and dig ditches. The plantation held about thirty head of cattle, fed by grazing in the swamp. Its stock of sheep and hogs was "not worth mentioning." John Washington, resident overseer, made the best of the company's failure to drain large stretches of the swamp. The slaves grew rice—seven tons, "equal in Quality to that of *South Carolina*." Unable to find a buyer in Virginia, Washington shipped fifty-five casks to Antigua, where people were building reserves of rice and beans.

At the meeting, Dr. Walker conveyed half of his share to Joseph Hornsby. As the number of owners of half-shares and quarter-shares grew, voting became cumbersome, with each full share casting one vote. The members thereupon changed all shares to quarter-shares, with each quarter-share casting one vote. An owner of an original full share, such as George Washington, Fielding Lewis, Francis Farley, or Secretary Nelson, would now cast four votes. Dr. Walker and his son-in-law each cast two votes. And David Jameson cast one vote for himself and three for Samuel Gist. Any member was free to sell some or all of his quarter-shares. John Washington, having lived on the outskirts of the Dismal Swamp for almost ten years, responded to Britain's attack on American liberty by entering the Virginia forces at the age of thirty-five. He "left the affairs of the Compa[ny] in a good deal of confusion." The partners employed Henry Riddick, whose land adjoined Dismal Plantation, to superintend its affairs in the swamp. Thomas Walker and David Jameson had the partners' appointment to act as "Trustees," conducting the company's business. Since the partners who met in Williamsburg were surrounded by people predicting an imminent invasion by the Royal Navy and Army, they adjourned without making new plans for improving the Dismal Swamp.

Taking the *Elizabeth* down the Thames on a clear, hot day, the last Friday in April, Captain James Barron conveyed letters and recent newspapers. His latest issue was dated Thursday, April 27, 1775. Articles and correspondence borne by vessels sailing since the first week of January dealt with a series of meetings held by London merchants trading with North America. Some opposed the ministry's policy; others thought first about debts of colonists, who would be even less likely to pay if war began. They proposed to petition Parliament. But Lord North also had supporters, who promised, through the

Earl of Dartmouth, to make sure that merchants met "not with any View to disturb the operations of His Majesty's Ministers but to take the head from a factious party." Two of the ministry's friends were Anthony Bacon and Samuel Gist.

At the first meeting, on January 4, 1775, Bacon suggested that they do nothing while the king and Parliament considered a petition from the Continental Congress. Bacon's proposal was obviously "a Ministerial manoeuvre" and was rejected. But the committee appointed to draft a petition was also a ministerial maneuver, loaded with supporters of coercion, such as Gist and four colleagues from Lloyd's: Frederick Pigou, Jr., William Neate, William Greenwood, and John Nutt.

Gist did not attend many of the committee's evening meetings, but when he took part, he showed "the most rancorous malignity agt. America & the people there, that you can possibly conceive." He opposed putting any words into the petition suggesting that merchants thought America oppressed or injured. He "always endeavor'd to get the most servile ideas introduced to flatter administration & implore their gracious protection." Lord North's merchant friends were Americans' "inveterate enemies," William Lee warned, "none more so than Mr. Saml. Gist." In its final form the petition described possible damage to Britain's trade and asked the House of Commons to give "most serious Consideration" to this subject and apply "healing Remedies." The House voted to refer the petition to what Edmund Burke called a "committee of oblivion."

Before the *Elizabeth* sailed, Gist wrote instructions to William Anderson. Reconciliation had not turned out the way Anderson expected. Instead of inviting his daughter and son-in-law to London to live in comfort, Gist had summoned a kinsman of his late stepsons, Thomas Smith, who had served as Gist's "collector." Gist treated his son-in-law as his resident representative for his Virginia holdings. In April 1775 he instructed Anderson to purchase a tract of about 550 acres adjoining his land in Hanover County. Anderson paid £1,600 of his own money for it. Gist also expected Anderson to find cargoes of tobacco for the *Mary*, the *Liberty*, and the *Elizabeth*.

Captain James Miller anchored the *Mary* in the York River just as residents of York Town learned of fighting outside Boston. The *Elizabeth* was leaving London. A week later, Captain William Outram anchored the *Liberty* in the York. On the same day, the *Virginia Gazette* published an anonymous letter informing the public that John Wilkinson, part owner of the *Mary*, had leased two of his ships to the British government to transport troops to Boston. The man who had sent the *Mary*—everyone knew he was Samuel Gist—"must have known of Mr. Wilkinson's crime." Gist had made himself "an accessory to the guilt," and the *Mary* ought to be sent back to London in ballast.

Captain Miller, in danger of facing Gist with no tobacco, put a rebuttal in the *Gazette*. He said that Gist was "innocent." Wilkinson owned a small share of the *Mary;* Gist was principal owner and sole manager. Gist recently had "proved himself a zealous friend to American liberty" by serving on a merchants' committee to petition the House of Commons. Captain Miller assured his readers that Gist would do whatever "will conduce the most to promote the glorious cause in which they are embarked." Gist's ship was allowed to remain in the York, but William Anderson found in June that "he cannot get the Mary loaded." He asked John Tabb to send hogsheads from Petersburg which Tabb had been saving for the *Elizabeth*.

Captain Barron and the *Elizabeth* made a swift passage. Less than four weeks after sailing from the Downs, she was about 330 miles north of Bermuda. There Captain Barron hailed a schooner. Her master told him that she was out of Marblehead, Massachusetts, and he had news. A battle had been fought between British regulars and the provincial militia, with small loss to the Americans. It had been bloody for the regulars. The *Elizabeth* resumed her voyage westward.

As the *Elizabeth* approached Cape Charles and Cape Henry, the House of Burgesses convened in Williamsburg. Lord Dunmore and the burgesses began their squabble. After Dunmore fled to HMS *Fowey* in the York, near the *Mary* and the *Liberty*, the burgesses voted to reject the North ministry's latest overture. It was a measure of coercion poorly disguised as conciliation, offering to forgo parliamentary taxation if the colonies agreed to pay the cost of the Crown's government and army in America. The House referred the offer to the Continental Congress. Virginians believed that Lord Dunmore had summoned a naval force which would arrive soon. Rumors spread, describing a plot among slaves in Norfolk, who had gathered gunpowder and "implements of war," planning "to rise and murder the white people in the night."

The *Elizabeth* arrived in the James River on June 14 after a voyage of forty-seven days. Fewer than ninety days remained before the ban on exportation would take effect. William Anderson and John Tabb hurried to find a cargo. The burgesses met to adjourn. Young men broke into the governor's palace to seize a large stock of muskets and pistols. Lady Dunmore and her children sailed for England in a Royal Navy schooner. The *Liberty* sailed for London, soon followed by the *Mary*. The *Elizabeth* was Samuel Gist's last hope for making the most of the coming shortage of tobacco.

Gist grew more eager. He wrote to Tabb: "for any Purchase you make on my acct I will pay your Bills no matter how soon they are drawn, how Large the Sum, or how low the Ex[chang]e." Tobacco filled warehouses on Tower Hill. Before the year ended, London merchants had imported almost 44,000 hogsheads—more than 44,000,000 pounds. Gist's colleagues at Lloyd's, James Dunlop and John Wilson, as well as eight other firms, brought in more than he did. Still, he was the tenth-largest importer in the City, with 1,434 hogsheads. Between the January meeting of the merchants and Christmas he acquired almost 1,500,000 pounds of tobacco. For the *Elizabeth*'s voyage in the summer he doubled the usual value of each hogshead as he insured them at Lloyd's. Sir Robert Herries, a buying agent for the Farmers-General of France, was speculating in tobacco privately, too. Learning that the French might drop him, he had to buy a great deal of tobacco on short notice at a higher price. Gist sold him some, but Gist intended to leave hogsheads brought by the *Elizabeth* in his warehouse, waiting for prices to rise still higher.

John Tabb and William Anderson had difficulty getting tobacco for the *Elizabeth*. As Gist had foreseen, the exchange rate was low: £100 sterling bought only £115 in Virginia currency, and tobacco prices were rising. Knowing they could not fill the hold with hogsheads, they also bought barrel staves, deerskins, and ginseng. During those weeks militia companies camped outside Williamsburg. Some men moved into the capitol and the governor's palace. When HMS *Mercury* stood up the York River in the second week of July, militiamen paraded along the bank in case she was the van of an invading fleet. A convention met in Richmond to create a new government for Virginia, assuming sovereign powers, establishing an armed force, regulating trade, and printing money. It authorized construction of a factory to make small arms in Fredericksburg, under the superintendence of Fielding Lewis and Charles Dick.

By Monday, August 14, Tabb and Anderson had loaded the *Elizabeth* with 463 hogsheads of tobacco and 13,000 staves. She was ready to sail, weeks before the deadline. The James River Naval Office cleared her out of port, and she dropped downriver. After she passed the capes, before she stood out to sea, it was time for the pilot to leave her. Captain James Barron announced that he was going, too—leaving the *Elizabeth* and quitting the employ of Samuel Gist. Virginia would need a navy as well as an army for Americans' fight against the British government, a force to capture or sink vessels of the Royal Navy and of British merchants. Barron chose to serve Virginia. He turned the *Elizabeth* over to the first mate and departed. The mate and the twelve seamen he now commanded sailed for London with the last of Gist's tobacco.

After the *Elizabeth* rode safely at her mooring in the Thames and the hogsheads had been carted to a warehouse, Gist wrote to Barron. He said that Barron had been a good captain in every way—except in joining the rebel cause. Gist urged him to return to the duty he owed his sovereign, and assured him that if he did so, he would receive command of "a fine ship in the transport service." Gist's partner in the *Mary*, John Wilkinson, owned two, the *Lion* and the *Brilliant*. Before a letter from Gist could reach Barron, his militia company was active in Hampton Roads, capturing vessels. Members of the Virginia Convention praised "his diligence & abilities." The Committee of Safety empowered him to fit out three armed vessels, one of which he commanded, naming her the *Liberty*. The committee said: "We . . . have great Confidence in his Prudence and Valour."

Writing a private letter on board HMS *Fowey*, Lord Dunmore warned the Earl of Dartmouth against Secretary Nelson, who had succeeded his late brother as president of the Council. Nelson's holding the secretaryship, "by much the best office" in the colony, still rankled in the fugitive governor's mind. He also resented Nelson's caution. In recent months the secretary had "shown nothing but a care to avoid giving offense either way." William Byrd, on the other hand, struck Dunmore as a loyalist, "averse from the violent proceedings in the country."

Dunmore read Byrd correctly. The conflict between the British government and Americans pained him. By July he believed that war was unavoidable and that Americans were deluded in expecting to hold out against British power. He asked Sir Jeffery Amherst "to inform His Majesty & his servants . . . of my attachment to them." He despised the colonists' "frantick patriotism," pushing them toward "inevitable ruin."

In April, Byrd's friend and Francis Farley's agent, Robert Munford, had agreed, deploring "the spirit for warfare" he saw in Virginians and their leaders. But Dunmore's seizure of the colony's gunpowder angered him, and, knowing he must choose a side, Munford joined the resistance.

Contrary to Francis Farley's assurances that his son took no part in rebellion, James Parke Farley was elected to the North Carolina Provincial Convention as a delegate from Guilford County. Byrd could see that his son-in-law disagreed with him. Byrd's son, Thomas Taylor Byrd, was an officer in the British Army. Another son, Francis Otway Byrd, was an officer in the Royal Navy. Though their letters sounded dutiful and loving, his relations with them were not happy. He did not wish Otway to leave the navy, and he did not wish Thomas Taylor to get married to Susannah Randolph, daughter of Attorney General John Randolph and niece of Peyton Randolph. If either son defied him, Byrd's will said, such disobedience would reduce his bequest to one shilling. Thomas Taylor obeyed, but Otway did not. After his father helped him get a leave of absence from the navy, Otway joined the Virginia militia, then went to the camp outside Boston and entered the Continental Army.

William Byrd and his second wife were close. He admired her "Goodness of Heart." Mary Willing Byrd also had wide reading, a good memory, and a gift for telling stories. One of her favorite stories carried a lesson bearing on her effort to persuade her husband not to disinherit Otway. She told about the wedding of her sister, Dorothy. At the age of eighteen, Dorothy had eloped with Captain Walter Sterling, a thirty-five-year-old officer in the Royal Navy. To be married in church without her family's approval, the couple stood at the altar in disguise. Dorothy, daughter of one of Philadelphia's leading merchants, was dressed as a cook, wearing a checked apron; Captain Sterling wore the uniform of an able seaman and put a black patch over one eye. When her father, Charles Willing, learned of the wedding, the shock caused him to fall, striking the back of his head. He died the following year at the age of forty-five. Only after his death did she have a proper wedding. Though his last illness was a fever, the family blamed his death on his fall. He had never forgiven Dorothy. Nor did William Byrd heed his wife's urgings to change his will. He had known his father only briefly; his mother had checked him in nothing. He had spent and gambled away a fortune. He would teach his sons prudence and obedience.

Byrd wished to pay his many debts, but his gestures did little to reduce them. The closed courts thwarted attorneys such as Benjamin Waller, who reported to his British clients: "Things are in so dismal a Situation here, that there is no getting any Thing." The return of Byrd's protested bills of exchange had grown routine. He had "kept no regular books," and he now regretted his "inattention to accounts."

As the General Assembly convened in Williamsburg on Thursday, June 1, to hear what Lord Dunmore would say about Lord North's conciliatory proposal, the *Virginia Gazette* published an attack on "the honourable W——m B——d, esquire." The author accused Byrd and his "abandoned faction" of plotting to alienate Virginians from the cause of liberty. The justice of this cause and the martial spirit of Americans attracted every virtuous man. Byrd was not virtuous. He had ruined himself with "the cursed thirst of lucre," and he was "publickly reputed a man of a very immoral character." The contrast between America's friends in Parliament and Byrd was as stark as the contrast between Cato and Caligula. Resentment of Byrd went back at least ten years to the days of Speaker Robinson's secret loans and John

Chiswell's murder of Robert Routledge. Now Byrd would have to read and hear censure without trying to put a printer or anyone else in jail.

The following Wednesday, Byrd wrote to a friend in Philadelphia: "You will see by our Papers how much I am abused." Rumor said that he had written to Virginia officers who had served with him in the 1750s, conspiring to raise an armed force to support Lord North's government. Byrd denied the charge: "no thought of raising a single Man for that, or any other purpose, ever enter'd into my Head. Nor have I, in any Instance whatever, interfered in any Publick transaction, except in disapproving of Men in Arms trampling all Civil Authority under Foot." Even if Virginians believed Byrd, his not raising soldiers for resistance to Britain gave offense. He declined to offer his military experience to Virginia by commanding troops that the summer convention in Richmond voted to mobilize. The other colonel of a Virginia regiment in the 1750s now commanded the Continental Army.

Byrd's life was crumbling. Around him at Westover lay a scene "most lovely, every thing in beautiful order." Acres of nearly perfect wheat stood ready to reap. The meadows and pleasure gardens, the terraces rising along the bank of the James, showed the careful work of more than seventy years. Scores of slaves tended crops, gardens, and livestock. In the pastures steers, horses, and sheep grazed. Near the house, one outbuilding was a nursery for plants that would later grow in the gardens. In the brick library, twenty-three black walnut cases held his father's great collection of books, to which he had added. The walls of the library and the house showed three portraits of his father, portraits of his father's noble friends in the days of Queen Anne, as well as portraits of Byrd and of each of his children. Sets of Hogarth prints ran along the walls, and in "poets corner" hung a picture of Pegasus and the Muses. Byrd had made Westover a reflection of his refinement. His son-in-law spoke of Byrd's "amenity of manners," while his neighbor at Maycox, David Meade, admired "the splendid dignified & highly polished Colo. Byrd of Westover." Byrd and his wife continued to entertain guests. Mary Byrd's "very noble bearing" and her seemingly effortless management of a house full of visitors made her a "most distinguished and charming" hostess. After patriots' censure and insults and threats began, she said: "many people who had been kindly treated at *good* Mr. Byrds were the most violent."

David Meade saw that his friend William Byrd had forfeited the good opinion of patriots. Byrd's stand, his son said, "exposed him to the resentment of the Contrary Party, who it appears are so numerous as to deprive him and the few who are of the same sentiments of all hopes of making any head against them." Byrd defied those he called "the brave heroes in hunting shirts." If any such "valiant volunteers" tried to carry out their frequent threats to visit Westover and punish him, they would find him "prepared for their reception" and ready "to try their courage." But his encounter with two of their leaders, he said, "convinced me I had nothing to fear from their resolution." In the summer Byrd thought that people rebelled because they had been misled by designing men; they greatly overestimated their power to win a war with the British. "I flatter myself the time is not far off," he wrote at the end of July, "when I shall be able to convince the Virginians of their error, & bring them back to their loyalty & duty." Achieving that "blessed purpose" would be the happiest event of his life. Two months later he had concluded that the rebels did not want peace on advantageous terms. They sought "a change of government." He concluded that war, suffering, and ruin must fall upon the deluded Americans.

On board HMS *William* in Chesapeake Bay, Lord Dunmore fulfilled a threat he had been making since spring. He signed a proclamation on November 7 and published it a week later, declaring martial law in Virginia, ordering every man able to bear arms to join him in putting down rebellion, and promising that all indentured servants and slaves in the service of rebels would be free if they fought for the king. This proclamation did for Byrd what Dunmore's seizure of the colony's gunpowder had done for Robert Munford, angering him and convincing him that he must join Americans' resistance to Britain. He offered himself to the Virginia Convention as commander of the new 3rd Virginia Regiment, but the delegates overwhelmingly rejected him in favor of Hugh Mercer. Byrd's friend Ralph Wormeley wrote: "Col: Byrd joined the popular party—he was not trusted—He lost every thing." Wormeley meant not that Byrd lost his property but that he lost the place among Virginians he had inherited from his father and his grandfather and had won for himself.

Lord Dunmore's schooners and his detachment of soldiers enabled him to use Norfolk as a base for raids along the shorelines. Militiamen crossed the James and moved downriver. New soldiers from Virginia and, later, North Carolina arrived in Nansemond and Norfolk counties. Firing on Royal Navy vessels became routine. Scottish merchants prepared to leave Norfolk, packing their trade goods and household furniture, loading departing vessels or standing ready to go on short notice. Norfolk held many people opposed to the British. Dunmore said that "this little dirty Borough" had "Sedition and Rebellion" in "all Ranks of People." But the merchants had given it a reputation among other Virginians as a center of loyalty to Lord North and the king. Many people in the borough took alarm both at "the elopement of their Negroes" and at reports that rebels intended to burn the city.

Dunmore learned in mid-November that militiamen had gathered at Great Bridge ten miles from Norfolk in the northeastern reaches of the Dismal Swamp. This long, low wooden bridge on trestles and piers connected two parts of a causeway crossing a stretch of the swamp. At one end of the causeway a road led to Norfolk; at the other a road led toward North Carolina. The bridge was the most important link in the land approach to Norfolk. Using a map drawn by Thomas Macknight, Dunmore, accompanied by another partner in the Campania Company, James Parker, took his 109 British regulars and two dozen black and white volunteers up the south branch of the Elizabeth River to secure the bridge. The militiamen withdrew; he pursued them northeastward into Princess Anne County and dispersed them easily, killing a few.

Dunmore marched to Norfolk and issued his proclamation summoning men to aid the Crown. He would no longer have thought that the president of Virginia's Council, Secretary Nelson, was equivocal if he could have heard "the language of the President" in Williamsburg when Nelson learned of the proclamation. One planter said of Dunmore's action: "men of all ranks resent the pointing a dagger to their Throats thro the hands of their Slaves."

Dunmore put a small garrison in a fort at Great Bridge and began fortifying Norfolk. Parker and Macknight supervised construction of earthworks. Dunmore, naval officers, and the remaining Scots thought the British could hold Norfolk indefinitely. Merchants sent word to Britain that they were free to ignore the rebels' nonimportation Association. One wrote to his brother: "be as Expeditious as possible and bring out as Many Goods in the Brig as She will hold. Now is the time to Strick a bold Strock depend upon it you will Never have such another to Make Money by dry Goods in this Country."

Much to the disgust of Virginians gathering near the British fort at Great Bridge, about 3,000 inhabitants of Nansemond, Norfolk, and Princess Anne counties and of the borough answered Dunmore's call. They swore loyalty to the king, though only a few hundred of them looked fit to bear arms. Many slaves joined the British. One of them, George, said when captured by Virginians that 400 blacks were with Dunmore in Norfolk. The governor armed black men in what he called "Lord Dunmore's Ethiopian Regiment." For white loyalists he organized "the Queen's Own Loyal Virginia Regiment."

The fort at Great Bridge held out against the Virginians. Learning that North Carolinians were coming with artillery, Dunmore decided, against the advice of army officers, to attack rebels' entrenchments on the south bank of the Elizabeth River. In addition to condemning privately "the Absurdity & extravagant Folly" of an assault, the officers blamed it on "the Scotch Pedlars" who had Dunmore's ear. On Saturday, December 9, at dawn, 121 soldiers and their officers crossed the bridge, advanced along the narrow causeway "through a Morass" toward the Virginians. Seventeen were killed and 49 wounded in a brief exchange of fire which left the Virginians unhurt. The British withdrew to Norfolk that night.

Notwithstanding their fortifications, Dunmore and the merchants suddenly saw that they could not remain in Norfolk. Soldiers and loyalists went on board naval and merchant vessels. Virginia and North Carolina forces entering the borough found only a few people. Warehouses stood full of shingles and planks. Empty streets were lined with unoccupied brick houses. Mahogany furniture, carpets, china, pictures on the walls awaited their owners' return. During the next two weeks the contest between Dunmore and the Virginians amounted to one question: who would burn Norfolk?

On Tuesday, January 1, 1776, Captain Henry Bellew of HMS *Liverpool*, "discovering," as Dunmore put it, that rebels were parading in the streets of Norfolk, began to shell the city. Other vessels joined him, then lowered boats and put men ashore to set fire to warehouses. Tuesday and Wednesday, after the boats withdrew, Virginia soldiers spread the fire and looted houses. A sailor trying to stop some of them received this answer: "the people in Norfolk were a parcell of Damned Tories and ought to have all their houses burnt, & themselves burnt with them." Joanna Tucker's home, emblem of Robert Tucker's success, was fired by soldiers. They took offense at a carpenter who refused to help; "they damned him for a Tory." The houses belonging to Robert Tucker's estate, to his son, Robert Tucker, Jr., and to his son-in-law, Thomas Newton, with most of the borough's other buildings, were destroyed. Almost all remaining buildings were burned before the soldiers abandoned the borough, leaving blackened brick walls and freestanding chimneys. Colonel Robert Howe of the North Carolina forces assured Virginia authorities that Norfolk would not again be a haven for loyalists or a trading station for Scottish merchants.

The three Scots of the Campania Company gave up their scheme to force the Dismal Swamp Company to share its success with them. James Parker and William Aitchison welcomed Dunmore to Norfolk. Their partner in North Carolina, Thomas Macknight, joined them in October.

The partners had done nothing with the North Carolina portion of the Dismal Swamp after Parker and Macknight and their slaves cut a pathway to Lake Drummond. They had never intended to spend money trying to drain,

as the Virginians did. The Campania Company, Parker said, was "a Speculation altogether." Their policy for swamp land was to "let it lay & take a
Chance." As merchants and landowners, they had flourished. Parker's residence, though not large, showed expensive tastes and overlooked an elaborate garden. He was part owner of a ropewalk and a distillery; his share of
stores and land in North Carolina, he said, was worth £14,000, and his five
houses and other holdings in Virginia even more. His open contempt for
"buckskins" and their rebellion had made him "most obnoxious" to Virginians. He approved of Dunmore's departure from Williamsburg. Parker said:
"What can a Governor do without a little force." Hearing that Speaker Peyton Randolph had died in Philadelphia after suffering a stroke, Parker said he
was sorry that Randolph "did not Live long enough to be hanged."

In seventeen years of working for Parker and Aitchison in North Carolina, Thomas Macknight had become one of the most important men in the
northeastern sector of the colony. He was clerk of Pasquotank County
Court. At his estate, Belville, he had more than one hundred slaves. Around
his house lay a ten-acre pleasure garden and large orchards. His store was a
big, two-story structure. He owned more than 8,000 acres, of which more
than 1,700 were cleared and in use. Governor Josiah Martin thought that
Macknight was worth £30,000 sterling. He had enriched himself by using his
partners' money and goods as if they were his own, calling on Parker and
Aitchison for more. After Parker learned of Macknight's misdeeds, he wrote
to a friend: "I am not at all surprized Mr. M deceives you by appearances, he
has me for 20 years by promises."

Early in October 1775, Macknight fled Belville on horseback "without a
servant or a change of clothes," riding more than 50 miles to Norfolk. He
said he had learned just in time that people plotting to kill him were about to
strike. Ever since April, when his colleagues in the North Carolina Convention had called him "Disingenuous and equivocal" and declared him "inimical to the Cause of American Liberty," many people had talked about killing
him. His friends, even his old Campania Company ally, Samuel Johnston,
turned against him after he refused to join in resistance to Britain. He defied
his critics in public and in print, saying that only by exports could he pay his
just debts in Britain. His critics called him "a pest of society."

Lord Dunmore gave Parker and Macknight the rank of captain of engineers. Parker's brother-in-law, Jacob Ellegood, took command of the
Queen's Own Loyal Virginia Regiment. As Dunmore abandoned Norfolk,
they went with him. William Aitchison took his family to the Eastern Shore,
leaving his "very elegant" and well-furnished house, one of seven he owned
in Norfolk. His country home, Eastwood, stood on a plantation in Princess

Anne County, and he owned land in North Carolina. Lord Dunmore often had visited Aitchison's home in Norfolk. In the fire on New Year's Day, Virginia troops began by burning it. Aitchison's slaves already had joined the British.

Aitchison, Parker, and Macknight believed the rebellion would not last long. They stood poised to act as soon as the British restored order. Macknight was to sail to London and persuade Alexander Elmsly to join them in "Commercial Speculation." Once the rebellion collapsed, Macknight would be "amongst the first in with a Cargo of Goods." A British Army officer sending a letter by him wrote: "he is the most spirited clever Fellow I have met with in this Country."

Nothing turned out right for the three partners. Not only did the rebellion continue, it became a revolution for the independence of America, with the colonies now renamed states. Everywhere Aitchison went—Princess Anne County, Northampton County, Pasquotank County—committees of safety treated him as suspect and let him know he was not welcome. He was sixty-three years old and infirm. This treatment "laid hold of his Spirits in a very strong degree." As they parted, James Parker did not expect to see Aitchison alive again. At Eastwood, Aitchison contracted a fever in October and died on the last day of the month.

Parker stayed with Lord Dunmore as his chief engineer while the governor roamed the waters of the Chesapeake for six months, accompanied by a flotilla of loyalists' vessels. They spent time ashore at Robert Tucker's mills and bakehouses, which they demolished, and on Gwynn's Island at the mouth of the Piankatank River. Smallpox and other diseases killed hundreds of Dunmore's white and black volunteers. Bodies washed ashore every day. A surprise attack on Gwynn's Island by rebels forced Dunmore's men to abandon it in a panic. After the remaining British and loyalist vessels set sail, a squall struck. Parker's armed tender, cruising in search of provisions, stranded on the Eastern Shore. He and the other seventeen men on board "immediately surrendered" to Virginia forces "and begged for quarters."

Thomas Macknight's voyage to London was deferred for several months after he met Governor Josiah Martin at Cape Fear, North Carolina. He accompanied the British expedition to Charleston and served for a while as an agent for prizes, obtaining for the army cargoes of American vessels seized by the Royal Navy. By the time he returned to Cape Fear in the summer, North Carolina's Provincial Congress had taken possession of his land and slaves. Reaching London in autumn, he heard that the 200-ton ship *Belville* he and Parker and Aitchison had dispatched to Cádiz laden with staves had been taken by a man-of-war off Cape St. Vincents and condemned as a rebel prize in a British Court of Admiralty at Gibraltar. Macknight had lost everything. The British government, he believed, owed him recompense not only for the value of the *Belville* but also for losses his loyalty had cost him: a plantation, many slaves, a store, and a large, valuable portion of the Dismal Swamp. Living in London "in the most frugal manner" on an allowance from the government, he spent much time drawing up petitions for compensation, attending cabinet ministers' levees in search of a hearing, and waiting in Whitehall to persuade officials to help him. In a state of "distraction" he accosted Earl Bathurst, president of the Council, in Green Park while the earl was taking his morning walk. Macknight explained his case and handed copies of testimonials to Bathurst, who, Macknight thought, "seemed to pity my distress."

Dr. Thomas Walker returned to Pittsburgh in the summer of 1776. He had visited in the autumn of 1775 to end the conflict known as Dunmore's War. In the presence of representatives of the Six Nations, the Wyandots, the Delawares, and the Ottawas, he had told representatives of the Shawnees: "we have before told you all that we had no intention of incroaching on your Lands which are the real Sentiments of our hearts." All present knew that, two days earlier, Flying Crow of the Six Nations had said to the Virginians: "we hope you will . . . make no Encroachments upon us that our Children may Continue to live in Peace and Friendship." Walker went back to Pittsburgh in 1776 as one of the Continental Congress's commissioners to Indians in the Ohio Valley. War between the Cherokees and the southern states already had begun. Walker and his colleagues were to report on the intentions of northern Indians.

Ever active, Dr. Walker turned a slow Tuesday into a picnic party of fourteen people, rowing up the Monongahela River in a large canoe to the site of General Edward Braddock's defeat. After eating a hearty meal, they walked over the battlefield, noting the bones and skulls of men killed by the Indians and the French more than twenty years past. The growth of trees scarred by musket balls and artillery fire had lifted the marks 20 feet above the ground. Dr. Walker gave the company a "warm and glowing narration" of the battle. His story reached a climax in the flight of Braddock's army, with "the hellish yells of the Indians, and the groans and shrieks of the dying and the wounded falling upon their ears."

Ten days after this excursion, Walker and his fellow commissioners warned western settlers to prepare for attacks by Chippewas, Ottawas, and Shawnees. In their report to Congress, the commissioners said that an Indian war was "by no means improbable." If it came, however, it ought to look different from the rout of the colonial settlers in the 1750s. Walker urged Virginians and Pennsylvanians to get ready to punish Ohio Valley Indians, as Cherokees were about to be punished. "We have sought only the security of the Frontiers against the Horrors of Indian Cruelty." Walker had warned Shawnees the previous October: "if you will Continue to do us Mischief you must not Expect to be treated with such Lenity as you were in the Year 1764 by Colo Boquet and by Lord Dunmore last fall."

Even as war spread over the continent and as General Washington's army abandoned New York City to retreat across New Jersey, Dr. Walker kept an eye on the Dismal Swamp. The company's slaves produced a good crop at Dismal Plantation in the autumn. Samuel Gist wrote to William Anderson, urging the company to invest in more slaves. Anderson explained that the war was "an insurmountable obstacle to the Companys advancing Money." Buying slaves, even were it possible, would not be prudent, lest "another Dunmore should appear on the Coast." Gist had hinted that he might visit Virginia, but of course, he did not. In August a sloop bearing Scottish factors sailed out of Chesapeake Bay, bound for New York. The summer of 1776 was not a good time for a merchant from Britain to travel in Virginia. Gist said he would trust "providence who I hope will in the end settle all things right." He told Anderson: "I must entirely rely on you in the mean while to do the best you can for me."

Dr. Walker visited Dismal Plantation and the swamp during the winter, a few weeks after Washington and his army revived their hopes by recrossing the Delaware River to attack the enemy by surprise. Walker still had faith in the promise of the Dismal Swamp Company's project, he said. He gave a favorable report to William Anderson, who wrote to Samuel Gist to reassure him that Walker and David Jameson "have as high an opinion of the value of the estate if it was properly conducted as you have." During the following spring, heavy rains flooded Nansemond and Norfolk counties. Waters of the Dismal Swamp rose and spilled over the surrounding land. On the route from Suffolk to Edenton, which skirted the swamp's western margin, long stretches of road lay under three feet of water.

Members of the Dismal Swamp Company took leading places in the new state government devised by the Virginia Convention and defined in a written constitution. The governor was to be elected annually by the House of Delegates and the Senate, but the first governor was chosen by the Convention. A minority voted for Secretary Thomas Nelson, partly in search of legitimacy through continuity, since the president of the colonial Council always became acting governor upon the death or departure of the royal governor. But most delegates chose Patrick Henry, Virginia's most popular politician. Henry moved into the governor's palace in Williamsburg. The furniture left by Lord Dunmore had vanished into the homes of patriots; the state bought replacements from William Byrd.

John Page served on the state Council, as he had on the colonial one. His colleagues elected him its president, thereby making him also lieutenant governor. For the first three months of his term, Henry was ill and Page did the work of governor, though he suffered debilitating attacks of vertigo, worsened by applying himself to accounts, reading, and writing.

As Page organized resistance to Lord Dunmore late in 1775 and early in 1776, his wife, Frances, was pregnant for the sixth time. Her delivery of their daughter, Alice Grymes Page, in February was difficult. Frances long seemed to lie near death, but she recovered and soon got pregnant again. She and John felt "crowded into a little House" after leaving Rosewell to live in Williamsburg. They had the lead stripped from their mansion's many window frames for Virginia to use in musket balls. It weighed almost 1,300 pounds. While Dunmore remained at large in the Chesapeake, their big house overlooking the York was not a safe place for one of Virginia's most important officials to live.

Almost all the former colonies adopted new state constitutions. Of Virginia's Page wrote: "I believe ours is the most perfect in the World." The tyranny of king and Parliament, by arousing resistance, inadvertently had resulted in "freeing Millions from Bondage." America would be "one of the noblest Republics the World ever saw." At work in Williamsburg, writing to St. George Tucker, Page warmed to his subject. With no advantages, Americans, though facing Indians' attacks and slaves' revolts, fought the empire the world held in awe, "rather than wallow in Peace & Luxury, if they must be deprived of the Privileges of free Men to obtain that Happiness." As he wrote "Happiness," Page was interrupted by a friend, Major James Innes, who had just arrived with a prisoner: James Parker. The little Scottish merchant had sold Virginians a great deal of luxury in peacetime, sneering at them all the while. He was held in Williamsburg for a month, then moved to New London in Bedford County. He soon escaped and joined the British in New York, offering his services for an invasion of Virginia.

Thomas Nelson, at the age of sixty-one, became secretary of the commonwealth of Virginia, taking an oath of loyalty to the new government. At the end of 1776, Dr. Walker and David Jameson were sworn in as members of the Council of Virginia. Three days after Walker joined the Council, the

General Assembly enacted a law prohibiting British subjects from recovering debts in Virginia. Under instructions from the Committee of Safety, given early in the year, Fielding Lewis not only produced small arms and provided ammunition but also fitted out armed vessels to cruise the waters of the Chesapeake. The 81-foot keel of the row galley *Dragon* was laid in Fredericksburg late in the autumn. He bought a schooner, a sloop, and a pilot boat.

In Paris, William Carmichael of Maryland heard that the Continental ship *Reprisal* had taken five British prizes. He wrote: "This will make a little noise at Loyd's." American vessels and others pretending to be American inflicted heavy losses on British merchant shipping. John Nicol, a seaman in a Royal Navy man-of-war protecting a convoy, said: "The American privateers swarmed around like sharks, watching an opportunity to seize any slow-sailing vessel." Every day at Lloyd's, new captures by Americans were posted in the big green arrival and loss book. Underwriters' estimates of the value of lost ships and cargoes had passed £300,000 in August and was nearing £600,000. After two years of American privateering, Lloyd's book showed a loss of 559 vessels, with a total value of more than £1,800,000. Insurance premiums on the Jamaica-to-London run rose to 15 percent. For some voyages on other routes, underwriters charged 28 percent. Anyone could see that some shrewd and lucky men would make fortunes at Lloyd's as long as war continued. Others lost everything.

The British condemned American vessels the Royal Navy apprehended. Nevertheless, the Philadelphia firm, Willing & Morris, insured some vessels at Lloyd's. Thomas Willing, Mary Byrd's brother, and his partner, Robert Morris, also envisioned making fortunes from the war. Offering to obtain supplies and arms in Europe for the American government, they intended to import merchandise to sell at a large profit. Morris was ready to pay a premium of 50 percent for insurance if necessary, though "vastly too high," because he could mark up European manufactures 500 percent to 700 percent for retail sale in America. The best commodity to ship to Europe was tobacco. Willing and Morris had "a considerable quantity" at Edenton, North Carolina, waiting for the company's agent in Martinique to send a fast sloop or schooner to Albemarle Sound, bearing dry goods in and tobacco out. Willing and Morris wrote to him: "dont loose a moment in executing this Scheme."

Willing and Morris had a representative in Paris: Silas Deane of Connecticut, who wrote to his wife: "I have been involved in one scheme and adventure after another." At the first Continental Congress, he and Patrick

Henry had discussed settling Connecticut farmers in towns "on the New England plan" along the Ohio River. In Paris, Deane represented not only Willing and Morris but also the United States government. He did the same things for the company and for the Secret Committees of the Continental Congress: obtain credit from the French government and merchandise and arms from Europe by importing commodities, especially tobacco. Morris wrote to him about shipments through the French West Indies: "You may depend that the pursuit of this plan deserves your utmost exertion & attention so farr as your mind is engaged in the making of Money for there never was so fair an opportunity of making a large Fortune since I have been Conversant in the World." About £250,000 sterling passed through Deane's hands. He fitted out privateers to seize British vessels and bring them into French ports. The men who purchased for the United States were his associates, as were the men who captured British cargoes and sold them. Deane suggested that Americans seize Bermuda to get a harbor from which to attack British shipping: "the whole West India Trade must be intercepted." Benjamin Franklin arrived in France at the end of the year. Arthur Lee, in London, received instructions to join Deane and Franklin.

France's aid and Deane's activities were supposed to be secret. Pierre Augustin Caron de Beaumarchais organized France's assistance, using the name "Roderigue Hortalez." Lee's letters to Beaumarchais from London were signed "Mary Johnston." Franklin's old friends in London, Samuel Wharton and Thomas Walpole, promoters of Vandalia, had the code numbers 176 and 177. Parts of some letters were written in invisible ink. These precautions availed little. Deane's secretary, Edward Bancroft, dividing his time between London and Paris, was a British agent. One of the letter drops used for communications between Deane and Bancroft was the office of Anthony Bacon in Copthall Court. After Arthur Lee moved to Paris, his secretary also was a British agent. Beaumarchais, on his way to Le Havre, posing as an iron dealer named "Durand," found that actors in *The Barber of Seville* had advertised that the author would attend the play. The ministry had other sources, who kept Viscount Weymouth, secretary of state for the southern department, better informed than his American spies did. The activities of Deane and his business associates were more hidden from the American government than from the British.

Deane realized that he could make money in London and Amsterdam, using information he and Franklin received from America. With Samuel and Joseph Wharton, Thomas Walpole, and Edward Bancroft, he tried to stay ahead of the bulls and bears on the stock exchange, and he took out insurance: "gaming policies" of the kind that Lloyd's underwriters formally deplored but still subscribed. As soon as American commissioners received word of events making war between Britain and France more likely, Deane and his friends in London paid premiums of 25 percent or more for policies enabling them to recover thousands of pounds if war broke out within a year. Bancroft was to warn the Whartons in case other news made war less likely so that they could buy "counter-insurance," betting the other way. Another British agent reported on Bancroft: "He is flush of mony. Has large share in the Cargoes going out—& I suppose has been bribed by W——le." Deane and Bancroft each took a one-fourth share of a policy paying £2,000 if France and the United States formed an alliance, an event they knew to be imminent. They told Samuel Wharton "to make his Speculations accordingly." As soon as two treaties were signed on the evening of February 6, 1778, an express messenger left Paris for London, bearing the news for the purpose of "advantageous speculation in 'Change Alley." He had a head start of "some hours" by the time the British ambassador received official notice. The messenger, booted and spurred, arrived by night at the residence of one of the Americans in London. The British ambassador's first dispatches from Paris were dated February 6. The express rider knew the treaties' terms; the ambassador did not. Deane also hoped to join Walpole and the Whartons in profiting from Vandalia by getting Congress to override Virginia's claims. He was versatile enough to talk with Patrick Henry about plans for Transylvania and with Samuel Wharton about plans for Vandalia. After Arthur Lee began to denounce Deane's corruption stridently, Deane wrote to Bancroft: "Mr. A.L. must be shaved, & bled or he will be actually mad for Life."

Congress recalled Deane even before delegates learned the scope of his enterprises. He had offended them by giving contracts and commissions to European officers seeking rank and pay in the American Army. He did not regain a position of trust. Nevertheless, his appetite for schemes remained strong. He wrote to his brother from Paris: "We have often talked of the Dismal Swamp. Pray inquire who the proprietors are, and what is their title; also at what price they estimate it. A good speculation may be made that way when peace takes place." The later insurance speculations by Deane and Bancroft failed as often as earlier ones had succeeded. Congress refused to reimburse Deane for his expenses. He needed money. He offered himself to the British government as an advocate of America's reunion with Britain.

Late in 1776, as Silas Deane drank champagne in his expensive rented house in Place Louis XV, William Byrd, at the age of forty-eight, gave up on the American Revolution and on life. His will, written two years earlier, contained phrases hinting that he did not expect to live much longer. Preoccupied with his many large debts, he attributed them to "my own folly." He wrote: "I . . . am unhappy I can do no more, which has shortened my days by many years." He blessed his wife and prayed that God would "continue her in health for many years." The will directed her to sell one hundred slaves, as well as part of their plate, furniture, and livestock. His father's library of almost 3,500 volumes also was to be sold to raise money to pay his creditors. Byrd could not bear to do these things. The law passed late in 1776 prohibiting Britons from collecting debts in Virginia did not relieve him because he thought of his obligations in Britain as "debts of honour."

Mary Willing Byrd spoke of her husband as "her good Mr. Byrd." They took pains in the education and upbringing of their children. At the end of 1776, Mary Byrd was five months pregnant. For her husband she had, she said, "heartfelt affection."

William Byrd's polished courtesy masked unhappiness. In his will he inserted a dig at his adult sons by praising "my son Charles, who never offended me." Charles was four years old. Byrd had disapproved when his son, Otway, joined the Continental Army and became aide-de-camp to General Charles Lee, an eccentric Englishman fighting for the Americans. Yet during Lee's visit to Westover in the spring of 1776, Byrd and his wife charmed the irritable misanthrope with "civilities and attentions," which at last had Lee playing with the Byrds' little daughters. Lee's letter of thanks concluded, "God give you all health and spirits," but God had not done so for William Byrd. His mind dwelt on how "greatly incumbered with debts" he was and on what he had suffered at the hands of estate managers "thro' carelessness of some . . . & the villany of others." Mostly he thought about his own folly in contracting this encumbrance, "which imbitters every moment of my life."

Describing William Byrd many years later, David Meade condemned gambling, the "inevitable consequences" of which were "poverty, want, misery and often suicide." Meade called this warning a "not unapt digression." On New Year's Day, 1777, William Byrd, in Meade's words, "resigned to his successors all his claims to temporal enjoyments and temporal honors." This was as close as Meade could bring himself to recording that Byrd had killed himself, and Meade came closer than anyone else.

For Mary Byrd, her husband's death was "her *great bereavement*." She displayed "extraordinary and almost inconsolable grief." He left her a thirty-six-year-old widow with seven children to rear, the oldest fifteen. She taught them and, later, her grandchildren to remember "the liberality of his heart," his "fidelity and activity" in public service, and the "warmth and sincerity of his soul." She gave birth four months after his death and named the boy William. She drew closer to Sarah Meade. Since Westover had two ferry boats, the women could fulfill their wish "to be together to cheer each other," Mary Byrd crossing the James to Maycox, or Sarah Meade crossing to Westover.

William Byrd's will was proved on February 5. It made his widow sole executrix unless she decided that the task was "too troublesome an office for her." He need not have worried. Mary Byrd threw herself into the project of ridding the estate of debt. Only by doing so could she secure for her children the legacies bequeathed to them. The will mentioned the possibility of selling Westover, but she meant to preserve it. Fifteen years earlier, upon first arriving, she had written to her family in Philadelphia: "This is the most delightful place in the world." She had believed that her new husband was rich and growing richer. Though she learned otherwise, she never swerved from maintaining Westover. Mary Byrd had "great wit." She enjoyed old Colonel Byrd's books, telling her sister: "The Library would delight you." These resources, with her "care and activity," sustained her as she faced "Colo Byrds Creditors daily coming upon her" and his debtors, who found many reasons not to pay. Her sister said of defaulters: "not contented with evading what is just they too generally become the Enemies of those they have injured."

On Thursday, April 24, the long road toward the James, passing through an oak grove and by Westover's vast meadows, leading to old William Byrd's monogrammed iron gate, filled with Harrisons, Randolphs, Carters, Pages, and many others attending the first of several auctions of effects from the estate of the recently deceased William Byrd. Joseph Hornsby and his brother, William, came from Williamsburg; John Tabb came from Petersburg to buy slaves. People bought horses, steers, calves, lambs, furniture, firearms, and utensils. Peter Lyons bought a backgammon table. Slaves from Westover and other Byrd plantations were sold. Black people whose families long had lived in two rows of whitewashed houses, the "village of quarters" just inside the main gate, were put on the block for a total of £6,790 10s. More followed in November. At sales in the fall and winter, Mary Byrd parted with paintings, etchings, Hogarth prints, and silver services. No one bid against her when she bought the family portraits and the portraits of old Colonel Byrd's friends for £1 each. The second sale brought in almost £11,000 in paper currency.

Mary Byrd said: "I hope to God it will be in my power to prevent any persons suffering by the Estate in any way what ever." She came from a family of merchants; she understood balancing accounts; her "singular intelligence" impressed others. She paid cash to people who had received from her husband worthless bills of exchange drawn on London merchants. This put her Virginia creditors in a tight place, testing their devotion to the American Revolution. An attorney explained to his client: "I did with the other Creditors receive your Balance from her in November 1777, in Paper Currency then declared by a Law of the new Commonwealth a lawful Tender in all Cases, with a Penalty on such as should make any Difference between Paper Money and Specie, the last of which had vanished. Besides at that time there was a danger of being accounted a Tory and treated accordingly in Case of refusing the Currency." Virginia had entered what David Jameson called "the age of paper." One of the most deeply indebted estates in Virginia moved closer to solvency.

In accordance with her husband's will, Mary Byrd advertised to sell "the very valuable LIBRARY." She found no buyer for almost a year. At last she sold all the books to Isaac Zane, Jr., owner of an ironworks in the Shenandoah Valley. He paid £2,000, expecting to resell them in the North at a profit. She kept old Colonel Byrd's manuscripts.

Some upstairs rooms in the Westover mansion fell out of use, permanently closed off. In those still open the house looked as it had in better times. Slaves made sure that gardens, groves, and meadows were "neatly kept." The first thing a visitor saw upon entering the house was a portrait of Mary Byrd's late husband. One of the portraits hanging in the drawing room showed the elder William Byrd looking out sardonically. Around the dining room table or in the drawing room, Mary Byrd encouraged her daughters to enjoy themselves. Guests found them "very witty and very lively company," full of "smart repartee." To help support the family, Mary Byrd had a brew house built; in it she "sat up brewing Beer."

Her stepdaughter and son-in-law, Elizabeth and James Parke Farley, stayed in their new house in the Land of Eden during the first year of the war. Elizabeth gave birth to a third daughter. James's father's slaves adapted from the work of growing cane and producing sugar to the different tasks and rhythms of growing and curing tobacco. Yet the only reduction in James's debt to the store owned by Dinwiddie, Crawford & Company came through shipments of rum and sugar from his father. James owed £1,700.

Francis Farley helped his son with rum and sugar until direct commerce between Antigua and the mainland stopped. James did not tell him about the debts. Just as Virginians rushed to send tobacco to Britain, they shipped food and lumber to Antigua. At least twenty vessels arriving from Antigua entered the port of Norfolk during 1775. By early August the island's markets were glutted with American grain. Prudent Antiguans such as Farley built reserves. After captures of vessels began early in 1776, he could buy little. He heard about his son rarely, through indirect channels. He knew that Elizabeth Farley was "an obliging good Wife" and that she and James had given him three granddaughters. He knew he had one hundred slaves working in North Carolina and Virginia, but he could not find out how they fared.

Although Farley denounced Americans' war for independence, he said the British could not win. He predicted an American alliance with France more than two years before one was formed. He wrote: "I know [th]at Continent prity well, I have been in eight different Provinces, and if the [Pe]ople continue united I do not think they are to be subdued by Land forces. The Sea Coast may, but I verily believe if the King of Prussia with the best 100,000 Troops he ever Commanded was 100 Miles in the Country they would be all cut off." Farley looked to the future with gloom, expecting war and American independence to destroy the world of sugar planters in the British West Indies.

The number of whites in Antigua had fallen to 2,600. They always worried about an uprising among the 38,000 blacks. A shortage of food would increase the likelihood of revolt. And if British troops were transferred from the island to North America, whites would have no trained defenders against a slave uprising or a French invasion. Antiguans were "high Loyalists," and they called on the Crown to protect them. The government sometimes seemed more preoccupied with preventing them from selling gunpowder to Americans.

In October 1775 drought settled on Antigua. Clouds drifting southward brought no rain. Hot, dry weather lasted for eleven months. Food crops did not grow. Stockpiles dwindled. Slaves were put on short rations, which they eked out by sucking sugar cane. Francis Farley foresaw starvation for many. As shortages grew more severe and prices rose, the island attracted speculators, who bought cargoes of foodstuffs after captured American vessels were condemned in a Court of Admiralty. Resale of these supplies on the open market made provisions still more expensive.

One of James Parke Farley's last transactions with Scottish storekeepers was to buy a gun on June 15, 1776. Not long afterward, many Scots left Virginia and North Carolina. James and Elizabeth Farley returned to Virginia, where James served as a soldier, apparently in the militia. Visiting North End, home of Elizabeth's cousin on a peninsula overlooking Chesapeake Bay not far from York Town and Rosewell, he fell ill and died "suddenly" on May 1, 1777. Elizabeth Farley was pregnant. She drew on the Byrd family's gift for sarcasm as she wrote that he died "a Victim to his country." The Byrds often blamed their troubles on the American Revolution. Her brother, Thomas Taylor Byrd, applying to the Council of West Florida for a grant of land, said that he had been deprived of a large fortune because his father had remained loyal to the king.

Months passed before Francis Farley learned of the death of his only son. A Scottish merchant who fled to New York mentioned it to a friend of Farley's, without details about how or when James had died. Knowing that Elizabeth was pregnant, Farley worried about her well-being and her children. He also feared for the security of his property in Virginia and North Carolina. Two of the three men to whom he had given power of attorney—James Parke Farley, William Byrd, and Robert Munford—were dead. His nephew, Jack, still served as an officer in the British Army. Farley thought that North Carolinians and Virginians, if they heard this, would confiscate his property. He urged Jack not to remain "a slave in the army of a very declining almost ruined country." Why not resign his commission and go to North Carolina to protect the family holdings? Francis Farley's son-in-law, Captain John Laforey, could not do so. He commanded a man-of-war, HMS *Ocean*. Farley wrote as if he hardly expected his nephew to heed his advice, and Jack did not.

Heavy rain fell on Antigua in September 1776. Reservoirs and ponds filled; people planted corn and other food crops. A few months later, however, drought returned. After nine months of dry heat, Antigua looked more "burnt up" than it had been for the past thirty years, "not a green thing to be seen." Early in 1777 the island began to depend primarily upon beans shipped from Britain. Farley was "extremely busy" trying to supply his six plantations and those he supervised for absentee owners. He cut some slaves to two-thirds of the usual ration "for fear of a total want." The sugar crop was stunted, but its owners thought more about the dangers of invasion and insurrection. Farley predicted that three out of every hundred slaves on the island would starve to death and that malnutrition would leave "a great many so reduced it will scarcely be practicable to raise them." As Antigua neared famine, Farley and his colleagues on the Council got permission from the navy to import food from St. Eustatius and other Dutch and French islands.

Despite these concerns, Francis Farley did not neglect his interests on the mainland or his daughter-in-law and grandchildren. Just after New Year's Day, 1778, he wrote to Robert Munford, requesting that cultivation of tobacco continue at the Land of Eden. Elizabeth Farley might detain some slaves in Virginia, but he knew that she was "very prudent" and would keep only a few. The rest, except those "employed in the Dizmal Swamp," should work his North Carolina land, with the proceeds going to his daughter-in-law. Farley saw speculators in prize cargoes pay 90 shillings per hundredweight for tobacco in St. Johns and make a good profit on it in England.

Munford ought to take advantage of these prices with tobacco shipped to France. Farley intended to visit Virginia as soon as the "unhappy dispute" ended. Elizabeth Farley lived at Nesting, about a mile upriver from Westover. Her fourth child was another daughter, named Mary Byrd Farley. The baby girl's maternal grandfather had killed himself before she was born; her paternal grandfather did not know she existed. Francis Farley hoped for a grandson to continue the name of Farley and inherit the Land of Eden and his share in the Dismal Swamp Company.

Robert Munford was forty years old when Farley asked for his help. In the decade before the war he had acquired more land and slaves in Mecklenburg County, bringing his holdings to 4,000 acres and ninety-one slaves. His home at Richland, like Dr. Walker's at Castle Hill and George Washington's at Mount Vernon, was built of wood, but the improvements he made gave it "the appearance of magnificence." To departing Scottish merchants Munford owed large sums. He had drawn £2,300 in unpaid bills of exchange, and his debts exceeded his assets.

Munford disliked "the intemperate warmth" Virginians had shown in opposing British measures before fighting had begun. Late in 1774 a petition circulated in Mecklenburg County. It advocated "expelling out of the country all *Scotchmen*." Two and a half years later, after most factors had left, 190 citizens of the county petitioned the House of Delegates to inflict "more severe punishment" on any remaining Scottish storekeepers who refused to accept the new paper money in payment of old sterling debts. This petition was signed by Sir Peyton Skipwith, Virginia's only baronet, and by such lesser men as David Royster, Joseph Royster, and Charles Royster, whose stridency showed that they were not "moderate & prudent" people of the kind Munford had hoped would forestall "the evils of a civil war." Munford did not sign.

After Munford sided with the Revolution, he recruited soldiers, served in the House of Delegates, and, late in the war, fought the British in North Carolina. But gleeful belligerence and ostentatious patriotism among Americans still offended him. At about the time the second Mecklenburg County petition against Scottish factors was signed by his neighbors—May 1777—he wrote a play: *The Patriots.*

How many of Munford's fellow planters, if they could have seen or read his play, would have recognized themselves in his fictional sketch of them? "Her father is a violent patriot without knowing the meaning of the word. He understands little or nothing beyond a dice-box and race-field, but thinks he knows every thing; and woe be to him that contradicts him! His political notions are a system of perfect anarchy, but he reigns in his own family with perfect despotism. He is fully resolved that nobody shall tyrannize over him, but very content to tyrannize over others." Asked to define the word "tory," one character, member of a Committee of Safety, replies: "All suspected persons are call'd tories." Munford's loyalty to the American cause had been "suspected" in March and April 1775. The voters of Mecklenburg County chose Bennet Goode, instead of their longtime burgess, Robert Munford, to represent them in the new House of Delegates. Goode also served on the county committee enforcing the Association. Munford's distaste for what his hero calls "the patriotic itch" and for politicians exploiting it recurs throughout his play. In Act II, just before the Committee of Safety denounces Scots as enemies, Munford's hero says of it: "I hate these little democracies." A Scot challenges the committee to prove that he is an enemy. One member answers: "We suspect any Scotchman: suspicion is proof, sir."

Munford ridiculed not only cant and bloodthirstiness among patriots but also a disposition in the American Revolution "to spurn at all government." He linked the "phrenzy of the times" with the decay of both "public virtue" and "the social virtues." Choosing as his hero one of two "gentlemen of fortune accused of toryism," he left little doubt of a connection between their being "gentlemen of fortune" and their being accused. A contemporary of Bennet Goode's later described Munford: "he was what they called an aristocrat." In *The Patriots*, the Revolution is, in part, a triumph of petty and ignorant men over educated and discerning men. Munford conveyed his disgust at this dimension of patriotism by having one member of the Committee of Safety say: "shew me a clever man, and I'll shew you an enemy." The play's happy ending was written by a man who did not appear to expect such an outcome in his own life. When he received Francis Farley's letter after writing *The Patriots* and read Farley's allusion to the war years—calling them "this unhappy time"—Robert Munford had reason to agree.

Virginia, with the other states, received from Congress in the fall of 1777 a recommendation that property of loyalists be confiscated to provide money for the war. Members of the House of Delegates would not yet go so far, in violation of international law. British officials had not seized the property in Britain of Americans they deemed rebels. The delegates instead sequestered the property of loyalists so that profits from these estates, as well as debts owed to loyalists, would not be paid. The proceeds were invested in Continental loan office certificates—that is, lent to the United States. Among the properties sequestered were five plantations and 149 slaves belonging to Samuel Gist.

Ever since Gist's departure from Virginia, Benjamin Toler had supervised overseers on Gist's plantations. He lived near the Pamunkey River, six miles from Hanover Court House. He traveled to Amherst and Goochland counties and within Hanover County to make sure that Gist's land remained productive, sending profits to Gist. His crop of 1777 yielded about 80 hogsheads of tobacco. In London they were worth at least £3,200; even in Virginia they would bring about £1,120. Gist's letters and instructions reached Virginia by way of Holland, France, or the French West Indies. In July 1777, Gist's agent at Petersburg, Thomas Shore, announced his intent to go to Europe. Anyone wishing to transfer money or order manufactured goods could apply to him directly or through Thomas Pleasants in Richmond or William Anderson in Hanover. Anderson offered the plantation of Gist's stepson, the late John Smith, for rent, and he bought land for Gist. In Virginians' eyes Gist was "an alien enemy who could not hold any property in this country." Yet, through Anderson, he did.

Late in November 1777, Gist and almost all leading underwriters and merchants at Lloyd's signed a memorial to the government, complaining about collusion by France and Spain in American raids on British commerce. Many privateers had few or no Americans on board. The merchants warned: "to such a Price has the Premium of Insurance already arisen, in Contemplation of these Hazards, that many of the most valuable Branches of the Navigation of the Kingdom cannot support so heavy a Charge." This memorial soon became irrelevant, as greater risks arose. On December 2 people in London learned that six weeks earlier General John Burgoyne had surrendered to the Americans in upstate New York. Although Sir William Howe had defeated George Washington's forces twice in Pennsylvania and occupied Philadelphia, the Northern Department of the Continental Army under Horatio Gates, with the help of militia, had captured an invading British Army. The value of stock fell, and one member of Parliament "said pleasantly and possibly truly enough that the insurers at Lloyds will have a good scuffle in Westminster Hall upon this Subject." Anyone could see that France's covert aid to the United States probably would soon become overt, in the form of diplomatic recognition and alliance in war on Britain. In that event Britain's merchant fleet risked not only Americans' piracy but also the French and Spanish navies. More underwriters faced bankruptcy.

By February 1778, Americans secured their alliance with France. Attempting to forestall it, Lord North's ministry appointed a peace commission to offer terms of reunion to the Americans. This commission had no chance of success, but Samuel Gist and other merchants formerly trading to America took care that reconciliation not come at their expense. They signed a memorial urging the ministry to provide in any agreement "the most effectual measures . . . to secure the debts due to them which have been contracted under the faith and sanction of the British laws." Americans' intent to evade paying was embodied, the merchants said, in "that most dangerous, accumulating, and overwhelming paper currency," which they made legal tender "in full discharge of book debts, bonds, and all other securities, without having any funds for its redemption." If the king did not protect "his much injured subjects," they expected "the loss of their fortunes."

Each sequestered estate in Virginia was assigned a commissioner to manage a loyalist's plantations in order to extract a profit for the benefit of the Continental loan office. Samuel Gist's old ally Peter Lyons persuaded the Council—Gist's partners in the Dismal Swamp Company, John Page, Thomas Walker, and David Jameson, were councillors—to make William Anderson commissioner for the holdings of Samuel Gist in February 1778. Lyons assumed that if Gist's property "fell into other hands, it would be much injured." Of course, everyone knew that Anderson was Gist's son-in-law. His appointment "subjected him to suspicion that he would not do as much for the public as an indifferent person." He was charged with "breach of duty, for not selling the crops soon and paying money into the treasury." He made his first payments in July. That year and the next he gave more than $21,750 in Continental currency to the treasurer of Virginia. Officially, this sum was the equivalent of almost £720 sterling. Anderson withstood suspicion and complaints, occasionally carrying a musket on militia duty to show that he was no loyalist. Mary Anderson's kindness and hospitality made her popular in spite of Virginians' dislike of her father. Benjamin Toler worked Gist's slaves, and Henry Riddick kept the Dismal Swamp Company's slaves at work with tools Gist had shipped before the war.

War gave Anthony Bacon little rest. The Ordnance Board, deliberating in private without taking competitive bids, awarded him contracts for cannon of various calibers at a price of £18 for each ton of dark gray iron. A single contract on June 17, 1778, one of many between 1773 and 1779, was worth £11,700. He received more orders than any other manufacturer of ordnance. Early in the war Bacon ended his partnership with John Wilkinson but still used and improved Wilkinson's method for boring cannon. He brought a new partner into his operations at Merthyr Tydfil. Buying out his first partner, William Brownrigg, and replacing him with Richard Crawshay, Bacon exchanged a man of science for a man of business. Crawshay worked forges, foundries, and laborers relentlessly. Bacon leased more land around Merthyr

Tydfil, as well as another furnace nearby in 1777 and still another in 1780. With more people working on iron, ironstone, and coal, new cottages rose to fill gaps between earlier ones in the town's cramped, crooked streets. The constant noise and heat of blast furnaces and iron wheels grew more intense, as did clouds of coal smoke. The forging, casting, and boring of Bacon's cannon surrounded their makers with flame, smoke, ashes, and soot. As his resident agent at the Cyfarthfa furnace, Bacon employed Richard Hill, husband of Margaret Bushby Hill, whose sister was Bacon's mistress. Bacon was a godfather of the Hills' daughter.

Taking account of the growing population of Glamorganshire, officials in Cardiff built a new jail. An improved turnpike ran from Merthyr Tydfil down the valley of the Taff 26 miles to Cardiff. It needed frequent repair as long teams of horses hauled wagons laden with iron guns, many with nine-and-one-half-foot barrels. At the edge of the neat walled town, guarded by a ruined castle overlooking the Bristol Channel, stood the Gwlat Quay. It became known as "Cannon Wharf." Cardiff's quiet was often broken as Bacon's guns were tested by firing 6-pound or 18-pound or 32-pound cannon balls from St. Mary's Street, at the end of the wharf, into the earthen bank of the south wall. Once approved, artillery pieces were shipped to the king's ordnance depots and on to America.

The Ordnance Board was only one of several contract-letting boards doing business with the member of Parliament for Aylesbury. Bacon owned a colliery in Cumberland County. He won contracts to supply coal to the British Army in America. One, in August 1778, was worth £18,000. Earlier agreements, under which he bought coal for the army and received a commission of 2½ percent, were even more lucrative, especially if he bought the coal from himself and took a commission.

Bacon also received contracts to supply provisions to the army. Although he was a lesser figure in this trade, he was paid more than £44,000 for Irish provisions in 1778. For 1779 the government stipulated a similar sum. The first agreements, setting a fixed, arbitrary price for the commodities Bacon's agents delivered, were "extremely favorable to the Contractors, & prejudicial to the publick." Bacon received overpayments even after a new system computed cost per ration.

Bacon bore the initial expense of furnishing food, coal, and cannon to the Crown, relying upon the government to fulfill its agreements. It was often slow to pay. The Ordnance Board gave him debentures, certifying its debt to him. The ministry, in turn, had to float large loans to finance the war. Delays mounted. In October 1780 debentures redeemable in August 1778 remained due. George Jeffery, a merchant in Throgmorton Street, around the corner from Bacon's offices, wrote: "an Ordnance Contractor applied to me for a parcel of Goods but could give me no other payment than ordnance Debentures." Reluctantly, Jeffery took the paper at a steep discount, making "such an exorbitant profit I was ashamed to ask for it. However I found I was still lower than other People." Bacon was only one of many who were circulating "an amazing fund for Commerce" created for carrying on the war. He was most resourceful when most beleaguered by his big risks, the husband of a relative said. "Once at least, if not oftener, his creditors were called together and his books shewn; and he has been heard to declare, that several times, even in the apparent zenith of his prosperity, had the same thing happened to him, he would have been found worse than nothing." Bacon survived and, with his fellow contractors, remained loyal to Lord North's ministry.

Opponents of Lord North censured corruption and waste in the contract system. The navy, the army, and the Ordnance Board spent far more than the sums voted by Parliament, relying on the members to cover these "extraordinaries" with new public funds. This practice, the clerk of the House of Commons later wrote, rendered the process of appropriation "ridiculous and nugatory," while the ministry tolerated "frauds and abuses." In debate Isaac Barré singled out the ordnance estimate: "The expence of the ordnance service for this year was above £470,000 and no man could tell to what the account might be swelled. . . . It had been all imposition from beginning to end, or some persons imagined they had an interest pretending to be deceived." Members criticized Bacon by name for the amounts he collected to provide slave labor to the government in the West Indies, calling the payments "a most shameful squandering of public money." The Treasury Board received complaints about late deliveries and inferior quality in Bacon's shipments of provisions. In the spring of 1778 the opposition tried to prohibit contractors from sitting in the House of Commons. One member provoked Bacon by denouncing them "for being private plunderers; for entering into a conspiracy with a corrupt administration to plunder their country." Bacon rose to defend himself. He said that he fulfilled his contracts "fairly and honestly," that he was not a tool of the ministry, and that he "could not conceive why contractors should be treated in so unbecoming, nay, contemptuous a manner—as if they were monsters and not fit for human society!" After the House divided on the question, the Treasury's secretary, Lord North's political operative John Robinson, reported from Downing Street: "We were hard run yesterday . . . and but barely threw out the Contractors' Bill." Less than three weeks after the vote, Bacon received a contract for sixty-three more cannons. The following year £1,500 was allotted from the king's privy purse to help re-elect him in Aylesbury.

Bacon did not let oratory in the House of Commons dispirit him. He enjoyed theatrical people. One of his critics in Parliament, Sir William Mayne, who owned large estates in Ireland and received an Irish peerage in 1776, was the brother of Robert Mayne, who shared Bacon's contracts to supply Irish provisions to the army. A satirist writing a mock epitaph for Sir William while he was still alive said that Lord North, "wishing to profit by his Connexions, and lamenting the Insignificance of an Instrument so wretched, implored the [king] to make a Lord of him." But even after Sir William became Baron Newhaven, he "for a long Series of tiresome Years, was neither distinguished by an Action or a Sentiment, which merited Observation." Anthony Bacon had no need to worry about what Sir William Mayne might say. Later in the war, Robert Mayne went bankrupt and killed himself.

Bacon cultivated other interests. In 1776 he helped David Garrick push a bill through Parliament incorporating a fund for the care of old and needy actors. In Wales, Bacon's "poetic and literary inclinations" led him to learn Welsh and to seek out "all the bards and educated men" within reach. He befriended the wild-eyed, drunken clergyman Evan Evans, or Ieuan Fardd, pre-eminent scholar of Welsh language and literature. In moments of liquored gratitude Evans sometimes gave away his most precious possessions. He gave or sold to Bacon his rare manuscript copy of the sixth-century epic poem *Y Gododdin* by Aneirin of the Flowing Muse, Prince of Bards, containing the story of Mynyddawg Mwynfawr and his host of men who feasted for a year before attacking Saxon invaders at Catraeth. It was "equal at least to the Iliad, Æneid or Paradise Lost." Compared to men Bacon knew, orators in Parliament talking about "what a mine of corruption government contracts were" cut a small figure. Bacon agreed with Samuel Rogers, a merchant writing from London: "Whatever be the Issue of the War in America, the Campaigns made there afford a good Opportunity for Business to People who are wise and skillful enough to keep their Affairs within their power."

Americans' war against Britain depended upon transatlantic trade. Virginia lay at the center of this trade. To purchase European arms, ammunition, and supplies for the war, as well as manufactured goods bought by citizens, and to repay loans, America's most valuable commodity was tobacco. During 1778 and 1779 a hogshead delivered to Spain, France, or Holland commanded more than three times its peacetime price. Delivered to Britain, it brought more than six times as much as the old price. The 22,012 hogsheads exported from Virginia yielded the equivalent of £990,083 sterling.

Robert Morris wrote to Silas Deane: "all Trading People do & must run Risques." Every master of a vessel bearing American tobacco knew this truth. Beyond the usual risks of the sea and danger of seizure by British privateers or Royal Navy vessels in distant waters, captains increasingly found that entering or leaving Chesapeake Bay was dangerous, almost prohibitively so. By 1777 the British Navy stationed fourteen ships of war in waters off Cape Henry and Cape Charles. Some vessels slipped past them in fog, and others outran them, but "Tis next to a miracle if a Vessel arrives within the Capes without being chased." At the end of 1778 beaches for 25 miles south of Cape Henry were littered with wrecks of trading vessels stranded while running from British cruisers. Shipping into and out of the bay fell to one-fourth its peacetime volume.

A safer route for getting tobacco out of Virginia and Maryland ran overland, along the northwestern reaches of the Dismal Swamp, into the waters of North Carolina. Tobacco vessels sailed out of the James River and up the Nansemond River, anchoring at Suffolk. Hogsheads were discharged into wagons to be hauled 25 miles to warehouses at South Quay on the Blackwater River. They were loaded on board sloops or square-riggers. These dropped down the Blackwater into the Chowan River and down the Chowan into Albemarle Sound. Vessels of almost 200 tons could call at South Quay. Smaller vessels also took hogsheads down the rivers to Edenton, where ships, schooners, and sloops rode at anchor. When ready to depart, they sailed out of Albemarle Sound and, protected by the Outer Banks, passed behind Cape Hatteras to Ocracoke Inlet, a break in the Outer Banks with a 12-foot draft. This was their passage to the sea. Vessels bringing munitions, rum, and manufactured goods to America entered at Ocracoke Inlet and followed the same route to Edenton and South Quay. Supplies for General Washington's army went from warehouses at Suffolk down the Nansemond River into the James and into Chesapeake Bay, then up the bay to its northernmost point: Head of Elk, Maryland, 12 miles from Pennsylvania.

Some vessels outward bound from Albemarle Sound or Chesapeake Bay sailed for Nantes or Cádiz or Bordeaux. But most headed for ports in the West Indies—French islands such as Martinique or the Danish island of St. Croix—or, best of all, the Dutch island of St. Eustatius. A dormant volcano rising steeply from the sea about 75 miles northwest of Antigua, St. Eustatius supported on its 15 square miles a rich mixture of visitors, "smugglers, adventurers, betrayers of their Country, and rebels to their King." Though the island's harbor was poor, it was ringed for a mile and a quarter with warehouses two deep. After these filled, hogsheads of tobacco and sugar covered the beach. Merchants routinely saw two hundred vessels anchored in the road. In 1779 more than 2,000 vessels brought cargoes to the island, almost 300 of them from the United States. At the peak of its wartime trade, St. Eustatius held goods and commodities worth more than £3,000,000.

The British naval officer who called some people on the island "betrayers of their Country" referred not to Dutch subjects but to British merchants, agents, and ship captains. Everyone knew that many goods passing through St. Eustatius came from Britain. Before the bench of the High Court of Admiralty the king's attorney said in October 1777: "Our own merchants, as well as the Dutch are concerned. The spirit of commercial adventure has seized all the world." English goods had "a prodigious Sale" in Virginia and other states. Many British merchants strove to profit. Vessels cleared from home port to a British island in the West Indies sometimes landed only part of their cargoes, then took the rest to St. Eustatius. Other captains were bolder. From a convoy escorted to St. Kitts by HMS *Leviathan* in the autumn of 1779, seven vessels "went down openly to St. Eustatius." British colonists and traders in St. Kitts sent Irish provisions to St. Eustatius. These found their way to Martinique to feed the French fleet. Commenting on British merchants' trade at the Dutch island, Vice-Admiral Sir George Brydges Rodney wrote to Captain John Laforey: "I . . . am fully convinced, by intercepting hundreds of letters, that if it had not been for their treasonable correspondence and assistance, the American war must have been long since finished."

Americans had followed this trade route during the previous war and in peacetime smuggling. They built a steady trade on behalf of independence more quickly than they built a reliable army. At St. Eustatius, European goods bound for America sold for 120 to 400 percent of cost. After they made the run to Edenton, South Quay, and Suffolk, they took another large markup. Worried about criticism from his associates Willing & Morris, Carter Braxton wrote defensively to justify charging customers only 300 percent more than he had paid for dry goods bought in the West Indies. His enemies the Lees said that he "from a ruined fortune is now amassing an immense Estate from the distresses of his country."

In Williamsburg, John Hatley Norton looked forward to getting rich. He told merchants in Rotterdam and Bordeaux: "European Goods particularly such as we used to receive from Engld, sell at an advance of 1500 pCent on sterling Cost." Many vessels were captured. Insurance at Amsterdam required a premium of 35 percent; French underwriters asked 45 or 50 percent or more. The transatlantic trade absorbed losses and premiums while remaining lucrative. Alarmed by high markups, state governments and Congress tried to control prices and regulate trade. Virginia named Fielding Lewis, Charles Dick, and James Mercer as commissioners to confer with North Carolina's commissioners on prices. Lewis served as chairman. In their meeting early in 1778, they concluded "that it is totally impracticable to regulate the general Imports & Produce of the States."

Fielding Lewis formed his opinion about importation not just from observation and report but also from experience. He and several other merchants and investors established Fielding Lewis & Company. Under the management of Joshua Storrs, the company pooled capital to send the schooner *Betsey*, laden with tobacco, to France and the French West Indies in search of profitable return cargoes: sugar, molasses, salt, coffee, cloth, china, and other goods. In Suffolk, Wills Cowper received tobacco for the *Betsey*. The company also brought cargo in the mail packet *Virginia*. The partners prospered. One wrote to another as they prepared a joint venture in January 1778: "May the good Luck of Fiel Lewis & Company attend us." A few months earlier a $\frac{1}{32}$ share in the company sold for £500 currency. Though Lewis spent the summer of 1778 at Berkeley Springs for his health, he gave advice about the *Betsey*'s voyage: "it's my opinion that Rum Sugr. & molasses are the best." The partnership dissolved at the end of the year; its substantial profits were divided in the spring of 1779.

John Page suggested a similar venture to St. George Tucker in the autumn of 1776. Bringing in rum, sugar, munitions, and medicine from the West Indies, Page wrote, "would put you into a way of making a very considerable Fortune." Five months later, Tucker allied with Maurice Simons of Charleston. The first leg of his trip to Charleston took him along the post road from Suffolk skirting the Dismal Swamp. In the still March evening unruffled brown water reflected vast trunks and high, moss-hung branches of old cypress trees, as in an "extensive looking Glass." He heard so many frogs that the ground seemed to be alive and croaking. The uneven road threatened to drop him into the swamp. Nightfall and chill came upon him. Seeking shelter in a house near the road, he found an old woman and a girl of sixteen. They let him use a bed. As he talked with them, they gave him coffee but no milk because their cows spent the winter in the swamp, foraging. The old woman explained her coffee's unusual "pungency" by telling him that she sweetened it with molasses: "we have no Sugar. No Sir, we poor people can not afford such Dainties as Rum and sugar." The next day Tucker reached Edenton, which was "nearly overrun by the busy sons of commerce."

After meeting Simons in Charleston, Tucker returned to Virginia. On his own and his partners' account he collected hogsheads of tobacco at South Quay and sent them in the brig *Dispatch* to Samuel and John Delap, merchants in Bordeaux. Early in 1779 the Delaps remitted about £2,000 sterling to Tucker through London and Bermuda. His share was more than £430. The return voyage of the *Dispatch* by way of Surinam was less happy. Off the Outer Banks two British cruisers gave chase. To save what he could, Captain William Hill Sergeant ran her on shore. Losing the vessel, Sergeant salvaged rum, molasses, and guns in her hold. Cargoes from Bermuda brought Tucker further profits. In April 1780 he bought a 100-acre farm.

A port town before the war, South Quay became a boom town. Virginia's two galleys built there joined other vessels in defending Ocracoke Inlet. Merchants traveling from Suffolk to South Quay had a "disagreeable journey." Whitefield's, the only tavern in Suffolk late in 1777, was "a bad one." The road leading westward from Suffolk and the Dismal Swamp passed small plantations and worn wooden houses. Sandy soil supported mainly short marsh grass and pine trees. Occasionally a traveler saw a gristmill or a tar kiln. Near the center of these silent pine barrens stood South Quay, a busy, dirty town of many kinds of transactions. American, French, and Spanish vessels were anchored near the wharves. The brig *El Sagrado Corazón de Jesus* brought twenty-two cannons. Full of sailors and teamsters, the town had little law and much rum. Early in 1778 hire of a wagon cost more than £4 per day. Pilferage from cargoes, routine in London, was rampant in South Quay. Masters of vessels, merchants, and agents made quick deals, trying to gauge how many hundreds of percent profit they could expect to turn. News of a cargo of salt attracted both merchants and local people. Essential for curing meat, salt was in short supply. Men furnishing rations to the army wanted it, as did people south of the James who supported themselves partly by curing hams. At one of the peaks of demand, a bushel of salt at South Quay brought £150 currency or 112 pounds of tobacco.

A traveler on roads out of Suffolk and Norfolk needed to take care—he might be robbed or killed by fugitives living in the Dismal Swamp. After Lord Dunmore left the region, some blacks and whites who had joined him, with others who had left their former homes, camped in dry sectors of the swamp, where militiamen did not relish pursuing them. It was safer to leave these runaway blacks, bitter loyalists, and bandits alone. Sporadically, some of them raided houses or attacked travelers, then "return'd into their strong swamps, from whence they will commit many daring outrages."

Despite dangers by land and sea, South Quay's trade flourished for the first three years of the war and revived during the last two. Demand for tobacco in Europe and for lumber and provisions in the West Indies, combined with Americans' eagerness for war supplies, liquor, sweets, and manufactured goods, drew vessels and speculators. A trader wrote to a partner in Fielding Lewis & Company: "You may guess my dislike at being engaged so long in such a Country as this." He could have said of South Quay what the master of the *Saucy Jack* wrote about its sister port in North Carolina as a warning to the same merchant: "I can fully assure you you have no friends in Edenton—(Vultures All)."

As men in other states did, Virginia's political leaders and moralists condemned behavior typical of wartime trade. John Page said that "the Demon of Avarice" had been "let loose upon us." Depreciation of paper money enabled Edmund Pendleton to make more rapid progress in settling accounts between the state and Speaker Robinson's estate. At the same time, he deplored "the graspers" and their greed, which "pervaded every breast almost." On the list of offenders were "Planters, Importers, Speculators, & monopolizers." Two years after Fielding Lewis & Company had dissolved, Lewis complained to George Washington that imported goods cost too much: "none can afford to buy except the Tradesmen and speculators." But the demon was not confined to a few classes or groups: "every man now, trys to ruen his neighbour."

Foretelling impending financial disaster for Virginians, moralists also deplored "luxury, and extravagancy." Prices were extortionate; yet, somehow, far too many people lived in "Indolence" and "dissipation," indulging themselves with costly objects. A list of goods in demand during August 1779 contained not only gunpowder, flints, earthenware, and cottons, but also gold leaf, blonde lace, white gloves, embroidered cambric waistcoats, brandy, and tea. A horse race in Caroline County late that year shocked Edmund Pendleton by the size of its purse: £30,000 in Virginia currency. Moral decline manifested itself both in gambling for such a large sum and in printing so much paper money that £30,000 would soon be worth only £240 sterling.

Censors of the times returned to the subject of "dirty paper," a currency almost of "no more value than Oak leaves." Inflation, they believed, brought the decay of ethics. George Washington complained that all but a few of his debtors paid him paper at face value under laws making currency legal tender. He thus received about 7.5 percent of the value of the money owed him. John Page said that "the Spirit of Traffic" spread among Virginians. He and Walter Jones saw this not as laudable enterprise and ingenuity but as "the licentious perfidy, fraud, pride and poverty which are the offspring of rags and paper, and are perfectly epidemic with us." Recalling stories of the famous bubble in France early in the century, Carter Braxton predicted in 1777 that, if prices continued to rise, "probably all our Money and Credit will end as the Mississippi scheme did."

Buying provisions at St. Eustatius, planters of Antigua regained indirectly some of their trade with North America, but not enough. Even if Antigua had enjoyed unfettered commerce, its condition would have remained desperate. Drought, beginning in 1777, continued in 1778 and 1779. The island's exports fell steeply. In a good year it produced at least 15,000 hogsheads of sugar. In 1779 and 1780 it harvested a "Dismal Crop," which yielded about 3,500 each year. Slaves' private vegetable gardens withered. The colony had to import water, which sold for 1s. 6d. per gallon. Even at that price, too little arrived. Some provisions from Britain turned out to be spoiled. In 1778 slaves began to die of starvation, "in the greatest agony." Many others were "exceedingly sickly." The following year "the Flux," dysentery, struck Antigua. As many as 7,600 black people, 20 percent of the population, died. No one knew the precise number.

Francis Farley believed that he was a humane slaveholder. He held a reserve of food on his plantations, yet feared that in a famine, "any of us that are provident and have a store of Provision by us for our own Negroes will have it forced from us." Soon he had new concerns: his wife's poor health and his own illnesses. Long a sufferer from gout, he came down with the flux in 1779. He hoped in March that a voyage to Tobago, about 900 miles round trip, would benefit him with sea air and a change of climate.

On Saturday, March 27, just before his departure, Farley, feeling "much Indisposed," wrote his will. To his wife he bequeathed lifetime use of one of his plantations, as well as personal possessions and household goods. After making a few monetary bequests, he left most of the rest of his property in Antigua, four plantations, to Captain John Laforey, trusting him to "act the part of a man of Honor by my Grand Children." Laforey also was eventually to inherit the plantation where Farley's wife lived.

Farley devoted a long section of his will to his property in North America: the Land of Eden, his plantations near Norfolk, and his share in the "Company known by the name of the great Dismal Swamp." He knew of three granddaughters in Virginia, but he had not learned the outcome of Elizabeth Byrd Farley's latest pregnancy. She had a fourth daughter, soon to be two years old, but Francis Farley provided for the possibility of a grandson. If one had been born, Farley wrote, he was to inherit the Land of Eden, the Virginia plantations, and the partnership in the Dismal Swamp Company. He also was to inherit Farley's Mercers Creek plantation on the north-eastern coast of Antigua. The granddaughters were to receive £2,000 sterling each, upon reaching the age of twenty-one. But if no grandson had been born, the granddaughters would inherit all Farley's property in Virginia and North Carolina and his Mercers Creek plantation jointly, share and share alike. Thus, by a roundabout way, the Land of Eden returned to the Byrd family. Old Colonel William Byrd's great granddaughters were to become partners in the scheme to drain the Dismal Swamp—a scheme, he had written fifty years past, which could be completed in ten years.

On Tuesday, March 30, Farley took passage on board a ship bound for Tobago. After two days at sea, he proved to be "too far gone to recover." He died on Thursday. The ship changed course to put back to St. Johns, intending to return Farley's remains to the burial grounds of other members of his family. Sailing for Antigua, her master and crew sighted French frigates to windward. The men-of-war bore down upon them to seize a prize. The ship bearing Farley's body ran before the trade winds, closely chased by the fast frigates. She "was very near being taken" as she approached the steep, wooded slopes of the British island of Montserrat, 27 miles southwest of Antigua. She sailed into Sugar Bay and dropped anchor under the guns of Fort Barrington. The remains of Francis Farley were buried in Montserrat.

When Captain Laforey learned of his father-in-law's death, he was commander of HMS *Invincible*. He had irritated the ministry by testifying for the defense in the court-martial of Admiral Augustus Keppel, another episode of the political fights in the navy and the capital. Keppel had been acquitted, to the delight of the fleet and of Lord North's opponents. Celebrators and rioters moved through London's streets at night. Keppel received the thanks of the City. He was honored with a dinner at the London Tavern, where toasts were raised to the Americans and to "Keppel and Liberty." Despite Laforey's politics, the Admiralty gave him a posting he wanted: commissioner of naval affairs in the Leeward Islands, with his office at English Harbor, Antigua. The appointment made him "extremely happy." He would be near his newly inherited plantations. The Admiralty welcomed a vacancy in the command of HMS *Invincible* as it reassigned senior officers. Leaving Eleanor Laforey and their children in England, John Laforey sailed for English Harbor.

As commissioner, Laforey oversaw the Royal Navy's most important harbor in the West Indies: a refuge from storms, a magazine of supplies, a shipyard for repairs, and a dumping ground for sick seamen. In the absence of an admiral, he had authority over all officers and vessels in the harbor. He found, however, that some newly promoted captains defied him—young men with no memory of the surrender of Louisburg in 1758 and with too little respect for their elders. He worked in a cramped office above a store-house, often staying late at his desk and sleeping on a field bed nearby. Around his building, drunken sailors wandered among hovels. Laforey had little time for plantations; he learned that Francis Farley had left them "under incumbrances" which could be lifted only with profits produced by plentiful rain and large crops of sugar.

As soon as Britain declared war on the Dutch, the British took St. Eustatius, ending the island's career as an entrepot for Americans. Almost two years earlier, in May 1779, a British force had gone to Virginia to strike South Quay and Suffolk. On Saturday, May 8, a fleet commanded by Commodore Sir George Collier sailed between the capes, into Chesapeake Bay. To the British, the spectacle looked impressive; to Virginians, frightening: five men-of-war, easterly winds filling their sails, accompanied by an armed galley, privateers, and 22 troop transports, bearing about 1,800 soldiers.

Commodore Collier and Major General Edward Mathew knew what they were after. In New York they had been told by William Franklin, royal governor of New Jersey, that a young man taken on his way from Virginia to Cádiz had let drop some information: Suffolk and Portsmouth held an unusually large concentration of provisions and other supplies. Loyalists told the British as much, hoping that the army would come to Virginia to stay. Accompanying Sir George as an advisor, James Parker returned to familiar scenes he had fled almost three years earlier. Sir George struck Virginia because it was "the province which of all others gives sinews to the rebellion from its extensive traffick." General Sir Henry Clinton allowed the army to raid but not to stay. If a permanent post around Norfolk looked advantageous later in the year, Sir George wrote, "the situation of the county of Norfolk is such as will require no very great force to keep possession, from its being covered by the Dismal Swamp and other difficulties in approaching it by land. I understand this part of Virginia carries on a great trade in tobacco and abounds in naval stores and in cattle." Loyalists tried to sell the strategic merits of the Dismal Swamp to the British as ardently as William Byrd or George Washington tried to sell the swamp's future to investors.

On the exposed point of land overlooking the Elizabeth River west of Portsmouth, among the ruins of Robert Tucker's mills and bakery, Virginians had built fortifications. As British troops landed on Monday, May 10, the commander of a small American force saw the uselessness of resisting. He withdrew along the eastern margin of the Dismal Swamp into North Carolina, returning northward on the western side.

Before withdrawing, Virginians burned a new Continental Navy frigate, but Sir George Collier still took rich prizes. In addition to vessels on the stocks in the shipyard, his seamen captured about 130 others in two weeks. In the yard he found large quantities of masts, sails, cordage, and seasoned timber. General Mathew's soldiers, surveying wharves and warehouses along the Elizabeth River, saw the first signs that Sir George's informants had told the truth. Almost 200 hogsheads of tobacco, more than 100 barrels of pork, more than 100 barrels of flour, as well as molasses, rum, salt—the list was long, and the proceeds of this booty, after it was taken away and sold, was divided among soldiers and sailors, according to rank. Rumor in New York the following month said that Commodore Collier and General Mathew each cleared £5,000 sterling.

Among those surprised at Portsmouth were two French vessels laden with tobacco. One, *Le Soucy*, out of Bordeaux, had brought a cargo of rum, sugar, and manufactured goods partly belonging to the Deane brothers, Silas and Simeon. Loading her with tobacco for an outbound voyage, Simeon had chosen Portsmouth as the safest port. He was there when the British appeared in the Elizabeth River. Captain Pierre Raphael Charlet, master of *Le Soucy*, tried to save her by withdrawing up the southern branch. When capture looked imminent, he put pitch and tar under the scuttles of her main deck and fired her before she could be taken. Deane tried to conceal bales of goods on shore, but the British, he said later, "came so suddenly upon us as to prevent saving anything. . . . I escaped the only Person in my Party of 30 Men." On the advice of local people, he fled westward along Deep Creek to hide in the northeastern reaches of the Dismal Swamp.

At dawn on Wednesday, May 12, he found himself trapped between a pond and a "terrible thicket." He feared he could not get out of the swamp, and he felt "almost kill'd by the Insects." He was not so lost as he thought. A little boy approached with instructions from his mother to guide Deane to the Suffolk road. He said that the English were asking for Deane by name. Simeon did not wish to become a trophy of war, the captured brother of America's former emissary to France.

With the boy's help, he reached the Suffolk road near Francis Farley's plantation. The route, however, was not safe. Too many British soldiers passed by, plundering farms and houses on their way to Suffolk. People piloted Deane from house to house, each person passing him on to another. He at last persuaded James Taylor to hide him "in the thick Swamp" until the British left. With a blanket for shelter and with food brought to him, he stayed more than a week "continually in the Swamp & almost ready to perish by such Millions of Insects." When he emerged, he had a beard, no stockings, torn clothing, and bare legs cut by briers. He had lost *Le Soucy*, her cargo of 360 hogsheads of tobacco, most of his merchandise, and £10,000 in currency.

While Deane waited under a blanket among the vines and stands of bamboo in the shadow of the swamp's big trees, the British destroyed Suffolk. A detachment of about four hundred men under Colonel George Garth marched to the Nansemond River. They found the unusually large collection of supplies which had attracted Sir George Collier to Virginia: more than 3,000 barrels, mostly pork, the rest flour and other provisions. With too little time and too few sailors to remove this hoard, the soldiers burned it. Stacked next to the wharves were hundreds of barrels of pine tar, pitch, turpentine, and rum. Men knocked the heads in and poured the contents over stockpiles of food, over wharves, and into the river. The fires they set consumed all but a few of Suffolk's one hundred frame houses, as well as its warehouses. Sheets of burning tar and pitch floated on the water. Exploding barrels of gunpowder threw burning timbers high into the air. Wind and water carried fire into the Dismal Swamp. For days, as flames moving through the swamp ignited tall reeds, people heard explosive bursts like running gunfire. On their way back to Portsmouth, soldiers drove ahead of them all the livestock they could find.

Sir Henry Clinton had ordered General Mathew to bring his troops back to New York by June 1. Seeking freedom, many slaves, perhaps five hundred, went to Portsmouth to leave with them. Some became seamen in privateers. One or more of the Dismal Swamp Company's slaves left Dismal Plantation. After the British were gone, the company paid "for carrying home a runaway Negro." Late on Monday, May 24, and in the dark morning hours of Tuesday, General Mathew's men went on board their transports. The British fired the shipyard. Keels, hulls, masts, and timbers sent up a bright flame as Commodore Collier's vessels set sail and left the Elizabeth River. The fleet spent one more day in Chesapeake Bay, then passed the capes and stood out to sea.

As the British departed, Williamsburg filled with people attending the spring session of the General Assembly. All rooms and beds were taken, if not by delegates and senators, by "Speculators and others of the same likeness," eager to witness the struggle over new land laws. Thomas Jefferson succeeded Patrick Henry as governor on June 1. Three times in 1777 and 1778 he had tried to win passage of measures to regulate the state's sales and grants of its western lands. Each time opponents deflected his proposal.

Jefferson wished to abrogate the vast colonial grants to companies and to groups of kinsmen and political allies. He envisioned a land office conveying public land to settlers more often, and to speculators less often, than in the past. He and George Mason had collaborated, dividing the labor of drafting bills to settle titles and to create a land office. These came before the delegates and senators in June 1779.

The legislators agreed upon rejecting the claims of the Indiana Company. Part of the urgency of fixing a policy came from a desire to thwart Pennsylvania speculators and others hoping to get Virginia's western territory. During the previous session, the General Assembly had made peace with Richard Henderson and his Transylvania scheme. Though claims based on private arrangements with Indian tribes, such as Henderson's purchase from Cherokees, were invalidated, the Assembly allotted to him 200,000 acres along the Green River in western Kentucky.

Jefferson's changes in the old system provoked more resistance. George Dabney, calling speculators "the greatest Enemies We have," explained: "the misfortune is the Example begins among our leaders." Jefferson later wrote about Mason's draft of a law: "His great object was to remove out of the way the great and numerous orders of council to the Ohio co. Loyal co. Mississipi co. Vandalia co. Indiana co. &c." This was Jefferson's wish, but Mason still worked to win confirmation of the Ohio Company's claim, with no more success than the Indiana Company had. Speculators and their friends were well represented in the Assembly. As the bills went through the House of Delegates and the Senate, Mason had good reason to fear that they would be "mutilated mangled & chop'd to Peices."

By the time the "act for establishing a Land office" emerged, it was almost a gift to speculators. It permitted purchase of public land with depreciated paper currency. Rules for surveys and conveyances favored speculators over settlers. Not surprisingly, after the Land Office opened in October, "People took out Warrants for vast Quantities of Land." Five months later, Fielding Lewis wrote: "I suppose five million acres are already granted, never was so fine a Country sold for so trifling a sum."

The "Act for adjusting and settling the titles of claimers" underwent fewer changes. Mason and Jefferson's draft declared void all orders of Council and entries for land west of the mountains except those already surveyed and patented. Only the Loyal Company and the Greenbrier Company would survive under this provision. But the act's wording cast doubt on the validity of all colonial grants of land not yet fully surveyed, and the Dismal Swamp Company's holdings were such a grant. The Assembly changed Mason and Jefferson's draft. The final act for settling titles omitted mention of the west and voided unsurveyed colonial grants. The act made one exception to this new rule: "except also a certain order of council for a tract of sunken grounds, commonly called the Dismal Swamp." The Assembly reserved to itself the power to determine the company's title. Obviously, the Dismal Swamp Company had friends in the legislature, and everyone knew that one of the partners was commander in chief of the Continental Army. Nevertheless, after the Land Office opened, many people took out warrants for acres of the Dismal Swamp, "knowing that the Company had lapsed the time allowed them by the Council under the former government."

With purchases, grants, settlements, and rival claims multiplying in the west, Virginians and North Carolinians agreed that fixing their boundary in the region had become a "necessary business." No one had more interest in the outcome than Dr. Thomas Walker, since the boundary of Virginia would also mark the southern line of the Loyal Company's tracts. Though "considerably beyond his grand climacteric," Walker said of himself, his wiry little body remained vigorous. His wife died in November 1778. Later that month the House of Delegates confirmed the Loyal Company's title to land already surveyed. In December he accepted appointment to serve as a commissioner to extend the line begun by William Byrd and continued by Joshua Fry and Peter Jefferson.

North Carolina chose commissioners led by Richard Henderson. The survey was to start in August 1779. During his visit to Williamsburg in the spring, Henderson saw Virginia's preparations for Walker's expedition: tents, utensils, provisions, arms and ammunition for chain carriers, line markers, packhorse men, and one hundred guards. Dr. Walker expected his fifteen-year-old son, Francis, to manage the Loyal Company's business someday. The boy accompanied the surveyors to get his first look at the west. Not relying solely on his own skills, Walker took another surveyor, James Michie, with him. But he spoke of "making great Haste, so that they may not wait to be very Accurate."

Early in August long lines of mounted men, with their packhorses, crossed the Blue Ridge. Pausing at Fort Chiswell, Walker wrote some letters about Loyal Company business. The men then rode into the mountains to meet Walker's fellow commissioner, Daniel Smith, and to find the North Carolinians "at the Beginning of the Line."

In 1749, Fry and Jefferson ended their survey at Steep Rock Creek, looking up at the Iron Mountains. Walker and Smith waited there for the North Carolinians, who came ten days late. Many trees had died in the preceding thirty years; no one could find markings by the earlier surveyors. The commissioners took observations with their Hadley's quadrants and azimuth compasses, then stipulated that they were on the line of 36°30′ of north latitude and that they were 329 surface miles or 319 air miles west of the beach above Currituck Inlet. On September 6 they began to extend their chains due west, they supposed, over the Iron Mountains, across the south fork of the Holston River, past Shelbys Fort, toward Moccasin Gap.

A week later, during a rainstorm, Richard Henderson sat in his leaky tent writing a letter. He warned the government of North Carolina not to grant Virginia's request that landholders' Virginia titles be confirmed by North Carolina wherever their property fell on the south side of the line. He already could see that the line ran north of settlements claimed by the Loyal Company. Here was a chance to overturn some of the "secret surveys" made long ago by "an old Land monger" who, even as Henderson sat writing, had his own tent pitched not far away. People who knew nothing of the Loyal Company, Henderson said, had settled in the region and started farms. Defying the company's claims, they had been treated with "Extreme Cruelty" by the "Damn'd Scotch-Irish Virginians in Office." He hoped that settlers, not the Loyal Company, would get title to land in North Carolina.

Henderson had predicted that news of the survey would cause "madness and rage" among Cherokees, Chickasaws, and Creeks. Walker and the Virginians also felt concern about Indians' reactions. The island in the Holston River, a customary place for meeting and trading by Virginians and Cherokees, fell on the North Carolina side of the line. In the last week of September, the commissioners met a delegation of Cherokees there. During the wait for the Indians' arrival from the valley of the Little Tennessee River, the North Carolinians began to complain that the boundary did not follow the proper parallel and ran too far south.

After Cherokee men from Chota reached the island, Dr. Walker addressed them, trying to put the best face on the surveyors' purpose. The next day, Onitositah, leader of the Upper Town Cherokees, replied. He said that he needed all his hunting grounds, extending northward from the Cherokee towns to the south bank of the Cumberland River and westward to its mouth on the Ohio. He hoped to keep his men away from the surveyors, but if this new line cut off any of his territory, he said, "'twill make me begin to think of what I was told some years ago by the Kings people." The British had warned him that if Americans won independence, "they would at last take all our hunting grounds and bring us to nothing." He hoped for "more compassion." Walker and Smith assured the Cherokees that Virginia "will not take any Land that you have a right to." The commissioners urged them to change from hunting wild game to raising livestock and to "live as we do." American independence promised not destruction but "a plentiful Trade." At the beginning of October, the surveyors resumed their progress westward.

After 5 miles, the parties stopped in Carter's Valley, 45 miles west of their starting point. Henderson and the North Carolinians insisted that the line ran about two and one-half miles south of its true course. Walker and Smith attributed his mistake to a change in the magnetic variation of the compass, perhaps caused by iron ore nearby. The Virginians tried to prove their case by letting Smith take two North Carolinians back eastward along the line they preferred, while Walker and Henderson continued westward. Every day's observation convinced Smith that the North Carolinians were wrong, but they remained adamant. On October 27, the parties were reunited as Smith caught up with Walker at Black Water Creek. Making more observations, Walker concluded not only that the North Carolinians erred in thinking the line too far south but that he too had miscalculated, running it too far north from the start. He proposed that they move the line two miles and ten seconds south. Henderson refused. Several days passed "in making observations, debating, and even abusing one another."

As the commissioners squabbled, they stood, without knowing it, more than 12 miles north of the line of 36°30′ of latitude. Walker's line was wrong, putting a strip of his own claim into North Carolina. Henderson's preferred line, two miles to the north, lay farther off a true course. Years later the surveyor and mathematician Andrew Ellicott wrote to the governor of Virginia about Walker's survey: "The accuracy of this work I have always considered at best but doubtful, owing to the mode and instruments made use of by those gentlemen." Since Walker failed to make correct allowances for magnetic deviation, his line did not run due west. The farther he went, the farther north of the true line he blazed his meandering boundary. Dr. Walker was in a hurry. He preferred a fixed, flawed line sooner to a perfect one later.

From Carter's Valley to Cumberland Gap, in the first two weeks of November, one file of chain carriers and packhorses followed Walker, while a little more than two miles away, another file followed Henderson. Crossing the Clinch River, they looked into water so clear they could see every fish and the river bottom at a depth of eight or ten feet. They climbed the long, steep range of Powell's Mountain. For the first time in thirty years Walker saw streams and heights he had named. In mid-November, they reached the well-traveled road running between steep cliffs—Cumberland Gap. Walker's line put it in Virginia; Henderson's put it in North Carolina. Henderson announced that the North Carolinians were quitting "this abortive undertaking."

Henderson went to Boonesborough for a few days, intending to keep his eye on the Virginia surveyors, then headed for French Lick on the Cumberland River. He and other speculators envisioned a town there, named for the dead war hero Francis Nash. Dr. Walker and the Virginians pushed their line westward from the Gap about 15 more miles, crossing Cumberland Mountain range and reaching Clear Fork. The guards began to complain about steep climbing; they sounded mutinous. Walker and Smith later reported to the House of Delegates that they considered giving up the survey at Clear Fork on November 22. But they knew that, farther west, settlers who thought themselves living in North Carolina held land reserved for Virginia's soldiers in the Continental Army. The commissioners wrote: "These, and some more of the like considerations, made us think it more conducive to the good of the State in general that we should keep on, than that we should return." They chose to skip a mountainous segment, make a detour using the Cumberland River, then resume their survey farther west on its bank, "where by reason of many People being about to settle, it might be of importance to run the line speedily." They turned north to reach the upper Cumberland. At the river's edge, they built canoes for themselves and their baggage, resting their thin, hungry horses. On New Year's Day snow began to fall.

The next day, hunters shot wild turkeys. On the third, under an overcast sky, snow on the ground rose above the men's ankles. Hunters killed six bison. More days of snow and bitter cold followed. Wind built deep drifts. The Cumberland froze—"a River," Walker said, "never known to be frozen before." The Virginians had no way to foresee in November, as they chose to push westward, that the first months of 1780 would bring to North America its coldest winter in forty years. In easternmost Virginia the waters of Chesapeake Bay froze "almost to the Capes," locking vessels in ice, which sank many. On January 15, Dr. Walker celebrated his sixty-fifth birthday. Daniel Smith reported: "The old Gentleman is in good health and stands fatigue surprizingly."

Unable to move downriver, they remained in camp for six weeks; out of deep snowdrifts they carved spaces for their tents. Large fires burned day and night; yet the surrounding snowbanks did not recede. To fish, they cut through a foot and a half of ice on the surface of the Cumberland. Each morning they found the hole frozen solid. Hungry opossums and raccoons entered their tents at night. The men lived on fish, venison, and other meat. In Walker's mess, his son, Francis, cooked, spending his days hunting game. Dr. Walker, lover of tall stories and practical jokes, allowed no gloom. He could not use one of his favorite stunts: boiling a rattlesnake in a coffeepot, serving coffee, then pulling out the dead snake. But he might retell his authentic account of a hard march in the last war, when commissaries went alongside cows following the army and cut out steaks as the cows walked. Francis never saw his father in better form, showing "all that life & good humour which we were kept alive by in the woods."

In mid-February a thaw let their canoes move downriver. A few miles north of the mouth of the Obey River, Walker and Smith chose a spot on the west bank of the Cumberland to resume their survey. They calculated that they were 109 miles west of the point where they had stopped in November; the true distance was 97 miles. They divided their labor. Smith continued overland with the survey while Walker's party went down the Cumberland to produce "a tolerable Map" of "a fine River." On his journey, Walker paused at French Lick to write William Preston about securing "such Lands as may bring me my money" and to say that he was "very Hearty," with hopes of returning east of the mountains in April.

Smith joined Walker at French Lick, having run the line 131 miles from the point where the Cumberland crossed it flowing southward to the point where the Cumberland crossed it again flowing northward. With some modifications, their irregular line remains the boundary between Kentucky and Tennessee. Together they floated down the Cumberland to their line and surveyed nine more miles to the bank of the Tennessee River. They did not know that on the Cumberland their survey had reached 36°40'—ten minutes of latitude off the true line. Their boundary continued to run erratically north of west until it struck the Tennessee.

The commissioners then headed homeward. But on April 7, 1780, they met a messenger bearing a letter from Governor Jefferson written nine weeks earlier, while they were snowbound. The state of Virginia wished to build a fort on the Mississippi River, near the mouth of the Ohio. Receiving instructions and assistance from George Rogers Clark at the falls of the Ohio, the commissioners were to find the point where Virginia's boundary met the Mississippi River and "fix it by some lasting immoveable natural mark" so that it could be found easily in the future, "which may perhaps be of importance."

Walker and Smith went down the Ohio to its mouth, then followed the Mississippi to a double set of switchbacks in its convoluted course. There, on May 9 and 10, they took out their quadrant and compass to end the line William Byrd, his fellow Virginians, and their surly counterparts from North Carolina had begun on the sand above Currituck Inlet in 1728.

Two months later, Walker and Smith stopped in Harrodsburg, just short of the Kentucky River, on their way eastward. They parted on July 22. By the time Dr. Walker and his son reached Castle Hill, they had been away from home for a year. Upon his return, Walker busied himself with establishing the Loyal Company's claims. In the midst of this paperwork, he concluded that two years as a widower were enough. The day before his sixty-sixth birthday he got married—as he put it, "I intermarried with Mrs. Elizabeth Thornton, an old sweetheart of mine."

As, in August 1780, Dr. Walker reacquainted himself with the comforts of Castle Hill, his longtime acquaintance and peacetime merchant in London, Samuel Gist, watched consternation spread through the underwriters' room at Lloyd's. Word arrived that the consolidated outbound convoy of East India and West India merchant vessels had been taken by the combined Spanish and French fleet under the command of Lieutenant-General Luis de Córdoba. Like the Stock Exchange, Lloyd's had a reputation for being "the Sport of False News & Fables." But this news was true.

Sailing before the wind, with the southerly set of the Canaries current, Captain John Moutray in HMS *Ramillies* escorted five large East India ships, as well as eighteen ships with troops, provisions, and equipment, and forty merchant vessels bound for the West Indies. Moutray also had two frigates: HMS *Thetis* and HMS *Southampton*. Ten days from Spithead, as the convoy was about 530 miles west of the Straits of Gibraltar, sailing for Madeira 230 miles to the south, seamen sighted at midnight the lights of strange ships ahead. Moutray signaled the convoy to change course and follow him westward, sailing close to the wind. The men-of-war and three merchant ships came round. Instead of following the lights of HMS *Ramillies*, the rest of the convoy continued to sail before the wind. At dawn on August 9 they found themselves near thirty-three Spanish and French warships. Only five merchantmen escaped. At the end of the month the people of Cádiz were treated to the spectacle of more than 2,800 British prisoners disembarking: soldiers, seamen, women of the army, and passengers, including "married and unmarried ladies of condition."

Two weeks after the capture, a visitor to the Royal Exchange wrote: "It has been a black week at Loyd's." Thirty years later, men still recalled the "many failures of Underwriters" following loss of that convoy. They spoke of a loss of £1,500,000. Even if that estimate looked too round and too large, the blow was severe. More bad news arrived on Monday, August 28. The outward bound convoy for Québec had been intercepted and dispersed in July by American privateers off the banks of Newfoundland. Somehow, a veteran privateering captain "had the most exact information concerning all our outward and homeward bound fleets, with the ships appointed for their convoy, and even in what longitude and latitude they were to part company." Twenty-two vessels were taken, most of them said to be worth £30,000 each. Underwriters' losses neared £400,000, rumor reported. London merchants asked Lord George Germain to provide better convoys.

Samuel Gist was not among the underwriters who became casualties of these disasters. As in his tobacco transactions, his skills as an insurer made him seem lucky. Early in 1778, Harry Clarke, a broker at Lloyd's, had worked the room in search of underwriters willing to insure cargo in the *Janet Laurie* for £1,500 from the Firth of Clyde to Jamaica. He had "much difficulty" because "our underwriters are very shy of West India risques," especially winter risks, beginning on August 1, the start of hurricane season. He eventually collected fourteen subscribers. Samuel Gist took a line for £100. John Sherer was one of two underwriters who took a line for £150. The following month Sherer subscribed for £200 on the *Jamaica Pollock* and £150 on the *Friendship*, both on the Clyde-Jamaica route. Gist did not join him. Before the war ended, everyone learned that Sherer had overextended. His name appeared on the list of bankrupts. The same fate befell John Walter, who had joined Sherer in taking lines on the policies of the *Jamaica Pollock* and the *Friendship*. Walter said: "I was 12 years an underwriter in Lloyd's Coffee House, and subscribed my name to 6 millions of property; but was weighed down, in common with above half those who were engaged in the protection of property, by the host of foes this nation had to combat in the American War." For some ruined by the war, the consequences were fatal. *The Gentleman's Magazine* published an obituary of "Mr. Delarive, a policy broker, whose death was accelerated by a run of ill success in the alley, a heavy loss in a large cargo of Irish provisions returned upon his hands from France, and the dangerous illness of a young woman who lived with him, and of whom he was doatingly fond." Some underwriters and brokers, though not facing bankruptcy, looked at their losses, then "quitted the Coffee-house."

Notwithstanding many failures, Lloyd's flourished during the war. By 1778 the number of men frequenting the rooms to "speculate in insurances" was said to be six hundred. Some, including Gist, made fortunes. In France, marine insurance premiums fluctuated around 50 percent. In Spain, underwriters often refused to insure transatlantic risks. At Lloyd's, premiums seldom ran so high as on the Continent. Even when they did, a "Merchant of Character" willing to pay could almost always get a policy, "every Risk having its Price." Of the 6,000 British vessels at sea during the war, almost 2,400 were lost to the enemy. But owners of the other 3,600 paid underwriters between 10 and 30 percent of the insured value of vessel and cargo for each voyage, as did owners of lost vessels. One merchant wrote: "the underwriters have had great losses, but they have had enormous premiums; and when the captains of merchantmen have done their duty, by sticking by the men of war appointed to convoy them, few have miscarried." Rates shipowners charged for freight rose at the same time that insurance premiums and seamen's wages did.

Shrewd underwriters shielded themselves. They largely abandoned a peacetime practice: accepting large premiums to insure vessels already at sea but late in arriving. They refused to pay policies on captured ships if the ship had left convoy, as many did in hope of a quick run to a good market. Almost five hundred vessels taken by the enemy were retaken. A vessel recaptured by the Royal Navy might become a prize for the man-of-war's officers and crew. Underwriters did not pay in such instances. Of course, the courts heard many cases between underwriters and policyholders.

Samuel Gist appeared in court sometimes as plaintiff and sometimes as defendant. After he refused to pay a policy on a captured vessel which, he said, had not joined a convoy as the owner had warranted she would, the owner sued him. The jury found for the plaintiff. Gist asked the Court of King's Bench for a new trial. After hearing testimony from masters of several ships, Lord Mansfield said from the bench, "This case is very clear," and ruled against Gist.

But Gist won another case when he sued several shipowners to force them to pay premiums they had agreed to pay but had withheld. The owners argued that Gist could not recover these premiums in court because the vessels, flying a flag of a neutral nation, were transporting provisions from Ireland to West Indian islands occupied by the French. The owners—the defendants—said that "this kind of trading was so notoriously illegal that the plaintiff must have known it to be so." The policy therefore ought to be void. But the jury found for Gist, and the Court of King's Bench refused to order a new trial. As did Gist, Lord Mansfield saw benefits in allowing men at Lloyd's to insure trade with the enemy "because," he said from the bench, "you hold the box, and are sure of getting the premiums at least, as a certain profit." Gist held the box throughout the war.

He kept his touch as a tobacco dealer. In July 1776, he held 195 hogsheads; in February 1782, he had 69. He also handled on consignment the sale of tobacco on behalf of loyalist merchants in American cities occupied by the British. He disposed of one shipment early in 1779 at twice the price the owners had paid in New York. Gist's chief rivals in profitable tobacco dealing were the firm of Champion, Dickason & Company. Despite its name, it no longer had a Champion in it because Alexander and Benjamin Champion had "left the Company & become Insurance Brokers."

The French made large purchases of tobacco in 1777 before they entered the war. When the price rose to 120 shillings per hundredweight—£100 per hogshead—Gist sold more of the hogsheads he had imported so eagerly in 1775. He did not report to Virginians who had consigned it to him that he received such high prices. He later told Moss Armistead & Company of Petersburg that in November 1777 he had sold their 20 hogsheads for a total of £406 4s. 2d. The firm of Jones & Watson fared still worse at his hands. Their 22 hogsheads, which he had acknowledged receiving, vanished from his records. He spared them the insult of the tuppence.

Across America Square from Gist, William Molleson was in trouble. His firm had imported more than four and a half times as much tobacco as Gist did in 1775. But in the following years Molleson suffered more from unpaid American debts, and the tobacco, or his method of turning it to account, did not serve the firm so well as Gist made his tobacco serve him. In the City, rumor said of Molleson: "it is supposed that instead of carrying on his mercantile business, he had commenced politician, and ruined thereby the fairest prospects." He gave up his business offices, then his home. Gist no longer saw him in America Square. In May 1778, Molleson stopped payment, called his creditors together, and opened his books. The creditors apparently did not force him into bankruptcy, but his days as London's leading tobacco merchant had ended.

Gist set aside more money to buy consolidated annuities, the most important vehicle for the British national debt and Gist's most secure investment. No one knew how much profit successful underwriters made during the war. Royal Exchange Assurance and the other chartered company, London Assurance, together did about 10 percent of the City's marine underwriting. Royal Exchange Assurance saw its average annual net income rise from £8,100 in 1771–75 to £29,700 in 1776–80. Gist and others at Lloyd's underwrote higher risks than the chartered companies accepted and charged premiums accordingly. With contractors, such as Anthony Bacon, they were among the most important subscribers to the growing public debt by which Lord North financed the war. Charles Greville, in May 1778, reported on their profit: "The distress of the public & the necessary douceurs raise the Loans of the year to 8 per Cent." While keeping much capital available for mercantile and insurance purposes, Gist, according to a man who knew him, had put £100,000 into government securities by the end of the wartime boom in business at Lloyd's.

· · ·

Samuel Gist, William Molleson, Anthony Bacon, and other London merchants trading to Chesapeake Bay before the war welcomed news that British forces had invaded Virginia again in the autumn of 1780. The merchants hoped that this time the army would stay.

On Friday, October 20, 1780, Admiral Sir George Brydges Rodney's four men-of-war and two galleys, with transports bearing 2,500 soldiers and with a flotilla of schooners, sailed into the bay. Major General Alexander Leslie expected to unite this force with the army under Earl Cornwallis moving northward through the Carolinas. Leslie "inwardly suspected" that Cornwallis would summon him away from the Norfolk region. Nevertheless, he brought from New York loyalist families seeking to reclaim their property. They began "settling themselves," trusting that they were secure. Their knowledge of the James, Elizabeth, and Nansemond rivers made them "very useful" to Rodney. Once more, James Parker saw the ruins of his former home and of his stores in Norfolk as he helped the British Army punish the buckskins. Loyalists who had stayed in Virginia were at first "shy" about welcoming Leslie, recalling how briefly the British had visited the year before. But they were told that Portsmouth would become "a military post." They expressed satisfaction; some men volunteered to take up arms. Leslie wrote: "it hurts me *once* more to come here, and then to forsake them; but I see the Necessity of it."

Cavalry and infantry ranged over Princess Anne County's flat, sandy expanses and along roads bordering the Dismal Swamp. They went to Suffolk and into Isle of Wight County; a detachment landed at Hampton. They plundered and burned houses, taking horses for new mounts and cattle to be slaughtered and salted. General Thomas Nelson, Jr., worked to assemble a force of militia, but Virginians' main hope was that the British "will soon Imbarke & leave our Capes Clair again." Black people accompanied the soldiers back to Portsmouth to leave with them.

General Leslie received orders to take his force to Charleston, and his men began to embark on Saturday, November 11. For four days Leslie pretended that he would leave a garrison at Portsmouth: "Refugees & followers of the Army were ignorant of my design to Evacuate the place." Wednesday, his last day ashore, loyalists and blacks knew that all the soldiers were about to go. Leslie reported: "The last twenty-four hours was an unpleasant time." Virginia troops entering Portsmouth Thursday morning met "Great numbers of negroes." Admiral Rodney's vessels remained in the bay another week. He felt sorry that the king's friends around Norfolk "will again experience persecution for their loyalty." On Thursday, the 23rd, he sailed for Charleston.

James Parker and two other loyalists in the king's service accompanied Leslie's "tedious and turbulent" three-week voyage to Charleston. Learning that another invading force had entered Chesapeake Bay five weeks after their departure, they headed back to Virginia "to be usefull in that part of America, from their Connections and Knowledge of the Country." But after Parker and his friends sailed back to the capes on board HMS *Romulus*, their frigate was captured by French men-of-war under the command of Captain Arnaud Le Gardeur de Tilly. Virginia's delegates in Congress asked French officers to hold these loyalists "in the most effectual manner" as "state Prisoners." Parker spent the next eighteen months in a series of cells: on board a French prison ship, in a dungeon in Saint-Domingue, and in close confinement in the citadel of Dinan, then in the castle of Saint-Mâlo on the northern coast of Brittany. He never again tried to control the Dismal Swamp.

The British soldiers arriving in the bay at the end of December 1780 were commanded by the newly commissioned Brigadier General Benedict Arnold. Three months earlier, while a major general in the Continental Army, he had narrowly escaped arrest after George Washington learned that he was in the pay of the British. Sir Henry Clinton gave the defector a British commission and sent him to attack Virginia. Arnold's first campaign in service to the king did not begin well. Still at sea, his force was hit by a northwest gale. Sailing into Chesapeake Bay, a man-of-war, HMS *Charon*, ran aground on the shoal which jutted from Willoughby Point east of the Elizabeth River. She spent the night on the mud, giving naval officers time to agree that "intelligent pilots" were "much wanted to conduct the ships and troops up James River." For the next seven months, British soldiers moved up and down the James, raiding into the countryside.

Until Major General William Phillips arrived three months later with 2,000 more men, Arnold and his 1,600 soldiers showed their flag. They could not do much to suppress rebellion, but they punished rebels. Arnold began with Mary Willing Byrd, harming her not by destroying Westover but by making it his base for a raid on the new state capital, Richmond. Arnold's wife, Margaret Shippen Arnold, colleague in his treason, was Mary Byrd's cousin. At Westover, his officers received "a very good breakfast." The force he took to Richmond demolished arms, ammunition, tobacco, other supplies, and several buildings, then returned. When the British departed, some of Mary Byrd's slaves went with them. Her light sufferings raised new suspicions that she was a Tory, which grew after Virginians heard that an officer serving in HMS *Swift*, Lieutenant Charles Hare, brother of a brother-in-law of Mary Byrd's, had brought in his cabin not only many letters from her but also a cache of merchandise obviously designed to support the Byrds at Westover: china, linen, broadcloth, port, brandy, and other goods. After his first raid, Arnold dropped downriver to reoccupy the familiar British lines around Portsmouth. His men entered the town, he reported, "to the great joy of the inhabitants." A junior officer wrote in his diary: "The whole town had been abandoned by its inhabitants, except for three families."

In February, some of Arnold's soldiers were "spreading ruin in the area and severely harassing the few good loyalists." About 250 black people entered his lines. He put them to work repairing earlier fortifications and erecting new ones. Militiamen did not rally in numbers large enough to endanger his force. On March 26, Major General Phillips arrived in the bay with 2,000 men. The following month Phillips and Arnold took a large force up the Appomattox River to Petersburg "to break up the communication from Virginia to Carolina." From the heights where Samuel Gist's agent, Thomas Shore, lived they dispersed the militia with expert artillery fire, then burned warehouses, vessels in the river, and 4,000 hogsheads of tobacco. Slaves showed the British where white people had concealed themselves and their property. British officers took spoils of war down the Appomattox and the James, but they soon had to return to Petersburg to meet Cornwallis. By the time this force arrived from North Carolina on May 20, Phillips had died of typhoid fever. Arnold returned to New York.

Ever since Arnold had left Westover in January, Mary Byrd had proclaimed her innocence of any loyalist sentiments or collaboration with the enemy. She knew that she was "much watch'd." An officer accosted her in her bedroom, seeking incriminating papers. Someone tried to burn the mansion at Westover. Her husband's last years had been embittered by such "persecutors." She wrote to Thomas Jefferson: "I cannot express violent, enthusiastic opinions, and wish curses [and] distruction on the meanest individual on earth. It is against my religion. I wish well to all mankind, to America in particular. What am I but an American?" Unluckily for her, the first stop for Earl Cornwallis's army after he left Petersburg on May 24, 1781, was Westover.

Almost 4,000 men camped in the once pristine meadows spread along the James. The soldiers tore down fences, turned horses loose in fields of ripening wheat, made Mary Byrd's garden nursery a stable for the general's horses, knocked her milk cows on the head and butchered them before her eyes. In her house, at the foot of the carved balustrade on the central staircase, Cornwallis posted guards to protect her "if she remained quiet and kept to the upper stories." He promised that she would be compensated by someone. He said he had no cash.

The Marquis de Lafayette arrived in Virginia with three Continental Army regiments—not enough to challenge Cornwallis but enough, with militia and new Continentals, to make the British notice. Since Cornwallis originally was supposed to secure Britain's hold in the deeper South, no one, not even his superior, Sir Henry Clinton, could tell what he expected to accomplish by marching here and there in Virginia. After three nights, his army headed northward. With the soldiers went forty-nine slaves from Westover. Although no one dared to say it to her face, Mary Byrd knew about "those who tauntingly say aye you see how well her good Friends the British has done for her & Laugh & say all she'll ever get will be promises." The following year she wrote: "extreme grief found its way to my heart— conscious rectitude, alone has saved me from the grave."

In the last week of May and the first week of June, Cornwallis sent raiding parties westward under Lieutenant Colonel John Graves Simcoe and Lieutenant Colonel Banastre Tarleton. Along the Pamunkey and Mattaponi rivers, Cornwallis's chief concern seemed to be destroying tobacco, supplies, and other property. Lieutenant James Hadden wrote from Westover: "Tobacco, alone has gained the Rebels Allies, and I hope the destruction of it will give the Rebellion a severe check." One detachment visited Samuel Gist's plantation in Hanover County. His agent, Benjamin Toler, watched as soldiers burned 12 hogsheads of tobacco and took away five horses and sixteen head of cattle, as well as brandy, bacon, and corn. About forty of Gist's slaves left with the British. By applying to higher-ranking officers, Toler got all but two of the black people returned to slavery on the plantation. To any officer who would listen he mentioned "in a particular manner" that "Samuel Gist then was a british subject residing in London."

The legislature had abandoned Richmond to convene in Charlottesville on Monday, June 4. Sunday night, at Castle Hill, Dr. Thomas Walker played host to Newman Brockenbrough, a member of the House of Delegates, Senator John Syme, former partner in the Dismal Swamp Company, and Judge Peter Lyons, who was still protecting Samuel Gist's interests. Early Monday morning, Walker came into the bedroom Brockenbrough and Lyons shared. He told them that the British had come to Castle Hill. If they lay still, Tarleton might not know they were in the house. Looking out an upstairs window, Lyons saw a yard full of soldiers. He went back to bed. Tarleton had come to Albemarle County in search of legislators and Governor Jefferson. Soon all Dr. Walker's guests were summoned downstairs.

Banastre Tarleton, by the age of twenty-seven, had shown himself to be arrogant and cruel. He had grown up in comfort, the son of a leading Liverpool slave trader. Contrary to his new prisoners' fears, he gave them "polite Treatment." Tarleton and his men ate breakfast at Castle Hill. A detachment rode to Belvoir, home of Dr. Walker's son, John. There the British found another partner in the Dismal Swamp Company, William Nelson, Jr., his brother, Robert, and John Walker's son-in-law, Francis Kinloch, a delegate to the Continental Congress. Tarleton released Lyons, Syme, the Nelsons, and other officeholders the same day, after they signed paroles promising not to act contrary to the interests of George III until exchanged for prisoners held by Americans. Kinloch and Brockenbrough were released a few days later. Tarleton's stay with Dr. Walker gave extra time for word of his approach to reach Charlottesville and Monticello. The legislators adjourned to meet at Staunton in the Shenandoah Valley. Jefferson left home to evade Tarleton's men. The British burned his tobacco, did the usual damage to his estate, and departed, accompanied by thirty of Jefferson's slaves. His term as governor had expired four days earlier, and the legislators had not found leisure to re-elect him or to choose a successor. He served no longer. On June 12, delegates meeting in Staunton elected Thomas Nelson, Jr. Ten years had passed since his father had so much enjoyed a stint as acting governor between the death of Lord Botetourt and the arrival of Lord Dunmore.

During late June and early July, Cornwallis's force moved down the James River, crossing it south of Williamsburg. With few exceptions, the slaves of "all those who were near the enemy" left plantations to accompany the British. As this slow column reached the Nansemond River and the Dismal Swamp in mid-July, soldiers and black refugees suffered from heat "so intense that one can hardly breathe," from thunderstorms, and from "billions of sand-[flies] and biting-flies." After horse flies dispersed, chiggers attacked. Some soldiers looked "like people who are seized with smallpox." For a week the army lay in and around the ruins of Suffolk.

Lord Cornwallis knew that Virginians had rebuilt part of their trade through South Quay. He ordered Lieutenant Colonel Thomas Dundas to take part of the 80th Regiment, the Royal Edinburgh Volunteers, on a day's march to South Quay to destroy it. The soldiers burned warehouses, tobacco, rum, sugar, coffee, wine, and other goods. They took every horse they found and "plundered the inhabitants in a most cruel manner."

Before Cornwallis moved to Portsmouth on July 21 and 22, British soldiers visited Dismal Plantation and left the Dismal Swamp Company's efforts in ruins. Eight draft steers used for heavy work, fifty-two head of cattle, two hundred barrels of corn, twenty-seven hoes, fourteen axes, eight dozen crosscut files and whipsaw files used in making shingles—all the company's means of working the swamp vanished with the raiding party. The soldiers did "great damage" to several buildings on Dismal Plantation, especially to barns. Almost all able-bodied slaves went out of the swamp with the British: a woman, a twelve-year-old girl, four small children, and twenty-two men. Eleven men, six women, and three children stayed on the plantation. The company's new agent, Jacob Collee, considered only five of them "fit for any kind of Labour." After Cornwallis withdrew into fortified lines around Portsmouth, Collee wrote to David Jameson about Dismal Plantation: "There seems a very promiseing crop Corn & a little Rice, but how its to be got in, I know not, as well as how matters are to be conducted in future, for want of help." Governor Nelson wrote to Lord Cornwallis about the large number of black people with the British, asking whether slaveowners could reclaim them. Cornwallis replied that any Virginian who had not borne arms or held office in the rebellion and who promised never to do so could come to camp and claim his slaves "if they are willing to go with him."

Sir Henry Clinton received from Lord George Germain, secretary of state for the colonies, an order to keep Cornwallis's army in the Chesapeake. Clinton directed him to establish a fortified base accessible to the Royal Navy. Cornwallis's engineers improved the elaborate works at Portsmouth, connecting redoubts and salient angles by deep trenches, erecting palisaded stakes surrounded with strong abatis, logs studded with long spikes. Within these lines, among burnt keels of unfinished vessels, skeletal remains of stocks in the shipyard, and the brick ruins of Robert Tucker's mills, more than 1,000 black people lived on army rations. After consulting with Captain Charles Hudson of HMS *Richmond*, Cornwallis decided that his fortified base should be at York Town. Evacuation of Portsmouth began on July 30. By then, smallpox was spreading among the black refugees.

In London, Samuel Gist, Anthony Bacon, and their fellow merchants formerly in the Virginia trade learned that Lord George Germain had ordered occupation of the Chesapeake and that Lord Dunmore had received the king's command to return to Virginia and resume his governorship. These merchants wished the ministry to remember them when drawing up Dunmore's instructions. In a memorial they reminded Germain that before the war they had given "large and extensive credits" to colonists, promoting a trade making the manufactures and commerce of Britain "the envy and admiration of all Europe." Interruption of trade since 1775 meant that "there remains large sums of money now due to your memorialists to their great loss and prejudice." They urged that Dunmore be instructed to assist them "in the protection of their property and towards the recovery of their just debts."

Lord Cornwallis moved his headquarters to York Town, leaving Brigadier General Charles O'Hara in command of the evacuation of Portsmouth. A flotilla of transports, escorted by HMS *Charon* and other men-of-war, plied between Portsmouth and York Town for more than two weeks, shifting soldiers and some black laborers to the new base. Loyalists from Norfolk and Princess Anne counties also went. The sufferings of "Hundreds of wretched Negroes" dying of smallpox distressed O'Hara. He shrank from "abandoning these unfortunate beings to disease, to famine, & what is worse than either, the resentment of their enraged Masters." In the last days of his stay, O'Hara moved the remaining four hundred black refugees to the Norfolk side of the Elizabeth River and left them with food for fifteen days, "which time, will either kill, or cure the greatest number of them." The last of the Portsmouth garrison left on August 20. Later, British officers drew up an inspection roll of "Negro emigrants" in New York. It included a number of black people who gave the word "Dismal" as part of their names, in the manner of the sometime slave of the Burwell family, Jack Dismal. If these people, like Jack Dismal, were former slaves of the Dismal Swamp Company, some of the company's laborers made their way out of the United States and out of slavery with the British evacuation in 1783.

Fielding Lewis's brother-in-law, the commander in chief, was planning a *coup de main*. Days before General O'Hara left Portsmouth, Washington learned that Rear Admiral the Comte de Grasse would bring twenty-eight men-of-war and more than 3,000 French soldiers to Chesapeake Bay. Having worked hard for American victory, Fielding Lewis could welcome the prospect of capturing Lord Cornwallis's army. But his declining health denied him the fullest enjoyment of his brother-in-law's greatest success.

During the hot months of 1780, Lewis traveled to the mountains for "a change of air." He had been ill since the fall of 1779. But his health did not improve in the mountains. Back at home, he remained indoors for seven months late in 1780 and early in 1781. From his windows he could see dark, undulating clouds of birds arrive in Fredericksburg, first on their way south late in autumn, then returning northward in spring.

Many worries offset in Lewis's mind his successes in the small arms factory, the little Virginia navy, and the cargoes of Fielding Lewis & Company. Beyond his old debt to Anthony Bacon, he had run up large new debts by operating the arms factory on his own credit, while the state failed to reimburse him. He also had borrowed money on Virginia's behalf—between £30,000 and £40,000, including £7,000 he lent to the state. Without his efforts the factory would have closed, he said; yet in February 1781 he found himself writing to the state treasurer: "I have distressed myself greatly, and at this time am not able to pay the collector my Taxes, and continue my business in the usual manner." Training and regulating skilled workers with a strict regimen, Lewis's partner, Charles Dick, turned out one hundred stand of new arms per month and repaired many old weapons. Displeased with the state's tardiness in paying, Lewis and Dick resigned at the end of 1780, but Governor Jefferson insisted that Dick continue to serve.

Fielding Lewis wrote gloomy letters to his brother-in-law. His second son, Fielding Junior, was still a spendthrift at the age of thirty. His fifth son, George, had embarrassed himself in the Continental Army by inattention to duty, for which he drew a brusque reprimand from his uncle the commander in chief; George Lewis resigned several months later. Fielding Lewis wrote about things of which George Washington already knew: "injustice, luxury, and extravagancy" throughout Virginia; Congress's admission of fiscal desperation by its devaluation of Continental currency, setting the value of $40 in paper at $1; high prices for imported goods, which only speculators could now afford; "the ignorance of our Assembly" and "the ignorance or villany of the Assessors," whose actions seemed to aim at "the destruction of the large Estates in Lands & Negro's," while people who once "were needy and had little or nothing to support them, are now the best able to live, they give greater prices at Sales than any other people, dress better & I believe keep as good tables." A chicken cost $1,000 in Virginia paper. Although in 1780 Lewis bought 30,000 acres in Kentucky, partly to acquire something tangible in exchange for his depreciating currency, he saw during his long confinement in his splendid new house that he would never be a King Carter. Looking back over the twenty years since he and George Washington first had taken an interest in the Dismal Swamp, he wrote: "I have generally been mistaken in my speculations."

In the face of censure in Parliament, Lewis's partner and creditor, Anthony Bacon, did not give up without a delaying action. The more difficulties the army and the navy encountered, the more troubles Lord North's ministry met in the House of Commons. Among its most vulnerable allies were the members who held government contracts. Bacon received contracts for provisions and artillery ammunition in 1779. He expanded his iron manufactures in Wales in 1780 by leasing the Hirwaun Works, six miles west of Merthyr Tydfil, repairing them and working them "vigorously." Bacon's beloved, illegitimate family continued to grow. In 1780, Mary Bushby gave him another son, whom he named for his late brother, the Reverend Thomas Bacon.

The opposition stepped up attacks on "those who have fattened on the ruins of the country by jobs and contracts." The Earl of Shelburne accused such men of prolonging the war in order to enrich themselves. In March 1781, John Sawbridge, member for the City of London, charged Lord North with buying support in the House by allowing members to take up part of the government's new loan. No one contradicted him or called him to order for unparliamentary speech. The ministry could outvote but not refute its critics. All knew that, when North lost his majority, the next ministry would at once exclude contractors from Parliament.

In 1781 and 1782, Anthony Bacon gave up some contracts by not seeking renewal and transferred others. The shifts, for example, to his cousin and former partner, Anthony Richardson, did not look convincing. One critic put Bacon's name in a list of contractors who made transfers, and wrote that by holding no contracts in their own names "they think to get re-elected; but can any person suppose that they have really & bonafide no concern in them. . . . It is impossible & absurd." Bacon withdrew from many business concerns at the age of sixty-five. Forty years had passed since his sailing days, when he commanded the *York*, with a cargo of felons bound for servitude in Maryland. Forty years after that voyage, Anthony Bacon and Fielding Lewis, transatlantic associates who apparently never met, understood that they would begin no new enterprises.

Growing angrier about property taxes, Fielding Lewis thought not only of his own assessment for his mansion in Fredericksburg, more than £2,500 Virginia currency, but also of the assessment on Mannsfield, the estate outside Fredericksburg where his friend Mann Page had settled after giving Rosewell to John Page. Mann Page and his son of the same name had to pay Spotsylvania County £4,000.

Less active in the Revolution than Lewis, Mann Page, who turned sixty-two in 1780, still owed debts inherited from his father and debts contracted to maintain Rosewell. If peace had returned at once, he could hardly have convinced John Norton that his debt ever would be paid. Page's contemporaries dwindled in number. Robert Carter Nicholas died in September 1780, fourteen years after offering himself as savior of Virginia's treasury from the malfeasance of Speaker Robinson. Robinson's critics, after taking power, had proven far more imaginative than the old speaker in their use of currency. Virginia's solvency now rested upon a law requiring creditors to receive depreciated paper money at face value. The new government had shown Charles Greville to be wrong in predicting America's failure at the start of the war, when he asked: "how can paper currency support its credi[t?] . . . people cannot for a long while give up reality for paper when its value diminishes dayly." Page's former partner in the Dismal Swamp Company, Robert Burwell, father of John Page's wife, had died in 1777, without having paid the dowry he had promised. The years after his death showed that his son and heir, Nathaniel Burwell, fared worse than Fielding Lewis, Jr.; "much addicted . . . to gambling," he soon dissipated his inheritance and later "died insolvent." As Robert Burwell's executor, his nephew, Thomas Nelson, Jr., assumed the burden of dealing with large debts owed by Burwell's estate.

Mann Page was pained by recriminations from his son, John. In 1779, Mann sold land around Tappahannock he once had promised to John. He did so, he explained, "to see if I cou'd pay off the Debts I had contracted" and still bequeath some money to his two younger sons. But John accused him of "injustice" and questioned his father's affection for him. Had Mann, his son asked, concluded that John was "less deserving"? Mann wrote: "I answer no & at the time I did it, had left you an equivalent by giving you my part of the Dismal & a Tract of Frying Pan, & after Christmas to give up those Plantations in Gloster." But John Page was not mollified by a gift of land in Gloucester County yielding too little tobacco, of King Carter's old copper mines near the Potomac, or of half a share in the Dismal Swamp Company.

Mann Page rightly suspected that his son suffered "great anxiety of Mind." John had led the Virginia Council since the beginning of the Revolution, burdened with the public's work, always in danger of prostration by an attack of vertigo. His familial obligations widened. His sister, Judith Burwell, died in September 1777, followed in March 1779 by her husband, Page's friend and neighbor, the gouty, fox-hunting Lewis Burwell, who left behind "a badly managed Estate." Page became executor of their "confused Affairs." He brought his four young Burwell nieces and nephews to live at Rosewell with the seven Page children. Large as his mansion was, so many children lived in it that he sometimes lost count and said he was caring for five little Burwells, whom he called "untractable Wards." Page resigned from the Council early in 1780, but he still performed the duties of "Executor, Guardian, Tutor, Vestry Man, Magistrate, Field Officer of Militia, & Delegate." Not to receive from his father the land and slaves at Tappahannock he had expected came as a blow at a difficult time.

Mann Page worried about bequests for his younger children because he had achieved no better success with his speculations than had Fielding Lewis. Hanover-Town on the Pamunkey River did not thrive. Twenty years after its charter, Page still owned two-thirds of the "valuable Lots on the principal streets." He died in November 1780, leaving an estate consisting chiefly of old debts.

The day after Lord Cornwallis's army surrendered at York Town, Fielding Lewis, knowing he was near death, wrote his will. His bequests divided his lands among his six sons, leaving his mansion and the land in and around Fredericksburg in the hands of his wife during her lifetime. In the past ten months Fielding and Betty Lewis had sold more than 2,200 acres in Spotsylvania County for almost £24,000 in currency. Their youngest sons, Robert and Howell, were twelve and ten years old. Fielding Lewis at last enjoyed some success with a crop of hemp, for which demand rose in wartime. It grew on his land in the Shenandoah Valley, not in the Dismal Swamp. He had no faith in the Dismal Swamp Company as a source of future income for his heirs. His will directed that his share in the company be sold "at the discretion of my Executors," for the purpose of paying his debts. His portion of the land he and George Washington and Thomas Walker had bought near the swamp was also to be sold. Two months later, Fielding Lewis died at the age of fifty-six.

Lewis's oldest son wrote to General Washington to explain the will, adding that his father had died "much indebted." Washington held out hope for the Dismal Swamp Company, but he agreed to the sale of land he, Walker, and Lewis's estate owned jointly. He warned: "I take it for granted, that you do not mean to sell these Lands unless you can get the value of them, or near it; because this would not only defeat the end *you* have in view but do injustice to Doctr. Walker and myself." In February 1784, when Washington visited Fredericksburg and talked with John Lewis, they concluded that an immediate sale would be "imprudent." A share in the Dismal Swamp Company and the jointly owned lands nearby remained in the estate of Fielding Lewis for years.

The French expeditionary force marched out of Philadelphia toward Head of Elk, Maryland, and Chesapeake Bay, but its commander, the Comte de Rochambeau, chose to go down the Delaware River by water with a small retinue of officers on Wednesday, September 5, 1781. They paused at Mud Island to study Fort Mifflin, then at Red Bank to study Fort Mercer. The fourteen-mile voyage to Chester was leisurely and pleasant to the eye. Beyond the river's marshy banks lay well-cultivated farmland. As Chester came into view on the right bank, the officers and Rochambeau discerned in the distance, standing near the water, a tall man in uniform, waving his hat in one hand and a white handkerchief in the other. Drawing near, they saw that he was General Washington, acting like a "child, whose every wish had been gratified." As soon as Rochambeau disembarked, Washington told him that, riding downriver three miles below Chester, the Americans had met an express messenger from the Comte de Grasse. The admiral and his fleet of twenty-eight ships of the line had arrived off the capes on August 26. The French were closing off Chesapeake Bay and patrolling the James River. Washington and Rochambeau "embraced *warmly* on the shore." As the news spread through the French and American armies in the following days, "soldiers from then on spoke of Cornwallis as if they had already captured him."

The generals reached the peninsula between the James and York rivers on Friday, September 14. By then they knew that de Grasse, with most of his men-of-war, had met Admiral Thomas Graves's squadron in battle off the capes on the same day that Rochambeau had wended his way down the Delaware. From York Town to Nansemond County people heard barrages of naval guns that afternoon. Facing a superior force, Graves could not enter the Chesapeake. He waited a few days, then gave up the attempt after receiving a report "of the French fleet being all anchored within the Cape, so as to block our passage." This fleet consisted not only of the ships Graves had fought but also of those de Grasse had waited outside the capes to cover as they arrived—a squadron of seven ships of the line bearing siege artillery, commanded by the Comte de Barras in his flagship, the *Duc de Bourgogne.* By Friday, September 21, most of the French fleet rode at anchor across the main channel below the mouth of the York. Sir Henry Clinton in New York wrote: "when the operation in Chesapeake was ordered, I was promised a Naval superiority, why we had it not, those who promised it can best tell."

Lord Cornwallis, knowing he was trapped within his semicircle of fortifications overlooking the York, made his headquarters with Secretary Thomas Nelson at the upper end of town. The tall, white-haired old man, flinching with gout, let nothing disturb him. He acted as if his garden and library were always open to any gentleman who cared to call. Nelson saw, as easily as his guest, that Cornwallis was encumbered in a way most military men wished to avoid. The prospect of a base in the Chesapeake had attracted loyalist refugees, black refugees, and British tobacco traders. Dozens of vessels now anchored in the river had come in search of rich cargoes of high-priced tobacco. Secretary Nelson could have told the forty-three-year-old general many stories about royal governance in Virginia during the past fifty years. If British officials had rested content with tobacco vessels, which even now outnumbered in the York those of the Royal Navy . . . but it was too late.

Washington and Rochambeau began their siege on Saturday, October 6.

Three days later their new batteries opened fire, General Washington putting the match to the first gun. For skilled artillerymen, York Town—sloping down from bluffs to the river and to an estuary filled with shipping—presented so many targets in so small a space that the bombardment hit everywhere. The second day it fell silent for a while, in response to a white flag. Secretary Nelson came out of town to enter American lines: "his House was no longer tenable he says." One shot had killed a slave by his bedside. Sitting at Washington's headquarters, surrounded by young officers, "he related to us, with a serene countenance, what had been the effect of our batteries, and how much his house had suffered from the first shots."

Cornwallis held out for another week. By then a person "could not take three steps without running into some great holes made by bombs, some splinters, some balls, some half covered trenches, with scattered white or negro arms or legs, some bits of uniforms." Rich furniture lay broken amid ruins. Decomposing corpses of men and horses were only partly covered by dirt. Among the ruins stood piles of books—Pope's works, Montaigne's essays, theology, history, and law. Like the secretary's house, David Jameson's house and outbuildings were destroyed. The night after Secretary Nelson left town, the unlucky HMS *Charon* was hit by a red-hot shell from a French battery. She went up in flames, fire running quickly up her masts, along her yards, into her sheets and furled sails. Cornwallis's last gamble—to cross the York and break through American and French lines around Gloucester—was thwarted on the night of October 16 by heavy rain and high wind. He could feed soldiers and refugees for one more week. The time to surrender had come.

Word of Cornwallis's surrender reached London in less than six weeks. A leading East India merchant described reactions among the king's ministers: "'Tis well, in the dejection it occasions, if we do not yield everything to France." The Earl of Shelburne, part of a fragmented but vehement opposition to Lord North, was fond of quoting his old acquaintance Benjamin Franklin, who liked to quote himself. "Dr. Franklin used to say," Shelburne wrote, "that Experience was the school for fools." Lord North must go, and the war must stop. Beyond those goals, the opposition split. But these enabled Benjamin Franklin, John Adams, and John Jay to secure American independence in negotiations among the belligerents.

Less than two weeks after word arrived from Virginia, the City of London urged the king to end the war and to dismiss his ministers. At the end of February 1782, the House of Commons voted on the war. Opponents of the ministry won by a majority of 19, Anthony Bacon voting with the ministry. Three weeks later, to forestall losing a vote of confidence, Lord North announced that the king would change his ministers. A kindly critic of Frederick North's overlong complaisance toward the king wrote of the outgoing minister: "He was an accomplished orator, an able financier, irreproachable in his individual character, and fully adequate to conduct the national affairs in ordinary times. His crime was the American war. In that abyss he became ultimately engulphed." One of the joint secretaries of the Treasury, Edward Chamberlayne, had become almost indispensable: "he made all Lord North's calculations, but . . . would never appear in it." Others attributed his attitude to diffidence. The new ministry begged Chamberlayne to continue in office: "he talked with great disgust of his place." Reluctantly, he agreed to serve, but after a friend "remonstrated with him on the absurdity of the apprehension with which he appeared to be actuated," Chamberlayne went up to his office in Whitehall, jumped headfirst out of a Treasury window, and broke his neck in the fall. Thirty-six hours afterward, he died.

The new ministry, led by the Marquis of Rockingham, lasted only a few months, until Rockingham's death. In it Shelburne became secretary of state for home, colonial, and Irish affairs. And, by Clerke's Act of 1782, government contractors could no longer sit in Parliament. Anthony Bacon arranged for Francis Homfray to take his contract to supply artillery, Homfray renting Bacon's iron mill and foundry and using only pig iron from Bacon's Cyfarthfa furnace. Before summer ended, Bacon's name appeared on no government contracts. He remained in Parliament and voted against the preliminary terms of peace a year after he had voted against ending the British war effort.

Forming a ministry after Rockingham's death, Shelburne gave the colonial secretaryship to Thomas Townshend. Both Shelburne and Townshend, during their brief tenure in that office, received petitions and memorials from merchants formerly trading to America. As usual, these reminded the government of large debts Americans still owed to British merchants. Many important names at Lloyd's appeared among the signers. One of the first memorials reached Shelburne three weeks after he became colonial secretary. It was signed by Samuel Gist and the heads of nineteen other firms. They said they were "anxiously looking forward" to the time "when the happy period arrives that restores peace between Great Britain and America." They trusted that Shelburne would make it his "peculiar care to protect & guard the legal demands of your Memorialists for such Debts as were contracted under the faith and sanction of the British Laws before the unhappy dispute commenced." The final treaty of peace gave British creditors the same legal recourse as creditors who were American citizens.

Such a promise did not inspire confidence. James Mercer's law practice in Virginia made him cynical. He not only expected a debtor to evade payment; he also expected a county justice to suggest to the debtor "the propriety of offering me Lands in the moon or some Hemp instead of money." British merchants hoped that this well-known, incurable evasiveness would move the ministry to help them collect. In 1783, William Jones, of Farell & Jones—creditors of William Byrd, James Parke Farley, and many others— said that the death of his brother-in-law and partner, Joseph Farell, during the war "was entirely owing to his anxiety of mind for our large property in Virginia." Lord North's ministry had created the war. The least his successors could do was repair some of its damage to Britons.

No one trusted the Earl of Shelburne. "The old Lord Holland used to say that many people were bred Jesuits, but that Lord Shelburne was born one." Amid the multiple attempted betrayals in negotiating a treaty of peace, Shelburne received messages from people hoping to win favor and to be of use. Silas Deane, taking the waters at Spa, devised a scheme to preserve "some Degree of Union" between America and Britain. Lord Dunmore proposed to arm and supply a force of loyalists to settle in the Mississippi Valley. There they would soon produce indigo, rice, tobacco, corn, lumber, hemp, flax, pitch, and tar. They would connect Canada to New Orleans, offering to Americans asylum from "the Tyranny and oppression of Congress." With assistance from Indians, Dunmore told the ministry, "you have it at any time in your power to drive the Thirteen united Provinces into the sea, besides securing the Fur Trade." Experience was not always a school for fools. Opening the session of Parliament on December 5, 1782, George III acknowledged that the treaty of peace must recognize American independence.

London in the summer of 1782 suffered from falling prices on its stock exchange and from an epidemic of influenza which killed many people. These concerns did not distract Samuel Gist from thinking about his property in Virginia. He wrote to William Anderson twice in October, saying peace was near. He intended to resume control of his plantations and slaves through Benjamin Toler. Gist told Anderson to send a list of slaves and livestock; he expected his son-in-law to visit the Dismal Swamp and report on the company's activities.

In subsequent months Gist wrote to debtors in Virginia. James Taylor was surprised to receive a demand for payment of more than £1,500 sterling due since January 1, 1776. True, Gist had sent goods to the firm Phripp, Taylor & Company in Norfolk for five years before the war. But, as Taylor reminded him, Norfolk now lay in ruins. He hoped that Gist had recovered his money through fire insurance on the stores and goods, since "little or Nothing will be Collected" from the defunct company.

Apparently dissatisfied with his son-in-law's reply, Gist wrote to Benjamin Toler, demanding detailed accounts and "wresting the estate out" of Anderson's hands. This left Anderson's feelings "much hurt" and brought Gist a reproof from Judge Peter Lyons: "I wish on many accounts the letter had not been wrote." Gist, he pointed out, would have lost all his property in Virginia if William and Mary Anderson had not rescued it from confiscation. In the spring of 1779 the General Assembly went beyond sequestering estates of Britons and loyalists. A new law prescribed seizure of real property, mainly land and slaves, by escheat and of personal property by forfeiture. The state would sell these to help pay for the war. When this bill came before the House of Delegates, Speaker Benjamin Harrison took an interest in William and Mary Anderson. He persuaded a narrow majority of delegates to exclude from the law the property of Virginians who were widows, wives, or children of British subjects. During a long, heated debate, Lyons heard some of the minority "rave" against such a "partial unjust" provision on Gist's behalf. They said that Gist was "reaping benefit from the war." They accused him of collusion with Hardin Burnley of Hanover in buying captured tobacco in New York. Harrison prevailed only by arguing that Gist was "dead to this country" and that the Andersons were a deserving, patriotic couple.

William Anderson made a point of "shewing a chearful disposition to oppose the enemy on all occasions." He also extended hospitality to his critics. Though people in Hanover County and nearby spoke "violent and insolent" words, he maintained a steady conduct. He became a vestryman, and he was elected to the House of Delegates. Anderson's demeanor proved helpful when resentment of the British reached new heights after Cornwallis's men did so much damage in Hanover County. Lyons thought that, if the war had continued, "not only british property, but half the great fortunes in this country belonging to suspected men, could have been confiscated and sold." In June 1782, William and Mary Anderson petitioned the House of Delegates to vest Gist's estate in Mary Anderson and her heirs. The law passed with "the strong assistance of his friends."

Lyons tried to impress upon Gist the risk Gist had run in writing to Toler to claim his land and slaves. If the letter had fallen into the hands of "some of our flaming patriots," it would have shown that Gist's critics in the House of Delegates had been right—that vesting the land and slaves in Mary Anderson had been a ruse to save this property for Gist. His letter might have led to confiscation of everything, including his three quarter-shares in the Dismal Swamp Company: "indeed my friend," Lyons wrote, "there is danger yet in talking of it." Throughout the war, Anderson and Toler treated the plantations and slaves as Gist's, paying profits to his order, as Gist knew by receiving Anderson's wartime letters. Anderson bought more land on Gist's behalf from Gist's brother-in-law, Thomas Massie, and from the state, which had confiscated land of the loyalist Samuel Martin. Lyons chided Gist: "is all this to be forgot in a moment, and a strict account of profits to be exacted?—surely not."

While Lyons fretted about Gist's indiscretion, William Lee, at home outside Williamsburg, warned a merchant in Ostend not to heed proposals from William Dolman of Westmoreland County. "Dollman is really Non Compis Mentis.—that is quite crazy headed," Lee wrote. "I hear that somebody has trick'd him out of all his right to the Estate." Dolman died five months later, bequeathing his property to his sons and daughters. The trickster turned out to be Samuel Gist, but he faced a rival claimant. Lee said: "*I will not pretend to decide whether either* of them have any legal claim to meddle in this business." Virginians' attempts to penetrate Gist's designs on Dolman's property by approaching another London merchant met this reply: "Mr Gist has studiously avoided giving me any information about the matter."

David Jameson reported to Gist on the condition of the Dismal Swamp Company, assuring him that the company would pay for the equipment and supplies he had furnished ten years earlier. Without tools for ditching, draining, or making shingles, Jacob Collee had settled for cultivation of rice and corn by the slaves remaining at Dismal Plantation. These crops brought little more than the cost of expenses and taxes. Nansemond County's assessors raised the tax bill in 1783 by setting the value of the company's land at 3s. 4d. per acre, rather than the previous assessment of 2s. 6d. To establish the company's tax bill during the war, Jameson and Dr. Walker had to specify a number of acres. The company had not done this in the past, simply claiming all the swamp on the Virginia side. Dr. Walker picked the figure 40,000 acres, which he "supposed was the whole," though it was only a corner of the swamp. Jameson reassured Gist: "The Land will be valuable." At that moment, Jameson wrote, "many" thought it worth £1 currency per acre. Land around Fredericksburg sold for about £10 per acre.

On Monday, October 6, 1783, peace was proclaimed in London. Large crowds gathered to see the formal procession and to hear the proclamation read at St. James's Palace, at Charing Cross, at the Royal Exchange, and elsewhere. Two days later, Samuel Gist started writing to Virginians, inviting them to resume sending consignments of tobacco and orders for manufactured goods. He pointed out that "by Death, and Misfortunes the old Virginia Merchts in this place are reduced to a very small Number indeed." He assured his correspondents that in his handling of their consignments, "your Interest shall be as much attended to in the sale as tho' it was my Own." He added: "I take this first safe Oppy, since the return of peace to Inclose your Acct. Currt. The Balance . . . I have no doubt on Examination you will find right, & that you will with your first Convenience, remit it to me, as well as the Interest due thereon."

Gist told his correspondents that William Anderson would take charge of shipping consignments from Virginia. Earlier in 1783, Gist had suggested that the Andersons move to London, and he offered financial support. They had made a good life in Hanover County and in Louisa County. They owned a prosperous plantation and used "very elegant" mahogany furniture. Mary Anderson, "a most amiable woman," was "in fine health and very fat." She rode in a "genteel carriage," while her husband acquired two "high blooded stud Horses." They had no children of their own, but they took into their home an orphaned two-year-old girl, Maria Anderson, and a boy, Francis Anderson, niece and nephew of William. He wrote: "I assure you we are very happy in our little boy & girl." Nevertheless, they were willing to live in London.

Fifteen years of experience with Samuel Gist had made William Anderson cautious. He would live in London and join Gist in business, "provided I can do it without becoming too dependant." He noticed "with great concern" that Gist's mention of support did not state a specific sum. Nor did it offer to settle upon the Andersons a fortune giving them their own permanent income. He saw that Gist reserved the right "to give them anything or nothing." With the most discreet wording he could devise, Anderson said he wished "to be equally guarded against extravagance and parsimony." He urged Gist to be definite about providing an income, "both with respect to the mode, and the Quantum." Otherwise, the Andersons would not cross the Atlantic in the summer of 1784, as Gist wished. And they did not.

At the end of the war, Robert Munford went the way of his friend William Byrd. On April 6, 1781, his daughter, Ursula Anna, was married to Otway Byrd. Elizabeth Farley said of her: "She is an amiable Girl & makes our Brother happy." Munford had just returned from the Land of Eden, where the Virginia militia paused after taking part in the battle of Guilford Court House on March 15. Munford commanded four hundred militiamen in General Robert Lawson's brigade. With bitter fighting, Lord Cornwallis's veterans forced the Americans under Nathanael Greene to withdraw, but British troops suffered twice as many casualties—almost one-third of Cornwallis's force. That night a cold rain fell on the battlefield and on dead and dying men of both armies. Cries of the wounded, a British officer wrote, "exceed all description." The Land of Eden lay 25 miles north of the battlefield. Munford left Saura Town for Virginia on Sunday, March 18.

After Cornwallis's surrender at York Town, Munford started to translate Ovid's *Metamorphoses* into English. Perhaps that work would distract him from thinking about Americans' behavior. He privately had written satirical verse more scathing than his two comic plays about cozening politicians and strident patriots. In "A Letter from the Devil to His Son" the devil describes plans for a new hell:

> *Nay More, to give you due content,*
> *I'll send you negroes to torment;*
> *An overseer, or two, besides,*
> *To help you cut and slash their hides,*
> *And if I did not know you well,*
> *(Tho' seldom any come to hell)*
> *Some women I might send; but then,*
> *I'm sure you'd whip them back again.*

Munford translated only Book One of *Metamorphoses*; he did not work steadily. Instead, he became a hard drinker.

As senior magistrate he attended sessions of Mecklenburg County Court so far gone in "excess of Drink & Intoxication" that his "profane swearing" and "indecent and disorderly behaviour" prevented other magistrates from doing the court's business. They reported his condition to the governor "with sorrow and regret"; it was an abrupt change from his previous "worthy and Judicious conduct." After a year of drunken disruption, Munford resigned. By the spring of 1783, his "most uncommon intemperance" had become so habitual that his brother-in-law said, "there can be no hopes of reclaiming him." Late in December, as George Washington resigned his commission to return to Mount Vernon, Robert Munford died. He left his son-in-law and executor, Otway Byrd, to deal with "the estate's noisey creditors." William Munford, his son, had to deal with "the embarrassment of my Mother's circumstances."

Fifteen years later, William Munford published his father's plays and poems. Reading *The Patriots*, he found passages in which his father's hero, Trueman, expresses scorn for his countrymen. In one of them, near the end,

Trueman says: "So in spite of all the malice and censure of the times, I am at last dubb'd a whig. I am not wiser or better than before. My political opinions are still the same, my patriotic principles unaltered: but I have kick'd a tory, it seems: there is merit in this, which, like charity, hides a multitude of sins." William Munford wrote a preface for his father's works to assure readers that *The Patriots* was ridicule of hypocrites, not "a satire on the conduct of America in the late revolution."

VI

———•———

THIS ELDORADO

ON CHRISTMAS EVE, 1783, George Washington returned to Mount Vernon, which he called "this retreat from all my public employments." He had heard nothing about the affairs of the Dismal Swamp Company for more than nine years; yet he still trusted that those "sunken lands . . . will in time become the most valuable property in this Country."

The first reports on the company were bad. They came to Washington from Dr. Thomas Walker, who in turn heard them from David Jameson. By express messenger Jameson warned that people were taking warrants at the Land Office in Richmond, encroaching on the company's grant. He urged Walker to seek legal advice from Thomas Jefferson. Walker promised to do so. They must act quickly to protect the company's title. There was talk in Richmond of cutting a canal through the Dismal Swamp to connect the Elizabeth River in Virginia with the Pasquotank River in North Carolina, creating a waterway between Chesapeake Bay and Albemarle Sound. Walker wrote to Washington: "the Company having Shewed the value of those Lands, many are so mean as to wish for what is undoubtedly their property"—that is, the partners' property. The next year, one of the men who had taken warrants with his eye on "a large Tract" in the Dismal Swamp made the mistake of calling at Mount Vernon to seek Washington's approval of running a survey in the swamp. Washington gave his opinion "unreservedly, that they had no right to." General Washington spoke "unreservedly" only on special occasions.

Jameson and Walker had taken earlier precautions. They paid property taxes and in October 1781 obtained an act of the General Assembly confirming the company's title to all land granted it by the colonial Council. The partners must file a survey in the Land Office, as they had promised twenty years earlier to file one in Secretary Nelson's office. After several delays, county surveyors marked the boundaries of the company's 40,000 acres in the summer of 1783. With some deviations on the western side, the lines formed a rough rectangle without its northwestern corner. Beginning about a mile and a half east of the road from Suffolk into North Carolina, the line ran eastward along the boundary dividing North Carolina from Virginia for about 5¼ miles. It ran due north just east of Lake Drummond for 14 miles, then west for about 3½ miles. From that point it ran southwestward to meet the western boundary about 11 miles north of the North Carolina line. These lines enclosed all of Lake Drummond and most of the northwestern quadrant of the Dismal Swamp. Dismal Plantation and the ditch to Lake Drummond lay about halfway down the western side of the company's tract. Suffolk lay just northwest of the missing corner of the rectangle.

David Jameson tried to assemble a quorum of partners in Richmond on Wednesday, November 5, 1783, hoping to get a decision about whether to file this survey with the Land Office and rest content with 40,000 acres or to press a claim to all the swamp in Virginia. Few partners gathered on the appointed day. Those present agreed to confine the company's holdings to the bounds of the survey. Jameson wrote apologetically to Samuel Gist: "I fear we shall not be able to support a claim to more—in truth if the matter is brought before a Court I wish we may be able to support our right to that quantity."

Dr. Walker did not fear courts. He said: "Lawyers are fond of Business on which I suppose their opinions are founded." He had won an important case in May. The Supreme Court of Appeals unanimously confirmed the titles of the Loyal Company and the Greenbrier Company to lands surveyed before 1776. Walker's bygone "secret Surveys," which everyone seemed to know about, were upheld.

Prodded by Samuel Gist, in search of payment for his past shipments to the Dismal Swamp Company and remittance of profits, David Jameson worked to interest his partners in revival and expansion of the work. He found this difficult. George Washington showed a keen concern for the company's success and for the proposed new canal. Yet, twenty years after first embracing a scheme to drain the swamp, he realized that "a considerable advance" of money beyond regular expenses still would be needed to "reclaim" the submerged acres and "render them fit for cultivation." He could not add to his present expenditures. Jameson wrote to Secretary Thomas Nelson, who was nearing his seventieth birthday, to remind him that he had owed the company one more slave since 1765. In 1771 the partners had imposed a charge of £7 per year on anyone failing to provide a full complement of slaves. Jameson called upon Nelson to pay the arrears of this fee—almost £150—to defray expenses of a survey and of getting title from the Land Office. Nelson said he had "no money," but he had an old bond for £100, signed by Dr. Walker on May 10, 1771, promising to repay Nelson for money advanced to the mother-in-law of Walker's son, John. Bernard Moore, the father-in-law, was supposed to redeem the bond. Though Moore was insolvent, if Jameson could get money from him the company was welcome to it. If not, Dr. Walker of course was liable.

From David Meade, Jameson received an opinion that the Dismal Swamp Company was "in a state of Bankruptcy," a view Jameson refused to share. One copy of his circular letter seeking to revive the company went to Rosewell. John Page, trying to ward off vertigo, still felt angry at his late father for sticking him with a failed copper mine and a half-share in the Dismal Swamp Company in lieu of a rich plantation. In search of more income, he advertised land in Gloucester County for sale, lease, or rent. He was not likely to make new investments in the Dismal Swamp.

Robert Tucker's share in the Dismal Swamp Company remained part of his estate, in the hands of his son-in-law, Thomas Newton, Jr. He stood ready to help Jameson protect the company's title. But he could hardly be expected to sink his own money into Tucker's estate, which of course still owed more than it held in assets. Newton offered for sale 170 acres adjoining Portsmouth, site of the ruins of Tucker's mill and bakery among remains of British and American fortifications.

John Lewis, executor of Fielding Lewis's estate, found himself in a predicament similar to Newton's when he received Jameson's letter. George Washington would not sell their jointly held land, yet the estate bore a heavy burden of debt. Early in 1784, John Lewis's half brother, Fielding Lewis, Jr., was held in confinement by the sheriff of Frederick County at the suit of unpaid creditors. The younger Lewis wrote to his uncle, George Washington, asking for money. In reply he received a lecture on the virtues of being sober and frugal.

Joseph Hornsby was prosperous when he received Jameson's letter. Between April 1781 and April 1784 he entered at the Land Office for 4,800 acres in Kentucky, south and east of Louisville. He displayed his success in Williamsburg most clearly in February 1783 after the death of Elizabeth Harrison Randolph, widow of Speaker Peyton Randolph. Hornsby bought the Randolph house for £1,800 in currency. His partners in the Dismal Swamp Company, Jameson and William Nelson, Jr., witnessed the sale and deed. Thereafter, Hornsby walked among rooms paneled in pine and oak, formerly a gathering place of Virginia's greatest men since the days when the elder William Byrd returned to Virginia from London. Decorative touches "in the Chinese taste" along the balustrade and elsewhere made this two-story frame house one of the most admired in Williamsburg. But despite his new comfort, Hornsby did not respond to hints that he should furnish money needed to get the Nansemond County surveyor's signature on the company's survey.

William Nelson, Jr., with his brother, Nathaniel, inherited President William Nelson's share in the Dismal Swamp Company. The younger William had his father's good humor without his father's application to business or desire for power. He served the company's interest as he served his own—intermittently, with good intentions. In September 1782, three years after he graduated from the College of William and Mary, Nelson was licensed to practice law. The following winter his wife, Polly Taliaferro Nelson, gave birth to their first child, a daughter. With the baby Betsey and "the pure, the modest, my affectionate Polly," Nelson found "perfect happiness." A sentimental lawyer, he did not aspire to rise to the top of his profession. He liked to read literature and philosophy amid "the calmness of the Lyceum." He was a loving husband, a loyal friend, and an inefficient partner.

The early months of 1784 brought Virginia another stormy, bitterly cold winter like the one four years earlier. In the lower James River, "great Quantities of Ice driving up and down" sank ships. Trees did not begin to bud until late in April. Slaves on Dismal Plantation went without meat after the company's hogs were killed by black people from other plantations and by bears and wildcats from the swamp. Jameson told Jacob Collee to buy pork to maintain the usual allowance. Early in the harsh winter two of the company's absent slaves, Tom and Lewis, who had been "lying out" for a long time, were locked up. These two skilled evaders came into Collee's custody at almost the same time. Apparently, the winter was too cold for them to remain free as fugitives.

Though Jameson's appeals to his partners yielded little, he refused to dismiss the Dismal Swamp Company as a failure. Clinging to its original scheme, he concluded that success required a large infusion of slave labor to drain the swamp. He talked with "surveyors and several others well acquainted with the swamp." They told him that effective drainage would need "a very great force" of laborers—one hundred slaves digging ditches "throughout in certain directions." The company had eleven adult male slaves, two of whom, enduring winter confinement to get shelter and food, would not stay on, much less work on, Dismal Plantation.

Having learned that his partners "cannot or will not advance any thing like a sum necessary to prosecute the work," Jameson put the question to Samuel Gist. Would Gist lend £5,000 or £6,000 sterling to the Dismal Swamp Company? For collateral he could have a mortgage on 40,000 acres of swamp. In words reminiscent of William Byrd's first proposal more than fifty years earlier, Jameson described to Gist the "healthy young men & women" the partners could put in the swamp to work and to produce more slaves through childbirth, thereby remedying the "great oversight" of originally ignoring Byrd's advice to combine procreation with drainage.

Appealing to Gist's vanity, Jameson wrote that Gist might "easily procure" the needed sum if he did not wish to furnish it from his own funds. Appealing to Gist's greed, Jameson said: "it is shameful to let an Estate of such value lie waste." But he tempted in vain. By the summer of 1784 he saw that the best the company could do was "hiring *at least* ten strong hands for the year." He told William Nelson, Jr., that "there was not a chance" of buying slaves.

Ever since Samuel Gist had established himself as a consignment merchant in London, he had provoked criticism in Virginia. Though his hostility to the American Revolution was widely known, his property in Virginia evaded escheat, thanks to the special law vesting it in his daughter. She and her husband intended to join Gist in London. His Petersburg agent, Thomas Shore, already had done so. Gist's dunning letters seeking payment of old debts started to arrive in Virginia in 1784. In the autumn the House of Delegates debated a bill to end further confiscations of loyalists' estates. Some "warm" delegates threatened to seize Gist's property on the grounds that in 1782 delegates had been "deceived by Mr. Anderson, who they insist holds it for Mr. Gists use." In September the *Virginia Gazette, or, the American Advertiser* published an unsigned defense of Gist, presented as a letter from London, urging readers: "Ship your tobacco to him, for my sake; persuade your relations to do so, and advise your friends to do it for their own advantage." The letter described Gist's "friendship and generosity," assuring Virginians that, among all the tobacco merchants in London, "Mr. Gist is the only one whose benevolence, whose humanity, and whose integrity I can speak of with truth and confidence." The letter could hardly have praised him more highly if he had written it himself. Gist's property again escaped confiscation, and some planters, Robert Beverley among them, consigned tobacco to him.

A few weeks after the date of the London letter in the *Gazette*, Gist testified before the Royal Commission for Enquiring into the Losses, Services, and Claims of the American Loyalists. He supported Thomas Macknight's request for compensation for his lost property in North Carolina. Since this included the Campania Company's claim to part of the Dismal Swamp, Gist appeared as an expert witness able to set a value on land in the swamp. He told the commissioners that he had been "a Joint proprietor of the whole of that part of the Swamp wch was in Virginia."

Experience with American loyalists made the commissioners cautious. They asked whether 2,000 acres of the Dismal Swamp would sell for sixpence per acre. Gist assured them that it would sell for "a great deal more." He said that in 1774 he would have been "puzzled" to decide whether to accept an offer of five shillings per acre for his share of the Dismal Swamp Company's grant. The commissioners asked what made the swamp so valuable—the soil or the timber growing on it? Gist replied: "the Timber is rather an Incumbrance." He estimated the value of the soil as almost 90 percent of the value of a tract in the Dismal Swamp. Gist had known Macknight twenty years earlier, while both of them were in America. Gist did not hold the Campania Company's futile attack on the Virginians against the luckless Scot. He tried in his testimony to induce the British government to pay more for land in the Dismal Swamp than anyone in Virginia or North Carolina ever had paid. Gist intended to apply for compensation himself, on the grounds that the state of Virginia had taken his property from him and given it to his daughter.

Leaving the governorship of Virginia in 1779, Patrick Henry wrote: "A long and painful attention to public matters obliges me to go for a while into retirement which is equally necessary to my health, finances and domestic life." He resumed the office in 1784. A proposal to dig a canal through the Dismal Swamp won his eager support. The spring and summer of 1784 seemed a good time to acquire part of the Dismal Swamp. In cooperation with others he chose 5,000 acres on the eastern side in the Green Sea, the broad tract of tall reeds where few trees grew. For a while Henry carried a few ounces of dirt wrapped in paper, showing it as proof of "the excellent quality of the Green Sea lands." He wrote: "My Land below is very rich in soil." The following year he and his associates acquired about 10,000 acres of the swamp in North Carolina. Henry also took more property in and near the swamp on the Virginia side. In 1787 and 1788 he paid taxes on 12,000 acres in Norfolk County. A critic wrote of Henry's acquisitions: "His Excellency then degenerated into the land-monger."

Taking out warrants in the Land Office for acres of the Green Sea was easy. Mongering them was not. Residents of Norfolk County knew that the Green Sea was "a low sunken Morass, not fit for any of the purposes of Agriculture, when dry will burn readily, little or no timber." Henry's new holdings had "no natural advantages except lying near the Canal" if one ever came. Allowing for some cutting down of nearby cedar trees and some past fires, the expanse of thickly massed green reeds looked much as William Byrd had seen it sixty years earlier.

The *Virginia Gazette* published on October 2, 1784, an advertisement by Dr. Thomas Walker, summoning partners of the Dismal Swamp Company to meet in Richmond two weeks later "on business of great importance." In Galt's Tavern on the appointed day, Walker found only David Jameson and one other member, presumably William Nelson, Jr., who lived in Richmond. Though they were not a quorum, they acted for the company. Three days later, Walker paid fees for the company's grant of 40,000 acres. A patent for the surveyed land was issued the next day in the names of William and Nathaniel Nelson, devisees of the late William Nelson, the only partner named in the Council's original grant. The money Dr. Walker paid came from David Jameson. Eager to placate Samuel Gist, Jameson reminded him that such fees and taxes were "not a trifling expence"; the company's title was now safe. The Nelson brothers made out deeds to other partners, apportioning 40,000 acres according to the number of quarter-shares each person held. Jameson told William Nelson "to make one in the name of Samuel Gist or rather in the name of Mary Anderson (following the act of assembly)."

The Dismal Swamp Company had a new neighbor on the North Carolina side of the line: the Lebanon Company. Hugh Williamson, a Pennsylvanian transplanted in North Carolina, was a delegate to the Continental Congress and a partner in the Lebanon Company. He and his associates claimed 40,000 or 50,000 acres—he left the total vague—adjoining the southern edge of the Dismal Swamp Company's tract. Unlike James Parker and Thomas Macknight, who had left the land almost undisturbed, Williamson put men to work in the swamp south of Lake Drummond, felling white cedar trees for shingles. Patrick Henry, looking for easy purchases in the swamp, found that "the Lebanon Company hold their lands higher" in value than he had supposed.

As George Washington had done, Hugh Williamson studied the Dismal Swamp closely. He, too, believed that "After the Timber is removed, such land cannot be exhausted by Agriculture." The two men also agreed—and Williamson urged Washington to use his influence in Virginia—that a canal giving North Carolina's products a waterway to Norfolk would enrich everyone with an interest in land between Albemarle Sound and the James River.

After his return to Mount Vernon, George Washington often said that his plantations and his affairs lay in disarray. During the war he fretted that his private concerns were "declining every day," threatening him with "capital losses, if not absolute ruin." At Mount Vernon his books showed that two-thirds of his Virginia tenants owed him back rent. He grew convinced that, whichever way he turned, people were cheating him.

Anxious to guard both title to and possession of his land along tributaries of the Ohio River, Washington spent the month of September 1784 traveling. With his nephew, Bushrod, his friend, Dr. James Craik, and others he went up the Potomac, along Braddock's road, down the watershed between the Youghiogheny and Monongahela rivers, to his land west of Pittsburgh. He asked men along the way about the lay of land and watercourses farther west; he took copious notes. On his property he found fourteen families with their houses, barns, and fences—members of the Seceders', or Associate Presbyterian, Church, who were, he sarcastically noted, "*apparently* very religious." They rejected his terms for their purchasing or leasing his land, and he rejected their offer to buy on long credit without paying interest. Having lived there for more than ten years, they said they would "stand suit, & abide the Issue of the Law." In a Pennsylvania court Washington began ejectment proceedings, which he later won.

Word that Shawnees were attacking settlers who had encroached on their land north of the Ohio convinced Washington to go no farther west. He had to forgo a visit to his tracts along the Ohio and Kanawha rivers. He returned to Mount Vernon by a more southerly route taking him up the Cheat River and across the Shenandoah Valley and the Blue Ridge. His trip confirmed his experiences before the war: he had trouble keeping his tracts free of people who would not pay; he did not find enough tenants who would pay on his terms. Learning that strangers were offering his lands for sale in Philadelphia and Europe, he prepared "to take measures for rescuing them from the hands of Land Jobbers & Speculators."

Completing a tour of 680 miles, Washington reached his home late in the afternoon of October 4. In his diary he wrote a long summary of the information he had gathered about routes and distances. And he put down his thoughts about keeping western settlers attached to the eastern states commercially and politically. He concluded: "The more then the Navigation of Potomack is investigated, & duely considered, the greater the advantages arising from them appear." His travels showed him that Virginians must act: "A combination of circumstances make the present conjuncture more favorable than any other to fix the trade of the Western Country to our Markets." The following week he sent his thoughts to Governor Benjamin Harrison. The time had come to revive an enterprise begun before the war.

The Potomac River could become the main channel of western trade only if a canal enabled vessels to pass rocks and rapids at the falls upriver from Mount Vernon. The House of Burgesses had adopted a proposal for a canal in 1772. When people spoke of resuming the project after the war, they linked it with George Washington. Thomas Jefferson wrote in February

1784 that Washington had the Potomac canal "much at heart. The superintendance of it would be a noble amusement in his retirement and leave a monument of him as long as the waters should flow." Washington wrote many letters to win support for investing in improvement of the Potomac to "draw the produce of the Western Settlers" and "bind those people to us by a chain which never can be broken." He assured his correspondents: "This is no Utopean Scheme." A guest at Mount Vernon heard Washington talk about his vision: "The General sent the bottle about pretty freely after dinner, and gave success to the navigation of the Potomac for his toast. . . . He never undertakes anything without having first well considered of it and consulted different people. But when once he has begun anything, no obstacle or difficulty can come in his way but what he is determined to surmount."

Virginians also revived their design for a canal around the falls of the James River at Richmond. Although ten years and more had passed since the first subscriptions, prospectuses, and diggings had been proclaimed for the James and Potomac rivers, Washington and his fellow promoters of interlocking routes of waterborne commerce still remembered John Ballendine, entrepreneur of canals in the 1770s. Washington had received warnings that this man was a "Lurking Scoundrel" with "superior Talents" in "the art of being a Villain." But a chance to open the Potomac route with his help proved too tempting to resist.

After the House of Burgesses voted for canals in 1772, Ballendine announced his intent to tour the great canals of Europe, then bring his new expertise back to Virginia. Creation of a separate western colony, Vandalia, seemed imminent. Virginia must compete with Pennsylvania for its trade. Early in 1773, Ballendine wrote from London to the *Virginia Gazette*, through a friend, to say that he had acquired "Plans and Models of all the necessary Machines." He had "engaged several ingenious Mechanicks to go out with me to Virginia." There was no doubt of passing the falls of the James, and the new proprietors of Vandalia would "contribute largely towards opening both James and Potomack Rivers." In London, he won the backing of Samuel Gist. Though he failed to raise money by subscription in England, he got from Gist a letter of recommendation saying that Ballendine "has not only been Countenanced by the first People here but has a very handsome Subscrip[tion]." Gist showed his confidence that work would "go on immediately" by furnishing Ballendine on credit tools and equipment worth more than £500.

Gist and the Virginians lost money on Ballendine, who returned to Virginia in the summer of 1774, proclaiming himself "fully qualified" to "remove the obstructions to the navigation of Potowmack river." Washington

and others invested. Though he failed on the Potomac, Ballendine advertised in the fall of 1775 his intent to dig a James River canal, financed by his
own capital, in anticipation of "large and generous contributions from all
who benefit" after its successful completion. During the war he linked his
work with an iron foundry the state needed. He tried to make himself Virginia's Anthony Bacon, producer of pig iron and cannon at government expense, until Benedict Arnold's raid on Richmond destroyed his operations.
He extracted money from the state for his canal on the grounds that his ironworks needed its water. In four years Ballendine completed only 5 percent of
his projected canal. He died deeply indebted to the state. Jefferson, Washington, and other promoters in the 1780s had dealt with Ballendine to their
cost. Yet his name vanished as they envisioned new successes.

Eager to begin, they found another entrepreneur in 1784. James Rumsey,
a builder and inventor living in Bath, at Berkeley Springs, went to Richmond
in the spring to seek the General Assembly's patronage of his design for a
new boat. He said he had conceived a mechanism of paddles, wheels, and un-
derwater poles which would propel a boat upstream, using the force of the
current it was moving against. The faster the river's flow, the faster his boat
would go upstream, needing little energy other than that of the current itself.
He offered to sell the secret of his invention to the state. The delegates made
fun of him.

Early in George Washington's trip to the forks of the Ohio in September,
he stopped at Bath. Rumsey explained his invention, and, swearing Washington to secrecy, showed him a model. Washington admitted he had
thought that making a swift current propel a boat upriver was "next to, if not
quite impracticable." Yet the model seemed to work, and he gave the inventor a certificate saying that there was "no doubt" of Rumsey's success and
that "the discovery is of vast importance—may be of the greatest usefulness
in our inland navigation." Rumsey then approached the General Assembly a
second time. It voted him a ten-year monopoly on his invention, the state re-
serving a right to buy it for £10,000. Rumsey wrote to Washington: "I Long
to have the Opertunity of Convinceing those that Remain Unbelievers." He
applied to other states and to Congress for protection of his invention.

During Rumsey's return to Richmond he already was talking about a different kind of boat, one moving against a current using energy from steam.
He turned his attention to bringing a steamboat "to the greatest perfection."
Enduring "the pelting of ignorance and ill-nature," he never perfected his
earlier invention. He learned that "dark assassins had endeavoured to wound
the reputation" of Washington for having endorsed it. In a pamphlet Rumsey told the public that he would have vindicated his supporters by building

successful mechanical boats had not a rival inventor stolen his ideas for a steamboat and tried to obtain a monopoly. Rumsey must defend his latest invention.

In the second week of January 1785, William Nelson, Jr., wrote from Richmond: "Opening a communication with the western-country, by extending the navigation of James River and Potomack, has lately engrossed much of the publick attention here." A visitor to Mount Vernon the following week listened to George Washington talk at length about the Potomac River and the interior. Washington went to both Richmond and Annapolis, persuading legislators to authorize the projects and fund them with a mixture of public money and private subscriptions. The James River company began with a capital of $100,000, the Potomac Company with $220,000. Dividends for investors were to come from tolls paid by users of the canals. Directors of the Potomac Company advertised for a manager. Meeting on July 1, they found that none of the applicants had furnished "proper Credentials." Washington suggested to his fellow directors that they consider James Rumsey. The next day he wrote to Rumsey: "I have imbibed a very favorable opinion of your mechanical abilities . . . I dare say if you are disposed to offer your services, they would be attended to under favourable circumstances." On July 14 the directors appointed Rumsey manager. Within three months he had "upwards of one hundred hands employed in blowing Rocks &c."

Promoters of the canal companies also wished to link the upper reaches of rivers flowing into Chesapeake Bay with rivers flowing into the Ohio. If all went as planned, they would reduce land carriage between eastern and western waters to 20 or 30 miles. A British visitor wrote: "the nation which, even in the first years of its political existence, has the genius to form such projects, and the patriotism to dwell upon them with confidence and enthusiasm, has already established the probability of their execution." Beyond improving commercial and political ties, such channels would swell the flow of people to Kentucky—"this Eldorado"—expecting to find there "the Richest Land in the World."

After Virginia's Land Office opened in 1779, Kentucky attracted even more migrants than in previous years. A European traveler said of Americans soon after the war: "they are always jabbering about the distant wonders of other provinces." As William Byrd had tried to sell his *Neu-gefundenes Eden* to Europeans, John Filson advertised Kentucky to easterners in 1784. In his account, getting title to land looked easy. He assured his readers: "scarcely any such thing as a marsh or swamp is to be found." He sent a copy of his book and his map to George Washington, saying: "these Sir I request and presume you will patronise." Kentucky seized many people's imaginations. A few years after Filson's book appeared, Moses Austin watched families passing through Cumberland Gap in December, walking in ice and snow, wearing too little clothing in the cold: "Ask these Pilgrims what they expect when they git to Kentuckey the Answer is Land. have you any. No, but I expect I can git it. have you any thing to pay for land, No. did you Ever see the Country. No but Every Body says it is good land." A traveler in eastern Virginia in 1785 heard reports of "a new Country Called Kaintuckey . . . affording almost all the necessities of life Spontaneously."

Unfortunately for pilgrims, surveys and Land Office warrants and other claims already covered Kentucky, often overlapping. Hardly any tract was free from dispute, and every transaction was open to suspicion. While being duped by land jobbers could happen anywhere in America, Caleb Wallace wrote from Kentucky, "Here it is reduced to a System, and to take advantage of the Ignorance or of the Poverty of a neighbour is almost grown into reputation." Though a political economist, such as Adam Smith, or a man of affairs, such as George Washington, insisted that in America owning land was a better investment than putting money out at interest, Kentucky showed that ownership was hard to establish; settling property's value depended upon "opinion, the art of speculating and long credit." Assessing the results of postwar migration twenty years later, a British traveler wondered how so many people had allowed themselves to be "abused by the dreams of enthusiasts and the falsehoods of knaves," who had led them "to this 'Land of Promise.' "

In 1781, Virginia offered to cede to the United States its land north and west of the Ohio River. The Continental Congress was slow to accept this cession on Virginia's terms, which confirmed the state's title to Kentucky and voided royal grants and purchases from Indians in the ceded region. Such conditions defeated the claims of land companies dominated by speculators from Pennsylvania and Maryland, including promoters of the Vandalia grant before the war. They urged Congress to assert its sovereignty over the west, ignore Virginia's title, and confirm theirs. Delegates in Richmond in the fall of 1783 heard that most western settlers hoped Congress would set aside Virginia's authority beyond the mountains, thereby voiding warrants and deeds. These pilgrims were "busied in building Huts on other Peoples Lands." Congress's need for revenue through sale of public land, as well as Continental Army veterans' expectation of grants in the new domain, proved stronger than the companies. Congress accepted the cession on March 1, 1784.

A canal through the Dismal Swamp looked like an easier project than the large undertakings on the James and the Potomac. In his first proposal to drain the swamp, William Byrd listed this commercial connection by canals as one benefit of his scheme. More than forty years later, the Dismal Swamp Company had made little headway in transforming the swamp. When the House of Burgesses approved other canals in 1772, it appointed commissioners to obtain surveys and choose a route for a canal to link the Elizabeth River with the North River, flowing into Currituck Sound. These men represented the borough of Norfolk and counties around it. Among them were Severn Eyre from the Eastern Shore, Lemuel Riddick from Nansemond, Peter Singleton—known as "Czar" in Princess Anne County—and Thomas Newton, Jr., of Norfolk. The committee submitted its report the day before the battle of Bunker Hill.

Before peace with Britain became final, a bill to authorize a canal through the Dismal Swamp appeared in the House of Delegates. A bill for the Elizabeth River–North River route passed in December 1783. Hugh Williamson and his North Carolina associates pressed upon George Washington a different route. Williamson said that getting into Virginia waters from Albemarle Sound by way of Currituck Sound would be "equal to an east India voyage, not quite so long but rather more troublesome." The course ought to run from the head of Pasquotank River to Lake Drummond, then to a navigable river in Virginia. This would take it through the sectors owned by the Lebanon Company and the Dismal Swamp Company. Washington said he long had thought a canal feasible and desirable; he approved of going by way of Lake Drummond. Washington sent copies of his and Williamson's letters to Dr. Walker, who sent copies to David Jameson. Jameson said that he supposed a navigable canal would facilitate draining and greatly benefit the public and individuals, "but there is very little probability that our present Compy. will ever engage in it."

Governor Henry and the Council could not easily find three men willing to go to the Dismal Swamp to choose a course for a canal. Those recommended in January 1785 declined to serve. A few months later, the Council named three friends of the Dismal Swamp Company: William Ronald, Robert Andrews, and David Meade. Meade wrote to Governor Henry, professing to believe that the governor and the councillors did not know that he was a member of the Dismal Swamp Company. Of course, he said, "that connexion evidently interests me in the question, with respect to the course" the canal would follow. Meade added that he had a new route in mind; he would be "obedient to your future commands." He remained a commissioner. Andrews, who had supervised the survey of the Dismal Swamp Company's boundary, said he would serve "very cheerfully," so much did he wish to increase Norfolk's trade with North Carolina. He believed the canal should run through the Dismal Swamp. Just before the commissioners visited the swamp, "a most tremendous gale" struck the Chesapeake on Thursday, September 22. The storm blew until Saturday. Water in the Dismal Swamp rose and spread, convincing the commissioners a few days later that they "could not take a very particular View of the Ground."

In October, Meade and Andrews recommended abandoning the route leading into Currituck Sound, pointing out "the great Dangers & Difficulties" in navigating it. A better course ran through the eastern side of the swamp, beginning just south of Portsmouth, passing within three and one-half miles of Lake Drummond, and joining the Pasquotank River north of Elizabeth City, North Carolina. Such a canal, 22 miles long, would lie near but not in the Dismal Swamp Company's tract. William Ronald presented to the House of Delegates in November a bill designating that course. The delegates deferred legislation until North Carolina was ready to pass a similar law.

Years before digging began, the prospect of a canal encouraged people to look differently at land in and near the Dismal Swamp. The Herberts of Norfolk County, with two associates, announced in 1783 that their 25 acres between the eastern and southern branches of the Elizabeth River had been "laid off into lots and streets for a Town by the name of Washington." It was "likely to become a place of considerable trade." Early in 1785 the state offered at auction three hundred lots in Gosport on the opposite bank of the southern branch, telling potential buyers: "the canal proposed to unite the waters of North Carolina, with the Chesapeak, will greatly enhance the value of those lands." From Paris, Thomas Jefferson replied to Hugh Williamson's description of the Lebanon Company and the canal route: "I am glad to find you think of me in the affair of the Dismal. It is the only speculation in my life I have decidedly wished to be engaged in. The uniting the navigation of Chesapeak and the sound renders the enterprise so interesting to the public as well as the adventurers that the embarking in it can never admit a reproach." Jefferson had no doubt that the Lebanon Company and the Dismal Swamp Company would "harmonize in their operations." He asked Williamson to buy shares in the canal on his behalf.

George Washington wrote to Jefferson, reporting on preparations for Virginia's canals. Eager for work to begin, Washington nevertheless warned that friends of the Dismal Swamp Canal were "better stocked with good wishes than money." Might Jefferson find "monied men" in Europe who could "be induced to become adventurers in the Scheme?" After Meade and Andrews reported their chosen route, Washington looked forward to the day when all the canals would be in use: "the conveniences to the Citizens individually, and the sources of wealth to the Country generally, which will be opened thereby will be found to exceed the most sanguine imagination— The Mind can scarcely take in at one view all the benefits which will result therefrom."

Hugh Williamson and George Washington had studied the Dismal Swamp. Washington estimated that its elevation did not vary more than two feet. He was almost right, the swamp's surface of peat varying between 15 and 20 feet above sea level. The two men agreed that a canal would need only one lock at the Virginia end to control movement of boats into and out of tidal waters in the Elizabeth River. Williamson concluded that the expense would be "inconsiderable." After Robert Andrews suggested the need for one lock at each end, Washington disagreed with the locations Andrews chose but not with his estimate of the number. No one guessed that a successful watercourse would require eight locks. Thirty years later, directors of the Dismal Swamp Canal Company, looking back at its early days, regretted that "So little . . . was then understood of the probable expense & difficulty of cutting a Navigable Canal 22 miles in extent, through a heavy timbered Morass."

Early in 1783, Virginians seeking to learn whether peace had returned did not wait for slow official news. They watched express messengers come to the Rappahannock, York, and James rivers from Philadelphia and New York. Arriving daily, sometimes hourly, riders brought orders to Virginia agents representing Northern merchants, telling them to buy tobacco. The war had shown how much money could be made from Europeans' desire for tobacco and Americans' desire for manufactured goods. Merchants raced to gratify these demands as soon as peace made trade lawful. Instructions to buy tobacco came to Virginia, and vessels sailed from British ports, laden with goods no one had ordered but Americans were sure to buy.

Officially, Virginia shipped 68,000,000 pounds of tobacco in 1783 and an equal amount in 1784. Prices were high, as much as 65 shillings currency for 112 pounds of the best James River leaf. The British government knew that smugglers evading customs duties brought tobacco and other products to "every accessible part of the coast of this kingdom." In Scotland in 1783 and afterward "vessels arriving directly from Virginia" were "landing their cargoes upon the coast." British merchants appeared in Virginia—not just old faces from the past but "Strangers" coming to Norfolk from all quarters and "modern adventurers, who now crowd every house and every shed" in Richmond.

These newcomers were selling as well as buying. Before the British government proclaimed the end of fighting, "Verry large Quantitys of dry Goods" left London and other cities for "every Port in America." Brook Watson went from Lloyd's to Whitehall to assure the Board of Trade that Americans would continue to buy British goods even if their new government tried to shift their commerce to other countries. He was right. His fellow underwriters, John Ewer and Abraham Hake, estimated that in the winter of 1783–84 more merchandise went from Britain to America than in any two-year period before the war. Through wartime trade and expenditures by the French and British armies and navies, Americans had amassed gold and silver. Virginians' specie quickly flowed to Britain; their tobacco shipments, though large, covered less than half the cost of their purchases. British merchants marked up goods for high return, but much of the profit on their books was new debt contracted by eager consumers. A veteran merchant in London calculated in the summer of 1784 that "more real value of goods have been Exported from Britain this Season than America will be able to raise of produce for Two years to come."

One eager young merchant arriving in Virginia was a large Scotsman, Alexander Macaulay. Still in his twenties, he had made money during the war by selling British goods in New York and in Philadelphia during the army's occupation. Demand for merchandise extended far beyond British lines. By 1780, New York imported at the same volume as in the years before the war. Macaulay already had a record of success when he visited the widow of the retired merchant, Francis Jerdone, in Louisa County in 1782. Macaulay and Sarah Jerdone's daughter, Elizabeth, were married in December. The couple left for York Town two months later, carrying letters from William and Mary Anderson addressed to Samuel Gist.

Macaulay was in a hurry to get "home" to New York. He feared that his business affairs "may be materially injured By my absence at the present critical Juncture," as lawful trade resumed. Reaching New York in the spring, he hoped to make money by shipping tobacco from Virginia to Britain. Well read, with a quick wit, he had little leisure to devote to science and the arts. He wrote to a friend: "I am doom'd to act the part of a mere drudge in Business; & not a Philosopher." The departure of the British left him little reason to stay in New York. In 1784, the year he turned thirty, he moved to Virginia, settling at York Town, where Francis Jerdone long had competed with William Nelson for business. There Macaulay met David Jameson and grew interested in the Dismal Swamp Company.

The expensive carriage with painted copper panels which Samuel Gist shipped to Sarah Jerdone in 1784 caused comment in Louisa County. People said that "a plain one would have done equally well." Macaulay's mother-in-law was one of many Virginians whose indulgences showed their love of luxury. British merchants could always rely on "a proper Buckskin" to be "fond of a Little Tinsell." They had flooded the state with "Feathers, Powder, Umbrellas &c &c &c." Moralists denounced the spreading influence of "British debts, British goods, British deceptions." Americans had been seduced into wasting their money and running into debt. In Paris, Thomas Jefferson heard from home that "Extravagance and dissipation has seized all Ranks of People. It has become fashionable to import even Hay from the Northern States and Coffins from Europe." After winning independence, Americans had restored the bulk of their trade to Britain. Many Virginians resumed the habit of spending more money than they possessed; while others newly experimented with buying more than they could afford. George Washington's cousin, Warner Washington, produced 100 hogsheads of tobacco a year but claimed to be unable to pay his debts. He "squanders the whole in profuse living."

Beginning early in 1785, British merchants curtailed shipments of goods. By October, London warehouses were filled with Virginia tobacco. They had no room for hogsheads still in the holds of vessels moored in the river. The price of tobacco fell below 20 shillings per hundredweight. Merchants who rushed to ship goods to America at the return of peace miscalculated the ex-

The Bank, Bank Buildings, Royal Exchange and Cornhill. Courtesy of the Henry E. Huntington Library. The Bank of England is on the left; the front of the Royal Exchange is on the right.

tent of a rise in demand after trade again became lawful. During the war, the flow of merchandise to the usual destinations had found new channels as well as familiar ones. Peace did not suddenly reopen a long-closed door. Instead, it made easy and direct a trade which in wartime had become clandestine and roundabout. Hence, peace did not yield a fortune to everyone shipping goods and importing tobacco.

Many Virginians blamed the collapse of tobacco prices on one man: Robert Morris. Serving as superintendent of finance in the war's last years, Morris had rescued the Continental government from the threat of insolvency, using, in part, his personal credit as a merchant. For peacetime, he formed far grander designs than privateering and running cargoes through the West Indies. He set out to control the sale of tobacco to France.

In April 1785, Morris contracted to supply the state tobacco monopoly of France, the Farmers-General, 20,000 hogsheads per year for three years. The Farmers-General agreed to buy no other American tobacco and advanced Morris 1,000,000 livres, the equivalent of about £670,000 in Virginia currency. The price he charged the French, about 24 shillings per hundredweight, was low. To make a profit he must buy tobacco at a still lower price. His agents offered 20 shillings, not in cash but in Morris's notes. Though his contract in France was later changed and was not renewed, the price of tobacco remained around 20 shillings through 1787. Since the French were not buying in Britain, merchants there bought less tobacco from Virginians. They took advantage of Morris's price to lower theirs. Virginians had begun to learn a lesson about Robert Morris which experience already had taught Joshua Johnson, a London merchant in the Chesapeake trade: "I have long known this Mans Commercial Character & I tell you that I never wishd any concerns with him he is a dangerous Friend."

A glut of tobacco in London—twelve vessels from Virginia arrived in ten days early in August 1784—and a decline in debtors' remittances as the last gold and silver ran out were followed by a run of stoppages and bankruptcies among merchants trading to America. Several, including Frederick Pigou, Jr., stopped payment in the first week of August. Pigou's failure "very much surprizes the City in general & it is much to be fear'd many others will follow." They continued for the next two years. Throughout 1785 tobacco was a drug on the market. Merchants were "tumbling to pieces every day"; bankers looked with suspicion on every man who owed money and who dealt with Americans.

A veteran merchant and underwriter, James Dunlop, went bankrupt in November 1785. Rumor said that his assets would not yield six shillings for each pound of his obligations. In 1775, Dunlop had imported more tobacco than all but four London houses. He had joined Samuel Gist and other London merchants in their wartime memorials to Lord North's ministry, then to the Marquis of Rockingham's ministry, urging the government to help merchants collect debts in America. After the war he continued to ship "Cloaths Silks Irish Linens Muslin Hosiery Haberdashery and Millinery Goods." But remittances in crops or cash were too few or worth too little. He no longer appeared on 'Change.

Samuel Gist imported tobacco in the summer of 1784. He dispatched a new ship, reminiscently named the *Planter*, to the James River in August. While she was loading for her return voyage, Philip Grymes wrote to Edmund Randolph: "What Tobacco have you for S. G[is]t or is any gone for London? The Planter takes all that can be obtained for him." Eager for his daughter and son-in-law to come to London, Gist established an income for Mary Anderson: the interest on £10,000—£500 per year. In the spring of 1785, William Anderson auctioned his property in Louisa County, and he and his wife sailed for London, presumably in the *Planter*, in July. Seventeen years after their elopement they were returning to live on Tower Hill. Gist gave Benjamin Toler instructions about the Virginia plantations the Andersons had preserved from confiscation. Judge Peter Lyons again warned that signs of his "interfering with the Estate here" produced "great clamour" in the House of Delegates, reviving the danger that the state would seize Gist's property.

While the Andersons crossed the Atlantic, a Virginian from the Eastern Shore sought out Gist at Lloyd's. Severn Eyre, Jr., had come to London to study medicine. His father, Severn Eyre, and his grandfather, Littleton Eyre, had known Gist in Virginia. The young man expected to derive "many advantages from such a connection" as rich Mr. Gist. To pay his way in London he had brought a bill of exchange for £400 drawn on Donald & Burton by Virginia's former governor, Thomas Nelson, Jr., who was generous but insolvent. In the crowded subscribers' room Gist told Eyre that Robert Burton would not accept the bill, and this prediction came true. Gist tried to educate Eyre by telling him that Burton's partner in Virginia, Alexander Donald, might have promised such an advance to Nelson only to obtain Nelson's crop of tobacco on consignment, without intending to honor the bill. Gist invited Eyre to dine with him the next day.

During their meal Gist extracted information about Virginia planters from Eyre, while Eyre tried to persuade Gist to lend him £100. Eyre pleaded that without money he would be compelled to give up his hope of becoming a physician and take the first vessel back to Norfolk. Gist said he knew of one that would sail in about a week. Back in his rooms, Eyre wrote of Gist: "you damned old Jew, Turk & infidel, worth upwards of £300,000 & will not lend one hundred to the child of him you call your friend, what do you intend to do with all of your money?" Nevertheless, Severn Eyre did not return to Virginia at once. A merchant gave him an advance. Americans new to London soon saw that "Every Thing is at high Charge in this Country, no Body ashamed to take Money." Eyre swallowed his resentment and continued his efforts to ingratiate himself with Gist.

A few days after dining with Gist, Eyre went to Drury Lane Theatre to see John Home's play *Douglas*, with Sarah Siddons in the role of Lady Randolph. It was a command performance, with the royal family in attendance. The king and queen admired the art of Mrs. Siddons, as everyone called her, who was far advanced in pregnancy. The queen sent her a box of powders of the kind the queen herself took when in that condition. Two weeks later, Eyre returned to Drury Lane and "saw Mrs. Siddons die" in a "soul-harrowing" performance of one of her most celebrated roles, Belvidera in *Venice Preserv'd*.

At the end of the American War and in the years following, Sarah Siddons established herself as the pre-eminent artist on the London stage. She appeared three times a week in a wide variety of roles. She was "the Empress of Tragedy." The king told her that he had never caught her in a false emphasis. A French traveler who recalled the greatest tragedienne of the reign of Louis XV said that Mrs. Siddons's acting reminded him of "les grands talents de l'immortelle Clairon." Drury Lane Theatre, decorated in crimson and gold, was always crowded. Her Shakespearean parts were Lady Macbeth, Rosalind in *As You Like It*, Isabella in *Measure for Measure*, and Desdemona. But audiences praised her most for her tragic heroines in more recent plays: Euphrasia in *The Grecian Daughter*, and Matilda, the Lady of Saint Valori, in *The Carmelite*. After seeing her create the latter role, the playwright, Richard Cumberland, said: "Mrs. Siddons was divine, and crown'd with unceasing peals of applause." A member of the audience wrote: "It seems to be contrived only for Mrs. Siddon's Powers. She does more Honor to the Author than the Work itself."

Amid these years of commercial trouble and financial ruin in the City, playgoers were transported by Mrs. Siddons in the title role of *Isabella; or, the Fatal Marriage*. Edward Gibbon thought it "a wretched play," but he watched her performance "with the most exquisite pleasure." She made people weep. Before the curtain rose, women in box seats spread their handkerchiefs on the front railing, in preparation for tears. Her mad scene in the fifth

Mrs. Siddons and Her Son in the Tragedy Of Isabella, J. Caldwell,
after William Hamilton. Courtesy of the Henry E. Huntington
Library. Sarah Siddons and her son, Henry, in the opening scene
of *Isabella; or, the Fatal Marriage.*

act was "terrifying": "she appears with the genuine pallor of death, with her
hair really dishevelled and her clothing in dire disorder. Her laughter and
certain tones of her voice are truly harrowing." In one audience, "Five ladies
were taken out fainting in the last act, and hardly a man could stand it."
Laetitia-Matilda Hawkins later recalled: "Physicians forbade patients to see
her in Isabella."

Lady Sarah Napier described herself as "Siddons mad." Crowds gathered
in the street to watch Mrs. Siddons as she arrived and departed. People surrounded her carriage. Early in 1783 she gave the rising artist George Romney several sittings with a wreath in her hair. The *Morning Chronicle* said that
he created a work "which Raphael would be glad of." In 1784, Sir Joshua
Reynolds completed his life-size, full-length portrait, *Sarah Siddons as the*

Tragic Muse. At her first sitting he said to her: "Ascend your undisputed throne and graciously bestow upon me some grand Idea of the Tragick Muse."

Early that year she and her husband and their children moved into one of the new houses that trustees for the young Duke of Bedford had built in a uniform row in Gower Street, extending from Bedford Square. This was the outer edge of northwestern London. The backs of these four-story brick buildings were "most effectually in the country, and delightfully pleasant." Strangers came to Gower Street to see the Siddonses' house, Number 14, which looked like all the others. Some only stared; others came to buy tickets for benefit performances in which the box office receipts went to her. Others, she complained, "forced their way into my Drawing-room, in spite of remonstrance or opposition." One woman who intruded into Mrs. Siddons's upstairs room told her: "I am in a very delicate state of health, and my Physician won't let me go to the Theatre to see you, so I am come to look at you here."

When Severn Eyre arrived in London, people of "the beau monde" had to see not only the acting of Mrs. Siddons but also the performance of the Amazing Learned Pig. In a building just off Whitehall near Charing Cross, gentlemen and "women of the first Fashion waited four hours for their turn" to enter and pay five shillings, later reduced to one shilling, for a thirty-minute exhibition. Using its mouth, a large trained pig arranged cards bearing letters and numbers to give the date and the time, to add and subtract, to tell people their names and their thoughts, and to answer questions. It enjoyed so much success in "the polite end of the town" that its owner took it on the stage in the summer of 1785. The Learned Pig became the headline act at Sadler's Wells Theatre. Skilled acrobats and tightrope dancers performing there "made great objections" to being reduced to a warm-up act for a pig. The manager did not try to keep them from leaving. He could readily find other tumblers; the Learned Pig was a star.

The *Planter* arrived in the Thames in the first week of September; the Andersons joined Samuel Gist in his home in America Square. Gist told his daughters, Mary and Elizabeth, their husbands, William Anderson and William Fowke, and his longtime clerk, Aiskew Birkett, that he planned to retire. He was sixty years old. The City had too many merchants shipping to America, as daily bankruptcies proved. Two years of effort to reopen trade and collect debts in Virginia had given him more vexation than it was worth. Instead of remittances he had received whining letters, such as John Tabb's: "really sir, for want of information & other disappointments, since the conclusion of the war you have lost me more than 2000 £, all was quite in your power to have prevented." Gist offered to turn over his trade, his goods, and the *Planter* to a new company in which Anderson, Fowke, and Birkett would be partners. It was established early in 1786. In mid-March, William Anderson & Company announced Gist's retirement and invited planters to benefit from "our knowledge, and experience in the Tobacco trade" by consigning tobacco to the new firm. With those letters to Gist's customers the *Planter* sailed from the Downs on April 6.

Gist remained available in the subscribers' room at Lloyd's. He was there on Monday, January 2, 1786, when a panic-stricken Severn Eyre, Jr., approached him to relate a long, complicated story about his former landlord in London. Though he had moved out of those lodgings after a short stay, the landlord was demanding payment of six months' rent, threatening him with a writ and daring him to go to court. He feared that he would soon be thrown into Newgate Prison. After hearing Eyre out, Gist laughed and said that Virginians "were not smart enough to live in London." He advised Eyre to see an attorney. After making inquiries and receiving more threats, Eyre paid in full. He then was visited by the wife of his hairdresser. Her husband had been apprehended while committing highway robbery. She asked Eyre to settle his account.

Seeking "a transitory respite to my depressed spirits," Eyre turned to the theater. After paying his hairdresser's wife on the last Saturday in February, he went to Covent Garden to see Mrs. Siddons a second time as Belvidera in Thomas Otway's *Venice Preserv'd*. No longer pregnant, she appeared in a benefit performance for the widow of an actor, John Henderson. The boxes and the pit were "lined with people of rank." In the first gallery Eyre was so tightly wedged among "an innumerable mob" that his hips were sore. But in the last act, during the mad scene, after Belvidera sees the ghost of her husband, who had killed his friend and himself on the scaffold rather than die at an executioner's hand, Eyre felt his tears on his cheeks as Belvidera says:

> *My love! my dear! my blessing! Help me, help me!*
> *They have hold on me, and drag me to the bottom.*
> *Nay, now they pull so hard—farewell—*

Belvidera's death looked so convincing that Eyre heard a man near him say that Mrs. Siddons was certainly dead and would never rise again. Later that year she played the title role in Robert Dodsley's tragedy *Cleone*. As Cleone in the third act walks with her child through a wood, the corrupted servant Ragozin, masked, attacks with a dagger. Mrs. Siddons cried "Help! Mercy! Save! Kill not my infant! Murder!" in "such a note of unison to the feelings of the house that in an instant everyone cried 'Murder' too, and ladies screaming and fainting were carried out by dozens."

Less than six months after William Anderson & Company went into business, Anderson learned that Samuel Gist's retirement consisted, in part, of second-guessing his son-in-law. Gist opposed an investment he thought too risky, and he told Joshua Johnson that he feared Anderson was "going too fast." Johnson said of Gist: "he is a tight hand."

A new system of tobacco duties announced by the British government in the spring of 1786 confirmed the wisdom of Gist's decision to quit the trade. In the old days, merchants made an extra profit of about £3 per hogshead on tobacco intended for the British market by charging planters full duties while taking advantage of a discount allowed by the government for payment in cash. The new system allowed no discount. The "old Merchants" of Gist's generation spoke of "giving the Business up" and predicted more smuggling.

After a few years of contending with a glutted market for tobacco in Britain and a market in France obstructed by Robert Morris's deal with the Farmers-General, Anderson had warehouses filled with unsold tobacco. He had to offer bargains, and he admitted to Joshua Johnson that William Anderson & Company had "lost a great deal of money."

In retirement, Samuel Gist frequented Lloyd's rooms and appeared in the Virginia Walk on 'Change, "a spruce little man." Meeting any new arrival from Virginia, he was "polite & particular" in his inquiries. In the summer of 1786 his onetime mentor in the slave trade, John Shoolbred, was elected to the governing committee of the Company of Merchants Trading to Africa. Shoolbred also was forming an alliance with James Hennessy and John Saule, brandy merchants of Bordeaux and Cognac, in their rivalry with the House of Martell.

Despite reverses in business, William and Mary Anderson lived well in America Square. They entertained visiting Virginians. While staying in London, Lewis Littlepage, newly appointed royal chamberlain to Stanislas II Poniatowski, last king of Poland, heard about his Virginia relatives from Mary Anderson. The younger Carter Braxton called after Gist spotted him on 'Change. The Andersons laid out an "elegant" dinner, with "fine wines, & pleasant fruits." After meeting Gist and dining with the Andersons, Braxton went to Drury Lane Theatre to see Sarah Siddons as Mrs. Beverley in Edward Moore's *The Gamester*, one of the roles in which "she outdid all description." He was struck by the "invariable stillness & attention" of her audiences. "We forget that she is Mrs Siddons, but believe her Mrs Beverley, Belvidera, Isabella." Seeing the "misery & anguish" to which the heroine was reduced by the gambling of her husband, played by Mrs. Siddons's brother,

John Philip Kemble, Braxton said: "no person with a particle of love or pity in his composition can refrain vowing, eternal abstinence from gaming."

Samuel Gist decided to leave the Andersons in possession of his house and counting room in America Square. His business address in the City remained Number 16, America Square, but for his residence in retirement he leased from the Duke of Bedford's trustees Number 37, Gower Street, and became Sarah Siddons's neighbor.

Crossing the Atlantic from Virginia in 1785, William Anderson took with him the Dismal Swamp Company's power of attorney, authorizing him to borrow £5,000 sterling on the company's behalf. The partners made this request at their first meeting in ten years. Anderson attended it a few weeks before he left Virginia.

By a newspaper advertisement George Washington summoned the partners to gather in Richmond on Monday, May 2. The company's affairs, he said, were "in a deranged state." The partners ought to take "some decisive measures." Reports from Dismal Plantation were gloomy: the company had only "a few old worn out Negroes," four of whom were retired, "incapable of labour." In wartime Jacob Collee had worked the plantation "without ever touching a Ditch." Drainage ditches begun before the war were "much broke & require a deal of Work"; the "Remnant of old Negroes" could not do it. Collee had not hired slaves to replace those who left with the British. While the partners worried about ways to drain the swamp, heavy rains flooded Dismal Plantation.

Near noon on Monday, May 2, members of the Dismal Swamp Company, walking through a cold east wind, entered the ugly capitol and assembled in the Senate chamber. George Washington had come from Mount Vernon. He had a dinner engagement with the Sons of Saint Tammany after the meeting. David Meade had come upriver from Maycox to represent both the Meade family's share and the share owned by the four young granddaughters of the late Francis Farley. John Page had come from Rosewell. From York Town, David Jameson represented himself and Samuel Gist. William Nelson, Jr., represented himself and his brother, Nathaniel. Neither Dr. Thomas Walker nor his son-in-law, Joseph Hornsby, was present, but Dr. Walker had sent from Albemarle County another son-in-law, Reuben Lindsay, to act on their behalf. Secretary Thomas Nelson, Anthony Bacon, and the estate of Robert Tucker had no one attending the meeting for them.

For three hours that afternoon and for another six hours on Tuesday, while a steady rain fell, the partners conferred. On Monday, they discussed paying for the survey of their 40,000 acres and paying Samuel Gist for tools and supplies. They voted to call Jacob Collee, who was leaving their service, "to a speedy and accurate settlement of his accounts." They discussed the possibility of dividing their 40,000 acres in proportion to the number of quarter-shares each partner held, a step that would end the dream of draining the swamp, but they voted that the work should still "be carried on jointly."

On Tuesday morning, the partners were joined in the Senate chamber by Nathaniel Nelson and William Anderson. They approved a change in operations in the swamp, one Washington wished he could make on his plantations: "get quit of Negroes," as he put it. In lieu of slaves the company ought to hire "German Redemptioners" or other laborers in Baltimore. If that effort failed, the company must hire slaves temporarily until the managers found as many as three hundred "Labourers acquainted with draining and other branches of agriculture" to be imported from Holland or Germany "or other parts of Europe." This scheme required money. For months David Jameson had urged his partners to borrow. Despite ten years of felling cedar trees for shingles before the war, the company's sector of the Dismal Swamp looked little changed from its appearance in the days when the dividing line's hungry surveyors rushed through it almost sixty years earlier.

Washington recommended skilled European workers, and Jameson's proposed loan seemed the best way to pay for them. Jameson and Anderson knew that Samuel Gist, though unwilling to lend, would question them closely to learn what they had done to make the Dismal Swamp Company profitable, especially since it owed money to him. The partners asked Anderson to borrow £5,000 for them when he reached London. They made themselves liable for repayment.

A few more matters remained to be settled before Washington left to dine with Governor Henry. The company's managers were to investigate strangers' encroachments on the company's property and get legal advice. They were authorized to purchase adjacent land or mills to support the company's operations. And Reuben Lindsay said that Dr. Walker was too old and infirm to continue in the management. George Washington also asked to withdraw. John Page took Washington's place, and Joseph Hornsby was appointed to the place of his father-in-law. Then the partners walked out of the capitol into the rain.

Back at Mount Vernon, Washington repeated that "reclaiming" the Dismal Swamp would make it "invaluable." In the following months he wrote letters and inquired in person about a loan and the possibility of getting someone "to deliver 300 able labourers, Germans or Hollanders, not more than eight women, at Norfolk" as indentured servants of the Dismal Swamp Company. He did not receive satisfactory replies. Once William Anderson settled at Number 16, America Square, and established William Anderson & Company, the partners of the Dismal Swamp Company heard no more about a loan in London.

To replace Jacob Collee as the company's resident manager in Suffolk, the partners chose John Driver, son and executor of John Driver, partner of David Meade's father. The firm of Meade & Driver, though defunct for decades, still owed more than £7,600 sterling to British merchants. The sons, unlike many other Virginians, acknowledged the debt after the war. With his second wife, a minister's daughter, Driver still lived in his father's house on the outskirts of Suffolk, surrounded by apple and peach orchards and "a good garden." He operated a store in Suffolk, priding himself on being "punctu-all" in paying his debts. But neither he nor David Meade contrived to pay their fathers' debts.

Nansemond County and Suffolk revived from the damage done by British invasion. Buildings increased so rapidly and the price of land rose so fast that in the autumn of 1785 inhabitants of Suffolk petitioned the General Assembly to add 16 acres of lots and streets to the town, giving more room for "mechanics and tradesmen." The General Assembly made Driver one of the trustees laying out new lots. This prosperity induced three "pirates" armed with muskets and cutlasses to board a schooner in the James River and sail off with her and her cargo of dry goods. They were soon "apprehended in the County of Nansemond, where they intended to open a store."

John Page urged David Jameson and Nathaniel Nelson to visit Dismal Plantation to "look into the Affairs of the Co. on the Spot & see what the Carolina Co. will be willing to do towards opening the Canals." Hugh Williamson of the Lebanon Company reassured his fellow physician and fellow native of Pennsylvania, Dr. Thomas Ruston, that the Dismal Swamp property in Virginia which Ruston had acquired was valuable, worth £1,500 sterling. And one could buy adjacent parts of the swamp at a price of $750 for 1,000 acres.

Dr. Ruston, after taking his degree at the University of Edinburgh, had lived in England for twenty years. Upon his father's death he decided to return to America. If he wished to continue "taking a slice at Physic," as Williamson put it, he might do so, but he expected to make a fortune by land speculation. In the spring and summer of 1785, Ruston took leave of England. At Drury Lane Theatre he saw Sarah Siddons in her last performance of the season, playing Rosalind in *As You Like It*. Ruston took most interest in watching the royal family. Later, he prevailed upon George and Sarah Fairfax to write a letter of introduction to George Washington. And he stopped at Number 16, America Square. He gave Samuel Gist power of attorney to manage his investments in England.

In the months after the company's meeting, Driver resumed production of shingles at Dismal Plantation. He could do little to repair drainage ditches. David Jameson still hoped that the company eventually would get "some white servants." He told Driver "to continue to manage as well as you can." He apologized for his partners: "I am truly sorry that the necessary steps have not been taken to put the Company's affairs on a better footing."

During John Page's stay in Richmond in May he paid Alexander Donald £300 for a thoroughbred stallion, a "beautiful bay" named Sampson. Page had just offered another "fine blooded stud Horse" for sale. His finances remained desperate. "Duns and Sheriffs" often called at Rosewell. He tried to sell "several young Negroes" and two tracts of land: 800 acres in Gloucester County and 1,300 acres in Loudoun County, inherited from his father-in-law, Robert Burwell.

For several months before the company's meeting, William Nelson, Jr., spent most of his time in Williamsburg, preparing to take over the law practice of Henry Tazewell, who became a judge of the General Court in Richmond. They advertised the change in June. Among Nelson's clients were John Norton & Son, still striving to get Virginians to pay for goods shipped them before the war, and Otway Byrd, executor of the estate of his father-in-law, Robert Munford. Byrd and Nelson paid as many of Munford's debts as his insufficient estate permitted. William and Polly Nelson enjoyed Williamsburg. They had met in the governor's palace while Thomas Jefferson lived there and William attended George Wythe's law lectures. Their happy return to the "peaceful city" lasted a little more than six months. Early in 1786, Polly Nelson died, apparently in childbirth, leaving a baby son, who did not live long, and a young daughter. William felt "a vacuum."

The health of William's brother, Nathaniel, was failing. He left the House of Delegates in January 1786 and wrote his will in March, bequeathing his interest in the Dismal Swamp Company to his son, William. If his children left no heirs, Nathaniel's half-share was to go to his brother, William, and their three brothers. Hoping to recover, Nathaniel sailed for Bermuda in April to visit St. George Tucker's father. He "seem'd very anxious to Live," but his condition grew worse. He died in June.

In those months William Lee contracted to buy John Page's Loudoun

County land for £1 currency per acre. In subsequent weeks Lee changed his mind, believing he had offered too much, but Page held him to the bargain. Then Page reconsidered the sale. Lee held him to the agreement, paying £676 sterling, but Page needed more. He asked Lee to lend him money, offering to pay 10 percent interest per year, twice the customary rate. Lee said he would not do so even if he were a moneylender. Such loans, he wrote, had "almost in every instance been followed by the ruin of the borrower and the disgrace of the lender."

After more than two years of practicing law in Williamsburg, making little money, William Nelson, Jr., took stock of his career at the age of twenty-seven: "Every day's experience the more confirms me in the opinion that I shall never be eminent at the bar, & shall not go beyond the line of mediocrity except by attention & length of standing." Still, he could read widely, one of his chief pleasures. And he found a new wife: Otway Byrd's half sister, Abby Byrd, fifth child of Mary Willing Byrd and William Byrd. She was twenty. Nelson began to spend more time at Westover.

At Nesting, upriver from Westover, the widow Elizabeth Farley lived with her four daughters. She was, a visitor said, "a very handsome woman." She looked at the youngest partners in the Dismal Swamp Company, ranging in age from six to eleven, and wrote: "I am Mother of four homely Girls. . . . They really are by no means pretty & I am silly enough to be sorry for it." She could not help having a discriminating eye, like that of her grandfather, old Colonel Byrd.

The five relied for support partly on the yield of the Saura Town plantation in the Land of Eden, where the slaves sent from Antigua still worked. After the return of peace she also received from Antigua rum and sugar worth £300 sterling per year, the annuity provided in Francis Farley's will. She and her daughters were served by four slaves borrowed from Westover. In December 1784, though she did not know him yet or know that he was coming, her second husband was crossing the Atlantic in search of a woman such as she.

John Dunbar was "an Irish minister." Sailing from London, he did not seek a parish in Virginia. He told a fellow passenger that "he was determined to have some of the rich Virginia widows." He went ashore at York Town in December or early in January. He struck people as "a genteel man." He and Elizabeth Farley were married on Sunday, February 27, 1785. Dunbar moved in with his wife and stepdaughters, Elizabeth, Rebecca—known by her middle name, Parke—Maria, and Mary. One of the people calling on the couple on the first anniversary of their wedding said that John Dunbar "seems to be very happily situated here."

Francis Farley's will stipulated that his daughter-in-law act as executrix only as long as she remained an unmarried widow. John Dunbar took steps to get courts in North Carolina and Virginia to make him administrator of Farley's estate within their jurisdictions. That estate and the Mercers Creek plantation in Antigua belonged to the four girls, subject to payment of their late father's debts. Farley's executors in Antigua had not yet begun to send them the profits of the plantation. Dunbar visited Antigua and arranged to get remittances. Only as administrator could he lawfully raise money to pay the estate's debts by selling some of the land the girls had inherited in Virginia and North Carolina. Only as administrator could he lawfully sell any of the slaves at Saura Town or buy more slaves with money from the estate. He retained St. George Tucker, a friend of Elizabeth Farley Dunbar's, as his attorney.

In the spring of 1786, Dunbar obtained an authenticated copy of Francis Farley's will. In the autumn the Court of Pleas and Quarter Sessions in Rockingham County, North Carolina, made him administrator of the Farley estate. Virginia law required a person seeking appointment as administrator to exhibit the original will, but Antigua law prohibited removal of the original will from Antigua. St. George Tucker drafted a bill for the General Assembly, authorizing Dunbar to administer the estate. He submitted it to the House of Delegates with a petition, which was referred to the Committee for Courts of Justice, apparently never to emerge. Dunbar turned to a new attorney: Patrick Henry.

At the beginning of this process, Dunbar published an advertisement, giving notice that he would apply to the General Assembly. Having applied, he acted as if his request had been granted, signing documents "Jno Dunbar Admr." A few years later he broke up the community of Antiguan slaves at the Land of Eden. Leaving about thirty people at the Saura Town plantation—most were either children or "old & infirm"—he brought thirty-eight people to Charles City County. He held a slave auction, buying some of the slaves for himself. They stayed with the Dunbars and the young heiresses.

More than a year after the Dismal Swamp Company's meeting and John Page's attempt to sell property, he still held land and slaves he had advertised. He owed money to John Norton & Son in London, to Alexander Donald in Richmond, and to tidewater merchants. Large obligations fell due on October 31, 1786. Page hoped that Robert Carter of Nomini Hall, heir to part of King Carter's Frying Pan Company tract, would buy the portion Page had received from his father. Page wrote that he had heard "there is a good Copper Mine thereon." Carter replied that his attorney, John Taylor, handled all such matters.

Page advertised for sale one-fourth of his interest in the Frying Pan tract, his Loudoun County land which William Lee was or was not buying, his 400 acres of the Green Sea in the Dismal Swamp, and one of his two quarter-shares in the Dismal Swamp Company. He assured the public that the company's land and the Green Sea tract were "equal in soil and timber to any lands in the State." He offered to sell thoroughbred mares and colts, as well as the stallion Sampson. He planned to have slaves taken from Rosewell to Petersburg to be auctioned, beginning on the first day of the racing season.

Too much Green Sea acreage came on the market. Patrick Henry tried to sell some to Mary Willing Byrd. She was suspicious. In 1784, Henry had written: "I have many offers for this land," but he still owned it. She replied: "as I understand your offer I should be making an absolute purchase of land, which there is no certainty of my selling for cash." She had struggled with her late husband's debts for almost ten years. She needed to make money, not lose it in paying more taxes. She felt "encircled with Difficulties," and she did not buy. Nor did anyone buy Page's holdings in the Dismal Swamp. A few months later, winter storms caused "overswelling of the swamps," flooding roads and breaking causeways. The Green Sea reeds stood in deeper water than usual.

John Page entered a long period of grief in January 1787 over the death of his wife, Frances Burwell Page. They had enjoyed twenty-two years of "sweet domestic Happiness," during which she had given birth to twelve children. For Page, the ensuing months "passed off like a Dream." He wrote to St. George Tucker in June: "Rosewell which was once my Paradise, is now less grateful to me than would be the Desarts of Arabia." Yet for the sake of his children, and the hope of keeping the estate and its grand mansion in his family, he must find money to pay his debts.

In March, Page placed his affairs in the hands of trustees: Matthew Anderson, his neighbor, and Mann Page, Jr., his son, who was twenty-one. Anderson and the younger Page advertised an auction at Gloucester Court House, to begin on Wednesday, May 1. They offered more than sixty—"probably 90"—slaves, including smiths, carpenters, sawyers, hostlers, spinners, "and an excellent laundress." They again offered Page's tracts of land, adding a few more. They failed. Their efforts produced £55 cash. John Page wrote: "I was disappointed cruelly in my Expectation." He said that his struggle with his money troubles distracted him from his grief. In June he advertised the property again, adding to it Claybank, a plantation adjoining Rosewell.

Since the days of John Page's grandfather, Rosewell and other Page estates had never produced enough to sustain the plantation above the York, its slaves, its owners, and the expense of building and maintaining its elegant mansion. In the spring of 1787, Page almost lost even the tobacco he shipped to London in the brig *Jolly Tar:* on June 10, sailing along the southern rim of the Grand Banks of Newfoundland, she struck a large iceberg. Though it broke away her bowsprit and foremast, the brig sailed on, arriving in the Thames on July 7 with Page's tobacco, consigned to William Anderson & Company.

As John Page grew more desperate, George Washington began efforts to sell some or all of his land in the west. Mount Vernon had not made ends meet since his departure for the Continental Army. He said he felt "exceedingly anxious" to clear himself of debt. He almost conceded that his terms for leases were too high. To a Frenchman considering a settlement of immigrants in the west he offered his tracts on the Ohio and Kanawha rivers, more than 32,000 acres, for £31,500 sterling. He believed, he wrote, his holdings were worth twice this sum, but he abated the price to sell everything at once. He knew his land would rise in value more rapidly than 5 percent per year, the amount the purchase price could earn if instead put out at interest. Washington also offered for sale Pennsylvania tracts reclaimed from squatters.

Early in 1787, Washington received a letter from Henry Emanuel Lutterloh, a former Continental Army officer living in North Carolina. Describing himself as "a German, and well-acquainted with all the different Principalities," he tendered his services in bringing Germans to Virginia as tenants, workers, miners, canal diggers. Washington at once thought of the Dismal Swamp Company. He consulted John Page, who wrote: "The Members are too Lukewarm to advance Money if they had it, & too indolent to attend to the Execution of any Plan which requires any Attention on their Part." Page agreed that the company ought to offer part of its 40,000 acres as payment for procuring such workers. Washington then told Lutterloh that the company's portion of the swamp was "capable of being made as valuable a tract of Land as any in the Country." Regretfully, Washington admitted that his partners were "in a manner, inattentive to the business." He knew they would not advance money, but they might give Lutterloh a portion of the company's holdings, which "would be highly advantageous to the Settlers" brought to the swamp. Upon receiving a good proposal, Washington wrote, "I would in that case use every endeavor to convince the Company that an agreement might be entered into." In reply, Lutterloh made clear that he sought a contract or subscription, payable in cash. He suggested that he visit Virginia to sell his idea to the partners in person, but Washington knew that his coming would do no good.

The summer of 1787 brought severe drought to Virginia. In the first week of April, Edmund Pendleton heard that "the good old women" in Caroline County were terrified by a report from Gloucester County, where "a Speaking Cow" had predicted a "dry, bloody & fatal" summer. London had a learned pig; Virginia had a clairvoyant cow. Pendleton thought this was an April Fool's joke that had taken on a life of its own. The cow turned out to be partly right. By the first week of July, the heat in and around the Dismal Swamp was "intollerable." A traveler doing no heavy work felt "almost Sweated to death." The rest of Virginia suffered similar dryness. George Washington's corn crop was "an almost total loss." At Dismal Plantation the greater part of the rice was "entirely blasted," and the corn looked "very indifferent." John Driver reported to David Jameson: "the place is getting much out of order."

Neither George Washington nor John Page found buyers for his land. The fall of tobacco prices, overextension of credit ending in unpaid debts, and great reduction of circulating gold and silver meant a commercial depression. The times did not favor selling good land for a high price with prompt remittance. Nor did Washington get many payments from his debtors. After the drought of 1787 and Washington's return from presiding over the convention which drafted a new Constitution for the United States, he said that those months "have caused me more perplexity and given me more uneasiness than I ever experienced before from the want of money."

Ten days after the meeting of the Dismal Swamp Company in Richmond, Anthony Bacon, at the age of sixty-seven, wrote his will in his home facing the Cyfarthfa blast furnace across the River Taff from Merthyr Tydfil. His wife, Elizabeth, lived with him. His and Mary Bushby's youngest son, William, was fourteen months old. In his will Bacon acknowledged that he was the father of all five of Bushby's children, four sons and a daughter named Elizabeth. A month later he signed and dated the will in the presence of witnesses, including Richard Crawshay, his partner managing operations at Cyfarthfa.

Across the Atlantic, the government of North Carolina advertised an auction of three tracts, totaling 660 acres, which the state had seized from Bacon by law the previous year. Before the war he acquired this land from Aquila Sugg, a merchant and justice of the peace in Tarboro, who owed him more than £3,380 sterling. Bacon's records showed more debts due from North Carolinians than from citizens of any other state: about £19,180 sterling. Virginia law prohibited foreigners from owning land in the state. Still, the partners of the Dismal Swamp Company treated Bacon's share as his property, though they had not heard from him in years. Bacon's debtors owed him more than £6,000 in Maryland and almost £5,400 in Virginia. Nearly half of the Virginia sum was due from the estate of Fielding Lewis.

Bacon's will disposed of his three ironworks—those at Cyfarthfa, the Plymouth furnace south of Merthyr Tydfil, and the Hirwaun furnace in the Cynon Valley just west of the Taff—by dividing them among his first three sons. The oldest, Anthony, was sixteen, attending school in Gloucester under the name William Addison. He was to receive the Cyfarthfa furnace and forge, with the land leases at Merthyr Tydfil. Thomas was to receive Plymouth, and Robert was to receive Hirwaun. The daughter, Elizabeth, who suffered from "lameness," and the baby, William, were to be supported by a fund consisting of profits from all his holdings. To Mary Bushby, Bacon bequeathed £1,000 and an annual payment of £50 for support of each of the four youngest children as long as they lived with her. To his wife he left an annuity of £700 per year and the use of his house, offices, and gardens at Cyfarthfa, later to go to his oldest son after her departure or death. She was also to receive his coach and the furniture and plate in his homes other than Cyfarthfa.

Bacon's bequest to his cousin and former partner, Anthony Richardson, was the unpaid money their partner Gilbert Francklyn owed Bacon. After a visit to England during the war, Francklyn had returned to Tobago in 1779 and lived there until 1789, when he moved to London. There he began a new career with the Society of Planters and Merchants. He wrote pamphlets defending slavery and denouncing humanitarians, egalitarians, and reformers.

Anthony Bacon bequeathed his share in the Dismal Swamp Company to his half brother, William Bacon. William's residence, Number 26, Thavies-Inn, was Anthony's last business address in London. Thavies-Inn was a street running south from Holborn just east of Hatton Garden, between St. Paul's Cathedral and the Inns of Court. On the site occupied until 1773 by ruins of an Inn of Chancery from the time of Edward III had risen a range of "handsome" new houses. Like Samuel Gist, William Bacon preferred to live in modern comfort. Anthony also left him a bequest of £500 and the proceeds of any North American debts he collected. Anthony asked him to pay one-fourth of that money to their nieces, the two daughters of the late Reverend Thomas Bacon. Rachel Bacon Harwood and Mary Bacon Passapae lived in Maryland.

Seven months after signing his will, Anthony Bacon died at Cyfarthfa on January 21, 1786. In an obituary the *Bristol Gazette* praised him: "Go to the mountains of Wales, and view his deeds—what roads, what industry, what civilisation, what sources of comfort and improvement he has opened in the once dreary and inaccessible district."

After Bacon's chosen executors declined to undertake the vast task, his estate was left in the administration of the Court of Chancery. William Bacon became receiver in Chancery for it; Richard Crawshay and William Stevens, a rich hosier in London, posted bond for him. The ironworks were leased until Bacon's sons each came into their inheritances at the age of twenty-four. For a rent of £1,000 per year the Cyfarthfa works went to Richard Crawshay, William Stevens, and James Cockshutt in partnership. Cockshutt managed production. For £650 per year, Richard Hill, Mary Bushby's brother-in-law, took a lease on the Plymouth furnace. Crawshay began to speak of Bacon's sons as "our young Landlords." Not long before the oldest turned twenty-four, he changed his name from Anthony Bushby to Anthony Bacon.

Richard Crawshay was an ambitious, peremptory man. His partnership at Cyfarthfa lasted only five years, after which he took sole control. He cultivated the heir. After the younger Anthony Bacon came into his inheritance, he turned the Cyfarthfa works over to Crawshay by lease or deed in return for an annual payment of £5,000. Bacon bought an estate overlooking the River Cynon and became a country gentleman. Crawshay and Stevens's capital expanded operations in Merthyr Tydfil; Crawshay said that in his first six years he put almost £50,000 into new facilities at Cyfarthfa. In the ten years after 1786, production of pig iron in South Wales rose from 12,500 tons per year to 34,000 tons per year. Of the latter, about 7,200 tons came from the furnaces at Cyfarthfa. Crawshay boasted to visitors "that at present he made more iron than probably any person in the *world.*" Merthyr Tydfil had three furnaces when the elder Anthony Bacon died. Twenty-five years later, it had seventeen.

In 1791, William Bacon's son, James, visited Dismal Plantation to get for his father "what information he can respecting the place." John Driver seemed chiefly concerned with raising money to pay the company's annual tax bill. The price of corn and rice had fallen so low that the plantation had not produced enough to meet an assessment of £101 currency. Driver said:

"the Sheriff will be anxious to get his money." He sent Bacon to York Town to learn more from David Jameson. William Bacon later divided his share of the Dismal Swamp Company: two-thirds to his son, James, and one-third to Gilbert Francklyn.

One of Virginia's last living ties to its old royal government fell away with the death of Secretary Thomas Nelson late in 1787, at the age of seventy-two. Forty-five years had passed since his father had bought for him the office of deputy secretary. Since leaving York Town during the siege, he had lived in quiet retirement in King William County, not far from Hanover Court House. He was surrounded by his sons, grandchildren, nieces, and nephews, as well as by good books in English and French. No longer making the careers of rising young men or overseeing land grants, he was "generally revered and esteemed," a tall, "noble figure" with white hair. After his death his share in the Dismal Swamp Company was divided evenly among his three sons: William, Thomas, and John, all former officers in the Continental Army. William and Thomas lived in Hanover County, John in Mecklenburg County. The Dismal Swamp Company was twenty-four years old. Only three of the original partners still held a share or part of a share: George Washington, Thomas Walker, and Samuel Gist.

After the Constitutional Convention in Philadelphia offered its new structure of government to the states for ratification, members of the Dismal Swamp Company differed in their opinions of it. Visitors to Mount Vernon heard George Washington say that he was "very anxious" to see all states ratify the Constitution. Alexander Donald wrote: "I never saw him so keen for any thing in my life, as he is for the adoption of the new Form of Government." Conversations at Mount Vernon touched on demagogues winning state elections to pursue "their own schemes," on the "impotence" of the Continental Congress, and on the danger of "Anarchy and civil war." Washington concluded: "it is more than probable we shall exhibit the last melancholy proof, that Mankind are not competent to their own government without the means of coercion in the Sovereign." By "sovereign" he meant not the people but the national government. Without a new, stronger government, he said, America faced "impending ruin."

Secretary Nelson's nephew, William Nelson, Jr., attorney in Williamsburg, did not support ratification. Nor did William's brother, Thomas, former governor of Virginia. John Page at first agreed with William that the Constitution should be amended before ratification to guard more effectively against too much power in the hands of the federal government. Page soon changed sides and supported ratification, though voters in Gloucester County passed him over to send stauncher Federalists to the state convention in June. Neither Nelson brother sought election. Instead of going to Richmond, William Nelson, Jr., got married to Abby Byrd, who soon was pregnant. Thomas Nelson, Jr.'s, daughter, Elizabeth, and John Page's son, Mann, were also married in June. This was the third wedding to join one of Nelson's children to one of Page's.

Voters who lived near the Dismal Swamp, as well as many others south of the James River, chose opponents of ratification as their delegates to the convention. After the new Constitution was adopted, these people still sent Antifederalists to the General Assembly and to the United States Congress. Outsiders often called the residents of Nansemond County stubborn and uncooperative. The flat terrain, tall trees, and scattered peach orchards for brandy-making struck visitors as "a long, dull, and insipid scene." Travelers could easily get lost but only with difficulty get directions from local people, who received them "with an ill grace." During the war, the Virginia authorities had thought Nansemond people were Tories, while the British had considered them rebels. Electing delegates to the ratifying convention, they did not expect impending ruin and anarchy in the absence of the new Constitution, or they did not care.

Writing from Richmond during debates over ratification, Archibald Stuart, a Federalist, reported: "The whole core of opponents to the paymt of British Debts are against us." The alignment was not so stark, but the man most hostile to paying British merchants, Patrick Henry, was also the leading critic of the Constitution. The merchants calculated that Virginians' debts to them contracted before the war had reached, with interest, a total of £2,305,408 sterling. A state law enacted in 1782 closed the courts to them. The treaty of peace overthrew that law, but Virginians, unlike debtors in other states, persisted in evasion. James Madison said that everyone knew "foreigners cannot get justice done them" in county courts. In 1787 the General Assembly repealed the law passed in 1776 prohibiting Britons' recovery of debts. But the new law also suspended their right to collect, on the grounds that the British Army kept garrisons on American soil south of the Great Lakes. A federal government established by the Constitution would create a system of federal courts. In these, Britons could seek enforcement of their claims against Virginia's recalcitrant debtors.

Debtors' evasions and state laws "benign to dishonest men" prolonged Virginia's reputation as a land of chicanery with too many "indolent, unindustrious, poor credit risks, big gamblers, tricksters." In London in the months between the Philadelphia convention and final approval of the Constitution, Joshua Johnson decided to close his firm's accounts in Virginia and send no more merchandise. He wrote: "I long to get rid of that State." Virginia reduced its public debt by devaluing wartime currency at the rate of 1,000 to 1. The state also accepted wartime certificates or vouchers, issued in lieu of cash, for payment of taxes and purchase of land from the state. Since no one knew how many of these had been drawn during the war, no one knew the size of the public debt.

The Richmond convention ratified the Constitution on June 25, 1788, by a vote of 89 to 79. Six of the delegates in the majority came from west of the Allegheny Mountains. Concerned about the presence of British forts and troops in the west, these delegates wished to deprive the British government of its excuse for that incursion, Virginians' refusal to pay their debts. The day after the convention voted on the Constitution, David Anderson wrote a letter to his brother, William, in London, giving him the news. The vessel bearing it made a swift passage, and William Anderson opened the letter on August 8. Samuel Gist could begin to prepare his cases against debtors for litigation in the federal courts soon to be established. In Virginia, William Nelson, Jr., foresaw that he and other lawyers could benefit from ratification: "The new constitution will open a wide field to us."

When members of the Dismal Swamp Company met in Richmond, with Reuben Lindsay attending in place of Dr. Thomas Walker, Walker was entering his seventies. His shoulders were rounded, his hair was gray. He took no more long journeys. He retained his good humor, but he was often ill. His memory had begun to fail.

Dr. Walker's youngest son, Francis, turned twenty-one in 1785. That summer he began to manage the affairs of the Loyal Company; he visited the grant in 1785 and 1786. Three years later the Walkers contracted with Francis Preston to act as subagent, collecting rents and dealing with tenants. Among the subjects Dr. Walker had difficulty remembering were the surveying fees the Loyal Company had left unpaid for twenty-five years.

Francis Walker had a warm heart and a quick mind. He taught law to Landon Cabell. The voters of Albemarle County elected Walker to the House of Delegates. Still, he lacked ambition, preferring to live at Castle Hill with his father and stepmother and more than eighty-five slaves. He knew he would inherit the house and the plantation. Dr. Walker and Francis sometimes rode across their rolling acres near the base of a chain of hills known as the Southwest Mountains. During one such ride with several guests, Dr. Walker suddenly galloped up to his son and lashed Francis with a horsewhip, giving him "several good cuts." Francis pulled away and asked his father why he had attacked him. Dr. Walker said: "My son, that is one of the corner-trees of your estate, & I wanted to make you remember it." Dr. Walker had devoted a large part of his life to land and its boundaries. If memory failed, those memories should fade last.

Francis Preston served the Walkers as subagent less than four years. He was subject to a difficulty of which many knew but few spoke: Francis Walker, with several of his brothers and sisters, was "liable to intoxication." On two visits to Castle Hill, Preston found Walker too drunk to deal with Loyal Company business. According to gossips, Dr. Walker himself "had a strong propensity this way, which however, his prudence & fortitude mastered, 'till he was old." Francis had a close attachment to his "good father" and dreaded the day death would "deprive his dependents of so inestimable a friend." One of the son's chief pleasures was to reminisce about the winter of 1779–80 and the adventures of Dr. Walker's surveying party as it extended Virginia's boundary westward. Recalling his father's vigor and humor while snowbound, Francis relived "some moments of the greatest happiness I ever enjoyed."

Shortly before delegates to the ratifying convention gathered in Richmond, Thomas Walker wrote his will. To his other sons and sons-in-law he left bequests of varying sizes in cash or livestock. Joseph Hornsby was to receive eight white steers. Dr. Walker and his second wife, Elizabeth Thornton Walker, had signed an agreement before their wedding, by which she retained control of her property and disavowed any claim on his. Castle Hill, Dr. Walker's adjoining lands, and all his possessions, including his two quarter-shares in the Dismal Swamp Company, he bequeathed to Francis.

In the years after Dr. Walker signed his will, Francis managed Castle Hill and his father's affairs, "closely engaged in Law suits and old accounts." In June 1789, Virginians learned that Gawin Corbin Tucker, the son whom Robert Tucker had planned to leave richly endowed with property in and near Norfolk, "drank himself to Death" at the age of thirty-four. Robert Tucker's insolvent estate still held his share in the Dismal Swamp Company. In June, Francis Walker saw the eldest of Elizabeth Farley Dunbar's four daughters in Albemarle County. Though only seventeen, she was already a widow. Walker's friend, John Banister, Jr., had died soon after he and Elizabeth Farley were married early in 1788. He left her "a very young gay widow." Walker had heard that she was "very rich," reported to receive £1,200 sterling per year from Antigua. Rumor apparently credited her with all the profits from the Mercers Creek plantation, though these were divided among the four sisters. He thought she was "sensible" and "handsome." Edward Carter escorted her to the springs. The younger William Aitchison looked ready to court her; James Parker's son wrote from Norfolk: "if he succeeds it will be the best Spec. he ever made." The same thought came to Francis Walker: "Had I not been extremely engaged should have joined in the escort & speculated in such a commodity."

Dr. Walker had helped his sons and sons-in-law with gifts of money, land, and other property. He apparently deducted these from the inheritance each was to receive, then used bequests in his will to reach his intended total. His will left his son, John, "seventy pounds twelve shillings and nine pence half penny to-gether with the sums heretofore charged him on my books." John felt aggrieved by his father's conduct. He wrote resentfully about "the pittance of a fortune I have received." The will was one more instance of how this "miserable" inheritance had been "dribbled out to me in shillings & pence, or trifles of that value, thro' the space of more than thirty years."

Dr. Walker, at the time of writing his will, had forty-four living grandchildren. Two years before his death, two of those grandchildren, Mildred Hornsby and Nicholas Meriwether Lewis, were married in Williamsburg. The first cousins made, a friend said, "an exact match." The bride enjoyed both minuets and reels. Joseph Hornsby treated his daughter and son-in-law and guests to two nights of dancing in the rooms in which Peyton Randolph and Speaker Robinson once had talked politics.

The couple's uncle, John Walker, had bitter thoughts about his own marriage, as well as about his father's bequest. Almost at the same time that his father wrote a will, his wife revealed to him that, twenty years earlier, Thomas Jefferson had tried to seduce her while John and Dr. Walker were at Fort Stanwix with men of the Six Nations and other tribes. His closest friend had betrayed him. Elizabeth Moore Walker had tried to dissuade her husband from making Jefferson executor of his will, but she did not explain her reason until Jefferson was on the other side of the Atlantic as American minister to France. She unfolded a lurid tale of his repeated attempts at seduction from 1768 until 1779, taking her story far beyond Jefferson's admission that he had "offered love" to her in 1768. John Walker believed the worst and remained angry until his last days. If Dr. Walker ever learned of the quarrel between his son and his former ward, he left no sign.

Notwithstanding Dr. Walker's dimming memory and uncertain health, he enjoyed himself at Castle Hill in his mid-seventies. A visitor might easily guess for whom the large leather easy chair was reserved. Walker was "very fond of telling anecdotes." The books in his library were those of a busy man, largely practical or devotional. He had spent much of his life outdoors. In his last years he still enjoyed "all kinds of sports." After snow fell at Castle Hill, Dr. Walker pressed everyone into a snowball fight—his children, grandchildren, and "all guests" in a general battle. Many years later, people said of his three sons, John, Thomas, and Francis: "None seems to have inherited the restless energy of the old Dr."

Panic and a collapse of credit again struck the City of London in 1788, beginning with the bankruptcy of Britain's largest firm of calico printers, Hargreaves, Anstie, Smith & Hall. Directors of the Bank of England spent their days sorting out bad bills of exchange. As usual, some people said that so many failures in so short a time had not occurred since the bursting of the South Sea Bubble. Firms trading to America looked especially vulnerable. On Friday, August 1, James Russell, longtime Chesapeake merchant, died at the age of eighty. Before the war he had been London's fourth-largest importer of tobacco. He left nothing for his grandsons to inherit except uncollected debts owed by Americans.

James Parker's son, Patrick, visited London at the height of the panic in June. He was trying to re-establish the family firm in Virginia and to recover some of his father's holdings in and near Norfolk. James reluctantly extended credit to his son for the purchase of trade goods. Patrick worried about repaying his father as he stopped in the subscribers' room at Lloyd's, where he met Samuel Gist. Gist offered to help; he promised to accept a bill of exchange for more than £140 sterling, drawn by a merchant in Northampton County, Virginia, who owed money to Patrick. The merchant had shown a letter from Gist which had convinced Patrick to take the bill in payment. With Gist's assurances Patrick Parker returned to Norfolk in August. In the following months, the bill of exchange came back protested three times. Parker delayed repaying his father, hired an attorney to sue the Northampton merchant, and admitted that he had been misled by "that Sneaking Lying Creature Sam Gists promise."

In the summer of the panic, Gist moved to his new home in Gower Street. Builders worked to extend the row of adjoining, almost identical dwellings northward from Bedford Square. Such austere, strict, symmetrically rectangular structures moved Thomas Jefferson to write: "Their architecture is in the most wretched stile I ever saw." New neighbors of Sarah Siddons's and Samuel Gist's were retired ship captains, physicians, a few members of Parliament, a builder, Joseph Kirkman, an important corn merchant, Claude Scott, and the Reverend William Morice, longtime secretary of the Society for the Propagation of the Gospel in Foreign Parts. When the celebrated fortune teller Mrs. Williams came to London from Bristol and Bath, she offered her clairvoyance at a half-crown per session in her house in Gower Street. John Scott, the Crown's solicitor general, moved into Number 42 not long after Gist took Number 37. The official residence of the lord chancellor stood just down the street in Bedford Square. Other former residents of the City besides Gist escaped smoke and grime by settling among the gardens of Gower Street. Gist's colleague at Lloyd's, Marmaduke Peacock, took Number 25. A newly married couple, Osgood Hanbury and Susannah Willet Barclay Hanbury, who united two banking families, became their neighbors. Charles Blagden, secretary of the Royal Society, lived nearby. Mrs. Siddons was not the only artist. The venerable organist and composer, John Worgan, lived at Number 65. In former times his playing had been mentioned in the same breath with that of Handel.

Behind his residence Gist kept a coach and horses in a coach house and stables. He employed a coachman and a full staff of servants. A visitor quickly saw that Gist lived "much in style," among pictures and books, his meals served on silver. His ink stood in a silver inkwell; big candles on pillar candlesticks were put out with a silver snuffer. To check the time he reached to a gold chain with pendant seals and pulled out a gold watch made by Mudge & Dutton.

On Tower Hill, in America Square, the three partners of William Anderson & Company struggled to turn a profit. For months at the end of 1788 and early in 1789 unusually harsh cold interrupted commerce in London. "The streets are a stratum of ice. The river is so hard frozen, that fairs are held upon it." Men who ordinarily worked on the river and along the quays were reduced to begging in the street. The *Planter* did not sail for the York River until March 12.

In June a wedding party came to America Square. John Shoolbred's daughter was married to the Andersons' neighbor, Jerome Bernard Weuves, a rising man in the Company of Merchants Trading to Africa. Shoolbred and his partner, Gilbert Ross, held two of the three London seats on the company's committee. Weuves had gone to the Gold Coast the year before the *Hope* sailed and served there fourteen years, the last six as governor, in turn, of Annamaboe Fort and Cape Coast Castle. He moved back to London in 1784. In the months before his wedding he helped the Company of Merchants by testifying to a committee of the Privy Council in defense of the slave trade.

In June 1788, William Anderson held too much unsold tobacco. A year later his agents in Virginia offered advances of seven to ten guineas per hogshead, while a rival firm, Donald & Burton, told its agents not to go above £6. A short crop came to market in 1789. The price in London rose above £9 per hogshead, with some speculators willing to pay more than £14. Anderson sold a hogshead of Dr. Thomas Walker's tobacco for £13 10s. As his fortunes in business turned better, William Anderson had to find new agents in Virginia because "unhappy family differences" led him to stop relying on some of his kinsmen.

Samuel Gist at last received £100 sterling from the Dismal Swamp Company in payment for tools and supplies sent long ago and lost in the British invasion. The company paid the remaining £54 5s. a few years later. Gist was eloquent on the subject of Virginia debtors. He told William Jones in the summer of 1789 "that he not only has not received anything from his old debts, but that he had shipped a good deal at the peace to men he considered as good as any on the continent, from whom he has received little or nothing since." Jones understood all too well. His firm, Farell & Jones, had been especially unlucky in its dealings with men linked to the Dismal Swamp Company. Among Jones's many large debtors were Dr. Walker, David Meade, John Syme, and the estate of William Byrd. Gist claimed to be owed £34,000. Jones claimed to be owed £80,000.

At home in Gower Street, Gist spent part of the summer of 1789 drawing up a memorial to the Royal Commission for Enquiring into the Losses, Services and Claims of the American Loyalists. Parliament had just extended the commission's inquiry for another year after receiving "strong applications from various persons" who said they had been prevented from applying for compensation earlier. A list of them in the act of 1789 contained the name of Samuel Gist. In his memorial he said he had lost all his property in Virginia. He asked for £23,051 19s. 5d. He told the commissioners that his daughter, Mary, had eloped while under age, married William Anderson "against your memorialists Approbation," and moved to Virginia. During the war, the state had vested all Gist's property in Mary Anderson, "whereby your memorialist is deprived of the greatest part of the Labour of the early part of his Life."

More than one-tenth of the sum Gist sought—£2,857 sterling—he set as the value of his three quarter-shares in the Dismal Swamp Company. He explained that since 1762 the company had been "expending Vast Sums of Money in Building draining & improveing." The swamp, he wrote, "is full of

Timber, & is among the Richest Land in the World." He calculated the compensation due him by computing his portion of the company's 40,000 acres at 2,857 acres and by setting on them a value of £1 sterling per acre.

In case the commissioners might think it odd that Gist, having lost such a large sum, waited until six years after the war to file a claim, he accounted for his delay. The "true cause" of it was "the extreme delicacy of his Situation & his Unwillingness to burthen his Country with any expence until his Friends in Virginia Assured him he had no Chance of relief in that Country." By the words "extreme delicacy," Gist apparently alluded to his relations with the Andersons. The commissioners must know that Mary and William Anderson lived in his former residence in America Square and that William Anderson had joined Gist's other son-in-law and Gist's former clerk in taking over his business as a tobacco and dry goods merchant. The Andersons remained American citizens. Gist's property in Virginia was theirs by law. But was it so in practice, the commissioners might ask. With his memorial he submitted documents designed to show that William Anderson "will not part with the Estate" unless Gist settled upon Mary Anderson a fortune equal to its value. This was out of the question. Thus, he explained, his Virginia property was lost to him, "as much as tho' he was Actually Dead & had no other Child." Of course, he did not tell the commissioners that the profits of the labor of his slaves on his Virginia plantations, nominally owned by the Andersons, came each year in a remittance from Benjamin Toler. The commissioners were not gullible men. Consideration of Gist's claim took many years.

The season of 1788–89 at Drury Lane Theatre brought another series of triumphs for Sarah Siddons: Lady Macbeth, Queen Katharine in *Henry VIII*, the title role in *Jane Shore*, her first London appearance in *Romeo and Juliet*, and her usual, ever popular roles in *The Gamester*, *The Fair Penitent*, *Venice Preserv'd*, and *Isabella; or, the Fatal Marriage*. A member of her audience for a later performance of *Macbeth* wrote: "In the sleepwalking scene the mere sight of her makes every drop of blood run cold."

At the end of the season, she temporarily retired from the stage to regain her health. She said she was "convinced if I could keep clear of these dreadful Theatrical exertions which enflame my blood and exhaust my Strength that I should be perfectly well in a fortnight." Though she liked her "nice house" in Gower Street, she and her husband decided to leave the neighborhood. They bought a house, Number 49, in Great Marlborough Street and moved in 1790. She soon returned to the stage; her admirers left Gower Street to follow her to her new address. Among them was a young Irish law student who said that "Mrs. Siddons had conceived *a passion for Him*. He fancied that she sent persons after Him to *drug* his victuals in order to inspire Him with love for Her." He repeatedly visited Great Marlborough Street and wrote "innumerable Letters" to Mrs. Siddons until he was taken into custody and sent back to Ireland. After 1790 the street in front of Samuel Gist's house was quieter than it had been during his first two years there.

A young British officer visiting Mount Vernon in 1788 admired the improvements George Washington had made: "He seems to be laying out his grownds with great tast in the English fashion." Washington's enthusiasm for details of agriculture showed plainly in his barns, livestock, and equipment; "he appears to be the compleatest Gentleman farmer I have ever met in America and perhaps I may Add England." Since the end of the war, Washington had enjoyed five years back at Mount Vernon. Then the first electors unanimously chose him as president of the United States. He moved to Manhattan.

At Mount Vernon one of Washington's most frequent guests was Henry Lee. A short, talkative man in his early thirties, Lee had won Washington's favor as a daring officer in the Continental Army. During the last years of the war he commanded a legion—a small force combining infantry and cavalry—in the Carolinas. He left the army in 1782. He was married to Matilda Lee, granddaughter of one of his uncles and daughter of Philip Ludwell Lee. She had inherited her father's plantation with its elegant brick mansion, Stratford Hall, overlooking the Potomac about 80 miles downriver from Mount Vernon. Henry Lee did not aspire to a retired life as a gentleman farmer. He sought public office, serving in the House of Delegates and the Continental Congress. He vehemently supported the Constitution as a delegate to the ratifying convention. He traveled often, and he took a growing interest in land speculation.

Lee admired an Arabian stallion Washington had bought from the estate of his late stepson, John Parke Custis. Sixteen hands high, with "a very beautiful shape," Magnolio was "in high health, spirits, and flesh"—"as fine a horse as any born in this country." Lee, a skilled horseman, coveted the stallion. Late in 1788 he offered Washington 5,000 acres of land in western Kentucky in exchange. After dinner on Tuesday, December 9, the two men closed the bargain.

Lee shared Washington's faith in the Potomac Company and its future canal at Great Falls as sure means to wider commerce and great wealth. In 1788 he bought 500 acres on the south bank of the Potomac, where the canal was to run. He envisioned a town there: Matildaville. In his mind's eye he already saw wharves, merchants' offices, warehouses, residences. After acquiring Magnolio, Lee told Washington that he wished to buy land in the Dismal Swamp. On the same principle by which a Potomac canal raised the value of Great Falls property, a Dismal Swamp canal would make property near Suffolk and Lake Drummond worth even more than it already was. Lee mentioned the tracts purchased jointly by Washington, Fielding Lewis, and Dr. Thomas Walker in 1764 and 1766, which he would be glad to get.

As Washington was inaugurated in New York, the April 1789 issue of *The Columbian Magazine* in Philadelphia published part of the elder William Byrd's proposal for draining the Dismal Swamp. This version included Byrd's description of the swamp and his argument for the benefits of draining it. The contributor, who could have obtained the text only by visiting Westover and copying it or by getting someone else to do so, omitted the last section of the manuscript. In that part, Byrd described how easily the project might expand in ten years from twenty slaves to three hundred, while financing itself, generating profits, and increasing the price of shares tenfold.

In remarks upon this text the "correspondent" cared less about Byrd's plan to drain the swamp than about Byrd's foresight in suggesting a canal to connect the Pasquotank River of North Carolina with the Elizabeth River of Virginia. The contributor used Byrd to endorse the projected new Dismal Swamp canal. "The advantages . . . must be obviously great to the community in general." One of America's leading periodicals in the nation's largest city in effect advertised that the Dismal Swamp and land along the Elizabeth River were about to become sites of a boom in commerce and real estate.

Busied with establishing a new government and disillusioned by the failure of his attempts since 1784 to revive the Dismal Swamp Company, George Washington no longer devoted time to promoting the Nansemond County prosperity he had predicted for the previous twenty-five years. The active partners were David Jameson, David Meade, Joseph Hornsby, and William Nelson, Jr. Jameson's nephew, John, called on Washington in New York during his first year as president, and they conversed about the Dismal Swamp Company. Washington said that he "did not expect ever to meet the Company again." He asked David Jameson to represent him. Late in the year, Washington appointed William Nelson, Jr., as United States attorney for the Virginia District. By giving the office to a man who had opposed ratification of the Constitution, Washington reassured Antifederalists that they would not be proscribed. Soon after moving back to Richmond, however, Nelson learned that the unsalaried office yielded little income in fees. He did not hold it long.

John Driver's reports to David Jameson, written from Suffolk, complained about the partners' neglect of the Dismal Swamp Company. Driver had difficulty finding a competent overseer for Dismal Plantation. In the spring of 1789 he dismissed one who would not "do right." For months no white man lived there. Driver gave the title "foreman" to "one of the old fellows" who had not left with the British. Driver visited the plantation two or three times a week. The small group of black people followed their annual routine of producing rice and corn, cleaning and mending ditches to increase the size of their crops. Driver wrote to Jameson: "If you think the owners of the Swamp do not intend to put any more hands there I wou'd wish to have nothing more to do with it. The place is so much out of order & such a heavy Tax to pay & nothing made I am tired of the business." Nansemond County encroachers entered the company's land, cut down trees, and hauled them away. Before the end of the summer, Driver chose Demsey Smith, a man he barely knew, as an interim overseer and warned Jameson to find another manager: "I have a very great notion of going next Summer to the Western Country." Four years of trips from Suffolk into the Dismal Swamp made Kentucky look inviting.

In the first days of 1790, Major John Simon Farley arrived in Norfolk from Antigua. He was forty-three. He had not heeded the urgent advice of his late uncle to resign from the British Army in order to protect his interest in the Land of Eden and in land along the northeastern margin of the Dismal Swamp. Nevertheless, he and his sister, Elizabeth Morson, remembered their father's claim and asserted it. Francis Farley's daughter-in-law, Elizabeth Farley Dunbar, and her four daughters ought not to keep for themselves all the riches of Norfolk County plantations and the Land of Eden. Major Farley believed that Francis Farley had refrained from giving his nephew and niece title to their share because he feared that all property of British subjects in America would be confiscated. The holdings stayed safely intact by remaining in the hands of American citizens, Farley's four granddaughters. The war was over; confiscations had ceased. If Elizabeth Dunbar and her daughters refused to divide the land, Major Farley stood ready to go to court in Virginia and North Carolina. He obtained a letter of introduction to a good attorney, St. George Tucker, and left Norfolk for Williamsburg.

In New York, on Thursday, March 4, 1790, George and Martha Washington gave a dinner for Vice President John Adams and the members of the Senate. The senators had deep disagreements over Secretary of the Treasury Alexander Hamilton's proposals for funding the public debts of the national and state governments. But Thursday afternoon's occasion was "a dinner of dignity." Senator Samuel Johnston of North Carolina had tried, twenty-five years earlier, to incommode the Dismal Swamp Company and force its partners to include the Campania Company in their huge anticipated profits. In the Washingtons' New York residence he drank excellent champagne and took after-dinner coffee with Martha Washington, "a most amiable Woman." At dinner the president looked grave. Between courses he played with his silverware, drumming on the table with a knife or fork. "The President seemed to bear in his Countenance a settled Aspect of Melancholy." The next day George Washington wrote to a kinsman in Virginia, describing his terms for selling some land in Gloucester County. He said that he wanted to sell, not lease to renters, "having found, from experience, that estates at a distance plague more than they profit the Proprietors of them."

The unaccountable failure of land in and near the Dismal Swamp to rise rapidly in value disappointed men who tried to emulate the foresight of the Dismal Swamp Company and to profit by the coming canal. Among these were Thomas Ruston and William Short. After coming into his fortune in 1785, Dr. Ruston returned to America to grow richer through land speculation. William Short, a friend and classmate of William Nelson, Jr.'s, went to France in October 1784 as secretary to the American legation. After Thomas Jefferson left Paris to become secretary of state, Short remained as chargé d'affaires. He, too, wished to grow rich. Ruston failed, while Short succeeded, but neither profited from Nansemond and Norfolk counties.

Before Ruston gave his power of attorney to Samuel Gist and sailed from London, he received Hugh Williamson's reports on the Dismal Swamp and on two stretches of land along the Nansemond River. Williamson said that buying into the Dismal Swamp Company was "impracticable. Several Gentlemen have told me that they had attempted in vain." But Ruston's tracts of 600 acres and 300 acres were said to be worth £1,500 sterling, and 1,000 acres of the Dismal Swamp adjoining these tracts went for 75¢ per acre. Neither Williamson nor Ruston suggested that this disparity in price looked odd. Ruston reached Philadelphia in 1785 and visited Virginia late in 1787.

Preparing to sail for France at the age of twenty-five, William Short needed money. He had inherited property in North Carolina, which he sold to John Harvie, head of the Virginia Land Office. Harvie paid half the price in interest-bearing Virginia land certificates and half in land—a two-thirds interest in 15,000 acres in Kentucky and a deed to 1,000 acres of the Green Sea in the Dismal Swamp. Short later wrote of the deal: "I think I must have been in a kind of delirium." In his mind's eye he saw "the best 15000 acres of all the western country." The Green Sea tract in Norfolk County, 1,000 acres of reeds adjoining Patrick Henry's holdings, Short pictured as "worth their cover in gold." He imagined the new canal cutting through his property. Harvie knew but did not say until years later that Green Sea lands were "Immense ponds of Water which probably will not be Drained in a Century." They had "little Worth." Almost thirty years after Short acquired the tract, its annual tax bill was $2.

Coming into money changed Dr. Thomas Ruston. He "lost all the habits of innocence, friendship, and benevolence of his early life." Instead of enjoying his freedom, he became greedy. He speculated wildly. By 1790 he had run through his fortune and was "a Bankrupt out of jail." His land adjoining the Dismal Swamp was occupied by tenants, who paid annual rents ranging from £1 10s. to £6 Virginia currency. The total payments for 1790 were less than £19. John Driver collected these, not charging Ruston a commission because the sums were "trifling." Even so, Ruston badgered both his attorney, William Nivison, and Driver with accusations and demands. He wished to sell the land, but he had difficulty understanding why tracts with an assessed value of slightly less than £1 per acre did not find buyers at a price of £6 per acre. In desperate straits, Ruston sought rescue through matrimony, courting two of Philadelphia's richest widows. They treated him with "every possible indignity. . . . He was the object of the contempt and pity of the whole city."

Cyrus Griffin was the new federal judge for the Virginia District. For sittings of the United States Circuit Court he was joined by one or two justices of the Supreme Court. They first sat alternately in Williamsburg and Charlottesville, but in 1791 they settled in Richmond. Griffin opened his court in the capitol in Richmond on Tuesday, December 15, 1789. This new venue offered an opportunity for John Wickham, a twenty-seven-year-old attorney, to move from Williamsburg to Richmond. When people spoke of him, the word "clever" came to mind. His uncle was Edmund Fanning, loyalist politician and soldier, who in 1771 had gone to New York with Governor William Tryon and endured the drunken wrath of Lord Dunmore. Wickham had held a commission in a loyalist regiment at the end of the war, and had been taken prisoner near Roanoke, Virginia, while carrying British dispatches from New York to Charleston. His "extreme youth" and "the interest of influential citizens" helped him escape punishment. In 1783 he feared that "the Disposition for Persecution" would prevent him from living in America, but in December 1785 he arrived in Williamsburg to study law with St. George Tucker and George Wythe. He remained there through 1789, practicing law, living next door to Tucker, building a library of law books.

John Marshall was eight years older than Wickham; he had practiced law in Richmond for six years when Wickham was admitted to the Virginia bar. To a person who needed an attorney in Williamsburg in 1789 he recommended Wickham as "a young man of great cleaverness." Marshall's lank, lounging, relaxed appearance did not look formidable at first sight. Yet he was a leader of the Richmond bar by the time the federal court opened and Wickham moved to Richmond.

Richmond, William Byrd's city at the falls of the James, was growing. In 1790 it held more than 3,700 residents—about 2,000 whites and 1,700 blacks. It looked raw. Dirt streets ran uphill from the north bank of the river. Wind raised clouds of dust and rain made thick mud. Wharves and buildings near the river were wooden structures, newly rebuilt after a recent fire. People in trade lived near the river; attorneys, state officials, and richer people lived up the hill. There a new capitol building was slowly rising, which would, Thomas Jefferson hoped, teach Americans classical taste in architecture. A British merchant visiting Richmond said of the structure: "I wish instead of laying out their money so ridiculously that they would first pay the British debts." The old capitol, near the river, looked like a barn. Delegates and senators attended their noisy sessions dressed in the same clothes they wore in their fields. To a resident of London, Richmond was "one of the dirtiest holes of a place I ever was in."

To the extent that a young attorney could afford to specialize, John Wickham devoted his practice to debts. He represented British creditors suing Virginians in federal court. His colleagues at the bar—John Marshall, Bushrod Washington, William Nelson, Jr., and others—also took such cases. Marshall represented debtors; Wickham found his best clients among creditors. After Wickham consented to pursue debts owed to the House of Norton, Charles Grymes, a collection agent, congratulated John Hatley Norton on his new attorney, saying: "he appears to be exceedingly cleaver." Unlike Marshall, Wickham stayed out of politics. Nevertheless, his early life as a loyalist earned him a reputation as a Tory, which served him well in attracting British clients. He had neither Marshall's ease and cogency nor Patrick Henry's dramatic voice and gestures, but he was witty, urbane, genteel, with beautiful elocution, able to "gild and decorate the darkest subjects." He thought fast on his feet, adjusting smoothly to surprises in court. William Nelson, Jr., called him "the most acute and quick man at the bar." Though Wickham looked younger than his years and seemed lighthearted, he knew how to make his meaning clear through the mask of his politesse. He wrote to a client's debtor: "I shall feel much pleasure if I find it unnecessary to have recourse to coercive measures."

Wickham successfully sued the estate of Robert Munford for more than £2,000 sterling. He represented many British firms, among them William Jones of Farell & Jones. While William Anderson & Company retained John Marshall, Samuel Gist chose Wickham. For receiving payment from debtors and transferring the money to creditors, he charged a commission of 5 percent. For collecting through litigation, he charged 10 percent. His practice in 1791 was "much more profitable . . . than it had ever been before." People spoke of him as "the famous lawyer." On Christmas Eve he and his cousin, Mary Smith Fanning, were married. In the following years his practice continued "to grow more and more profitable." He and John Marshall built large brick houses on the hill.

In June 1790, William Jones, acting through his Virginia attorney Jerman Baker, later joined by John Wickham and others, brought suit against Dr. Thomas Walker in the United States Circuit Court for the Virginia District. This was one of thirty cases Jones began in the court's first three terms. The suit alleged that Dr. Walker owed Farell & Jones £2,903 15s. 8d. sterling. In December, Francis Walker and John Walker appeared in court for their father. Arguments did not take place until the last week of November 1791. The federal courts' decision on Dr. Walker would govern pending and future suits for debts to British merchants contracted before the war. On the bench were Judge Cyrus Griffin and two justices of the Supreme Court, Thomas Johnson and John Blair. Each side was represented by four attorneys. For the plaintiff: John Wickham, Jerman Baker, Andrew Ronald, and Burwell Starke. For the defendant: Patrick Henry, John Marshall, Alexander Campbell, and James Innes. Arguments lasted more than a week. Dr. Walker's attorneys resorted to the usual pleas: that the dissolution of the colonial government ended the obligation; that British property was forfeit to the state; that Virginia law prohibited recovery; that, in accordance with wartime state law, he had paid his debt to the Virginia Loan Office rather than to his creditor; that the British still owed Virginians compensation for slaves who had left with the British Army; that the British violated the treaty of peace by keeping troops south of the Great Lakes. Patrick Henry, after uncharacteristically vigorous research, went further, giving a long, erudite, impassioned argument designed to raise the matter of Dr. Walker's debt to a question of the nature of man and of nations. Although the Court gave no decision, the attorneys impressed even the skeptical. William Nelson, Jr., wrote: "I did not think so much could have been said against their payment." While others praised Henry's eloquence and scholarship, Nelson noticed the attorneys of the future: "Campbell & Wickham are young men of great talents." Most listeners, even those who owed nothing to Britons, "thought there could not be a recovery."

The court delayed its ruling. Patrick Henry returned to Richmond with his little brown wig in May 1792, ready "to harangue 'em on the impropriety of paying." Justice James Wilson of the Supreme Court and Judge Griffin sat for only a week, ignoring more than one hundred debt cases. A creditor's attorney heard Wilson say to Henry in a hall of the capitol: "Mr. Henry it will not be necessary for you to attend longer, as we decline going into the general question."

In the spring of 1793, Judge Griffin, Chief Justice John Jay, and Justice James Iredell heard arguments in another suit for a debt owed to Farell & Jones. William Jones had died, waiting for his money. John Tyndale Warre, or Ware, pursued the firm's debtors. In the case of *Ware* v. *Hylton*, the court struck down all but one of the debtors' arguments. Griffin and Iredell outvoted Jay in accepting the plea of wartime payment into the state Loan Office. Since few debtors had made such payments, creditors could win many cases. In 1793 verdicts were given in sixty-eight cases of British debts; plaintiffs won fifty-two. Three years later the Supreme Court reversed Griffin and Iredell on the Loan Office question, disallowing Virginians' last defense. By then Dr. Walker had died.

Many debts went uncollected for lack of proof. Nor did winning verdicts necessarily mean receiving money. But John Wickham did well for Samuel Gist, as did Gist's agent for collections, Thomas Shore. Wickham and Shore recovered and remitted "large sums." These did not appear in the ledgers Gist submitted in pursuit of compensation from the Crown for his losses in America as a loyal subject of the king.

The race for the hand of the first of Francis Farley's four Virginia granddaughters, the young widow Elizabeth Farley Banister, ended in victory for Thomas Lee Shippen. Though a Pennsylvanian, he was also a Lee. His mother, Alice Lee Shippen, was a sister of the well-known Lee brothers— William, Arthur, Richard Henry, and Francis Lightfoot—and the aunt of Henry Lee's wife, Matilda. Thomas Shippen toured Virginia after the war, visiting Williamsburg, Rosewell, Westover, and Richmond.

Shippen's father sent him to London in the summer of 1786 to study law at the Inner Temple, but he showed more interest in women. On Tuesday, October 3, he went to Drury Lane Theatre for a performance of *Venice Preserv'd*. Lord North, his wife, and their two daughters sat in one of the boxes. Seeing Sarah Siddons in a gray satin gown, a woman in the audience thought: "Belvidera takes the stage in the part of wife and daughter, and acts with a truth which charms and ravishes." After Belvidera went mad, Shippen could hardly contain himself. He wrote of Mrs. Siddons: "I have indeed beheld, I have heard, I have felt, through my whole system felt her. . . . In the mad scene she was particularly great, and in the cry of murder, piercing to the most phlegmatic breast." Returning to Philadelphia, Shippen nominally practiced law, but he welcomed an opportunity to visit Virginia in the autumn of 1790.

Shippen's uncles entertained him on the Northern Neck, between the Potomac and the Rappahannock. With them he visited Stratford Hall, where they and Shippen's mother had lived as children. Matilda Lee had died the previous month, and Henry Lee was not at home. At the center of the mansion Shippen sat in the elegant room that connected its two wings. He looked at portraits of his late uncle, Philip Ludwell Lee, of his grandfather and grandmother, Thomas and Hannah Ludwell Lee, of his great-grandfather and great-grandmother, Richard and Laetitia Corbin Lee, and of the first Richard, one of Virginia's largest landholders at his death in 1664, and of his wife. Shippen wrote to his father: "I dwelt with rapture on the pictures of Stratford and felt so strong an inclination to kneel to that of my grandfather." In his travels along the James River, among Carters and Byrds, he met Elizabeth Banister, the Antigua and Dismal Swamp Company heiress. She had held out against her suitors for more than a year. She accepted Thomas Lee Shippen. He need no longer pretend to practice law. He wrote to his father: "We shall be comfortably independent I think at least."

Shippen returned to Virginia early in 1791 for the wedding, which took place at Nesting on the evening of Thursday, March 10. Bishop James Madison, president of the College of William and Mary, came from Williamsburg to perform the ceremony. The bridegroom called himself "the happiest of men," married to "the loveliest and best of women." Within six weeks Elizabeth Shippen was pregnant. Mary Willing Byrd felt sorry to see the young couple leave for Philadelphia, but she knew that Thomas would be happier there "than he possibly can be in this unpolished Country."

Thomas Lee Shippen took an interest in the Dismal Swamp, the Land of Eden, Major John Simon Farley's lawsuits, and the Mercers Creek plantation in Antigua. During the 1790s the labor of the Mercers Creek slaves on cane fields, sugar boilers, and rum distilleries yielded an average annual payment of more than £430 sterling to each of Francis Farley's four granddaughters. Elizabeth and Thomas Shippen bought a country estate about 17 miles northeast of Philadelphia on a hill overlooking the road to Trenton and the toll bridge across Neshaminy Creek. She named the place "Farley." Their first child, a boy named for Thomas Shippen's father, was born in January 1792. Planning for his son's future, Thomas Shippen paid $750 for three shares in the Dismal Swamp Canal Company.

The legislatures of Virginia and North Carolina passed laws in 1790 authorizing the Dismal Swamp canal and creating a company to dig it. Shares cost $250 each. Shareholders' prospect for future profits lay in the company's right to charge tolls on vessels, people, livestock, and commodities transported through the canal.

Some North Carolinians protested in vain, warning that a canal would make Norfolk "the Emporium of commerce, of the Southern States" at the expense of North Carolina. "The contract carries with it the face of a Jobb" in "the evident advantage, which the Canal will bring into the hands of a few Land Speculators, who hold property contiguous to it." Patrick Henry hoped this was so obvious that he could get rid of his Green Sea tract and his acres near the Dismal Swamp Company's property. As soon as North Carolina's law passed, he advertised his willingness to exchange his holdings for acreage in the piedmont. He said: "The proposed canal which is to connect the navigation of the Chesapeake with that of Albemarle Sound, it is supposed must necessarily pass through these lands." He had been governor when the canal's course was chosen; he had reason to know that it lay east of the Dismal Swamp Company's land and west of the Green Sea.

George Washington and John Lewis sold the roadside tract south of the North Carolina line. Washington thought that in May 1791 "the moment was not favorable" for getting the best price; yet he consented, he told Lewis, "as the Affairs of your fathers Estate pressed, and my own want of money was great." He was drawing his salary as president in advance. He and his brother-in-law had paid about £1 per acre in Virginia's colonial currency for the land. John Lewis sold it for £1 per acre in Virginia state currency to John Cowper, a manager of the Dismal Swamp Canal Company.

Subscription books for the new canal company's stock were open in the spring and summer of 1791. By the first week of September, men in Norfolk and Portsmouth had bought about 140 shares. Two weeks later the managers compiled a list of subscribers. It contained 142 names, representing an investment of $47,000 in 188 shares. More soon joined, and the General Assembly invested $12,500 of public money in fifty shares. Francis Walker, Henry Lee, and delegates from Nansemond County voted for the purchase. Thomas Newton, Jr., bought four shares; Dr. Thomas Ruston's attorney,

William Nivison, bought two; St. George Tucker bought one. William Aitchison and Patrick Parker, sons of the unlucky loyalists, bought shares. Few North Carolinians invested.

The list had a 143rd name on it, that of David Jameson, acting for the Dismal Swamp Company. The company ought to take an interest in the canal, but getting the partners to do anything was difficult. William Nelson, Jr., about to become a judge of the General Court, asked for a meeting in August. David Jameson lay ill in York Town. Joseph Hornsby and his daughters were visiting Dr. Walker at Castle Hill. Hornsby's wife, Mildred, had died in childbirth in Williamsburg on Friday, June 11, 1790, "very much lamented by myself," he wrote in the family Bible, "& all our dear children." The summer trip to Castle Hill was his second that year. Dr. Walker was in good spirits but fading. Hornsby gave him several opportunities to see his grandchildren. Nor did Thomas Newton, Jr., come from Norfolk to represent Robert Tucker's share. He said he was "prevented by business here that I cannot leave." Robert Andrews, after waiting so long for the company to pay him for supervising its survey, had foreseen that Nelson would not manage to convene a meeting: "I knew he was not prone to activity in business."

Dismal Plantation produced little for sale in 1791. The overseer said that no shingles could be made until late in the year. Slaves had not opened ditches or built new fences. The plantation yielded a little more than £51 in 1790. The total for 1791 was £16 2s. currency. In the northeastern sector of the company's holdings, "strangers from the North[war]d" worked the swamp, and other people made "many unwarantable incroachments." Without a meeting, the managing partners—Jameson, Hornsby, and David Meade—subscribed on the company's behalf for twenty shares in the Dismal Swamp Canal Company, at a cost of $5,000. Jameson's letter to Francis Walker about the assessment on Dr. Walker's two quarter-shares sounded peremptory: "I . . . shall be much obliged to you to have something done speedily." Three years later, the partners had paid about half of their subscription to the canal company's stock.

In the six months after the canal company drew up its first list of subscribers, twenty-five men bought another 112 shares. Thomas Lee Shippen subscribed for three; his wife's stepfather, John Dunbar, for two. The estate of Secretary Thomas Nelson bought a share. So did Patrick Henry. Alexander Macaulay, merchant of York Town, had his eye on the Dismal Swamp Company, and he subscribed $2,500 for ten shares in the canal company. Except for the state's fifty shares, the Dismal Swamp Company was the largest shareholder in the Dismal Swamp Canal Company.

The canal company organized for work in 1792 and 1793, led by Robert Andrews. It had a capital of about $80,000, soon increased to $100,000. Writing in 1793, the Reverend John Jones Spooner, rector of a parish near David Meade's plantation, told readers of the Massachusetts Historical Society's *Collections* that the new canal was "in considerable forwardness." Yet digging had just begun. One end of the ditch began in North Carolina, seven miles south of the dividing line, at South Mills, where Joyce's Creek flowed into the Pasquotank River. The other end began near the head of navigation on Deep Creek, a tributary of the Elizabeth River, about 7 miles south of Portsmouth and more than 11 miles by water from Norfolk. Moving up the Elizabeth River and into Deep Creek, a vessel passed between thick growths of timber, broken in some spots by a patch of two or three acres of cleared land on which stood a house, "small and mean in appearance."

Laboring on the canal trench, hired slaves used saws, axes, and picks more often than shovels. Pine, cedar, and hardwood trees had to be felled; canes, briers, and other undergrowth cut away. For at least ten feet below the peat surface, men sliced through peat, roots, fibers, and white sand. As they deepened the trench, they always stood in water. About a yard below the surface in many places, streams of brandy-colored water flowed ceaselessly down the walls of the canal from the surrounding swamp. The finished canal was supposed to accommodate vessels with a 15-foot beam and a 3-foot draft; it must be at least 8 feet deep.

John Sparling and William Bolden, merchants of Liverpool, were surprised to learn that John Lawrence, their man in Suffolk, Virginia, had subscribed for only one share in the Dismal Swamp Canal Company. They ordered him to buy at least twenty more "if it can be done at Par, or without much advance from the original subscription." They did not see why the canal company expected to take three or four years to cut a short canal through "a level soft Country," but they predicted that the project would cost more than twice the allotted $100,000. Even so, they said, once it was completed, North Carolina's trade would make the canal "a beneficial thing to the Proprietors."

David Jameson, David Meade, and Joseph Hornsby summoned their partners to meet at Suffolk on May 13, 1793, so that members of the Dismal Swamp Company could visit Dismal Plantation and the swamp to "form a just idea of its value, as well as the mode of draining and improving it." That planned meeting apparently did not occur, but a quorum of members gathered in York Town on Wednesday, May 22. After a recent attack of violent spasms, David Jameson lay motionless, near death. His quarter-share and Samuel Gist's three quarter-shares were represented by his nephew, David

Jameson, Jr. In all, seventy-two quarter-shares were voted by their owners or by proxy. During the session, the executors of Fielding Lewis's estate conveyed his share to Alexander Macaulay and John Brown, clerk of the General Court in Richmond, for £1,000. In return for this show of confidence in the company's future, their partners made them managers, with William Nelson, Jr., Joseph Hornsby, and David Meade. The meeting's only resolution, except to meet again, was to assess each full share £24 to pay an installment on the price of the twenty shares in the canal company. The younger Jameson soon learned that collecting would not be easy. On Thursday he wrote to Thomas Newton, Jr., to get £24 from Robert Tucker's estate. The next day Newton replied: "I cannot pay it without the risque of loosing it altogether. This share must be sold. There are so many concerned in it that no division can take place."

The canal advanced slowly. A day of hard work moved the ditch forward less than ten yards. Those digging from the north and those digging from the south each had to cover 11 miles. No one knew or tried to determine how many locks the canal would need. No one knew whether the Joyce's Creek end lay higher or lower than the Deep Creek end. The company's managers had no way to estimate future costs. By the end of 1793 the company had made four assessments on its shareholders. On November 16 it called on the Dismal Swamp Company for another $500. Sparling and Bolden had no cause for worry that the price of shares would rise above par. Instead, it fell. After six years of digging in the swamp by the company's hired slaves, a share originally purchased for $250 sold for $100.

John Page and his daughter, Alice, who was eighteen, visited York Town on Monday and Tuesday, October 8 and 9, 1792. Rather than return to Rosewell for the night, they stayed in town. John Page had much on his mind. He had been happily remarried for more than two years. While serving in the House of Representatives during the first session of Congress he met Margaret Lowther in New York. Fifteen years younger than he, she was a poet with a "happy Temper." Within a month of their wedding she was pregnant.

Page's re-election to Congress in 1790 had not come easily. Francis Corbin opposed him, treating the voters to "strong grogg & roasted piggs" while telling them that in March, after Quakers petitioned Congress in opposition to slavery and the slave trade, Page had viewed the petition favorably. Corbin accused Page of being "principled against Slavery." Page denied the charge. He privately said that, if defeated, he would "enjoy the Luxury of Retirement, made sweet by the sweetest Partner of domestic Happiness."

Many people thought he would lose the election, but he won. He won again in 1792.

Page found service in Congress wearing. He had no time for rest or exercise. He worried about the new government. Calling himself "a Democratical Member," he saw the Washington administration "moving headlong into Monarchy." George Washington had been "taken in by the Aristocrats"; Page wished that he had not accepted the presidency. Perhaps only the French Revolution could keep liberty and republicanism alive.

By October 1792, John Page's money troubles had worsened. A suit was pending against the estate of his late brother-in-law, Lewis Burwell, for which he was executor. The British merchant Wakelin Welch threatened to foreclose a mortgage Burwell had given in 1768. Men to whom Page owed money, John Hatley Norton and John Jameson of Culpeper County, were pressing him. He called them "unreasonable impatient creditors." He again tried to sell land, without success. Early in 1792 he almost persuaded Thomas Lee Shippen and William Bingham that his two quarter-shares in the Dismal Swamp Company and his 500 acres of Green Sea land were cheap at a price "about £300 more than would pay every Debt I owe." But the sale did not go through. In May he asked to borrow money in Philadelphia at 20 percent interest to pay Jameson. Page knew in October that, upon his return to Philadelphia to attend Congress, he must again ask his oldest friend, Thomas Jefferson, to sign as his security for a short-term loan. He felt "unhappy and ashamed."

The summer of 1792 brought heat and drought. Crops fell short. The firm of Donald & Burton refused to accept Page's bill of exchange, and he commented: "justly enough I confess." Robert Andrews pressed Page to confer with David Jameson about the condition of Dismal Plantation and the company's affairs, but Page had too many worries to devote much attention to the company he was trying to leave.

In York Town, on the morning of Tuesday, October 9, as Page was dressing, a letter was handed to him. It came from young Dr. Augustine Smith, a frequent guest at Rosewell. Smith lived in York Town, but he wrote a letter, fearing that if he spoke in person he would be "confused." Page read: "I have long been tenderly attached to your amiable Daughter, & flatter myself that your sanction wou'd induce her to approve of my attentions." The letter acknowledged that Smith had too little income as a new physician to support a family. He promised: "Industry, care & attention may considerably remedy this inconvenience—and every thing shall be willingly sacraficed to the happiness of your accomplished Daughter."

This request seemed odd, since John Page, four weeks earlier, had ordered wedding apparel for Alice and her bridesmaids. Of course Alice was going to be married to Augustine. He had been courting her for more than two years. Yet only after wedding arrangements had begun did he work up the courage to seek her father's consent.

Augustine Smith loved literature and wrote verse. He had all the marks of one who took *The Sorrows of Young Werther* to heart. From an early age he depended upon Thomas Nelson, Jr., who sent him to Edinburgh to study medicine. Smith returned to York Town in time to care for Nelson during his final illness in December 1788. Smith fell in love with Alice Page at first sight when she was almost sixteen. In the summer of 1790 he invoked the god of love in secret verse:

> *When first Alicia's form was seen,*
> *Her genteel air and graceful mien,*
> *Her lovely winning Face;*
> *I saw th'almighty God of love*
> *Around the Maid with rapture move*
> ***
> *O make Alicia mine!*
> *Two tender Doves, a milk-white pair,*
> *With silken downe, I'll then prepare*
> *An off'ring at thy shrine.*

He wrote to a friend: "I have lately felt all the perturbations of a lover whom prudence wou'd persuade to be silent on the theme that engrosses his whole soul."

After that first meeting, Smith visited Rosewell off and on for a year, seemingly just one among many guests. Yet he knew that his behavior gave him away. He took heart and declared his love. In July 1791 he wrote to Alice: "Connections commencing in fraud and dissimulation I concieve, must end in hatred and contempt.—I love you Miss Page!—I have loved you from my first acquaintance with you.—And had niggard Fortune enabled me to offer you a competency of wealth, my faithful Heart had long ago been opened to you. . . . I blush at my presumption in offering you a hand almost shrivelled by the hard gripe of indigence."

Augustine made more visits to Rosewell. Alice, remaining poised and modest, made him welcome. On Monday, August 29, she invited her suitor to stay until evening, but she agitated him by speaking not of love but of her

"Gratitude, Esteem, and Friendship." He rushed away, crossed the York River to his home, and sat up until midnight writing a letter to her: "I thought I had reduced my mind to some thing *like* reason—but feel every emotion of my soul verging toward insanity. . . . I feel that my amiable Alice is alone capable of making me happy, & interest, mere self interest so blinds me as to make me believe, in spite of reason & truth, that I cou'd make *her* happy—I feel myself, at this instant, degraded even below your *compassion;* yet nothing short of your *love,* your unreserved, warm ingenuous affection can possibly content me—Great God! I am mad."

She carefully saved his letters. Augustine was back at Rosewell for her birthday, writing impromptu verse after the sun broke through the clouds, shining on the huge mansion, its gardens, and the river.

> *Go Nymphs! and sound the tuneful shell,*
> *Let all be jocund, pleas'd & gay—*
> *Go, to each mortal loudly tell*
> *That this is Alice' natal day.*

Looking at Augustine Smith's letter in York Town, John Page knew all this. In his day he had written similar verse. The only mystery was Smith's delay in asking him for his daughter's hand. The young man worried that he might have "committed an impropriety in not having spoke to him."

After returning to Rosewell, John Page replied to Smith. He explained that he could not give money to the young couple: "my own Circumstances are in such an unhappy State at present, & my future Prospect so gloomy, that I cannot even hope to see the Day when I may be able to give my Daughter any thing which could in even a moderate Degree contribute to her Support." With a hint of a joke about Smith's suggestion that Page might at this late date induce his daughter to accept a proposal, Page added: "She is capable of judging for herself, & if your Attachments are mutual & fixed, neither of you will be more unhappy than I shall be should prudential Motives induce you to make a painfull Sacrifice."

The wedding took place a few months later. John Page took pride in Rosewell, calling it "the most beautiful Seat in Virga. with the most elegant House in America thereon." Fifty-five years past, William Nelson had crossed the river from York Town to be married to Elizabeth Burwell. Now John Page was fifty years old, giving his daughter in marriage. Though he was seeking money desperately, he stinted her in nothing for the wedding. The bridal party made a display of white silk, pink silk, embroidered muslin, white and pink ribbons, white kid gloves, satin slippers, and white ostrich plumes. John Page was at the head of Gloucester County gentry, and in entertaining they vied with one another in offering lavish hospitality—turtle feasts, fish feasts, a party of forty dining under an arbor erected a few yards from the beach, bushels of ice from an icehouse in summer to chill cider and punch and wine, a fiddler with dancing on the green. Augustine Smith and Alice Page Smith settled in York Town. His practice improved. They were attended by household slaves; they acquired mahogany and walnut furniture and many volumes of Latin and English literature. In twelve years they had six children.

John Page at last sold one of his quarter-shares in the Dismal Swamp Company to his son-in-law, William Nelson of York Town, son of Augustine Smith's benefactor, Thomas Nelson, Jr., and nephew of William Nelson, Jr. The price he received in May 1793, £250 in Virginia currency, was much less than he had expected to get from Thomas Lee Shippen and William Bingham. A year later he sold the other quarter-share for the same price to Philip Tabb, a neighbor in Gloucester County. In the time between these transactions he advertised other land. His old enemy, vertigo, returned. In the autumn of 1793 he suffered an "extreme low state of health." To raise money he turned to a planter's last recourse: putting slaves on the auction block. Sixty-eight slaves over the age of twelve worked at Rosewell in 1791. By 1795, thirty-six remained to grow and cure tobacco, to tend horses, hogs, one hundred cattle, and twenty-nine sheep, and to work in and around the brick outbuildings and the ornate mansion standing at the end of a long double avenue of cedar trees—the house John Page's grandfather had built for King Carter's daughter.

Writing to his father, who received his mail at Lloyd's, Patrick Parker sent a warning to underwriters. They ought to have an agent at Norfolk, as they did on the Rappahannock River. Norfolk's trade was reviving rapidly. Sometimes a captain of a vessel in distress played "Slippery Tricks" to enable owners to recover insurance on a total loss when a loss need not have been or had not been total. An agent investigated and made sure of the best salvage, with a fair sale of damaged goods. Without such protection, "some of the underwriters at Loyds will Probably be Sweated."

William Anderson & Company took pride in their new 205-ton ship *Powhatan*, which, they said, "stands A1 at Lloyd's." At Norfolk in March 1792, Captain Mills Riddick welcomed consignments of tobacco to Anderson or shipments of hogsheads to any house upon payment of freight charges. Anchored in the roadstead or moored at the log wharves were many sloops, schooners, and ships. The traffic increased so rapidly that Naval Office clerks issuing entries and clearances hardly had time to eat. Impatient captains often insulted them for their delays. The searcher of the Port of Norfolk, responsible for preventing smuggling, knew that some vessels entered the bay and dropped anchor off Sewell's Point to discharge their cargoes, rather than come up the Elizabeth River to Norfolk. He had no way to stop them. Because the port sent foodstuffs to the West Indies, Norfolk attracted wheat and flour speculators. Shipyards and a ropewalk revived and expanded. A new vessel of the *Powhatan's* burden sold off the blocking for about $8,000 in 1792, and the price was rising.

In the borough of Norfolk new houses built with pine boards and roofed with cedar shingles spread among the ruins of free-standing chimneys and crumbling brick walls left by the fire of 1776. Flimsy new buildings lined crooked, narrow, dirt streets. Owners of land near the river leased it at high rent but would not sell; renters did not bother to erect substantial buildings. Carpenters and bricklayers found steady work at high wages. New clapboard warehouses among the wharves—some stood three stories high—were bigger than most residences and stores but just as ugly. Construction followed no design, creating a maze of lanes and alleys. Raw sewage ran in open ditches bridged by narrow planks. Near the river a stench hung over the city, especially at low tide. Norfolk had more than 3,000 people in 1792, whites outnumbering blacks by a few hundred. A newly established merchant wrote: "There is Certainly a great field for Speculation at this Market." Thomas Newton, Jr., told George Washington: "this place is growing fast & of consequence in trade & whenever the canal is finished it will have great advantages."

Beginning late in the summer of 1791, Virginians received reports of violence in the French colony of Saint-Domingue. There 40,000 whites and 28,000 free people of color, mostly mulattoes, lived among 500,000 slaves. Divisions among whites and the free people of color arising out of political and constitutional changes made by the French Revolution expanded into revolt by slaves. In the North Province whites fortified themselves in the city of Cap Français on the coast. Beyond the city's entrenchments bands of insurgents controlled the countryside.

In the spring of 1792, as Jacobins in Paris proclaimed equality for free persons of color in Saint-Domingue, Virginians reported rumors of plans for slave insurrections in their own state. The new governor, Henry Lee, received accounts of a conspiracy for a general uprising in Northampton County on the Eastern Shore. Supposedly, nine hundred slaves acting in concert with slaves in Norfolk and Portsmouth intended to attack Norfolk, blow up the gunpowder magazine, set fire to the city, and "massacre the inhabitants." Lee assumed that they were following "the example of the West Indies." Upon closer scrutiny, the rumored conspiracy vanished. Three slaves were expelled from the county; several others were flogged. In Norfolk, Thomas Newton, Jr., ordered Methodist and Baptist preachers to stop holding "nocturnal meetings." In July three slaves—Jack, Daniel, and Matthew—were tried and hanged for attacking a slave patrol in Northampton County.

In London, both houses of Parliament held debates in April on abolishing the British slave trade. To supplement evidence given in hearings, opponents of slavery gathered and published testimony about the cruelties of the African trade given by men formerly employed in it. Francis Jerdone, in Louisa County, received a letter late that summer from his brother-in-law in England: "Liberty Notions are spreading all over Europe & I hear amongst the Negroes of North America. . . . Many ignorant People here have left off the Use of Sugar on the foolish Supposition that every Pound that is consumed costs the Negro that makes it an ounce of Blood." The men governing Virginia took steps to prevent liberty notions from becoming actions like those in Saint-Domingue. The General Assembly passed new laws regulating free black people, restricting the movements of slaves, and making conspiracy to rebel punishable by death.

In the first week of July 1793 more than one hundred French vessels— men-of-war and merchant craft—sailed into Chesapeake Bay bearing thousands of refugees from Cap Français. These people told of their fight, aided by French soldiers and seamen, against French Jacobin officials with allies among the free people of color. The Jacobins offered freedom and the rights of French citizenship to insurgent slaves who would help them. More than 3,000 attacked the city. Most of Cap Français went up in flames; many whites were killed. The refugees fled to the shoreline, escaping in vessels which sailed for the Chesapeake on June 23. As the French disembarked in Norfolk, seeking shelter and searching for relatives separated from them in flight, Thomas Newton, Jr., reported to Governor Lee that they had brought "too many negroes."

France had been at war with Britain and the Continental powers since February. In April, President Washington had proclaimed the neutrality of the United States, but the French Revolution had many sympathizers in Norfolk. Most refugees were royalists, hoping for restoration of the monarchy in France. Nevertheless, Virginians and people in other states collected funds for their benefit. The convoy from Cap Français did not stay long in Hampton Roads. Many exiles remained in Norfolk; others moved to cities farther north. Those who had brought slaves were allowed to keep them, despite Virginia's law prohibiting such importation.

During the summer Governor Lee received reports of plots and "insolence" among slaves. These stories routinely connected the conduct of blacks with the revolt in Saint-Domingue. John Randolph said that he had heard one black man say to another: "you see how the blacks has killed the whites in the French Island and took it a little while ago." Lee was told that in Portsmouth slaves from Saint-Domingue were attacking one another at night, household slaves against those who supported the insurgents. Rumors of plots for an uprising came from Petersburg, Hampton, Richmond, and Norfolk. If Lee believed all the letters reaching him, he would have concluded that hundreds of black conspirators were armed, while the militia had no muskets or ammunition. After the House of Delegates convened in October, Governor Lee reported that he had distributed arms among tidewater towns and cities upon learning of "a design in our domestics to imitate the example exhibited in saint Domingo." He suggested that these weapons be issued to the militiamen and that training be improved. Yet the annual grand review of the Norfolk militia on Thursday, May 1, 1794, presented the customary scene. Most companies wore street clothes rather than uniforms; they were poorly armed and untrained. The men in green uniforms, with plumed and ribboned caps, "look like toy soldiers." Spectators celebrated May Day by wearing a tuft of deer's tail in their hats. After the review, everyone ate barbecue. "The combination of May 1 with the reunion of brothers-in-arms results in boisterous joy, with the usual finish: not every citizen-soldier is able to conquer the charms of the bottle."

Thomas Newton, Jr., did not stop fretting. He wished that all "French negroes" could be "sent off, as I apprehend they may be troublesome some time or other." A traveler passing northward through Virginia reported that, farther south, free blacks and mulattoes from the French West Indies were inspiring Carolina slaves "with the notion of freedom, and the possible success of an insurrection." Upon hearing this, a writer in the *Virginia Herald and Fredericksburg Advertiser* warned slaveholders to prevent slaves from "having barbacues, harranguing each other publicly, exercising, appointing their officers, and in every respect getting qualified for something more important."

The demands of the governorship and the Saint-Domingue scare did not distract Henry Lee from his interest in buying and selling land. In Philadelphia he had met Théophile Cazenove, recently arrived in America as agent for the Dutch bankers Pieter Stadnitski & Son and other Amsterdam firms ready to invest in American public securities and land. Cazenove made clear that he "had a large monied capital at his disposal." Lee offered to introduce him to good opportunities for investment. One of these was a share in the Dismal Swamp Company. In February 1793, two weeks before starting his second term as president, George Washington wrote a memorandum for Lee's use, describing the company and setting a price on his share.

Washington said that the Dismal Swamp "in fertility of Soil, cannot be exceeded." He assured Cazenove: "it may be easily drained." Then it would be "equal to the richest rice land of So. Carolina," which, ready for cultivation, sold for £30 to £50 sterling per acre. Its location near the Nansemond and Elizabeth rivers gave the company's tract "advantages over almost any other of equal quantity in the United States." The new canal "adds infinitely to its worth." Washington offered to sell his four quarter-shares for £5,000 Virginia currency, five times the amount Fielding Lewis's estate received for his.

Bold in other transactions, Cazenove seemed "timid" in this one. While waiting, Lee turned to Washington's friend Bryan Fairfax, urging him to relocate some of his tenants living near the falls of the Potomac to clear the way for development of Matildaville. Lee looked forward to the day when commissioners started to sell lots in his "manufacturing town."

Americans learned in mid-March of the declarations of war in Europe. For the past year, Lee had thought of leaving the governorship to go to France and become a major general in the Revolutionary army. He said that a return to soldiering would be "the best resort to my mind in its affliction"—his bereavement by the death of Matilda Lee in 1790. While weighing this notion he took time to assure Armistead Burwell: "I will try to place you in comfortable business on the potomac for I have a regard for you & a confidence in you."

Lee's thoughts also turned to remarriage. His eye fell upon the Dismal Swamp Company heiress Maria Farley, second of Elizabeth Farley Dunbar's four daughters. So ran the story her family told long afterward. He was thirty-seven years old; she was twenty. She was about to receive a large increase in her income: the price of sugar shot up in 1792. The next year the Mercers Creek plantation in Antigua made a gross income of £10,341 8s. 4½d. sterling. Lee was a small man, and he talked too much, as if he were always addressing a public meeting. Still, he was a war hero, governor of Virginia, and a friend of the president of the United States. Maria Farley rejected him. Soon afterward, on May 1, 1793, she and William Champe Carter were married.

Reports of Revolutionary terror in France, added to letters of advice from George Washington and William Lee, led Governor Lee to give up his notion of fighting in Europe. A few days after the wedding of Maria Farley and Champe Carter, Lee wrote: "I mean now to become a farmer & get a wife as soon as possible." He apparently had noticed that Champe Carter's cousin, Ann Hill Carter, daughter of Charles Carter of Shirley and Anne Butler Moore Carter, was more impressed by him than Maria Farley had been. She, too, was twenty years old, and she quickly accepted his proposal of marriage. To gain her parents' approval, Lee had to declare upon his honor that he would not go to France. Then Charles Carter wrote to him: "we certainly know that you have obtained her consent. . . . Mrs Carter and I, are perfectly persuaded that our dear Girl will make you a dutiful and loving Wife." The wedding took place at Shirley on Tuesday, June 18.

Théophile Cazenove purchased vast tracts for Dutch investors, but he did not buy George Washington's share in the Dismal Swamp Company. Washington wrote: "Mr. Casenave expected, probably on good ground, that a purchase from others might be made on lower terms than I had affixed to mine." Washington turned in the spring of 1794 to Robert Morris, who was launching land speculations surpassing the grandest designs of companies in colonial days. To Morris, Washington described the Dismal Swamp Company with more restraint, saying that the canal would add "immensely," rather than "infinitely," to the value of the company's land. He wrote about the tract's suitability, once drained, for rice, tobacco, corn, and oats. He concluded: "The value of so much land, of this quality within a few miles of Norfolk, Suffolk and Portsmouth; and along side of Nansemond River (at a very small distance therefrom), cultivated in these articles or laid to grass for mowing or grazing is almost incalculable." His price remained £5,000.

As Washington dealt with Morris, Governor Lee, no longer serving as a go-between for Cazenove, decided to buy part or all of Washington's four quarter-shares for himself. He wrote to one of the investors in Matildaville—presumably, Morris—"can you venture on the dismal swamp, you will join me and me only in that purchase I hope." Lee also bought Belvidere, the house overlooking the falls of the James River, where the younger William Byrd had begun his unhappy first marriage.

Lee's third one-year term as governor ended in an embarrassing manner. In the autumn of 1794 he commanded a federal force mobilized by President Washington to demonstrate the government's power to suppress defiance of excise taxes in Pennsylvania. This show of strength was unpopular in Virginia. In Lee's absence the General Assembly invoked a state law forbidding officials to accept federal office and declared the governorship vacant before the end of his term. Back in Virginia and out of office, Lee's mind dwelt more and more upon land transactions promising wealth. He wrote to Patrick Henry: "there are individuals of character & gold daily arriving in Philada. & N York from G Britain & other European nations whose sole object is the purchase of lands." He wished to oblige them: "A million or two of acres may be contracted for . . . as easy as so many thousands . . . a small profit on that quantity will form a handsome aggregate sum."

Late in 1790 or early in 1791, William and Mary Anderson moved out of Samuel Gist's City residence in America Square. Their new home and the offices of William Anderson & Company were in Crosby Square northeast of Tower Hill, a short walk along Threadneedle Street from the Royal Exchange. They lived in the shadow of the great Gothic mansion Crosby Hall, once the residence of Richard, Duke of Gloucester, before he became King Richard III, and later the property of Sir Thomas More. Still elegant in decay, it served merchants as a warehouse. The Andersons were in Number 10, Crosby Square, by March 1. Gist kept America Square as his business address. William Anderson pursued the old-fashioned consignment trade in tobacco and dry goods. In Virginia he had representatives at Gloucester, Fredericksburg, Petersburg, and Richmond. In January 1793 he added Richard S. Taylor in King William County.

The onset of war early in 1793 brought panic and bankruptcies to some underwriters at Lloyd's and to other merchants and financiers in the City. As more and more men frequented Lloyd's rooms, trying to make easy money by subscribing policies, underwriting had grown more competitive late in 1792. "The premiums are run down so low & so many Averages occur that few People now get any thing by it, & unless a man has much Influence in the Coffee house & Policies of his own to shew in Return, he will have nothing shewn him but indifferent Risks, & such as others are glad to be free of." War suddenly brought danger to many insured vessels. Long delays in the arrival of many ships meant late remittances and deferred obligations, raising doubts about firms' ability to collect money. A crisis of confidence in the credit even of large banks and mercantile houses spread with stoppages of payment and bankruptcies: "the bubble is now burst, & thousands will be involv'd in ruin by it." Failures of big companies "must occasion lesser ones, and so on, and it is impossible to foresee where the evil will be arrested." Twice as many bankruptcies occurred in 1793 as in 1792. Importation stagnated. Construction companies underwent one of their worst years of ruined firms. The early months of 1793 became a benchmark at Lloyd's: the year of "the great failure among the Underwriters."

As in the period before the panic of 1772, many merchants and banks had expanded credit by covering bills of exchange with other bills of exchange. Merchants who had speculated in large shipments overseas were exposed when trade fell off and remittances declined. The government met this crisis by increasing the money in circulation and by extending credit to merchants. Issuance of £2,200,000 in Exchequer bills lent at 5 percent interest helped end the crisis in credit by summer.

William Anderson & Company did not survive the year in its original form. Anderson's brother-in-law, William Fowke, dropped out. The original three-way partnership became known as the Old Concern. The new William Anderson & Company retained two original partners—Anderson and Aiskew Birkett—and added two new partners: Henry Smith Shore and Thomas Reeves. Reeves was a British merchant in Virginia; Shore was a Virginian in London. In the New Concern, Anderson held a one-half interest, Birkett one-quarter, and Shore and Reeves one-eighth each. Leaving Shore in the house in Crosby Square, the Andersons moved across the Thames upriver from Westminster Bridge to lease Belmont House in Vauxhall.

That summer William Anderson wrote his will. In it he made his wife and Samuel Gist trustees for his nephew, Francis, until the age of twenty-two. He called Gist his friend, but he showed displeasure at Gist's refusal to pay for land in Virginia he had bought at Gist's instructions. The will ordered his executors to convey title only after Gist paid to the estate the purchase price, twenty years' interest, and the cost of improvements, taxes, and titles. Anderson bequeathed to his wife "all my right title, and interest in and to the whole, and every part of the real and personal estates formerly the property of Samuel Gist Esqr. which was vested in my wife by an act of the General Assembly of Virginia." He bequeathed his slaves to his mother, ordering that they be treated "humanely and kindly." Upon her death, they were to be emancipated, "any law usage or custom to the contrary notwithstanding." The proceeds of sales of his property in Virginia were to be divided among his Anderson relatives. He appointed his wife, Gist, Shore, Birkett, and two other men to execute his will. Two months later, the "New Concern" William Anderson & Company dispatched the *Powhatan* from London, bound for Virginia in search of consignments and freight. Anderson shipped tobacco to Le Havre. The French had not stopped smoking when they became republicans and went to war. Anderson was willing "to run the Risk of that market, Remittance &ca."

War promised benefits to "the monied men," those like Samuel Gist with large reserves of cash and stocks. War offered "the hope of finding some opportunity to take advantage of either public or private distress & speculate with a certainty of immense gains." They were "laying by," holding their money, waiting for governments to borrow and for scarcities to raise prices. This was not a good time for Henry Lee or Robert Morris or others to offer American forests and swamps. After the panic abated in the summer of 1793, a letter from London warned an American speculator: "they say here that Money is worth too much to be laid out in Lands."

The gloom at Lloyd's soon lifted. War brought high premiums for marine insurance; overseas trade rose to levels like those of the boom year 1792. George Rose, secretary to the Treasury, said that in 1794 property worth £80,000,000 was insured at Lloyd's. The cautious chartered companies, London Assurance and Royal Exchange Assurance, took in more than twice as much in premiums as they paid out in losses. A similar pattern at Lloyd's would have yielded to its underwriters that year a total profit of perhaps £10,000,000 to £15,000,000. After a few such years, one could say: "Lloyd's coffee-house is now an empire within itself."

Surrounded by opportunities for moneyed men and veteran underwriters, Samuel Gist kept his Virginia debtors in mind. He wrote to Joseph Jones of Petersburg, renewing a demand that Jones pay through Thomas Shore an old debt of more than £500, with interest. Gist warned: "On failure he will be under the disagreeable necessity of bringing Suit against you immediately to recover the same." Gist sued and won. Jones begged Shore for a little more time: "I will pay it to you when you say that you must have it—therefore I hope you will not put the execution in the hands of the Marshall."

In Philadelphia, Robert Morris learned that his far-flung investments had suffered losses in the panic of 1793, perhaps $500,000. His friend Gouverneur Morris, of the New York Morrises, had been in London early in 1792 before President Washington appointed him minister to France. He often went to the King's Theatre in the Haymarket to see Sarah Siddons and the Drury Lane company perform. She appeared as Mrs. Beverley in *The Gamester* on Saturday, February 4. "The Piece is very bad," Morris said, "but her expressive Countenance draws Tears and even Groans from many of the Audience." Watching the French Revolution unfold and war approach, Gouverneur Morris warned Robert Morris late in the year that war would deter

Europeans from putting their money into American investments. But dangers and losses stimulated Robert Morris's imagination, pushing him toward grander, riskier designs to recoup his fortunes with a single master stroke.

Late in August 1793 a twenty-seven-year-old man from Massachusetts, James Greenleaf, a merchant in New York and Amsterdam, approached Robert Morris with a plan to profit from the projected new capital city on the banks of the Potomac—Washington, in the District of Columbia. Greenleaf was a persuasive man, the kind of person a loyalist had in mind in 1786 as he told a London dinner party "that the Americans were trying to sell the lands beyond the Alleghany Mountains to the English and Dutch; that they had agents here, who had already received large sums and that they were finding dupes every day." Within three months of his arrival in Holland, Greenleaf had won the hand of Baroness Antonia Cornelia Elbertine Scholten van Aschat et Oud-Haarlem. He soon began to complain about his wife. A few years after Greenleaf's departure for the United States, she saw that he had deserted her and their child, and began proceedings for divorce. Greenleaf had obtained loans from the Dutch firm of Daniel Crommelin & Sons. He said he could approach a firm in Rotterdam: Rocquette, Elsevier & Beeldemaker. He invited Morris to join him in buying thousands of lots in the new Federal City, using money to be borrowed from the Dutch with the lots as collateral. Upon reselling these at a much higher price, they would repay the Dutch and keep the profit. Morris later said that Greenleaf "tempted" him

The City of Washington in 1800, George I. Parkyns. Courtesy of the Henry E. Huntington Library

The Great Falls of the Potomac, George Beck. Courtesy of the Mount Vernon Ladies' Association. A painting owned by George Washington, depicting the obstacles to commercial use of the Potomac River.

into this undertaking. Just after talking with Greenleaf, Morris wrote to his partner John Nicholson: "Washington building lots will continue rising in price for one hundred years to come!"

Virginians worked hard to bring the capital city to the Potomac, speaking darkly of disunion if the nation's most populous state were neglected and if western settlers were left remote from the seat of government. They had offered land for the District of Columbia. Henry Lee wished to place the capital upriver from the canal and Matildaville. He and other advocates of the Potomac assumed that the capital would become a center of commerce and that the river would become the most important channel of trade with the west. Much as Virginia politicians disliked Alexander Hamilton's legislation for the federal government's assumption of states' public debt, they enabled it to pass in order to get the District of Columbia on the banks of the Potomac. They achieved their purpose "with uncommon difficulty."

No one did more than George Washington to bring the city named for him to a site near his home. He appointed commissioners to oversee design, construction, and sales. He took a keen interest in all aspects of the creation of the Federal City. Surveying and marking the district's boundaries began in February 1791. It contained a town, Georgetown, and other houses and structures, but it consisted largely of gentle hills covered with woods. President Washington visited Georgetown on Tuesday, March 28. Andrew Ellicott, the surveyor, showed him a newly completed plat. Two weeks later, Samuel Davidson, a merchant in Georgetown, wrote to Thomas Shore that "the Grand Federal City" had begun: "several Speculations have of late taken place on the occasion; nor have I been able to withstand the temptation, having recently made a purchase therein, to amount Six thousand pounds." Later in the year, one investor said that he looked forward to "the pleasure of viewing, in the course of a few years, the rise of the first city in the world."

In August, Pierre Charles L'Enfant submitted to the president a design for the city—a bold scheme of broad radial avenues superimposed on a grid of streets. The capitol and the presidential mansion, on eminences a mile apart, stood out as foci of the city. To pay for construction of these and other public buildings, the commissioners were to sell lots at auction. The first sale on Monday, October 17, disposed of 35 lots, each containing 5,265 square feet. A year later a second sale aroused little interest. James Greenleaf arrived on the day of the third sale, Tuesday, September 17, 1793. President Washington bought four lots, but he had few imitators. The next day the president went to Capitol Hill to lay the cornerstone of the capitol. He had to admit that matters were "in a stagnant state."

James Greenleaf brought a letter of introduction from President Washington to the commissioners of the District of Columbia. It invited them to consider Greenleaf's proposals, which "promise to promote the growth of the City" on an "extensive Scale." Washington concluded: "I have reason to believe that if you can find it consistent with your duty to the public to attach Mr. Greenleaf to the federal City, he will be a valuable acquisition." Less than a week after his arrival, Greenleaf and the commissioners agreed that he would buy 3,000 lots at $66.50 per lot. He promised to pay in seven annual installments and to build ten two-story brick houses per year for ten years. He also agreed to lend the commissioners $2,600 per month for construction of the public buildings.

In November, Robert Morris and John Nicholson each took a 50 percent share of Greenleaf's purchase. On Christmas Eve, Morris and Nicholson joined him in a second purchase of 3,000 more lots. They combined this contract with Greenleaf's earlier one and averaged the different prices per lot in the two. Thus, the consortium promised to pay about $480,000 for 6,000 lots.

Within eighteen months, Morris disposed of about 1,000 lots. Among the new owners was Henry Lee. He offered $300 per lot for 150 lots—slightly more than 5½¢ per square foot. Morris called this offer "too low" and urged Lee to buy at once, before the partners raised the price above 10¢ per square foot. He said that in 1800, only a few years away, "Lots and Houses in the City of Washington will command prices that will astonish those who might now buy at low rates and neglect to do it." He foresaw a price of $1,500 to $3,000 per lot. Having paid ⅔¢ per square foot, Morris sold the best sites for 25¢ per square foot. Lee bought "well situated" lots.

Visitors to the inchoate Federal City were struck by the sight of Pennsylvania Avenue and other avenues—a broad, straight stretch of cleared land, where trees had been felled and removed, leaving walls of forest on either side. Three years after construction of the capitol began, about half the city remained woods. The residents were chiefly workers cutting streets and avenues or erecting buildings. Even so, an English traveler was told in the summer of 1794 that "The value of each lot is from forty pounds to two hundred pounds sterling." In the mind's eye the Federal City looked impressive, but "were it not for the President's House and the Capitol, you would be ignorant that you were near the spot intended for the metropolis of the United States."

James Greenleaf lingered in Philadelphia and New York through the summer of 1794, rather than sail for Holland, where the large loans he had promised to Morris were attracting few subscribers. He wrote to his agent in Amsterdam: "in case you should not have succeded in the first instance you must immediately bring forward a plan for raising from 600,000 to 1,000,000 Drs. & in the execution of which I hereby give you in our joint behalf a *Carte blanche.*" Greenleaf had not lost his gift for talking people out of their money. Though William Duer, a broken speculator, was in debtor's prison, Greenleaf convinced him to divert as much as $80,000 into new speculations, promising him one-fourth of the future profits. In August, Thomas Law arrived in New York from India by way of London. After twenty years with the East India Company, he took his fortune to America, eager to add to it by "commercial Speculation." Using only a map and powers of persuasion, Greenleaf got Law to spend almost half his money on 445 lots in the District of Columbia. Greenleaf and his associates had contracted to pay $80 per lot. He charged Law almost $300. Upon learning of this transaction, President Washington chided the commissioners, not because Greenleaf had duped Law but because Greenleaf stood to make "immense profit" from the city's certain growth, while the commissioners raised too little money by their sales. One of them, Daniel Carroll, assured Washington that Law's money would make Greenleaf and Morris more punctual in their payments and that property values would rise as a result of the 166 houses Law had agreed to build—a provision of the contract which Greenleaf had not mentioned and Law had not noticed.

Far from making large profits in the Federal City, Greenleaf's speculation was failing. He and Morris found too few Thomas Laws and Henry Lees. The Dutch loans raised only $190,000. Greenleaf diverted this money to cover his personal expenses and notes. The partnership dissolved in July 1795; Morris and Nicholson bought out Greenleaf at a price of $160 per lot. Since they had too little money to meet their obligations to the commissioners, Greenleaf was even less likely to get paid.

Thomas Law settled in Georgetown, where his neighbors and guests enjoyed his company. He was "a man of very superior understanding." On Tuesday, February 9, 1796, President Washington and his wife were surprised to receive a letter from Martha Washington's granddaughter, Elizabeth Parke Custis, announcing that she and Thomas Law soon would be married. She was nineteen; he was forty. Her stepfather, David Stuart, one of the commissioners of the District of Columbia, wrote to George Washington: "Betsey as I suppose she informed you, made entirely her own bargain in a Husband."

During the year after his wedding, Law struggled with the consequences of his investment in the Federal City. He protested that the terms of his purchase were extortionate and suggested that Robert Morris build the brick houses Law's contract required. Morris replied: "I cannot get the means fast enough to build what I am bound to build for myself." Since city lots were a glut on the market, Law had to compete for buyers. Rival speculators promoted different neighborhoods: Georgetown, Capitol Hill, the riverfront, and the East Branch—that is, the Anacostia River. Law's holdings lay between the Capitol and the Anacostia River. A visitor said of him: "he has wilfully plunged himself into an abyss of cares, and all the contentions of this distracted city. . . . every day his obstinacy on this subject increases, continually leading him to new expences in this vexatious speculation."

Charles William Janson arrived in America from England in the summer of 1793. Thirteen years later, he realized that he had been duped at every turn. Early in 1795, "about the time he was planning his return to Europe, specious and tempting offers induced him to risk a considerable sum in a land-speculation, (a fatal snare for every emigrant)." Over the next ten years he saw much of the United States. In the streets of Norfolk he waded knee-deep in mud. He accompanied a deer hunter into the Dismal Swamp, which he later called a "vast tract of useless land." He visited Washington, D.C., and said of it: "Speculation, the life of the American, embraced the design of the new city. . . . How very beautiful a city Washington appeared when laid out—on paper!" Upon returning to England he published a book to warn others against Americans by the example of his sufferings: "Placing confidence in the reports of interested men, he was led to believe, that the dismal swamps, barren desarts, and pine woods of the new world, flowed with milk and honey."

George Washington had lost interest in land as a source of profit for himself. In the spring of 1794 he set out to sell his holdings and put the purchase money into safe securities. He wished to "draw the interest regularly as it comes due" so that "the remainder of my days may, thereby, be more tranquil and freer from cares." He told his former secretary Tobias Lear that the strongest motive for taking this step was his wish to free his slaves. He owned them, he said, "very repugnantly to my own feelings." He blamed his keeping them on "imperious necessity," which could be reduced or removed by selling land he had bought as an investment and by leasing his Mount Vernon farms to tenants. On the subject of slaveholding he wrote in the fall: "I do not like to even think, much less talk of it. Were it not then, that I am principled agt. selling negros, as you would do cattle in the market, I would not, in twelve months from this date, be possessed of one, as a slave. I shall be happily mistaken, if they are not found to be a very troublesome species of property 'ere many years pass over our heads."

In Philadelphia early in 1795, George and Martha Washington appeared to be in "perfectly good health & spirits." True, the president's temper had not been improved by receiving a letter concerning the Dismal Swamp Company. John Jameson reminded him of an unpaid assessment of £24 to meet an installment due on the company's purchase of shares in the Dismal Swamp Canal Company. Jameson had just returned to York Town after a visit to Dismal Plantation. He explained that repeated theft of timber from the company's land had given the managers an idea. The company ought to give up its effort to drain the swamp and instead hire slaves and "get the Timber ourselves" after clearly marking the boundary of its tract. "If the proprietors would advance one hundred pounds for each Share I am confidant it would render the Estate profitable and also pay the remainder of the Shares in the Canal Company."

Washington replied that the last report he had received from Jameson's late uncle showed the company with a balance on hand. "Having never received an iota from the company for more than twenty years nor never having heard of any appropriation of the sum acknowledged to be in hand, I was in hopes of receiving, instead of being called upon to advance." Nevertheless, Washington approved of turning to timber, and he paid his portion for shares in the canal company. He asked Jameson to send an account of their company's affairs and an estimate of the going price of four quarter-shares. He gave Jameson power of attorney to represent him, but he intended to sell.

Henry Lee enlisted Patrick Henry in his land schemes. Patrick Henry had not yet disposed of his worthless Green Sea tract. Lee offered to help, suggesting that the convening of the United States Circuit Court in Richmond on Friday, May 22, 1795, would be a good time to act. James Wilson of Pennsylvania, a justice of the United States Supreme Court, sat on the Circuit Court. He also speculated extensively in land.

Justice Wilson was a scholar and a teacher of law who had played a leading role in writing the United States Constitution. He devoted his great powers of reasoning to constitutional thought and jurisprudence. In land transactions he was a visionary. In June 1795 his imagination turned to swamps. He received a note from Henry Lee, offering him land—apparently, Patrick Henry's tract—at a bargain price. Wilson wrote to Hugh Williamson, a well-known expert on swamps, seeking information. Williamson described the Dismal Swamp, adding that even where the soil was poor the timber was valuable. He said of North Carolina: "I am induced to believe that a great Part of our swamp land will presently become the most valuable Property in our State, because late Experience has shewn that it may be drained with more Ease than had been expected and because the Course of Nature in that Country is obviously making the Swamps dry." Justice Wilson, already overextended in his investments, borrowed money, $8,000 of it from Henry Lee, and bought land, including Patrick Henry's in the Green Sea. While in Richmond, Lee sold the Belvidere estate to Bushrod Washington, whose law practice brought him before the Circuit Court.

George Washington did not receive from John Jameson an estimate of the value of his four quarter-shares in the Dismal Swamp Company. While at Mount Vernon in September he wrote to Thomas Newton, Jr., and to John Page, asking them to estimate the "highest price." Both told him that he could not get more than £1,000 Virginia currency. Newton enclosed a letter from Isaac Sexton, predicting success for the company's lumber operations. He wrote: "the land in a few years will be very valuable far exceedg the present prices or £1000 per Share." The company, if it applied "activity," would return profits of at least 25 percent per year.

Isaac Sexton was a partner with John Cowper in the lumber business in Nansemond County. He knew the value of the Dismal Swamp Company's timber because he was stealing it. He had proposed to bargain for white cedar. When told that the managers "wished the Land to remain undisturbed," he cut down trees anyway. John Driver reported: "with the number of hands employed by Mr. Cowper & himself they get a very considerable quantity." The Dismal Swamp Company in 1795 had nine slaves—eight men and one boy—hired to fell trees and cut shingles.

Sexton developed his methods in the 1780s, using them in Norfolk County's part of the swamp, along the North Carolina line. Professing to be resurveying Byrd's dividing line in order to enter claims, he admitted knowing that the land already had been patented. He said the earlier titles were not good. So pleased with his own cleverness that he could not conceal it, he added "that the soil was not his object, but that the timber was his object, and that he was determined to establish his survey if he could and that if they did sue him, it might so happen that he could get the Timber off first, and then he did not care what became of the Swamp." While Sexton gave advice to George Washington, John Cowper surveyed new claims along the western line of the company's tract. It was easy to see that he intended to use Sexton's method of encroachment for timber. Agents and partners of the Dismal Swamp Company denounced "that bad man, Sexton."

Predictions of a bright future for the Dismal Swamp Company did not alter George Washington's intent to sell. He looked back on what he called "the injury they had received by the effects of the war, and the still greater, which their inattention to their own concerns had done them." His "many attempts" to stimulate his partners had failed; he "gave up all further hopes of any thing effectual being done for their interests." With Jameson calling for more money, Washington's share in the company was, he said, "rather expensive than productive."

To Henry Lee, Washington set the price of his four quarter-shares at a total of $20,000, or £4,000 Virginia currency. Lee took it. This was four times market price but £1,000 less than Washington had been asking. Lee hoped to make his first payment, about $7,000, not in cash but in Justice James Wilson's bonds, payable in one and two years. Having lent money to Wilson to buy Patrick Henry's thousands of acres of reeds in the Dismal Swamp, Lee expected to use Wilson's debt to him to pay Washington. Lee assured Washington that he had inquired into the justice's affairs. There was "not a doubt" that Wilson could meet his obligations. Washington retained title to his four quarter-shares, pending Lee's payments, but he told his former partners that

Lee would henceforth "receive the profits" and "pay all unsatisfied demands upon me."

Not until he neared his eightieth birthday in the 1790s did Dr. Thomas Walker grow infirm. He and his wife, who was approaching seventy, kept a permanent guest at Castle Hill: Weston Alcock, a former officer in the British Army who had come to Charlottesville as a prisoner of war and remained in peacetime with no means of support except the Walkers. Alcock signed Dr. Walker's will as a witness in 1788. He became "a dependant" and took care of Thomas and Elizabeth Walker.

Francis Walker turned twenty-nine in 1793. He had just won election to the United States House of Representatives. James Madison talked with him in April to make sure that he was "right" on political questions, that he would join the gathering opposition to any increase of the federal government's power. Unless forestalled, they believed, the Washington administration would make the United States more and more like Britain, almost a British dependency. Three weeks before Congress convened in Philadelphia, Francis Preston called at Castle Hill on Friday, November 8, to resign as agent of the Loyal Company. He found Francis Walker drunk. The "extensive circle of acquaintances who respected and friends who loved him so dearly" could not find a reason for Walker's drinking, unless it was "an hereditary fever in the blood or itch upon the palate."

A year later, on Monday, November 9, 1794, Dr. Thomas Walker died. His body was buried at Castle Hill. The following month Weston Alcock and another witness proved the will in Charlottesville. Francis Walker came into his inheritance.

He was challenged for re-election to Congress by Samuel Jordan Cabell, veteran of Saratoga, Valley Forge, and the siege of Charleston. Cabell, a kinsman wrote, "was a magnificent man before the people, the greatest man on a court green, in a crowd, or on the electioneering arena that I ever met with, except, perhaps, John Randolph of Roanoke." On public questions important to Madison and Thomas Jefferson, few men were so "right" as Cabell. He denounced "the speculating monied interest growing out of banking and funding systems, &c. which I consider the two great political curses of my country." He praised "our dear and magnanimous allies the French," and he predicted a revolution in Britain to overthrow "the maddening spirit of her Ministry for coercive measures to stifle the principles of liberty."

Francis Walker "lacked ambition," as did "most of Dr. Walker's descendants," one of them wrote. Six weeks before the election, Thomas Jefferson foresaw that Walker would lose. Cabell was "indefatigable attending courts &c. and wherever he is, there is a general drunkenness observed." A shrewd candidate kept the voters drunk, not himself. Jefferson disapproved of Cabell. He wrote of Walker's impending defeat: "The low practices of his competitor though seen with indignation by every thinking man, are but too successful with the unthinking who merchandize their votes for grog." Walker's career in Congress ended after one term.

Ten weeks after the election, Francis Walker's niece, Mildred Gilmer, was married. She was the oldest daughter of the first cousins, George Gilmer and Lucy Walker Gilmer, who had eloped in 1767 and who now had eight children. Mildred's new husband was William Wirt, an ambitious twenty-two-year-old attorney, newly arrived in Virginia from Maryland to make his fortune.

Dr. Walker was the third but not the last husband of his second wife. Elizabeth Thornton Walker had her own property in her third widowhood. In July 1795 she wrote a will, bequeathing all her estate to Weston Alcock in gratitude for "great attention and care." At her suggestion, the Walkers believed, she and Alcock were married early in 1796. She died in August.

Elizabeth and Thomas Lee Shippen visited Virginia late in the summer of 1792, giving Elizabeth Farley Dunbar a chance to see her first grandchild. Champe and Maria Carter arrived at Nesting for a reunion of the four sisters. Mary Willing Byrd came up from Westover. Though John Dunbar was sick, all were happy to hear from Antigua that the Mercers Creek plantation promised a bumper crop of sugar cane. The Shippens expected their share of the profits in 1793 to be £1,000 sterling. John Dunbar recovered his health by October, but in that month fire broke out at Nesting, destroying the house, furniture, and offices.

The Shippens, the Carters, and John Dunbar, as guardian of the two younger sisters, were defendants in Major John Simon Farley's suit in Chancellor George Wythe's High Court of Chancery. Farley and his sister, Elizabeth Morson, as heirs of their father Simon Farley, demanded one-half of the Land of Eden and one-third of the holdings in Norfolk County, Virginia. They asserted that the defendants, Francis Farley's heirs, held Simon Farley's share in trust for them, as Francis had done, and they now claimed their legacy.

The Shippens, the Carters, and John Dunbar replied through their attorney, John Wickham, that Francis Farley had owned all the land as his brother's surviving heir, that he had bequeathed it to his granddaughters, and that the law prohibited aliens from owning land in Virginia. The case had not yet been argued before Wythe. Thomas Lee Shippen and Champe Carter disliked the delay and suspense, eager as they were to divide and sell the Land of Eden. Their attorneys, however, said they could not do so while the suit was pending. Shippen had to content himself with bright prospects for sugar.

After the fire at Nesting, John Dunbar settled in Williamsburg. Shippen accompanied him from Berkeley plantation to choose a home. In the former capital uninhabited houses were falling to ruin, covered with moss and mildew, among the neat dwellings of its remaining residents. About 1,300 people, half of them blacks, lived in the city—fewer than at the end of the war ten years earlier. Politicians and merchants no longer gathered from all parts of Virginia. Grass grew in some streets. The brick college building looked ill kept. The governor's palace had caught fire and burned down on Christmas Eve, 1781. Some ruins still stood on the site; people had stripped the grounds of timber. The capitol was slowly crumbling, especially the part where the House of Burgesses once sat. The old chamber in which the Council sat as the colony's General Court was used as a courtroom; another part had become a grammar school. The wooden pillars of the portico were twisted awry. Among them stood the marble statue of Lord Botetourt, much defaced, its nose broken off, a hand missing. During the Terror in France, college students decapitated it. The Dunbars moved to what William Nelson, Jr., called "the peaceful city of Wmsburg." It was so peaceful that to visitors it seemed near death.

Upon getting married, each of the Farley sisters convinced her husband that her stepfather, John Dunbar, had been looting her legacy for his own benefit while acting as her guardian. At the time he came to Virginia and so quickly got married to their mother, it was a matter "of public Notoriety" that he had "no Property." Their mother received an annuity of £300 sterling from Francis Farley's estate. Yet John Dunbar lived "in all the Comforts and Luxuries of Affluence—he purchased Farms, Houses, Slaves—he remitted large sums of money to Great Britain." Thousands of pounds sterling came from Henry Benskin Lightfoot, their representative in Antigua. At Mercers Creek two hundred slaves worked 165 acres; a good year yielded 140 hogsheads of sugar and 80 hogsheads of rum. Rents from the Land of Eden were $1,500 to $2,000 per year, and the plantation agent at Saura Town paid more than £1,200 Virginia currency to Dunbar's order in a five-year period. Yet the old debts of James Parke Farley's, which Francis Farley's will ordered to be paid, remained outstanding on the books of Dinwiddie, Crawford &

Company. No wonder John Dunbar could walk away from the ruins of Nesting and take a house in Williamsburg.

Chancellor Wythe heard arguments in the case of John Simon Farley and Elizabeth Morson against the Shippens, the Carters, and Dunbar on Tuesday, March 18, 1794. His decision awarded the plaintiffs everything they sought. The evidence was clear: Francis Farley always had acted as trustee for his brother's children; their right to the land had accrued to them before Virginia law prohibited aliens from owning land—indeed, before they were "aliens." Wythe ordered the defendants, "at their costs," to convey half of the Land of Eden and one-third of the Farley property in Norfolk County to the plaintiffs and to pay the plaintiffs the appropriate share of rents and profits received since the suit had begun. Just as the four sisters were coming into their legacy, they lost half of the Land of Eden. John Dunbar was in failing health at this time, and died in October 1794.

A few weeks later, Elizabeth Dunbar's third daughter was married. Rebecca Parke Farley—known as Parke—took as her bridegroom Richard Corbin, namesake and twenty-three-year-old grandson of the last deputy receiver general of the king's revenue in Virginia. Corbin's father had died in April, and he avoided his mother, who lamented her widowhood at every opportunity, talking and writing about herself at length. She was the daughter of Benjamin Waller, Speaker Robinson's right-hand man. She was distressed by the prospect of a life as "a Hermitess with a bare Subsistence," scrimping in the largest house in King and Queen County. She wrote to her son just before his wedding: "How then my Beloved Richard can you invite or wish such an object as I now am to your gay City—Such a Visitor could only Damp your good Spirits and throw a Gloomy Sadness over your bright and fair Prospects." Elizabeth Dunbar strove to cheer Richard's brothers and sisters during their visit to Williamsburg for the festivities. She wrote a "polite Letter" to his mother after the wedding on Saturday, November 15.

Richard and Rebecca Parke Corbin lived in the mansion at Laneville plantation, 2,400 acres in King and Queen County. The two-story brick house, with its single-story wings, presented a front almost 200 feet long on a hill overlooking the Mattaponi River and a terraced front lawn descending to the water. About seventy slaves worked on the plantation.

Within three months of his wedding, Richard Corbin had learned to suspect that his wife had not received and was not receiving the full amount of her one-fourth of the profits of the Mercers Creek estate. John Dunbar was dead, but Thomas Lee Shippen and Elizabeth Shippen had corresponded with Henry B. Lightfoot for years, receiving payments and sugar from him, perhaps more than they were entitled to. The Corbins wrote to Thomas Lee Shippen, asking how much money they could expect.

Shippen suffered from consumption—tuberculosis. He dosed himself with opiates and spent much time brooding. His wife unfailingly helped him and tried to cheer him, but he saw around him false friends and real enemies. A few days after receiving the Corbins' letter, he wrote his will. By law, his wife's property was now his. He bequeathed to her for her lifetime the proceeds of the Mercers Creek plantation and the Land of Eden. He left the quarter-share in the Dismal Swamp Company and the interest in Norfolk County land to their sons. To his wife and each son he bequeathed one share in the Dismal Swamp Canal Company. His younger son was to inherit his lot in the District of Columbia.

Richard Corbin refused to quarrel with Shippen. They shared a wish to sell the Land of Eden and the Antigua estate. Finding that his wife was a partner in the Dismal Swamp Company, Corbin wrote: "what has been done with this Land I know not, nor do I know who are in actual possession at present." The four sisters appealed Chancellor Wythe's decision to the Court of Appeals. Even if they lost the case they would each own one-eighth of the Land of Eden. Corbin and Shippen planned to divide half the tract among the sisters so that they could get some money by sale at once.

John Dunbar had not lived a life of affluence alone. Accusing him implied censure of his wife. Elizabeth Dunbar was pained by the preoccupation of her daughters and their husbands with lost Farley riches. She believed Francis Farley's estate, in other words, her daughters, owed her, rather than the reverse. She wrote to Elizabeth and Thomas Shippen: "be that as it may, my sons and Daughters must and shall love me, and whether creditor or debtor, We will be forever friends." In the summer of 1795 the Shippens moved to their retreat in Bucks County, Pennsylvania, called Farley. Their "finely situated" large house on a hill above Neshaminy Creek impressed visitors with its elegance and neatness. Elizabeth managed it while Thomas, an invalid, spent much of his time reading and devising ways to extract cash from the Farley bequest. At the end of the summer Richard and Rebecca Parke Corbin received their first remittance from Henry B. Lightfoot: a bill of exchange for £100 sterling.

The Farley heirs in Virginia compromised with John Simon Farley and Elizabeth Morson, ending their appeal in the courts early in 1796. The sisters and their husbands gave up the land Chancellor Wythe had awarded to Francis Farley's nephew and niece. John Simon Farley and Elizabeth Morson gave up their claim to arrearages of rents and profits. Unlike the Corbins and the Shippens, Champe and Maria Carter had not devoted themselves to pursuing John Dunbar, Henry B. Lightfoot, a larger share of the Land of Eden, and the riches of the Dismal Swamp. They got rid of their right to a portion of the Land of Eden at once, without waiting for North Carolina courts to order surveys and a division. Champe Carter sold it in June for $2 per acre.

William Nelson, Jr., became a judge of Virginia's General Court at the same time that Henry Lee was elected governor. The new position suited him. In his law practice, he said, "neither my profits nor my reputation equal'd my wish, tho' they at least equal'd my abilities." The judges sat for three weeks in Richmond twice a year, then rode circuit, taking about half of Nelson's time. This schedule left him "more time to read, & to enjoy domestick tranquillity." When not on the bench he lived at Westover, where Abby Byrd Nelson stayed with her mother and sisters. Each year she had another pregnancy and a new baby—all girls.

Nelson's friend John Page brooded about the movement of Federalists in Congress toward Britain and toward British political repressiveness. His health remained fragile, and none of his efforts freed him from debt. He refused in October 1793 to give John Hatley Norton's representative a deed of trust for slaves worth the amount of his debt, but in December he relented and signed. Noah and Betty and their children, Bob and Bridget and their children, and Will and Hannah would leave Rosewell if Page could not raise almost £260. Fifteen months later, his predicament had grown worse, and he feared that he would have to sell Rosewell. At best, he might keep the mansion and 500 acres around it. He resigned his post as commander of the Gloucester County militia, traditionally held by the county's leading citizen.

Serious illness struck Abby Byrd Nelson in November 1795. A violent cold gave way to a debilitating disease, depriving her of the use of her lower legs. She could cross a room only with a person on each arm, holding her up. While her husband, her mother, and her sisters at Westover watched over her anxiously, at Rosewell, John Page sold some of the deeded slaves to Norton's representative to pay part of his debt. Page did not attend the opening of Congress in Philadelphia because he had promised a creditor that he would not leave the state until he paid in full. By early December, Abby Nelson knew that she lay on her deathbed. She said that she wished her daughters reared in the Christian faith. She told her sisters which daughter should receive each of her most prized rings, her watch, and other mementoes when the girls became young women. Not long afterward, she died. William Nelson, Jr., went into mourning for his second wife. Sarah Meade crossed from Maycox to spend time with Mary Willing Byrd. A "feeling letter" to Mary Willing Byrd arrived from her stepdaughter, Elizabeth Dunbar. Sarah Meade carried a message in reply from Westover to Williamsburg. Nelson asked St. George Tucker to convey his thanks and love to Elizabeth Dunbar. Nelson's daughter by his first marriage was now a ward of George Wythe's. At Westover, Mary Willing Byrd, "honored grandmama," looked at an infant and girls aged two, three, four, and five.

The crisis kept Nelson away from the December session of the United States Circuit Court in Richmond, where he formerly had practiced and sometimes still listened to arguments as a spectator. He was absent when the court announced verdicts in Samuel Gist's four suits for debt against his one-time agent, John Tabb. In years long past, Tabb had loaded Gist's vessels with tobacco and had waited for the *Hope* to arrive from the Gold Coast with slaves for him to sell. Gist won all four cases. Since the start of the suits, Tabb had been in "a state of mental derangement."

John Page reached Philadelphia later in December. The day after New Year's he tried to sell his gold watch for $60. The treaty with Britain approved by Washington's administration and by Federalists so distressed him that he contemplated not seeking another term in Congress. He was not reelected. He later wrote: "John Adams and A. Hamilton shut me out." Page saw both his country's fortunes and his own in decline. His financial straits had forced him to sell for too little the interest in the Dismal Swamp Company given him by his father. "No doubt," he wrote, "the Value of Shares must have encreased" in the eighteen months after he left the company. He would not benefit, but the company's bright prospects must be obvious to "all who know anything respecting the Dismal Swamp & the intended Canal." William Nelson, Jr., one of the managers, believed that he and his partners at last had found the way to succeed: lumber.

Visiting Westover to console Mary Willing Byrd, Sarah Meade knew that she and her friend must soon part. David Meade took stock of his finances in the fall of 1794, "by which enquiry I discover," he wrote to John Driver, "that I cannot provide even a decent subsistence for my large family beyond the Spring of 95, unless money is raised by a very disadvantageous Sale of more property, & that what Estate yet remains to me is so reduced in quantum that no kind of application of it within my power can be nearly adequate to that purpose." He preferred to sell all his property in Virginia, then move to Kentucky, where he could live comfortably at less expense. Much of 1795 he devoted to arranging his affairs, preparing to go west in the spring of 1796. He said: "there has not been a time for some years past that I have been free from care." Kentucky promised fewer cares, perhaps freedom.

Meade had sustained his interest in the Dismal Swamp Company as one of its managers. He voted all four quarter-shares once the property of his wife's father, William Waters. Two now belonged to his brother, Richard Kidder Meade. After service as one of Washington's aides during the war, Richard settled on 1,000 acres in Frederick County. David Meade had not made the Dismal Swamp Company profitable for himself and his brother. In June 1795, John Driver gave him an advance of £30 from the company's small reserve of funds. The slaves working in Meade's intricate pleasure gardens at Maycox ate rice grown by slaves working on Dismal Plantation.

Hoping to close the forty-year-old debts contracted by his father and John Driver's father, which with interest had mounted to £4,500 sterling, Meade negotiated with Benjamin Waller in Williamsburg, agent and attorney for Wakelin Welch & Company. Each man brought in another lawyer: Joseph Prentis and Littleton Waller Tazewell. Meade offered to clear the debt by conveying land at a valuation of £10 per acre and by covering the balance with his bond and Richard Kidder Meade's. He thought Waller had accepted this arrangement. Yet, after several meetings and much discussion, Waller and Tazewell's version of the terms differed from Meade and Prentis's version. Each side accused the other of bad faith. Meade paid nothing.

Richard Kidder Meade kept his two quarter-shares in the Dismal Swamp Company and remained in Virginia. He felt constant anxiety that his wife would learn why her brother was confined in the Lunatic Hospital in Williamsburg. Mary Grymes Meade and Benjamin Grymes were children of Elizabeth Fitzhugh Grymes and Benjamin Grymes, a partner of Anthony Bacon's in Fredericksburg from 1756 until 1758. The younger Benjamin had shown "a derangement of his brain" since childhood, worsening in adulthood with "the inflamation brought on by the use of ardent spirits." Richard had "long since" told Mary that her brother was in the Lunatic Hospital but dreaded that she would find out about "the murder, & trial" which had put Grymes there. He said he shuddered at the thought that Grymes might be released. "My earnest Prayer," he wrote, "is, that it would please Heaven to put an end to *his* miserable existence."

To dispose of his quarter-shares in the Dismal Swamp Company, David Meade turned to George Keith Taylor, agent for Justice James Wilson. Wilson desired more of the Dismal Swamp than the Green Sea land he had bought from Patrick Henry. He contracted with Taylor to buy on his behalf. Taylor asked repeatedly: "are you certain that your funds will enable you to go through with this contract?" Wilson led him to believe that "immense" resources backed his purchases, an assurance passed on to sellers. Meade sold Wilson two quarter-shares and 1,450 other acres in and near the Dismal Swamp for £1,200 Virginia currency. Meade received no cash. He gave Wilson a deed, and Wilson gave him a mortgage on the land and on the shares as security for future payment. Even before the deed and the mortgage were exchanged, Taylor began to have doubts. The first bill of exchange he drew on Justice Wilson for $1,000 was returned protested.

In May 1796 the Meades, their children, their slaves, and George Royster headed for Kentucky. David and Sarah Meade were two years short of the thirtieth anniversary of their wedding. He predicted a bright future for the region: "in less than twenty years there will not be a tree left on the banks of the Ohio but such as are left for ornament—in half a century the population will equal any part of the world except (perhaps) China."

David Meade's prediction had no advocate more ardent than Robert Morris. With his partners John Nicholson and James Greenleaf, Morris devised a land scheme embracing 6,000,000 acres in Kentucky, Pennsylvania, Virginia, the Carolinas, and Georgia. If successful, it would repay Morris's creditors and recoup his fortunes. The financing was tricky, but the idea was simple: make contracts for huge swaths of unoccupied land, then sell in bulk, at a large profit, to European investors who believed with Adam Smith that in America "purchase and improvement of uncultivated land is there the most profitable employment of the smallest as well as of the greatest capitals." The population of the United States doubled every twenty years; people moved westward over snow and ice; they sought small farms; each new farm raised the value of property near it. Who could decline an opportunity to make so sure a profit from America's growth?

Between 1793 and 1795, Morris and his partners bought land. They committed themselves to pay almost $1,250,000 for 6,000,000 acres. More than 2,300,000 lay in Georgia, which then extended to the Mississippi River. Almost 1,000,000 lay in western Virginia, and more than 400,000 were in Kentucky.

Morris's purchases attracted the attention of Thomas Blount, a new member of Congress from North Carolina. After talking with Dr. John Hall, a veteran land speculator and "a genteel, respectable & polite man & my friend," Blount saw how North Carolinians could benefit. From the state Dr.

Hall would obtain grants in unclaimed regions, then sell them to Morris. Blount explained Hall's plan to his brother, John Gray Blount: "it is calculated to afford to the State, at present the *advantage* of Selling her worst Lands, which in reality have no value at all, for ready Money at the price of her best." Hall offered John Gray Blount one-eighth of his profits in return for help in North Carolina. Another speculator, David Allison, followed the same course in cooperation with Blount. Almost all the 700,000 acres Morris and Nicholson bought in North Carolina came from these two men.

Hall sold the partners 200,000 acres of swamp in Beaufort and Hyde counties, west of the Outer Banks and south of Albemarle Sound and the Dismal Swamp. As soon as Morris was ready to sign in June 1794, Hall wrote to Blount: "I wish you would engross all the Swamp in North Carolina—a little Marsh would answer." He added a warning: "every thing had better be kept a Secret."

Morris's purchase would not become final until October, allowing him time to learn about the swamp. Blount assured the partners that the land was of "good quality." When drained, it "will become the garden spot of North Carolina." Morris's agent, William Swansey, went to North Carolina to check this description. Dr. Hall wrote ahead to Blount: "you had better prepare the Gentlemans mind Who is employed to inspect the Land." Blount smoothed Swansey's visit to the forks of the Tar River and the swamp. Morris afterward was told "that fully one half of it was worth Ten Guineas P Acre & could be reclaimed for one Dollar P Acre."

Morris and Nicholson contracted to pay $40,064 for 200,320 acres. The flaw in Hall's plan to dupe the partners lay in the form of payment he accepted. Neither Hall nor John Gray Blount received "ready Money"; instead, Hall was to be paid in installments spread over twenty-two months. For half of the sum, Morris drew a bill of exchange on Nicholson, which Nicholson accepted and promised to pay. For the other half, Nicholson drew a bill on Morris, which Morris accepted. Thus Dr. Hall and David Allison joined the many holders of an "amazing quantity" of paper issued by Morris and Nicholson.

Morris hoped that war in Europe would soon end and that capital would flow to America. One of the London firms he had in mind as investors was Bourdieu, Chollet & Bourdieu. James Bourdieu and David Chollet had been among the founders of New Lloyd's. Bourdieu was the "positive and peremptory" partner; Chollet was the "vastly civil" partner. Unlike Samuel Gist, Bourdieu had stood by the Americans during the Revolutionary War. The British government had intercepted his mail. But unpaid debts soured the partners' opinion of the United States. Independence had created a country that attracted the kind of people they knew all too well, such as a bankrupt French hatter seeking to make a fortune in trade: "he seems full of projects, and having nothing to lose, runs no risk in the event. He faild at Paris, and went to America as to the Land of Canaan." Even the obliging Mr. Chollet had to tell a visiting American not to bother trying to get a loan in the City because "the Name of America terrifies the mercantile Part of the Community." Bourdieu and Chollet looked at Morris's activities with the same skepticism that all American schemes provoked in them. The partners wrote about merchants in the United States: "While they were subject to our laws their salutary force impressed a character of honesty, which the said merchants have abandoned in their revolution to return to their natural habits of ruse to attack the welfare of others.... Unless we had surplus money which could await the progress and advantages of a natural population growth, it would not be in these distant wilds that we would place it." The partners foresaw that in wartime European investors would lend their money to belligerent governments, not hand it to Robert Morris to enable him to redeem his notes and bills.

By January 1795, Morris had trouble raising money. He borrowed "at a dreadful interest," looking more and more like "a desperate gambler." That month he sent an agent to Kentucky: Charles Willing Byrd, twenty-four-year-old son of Mary Willing Byrd and nephew of Morris's longtime mercantile partner, Thomas Willing. A few years earlier, a visitor at Westover had found him "a very pretty youth Lounging at home." Morris instructed him to secure title to the large tracts the partners had agreed to buy for 25¢ per acre. Morris had to learn the same lesson that experience taught others: "a purchaser in Kentucky buys a lawsuit with every plot of unoccupied land he pays for there." He ordered Byrd to scrutinize closely any claims to title competing with his.

Five years before Byrd went west, Kentucky held about 74,000 people; five years after he arrived in Lexington, the new state had 221,000. A traveler saw people walking "hundreds of Miles, they know not for what Nor whither, except its to Kentucky," a place they deemed "the Promised land . . . the Land of Milk and Honey." Once in the state, many turned to the practice of its "two principal Evils"; they began "to Quarrel about religion" and "go to Law about Land."

Kentuckians called Morris's purchases "the speculating lands." At a price of 25¢ per acre, he could hardly expect to get good soil. Since a "Barren mountain would command as much as a fertile valley," sellers furnished chiefly the former. Only later did one of Morris's partners learn that "almost every large tract then sold, was *generally* of land *then* intrinsically worth nothing, & will be worth very little to the Resurrection." Sellers cheerfully gave a general warranty that they were conveying a secure title "when they knew the title was either not good, or at least doubtful." These were the men whom good-looking young Charles Willing Byrd went from Westover to Lexington to outwit.

On Friday, February 20, 1795, Robert Morris, John Nicholson, and James Greenleaf created the North American Land Company. They announced that investors could join them in "extreamly profitable" resale of property they had amassed. Their 6,000,000 acres were held by the company's trustees. Capitalized at 50¢ per acre, 30,000 shares would sell for $100 each. Dividends were to come from profits on sales of land. The founders guaranteed 6 percent per year. Their security for paying dividends was the 9,000 shares they held. They assured potential investors that the company's title to its land was secure. Its agents would fan out to survey farms, lay out towns, erect mills, make roads, and establish stores to sell tools and stock. The first settlers would "readily agree" to pay $2 per acre. As farms multiplied and land values rose, shareholders' dividends would exceed 6 percent, and the value of shares would grow to "four or five, or more likely ten times" the original purchase price. All this, Morris said, "without either Risque or trouble."

The North American Land Company at once attracted critics and satirists. In Paris, newspapers published warnings from France's minister to the United States, Jean Antoine Joseph Fauchet, naming Morris as the archvillain of fraudulent land sales. In Baltimore a satirist signing himself "TIM. BROADBACK"—a play on the name of Morris's associate Daniel Brodhead, surveyor general of Pennsylvania—proposed a mock scheme to rival that of the North American Land Company. He would get claims to 20,000,000 acres at twopence per acre, then capitalize his land company at two shillings per acre. Although he would have a nominal capital of $5,333,333.33, he calculated that $50,000 cash would be enough to make a start sufficient to attract subscribers, who would buy shares to keep him afloat because they already held so many of his notes. "Thus, with a little address we may make a South Sea SCHEME of it."

Morris scattered copies of his company's prospectus and blocks of 1,000 shares among merchants on the other side of the Atlantic, calling his plan "the best that ever was devised in America." He told London merchants: "the uncultivated Lands in the U States now afford the safest and most profitable speculation of any thing in this world." People in Britain who picked up a pamphlet entitled *London Considered as the Metropolis of Europe for the Operations of Commerce and Finance* gradually realized as they read that its chief purpose was to encourage investment in American land. The author conceded that speculations might "miscarry" but added: "European speculators, properly guided by men of judgment and integrity, can wish for no more rapid means of enlarging their property." As an example of the rapid rise in value, the author told a story of Francis Farley's purchase of the Land of Eden from William Byrd. Farley had paid 1,000 guineas, then eleven years later had refused an offer of 28,000 guineas for the tract. Through his investment, "his capital had been placed at the compound interest of 25 per cent. . . . Many fortunes, which could be considered as immense in Europe, have been acquired there through similar speculations."

Four months after the North American Land Company was established, bills of exchange James Greenleaf had drawn on Dutch financiers began to come back protested. Greenleaf could not keep his commitments to Morris and Nicholson for District of Columbia lots or the North American Land Company. Morris's notes and bills drawn in 1793 and 1794 were, he said, "daily falling due." His only recourse was quick resale of land.

To this end Morris sent his son-in-law, James Marshall, younger brother of John Marshall, to London. Morris had interested the Marshall brothers in purchasing 160,000 acres, the residue of the Fairfax proprietary, from the Fairfax heir in England. Those negotiations had included Henry Lee. Morris turned to Lee again as James Marshall prepared to leave for London in October 1795. Lee was just about to buy George Washington's share in the Dismal Swamp Company. If he could afford $20,000 for that venture, he could afford to help Morris. Although Morris and Nicholson already owed Lee $21,500 for land in and around Matildaville, Morris asked Lee to lend him $40,000 in cash. Morris would draw bills of exchange for that amount on William Temple Franklin, his agent in England for the sale of New York land. Marshall would take them to London, where they "would be duely paid." For the safety of this loan Lee could rely "on the promises of Judge Wilson." Lee produced the cash. Morris drew up bills, payable to Lee, and entrusted them to James Marshall.

Morris wrote letters of introduction for Marshall to Bourdieu, Chollet & Bourdieu, as well as to other merchants in London, Amsterdam, and Leipzig. To William Temple Franklin, he wrote: "The Lands are daily increasing in Value, there is no possibility of Loss, on the Contrary immense profits are certain." Morris drew up instructions for selling North American Land Company shares and tracts. Marshall was to investigate the Amsterdam and

Rotterdam loans that Greenleaf had promised for lots in the Federal City. Morris gave Marshall a packet of papers: copies of deeds, testimonials about Georgia land, a copy of William Swansey's report on North Carolina swampland, and "a description of Kentucke Lands." Armed with these, Marshall sailed for London. The men he went to meet did not need the warning a young Englishman sent from Virginia to his friend in Lancashire: "Let every man beware of those who go to England to sell land."

VII

TERRAPHOBIA

ON NEW YEAR'S DAY, 1796, Alexander Macaulay, merchant of York Town and a manager of the Dismal Swamp Company, signed an agreement with Thomas Shepherd of Nansemond County. Shepherd contracted to make the company's affairs his sole occupation for five years as agent and business manager.

Macaulay, now forty-one, had grown heavy in ten years in York Town. He looked prosperous, but he was not. For the preceding four years he had drawn large bills of exchange which were returned to his creditors, protested. He "suffered greatly" by the financial panic in London in 1793. In the following year, John Jameson, fellow manager of the Dismal Swamp Company and fellow resident of York Town, consented to Macaulay's drawing on the company's funds for "his own use." By the time Shepherd signed, Macaulay had taken $2,000. In 1796 he drew much more. One entry in his accounts showed that he paid "Self per receipt $8040.34."

Macaulay wished 1795 to be the year he freed himself from debt. Instead, he lost a suit in the United States Circuit Court. He heard from John Wickham, acting on behalf of people stuck with his bad bills. In August his brig *Helen*, laden with a valuable cargo, ran aground near York Town during a hurricane. Another brig, homeward bound from Madeira, he lost to a British privateer. He thought it best to send his daughter, Helen, and his son, Alexander, to Scotland for education because the teaching of boys and girls in Virginia was contaminated with "French principles." But he could not afford a proper education for them. In January 1796 he had not yet paid for 280 barrels of corn purchased two years earlier. He must soon stop pretending that he was going to repay the money he had taken from the Dismal Swamp Company.

Thomas Shepherd was "an intelligent young gentleman," who owned a broken-down sawmill and a gristmill near the northeastern margin of the swamp, not far from the unfinished Dismal Swamp canal. He was to lead the company in its new direction—profits from lumber. The Dismal Swamp Company bought a half interest in his mills and shared the expense of repairing them. At the joint charge of the company and Shepherd a canal was to be cut in the heart of the swamp to connect the eastern boundary of the company's land with the Dismal Swamp canal, as well as another feeder to run from the Dismal Swamp canal to Shepherd's mill pond. After getting approval from the company's managers, he could cut roads and ditches into its tract to bring out timber and transport it by water to the sawmill. There the logs would be cut into boards or shingles. If he and the company did not renew their agreement in 1801, the company could buy his interest in the mills.

The partners had largely abandoned both of William Byrd's proposals: draining the swamp and making the enterprise self-supporting by farming. Only a few slaves remained at Dismal Plantation. A member of the Riddick family acted as overseer. Making shingles would require hiring slaves, and the price of shingles was so low that Shepherd did nothing but "hold possession." By allowing others to take trees in return for half the profits, the company in 1795 and 1796 cleared £219 6s. 7d. Virginia currency. The sum would have been £519 if Alexander Macaulay had not withdrawn £300 in cash. The company's new plan for a water route to the sawmill met difficulties. The Dismal Swamp Canal Company had cut off water to Shepherd's pond. The mills needed repair partly because they had been idle since 1795. Shepherd soon learned that holding possession required much effort to ward off timber thieves.

David and Sarah Meade, their seven children, and about forty slaves paused on their way to Kentucky to spend time at Richard Kidder Meade's plantation in the Shenandoah Valley near the foot of the Blue Ridge. As they prepared to leave, David Meade saw that three slave men had run away. He was not surprised by the "defection" of his postilion Syphax and of Boddow, but the departure of the elder Billy, he said, "vexes my spirit." Meade assumed that they would return to the vicinity of Maycox. If caught, they were to be sold. Billy was taken at the Shenandoah ferry, trying to cross the river. Once he was back with the Meades, he expressed "much contrition," and he was not sold. The next day, June 8, 1796, the Meades' coaches and horses, accompanied by the slaves, followed their three hired wagons full of baggage to Winchester on their way to Pittsburgh.

Nine days later their wagons and coaches rolled over the unmarked grave of General Edward Braddock, whose body had been buried in the road so that Indians and Frenchmen could not find it. From Pittsburgh they went down the Ohio River by boat. The last leg of their journey took them over-land from Limestone on the Ohio to Lexington, 60 miles southwest. They reached their destination a month after leaving Richard Kidder Meade's plantation.

About 1,600 people lived in a growing town of frame houses, log houses, some stone structures, and new two-story brick homes. Charles Willing Byrd welcomed the Meades to Lexington. He had just told Robert Morris that he was fixed there for life. He helped them find lodging. The first per-son to call on them was a granddaughter of Speaker Robinson's. She came with her husband, "Mr. West an Irish Man, who proves a very attentive, friendly & agreeable acquaintance." Otway Byrd visited his half brother in the summer. Returning to Virginia, he could report to Mary Willing Byrd that her son and her friend Sarah Meade were doing well.

David Meade bought about 550 acres at the mouth of Jessamine Creek nine miles southwest of Lexington. He designed a comfortable house and pleasure gardens far more extensive and elaborate than those at Maycox. In the summer and early fall the family remained in Lexington while slaves and a few white workmen began a one-story cluster of rooms Meade called "our Cottage." Its centerpiece was a square dining room, 20 feet on each side, wainscotted in black walnut, with deep window seats. In the last week of Oc-tober, after the leaves in his "noble" stands of sugar maple had turned yellow, the family moved from Lexington to the estate, living in a small log house through the winter while work continued, even in snow. They occupied their unfinished five-room house in April. Meade was eager to add new rooms, some frame, others stone and brick. The house spread into a villa.

Meade began his gardens in the spring. His imagination saw a stone fence with red and white roses, hedges covered by honeysuckle, with an outer gate that opened to a winding road through a park, opening onto a broad, sloping expanse of smooth bluegrass in front of his house. He designed vistas leading the eye into the distance, as well as bowers, nooks, and alcoves concealing a comfortable bench or a small Chinese temple. Except for corn, which almost every Kentucky farm seemed to produce in abundance, Meade did not work food crops. Any farming was done by others, who rented some of his land. He did experiment with growing hemp. Above his gate Meade put the name he gave his new home: Chaumière des Prairies—Cottage in the Meadow.

On Easter Sunday, April 16, the Meades' oldest daughter, Sally, was mar-ried to Charles Willing Byrd. Growing up at Maycox and Westover, the bride and bridegroom had known each other all their lives. David Meade said that the match "adds one more to our family." Before the summer passed, Sally Meade Byrd was pregnant.

In 1796, John Tyndale Warre, executor of the estate of the Bristol firm Farell & Jones, sued David Meade in United States Circuit Court in Richmond for an old unpaid debt of £115 sterling. Warre's attorney won a verdict, and a writ of execution against Meade's property was given to the United States marshal. Richard Hanson, Warre's agent in Virginia, reported this outcome but added that Meade had moved 800 miles away. The distance in a straight line was about half that, but with a large number Hanson conveyed his disappointment. At the end of 1797, Meade wrote to his largest creditor in Britain, Wakelin Welch, accusing Benjamin Waller of "extreamly faithless" conduct in their negotiations for clearing the old debt. If Welch and Waller imitated Warre and Hanson by pursuing Meade in federal court, he warned, "I will avail myself of the vicinity of a foreign government and avoid unjust persecution." Meade had not yet received any money from James Wilson in payment for land in the Dismal Swamp and two quarter-shares in the Dismal Swamp Company. He began to think about foreclosing Wilson's mortgage, reclaiming the shares and the land.

To friends and relatives in Virginia, Meade praised Kentucky. Of the estate of Governor Isaac Shelby, he wrote: "the fabled Golden age seems to be here revived." He often mentioned the soil's fertility, predicting that his would yield at least twelve barrels of corn per acre. He told everyone that his change of homes had proven wise: "I regret nothing I have left behind me but a few valuable friends . . . as to everything else—I would scarce change my present situation for wealth in Virginia."

After the state capital moved to Richmond, Williamsburg offered fewer rewards to a storekeeper. Joseph Hornsby led the life of a country gentleman, dividing his time between his house in town and his 3,000-acre plantation, Yarmouth, in James City County. He had ten slaves in town and twenty-seven on his plantation. He kept a carriage in Williamsburg and thoroughbreds at Yarmouth.

Hornsby gave up his positions as a manager of the Dismal Swamp Company and treasurer of the Court of Directors of the Lunatic Hospital in 1794. He was preparing to move to Kentucky. He disposed of his blooded horses. During his last year in Virginia, 1796, only four slaves remained at Yarmouth. By agreement in Williamsburg District Court, he and Mary Willing Byrd settled William Byrd's old debt to Hornsby's uncle.

In November 1796, Hornsby was ready to say good-bye to his brother, William, and head westward. His slave James, a large man in his late twenties with "some scars about his neck," took this opportunity to leave Hornsby's service. James was still at large eighteen months later. Hornsby, with two daughters and three sons, apparently spent the winter in Albemarle County with his married daughter and the Walker brothers. In March his daughter Sarah died at the age of sixteen.

In the spring Joseph Hornsby and his family crossed the mountains to his property near Floyds Fork, 47 miles northwest of Lexington and 17 miles from the Ohio River. He irritated David Meade by not making a 20-mile detour to visit Chaumière des Prairies. Hornsby made a return trip to Virginia almost at once, and stopped at Meade's home on his way eastward in the last week of July. Meade prided himself on his hospitable entertainment of unexpected guests. That spring he had added two more bedrooms to his house.

Hornsby spent the late summer and early fall of 1797 in Williamsburg, visiting his brother, whose health was uneven. He bought slaves. He collected peach stones and vegetable seeds to reproduce his Williamsburg garden in Kentucky. And he sold his two quarter-shares in the Dismal Swamp Company to the Reverend John Bracken, rector of Bruton Parish in Williamsburg, who already held two shares in the Dismal Swamp Canal Company. In October, Joseph Hornsby headed westward again. The following month David Meade wrote to a friend: "Mr. Hornsby, we hear is returned to His new settlement in Shelby County—bringing with him it is said a hundred Negroes."

A visitor to Hornsby's plantation saw fields of clover, flocks of sheep, a herd of cattle, and a large hogpen. In addition to corn, wheat, and ordinary garden vegetables, Hornsby and his slaves cultivated asparagus, artichokes, and cantaloupes. Hornsby also grew hemp. Suffering from rheumatism in his late fifties, he could not do much work. He kept his house well stocked with whiskey. From cut flint glass bottles bearing his name, he could pour for a guest into a silver rummer or use a silver ladle to draw punch from a large china bowl. When absent from the plantation, he was usually in Louisville to take communion or in Shelbyville to vote Republican.

James Marshall's stay in London on behalf of the North American Land Company did not go smoothly. He found few buyers; he had no prospects. An American in London explained that British capital for investment was "compleatly employed in commercial & other speculations, connected with Government securities &c." Though Robert Morris blamed his difficulties on these wartime opportunities for profit, all efforts to sell American property met suspicion. A Pennsylvanian decrying land speculation described it as "that horrid disorder which some call the terra-phobia." He meant speculators' ravings about their future profits. But British moneyed men had true terraphobia—fear of buying American land. The result in Philadelphia was "that every land jobber here is out of money."

Robert Morris pressed on. At his behest, in January 1796 the board of directors declared a dividend on North American Land Company stock for the year 1795: $6 per share. Fewer than five hundred shares had been sold that year. Only two people outside the United States bought any. Morris urged James Marshall to keep trying: "The North American Land Compy Shares are now worth double or treble what they were when you left this place. . . . The Shares in the North American Land Compy are by far the best Object for an European to vest money in."

Troubles multiplied. John Nicholson's creditors won judgments against him in Pennsylvania courts. In 1795 the two partners had fallen behind in payments to the commissioners of the District of Columbia. Their repeated promises went unfulfilled. Their failure to pay threatened to force a halt in construction of the Capitol and the president's house. At the end of the year, Morris gave up hope of obtaining Dutch loans, on which his large venture into Federal City lots had been based.

George Washington, beginning the last full year of his presidency early

Gouverneur Morris and Robert Morris, Charles Willson Peale. Courtesy of the Pennsylvania Academy of the Fine Arts

in 1796, again offered his western land for sale. He needed money; he insisted on prompt payment and on receiving what he called "the real value of the Land." These conditions made finding a buyer difficult. He refrained from advertising in Europe, where, he said, "land jobbing is in much disgrace."

Washington had lived away from Mount Vernon for almost sixteen years during the war and his presidency. His home had fallen into disrepair. Except in its setting above the Potomac, it was not a grand mansion—an outer wall of wood chamfered, painted, and sanded to give the appearance of stone, an inner passageway wall of pine painted to look like mahogany. The rooms were plainly furnished. A visitor might awkwardly discover that "the furniture is dropping to pieces." Washington put joiners, masons, and painters to work as soon as he returned from Philadelphia. He looked forward to spending his retirement amusing himself with "Agricultural and rural pursuits" and repairing a house "going fast to ruin." To this end he sought to turn his land into money.

Washington's sale of his four quarter-shares in the Dismal Swamp Company to Henry Lee did not yield prompt payment. By December 1, 1796, Lee was supposed to pay $6,666, one-third of the total price, with interest on the sum yet to be paid. Lee's hope to use Justice James Wilson's bonds or to draw notes on Wilson failed when Washington refused to accept them, knowing that he "could not depend upon converting them into cash." Then the bills of exchange drawn on William Temple Franklin by Robert Morris to repay Lee's loan of $40,000 came back from London, protested. Lee resubmitted them; they were returned protested again. Franklin had completed his work for Morris; he had other worries, such as a report that the Directory in Paris ordered his arrest if he returned to France. Two months after Lee's first payment to Washington fell due, he came up with only $700 in cash.

Morris could not repay Lee. Morris and Nicholson missed a payment to the commissioners of the District of Columbia in April 1796. Nor did they construct more new houses in the Federal City, as their contract stipulated. They blamed their difficulties on James Greenleaf, failed wizard of the lost Dutch loans. If Greenleaf was at fault for their problems in the Federal City, he must also be responsible for the North American Land Company's troubles. He was supposed to have the power to tap European capital; and the North American Land Company, despite its pretense of development and settlement, had no other purpose. Morris and Nicholson bought Greenleaf's 10,000 shares. They gave him in May a generous settlement of $1,150,000 in the usual form, Morris promising to redeem Nicholson's notes and Nicholson promising to redeem Morris's. Greenleaf's security, if his former partners did not pay, was a right to sell his shares of the North American Land Company on the open market.

Desperate for cash, Morris ordered Charles Willing Byrd to sell land in Kentucky that Morris had bought for himself, not his company. Byrd thus had instructions to persuade other people to put money into the company's land while he turned Morris's into money. In response to Henry Lee's complaints about protested bills of exchange drawn on William Temple Franklin, Morris drew a new bill on James Marshall in London, suggesting to Marshall that he meet this bill by compounding with London bankers, using shares in the North American Land Company to get credit. As Morris drew his bill for Lee and sent instructions to Marshall in September 1796, Morris's and Nicholson's notes changed hands in Philadelphia at a valuation of 17¢ on the dollar. After a year in London, James Marshall had sold forty shares in the North American Land Company. The venture had failed. Morris held a reserve of what he called "Blanks." The time to use them had come. He wrote to Nicholson: "we must depend on ourselves, put the world at defiance and set ourselves on the Front Seats of the Worlds amphitheatre."

During the last months of 1796 the collapse of the American land market became clear in Philadelphia. A Richmond merchant wrote: "I am informd that every confidence between man and man is at an end." At the suits of creditors, the sheriff put broken speculators into debtors' prison until they were declared legally insolvent. Dr. Benjamin Rush heard that 150 people had failed within six weeks, and 67 went to jail. Dr. Thomas Ruston, still holding 800 acres near the Dismal Swamp, had sold 136,000 acres of Pennsylvania land to Morris and Nicholson two years earlier, but he could not collect. He had debts, rumor said, of $200,000. He entered prison in September. Justice James Wilson, aware of his own impending fate, looked "deeply distressed," and to distract his mind read novels constantly. The sheriff came for him on Thursday, December 8. A Virginian summoned to Richmond for service on a federal Circuit Court grand jury wrote in his diary: "no Court for want of a Judge who was Speculating." Morris heard that people expected him to go next. His and Nicholson's notes, reported to total $10,000,000, were traded for 12¢ on the dollar.

Morris tried to keep up the credit of the North American Land Company by announcing a dividend early in January 1797, but he had no money. He called for Nicholson to pay it, a vain hope. Nicholson's creditors also pursued Morris, who had endorsed his partner's notes. Morris wrote: "I consider you as the sole Author of all the perplexities about Laws Titles & you must extricate them." He admitted on February 1 that the company could not survive: "The money for dividends is run out & I have no more, so that I suppose its credit will be dissolved." Three weeks later a broker told Nicholson that he could dispose of Morris's and Nicholson's notes at 10¢ on the dollar.

Morris and Nicholson still owed Henry Lee $21,500 for property in and around the illusory city of Matildaville. Unable to pay, they tried in March to sell their holdings to James Greenleaf, who declined to buy. Morris then offered to sell the land back to Lee. Lee needed to raise money to pay George Washington; he wished to sell, not buy. The partners forfeited their interest and wrote off their investment as a loss. By April 13, Greenleaf was in the custody of the sheriff at the debtors' prison. He wrote to a consortium of creditors: "take my Books, my papers, my Property & do with them what you please. . . . *I am distroyed solely by having suffered myself to be led on by too ardent a desire of saving others from destruction.*"

To placate George Washington, Henry Lee gave him in the early months of 1797 a document from the firm Reed & Forde obliging them to transfer to Washington seventy shares of stock in the Bank of Columbia. Washington reluctantly accepted, only to find that the shares, nominally worth $40 each, were selling on the open market for $33. Lee's remittance not only fell short by $500 but came late. Reed & Forde lacked the cash needed to buy bank stock for Washington, partly because Robert Morris had not repaid $5,000 he had borrowed. Morris wrote to them: "My mind is continually on the rack and I am daily employed in Search of ways and means."

Of course, the bill of exchange Morris drew on James Marshall to repay Lee's large loan came back protested. Morris said in July that he hoped to be able to pay soon. Two months later he admitted that he could not send Lee anything. Lee kept writing for four years, to no avail.

In Williamsburg, at Christmastime, 1796, and in the first weeks of the new year, St. George Tucker wrote a play about Robert Morris. He called it *The Wheel of Fortune: A Comedy.* The character resembling Morris is "Buckeye, a Land Jobber." He cheats foreign investors and sells vast tracts of land, as well as lots in the Federal City. Tucker's hero, Freeman, explains the play's title: "Some favorite plan of Speculation presents itself—money is wanted and must be had, at any price. One purchase is made upon a Credit of sixty days, to enable the purchaser to pay another sum of money in thirty; the Wheel is kept continually turning till it either ruins, or makes, the party engaged in the Operation." Of course, the traditional wheel of fortune would bring low those who once rode high. One character, a defrauded land buyer, reveals Buckeye's methods: he sold 20,000 acres, "which he described as an earthly paradise, uniting every advantage soil, climate, Waters, Rivers, and intercourse with a populous Country. Here is a map in which it is described.

Would not one suppose it was the Garden of Eden! This is the description of that miserable spot." Amid the drama's conventional schemes, plot complications, and recognition scenes, Tucker's denunciation of speculators is the recurrent leitmotif. In the banal and predictable ending, lovers are united and speculators are ruined.

In hopes of getting his play produced in Philadelphia during the spring of 1797, Tucker submitted it to Thomas Wignell, manager of the Chestnut Street Theatre, the best house with the best actors in the United States. The ornate building, modeled on Covent Garden Theatre and the Theatre Royal in Bath, with 1,165 seats, had been constructed with financial aid from Robert Morris. Wignell's season lasted until May 6. He was running a deficit. He declined to produce *The Wheel of Fortune*, saying that Morris and Greenleaf were "suffering so severely for their Speculations" that they ought not to be "exhibited to Ridicule on the Stage" in Tucker's characters Buckeye and O'Blunder. He added that the play was too long and needed revision.

Wignell was actually letting Tucker down gently, sparing him the truth. The play was old-fashioned, differing little from Samuel Foote's *The Bankrupt* of twenty-five years past or from satirical plays about the South Sea Bubble seventy years past. The modern public preferred a different kind of drama, not moralizing about political economy and civic virtue. At Drury Lane Theatre in 1797, Matthew Lewis began a successful run of his new play *The Castle Spectre: A Dramatic Romance*. Robert Merry, husband of Thomas Wignell's lead actress, Ann Brunton Merry, had written *The Abbey of St. Augustine* for the 1797 season. He again tried to capture the new fashion in a play he submitted to Wignell a few months after Tucker's. It was *The Tuscan Tournament: A Tragedy in Five Acts*. The last act was almost all pantomime. The public enjoyed excitement and sentiment and mystery. In *The Tuscan Tournament*, the curtain rises to reveal "Scene—The Appenines—A Ruin'd Castle—A Storm—Thunder & Lightning. Enter Ximenes disguised as a Friar." Wignell moved to New York for the summer and fall to repair his company's fortunes. In the Greenwich Street Theatre he presented *Isabella; or, the Fatal Marriage*, with the title role played by Elizabeth Whitlock, Sarah Siddons's sister.

Robert Morris no longer left his house in the autumn of 1797. He avoided the sheriff by remaining indoors, except when he took the air by going out on his roof. But he was only buying time. He said: "property will not command money and the world have shut me out of their confidence."

After his release from prison in Philadelphia, Justice James Wilson spent some time in jail in Burlington, New Jersey, in September until he raised $300 to pay a judgment. He took refuge in Edenton, North Carolina. There he was jailed in April 1798 at the suit of the holder of a note he had endorsed. Once released, he stayed in Edenton, refusing to declare himself insolvent and give up all his property so that he could return to Philadelphia. From Kentucky, David Meade sent word that unless Wilson soon paid the arrears of his purchase of two quarter-shares in the Dismal Swamp Company and of nearby land, Meade would foreclose his mortgage and resume possession. Meade had no sympathy with Pennsylvania speculators. His son-in-law, Charles Willing Byrd, had gone unpaid by Robert Morris throughout 1797. Wilson did not care what Meade did. Dressed in shabby clothes, he sat listlessly in his tavern room, looking out the window at the waves of Albemarle Sound, facing away from the Dismal Swamp.

George Washington had grown exasperated with Henry Lee. None of Lee's extemporized devices yielded cash. Lee gave Washington what he called "a negotiable note" for $1,000, drawn on Jesse Simms, in the summer of 1797. Washington sent it to his banker, who told him in January 1798 that Simms refused to pay. Washington wrote to Lee: "Let me entreat you to believe, that at the time I entered into the contract with you for the property I held in the Dismal Swamp, I had no conception of such disappointments, and that it is a mode of dealing to which I am not accustomed." Washington grew angrier upon hearing that Simms spread rumors that Washington was speculating in Simms's notes. Every step Lee took seemed to make matters worse.

Leaving Washington unpaid, Lee acquired Champe and Maria Carter's portion and Richard and Rebecca Parke Corbin's portion of the Saura Town property in the Land of Eden. Champe and Maria Carter had sold their one-eighth interest for $2 per acre; Lee paid more than twice as much. He offered this one-fourth of the Land of Eden to Patrick Henry. Henry still held the note James Wilson had drawn on Lee as Lee lent Wilson $8,000 to buy Henry's worthless Green Sea tract. Lee had no cash with which to pay Henry and redeem the note. James Wilson, sitting in Edenton, could not repay Lee. So Lee urged Patrick Henry to take, instead of cash, one-fourth of the Land of Eden, assuring him that it was worth $4 to $6 per acre.

Robert Morris knew on Thursday, February 8, 1798, that he must enter debtors' prison the following week. He wrote: "The Punishment of my imprudence in the use of my Name and loss of credit is perhaps what *I* deserve, but it is nevertheless severe on my Family and on *their* account I feel it most tormentingly." In the past two years he had watched his wife, Mary White Morris, change from "a remarkable well looking woman . . . blooming as a rose in June" to her present state, "pale, wan, dejected & spiritless." He entered the Prune Street prison on Friday, February 16. He lived in a furnished room, an "ugly whitewashed vault," in which he received visitors, and he dressed as usual in neat, old-fashioned suits. Every morning from six until eight he walked in the garden, counting his turns by dropping a pebble at the end of each lap. He knew that he must surrender all his property to gain release. He wrote: "I confess I do not like the idea of dieing here." The North American Land Company had no offices. If it had managers, no one knew who they were. In the subsequent liquidation of Morris's assets, the company's shares sold for 7¢ each.

James Wilson went into his final decline in July and August. He contracted malaria. In the Edenton tavern overlooking Albemarle Sound he lay in bed, talking about returning to his circuit duties as a justice of the Supreme Court. After suffering a stroke in August he spoke deliriously of debts, bankruptcies, and jails. On Tuesday, August 21, he died.

"I shall be able to close my contract," Henry Lee promised Washington that week; "this is an object I have much at heart, & which if Judge Wilson had not treated me very illy would have long ago been compleated." Lee's latest idea for remittances was to ship corn up the Potomac from Stratford to Mount Vernon and to offer Washington houses and lots in the Federal City. Lee added: "the time is fast approaching when property like mine must be in great demand."

"You know perfectly well what my inducements were to part with the property you purchased of me," Washington wrote. But Lee refused to understand that he was supposed to furnish cash or property of unquestioned title convertible to cash. Washington already had a supplier of corn. He held no illusions about the value of lots in the Federal City: "it is a question of very equivocal solution." He grew tired of Lee's improvisations, assurances, and excuses. He entrusted the matter to his nephew, Bushrod Washington, who would give a deed to the Dismal Swamp Company quarter-shares or not give it, as he thought best after dealing with Lee.

The death of James Wilson left Patrick Henry holding Wilson's note for purchase of the Green Sea land, payable by Lee. Lee had little prospect of recovering from Wilson's estate the $8,000 Wilson had borrowed. Patrick Henry had little hope of getting money from Lee. Even so, Henry did not wish the Green Sea tract returned to him by default. The two men agreed to an exchange. Patrick Henry deeded his acres of reeds in the Green Sea to Lee, and Henry Lee deeded about 6,300 acres of the Land of Eden to Henry.

Two and a half years after Henry Lee's first payment to George Washington ought to have been made and six months before his last payment was due, he had made no more headway in finding $20,000 for four quarter-shares in the Dismal Swamp Company. He wrote: "all my endeavors are vain.

I shall never recede from my exertions till I do accomplish the end, for no event of my life has given me more anguish." He found that conversations with Washington intensified his feelings of regret. He offered to return the quarter-shares and forfeit payments he had made. "The loss of money I am used to," he said; "the loss of mental quietude I cannot bear & pained as I am, I wish to regain tranquility." Lee resolved not to see Washington again until he could pay everything. He said he was sure he could do so in the next few months.

Aiskew Birkett, William Anderson's partner, did some work for his former employer, Samuel Gist, in 1795. To help John Wickham pursue Gist's suits in United States Circuit Court in Richmond, Birkett gave depositions and affidavits in London. As Gist's former clerk, he swore under oath to the validity of accounts showing the debts Wickham sued to collect. Gist meant to miss no opportunity. As sons of the late Governor Thomas Nelson, Jr., strove to settle his indebted estate, Gist filed a claim. Nelson owed money to William Anderson & Company, but that did not mean he owed Gist. Robert Andrews, agent for Nelson's creditors, wrote in his list of claimants: "Gist no Evid of any sort furnished." By the summer of 1795, William Anderson & Company had disbanded for the second and last time. Aiskew Birkett sent his ship *Ceres* to the James River in search of a cargo of tobacco. He now belonged to the firm Birkett, Shore & Reeves.

Early that year in Richmond, Nathaniel Anderson complained that his brother William's letters from London were "Crusty & harsh." William Anderson's health was failing. He had reason to feel bitter. Events had not gone his way. At the age of fifty-four, he was sick, while his father-in-law remained vigorous and sharp at seventy. Anderson had lived comfortably in London with his wife and niece and nephew, but he had never obtained an independent fortune from Samuel Gist. Nor had he succeeded as a merchant.

Anderson's condition worsened during the summer. He and his wife and her sister went to Chesterfield in the hills of northern Derbyshire. There he lay "in a low state of Health" until New Year's Day, 1796, when he died. With him died the last threat to Samuel Gist's control of the property he had left behind in Virginia thirty years earlier—plantations, slaves, and three quarter-shares in the Dismal Swamp Company. Edward Jacquelin Smith, son of Gist's late stepson, Joseph Smith, had died in 1794. Except for nagging from Thomas R. Rootes, son by an earlier marriage of Joseph Smith's widow, Gist faced no challenger.

Three weeks after Anderson's death, Gist proved his son-in-law's will in the Prerogative Court of Canterbury. He made himself "the chief, if not sole acting" executor of the estate. Its main assets were outstanding debts Virginians owed to the Old and New Concerns known as William Anderson & Company. The executors commissioned a partner in the defunct company, Henry S. Shore, and George Syme in Virginia to collect from debtors and remit to Gist. Within six years they sent almost £1,500 sterling. On Gist's behalf, John Wickham won more suits in federal court. John Lyons, Gist's attorney in Hanover County, went to court to seize forty-nine slaves, collateral for an unpaid bond. They were to be sold to satisfy Gist's demand for more than $3,000.

Despite a financial crisis in 1797, Gist's investments in government funds and in stocks yielded a large income in his retirement. If he read Adam Smith, he could chuckle over one sentence: "though many people have made a little money by insurance, very few have made a great fortune." Gist had bought some land in England after the American War. He now stepped up his purchases. Other moneyed men in the City transformed themselves into landed gentry; he could do so as well. His favorite holdings lay in northern Gloucestershire, in the upper division of Tewkesbury Hundred and the lower division of Kiftsgate Hundred, midway between Gloucester and Stratford-upon-Avon. Gist bought the crumbling manor house at Wormington and with it the lordship of the manor and the patronage of the parish church. The parish held about ninety people. The occupants of one farm and of six cottages in the village became his tenants. A little more than a mile from the church Gist began a new house, Wormington Grange, a two-story masonry building with bay windows. In the small fourteenth-century church, against the chancel's north wall, near a later Tudor arch, Gist added a plain monument:

Sacred to the Memory of

WILLIAM ANDERSON, ESQR.

WHO DEPARTED THIS LIFE,
THE 1ST DAY OF JANUARY 1796,
AGED 54 YEARS.

Later, Gist bought the lordship of the manor of Dixton, a few miles southwest of Wormington. His purchases in Gloucestershire amounted to 2,180 acres.

Aiskew Birkett died in September 1798. His sister, Elizabeth Birkett, was his executrix and heir. His estate had a right to one-fourth of the money owed to William Anderson & Company, collected under the direction of Samuel Gist. Remittances kept coming from Virginia, eventually nearing a total of £4,000. Gist once paid Elizabeth Birkett £150. Three other times he gave her small sums totaling £50. Through a broker, formerly Aiskew Birkett's clerk, she repeatedly pressed Gist to make further payments. He refused, saying that she had not yet settled with her late brother's creditors. Gist would "retain the Money in his Hands until some Arrangements had been made."

In the same year that Aiskew Birkett died, William Anderson's brothers and sisters brought suit against Gist in the High Court of Chancery in Richmond. They accused him of violating Anderson's will by neither paying the estate for the plantations Anderson had bought at Gist's instructions nor returning these plantations to the estate. Instead, he still cultivated them for his own profit. John Wickham filed Gist's answer with the court in 1799. He said that one of the plantations belonged to Mary Anderson, not William Anderson, and that the estate of William Anderson owed money to Gist.

The treaty between Britain and the United States ratified in 1795 provided for establishment of a joint commission on debts owed by Americans to Britons. The commission met only once and resolved nothing. But in 1798 and 1799 it compiled a register of claims. These included a memorial and claim from Samuel Gist, with a list of 545 debts for which he sought recompense.

A young Virginian, Littleton Dennis Teackle, traveled in England in 1799. His father, John Teackle, had done business with William Anderson & Company. The son carried letters of introduction, one from George Syme to Gist. Gist invited Teackle to dine at Number 37, Gower Street on Sunday, May 26. There he met Mary Anderson and young Maria Anderson with two other women. Teackle enjoyed their sprightly conversation around the silver-laden dinner table. He had heard that his host's yearly income was £10,000. Gist, he noted, liked to let people see that he was rich. Teackle had been told that he was "parsimonious," but the old man did not stint himself. Soon after dinner the ladies withdrew, and Teackle and Gist chatted for several hours. That night Teackle wrote in his diary: "upon the whole I form'd no very favorable oppinion of him. I thought I perceiv'd more of *design* in his countenance, than any person I had been in company with in England."

In subsequent months Gist bought from the Duchess of Dorset the manor of Hardwick in Oxfordshire, as well as several farms in Neithrop Parish. He acquired more than 1,000 acres in the county. As leases on these fields of wheat, barley, turnips, and beans expired, he raised rents.

. . .

Managers of the Dismal Swamp Company summoned their partners to gather in Suffolk for a "full meeting" on October 15, 1796. A meeting took place on Friday, November 18, but only the managers attended: William Nelson, Jr., Alexander Macaulay, and John Jameson. They approved the company's contract with Thomas Shepherd and purchase of sawmills as an aid to the company's drive to profit from timber. They authorized Macaulay to hire an overseer for Dismal Plantation and to buy six young male slaves. They resolved to invest $10,000 in United States government bonds bearing 6 percent interest. And they declared that no single partner—meaning, Alexander Macaulay—would be allowed to draw money from the company's assets. Macaulay signed the minutes. Three weeks later, he made his largest withdrawal, more than $8,000.

John Driver died in the last week of April 1797. To succeed him as the company's resident agent in Suffolk, the managers chose his son-in-law, Thomas Swepson, a resident of Nansemond County and surveyor of customs for the Port of Suffolk. Thomas Shepherd still supervised hired slaves felling trees and cutting shingles.

The company needed to exclude trespassers who were stealing trees. It must repair its mills and cut canals to float logs to them. In Richmond, Alexander Macaulay met a newly arrived young English architect and engineer, Benjamin Henry Latrobe, who knew about "the old dismal Swamp Company," as he called it. On a visit to Mount Vernon in the past summer, Latrobe had heard George Washington give "a detailed account" of it, saying that he "gave up all further hopes of any thing effectual being done for their interests, and sold out his shares in the Proprietary at a price very inadequate to their real value." In the first week of June 1797, Latrobe accepted Macaulay's invitation to work for the company. On Tuesday, June 6, the large Macaulay and the slender, curly-haired Latrobe entered a stagecoach and headed down the James River, toward the Dismal Swamp. Their traveling companions were two Frenchmen who spoke no English, an actress, Margaretta West, and a Virginian who started drinking mint juleps at six-thirty in the morning.

Macaulay commissioned Latrobe to resurvey the company's tract and to cut a lane around the edge of its 40,000 acres, clearly marking a boundary. He was also to select the courses of canals leading to the sawmills. At dawn on Friday, June 9, Macaulay, Latrobe, and Thomas Swepson left Suffolk. After breakfast at Dismal Plantation, they went into the swamp, accompanied by two black men. The group walked along the narrow canal or ditch leading to Lake Drummond until the water in it became deep enough for canoes. "Millions of Muskitoes surrounded us," Latrobe said. Trees, both "immensely large" and "younger and smaller" enveloped them—gums, maples, elms, bald cypress, and white cedar—and, as they advanced, stands of bamboo grew taller and thicker. Latrobe was impressed by Lake Drummond, its silent immobility ringed by "the most gigantic trees in the world." He said of the lake: "It absorbs or expells every other idea, and creates a quiet solemn pleasure, that I never felt from any similar circumstance." On their way back to Dismal Plantation, the five men were drenched by a thunderstorm.

Over the weekend and in the following week Latrobe and Macaulay visited the mills. Latrobe met Thomas Shepherd and identified repairs the mills needed. He stayed in Suffolk for two weeks, then went to Norfolk to order tools and supplies. Joining him, Macaulay brought a letter from Governor James Wood. Latrobe had submitted designs for a new state penitentiary. Governor Wood wrote that these had been accepted; Latrobe must return to Richmond at once. Macaulay released him from his engagement with the Dismal Swamp Company. Latrobe later returned $200 he had received from the company, and he refunded the cost of his expenses in Norfolk and in traveling to Richmond, another $100. As the summer's work on the penitentiary advanced, he encountered criticism from the superintendent of construction and received little cash from the state. He lived in a "Doghole," paying high rent. Looking back on his lost opportunity to work for the Dismal Swamp Company, he said: "I had a choice of difficulties, & I fear I chose wrongly."

Two months after Latrobe left the swamp for Norfolk, Thomas Shepherd sent Alexander Macaulay an estimate of the cost of rebuilding his sawmill. Macaulay had other things on his mind. He owed a great deal of money, almost $13,400 of it to the Dismal Swamp Company, and his creditors' suits moved through the courts. Knowing that his assets would not suffice, he tried to protect some of his creditors by executing a deed of trust on November 15, 1797. Those named in the deed were to have first rights to the proceeds of his land, his shares in the Dismal Swamp Canal Company, his two quarter-shares in the Dismal Swamp Company, his livestock, vessels, household goods, and slaves, all held by trustees. Among the preferred creditors were his brother-in-law, Francis Jerdone, and John Jameson, who understood, without anything in writing, that £5,000 Virginia currency owed to him included Macaulay's debt to the Dismal Swamp Company.

Benjamin Henry Latrobe, passing the winter of early 1798 in his ugly, expensive rooms, worrying about money, tried to cheer himself by writing a play, a comedy. He had drawn designs for a new theater which the impresario Thomas West hoped to build in Richmond. In the old theater, West's company performed Latrobe's comedy on January 20, 1798, as a benefit for one of West's actresses, Mrs. J. J. Green. *An Apology* was a satire on Alexander Hamilton and his newspaper ally "Peter Porcupine"—that is, William Cobbett, represented by the character Skunk. Latrobe's title alluded to Hamilton's recent admission that he had had sexual relations with Maria Reynolds, a married woman whose husband tried to blackmail him while he served as secretary of the treasury. Apologizing for adultery, Hamilton denied that he was guilty of malfeasance or speculation. Latrobe intended his comedy for the friends of "liberty and morality." His audience showed charity, but the performance was a fiasco. The actors had not learned their lines, and the evening's biggest laugh came when five actors stood on stage, none knowing what to say next, whereupon all walked off. Latrobe said: "You may guess at my feelings." Three days later, after a bad performance of Shakespeare's *Richard III*, the theater burned down.

Thomas Shepherd felt the lack of Latrobe's services in protecting the Dismal Swamp Company's boundary. Some residents of Nansemond and Norfolk counties grew bolder in stealing timber from the company's tract in 1798. Among them were men who had claimed land in the swamp, then lost it to the company in the new survey for the grant of 1784. They said the title was not good, offering as proof the company's failure to stop them from taking trees. They "bid defiance" to the Dismal Swamp Company and to Shepherd, passing "boldly over the line, a running main bridges to & fro as they think proper" and "cutting and a Slaying the Timber in a most horrid manner." Shepherd knew who they were: William and John Bartee, the Butt brothers, Willis Wilkins, and others. He reported to the company's managers: "I prepared to drive them off, but my friends advised me to desist, otherwise I would certainly be killd, as they so frequently threaten my life." There was money in shingles and lumber. Although wartime seizures of vessels on the high seas interrupted trade with the West Indies, construction of new buildings in Boston, New York, Philadelphia, Baltimore, and the Federal City kept up demand. Shingles sold for $10 per thousand. Shepherd wrote: "Every persons, Owners of the lower Swamps is Opposed to the Dismal Swamp Company I believe they hate me upon the Earth."

Writing to an English friend in May 1798, Alexander Macaulay said that he long had been ill. He could neither defend himself against his creditors' lawsuits nor pay judgments issued against him. In the summer a writ of execution hung over his property, threatening him with a general auction. His trustees hoped to save his plantation and slaves. Before the sheriff came to carry out the court's order, Macaulay died.

After the estate auction, Elizabeth Jerdone Macaulay felt bitter. She had not received protection and consideration of the kind extended to Joanna Tucker under similar circumstances thirty years earlier. She wished to keep the plantation, livestock, furniture, and tools, as well as slaves "for the crop that is now growing." To raise money to "get this burthen of Debt Settled," she hoped to sell some of her late husband's land, including his two quarter-shares in the Dismal Swamp Company and his lots in Hanover-Town, the late Mann Page's city that refused to grow. But that property did not attract bidders, while property she expected to save with a token bid attracted competitors. "Negroe buyers" with rolls of cash "bid on every Negroe." She bought nineteen and lost four. Neighbors in Gloucester and York counties, "who had profest the greatest friendship for poor Mr. Macaulay," bid against her for furniture, livestock, and slaves, "expecting I should be discouraged & give over." At a cost of almost £1,300 she kept the plantation intact. The only concession to her was a low price for the house and lots in York Town, "which was sold rather in a private manner."

Just before Christmas, William Nelson, Jr., John Jameson, and John Brown held another meeting of the Dismal Swamp Company. They resolved to put its accounts in order and to sort out Macaulay's land transactions. They believed that the company ought to buy Macaulay's two quarter-shares if Thomas Swepson said that "the funds in hand will justify it." Elizabeth Jerdone Macaulay thought she had made a sale. Eight months later, however, she had received no money. Through a friend, she asked to be paid. The company's managers were still considering the purchase ten years later.

Swepson advised the managers to combine Jericho Mills west of the company's tract with a purchase of 600 acres adjoining the tract's western boundary—Lemuel Riddick's Paradise Plantation, for sale at a price of $3,000. They could take oak and "excellent pine" from Paradise Plantation, then cut a canal through it, connecting Jericho Mills to thick stands of white cedar in the swamp's interior, drawing water from Lake Drummond to float logs to the mill. Swepson tempted them with images of tree trunks 6 feet in diameter rising as much as 70 feet above the ground before putting out their lowest branches. The managers followed his advice in 1799.

On the eastern edge of the company's land, trespassers worked faster. Thomas Shepherd guessed that each month they were cutting 100,000 shingles, which they sold to George Capron, contractor for the Dismal Swamp Canal Company, the same man diverting water away from Shepherd's mill pond. As a further insult, Capron built "a very Elegant Saw Mill" along Deep Creek at the canal's northern end. Trespassers also were "selling the Timber to people by the thousand which makes prodigious destruction." The company's hired slaves, working the western reaches of the swamp, cut shingles, but in the spring much was lost in a fire set by "incendiaries." Nevertheless, Thomas Swepson invested in the company's future. After Chancellor Wythe decided in David Meade's favor in his suit against the estate of Justice James Wilson, Meade's two quarter-shares were each sold for £1,000 Virginia currency, one to Swepson and one to Richard Willing Byrd, brother of Charles Willing Byrd. They paid the same price George Washington had charged Henry Lee.

In the last year of his presidency, a letter from Liverpool reached George Washington. It came from Edward Rushton, a poet and tavern-keeper. Rushton had served as mate in a slave ship years earlier, an experience that turned him against slavery and cost him his sight in an outbreak of ophthalmia. He had opposed Britain's war against American independence. In his letter, which was written for publication, he praised Washington both for his services in the Revolution and for his voluntary retirement from power; but he then went on to reproach the president for continuing to own slaves. Having "conquered under the banners of freedom" and having served as "the first magistrate of a free people," he ought to serve liberty. "Your friend Jefferson" Rushton wrote, "has endeavoured to show that the negroes are an inferior order of being, but surely you will not have recourse to such a subterfuge. Your slaves, it may be urged, are well treated—That I deny—man never can be well treated who is deprived of his rights."

Rushton could hardly have contrived a series of remarks better suited to irritate Washington. People said that he disliked slavery and wished it to end. "If your feelings be actually repugnant to slavery," Rushton argued, "then are you more culpable than the callous-hearted planter, who laughs at what he calls the pityful whining of the abolitionists, because he believes slavery to be justifiable; while you persevere in a system which your conscience tells you to be wrong." Having thus impeached Washington's integrity, Rushton then attributed this lapse to a base motive. "Now, Sir, are you sure that the unwillingness which you have shewn to liberate your negroes, does not proceed from some lurking pecuniary considerations? If this be the case, and there are those who firmly believe it is, then there is no flesh left in your heart; and present reputation, future fame, and all that is estimable among the virtuous, are, for a few thousand pieces of paltry yellow dirt, irremediably renounced."

Publishing his letter in Liverpool just before Washington left the presidency, Rushton added a note, telling his readers that "a few weeks ago it was returned under cover, without a syllable in reply."

George and Martha Washington owned 316 slaves in 1799, dispersed among five Mount Vernon farms. This was twice as many as the farms needed, he said. "To sell the overplus I cannot, because I am principled against this kind of traffic in the human species. To hire them out, is almost as bad, because they could not be disposed of in families to any advantage, and to disperse the families I have an aversion. What then is to be done? Something must or I shall be ruined." In the four years since he had advertised his lands for sale, Washington had received from purchasers a total of $50,000. That sum, he said, "has scarcely been able to keep me afloat." He must consider establishing more plantations on his land elsewhere to make his slaves productive. He said of his retirement: "A mind that has been constantly on the stretch since the year 1753, with but short intervals, and little relaxation, requires rest, and composure." At Mount Vernon these still eluded him.

Washington wrote a new will in July 1799. It opened with the customary injunction to pay his debts, "of which there are but few, and none of magnitude." Then came the major bequest to his wife of a life interest in all his estate. After these, his first concern was the future of his slaves. The terms of the dower right by which Martha Washington inherited her first husband's slaves and their descendants prevented George Washington from freeing them lawfully. He said that he "earnestly wished" to free all slaves he owned. He thought that doing so would "excite the most painful sensations, if not disagreeable consequences" among the people inherited by his wife, owing to "intermixture by Marriages" among the two groups. His will directed that his slaves, 124 of the 316, be freed upon Martha Washington's death, with provision for support of the old and infirm and with tenancy or apprenticeship for the others. He added: "I do hereby expressly forbid the Sale, or transportation out of the said Commonwealth, of any Slave I may die possessed of, under any pretence whatsoever."

The will ordered the sale of his property other than Mount Vernon, dividing proceeds among members of his and his wife's families. He added to the will a "Schedule of property . . . with discriptive, and explanatory notes." Again and again his notes read "valuable," "extremely valuable," "no richer or more valuable land in all that Region." For tracts sold by the estate within three years of his death, his estimates proved reasonable, even conservative. Not all of his property found buyers, however, and his executors heeded the will's advice "not to be precipitate" in selling at a lower price. Washington defended his longtime confidence in the Dismal Swamp. He said of the land east of Suffolk bought jointly with Fielding Lewis and Dr. Thomas Walker: "comprehends part of the rich Dismal Swamp; is capable of great improvement; and from its situation must become extremely valuable." He set its worth at $8 per acre. Long afterward, Bushrod Washington noted: "5$ is the best offer the Executors have had for this land."

After contracting a severe inflammation of the throat and submitting to unhelpful medical treatment, George Washington died on December 14, 1799. Fourteen years later, Walter Jones, a Virginian appointed United States attorney for the District of Columbia by President Thomas Jefferson, wrote an essay on a "perilous" topic: George Washington. Jones saw flaws in both political parties. Federalist polemical writers were worse than Republicans, he thought, in "gross, brutal, and unsparing . . . calumny & detraction." He wished to rescue Washington from their embrace. In his essay, sent to Thomas Jefferson for comment, Jones tried "taking Genl Washington on my shoulders, to bear him harmless through the federal Coalition." Jefferson praised his endeavor and described Washington's bearing and demeanor, the workings of his mind, his integrity. "He was, indeed, in every sense of the words, a wise, a good, and a great man." If pressed to name the strongest feature in Washington's character, Jefferson would choose, he wrote, "prudence, never acting until every consideration was maturely weighed." And, in promoting development in America, Washington was, Jefferson recalled, "liberal in contributions to whatever promised utility; but frowning and unyielding on all visionary projects."

In the last year of the Revolutionary War, the General Assembly of Virginia made private emancipation of slaves easier. About 15,000 black people eventually were freed under the new law. But emancipation on the scale undertaken by George Washington remained rare. In 1790, Virginia held about 306,000 black people, of whom almost 13,000 were free. Five years later, in connection with his lectures on law and policy at the College of William and Mary, St. George Tucker began to think about general emancipation in Virginia. He said that he would "endeavour to do justice to the rights of human nature, and to banish deep-rooted, nay, almost innate, prejudices." But he acknowledged that this was "a task, perhaps, beyond the power of human nature to accomplish." He suspected that continuation of slavery was "now perhaps unavoidable." Nevertheless, he offered the General Assembly his proposal.

Tucker published it in Philadelphia in the fall of 1796. It opened eloquently: "Whilst America hath been the land of promise to Europeans, and their descendants, it hath been the vale of death to millions of the wretched sons of Africa." His system was complex, and his approach cautious. Slaves would be freed gradually; blacks would still be held to forced labor in their youth; former slaves would not have the same civil rights enjoyed by whites. Slavery would last another one hundred years. Tucker sought to end it, yet avoid the fate of whites in Saint-Domingue. "The calamities which have lately spread like a contagion through the West India Islands afford a solemn warning to us of the dangerous predicament in which we stand." Oppression invited war of blacks against whites, but so did the idea that blacks could be equal to whites. Tucker hoped to end one danger without running into the other.

He sent a copy of his proposal to the House of Delegates and a copy to the Senate. From the Senate he received bland congratulations. In the House he met sharp criticism, though he doubted that anyone had read the document before denouncing it. Some delegates wished to send his pamphlet back to him; the House voted to table it. Tucker said he did not have "the smallest hope of advancing a cause so dear to me as the abolition of slavery. Actual suffering will one day, perhaps, open the oppressors' eyes. Till that happens, they will shut their ears against argument."

The General Assembly heard from some constituents on the subject of emancipation. A petition from 214 citizens of Mecklenburg County said that a right to own slaves was part of the liberty won in the Revolution and secured by the new American government. An attack on that right was an attack on America: "a very subtle & daring Attempt is on Foot to dispossess us of a very important Part of our Property. An Attempt made by the Enemies of our Country, Tools of the British Administration, and supported by certain Men among us of considerable Weight, to effect our Destruction by Subtlety & Craft." The text cited scriptural authority in defense of slavery and argued that emancipation would bring poverty and ruin to whites, famine and death to infants and the aged among blacks. It would lead to "the Horrors of all the Rapes, Robberies, Murders, and Outrages, which a vast Multitude of unprincipled, unpropertied, vindictive, and remorseless Banditti are capable of perpetrating." The petitioners also disapproved of the new law facilitating private emancipation and asked that it be repealed. They said: "many of the Slaves liberated by the said Act, have been guilty of Thefts, & Outrages, Insolence & Violences."

Thomas Swepson's father Richard Swepson signed the petition. Familiar names appeared among the signers—the same men who had irritated Robert Munford twenty years earlier by demanding harsher punishment of Scottish storekeepers—names such as Reuben Vaughan, Philip Poindexter, Sr., Philip Poindexter, Jr., and Joseph Royster. The petition originally held 215 signatures, but the name of John McCann was scratched out. Next to it, Samuel Dedman wrote: "McCann is condemned a Tory and his name ought to be Erased." A friend of Britain could not be allowed to join this exposure of a British plot to destroy American liberty by freeing Virginians' slaves.

Whites learned at the end of the summer of 1800 that hundreds of slaves, especially in and near Richmond and Petersburg, had plotted an uprising. Thomas Prosser's slave Gabriel, with help from others, recruited followers for months. He envisioned a military campaign, beginning with seizure of arms in Richmond. His brother afterward described Gabriel's intent: "we might conquer the white people and possess ourselves of their property." On the night chosen for rendezvous and an attack on Richmond by 1,100 men— Saturday, August 30, 1800—a severe thunderstorm dispersed or disoriented the insurrectionists. Whites discovered the plan; militiamen mobilized. Trials, thirty-five executions, and other punishments followed through September, October, and November. A letter from Richmond late in September said: "The conspiracy of the Negroes occupies all our thoughts." Two years later, another alarm led to more executions in Virginia and northeastern North Carolina, though evidence of an intent to burn Norfolk was thin. Writing from Williamsburg early in 1802, Chapman Johnson asked: "Is it not miserable, is it not shameful, is it not unworthy the character of Virginians, or of men, thus to live the unsafe trembling tyrants of an unhappy people?"

Republicans held a majority of seats in the House of Delegates in November 1799. They elected one of their own as speaker and removed the previous clerk from office "for his federal politics." On the recommendation of Thomas Jefferson, they replaced him with young William Wirt. He later wrote of those days: "You know how high parties then were—& how they hated each other." The contests were bitter during the administration of President John Adams. Federalists' hostility to France, leading to augmentation of America's army and navy, convinced many Republicans that the administration, as a tool of Britain, wished to go to war with France. Federalists' laws and arrests directed against agents of sedition, as they called it, showed Republicans that the administration threatened to destroy liberty and self-government. After Bushrod Washington demonstrated his "zeal against *the subverters of all Government*," President Adams appointed him to the Supreme Court. John Page called Federalists "the Anglo-monarchico-

John Page, After Gilbert Stuart. Courtesy of the Henry E. Huntington Library. Page while he was governor of Virginia and his friend, Thomas Jefferson,was president of the United States.

aristocratic Faction," supported by "british Merchants, old Tories, Specula-tors, & place-hunters." William Wirt knew that, by winning the clerkship, he had made enemies of the Federalists and their leader, John Marshall. This did not prevent his election to the Buchanan Spring Barbecue Club, whose members, Richmond's leading men, gathered on summer Saturdays to eat and drink well. The rules forbade talk of politics.

William Nelson, Jr., did not agitate himself about the course of politics, as his friend John Page did. He rode circuit in eastern Virginia, then spent time with his daughters at Westover. Under the guidance of their grand-mother, Mary Willing Byrd, and their unmarried aunt, Anne Byrd, Nelson's four youngest daughters, as well as their half sister, were growing into "a groupe of sweet interesting girls." Nelson's preference for the company of women and books at Westover—his love of pondering and joking, rather than "boldness and promptitude"—confirmed in some minds his reputation for "slowness, or want of power." William Wirt said that if Nelson's mind had been "less comprehensive & fertile" and his "heart less delicate and scrupulous," he "would have made a much more distinguished figure in the public estimation than he did." After a stay in Virginia a French officer

John Wickham, A. Rosenthal, after Charles Balthazar Julien Févret de Saint-Mémin. Courtesy of the Henry E. Huntington Library

wrote: "The Americans are phlegmatic, extremely serious, always engaged in their business, and that of the state. They are with their wives only to take tea or some other drink."

In December 1802 the General Assembly elected John Page governor. He dedicated himself to "the Republican Cause, & the constitutional Independence of the State-Governments." Grateful to receive a salary, he paid his outstanding bills at stores and cleared up some of his old debts. The Pages lived more comfortably in the governor's house in Richmond than in the mansion at Rosewell.

As Page took office, William Wirt left the clerkship of the House of Delegates to become a judge of the High Court of Chancery for eastern Virginia, sitting in Williamsburg. Contrary to his expectations when he accepted the post, Wirt moved to Williamsburg a married man. A widower, he had earlier declared his love to Elizabeth Washington Gamble, eighteen-year-old daughter of Catharine Gamble and Robert Gamble, a leading merchant in Richmond. Elizabeth returned his love, but, William said, "for certain reasons *of state*, I was discarded." In his early days in Virginia, Wirt had acquired a reputation as "a hearty good fellow" around town; but he had reformed, and in the summer of 1802 his courtship prevailed. Elizabeth and William were married on Tuesday evening, September 7.

Arriving in Williamsburg, the Wirts entered a hospitable society. Residents fond of parties held frequent balls, striking visitors as "gay and extravagant." The town nevertheless slowly decayed. The value of property did not rise. St. George Tucker, wishing to speak well of the place, said: "Williamsburg has seen its worst days." Bishop James Madison rescued the statue of

St. George Tucker, A. Rosenthal, after Charles Balthazar Julien Févret de Saint Mémin. Courtesy of
the Henry E. Huntington Library. Professor of
law, judge, and counsellor.

Lord Botetourt from its indignities. He and the professors in the college
bought it from the state for $100. Removing it from the ruins of the old capi-
tol, they set it in front of the college building. An iron plug reattached Botetourt's head, and his lost marble nose was *"scientifically* renewed." The
encomiums carved into the faces of the pedestal were reunited with their
subject. The suave form of the dead courtier looked down Duke of Gloucester Street, cutting "a very handsome figure indeed." This was Williamsburg's
idea of exciting news. The town's presiding deity seemed to be the "Goddess
of Dullness." Even so, a Virginian who reluctantly followed her husband to
the Mississippi Valley wrote home: "Williams[bur]g is Paris compared with
Baton Rouge."

William Wirt decided to resign his judgeship and return to practicing
law. He thought first of moving to Kentucky. His pregnant wife wept at "the
idea of such a distant, and most probably final, separation from her parents
and family." He soon learned that money did not flow in Kentucky, as he had
supposed. A shortage of coin led to clients' paying their legal fees with livestock. An able young attorney, Littleton Waller Tazewell, having learned law
under John Wickham, invited Wirt to share his new practice and attain
wealth "through the progressive prosperity of Norfolk." Wirt wrote to Governor Page, resigning from the Court of Chancery in the last week of April
1803. The Wirts left Williamsburg that summer.

Edmund Pendleton died in October 1803, at the age of eighty-two. His
seat on Virginia's Supreme Court of Appeals went to St. George Tucker in
January 1804. Though Tucker continued to teach law, he resigned his pro-
fessorship at the College of William and Mary. His successor was William

Nelson, Jr. Working at Westover in the late summer heat, Nelson put together 115 pages of lectures "on Law and right of Nature, of Nations and in government in general." Acting as agent of the Dismal Swamp Company, he at last reached an agreement with trespassers taking timber from the swamp. The Butts and the Bartees conceded "that many trespasses and encroachments may unintentionally heretofore have been committed." They promised to respect a newly surveyed boundary. The company released them "from all suits, actions and damages" connected with their past conduct. Nelson began lecturing on Tuesday, November 20, 1804. Seventeen days later, John Page was re-elected governor for a third and final year.

William Wirt's ten breezy essays, thinly disguised as letters from a British spy, began to appear in *The Argus* just after his wife gave birth to their daughter, Laura Henrietta, namesake of Petrarch's ideal and William Wirt's mother. The *Norfolk Herald* started reprinting them a few weeks after the Wirts arrived in the city. The pieces attracted more attention than their author had expected. The spy commented on a range of subjects: William Byrd and rich Virginians' "aristocratic" pretensions, geology, oratory, unjust treatment of Indians, and the virtues of *The Spectator.* The passage provoking most reaction sketched well-known Virginians, unnamed but easily recognizable: James Monroe, John Marshall, John Wickham, and Edmund Randolph. Though free from malice, these portraits did not flatter. Wirt heard that Mary Ambler Marshall "was exceedingly angry" about his description of her husband. Once one knew, as readers soon did, that the letters came from the pen of an ambitious young attorney, it was easy to guess why he chose these four. Wirt had studied most closely men who had risen to wealth (Wickham), to the nation's highest judicial office (Marshall), or to high political office (Monroe and Randolph), beginning as attorneys. Wirt sought to detect their gifts and frailties. Exposing these with an air of condescension, he seemed to be making light of his subjects' eminence, which he privately envied. As his work in book form went into a third edition within two years, he contemplated writing a series of "lives of our Virginian revolutionary characters of eminence." If this succeeded, he said, "it will pay a just tribute of honor to the dead, will perpetuate their memory, stimulate the rising generation and present them with the best models by which to form their own characters, besides offering to myself a decent harvest of reputation and— *cash!*"

John Wickham did not hold a grudge against Wirt. *The Letters of the British Spy* was a slight irritant to one enjoying Wickham's success. His practice embraced "every variety of cases"; for his legal opinion he charged a fee of $100. His offices held "a most extensive and judiciously selected library." His house became the most hospitable in Richmond: "All the world was at Mr. Wickham's last night—and we had a profusion of rarities & dainties." Upriver from Richmond, in Goochland County, he bought part of the plantation Tuckahoe, 2,100 acres overlooking the James River. There his slaves grew wheat, corn, and oats, while he kept the best thoroughbred horses in the county. A British visitor said that Wickham's "manners and mode of life would do honour to the most cultivated societies."

Wickham wrote periodically to Samuel Gist, reporting on his progress in extracting payment of old debts. In May 1803, Wickham filed a bill against the attorney general of Virginia and the state auditor in the High Court of Chancery. He demanded that the state repay to Gist profits sequestered from his Virginia plantations during the Revolutionary War and paid into the state treasury by William Anderson. Wickham's careful search of public records yielded evidence convincing Chancellor George Wythe to rule in Gist's favor. Wickham collected more than $7,500 in principal and interest. This money, less Wickham's $750 commission, soon lay in Gist's hands.

For eight years, beginning in May 1803, Samuel Gist enjoyed a new hobby: pursuing another claim for compensation. In the first year of Jefferson's administration, the British and American governments concluded an agreement to settle the question of prewar debts. The United States paid Great Britain £600,000—$3,000,000—in installments to discharge all remaining private debts owed by Americans before 1776. To disburse this money among creditors, the British government appointed three commissioners: Thomas Macdonald, Henry Pye Rich, and John Guillemard. At their offices in Great Marlborough Street they accumulated rooms full of documents— claims, with reams of evidence, seeking, in all, eight times as much money as the American government paid. Gist filed a memorial asking for £45,896 8s. This, he wrote, was the total of his debts lost as a consequence of the American War, with accrued interest.

The commissioners worked with "assiduity and intelligence." If they were not cynical when they began, they soon became so. They rejected almost 80 percent of the claims. Among the papers lying before them were reports from special agents in America, men hired to investigate claims submitted by American loyalists seeking compensation for losses. In Virginia, William Waller Hening tried to verify debts in Samuel Gist's schedule of losses. Hening found many "Suspicious Circumstances." Some debts had been paid before the war; some debtors had died before the war. For other debts, Gist had won court judgments before leaving Virginia, but debtors had absconded or turned up insolvent. These were ordinary bad debts in business in peacetime, not losses inflicted upon Gist by reason of his loyalty to the Crown. Hening reported on Gist's claims: "some of his lists appear to be the mere sweepings of his compting room."

Gist turned eighty at the start of 1805. He enjoyed "very good health," his faculties "perfectly sound & as good as ever they were." To handle his business in the City he employed Leighton Wood, Jr., who had come to London from Virginia after working for William Anderson & Company. Gist set up Wood in offices at Number 12, Copthall Court, off Throgmorton Street, formerly the home and offices of Anthony Bacon. With safe, productive investments in land, Bank of England stock, East India Company stock, and government funds, Gist had ample leisure to pester Thomas Macdonald, Henry Pye Rich, and John Guillemard. He sent them a deposition by Leighton Wood, Jr., attesting to the solvency of his debtors in Virginia. He reminded the commissioners: "time with me is precious." But they refused to be rushed. Their deliberations went on for years. Gist wrote to them in the last week of April 1808: "I hope my time is come."

On Monday, May 9, Gist was called to Great Marlborough Street to testify under oath about his claim. The commissioners told him that ledgers he had submitted as evidence did not support his list of losses. The disparity was so obvious that they asked: "Have you examined the books which have been produced by you at this office—so as at least to know the general nature of each of them?" Gist replied: "I have—and I do not know that there is any error in them." Instead of submitting records of daily business, he had given the commissioners some journals and two ledgers, "one of which," they told him, "appears to have been in many instances recently made up." Entries in the ledgers did not match those in the journals. Where were the original records? Gist said that he might still have them somewhere, or they might have been destroyed. If he found any, he would submit them.

Then the three commissioners addressed specific entries. Gist's representatives in Virginia had collected old debts in recent years and had sent money to Gist. Yet his books given to the commission did not deduct these payments from the losses for which he claimed compensation.

Q: How do you account for this?
A: By money paid to Thos Shore as Collector not entered in my books.

Q: Have large sums been recovered and remitted to you by Thos Shore, John Wickham & others in payment partly of the debts claimed on & partly of others?

A: Yes.

Q: The Board observe that there is no account in your Le[d]gers produced, for Thos Shore later than June 1782. Have those remittances been subsequent to that period?

A: Yes.

Q: How does it happen that no account is to be found in your Le[d]gers of those remittances?

A: The Books have lain by & no entries of such credits or remittances have been made, but accounts have been rendered of the payments made to them.

To close their questioning, the commissioners asked why fifty folios had been inserted into Ledger Number 1. Gist said that the volume had been filled with entries and needed more folios. The commissioners noted that entries in the fifty new folios did not correspond to the ledger's original index.

Q: How do you account for this?

A: By supposing it a mistake in the Index.

The commissioners had no more questions.

Samuel Gist went home to Gower Street unhappy. He was not accustomed to this sort of treatment. He protested to the commissioners several times in the weeks after his testimony. He said that he felt "Hurt at your repeated observations at the defective state of the Accounts." He assured them: "I would not for all the Money in England lay a single Accot. before you that I knew there was an error in." He reminded them that he was no ordinary memorialist trying to wheedle the commission into doing him a kindness. "I trust my reputation stands as high as any Merchant's in London exceptg. none." He sent them some letters from Thomas Shore, just found, he said, among his papers. He promised to render a full account of any further remittances from Virginia. In July, Gist wrote: "I should hate myself if I did not act by the nicest principles of Justice, Honesty & Honor in all my transactions." Two days later he returned to the offices in Great Marlborough Street. He waited for ninety minutes but did not see the commissioners. They had found another remittance of more than £300 which he had received without deducting it from his claim. He attributed his lapse to "the almost total decay of my memory."

In the following year, after receiving a report from their agent in Richmond confirming many of their doubts, the commissioners stopped answering Gist's letters. He demanded an explanation of their delay. He knew that they must soon close their accounts. He hinted, with menace: "it would give me pain to proceed by any ot[her] than friendly measures against you." In the end the commission awarded Gist £2,415 os. 1od.

The youngest of Francis Farley's and William Byrd's four granddaughters, Mary Byrd Farley, was married in Williamsburg on Thursday evening, April 20, 1797. Her husband, George Tucker, was a twenty-one-year-old kinsman of St. George Tucker's. He had imitated St. George Tucker by emigrating from Bermuda to study law in Williamsburg. When Mary Farley accepted George Tucker, her health was poor. She suffered from several complaints, the most serious apparently being tuberculosis, the same disease steadily weakening her sister's husband, Thomas Lee Shippen.

The Shippens visited Williamsburg for ten days at the time of the wedding, after a stay in North Carolina. In that state they had begun a suit in Salisbury District Superior Court: *Thomas Shippen et ux* v. *Devisees of Francis Farley, Deceased.* This friendly suit asked the court to order and supervise a division of Francis Farley's half of the Land of Eden among the four sisters. On November 4, the court ordered a division and appointed surveyors to mark lots. George and Mary Tucker sailed for Bermuda, hoping that a voyage would restore her health. Spending the winter in South Carolina gave Thomas Lee Shippen some comfort but did not arrest his disease. He died on Sunday, February 4, 1798.

Rebecca Parke Corbin was the first sister to get out of the Dismal Swamp Company. She and Richard Corbin, to clear a debt of about £324 currency, transferred their quarter-share to Dr. Corbin Griffin of York Town in June 1798. Richard Corbin sold for more than £1,900 their portion of the Land of Eden, acquired by Henry Lee the next year and transferred to Patrick Henry.

George and Mary Tucker stayed in Bermuda until May 1798, but, back in Virginia, her health declined. As spring arrived in 1799, she knew that she did not have long to live. She and her husband worried that upon her death he would lose all claim to share in Francis Farley's estate. Hoping to secure her one-fourth for him, they signed a deed of trust conveying it to St. George Tucker. They retained use of the property, and the survivor could revoke the trust and own the property outright. They signed on Wednesday, March 27. Two months later, Mary died at the age of twenty-two.

Early in the new year the mother of the four Farley sisters was married for the third time at the age of forty-five. For twenty-seven years Henry Skipwith had been married to Anne Wayles Skipwith, sister of Thomas Jefferson's wife. Soon after his wife's death, Henry Skipwith approached Elizabeth Farley Dunbar; she accepted him, and he joined her in Williamsburg.

From Antigua, Henry Benskin Lightfoot reported a successful crop at Mercers Creek in 1799. He wrote to the heirs, offering to buy the plantation for £20,000 sterling, the equivalent of seven years' average profits from it. In case the owners thought this a low figure, he reminded them that abolitionists were trying to end the African slave trade, as well as slavery in the British empire.

George Tucker visited Antigua in the summer and fall of 1799. Though he enjoyed planters' hospitality, he received bad news from an attorney: his Virginia deed of trust did not conform to Antigua law. He had little prospect of prevailing in a court of equity. He could not establish his claim to one-fourth of the Mercers Creek plantation. He wrote: "I have therefore relinquished my pretensions for ever."

Champe Carter sailed to Antigua in June 1800. On behalf of the three surviving sisters, he sold the Mercers Creek estate to Lightfoot for £20,000, with payments spread over four years. Three months after his return to Virginia, Champe and Maria Carter went to Richmond to prove the deed of conveyance. George Tucker spent much time with them and their sixteen-year-old "fair niece Maria," suspending his recently begun regimen of "study and sobriety." Much as he enjoyed the Carters' company, he kept thinking about the $100,000 from Antigua, to be divided three ways, not four. With encouragement from St. George Tucker, he pursued a claim for one-fourth of the sum. Champe and Maria Carter sold their quarter-share in the Dismal Swamp Company to the company.

George Tucker and Champe Carter's niece, Maria, soon were married. In Richmond he put up an office building which looked like a Greek temple. He speculated in bank stock and real estate; he contracted gambling debts. In need of money, he sold his quarter-share in the Dismal Swamp Company for £500 currency. Richard Willing Byrd, with help from Thomas Swepson, bought it on behalf of his mother. As the scheme to drain the Dismal Swamp faded, Mary Willing Byrd became a partner.

In Philadelphia, Elizabeth Farley Banister Shippen entered her third marriage. After Thomas Lee Shippen's death, she had "a numerous band of suitors" following her "through places of fashionable resort." Other women said that she led the men on, using "flirtations." She chose a South Carolin-ian, Captain George Izard, until recently an officer in the United States Army. He was a "fine-looking, portly man, of rather haughty demeanour, but polished manners." A year had passed since Izard attracted unwanted atten-tion by crossing the Delaware River to Gloucester Point, New Jersey, for a duel with a Frenchman whose family had fled Saint-Domingue. His oppo-nent was the brother of a woman of "considerable attraction," with whom Izard had reached "a perfect understanding" in Charleston two years before. The couple inadvertently had revealed their "mutual attachment" by com-mitting what Izard called "an act of unpardonable imprudence." Though neither wished to be married to the other, Izard let her family rescue her honor by announcing an engagement. Now her brother had come to Philadelphia to save the family honor by forcing Izard to choose between marriage and a duel. Not wishing to kill his opponent, Izard put a light charge of powder in his pistols. In the exchange of fire the Frenchman suf-fered only a contusion on his leg, while Izard took a ball in the chest. He barely recovered, but he at last escaped "an embarrassing yoke."

Later that year he visited Elizabeth Shippen at her country estate. She gave him permission to call again after his winter stay at West Point. He asked for her hand, "which she unaffectedly and kindly promised me for the month of June." After becoming Elizabeth Izard, she said she had fulfilled the prophecy of a black woman who had told her fortune, predicting "that in the course of her life she should have eighteen feet of husband." The com-bined heights of John Banister, Jr., Thomas Lee Shippen, and George Izard totaled 18 feet 2 inches. Izard adjusted easily to the "elegance, neatness and abundance" of the country house at Farley.

Division of the Land of Eden was complete in 1803. In fall term the Salisbury District Superior Court, at her attorney's request, dismissed the suit begun by Elizabeth Izard four years earlier. The survey completed under the court's order also brought nearer to an end a suit begun in March 1802 on behalf of Patrick Henry's sons, Alexander Spotswood Henry and Nathaniel West Henry. At his death in June 1799, Henry in his will allotted to each boy one of the two portions of the Land of Eden he had received from Henry Lee. Lee made a claim against the estate; Patrick Henry's widow wrote: "I think it unjust and I do not intend to pay one shilling unless he can recover it by law." Through her attorney, she asked the court to assign to the Farley and Henry claimants an appropriate share. The court's decree on April 10, 1804, divided the land among John Simon Farley, Elizabeth Mor-son, Elizabeth Izard, George Tucker, and the Henry boys, one-fourth each to Farley and Morson, one-eighth each to the others.

Dorothea Henry, second wife of Patrick Henry, outlived him by more than thirty years. Against his dying wish, she afterward took another husband: Patrick Henry's cousin, Judge Edmund Winston. In later years Henry's son-in-law, Spencer Roane, called on Dorothea Henry Winston to talk about the dead patriot. Roane said that Henry had hurt himself in the eyes of Republicans by his collaboration with Federalists in his last years. Roane blamed this apostasy on the wiles of Henry Lee. Dorothea Henry Winston did not disagree, but, remembering the Land of Eden, she "concluded, with a laugh, that Henry Lee had been a great friend to their family, for that Mr. Henry had got two fine tracts of land from him!" She did not mention that, in the process, her late husband had left Lee holding a broad stretch of reeds in the Green Sea in the Dismal Swamp.

Shortly before she took her third husband, Elizabeth Izard received helpful advice from some North Carolinians. They told her that North Carolina law, like Antigua law, recognized a deed of trust such as George and Mary Tucker's only if the governor had witnessed its signing. She wrote to Judge Edmund Winston, who acted for the Henry boys. If Winston and the Izards cooperated to invalidate George Tucker's claim, they could, under the terms of Francis Farley's will, divide Farley's half of the Land of Eden three ways, rather than four. Judge Winston approved. The Izards and Tucker began litigation in North Carolina and Virginia, some of which lasted the rest of the Izards' lives.

The greatest burden on all three sisters and their husbands, on their mother and Henry Skipwith, and on George Tucker was a suit in United States Circuit Court in Richmond, begun in 1802 by Dinwiddie, Crawford & Company to recover James Parke Farley's unpaid debts contracted in the 1770s. In May 1805, John Marshall and his colleagues of the Circuit Court issued a decree in the case *Dinwiddie, Crawford & Co.* v. *Henry Skipwith, Elizabeth Hill Skipwith et al.* Working from a commissioner's report, the court allotted to each husband of James Parke Farley's daughters a share of the debt owed by Farley's estate. Since George and Mary Tucker had received less income from Francis Farley's bequest, Tucker owed half as much as the others—slightly less than $2,000. Izard, Carter, and Corbin were each assessed about $4,000. The commissioner had calculated Elizabeth Skipwith's income from Francis Farley's estate and her expenditures on her daughters' behalf while they lived with her. He found that the daughters and their husbands were entitled to recover almost $1,000 from the Skipwiths.

Elizabeth and George Izard were the last of the Farley heirs to leave the Dismal Swamp Company. They sold out soon after the court issued a slightly revised decree in the fall of 1805. They thought the commissioner's apportionment of James Parke Farley's debts inequitable because it overstated the amount Elizabeth Izard had received from Francis Farley's estate. As an example, George Izard showed that the commissioner had assigned a value of £500 currency to one quarter-share in the Dismal Swamp Company and had computed the value of this asset as if Elizabeth Izard had received a yearly dividend of 6 percent on £500 since February 1788. By this calculation, one quarter-share appeared in a list of her income from her grandfather's estate as £1,070. But in selling the quarter-share to Richard Willing Byrd, Izard received £450. Of course, there had been no dividends. Thus the Izards lost £620 by being ordered to make a proportionately larger payment to Dinwiddie, Crawford & Company. They did not intend to take these losses quietly. George Izard, Champe Carter, and Richard Corbin turned to John Wickham. Izard wrote: "The Question will now be, to whom must I apply for Reimbursement?"

Francis Walker attended his last meeting of the Dismal Swamp Company in Richmond on Friday, January 9, 1801. He was then in the capital to represent Albemarle County in the House of Delegates. The year before, he had voted for a restatement of the Virginia Resolution, expressing the state's repudiation of federal laws known as the Alien and Sedition Acts. His subsequent re-election pleased James Madison, who assured Thomas Jefferson that such victories showed that "the patrons of usurpation and aristocracy will have little encouragement in this quarter." Walker needed money. In the fall of 1800 he thought that John Brown, acting for the Dismal Swamp Company, had agreed to buy his two quarter-shares for £900. Brown called this "A mistake in mr Walker." So Francis Walker participated in the January meeting and in the election of a new board of managers: William Nelson, Jr., John Jameson, the Reverend John Bracken, Dr. Corbin Griffin, and George Tucker. The only original partner of the company still active was Samuel Gist.

Francis Walker waited until he turned thirty-four to get married. His wife, Jane Byrd Nelson, was more than ten years younger. One of her uncles was William Nelson, Jr.; her paternal grandfather was President William Nelson; and one of her maternal great-grandfathers was the elder William Byrd. She and Francis Walker had two daughters and a son. A woman of "extensive reading and reflection," she drew up a plan of education for her daughters.

Francis Walker disposed of his quarter-shares in the Dismal Swamp Company separately. He sold one to the Reverend John Bracken, owner of the two quarter-shares Dr. Thomas Walker had given to Joseph Hornsby.

The other went to the Reverend James Henderson, a new convert to the Dismal Swamp Company. He also bought the one-third portion of Anthony Bacon's share owned by Bacon's former partner, Gilbert Francklyn. Earlier problems in developing the swamp arose from a simple cause, Henderson said: "the affairs of the Company had been managed very loosely."

More than a mile of swamp still lay between the converging ends of the trenches of the Dismal Swamp canal in November 1804. The canal company completed a road through the swamp passable by foot and horseback, soon to be wide enough for carriages. The Virginia sector of the canal attracted some commerce, but the company made more money from its sawmill, gristmill, and shingles than from tolls. Its largest private shareholder, the Dismal Swamp Company, awaited growing revenue impatiently. Francis Walker could not wait.

Marriage, fatherhood, outward marks of comfort at Castle Hill notwithstanding, Francis Walker remained "a victim to the bottle." In March 1806 he escorted his wife and children to York Town, leaving them for a visit among their Nelson kin. He headed back to Castle Hill in his carriage with a driver and a household servant. Sometime during their passage through Hanover and Louisa counties, Walker died, apparently of a stroke, so quietly that neither man with him knew until they started to help him leave the carriage at the end of the day. He was not quite forty-two years old. The news brought Jane Nelson Walker to "the point of distraction."

During Francis Walker's last journey from York Town, the Dismal Swamp was burning. Summer in 1805 and winter and spring in 1806 brought severe drought to Virginia, leaving the swamp drier than usual. Though fires often had spread through parts of it, "the great fire of 1806" swelled so large and lasted so long that people still talked about it thirty years later. No one knew how it began, but some suspected unsafe methods of clearing the land used by men in a hurry. For weeks shingle-getters and canal diggers saw smoke rising from the interior of the swamp. Flames moved rapidly through thick, dry undergrowth, encircling the tall trees. Winds spread fire first in one direction, then another. In the distance, workers heard huge old trees crashing down in quick succession. Thick clouds of smoke enveloped Norfolk and a rain of black cinders fell on the city. As the fire neared their camps, lumbermen saw bears and other animals fleeing through the woods, some with burns from passing through flames. The fire overtook buildings and bridges, dropped large, half-burned obstructions across the canal, and destroyed more than 2,000,000 shingles ready for market. In the first week of May, after the fire had burned for two months, the printer of the *Norfolk*

Gazette and Publick Ledger wrote: "Without rain, there is no hope of its stopping, short of the entire destruction of all the timber in this great tract of country." A week later, rain began to fall, continuing for several days. At the start of winter in mid-December a blizzard swept over the tidewater, leaving the swamp's blackened trees, charred fallen trunks, tangled branches, and ashen remains of undergrowth covered in white. Beyond Lake Drummond and the bounds of the spring fire, for miles in all directions, the Dismal Swamp lay under snow and frost.

After John Page's third term as governor ended, he and Margaret Lowther Page and their children left Richmond in the first week of January 1806. They traveled to Rosewell by way of Westover and Williamsburg, where they stayed with St. George Tucker and his family. Mary Willing Byrd and Lelia Tucker enjoyed Margaret Page's company, but behind her back they pitied her. Mary Willing Byrd said: "I wish her more happiness, than I fear awaits her at Rosewell." Noticing that Margaret Page was pregnant again, Lelia Tucker thought: "Poor Lady! she is in the way to increase her family, already too large for their means of support."

John Page let go of more land in Gloucester County during his last year as governor. His estate shrank to 800 acres, most of it uncultivated. With fifteen slaves over the age of twelve, Rosewell could do little more than produce food to support its inhabitants and some surplus commodities. These seldom commanded cash; the plantation cleared, at most, $500 in a year. In his first summer back at Rosewell, Page mused about Virginians and wealth. He told himself that he could have left his family rich if he had refused to pay his debts, perhaps borrowed still more, and died in debtors' prison after conveying his property to his wife and children. His default would not have harmed them, as he had learned from sixty-three years of living in Virginia: "they would always be respected in proportion to their riches, and . . . both I and they would have been despised had I left them poor." He refrained from following this course, he believed, only because he had a strong Christian faith, expressed through the Church of England, later the American Episcopal Church. If he had taken no thought for his soul, he could have told his family "that they ought to enjoy their hearts desire in all things and say 'let us eat & drink for tomorrow we die.' " If he were not a Christian, Page concluded, he would not be a republican. He would prefer "a despotic Prince to preserve a greater degree of Order, & security of life & Property." Appeals to morality would be merely "a good Countenance to restrain others from injuring me, and mine, & from interfering too much with me when in pursuit of favorite Gratifications." Only Christian faith had rescued him from such egotistical materialism.

Page recently had heard of a terrible example of the consequences of irreligion. Chancellor George Wythe, still active in court at the age of eighty, was murdered by his sister's grandson, who lived in Wythe's home in Richmond. Wishing to hasten the day of coming into his inheritance, George Wythe Sweeney put arsenic in the old man's coffee. Wythe long had been a deist, Page said; this meant that he had raised young Sweeney without Christian morality. The young man wanted money. Nothing restrained him. He forged checks. He killed his guardian. An irreligious Virginia, Page suggested, risked becoming either a despotism or a commonwealth of Sweeneys.

John Page spent the last two years of his life holding a federal patronage appointment under the Treasury Department as commissioner of loans in Richmond. His duties were light, consisting chiefly of signing his name. He borrowed more money to support his family. He wrote to Thomas Jefferson, who gave him the position: "Rosewell is all I have left, of Land, & by Sales & Deaths of Negroes, I have not enough to Work *it!*" He and his wife worried about the future education of their children, requiring money they did not have. Margaret Lowther Page confided to St. George Tucker: "I am very unhappy." John Page knew. He wrote to Jefferson of "my dear unhappy Wife."

In the last summer of John Page's life, Skelton Jones of Richmond, collecting material on the history of Virginia, submitted biographical questions to him. Writing answers took him back to happier times. He recalled the learning and the virtue of his ancestors. His "dear, pure minded and American patriotic" grandfather, Mann Page, creator of the mansion at Rosewell, had "checked the British Merchants from claiming even freight on their goods from England." His father, Mann Page, had received encouragement to pay court to Sir Gregory Page, a baronet in England, in expectation of becoming his heir. "But he despised titles sixty years ago, as much as you and I do now; and would have nothing to say to the rich silly Knight, who died, leaving his estate and title to a sillier man than himself, his sister's son, a Mr. Turner, on condition that he would take the name and title of Sir Gregory Page." Family tradition had garbled the story: Sir Gregory Turner was already a baronet in his own right when he inherited Sir Gregory Page's landed estates in 1775, becoming Sir Gregory Page-Turner. But John Page had learned from his father's independent spirit that the Virginia Pages did not sacrifice self-respect for titles and riches.

John Page fondly described his grandmother, Judith Carter Page, who introduced him to the world of books. He remembered "our highly enlightened Governor Fauquier." From the age of fifteen through the completion of his studies at the college, Page had lived in Williamsburg while Fauquier made the governor's palace a center of learning, science, and music. Page proudly recalled standing by his "Whiggish principles" in openly challenging the Tory governor, Lord Dunmore, while serving on the college's board of visitors and on the king's Council. Page listed public offices he had filled. He said that, if he lived, he would write his memoirs. On Tuesday, October 11, 1808, John Page died. Two months later, Margaret Lowther Page and her children again visited the Tuckers in Williamsburg on their journey from Richmond back to Rosewell.

Within days of her return to the neglected mansion she wrote to St. George Tucker: "To clear the Estate from Debt is my first Object." She lived for another thirty years, apparently spending most of her time in Williamsburg and Richmond. Following the example of Mary Willing Byrd, she brought order to her late husband's tangled affairs. After eight and a half years of effort she wrote to Tucker: "I know it will give you pleasure to learn that I am entirely free from Debt, and have no Extravagance to regret in the Past—nor dread anticipation of the privations of the Future." By that time the big brick mansion at Rosewell was "in bad repair." Margaret Lowther Page, a New Yorker, and her children were the last Pages to walk as owners across the black-and-white marble floor of the great hall and climb the mahogany staircase to move among more than a dozen rooms paneled in different woods. At her death, the Page heirs sold the Rosewell estate and the decaying mansion—with its leaking roof, broken windows, and rats—for $12,000.

Henry Lee received a letter from Robert Morris late in the summer of 1801, a reply to "two distressing letters" he had written. Lee was still trying to get repayment of at least part of his $40,000 loan. Morris informed him that his letters had arrived while commissioners of bankruptcy and creditors were going through Morris's papers to make sure they had seized all his assets before releasing him from the Prune Street prison. His "good wishes," Morris told Lee, "is all that is left in my power. those you have & ever will have." From that day, if not before, Lee's own insolvency or imprisonment became certain.

Lawsuits, foreclosures, insistent creditors attacked him on all sides. Though Lee had been too young to contract debts with British merchants before the Revolutionary War, John Wickham took him to court on behalf of the House of Hanbury, seeking payment of the debts of Matilda Lee's father,

Philip Ludwell Lee. In his customary manner Wickham wrote: "You will naturally suppose that no further Indulgence can be granted." But by 1804, Wickham had to report on Lee to his client: "he & all his sureties had become insolvent." Lee sold more and more land in Westmoreland County. The Stratford estate was not his to sell, since he had only a widower's life interest in it. Elsewhere in the county his holdings fell from 2,049 acres to 236. Lee's western purchases, like Morris's, had been indiscriminate. Too much property fit the description of his tracts in the mountains above the Shenandoah Valley: "the situation is very unfavorable, in most places too steep for cultivation; whenever you meet with a level spot, there the soil is very fine, but very few of these spots have I met with that are called General Lee's land."

Lee had acquired a reputation for deeding the same property to two different people, for conveying to others land he did not own, for promising to convey title yet not sending deeds. An agent for one of his creditors warned in April 1805: "as all titles of land held under Genl. Lee may be supposed as precarious, these that he cannot shew any evidence of title for, must be doubly so." Sometimes Lee took offense at complaints. After receiving seven letters from William Hodgson pressing him to pay, he replied that he did not like to be addressed as if he were a professed cheat. To which Hodgson rejoined that his letters only stated facts without imputing motives; an unpaid creditor remained unpaid whether or not his debtor intended to cheat him. In July 1805, Nathaniel Pendleton wrote: "I would give $250 to have General Lee arrested in Fairfax."

Lee evaded sheriffs for several more years, but by early 1809 he could no longer raise enough cash to fend off his creditors. Yet he did not wish to imitate Robert Morris and give up all his property by declaring himself insolvent. He wrote on March 4: "I am miserable [in]deed, as I must prepare for jail." Just before he surrendered to the sheriff of Westmoreland County, he wrote to Bushrod Washington. He said that he was willing to return George Washington's four quarter-shares in the Dismal Swamp Company to Washington's estate without demanding a refund of payments he had made. He had many reasons for regret, but he had it in his power to clear himself of his most embarrassing failure to pay.

Henry Lee entered the Westmoreland County jail on April 24, 1809. During his brief stay there, he and his wife signed a deed conveying all their "right, title and interest" in the Dismal Swamp Company to the estate of George Washington. Lee was transferred to the Spotsylvania County jail on May 13. Jailer Thomas Hicks signed a receipt for "the Body of Henry Lee," confined at the suit of Nathaniel Pendleton and others. Virginia law did not require that Lee stay locked in a cell. He moved within Spotsylvania County's equivalent of "prison bounds." After one year, however, he must pay his debt or give up his property and take an oath of insolvency or go into close confinement. Lee waited eleven months before making his choice.

He devoted his time not to sorting out his confused transactions but to writing his memoirs. He filled long sheets of paper with his sprawling, sometimes barely legible handwriting. He was telling his story of the last years of the Revolutionary War in the Carolinas. His main character was twenty-five years old: Light-Horse Harry Lee, commander of Lee's Legion—a special unit of 100 cavalrymen and 180 infantrymen—repeatedly outwitting the forces of Lord Cornwallis. For good measure he added an account of the last invasions of Virginia, with their climax in the surrender of Cornwallis's army to George Washington at York Town. George Washington Parke Custis, Martha Washington's grandson, later said of Lee's behavior in the days of his financial ruin: "The fame and memory of his chief was the fondly-cherished passion to which he clung amid the wreck of his fortunes—the hope, which gave warmth to his heart when all around him seemed cold and desolate."

As the first anniversary of Lee's confinement neared, he reluctantly surrendered his property, drawing up a list of his holdings and specifying to which debts they should be applied. His life interest in Stratford Hall he conveyed to his oldest son, Matilda Lee's heir, the last Lee to own the mansion. Henry Lee took the oath of insolvency; Sheriff Edward Henderson and Jailer Hicks released him on Wednesday, March 20, 1810.

Shareholders in the Dismal Swamp Canal Company received from the management repeated calls for money. Each year its sometime president, Thomas Newton, Jr., said that the northern and southern trenches were about to meet at a proper width. But hiring and feeding slave laborers was expensive. Work often stopped as the company ran out of money. The canal made little headway in the summer of 1802. Yet Newton wrote to Governor James Monroe: "I think the boats may pass through by next summer." Two years later Newton wrote to Governor Page: "I think the boats may pass through by next summer."

The Dismal Swamp Company also relied on the labor of hired slaves for its lumber business. White men and black men came to an understanding: the blacks turned out enough shingles; the whites left them to do it in their own way. Workers spent most of each week in the swamp, felling white cedar trees and cutting shingles. The men were spread out, a few in each camp, sleeping on cedar chips in low, flimsy shanties built on mounds of leftover wood. If they produced their shingles in five days, they took two days for themselves outside the swamp. Some weeks they took three. Their owners and other whites in and near Suffolk complained that the shingle-getters had "too much leisure time," which they spent "improperly." The black men's labor in the swamp furnished the company with hundreds of thousands of shingles each year through a system which lasted for decades.

At a meeting in May 1804 the managers of the Dismal Swamp Company resolved: "The Negroes & etc to be sold." This decision ended all vestiges of the original scheme devised by the elder William Byrd and afterward persuasively presented to the accommodating Governor Francis Fauquier. The partners at last admitted that for years they had not envisioned a self-supporting, growing population of company slaves who would turn the Dismal Swamp into farmland to make shareholders rich. Their true source of profit always had stood fully grown in the swamp. In 1807 the company's hired slaves made 928,700 three-foot cedar shingles; in 1808 they made 1,285,900. Anticipating larger dividends, the partners bought for the company as many quarter-shares as they could. The two-thirds of Anthony Bacon's share which had come to James Bacon were sold to the company. The namesake cousin of William Nelson, Jr.—William Nelson of Caroline and King William counties—had inherited one-third of the share owned by his father, Secretary Thomas Nelson. Writing his will on Christmas Day, 1806, he said that "it is now likely" this share "will be very valuable." He bequeathed it to his four sons. Of these four-twelfths of a share, the company managed to buy one. A subsequent owner of another twelfth replied to an inquiry: "should I be disposed to sell hereafter I shall most certainly give the Company the refusal."

William Nelson, Jr., almost missed the company's meeting in Suffolk on May 10, 1810. He had fallen ill in March, and St. George Tucker had feared that Nelson would die. "The loss of such a friend is to me irreparable. He was my other self." But Nelson's health slowly returned during a stay in York Town in April. He walked along the riverbank, picking up shells. Back at Westover, he did not yet look well. This was not a good way to turn fifty.

The new managers were eager to make money. Writing to Samuel Gist in 1811, the Reverend John Bracken found Gist ready to help him. The Reverend James Henderson pushed his colleagues to make the company more efficient. It ought to stop allowing partners to serve as managers for life, as William Nelson, Jr., had done. Instead, the company ought to choose a president, who would, with managers' advice, "direct all the Operations of the Company." Henderson felt frustrated by partners' "stinginess & indecision." He urged onward the new Jericho Canal through the swamp, establishing a narrow water course for cargoes of shingles, connecting Lake Drummond with the Nansemond River. He looked forward to charging tolls for floating other people's shingles on the company's canal.

Beginning in 1810, the Dismal Swamp Company paid steady dividends to shareholders. That year a quarter-share drew $333. In 1811 a quarter-share drew $500—in 1812, $400; in 1813, $300; in 1814, $600. The estate of George Washington, with four quarter-shares, received a dividend of $2,000 in 1811. Before the partners' meeting, Justice Bushrod Washington wrote to James Henderson: "The handsome dividend which you anticipate in May furnishes a strong evidence of the prosperous state of the Company's affairs & of the good management of those to whom they have been & are committed." He approved of Henderson's proposal to seek a charter of incorporation from the General Assembly. Henderson wished that the partners were less delighted with their dividends. They did not heed his advice to reinvest some of their profits. "Among the Proprietors," he complained, "there are some who would not expend one Dollar to receive 20 per Cent Interest." Their notion of a good report was news of fifty black men working in the swamp, bringing out 20,000 of the 80,000 shingles coming from the swamp each week to meet a high demand at a price of $16 per 1,000. Years later, warned about "a waste of Timber," their minds had not changed. A new shareholder wrote to Bushrod Washington: "Our partners seem to prefer present profit to any advantage in the future. . . . Our Attention is now exclusively applied to the shingle-getting."

William Nelson, Jr., again fell ill in the autumn of 1812. He did not recover. Weakened by intestinal disease, he stayed at Westover, asking St. George Tucker to lecture to the law students. Nelson seemed in good spirits, joking as usual. He did not let his daughters, their aunt Anne, or Mary Willing Byrd know that he was near death. As his condition worsened early in the new year, he moved to Williamsburg, staying in the house he had shared with his friend William Short almost forty years earlier. In the first week of March he could not get out of bed. He died on the morning of Monday, March 8. His body was placed, as Lord Botetourt's had been, in the chapel of the college. An obituary in the Richmond *Enquirer* said of Nelson: "He passed through life, it is believed, without an enemy; but, at every turn met with those who loved, respected, and esteemed him."

Eight months later, Mary Willing Byrd suffered another loss. Her daughter, Anne, died at the age of fifty. Anne Byrd lived at Westover all her life. Judge Nelson's five daughters called her "Mother," later remembering her as "a truly pious well educated dear creature." After her death, the family went into "the deepest dejection." Within a few weeks Mary Willing Byrd was very sick. She wrote her will in December 1813, dividing the contents of her mansion among her children, stepchildren, and grandchildren. William Wirt, gathering material on Patrick Henry, wrote of "poor Mrs. Byrd": "when she dies, adieu to the glories of Westover. . . . Look at the apparently inexhaustible mines of opulence to which Colo. Byrd was born—and see his family already in decay and ruin: a magnificent prince himself—his children & grand children beggars!" To his surprise, Wirt received from Mary Willing Byrd and the other executors of William Byrd's estate an offer of employment. He had represented them in their litigation with the administrators of Speaker Robinson's estate. Byrd's executors now said that if Wirt could establish in court the estate's claim to two hundred or three hundred city lots in Richmond and to 630,000 acres along the Roanoke River, they would pay him 10 percent of all he recovered. He calculated: "if 100 lots are recovered, I get, at an average, property worth, at least, $50,000. You see this is a pretty splendid bubble." Mary Willing Byrd died in March 1814. She had been a widow for thirty-seven years.

The spring of 1814 was a time of celebration for shareholders in the Dismal Swamp Canal Company. A 20-ton boat made a voyage from Scotland Neck, North Carolina, down the Roanoke River into Albemarle Sound, up the Pasquotank River, through the length of the canal, then down the Elizabeth River to Norfolk. She was the first vessel other than shingle flats and the like to use the canal. Even after the canal's two ditches had met, much work remained to be done. With the labor of twenty or thirty slaves in summer and half as many in winter, the last segments did not reach a width of 20 feet until 1809. The canal still needed locks. The first were temporary, made of wood. The company borrowed money to continue work, mortgaging future revenue from tolls.

As the canal company began a three-and-one-quarter-mile feeder ditch to Lake Drummond in 1812, the Dismal Swamp Company extended and brought into use its Jericho Canal. Twelve feet wide, four feet deep, and ten miles long, it began near Suffolk, ran southeastward across the company's tract, then turned almost due south to Lake Drummond. James Henderson insisted upon faster progress than the hapless canal company had achieved. Suffering, disease, and deaths among slaves working on the Jericho Canal appeared in stories told by people in Nansemond County for generations—stories of "chain-gangs of slaves": "They say the poor creatures died here in heaps from swamp fever. But that didn't make any difference to their owners. They was made to dig right into the heart of the swamp to get at the juniper trees." Early in the twentieth century, a tourist entering the Dismal Swamp by the Jericho Canal asked her guide, a young white Virginian, why a swamp so filled with color, sunshine, and bird calls was named "dismal." " 'There's more to it than shows just at first, ma'am,' he answered. 'There are more sad stories about this swamp than all the sunshine can make bright.' " Among many accounts of the origin of Lake Drummond, one was a tradition begun in Nansemond County: "The black folks around here say that the lake belongs to the devil."

Shingle-getters for the Dismal Swamp Company cut their way into the interior of the swamp. In addition to felling stands of white cedar, they found many large trunks of trees lying on top of one another, covered by water and layers of peat. The great fire of 1806 and other fires left many blackened trees but also "brought to view and into use, more good timber than they injured, by burning the soil down to where numerous trees had lain perhaps for a century concealed, and their existence unsuspected." After twenty-five years of cutting millions of shingles, the company's workers were felling cedar trees with a diameter of 12 inches. Dismal Plantation lay unused, its fences broken. In October 1813 the managers leased it at a rent of $60 per year to Thomas Bains and Benjamin Lassiter, who signed with their marks.

The old Dismal Swamp Company came to an end two days before Christmas 1814. The General Assembly passed an act of incorporation for the Dismal Swamp Land Company. James Henderson became its president. In the years 1817 to 1825 a quarter-share drew an average annual dividend of $285.

The Dismal Swamp Canal, newly enlarged, reopened on the last day of 1828. Stage coaches used the parallel road. Early in 1830, Isaiah Rogerson announced the opening of his Lake Drummond Hotel adjacent to the canal. A building 128 feet long, it had eight chambers, four in Virginia and four in North Carolina. The bar was "furnished with the choicest wines and liquors of every description." North Carolina law made getting married easier than did Virginia law. For this and other reasons, the Lake Drummond Hotel boasted about the convenience of guests' being able to cross the state line without leaving the building. It was an establishment in the heart of the Dismal Swamp "fully applicable for all the purposes of life, as eating, drinking, sleeping, marrying, duelling, etc., etc., in all its varieties."

Nearing his ninetieth birthday, Samuel Gist bought more farms in Oxfordshire, Gloucestershire, and Warwickshire in 1810 and 1811. In subsequent years his annual income from leaseholds was almost £6,000. His stock, consolidated annuities, and other personal property yielded at least another £6,000 each year, apart from investments set aside for his daughters and their husbands. His daughter, Mary, was now the wife of Martin Pearkes, a tobacconist in London. Between July 1810 and February 1812, John Wickham sent Gist more than £2,000 sterling in debtors' remittances from Virginia. The dividend in 1810 on Gist's three quarter-shares in the Dismal Swamp Company was $1,000. He collected it by authorizing the Reverend John Bracken to receive it in return for Gist's securing a bill of exchange Bracken had sent to London for another purpose.

Gist began to prepare for his death. He wrote his will. He ordered a vault to be readied for his remains in Wormington's small church. He bought a white marble coffin, which he kept in a case in the stables behind his house in Gower Street. In his eighties Gist thought much about carrying on his family name. Beginning life in a charity school, a kinsman of weavers, he had made the name of Gist feared and respected in the City. He owned more than 4,000 acres in England. He had aspired not just to amass wealth but also to found a line of Gists, a great family, yet he had no son, no grandchildren, no brother or sister, no nephews or nieces. He did not keep his concern secret. He "sought with great anxiety for any family of his own singular name, in the hope of fixing upon a male inheritor the bulk of his vast property."

The closest male relative of whom he knew was his cousin, James Gist. In 1764, as Samuel prepared to move from Virginia to London, James, at the age of thirty-six, gave up his trade as a weaver and enlisted as a private in the army of the East India Company. He was shipped to Bengal. Perhaps he had married "an European woman" and fathered sons. If so, Samuel Gist wished to make the oldest son heir to the Gist fortune.

But James had died a bachelor in the fall of 1774. His remains were buried in Calcutta. The year after James's death, as Samuel rushed to get the last peacetime shipments of tobacco from Virginia, his uncle, Thomas Gist, James's father, was living in another part of London with Henry Rogers, a kinsman. Thomas Gist, long a weaver, was eighty-seven years old, dependent upon the Rogers family. While working in the City, Rogers learned of James's death in India. At home that evening, he asked Thomas Gist whether he wished to hear what had become of his son. The old man replied: "Oh Harry I shall never hear of him any more." Rogers worked the conversation around to breaking the news of James's death. Long afterward Rogers's children remembered that "Thomas Gist wept much upon receiving the intelligence." Of these events Samuel Gist knew nothing in 1775, or forty years later.

Samuel Gist thought that if James had died leaving no sons, his closest male relative was a second cousin living in Bristol. Josiah Sellick was an accountant, forty-five years old in 1810. He was married; he had a daughter and, more important for Gist's purposes, a son. In the absence of male descendants of James Gist, Samuel Gist bequeathed all his land in England and the bulk of his stock, annuities, and cash to Sellick in trust, and after Sellick's death to his oldest son, and so on in each generation. To this inheritance he attached a condition. Anyone receiving it must adopt "the Surname of 'Gist' and in and by the Surname of Gist only and no other thenceforth for ever continue." Any person eligible to receive the inheritance who refused or neglected to abide by this requirement, Gist wrote, "shall thereupon be considered as dead."

In *The Times* and the *Morning Chronicle* on January 20, 1815, lists of deaths included: "On Monday last, at his home in Gower-street, Bedford-square. Samuel Gist, Esq. in the 91st year of his age." A list of January deaths in the *Monthly Magazine* read: "In Gower-street, Bedford square, 90, *Samuel Gist, esq.* leaving immense wealth." *The Gentleman's Magazine* gave a fuller obituary, adding that Gist "is said to have amassed more than half a million of money." He had "entered Lloyd's Coffee-house, and was one of its most fortunate adventurers." Josiah Sellick of Bristol looked "likely eventually to possess the bulk of his fortune, which is most unexpected, he having only occasionally had any communication with the deceased."

The bequest to Josiah Sellick was not the only surprise in Gist's will. He named as executors his sons-in-law, Martin Pearkes and William Fowke; his attorney, Francis Gregg; and his banker, George Clarke, of Walpole, Clarke & Bourne in Lombard Street. He bequeathed annuities, £50 or £100, to several relatives, and he established a fund for any relatives of his mother or father who might come forward. He ordered payments to the estates of three former associates in business—John Hiscox, John Wilkinson, and John Tabb—each of whom had accused him of unjust dealings. To his servants, Gist gave £20 or £30 each, depending upon length of service. To eight charities—the Bristol Infirmary, Christ's Hospital in London, London Hospital, the London Lying-in Hospital, the Welsh Charity School, the Hospital for the Reception of the Blind, the Vaccine Institution, and the Hospital for the Maintenance and Education of Exposed and Deserted Young Children—he bequeathed £100 each. His largest charitable bequest was £10,000 in 3 percent consolidated annuities, the proceeds of which were to be used by the Corporation of the City of Bristol to support six poor men, six poor women, six poor girls, and six or more poor boys attending charity school at Queen Elizabeth's Hospital, as he had done.

Gist's trust was to give each of his daughters £2,000 per year. To receive hers, Mary Pearkes must renounce all claim to the three quarter-shares in the Dismal Swamp Company and to all land and slaves in Virginia vested in her by act of the General Assembly. Gist wrote in his will: "Now I do declare that the same act was obtained only for the purpose of vesting such my Estates in Virginia in the same Mary Anderson (now Mary Pearkes) as being a native of and resident of that State In trust for me and my use and to be disposed of at any future period in the manner I should direct." If his daughter refused to surrender the Virginia property to his executors, "all and every sum and sums of money which she the said Mary Pearkes would have been entitled to and which I may give her by this my will shall not be paid and in lieu thereof I give to her the sum of one shilling only." A similar condition and threat applied to Elizabeth Fowke if she asserted any claim to the Virginia property. As a further incentive to cooperate with his will, Gist bequeathed to each daughter £1,000 in East India Company stock and £1,000 in Bank of England stock, "recommending it to them to be the last Stock they part with believing it to be the best."

All these bequests left Josiah Sellick—who became Josiah Gist within five weeks of his benefactor's death—with a fortune in trust totaling £153,686 4s. 6d. in personal property and 4,000 acres of farmland bringing in annual rents equal to about 4½ percent of their value.

Perhaps those most surprised by Gist's will were more than three hundred black people in Hanover, Goochland, and Amherst counties in Virginia. Having declared that these slaves belonged to him, Gist directed that they be freed. John Wickham had not heard from Gist since 1812, when the United States declared war on Britain. Not long after the war ended in 1815, Wickham learned that Gist was dead and that the will appointed himself and Matthew Toler, son of the late Benjamin Toler, Gist's longtime estate manager in Virginia, to the task of emancipating all Gist's slaves. A codicil to the will said that, if the General Assembly of Virginia deemed it "impolitic and perhaps improper" to fulfill his wish, the slaves were to work his plantations as before, with profits remitted to Mary Pearkes and Elizabeth Fowke until their deaths, thereafter to Josiah Sellick and his heirs.

Mary Pearkes and Elizabeth Fowke, with their husbands, sent a petition to the General Assembly in 1815. They said they thought their father's bequests to them were "very inadequate to their reasonable expectations, considering his very great estate." They were unhappy that the bulk of his wealth "has passed into the hands of strangers." Mary and Martin Pearkes denied that the property in Virginia belonged to Gist. Nevertheless, the sisters assented to Gist's will and asked the General Assembly to decide whether it would free the slaves. Gist had arranged his bequests so that if the slaves were freed each sister received £500 per year in lieu of profits from the plantations and the Dismal Swamp Company.

Gist apparently did not know that after 1806 Virginia law required any black person freed from slavery to leave the state within a year. Those who did not leave could be sold back into slavery, though this provision sometimes went unenforced. Gist knew that slaves would not be freed unless he provided for their support. To this end he left all his property in Virginia, "including my proportion of the Great Dismal Swamp," in trust to John Wickham and Matthew Toler, with instructions that its proceeds be devoted to support of these newly freed people, to schools for them, and to instruction in Christianity as taught by the Church of England. Manumission of his slaves, Gist wrote, was to occur within a year of his death.

John Wickham agreed to support the petition of Gist's daughters and to help win manumission for the slaves. The task of fulfilling the rest of Gist's instructions he entrusted to his son, William F. Wickham. John Wickham's friends in the General Assembly told him that the slaves would not be freed unless delegates and senators believed that these black people would leave the state. Sponsors of enabling legislation hinted that Gist's slaves might join the colony for free blacks established by British abolitionists in Sierra Leone. A law freeing Gist's slaves on condition of their departure from the state passed the General Assembly on February 26, 1816.

In a series of removals from 1818 until 1831, most of the freed blacks settled in southern Ohio, on tracts purchased with money from sales of Gist's land in Virginia. In May 1818 one of his quarter-shares in the Dismal Swamp Company was bought by the new Dismal Swamp Land Company, another by the younger Fielding Lewis, and the third by the College of William and Mary. These three quarter-shares sold at auction for a total of $10,849.87½. The buyers paid cash.

Gist's slaves gained their freedom more slowly than he had directed partly because the General Assembly's act left his Virginia estate subject to suits. The chief litigants were relatives of William Anderson and relatives of the widow of Gist's stepson, Joseph Smith. The Andersons believed that Gist had cheated his daughter's first husband. The Rooteses believed that Gist had stolen the patrimony of his wife's sons by her first marriage. He had grown rich through his unscrupulousness, then devised a will by which they would receive no land, no cash, and no slaves. His only bequest to any kinsman of his wife's was a gold watch. What did he mean that gift to suggest? In John Marshall's Circuit Court, William Anderson's legatees, represented by William Wirt and others, eventually won a judgment of more than $17,000 against Gist's Virginia estate at the expense of Gist's legatees, the free blacks.

In later years the black people who moved to Ohio underwent hardships and complained of injustices at the hands of William F. Wickham's agents.

Stories gathered around Gist's bequest. At best, they said, his trustees had not disbursed proceeds of his Virginia estate as he had directed. At worst, Gist's freed former slaves and their descendants, rightful heirs to all his vast fortune in England and America, had been denied their rich legacy by the Wickhams, John Marshall, and other Virginians.

In London, Samuel Gist's heirs sued one another in the Court of Chancery. Suits by Josiah Gist, formerly Josiah Sellick, against Gist's daughters overlapped suits by Mary Pearkes, joined by her sister and brother-in-law, against Martin Pearkes and Gist's attorney Francis Gregg. In the end, Gist's wishes prevailed. The Bristol accountant Josiah Gist became a landed gentleman, moving to his seat at Wormington. He was succeeded by his son, renamed Samuel Gist Gist. Nine years after Samuel Gist's death, his namesake was married to Marianne Westenra, daughter of Baron Rossmore of Monaghan. The baron's son and heir was married to Anne Douglas-Hamilton, illegitimate daughter of the eighth Duke of Hamilton. The son of Samuel Gist Gist and Marianne Westenra Gist—Samuel Gist—inherited the Gist estate.

Long afterward, tourists with an interest in Gothic architecture visited the church dedicated to St. Catherine in Wormington. It was a mixture of elements, mostly fourteenth-century Perpendicular but with eighteenth-century additions, a Tudor arch, fragments of medieval stained glass, and an Anglo-Saxon or Norman crucifix. Beyond its narrow nave, in the chancel, stone tablets on the wall commemorated Gists. One blue stone read: "Sacred to the Memory of Samuel Gist, Esqr. Patron of Church and Lord of Manor, who died Jany 15, 1815, Aged 92 Years." This inscription was not quite accurate, but hardly any visitors would know. Nor would connoisseurs of architecture care that they stood not far from Gist's marble coffin. They saw heraldic devices on hatchments in the church. Among these were the three blue fleurs-de-lis and three silver swans in the arms of the House of Gist, with its motto: *Benigno numine*—Beneficent by divine will.

Four weeks after Samuel Gist's death, Sally Meade Byrd died. Since 1800 she and her husband had lived in Ohio. Early in their life together, David Meade worried about his daughter and her husband, "whose prospects have not been very promising since the bankruptcy of Mr. Morris." But in 1800, "thro' the interest of his friends in Philadelphia," Charles Willing Byrd was appointed secretary of the Northwestern Territory. In the fall of 1802 he reported to President Jefferson that Governor Arthur St. Clair, a Federalist, was obstructing his work and preventing him from appointing Republicans to territorial offices. Jefferson removed St. Clair. The following year Ohio became a state, and Jefferson rewarded Byrd with an appointment as judge of the United States District Court. In 1814, by Mary Willing Byrd's will, Charles and Sally Byrd's three sons, as well as the boys' male first cousins, became joint owners of their grandmother's quarter-share in the Dismal Swamp Company. Three years after Sally Byrd's death, Charles Willing Byrd was married to Hannah Miles.

David and Sarah Meade lived contentedly at Chaumière des Prairies. With "refined courtesy" David Meade received guests in an octagonal wainscotted drawing room. He still wore a square-cut coat with big cuffs, long vest, knee breeches, and black or white stockings in the fashion of the days when he had published an acrostic love poem to Miss Waters. Sarah Meade wore stays, a long-waisted dress with ruffles, and a white apron and cap. She greeted guests in "a very mild and pleasant" way. She entertained them by expertly playing her pianoforte "with the cheerfulness of a girl of 16."

Among the Meades' forty slaves were cooks, dining room servants, footmen, a coachman, a butler, valets, housemaids, and the people whose labor carried out David Meade's fanciful designs for his gardens and grounds. With shaded avenues, bridges over streams, a lake with an artificial island reached by an arched white bridge, a Grecian temple along the lakeshore called the Temple of the Naiads, Chaumière des Prairies occupied Meade for thirty years. He wrote: "I may with confidence assume that my gardens containing forty acres including ten acres of native wood are more extensive than any other in the United States."

In 1826, David Meade at the age of eighty-two, and Sarah Meade at the age of about seventy-seven, took in their granddaughter, Mary Willing Byrd Randolph, and her daughters. Her husband, Patrick H. Randolph, had proven irresponsible, and her father, Judge Byrd, rejected her, saying that if the Meades sent her to him, he would send her back. David Meade could hardly believe the transformation in "the son of the splendid dignified & highly polished Colo. Byrd of Westover." Charles Willing Byrd had not "cohabited" with his wife for some time. He spoke of resigning his judgeship. And, "most extraordinary," Meade said, "He and His youngest Son William have joined the Shaker community in Marion County." Upon reaching the society at Pleasant Hill, Kentucky, William S. Byrd, twenty years old, obeyed Shaker teachings about property. He arranged for his sister, Evelyn, to receive dividends from "my dismal swamp interest, which is likely to become much more valuable than it has been."

William Wirt completed his study of Patrick Henry in September 1817, and the book was published in November. He began gathering material in 1805, asking for written recollections by those who remembered Henry during the Revolution. Wirt had thought about writing a series of biographical volumes, but the first one gave him so much trouble that he did not try another.

In his years of intermittent work on *Sketches of the Life and Character of Patrick Henry*, Wirt made his name, as Henry had done, in the practice of law. In 1807 he served as a prosecutor in the trial of former Vice President Aaron Burr on charges of treason. John Wickham and others won the case for the defense, but Wirt won new fame. William and Elizabeth Wirt moved to Richmond in 1810, a sign that he had reached the top rank of the Virginia bar.

Looking at letters from old men describing Henry and at documents from Henry's day, Wirt complained about the difficulties of his task. The old men's memories disagreed with one another and sometimes with official records and newspaper accounts. Thomas Jefferson at first thought that Speaker Robinson and his allies had tried to enact a loan office "in 1762, or a year sooner or later," rather than in 1765. Wirt wished to write expansively, letting his imagination and his rhetoric flow freely, but he felt constrained by the requirements of a chronological narrative and by the limits of evidence. He called it the "business of stating facts with rigid precision, not one jot more or less than the truth." "[W]hat the deuce," he protested, "has a lawyer to do with truth." He fretted that political partisans would find fault with him for either excessive praise or excessive censure of Henry. He feared that literary men would think his book trivial.

When *Sketches of the Life and Character of Patrick Henry* was published, it fell short of a biography. Wirt called it "these crude sketches," which he intended to be didactic—"a discourse on rhetoric, patriotism and morals." He dedicated the book to the young men of Virginia. With his political story, containing his attempts to reconstruct Henry's speeches and to describe their effect on listeners, Wirt celebrated Virginia's leaders of the American Revolution, holding them up for emulation. He wrote to a friend about the General Assembly in 1808: "you will see how wofully the legislative council has fallen since the days of Pendleton, Wythe, Henry, Jefferson, Richard Henry Lee, etc." His book invited young men to take such great men as their exemplars. In an essay published in 1814 he wrote: "Were not these men, giants in mind and heroism? Compared with them, what is the present generation, but a puny race of dwarfs and pigmies?" In his portraits of society Wirt drew on his imagination to dramatize the difference between colonial Virginia and democratic Virginia.

The foils for both of Wirt's contrasts—of great revolutionaries with modern politicians and of the old colonial order with modern life—were the "aristocrats" of the days before the Stamp Act. Wirt embodied the rule of "aristocrats" in his version of the colonial capital. In Williamsburg, "fashion and high life" prevailed: Governor Fauquier lived in "royal state"; the burgesses followed "stately modes of life" in houses of "costly profusion." Amid this "general elegance" there abruptly appears Patrick Henry, an awkward man in threadbare clothes. On his first page Wirt portrayed Henry's parents living "in easy circumstances . . . among the most respectable inhabitants of the colony." Yet, for dramatic and didactic purposes, Henry must be a man of the people. Describing his book, Wirt wrote: "It was from the body of the yeomanry, whom my correspondent represents as looking askance at those above them, that Mr. Henry proceeded." Wirt's correspondent was Thomas Jefferson. Alert to the possibility of criticism, Wirt suspected that "the descendants of our landed aristocracy" might resent strictures on their ancestors which he had borrowed from Jefferson. Wirt meant nothing personal. He only used those dead "aristocrats" to edify young men entering public life. His closest friends in Virginia were descendants of colonial "aristocrats."

Thomas Jefferson knew the difference between aristocrats in Britain or France and the men who ran the Council and the House of Burgesses in his youth. He acknowledged to Wirt that in politics during the contest with the British ministry after the Stamp Act was repealed, "the old leaders of the house being substantially firm, we had not after this any differences of opn in the H. of B. on matters of principles." Jefferson's chief concern was "the spirit of favoritism" pervading John Robinson's speakership and alliances. The proposed loan office in 1765 epitomized for Jefferson the evils of the old system. He remembered and described for Wirt a withering speech Patrick Henry had made against the proposal, with the result that "it was crushed in its birth." In fact, the loan office passed the House of Burgesses but was rejected by the "aristocrats" on the Council. As a convenient word for the method by which Virginia was governed in Speaker Robinson's day and for the men who governed it, Jefferson chose "aristocracy," and William Wirt followed his example. Francis Lightfoot Lee, praising John Adams as a "genuine" republican, turned the tables by writing: "Jefferson in my opinion, is a very good Aristocrat."

Patrick Henry's son-in-law, Spencer Roane, who had been three years old when Henry spoke against the loan office and the Stamp Act, described for Wirt his father's admiration of Henry: "That a plain man, of ordinary though respected family, should beard the aristocracy by whom we were then cursed and ruled, and overthrow them in the cause of independence, was grateful to a man of my father's Whig principles." Roane treated the election of Henry rather than Secretary Nelson to the governorship in 1776 as a triumph over "the aristocracy." Roane explained to Wirt that Patrick Henry had not really become a Federalist in his last years but had remained "a true and genuine Republican." Only his "debility" and the "seductions" of a Federalist aristocrat, Henry Lee, with his offer of tracts in the Land of Eden, had made Henry temporarily weak.

Wirt believed that the purposes of his book justified his passing lightly over Henry's "aberrations," such as collaborating with Federalists and amassing land and money. Wirt asked Jefferson: "Will not his biographer then be excused in drawing the veil over them and holding up the brighter side of his character, only, to imitation?" Jefferson's answer, given to others, not to Wirt, was no. He said: "it is a poor book, written in bad taste, & gives so imperfect an idea of Patrick Henry, that it seems intended to show off the *writer*, more than the subject of the work." John Randolph of Roanoke, no democrat, wrote: "I have seen, too, a romance, called the Life of Patrick Henry—a wretched piece of fustian." Spencer Roane, on the other hand, praised Wirt's book. The public attention it received was generally favorable, and it went through many editions. St. George Tucker encouraged his friend during the years that Wirt did research in hours taken from the practice of law. Tucker tried to re-create Henry's oratory for Wirt. Nevertheless, Tucker doubted that anyone could capture in prose the dead leaders of Virginia. And he thought that few would care to read an attempt. "Who knows any thing of Peyton Randolph once the most popular man in Virginia, Speaker of the House of Burgesses, & President of Congress, from its first assembling to the day of his Death?" Unlike Wirt, Tucker did not have to rely on documents and other people's reminiscences for his knowledge of men such as John Blair, General Thomas Nelson, Jr., and Beverley Randolph. "I knew them all well, nay *intimately*. Yet for the soul of me, I could not write ten pages of either, that would be read by one in fifty." Tucker admired the great men of his youth in Williamsburg. He agreed that their virtues deserved emulation. He wrote to Wirt: "I think it much to be regretted that such men as I have mentioned above should descend to the Grave, and be forgotten, as soon as the Earth is thrown upon their Coffins. But so it is, my friend."

. . .

In the autumn of 1803, after the birth of her daughter, Elizabeth Wirt read Gothic novels—fiction in the vein of Horace Walpole's *The Castle of Otranto* and Ann Radcliffe's *A Sicilian Romance* and *The Mysteries of Udolpho*—tales of dark castles with abandoned chambers and underground passageways, eerily lit rooms hiding ancient manuscripts revealing guilty family secrets, halls in which perturbed spirits of the dead walk by night as ghosts.

William Wirt was traveling between Richmond and Norfolk in the first week of November. He stopped for the night at Westover on Wednesday, November 8, not long before sunset. He turned his horse and gig out of the road, passing through the first gate. For more than a mile his gig rolled through an oak grove. Around the trees the ground was a smooth, clean turf. Beyond a second gate, he entered a broad lane lined with rail fences. Emerging from the oak grove, he saw the last sunlight glinting in the windows of the Byrd mansion. On his left lay the vast expanse of Westover's famous meadows. To his right he had a view of the James River, a sloop moored near the house, and, in the distance on the south bank, the gardens and house of Maycox.

Two rows of uniform, whitewashed log cabins facing each other across a street were the quarters of Mary Willing Byrd's slaves. Close to the house lay the garden, with its statuary and ponds. A circular road passing stables and other buildings took Wirt's gig to the ornate north door of the mansion. Mary Willing Byrd, her daughter and granddaughters, and Judge Nelson were away on a pleasure trip. Wirt was met by a dignified old black man wearing a wig. He was Jack White, who had been body servant to Mary Willing Byrd's husband during the war against the French and the Indians. Her husband, in the last years before he killed himself, used to say that Jack White "on different occasions saved me from the grave." Now, family legend said, her husband's spirit returned nightly to the room in which he had died, "there to sit by the fire and meditate." Jack White took care of Wirt's needs. At night, Wirt had the house to himself.

Trying to do some work before going to bed, Wirt needed a few of Judge Nelson's law books. The bookcase was upstairs, where not all rooms were in use. Since sunset the wind had picked up. Wirt heard shutters rattle.

Almost every occupied room in the mansion had portraits hanging along the walls. In his movements Wirt could see likenesses of Mary Willing Byrd, of her late husband, of her mother Ann Shippen Willing, of Judge Nelson, of Elizabeth Byrd, who had married, in turn, James Parke Farley, John Dunbar, and Henry Skipwith. There were several portraits of old Colonel William Byrd, whose expression suggested that he was enjoying a joke not understood by the onlooker. His body lay buried in the garden just outside the west end of the house. One of the portraits from Queen Anne's time showed that fierce rake, old Colonel Byrd's first father-in-law, Colonel Daniel Parke, who had been murdered by the queen's subjects in Antigua.

Judge Nelson was not a systematic man, but Wirt found the law books and made his way back downstairs. As he worked, the wind roared and sighed around the house. The last thing he did that night was to write a letter to his wife. He never could resist making a little fun. Had he not just won celebrity by writing a volume of fun, *The Letters of the British Spy*? He wrote to Elizabeth Wirt: "I have been about a mile and a half up the stairs to look for a couple of law books. It reminds me of the old castles you are reading about. I dare say it is as full of ghosts as any of them—& as the family is all gone, & left the house to them, I suppose we shall have a carousal tonight—Maybe old Colo. Byrd will come & give me a little more information about the dismal swamp against the next edition of the British Spy."

NOTES

Since many of the stories in this book are not well known, these endnotes identify the sources of quotations and the main evidence for the narrative. Page numbers and key words indicate passages in the text to which the notes refer. Throughout, I have tried to record my many obligations to the work of other scholars. The citations do not differentiate between manuscripts in archives I visited and manuscripts I read in the form of photocopies—chiefly, though not solely, in the microfilm collection of the Colonial Williamsburg Foundation Library.

Rather than cite repeatedly a number of widely read scholars of Virginia's history, I list their books here, with the understanding that their works bear on many aspects of my narrative:

Warren M. Billings, John E. Selby, and Thad W. Tate, *Colonial Virginia: A History* (White Plains, 1986); T. H. Breen, *Tobacco Culture: The Mentality of the Great Tidewater Planters on the Eve of the Revolution* (Princeton, 1985); Richard Beale Davis, *Intellectual Life in the Colonial South, 1585–1763* (Knoxville, 1978); Jack P. Greene, *Pursuits of Happiness: The Social Development of Early Modern British Colonies and the Formation of American Culture* (Chapel Hill, 1988); Jack P. Greene, *The Quest for Power: The Lower Houses of Assembly in the Southern Royal Colonies, 1689–1776* (Chapel Hill, 1963); Rhys Isaac, *The Transformation of Virginia, 1740–1790* (Chapel Hill, 1982); Allan Kulikoff, *Tobacco and Slaves: The Development of Southern Cultures in the Chesapeake, 1680–1800* (Chapel Hill, 1986); Kenneth A. Lockridge, *The Diary, and Life, of William Byrd II of Virginia, 1674–1744* (Chapel Hill, 1987); Pierre Marambaud, *William Byrd of Westover, 1674–1744* (Charlottesville, 1971); Drew R. McCoy, *The Elusive Republic: Political Economy in Jeffersonian America* (Chapel Hill, 1980); Drew R. McCoy, *The Last of the Fathers: James Madison and the Republican Legacy* (Cambridge, 1989); Arthur Pierce Middleton, *Tobacco Coast: A Maritime History of Chesapeake Bay in the Colonial Era* (Newport News, 1953);

Notes

Edmund S. Morgan, *American Slavery, American Freedom: The Ordeal of Colonial Virginia* (New York, 1975); and Charles S. Sydnor, *Gentlemen Freeholders: Political Practices in Washington's Virginia* (Chapel Hill, 1952).

ABBREVIATIONS

Add MSS	Additional Manuscripts
Adm	Admiralty
AfEcH	*African Economic History*
AHR	*American Historical Review*
AN	*American Neptune*
AO	Audit Office
C	Chancery
CaOTP	Toronto Public Library, Metropolitan Reference Center
CHR	*Canadian Historical Review*
CO	Colonial Office
CSmH	Henry E. Huntington Library, San Marino, California
DeWint-M	Henry Francis duPont Winterthur Museum—Joseph Downs Manuscript Collection, Winterthur, Delaware
DLC	Library of Congress, Washington, D.C.
DNA	National Archives, Washington, D.C.
E	Exchequer
EcHR	*Economic History Review*
EnHR	*English Historical Review*
ExEcH	*Explorations in Economic History*
FCHQ	*Filson Club History Quarterly*
HCA	High Court of Admiralty
HIJES	*Hampton Institute Journal of Ethnic Studies*
HJ	*Historical Journal*
HLQ	*Huntington Library Quarterly*
HO	Home Office
HR	*Historical Research*
JAfH	*Journal of African History*
JAmS	*Journal of American Studies*
JBS	*Journal of British Studies*
JCarH	*Journal of Caribbean History*
JEcBH	*Journal of Economic and Business History*
JEcH	*Journal of Economic History*
JMH	*Journal of Modern History*
JNH	*Journal of Negro History*
JSH	*Journal of Southern History*
KHSR	*Kentucky Historical Society Register*
KyLoF	Filson Club Historical Society, Louisville, Kentucky
KyU	University of Kentucky, Lexington
LU	Louisiana State University, Baton Rouge

MACH	*Magazine of Albemarle County History*
MdAA	Maryland Hall of Records Division, Annapolis
MdBHi	Maryland Historical Society, Baltimore
MH	Harvard University, Cambridge, Massachusetts
MHM	*Maryland Historical Magazine*
MiU-C	William L. Clements Library, Ann Arbor, Michigan
MM	*Mariner's Mirror*
Nc-Ar	North Carolina Division of Archives and History, Raleigh
NcD	Duke University, Durham, North Carolina
NCHR	*North Carolina Historical Review*
NcU	University of North Carolina, Chapel Hill
NN	New York Public Library, New York
NNHi	New-York Historical Society, New York
NNPM	Pierpont Morgan Library, New York
NYH	*New York History*
PaH	*Pennsylvania History*
PHarH-Ar	Pennsylvania Historical and Museum Commission, Division of Archives and Manuscripts, Harrisburg
PHi	Historical Society of Pennsylvania, Philadelphia
PMHB	*Pennsylvania Magazine of History and Biography*
PP	*Past and Present*
PPAmP	American Philosophical Society, Philadelphia, Pennsylvania
PRO	Public Record Office, London
RIH	*Rhode Island History*
RPJCB	John Carter Brown Library, Providence, Rhode Island
SA	*Slavery and Abolition*
SCHM	*South Carolina Historical Magazine*
SHR	*Scottish Historical Review*
SP	State Papers
SRO	Scottish Record Office, National Archives of Scotland, Edinburgh
T	Treasury
TQHGM	*Tyler's Quarterly Historical and Genealogical Magazine*
Uk	British Library, London
UkENL	National Library of Scotland, Edinburgh
UkEU	Edinburgh University Library
UkSh	Sheffield City Library
USCCVD(EC)	United States Circuit Court, Virginia District, Ended Cases
VG	*Virginia Genealogist*
Vi	Library of Virginia (formerly Virginia State Library), Richmond
ViFreJM	James Monroe Museum, Fredericksburg, Virginia
ViRHi	Virginia Historical Society, Richmond

ViRVal	Valentine Museum, Richmond, Virginia
ViU	University of Virginia, Charlottesville
ViW	College of William and Mary, Williamsburg, Virginia
ViWC	Colonial Williamsburg Foundation Library, Williamsburg, Virginia
VMHB	*Virginia Magazine of History and Biography*
WHi	State Historical Society of Wisconsin, Madison
WHR	*Welsh History Review*
WMQ	*William and Mary Quarterly*
WO	War Office

PROLOGUE

PAGE

ix Thomas Moore, *Epistles, Odes, and Other Poems* (London, 1806), 38–40, 21n; Thomas Moore to Anastasia Moore, Nov. 7, 28, Dec. 2, 1803, *The Letters of Thomas Moore*, ed. Wilfred S. Dowden (Oxford, 1964), I, 50–55; Frederick Horner, *The History of the Blair, Banister, and Braxton Families* (Philadelphia, 1898), 108–109; Benson J. Lossing, "Tom Moore in America," *Harper's New Monthly Magazine*, LV (Sept. 1877), 537–541; entries of March 16–17, 1853, Diary of Benson J. Lossing, LS 1116, CSmH; *Norfolk Herald*, Oct. 6, 1803; Hoover H. Jordan, *Bolt Upright: The Life of Thomas Moore* (Salzburg, 1975), I, 92–95; Howard Mumford Jones, *The Harp That Once—A Chronicle of the Life of Thomas Moore* (New York, 1937), 68–70; Thérèse Tessier, *La poésie lyrique de Thomas Moore* (Paris, 1976), 90.

I: THE LAND OF PROMISE

3 Great Dismal Swamp: [William Wirt], *The Letters of the British Spy* (Richmond, 1803), 3–4.

5 "a sly" . . . "parts": [James Kirke Paulding], *Letters from the South* (New York, 1817), I, 21–29. See also Kevin J. Hayes, *The Library of William Byrd of Westover* (Madison, 1997), 3–103; Margaret Beck Pritchard and Virginia Lascara Sites, *William Byrd II and His Lost History: Engravings of the Americas* (Williamsburg, 1993), chap. 2; Peter Martin, *The Pleasure Gardens of Virginia: From Jamestown to Jefferson* (Princeton, 1991), 64–77; C. Allan Brown, "Eighteenth-Century Virginia Plantation Gardens: Translating an Ancient Idyll," in Therese O'Malley and Marc Treib, eds., *Regional Garden Design in the United States* (Washington, 1995), 125–162; Mark R. Wenger, "Westover: William Byrd's Mansion Reconsidered" (M. Arch. Hist. thesis, University of Virginia, 1980); Daniel D. Reiff, *Small Georgian Houses in England and Virginia: Origins and Development through the 1750s* (London, 1986), 241–246.

effects of the plague: [William Byrd], *A Discourse Concerning the Plague* (London, 1721).

"a great" . . . Profitable": William Byrd, *The Writings of "Colonel William Byrd of Westover in Virginia Esqr.,"* ed. John Spencer Bassett (New York, 1901), 72.

a petition: [William Byrd], "To the Kings most Excellent Majty," [1729], BR Box 256(29), CSmH.

PAGE

7 "the old . . . Company": B. Henry Latrobe to James Wood, Feb. 14, 1798, *The Virginia Journals of Benjamin Henry Latrobe*, ed. Edward C. Carter II *et al.* (New Haven, 1977), II, 364.

9 "old Colo. Byrd": William Wirt to Elizabeth Wirt, Nov. 8, 1803, William Wirt Papers, MdBHi.

   city of Richmond: Sarah S. Hughes, *Surveyors and Statesmen: Land Measuring in Colonial Virginia* ([Richmond], 1979), 135.

   south of the James: H. R. McIlwaine, ed., *Legislative Journals of the Council of Colonial Virginia*, 2d ed. (Richmond, 1979), 80–81; H. R. McIlwaine, ed., *Executive Journals of the Council of Virginia* (Richmond, 1928), III, 49, 80, 107, 131–133, 136; William L. Saunders *et al.*, eds., *Colonial Records of North Carolina* (Raleigh, 1886–), I, 357–358, 740; Michael L. Nicholls, "Origins of the Virginia Southside, 1703–1753: A Social and Economic Study" (Ph.D. diss., College of William and Mary, 1972), 72–79.

10 "no . . . Dismall": Entry of May 24, 1710, "A Journall of the Proceedings of Philip Ludwell and Nathll Harrison," *VMHB*, V (July 1897), 9; Saunders *et al.*, eds., *Colonial Records of North Carolina*, I, 735–746.

11 "our land . . . innocence": William Byrd to Earl of Orrery, Feb. 2, 1727, *The Correspondence of the Three William Byrds*, ed. Marion Tinling (Charlottesville, 1977), I, 358. Most of the sources for a description of the Dismal Swamp are listed in the bibliography of Paul W. Kirk, Jr., ed., *The Great Dismal Swamp* (Charlottesville, 1979). See also Gerald F. Levy, "Atlantic White Cedar in the Great Dismal Swamp," in Aimlee D. Laderman, ed., *Atlantic White Cedar Wetlands* (Boulder, 1987), 57–68. Other sources, primarily manuscripts, are cited below.

   "no difference" . . . "men": John Urmston to the Secretary of the Society for the Propagation of the Gospel, July 7, 1711, Saunders *et al.*, eds., *Colonial Records of North Carolina*, I, 770, 767.

   "Borderers": Byrd, *Writings of Byrd*, ed. Bassett, 47.

   "The Inhabitants . . . admiration": George Burrington to Board of Trade, Feb. 20, 1732, Saunders *et al.*, eds., *Colonial Records of North Carolina*, III, 337–338.

12 "the disputed bounds": Hugh Jones, *The Present State of Virginia*, ed. Richard L. Morton (Chapel Hill, 1956 [orig. publ. London, 1724]), 89. See also A. Roger Ekirch, *"Poor Carolina": Politics and Society in Colonial North Carolina, 1729–1776* (Chapel Hill, 1981), 4–36.

   "The fire . . . streets": John Perceval to William Byrd, Oct. 15, 1720, *Correspondence of the Byrds*, ed. Tinling, I, 330.

13 "the opinion of mankind": Malachy Postlethwayt, *The Universal Dictionary of Trade and Commerce*, 4th ed. (New York, 1971 [orig. publ. London, 1774]), II, "South Sea Company."

   "Five hundred . . . paper!": [Lewis Saul Benjamin], *The South Sea Bubble* (Boston, 1923), 148. See also entries of June 2, July 14, Sept. 23, 30, 1720, Diary, in *The Family Memoirs of the Rev. William Stukeley*, Surtees Society, LXXIII, LXXVI, LXXX (1880–85), I, 59–61.

   "the ruinous" . . . "times": Robert Carter to John Carter, Feb. 14, 1721, *Letters of Robert Carter, 1720–1727*, ed. Louis B. Wright (San Marino, 1940), 79; John Custis to "Gentlemen," [ca. 1721], John Custis Letter Book, DLC; entries of Dec. 11, 12, 1720, William Byrd, *The London Diary (1717–1721) and Other Writings*, ed. Louis B. Wright and Marion Tinling (New York, 1958), 485.

PAGE

13 "the author . . . Alley": Thomas Mortimer, *Every Man His Own Broker; Or, A Guide to Exchange Alley*, 6th ed. (London, 1765), v. See also John Carswell, *The South Sea Bubble*, rev. ed. (Stroud, 1993); P. G. M. Dickson, *The Financial Revolution in England: A Study in the Development of Public Credit, 1688–1756* (New York, 1967), 33–159; E. Victor Morgan and W. A. Thomas, *The Stock Exchange: Its History and Functions*, 2d ed. (London, 1969), chap. 2; R. S. Neale, *Bath, 1680–1850: A Social History* (London, 1981), 121–129.

14 "cast . . . Sigh'd": William Byrd, *William Byrd's Histories of the Dividing Line betwixt Virginia and North Carolina*, ed. William K. Boyd (New York, 1967 [orig. publ. Raleigh, 1929]), 45.
"Criminals . . . State": Byrd, *Writings of Byrd*, ed. Bassett, 41.

15 "so barren" . . . "publick": Saunders *et al.*, eds., *Colonial Records of North Carolina*, II, 779–780.
"strange": *Ibid.*, 788–790. See also 2d ser., VII, 554–569.

16 commissioners: Ekirch, *Poor Carolina*, 57–59; Hugh T. Lefler and William S. Powell, *Colonial North Carolina: A History* (New York, 1973), 87–88, 116–118; Robert J. Cain, ed., *North Carolina Higher–Court Minutes, 1724–1730* (Raleigh, 1981), xii–lviii.
20,000 acres: William Byrd to Gabriel Johnston, [1735?], *Correspondence of the Byrds*, ed. Tinling, II, 449.
"the most . . . saw": William Byrd to John Perceval, June 10, 1729, *ibid.*, I, 404.
"the Land of Eden": William Byrd to Johann Rudolph Ochs, [1735?], *ibid.*, II, 451.
"to add . . . Characters": Byrd, *Writings of Byrd*, ed. Bassett, 314; David Smith, "William Byrd Surveys America," *Early American Literature*, XI (1976–77), 296–310.

17 Parke's will: Helen Hill Miller, *Colonel Parke of Virginia: "The Greatest Hector in the Town"* (Chapel Hill, 1989); Jo Zuppan, "John Custis of Williamsburg, 1678–1749," *VMHB*, XC (April 1982), 177–197; Paula A. Treckel, " 'The Empire of My Heart': The Marriage of William Byrd II and Lucy Parke Byrd," *VMHB*, CV (1997), 125–156; Jacob M. Price, *Perry of London: A Family and a Firm on the Seaborne Frontier, 1615–1753* (Cambridge, 1992), 68–69; Douglas Southall Freeman, *George Washington: A Biography* (New York, 1948–57), II, 280–291.
"that little bastard": John Custis to William Byrd, [ca. Jan. 1725], *Correspondence of the Byrds*, ed. Tinling, I, 351.

18 "no longer . . . Land": Wilmer L. Hall, ed., *Executive Journals of the Council of Colonial Virginia*, 2d ed. (Richmond, 1967), V, 38. See also John Bartram to William Byrd, [Nov. 1738], *The Correspondence of John Bartram, 1734–1777*, ed. Edmund Berkeley and Dorothy Smith Berkeley (Gainesville, 1992), 98–99; Albert B. Faust, "Swiss Emigration to the American Colonies in the Eighteenth Century," *AHR*, XXII (Oct. 1916), 42; Ned C. Landsman, *From Colonials to Provincials: American Thought and Culture, 1680–1760* (New York, 1997), 41; Michael J. Rozbicki, *The Complete Colonial Gentleman: Cultural Legitimacy in Plantation America* (Charlottesville, 1998); Richard Godbeer, "William Byrd's 'Flourish': The Sexual Cosmos of a Southern Planter," in Merril D. Smith, ed., *Sex and Sexuality in Early America* (New York, 1998), 135–162; Dana D. Nelson, *The Word in Black and White: Reading "Race" in American Literature, 1638–1867* (New York, 1992), 29–37; Donald T. Siebert, Jr., "William Byrd's *Histories of the Line*: The Fashioning of a Hero," *American Literature*, XLVII (Jan. 1976), 535–551; Norman S. Grabo, "Going Steddy:

William Byrd's Literary Masquerade," *Yearbook of English Studies*, XIII (1983), 84–96; Susan Manning, "Industry and Idleness in Colonial Virginia: A New Approach to William Byrd II," *JAmS*, XXVIII (Aug. 1994), 169–190; Richard Beale Davis, *Literature and Society in Early Virginia, 1608–1840* (Baton Rouge, 1973), 98–132; David Bertelson, *The Lazy South* (New York, 1967), 68–85.

19 "that plague . . . Company": Robert Carter to John Pemberton, May 26, 1721, *Letters of Carter*, ed. Wright, 93.

"plain" . . . "us": Robert Carter to William Dawkins, Feb. 23, 1721, *ibid.*, 80–81.

"lay . . . well": Entries of Sept. 28–Oct. 1, 1720, Byrd, *London Diary*, ed. Wright and Tinling, 456–457; William M. S. Rasmussen, "Drafting the Plans," in Charles E. Brownell *et al., The Making of Virginia Architecture* (Richmond, 1992), 8.

"a dunce . . . blockhead": Robert Carter to Richard Perry, July 13, 1720, *Letters of Carter*, ed. Wright, 4.

"one of . . . knew": John Page, Memoir, *Virginia Historical Register*, III (July 1850), 144.

"Walpool": Robert Carter to Thomas, Lord Fairfax, June 24, 1729, Papers of the Fairfax Estate, Add MSS 30306, f. 91, Uk.

20 "dear friend": Mann Page, Will, Jan. 24, 1730, *VMHB*, XXXII (Jan. 1924), 41.

"great tract": Robert Carter to Thomas Hooper, July 3, 1720, *Letters of Carter*, ed. Wright, 49.

"the best . . . Virginia": Entry of June 28, 1732, "Virginia in 1732: The Travel Journal of William Hugh Grove," ed. Gregory A. Stiverson and Patrick H. Butler, III, *VMHB*, LXXXV (Jan. 1977), 26. See also Richard L. Bushman, *The Refinement of America: Persons, Houses, Cities* (New York, 1992), 113–114; Reiff, *Small Georgian Houses*, 288–294.

21 "very angry": John Carter to Micajah Perry, July 2, 1737, Carter Family Letterbook, ViU. George Washington: George Washington to John Posey, June 24, 1767, *The Papers of George Washington, Colonial Series*, ed. W. W. Abbot *et al.* (Charlottesville, 1983–), VIII, 3. On Carter, see also Edmund Berkeley, Jr., "Robert 'King' Carter" (M.A. thesis, University of Virginia, 1961); Louis Morton, *Robert Carter of Nomini Hall: A Virginia Planter of the Eighteenth Century* (Williamsburg, 1941), chap. 1; Manning C. Voorhis, "Crown versus Council in the Virginia Land Policy," *WMQ*, 3d ser., III (Oct. 1946), 499–514; Robert D. Mitchell, *Commercialism and Frontier: Perspectives on the Early Shenandoah Valley* (Charlottesville, 1977); Kenton Kilmer and Donald Sweig, *The Fairfax Family in Fairfax County* (Fairfax, 1975), chap. 1; Victor Dennis Golladay, "The Nicholas Family of Virginia, 1722–1820" (Ph.D. diss., University of Virginia, 1973), 1–37; Clifford Dowdey, *The Virginia Dynasties: The Emergence of "King" Carter and the Golden Age* (Boston, 1969), chaps. 5–10; Holly Brewer, "Entailing Aristocracy in Colonial Virginia: 'Ancient Feudal Restraints' and Revolutionary Reform," *WMQ*, 3d ser., LIV (April 1997), 328–332; William Keith, *The History of the British Plantations in America* (London, 1738), 184–185.

"Examine . . . Choose": Entry of June 28, 1732, "Journal of Grove," ed. Stiverson and Butler, *VMHB*, LXXXV (Jan. 1977), 31–32.

21 "a man" . . . "by them": William Byrd to John Perceval, July 12, 1736, *Correspondence of the Byrds*, ed. Tinling, II, 487–488.

25 "drained . . . Cash": Charles Steuart to Thomas Ogilvie, July 25, 1752, Charles Steuart Letterbooks, PHi.

PAGE

25 John Custis: John Custis to Mr. Loyd, 1736, Custis Letter Book, Custis-Lee Families Papers, DLC. On expansion of slavery, see Lorena S. Walsh, "Slave Life, Slave Society, and Tobacco Production in the Tidewater Chesapeake, 1620–1820," in Ira Berlin and Philip D. Morgan, eds., *Cultivation and Culture: Labor and the Shaping of Slave Life in the Americas* (Charlottesville, 1993), 170–199; James A. Rawley, *The Transatlantic Slave Trade: A History* (New York, 1981), 164–183, 400–405; Herbert S. Klein, *The Middle Passage: Comparative Studies in the Atlantic Slave Trade* (Princeton, 1978), chap. 6; Susan Westbury, "Slaves of Colonial Virginia: Where They Came From," *WMQ*, 3d ser., XLII (April 1985), esp. 235–236; Walter Minchinton, Celia King, and Peter Waite, eds., *Virginia Slave-Trade Statistics, 1698–1775* (Richmond, 1984).

26 "a monotonous ... life": David Meade, "Family History," in Henry J. Peet, ed., *Chaumiere Papers, Containing Matters of Interest to the Descendants of David Meade* (Chicago, 1883), 7; P. Hamilton Baskervill, *Andrew Meade of Ireland and Virginia* (Richmond, 1921), chap. 2.

tobacco: Jacob M. Price, *Capital and Credit in British Overseas Trade: The View from the Chesapeake, 1700–1776* (Cambridge, 1980); Jacob M. Price, *France and the Chesapeake: A History of the French Tobacco Monopoly, 1674–1791* (Ann Arbor, 1973); Price, *Perry of London*; Robert C. Nash, "The English and Scottish Tobacco Trades in the Seventeenth and Eighteenth Centuries: Legal and Illegal Trade," *EcHR*, 2d ser., XXXV (Aug. 1982), 354–372; Jacob M. Price and Paul G. E. Clemens, "A Revolution of Scale in Overseas Trade: British Firms in the Chesapeake Trade, 1675–1775," *JEcH*, XLVII (March 1987), 1–43; Kenneth Morgan, *Bristol and the Atlantic Trade in the Eighteenth Century* (Cambridge, 1993).

"no Promises ... upon": Richard Corbin to Robert Dinwiddie, July 10, 1761, Letterbook, Richard Corbin Papers, ViWC.

27 "there's ... Note": [George Fisher], "The Fisher History," in Louise Pecquet du Bellet, *Some Prominent Virginia Families* (Lynchburg, 1907), II, 773.

"this may ... Performing": Edmund Wilcox to James Russell, May 6, 1760, Hubard Family Papers, NcU.

a "great part": William Byrd to [Jacob?] Senserff, [ca. June 25, 1729], *Correspondence of the Byrds*, ed. Tinling, I, 410.

"scheme of a project": William Byrd to Martin Bladen, June 13, 1729, *ibid.*, 407–408. The copy Byrd sent to Wager is in the Vernon-Wager Manuscripts, Peter Force Collection, DLC.

"running ... did": William Byrd to Micajah Perry, [ca. July 3, 1728], *Correspondence of the Byrds*, ed. Tinling, I, 378.

"National" ... "for ever": F. Hall, *The Importance of the British Plantations in America to this Kingdom* (London, 1731), iii, 75–76.

hemp: Byrd, *Writings of Byrd*, ed. Bassett, 366–367; William Byrd to Hans Sloane, May 31, 1737, *Correspondence of the Byrds*, ed. Tinling, II, 513; George Melvin Herndon, "The Story of Hemp in Colonial Virginia" (Ph.D. diss., University of Virginia, 1959); Joseph J. Malone, "England and the Baltic Naval Stores Trade in the Seventeenth and Eighteenth Centuries," *MM*, LVIII (Nov. 1972), 390; Alexander Garden to John Ellis, May 6, 1757,

PAGE

in James Edward Smith, ed., *A Selection of the Correspondence of Linnaeus and Other Naturalists* (London, 1821), I, 403.

28 "a thousand shifts": Mr. Allen's Letter, 1743, James Abercromby Letter Book, Nc-Ar; Ekirch, *Poor Carolina*, 16.

29 "Schemes" . . . "*Virginia*": [Edward Kimber], *Itinerant Observations in America* (Savannah, 1878), 60. See also Thomas C. Parramore, Peter C. Stewart, and Tommy L. Bogger, *Norfolk: The First Four Centuries* (Charlottesville, 1994), chaps. 5–6; Thomas M. Costa, "Economic Development and Political Authority: Norfolk, Virginia, Merchant-Magistrates, 1736–1800" (Ph.D. diss., College of William and Mary, 1991), chaps. 1–2; Joseph A. Goldenberg, *Shipbuilding in Colonial America* (Charlottesville, 1976), 117–120.

"intire . . . Business": William Lux to John Norton, Aug. 20, 1766, William Lux Letterbook, NNHi.

"Marriage is honourable": Notes to "Charges Against Spotswood," *VMHB*, IV (April 1897), 361–362.

"new Negroes": Minchinton *et al.*, eds., *Virginia Slave-Trade*, 125, 131, 137, 139, 143. See also David H. Makinson, *Barbados: A Study of North-American–West-Indian Relations, 1739–1789* (The Hague, 1964), 43.

30 "Assiduity . . . Business": William Nelson to Edward Hunt & Son, May 29, 1767, William Nelson Letterbook, Vi.

mills and bakeries: Purdie and Dixon's *Virginia Gazette* (Williamsburg), Oct. 8, 1767; depositions of Philip Carbery and Richard Taylor, Commissioners to Examine Claims in Norfolk, Entry 235, Auditor of Public Accounts, Public Claims, General Records, Vi; George Washington to John Carlyle and Robert Adam, March 9, 1765, *Papers of Washington: Colonial*, ed. Abbot *et al.*, VII, 360; William Lux to Robert Tucker, Oct. 3, 1765, Lux Letterbook, NNHi. On skilled slaves, see Philip D. Morgan, *Slave Counterpoint: Black Culture in the Eighteenth-Century Chesapeake and Lowcountry* (Chapel Hill, 1998), 225–244.

31 "all" . . . "Opulence": Kimber, *Itinerant Observations*, 59–60; Francis Jerdone to Buchanan & Hamilton, June 28, 1748, "Letter Book of Francis Jerdone," *WMQ*, 1st ser., XI (Jan. 1903), 154.

"choice young Slaves": Parks's *Virginia Gazette*, April 8, 1737, June 8, 1739.

32 "When . . . England": Thomas Nelson to Andrew Stone, Sept. 21, 1747, Newcastle Papers, Home Correspondence, Vol. XXVIII, Add MSS 32,713, f. 98, Uk.

"remove . . . expedition": Fisher, "Fisher History," in Pecquet du Bellet, *Some Prominent Virginia Families*, II, 765.

an "agent": Duke of Richmond to Duke of Newcastle, July 17, 1747, *The Correspondence of the Dukes of Richmond and Newcastle*, ed. Timothy J. McCann, *Sussex Record Society*, LXXIII (1982–83), 250.

became secretary: William Byrd to Francis Otway, Feb. 10, 1741, *Correspondence of the Byrds*, ed. Tinling, II, 578, 579n.4; Charles Carter to Foster Cunliffe, Aug. 1, 1742, Foster Cunliffe to Charles Carter, recd. Jan. 14, 1743, Carter Papers, ViFreJM.

"make" . . . "match": John Lewis to Lawrence Washington, June 28, 1742, in Moncure Daniel Conway, *Barons of the Potomack and Rappahannock* (New York, 1892), 161–162.

33 Elizabeth Burwell: Parks's *Virginia Gazette*, Feb. 10, 1738; William Meade, *Old Churches, Ministers and Families of Virginia* (Philadelphia, 1900 [orig. publ. 1857]), I, 26n, 206; William Nelson to R. C. M. Page, April 3, 1883, in Richard Channing Moore Page, *Genealogy of the Page Family in Virginia*, 2d ed. (Bridgewater, 1965), 158.

Thomas Nelson built: François-Jean, Marquis de Chastellux, *Travels in North America in the Years 1780, 1781 and 1782*, ed. Howard C. Rice, Jr. (Chapel Hill, 1963), II, 385; Ernest McNeill Eller, ed., *Chesapeake Bay in the American Revolution* (Centreville, 1981), 313; *Virginia Independent Chronicle* (Richmond), April 9, 1788.

a 110 percent markup: T. West to Esther West, Nov. 12, 1756, HCA 30/258, PRO. Compare Francis Jerdone to Samuel Richards, Israel Mauduit & Company, Dec. 14, 1754, "Letter Book of Jerdone," *WMQ*, 1st ser., XIV (Jan. 1906), 142–143.

"Nelson . . . money": John Syme to Farell & Jones, May 10, 1763, *Jones' Exor.* v. *John Syme*, 1799, USCCVD(EC), Vi; Fisher, "Fisher History," in Pecquet du Bellet, *Some Prominent Virginia Families*, II, 770.

"conscious Dignity": Fisher, "Fisher History," in Pecquet du Bellet, *Some Prominent Virginia Families*, II, 765.

"except . . . Country": Graham Frank to Ellen Frank, Nov. 10, 1756, HCA 30/258, PRO.

"As to . . . Time": William Nelson to Thomas Jones, Dec. 22, 1753, Roger Jones and Family Papers, DLC.

34 "There . . . that!": Fisher, "Fisher History," in Pecquet du Bellet, *Some Prominent Virginia Families*, II, 770, 783.

"pleasant and entertaining": Jack P. Greene, ed., "A Mirror of Virtue for a Declining Land: John Camm's Funeral Sermon for William Nelson," in J. A. Leo Lemay, ed., *Essays in Early Virginia Literature Honoring Richard Beale Davis* (New York, 1977), 197.

"prudent & sensible": "Characters of leading Men & Descriptions of Places in Virginia," Peter Russell Papers, CaOTP.

"squandered . . . health": Thomas Nelson to Henry Tucker, Jan. 21, 1774, Tucker-Coleman Papers, ViW.

"in making . . . place": John Waller to Benjamin Waller, Dec. 9, 1751, Andrew Lewis Riffe, "The Wallers of Endfield, King William County, Virginia," *VMHB*, LIX (Oct. 1951), 474; Henry Tucker to St. George Tucker, April 13, 1774, Tucker-Coleman Papers, ViW.

"has . . . friends": John Rutherford to William Adair, March 26, 1773, MSS 18741, Sir Thomas Phillips Collection, DLC.

Robert Dinwiddie: Robert Dinwiddie to Board of Trade, June 16, 1753, Board of Trade to Earl of Loudoun, March 17, 1756, *Robert Dinwiddie Correspondence*, ed. Louis Knott Koontz (Berkeley, 1951), 417–418, 911, 916–919; Robert Dinwiddie to Horace Walpole, Oct. 25, 1754, Robert Dinwiddie to James Abercromby, Oct. 23, 1754, *The Official Records of Robert Dinwiddie*, ed. R. A. Brock (Richmond, 1883), I, 370, 374–376.

35 "upright Character": John Hook to Gertrude Gresley, Jan. 20, 1774, John Hook Letterbook, Vi.

"that . . . imposed on": Thomas Nelson to Francis Fauquier, enclosed in Francis Fauquier to Board of Trade, Nov. 23, 1764, *The Official Papers of Francis Fauquier*, ed. George Reese (Charlottesville, 1980–83), III, 1177.

a list of grants: McIlwaine, ed., *Executive Journals*, VI, 274; Thomas Nelson to Francis

PAGE

Fauquier, enclosed in Francis Fauquier to Board of Trade, Dec. 27, 1764, Thomas Nelson to Francis Fauquier, enclosed in Francis Fauquier to Earl of Shelburne, May 20, 1767, *Official Papers of Fauquier*, ed. Reese, III, 1210–1211, 1457; "A true and full Acct," enclosed in Baron de Botetourt to Board of Trade, July 31, 1770, CO 5/1333, ff. 48–56, PRO.

36   "it would . . . Secretary": George Seaton to Edmund Wilcox, Sept. 7, 1765, Hubard Family Papers, NcU. On the Nelson brothers, see also Emory G. Evans, "The Nelsons: A Biographical Study of a Virginia Family in the Eighteenth Century" (Ph.D. diss., University of Virginia, 1957); Emory G. Evans, "The Rise and Decline of the Virginia Aristocracy in the Eighteenth Century: The Nelsons," in Darrett B. Rutman, ed., *The Old Dominion: Essays for Thomas Perkins Abernethy* (Charlottesville, 1964), 62–78.

"there . . . do": Entries of March 13–14, 1752, *The Diary of Colonel Landon Carter of Sabine Hall, 1752–1778*, ed. Jack P. Greene (Charlottesville, 1965), I, 85–86.

37   "at their beck": Thomas Jefferson to William Wirt, Aug. 5, 1815, Papers of Thomas Jefferson, DLC.

"To committees . . . column": Edmund Randolph, *History of Virginia*, ed. Arthur H. Shaffer (Charlottesville, 1970), 174.

"He was . . . man": Thomas Jefferson to William Wirt, April 12, 1812, *The Writings of Thomas Jefferson*, ed. Paul Leicester Ford (New York, 1892–99), IX, 339.

"had a" . . . "happy": William Nelson to Edward and Samuel Athawes, Nov. 13, 1766, Nelson Letterbook, Vi.

"universally Esteemed": "Dinwiddianae," in Richard Beale Davis, ed., "The Colonial Virginia Satirist," *Transactions of the American Philosophical Society*, new series, LVII, Part I (1967), 24.

"beloved": Francis Fauquier to Board of Trade, April 10, 1759, *Official Papers of Fauquier*, ed. Reese, I, 205; Robert Carter Nicholas to the Printer, Sept. 1, 1766, Purdie's *Virginia Gazette*, Sept. 5, 1766.

"thousand . . . attentions": Randolph, *History of Virginia*, ed. Shaffer, 174.

"warm . . . friendships": David Boyd to Richard Henry Lee, Nov. 17, 1766, Lee Family Papers, ViU.

"undue influence": Robert Carter Nicholas to the Printer, Sept. 1, 1766, Purdie's *Virginia Gazette*, Sept. 5, 1766; William Nelson to Edward and Samuel Athawes, Nov. 13, 1766, Nelson Letterbook, Vi.

"indirect methods": [Richard Bland], "A Freeholder," Purdie's *Virginia Gazette*, Oct. 17, 1766.

"unnatural . . . House": Richard Bland to Richard Henry Lee, May 22, 1766, Lee Family Papers, ViU.

Pleasant Hill: George Washington to Robert Cary & Co., Nov. 10, 1773, *Papers of Washington: Colonial*, ed. Abbot *et al.*, IX, 378n.4; entry of June 28, 1732, "Journal of Grove," ed. Stiverson and Butler, *VMHB*, LXXXV (Jan. 1977), 27–28; Purdie and Dixon's *Virginia Gazette*, Dec. 21, 1769, Oct. 14, 1773.

38   John Chiswell: Andrew Burnaby to George Washington, Jan. 4, 1760, *Papers of Washington: Colonial*, ed. Abbot *et al.*, VI, 381; Carl Bridenbaugh, "Violence and Virtue in Virginia, 1766: or, the Importance of the Trivial," Massachusetts Historical Society, *Proceedings*, LXXVI (1964), 10–14; Account of the Lead Mine Company with John Robin-

son, 1760–1768, William Byrd, III, Papers, Section 8, ViRHi. On Robinson, see also Carl Bridenbaugh, *Seat of Empire: The Political Role of Eighteenth-Century Williamsburg* (Williamsburg, 1950); William Minor Dabney, "John Robinson: Speaker of the House of Burgesses and Treasurer of Virginia" (M.A. thesis, University of Virginia, 1941); Jack P. Greene, "The Attempt to Separate the Offices of Speaker and Treasurer in Virginia, 1758–1766," *VMHB*, LXXI (Jan. 1963), 11–18; Jack P. Greene, "Foundations of Political Power in the Virginia House of Burgesses, 1720–1776," *WMQ*, 3d ser., XVI (Oct. 1959), 485–502; David Alan Williams, "Political Alignments in Colonial Virginia Politics, 1698–1750" (Ph.D. diss., Northwestern University, 1959), 101–109, 329–337.

38   "mental Qualifications": Francis Fauquier to Board of Trade, July 31, 1762, *Official Papers of Fauquier*, ed. Reese, II, 782.

"a shallow weak man": "Characters of leading Men," Russell Papers, CaOTP; entry of Sept. 2, 1772, *Diary of Landon Carter*, ed. Greene, II, 720; George Washington to Jonathan Boucher, Oct. 2, 1772, *Papers of Washington: Colonial*, ed. Abbot *et al.*, IX, 113.

"of a . . . Family": Francis Fauquier to Board of Trade, July 31, 1762, *Official Papers of Fauquier*, ed. Reese, II, 782; McIlwaine, ed., *Executive Journals*, VI, 229.

Their home estate: Purdie and Dixon's *Virginia Gazette*, May 16, 1771; *WMQ*, 1st ser., XXVII (Jan. 1919), 210. On Burwell, see also Robert Burwell to John Norton, May 9, 1770, John Norton & Son Papers, ViWC; Nathaniel Burwell, Will, Aug. 20, 1721, Berkeley Family Papers, ViU.

39   Micajah Perry: John Carter to Micajah Perry, July 2, 1737, Aug. 1, 1738, Carter Family Letterbook, ViU.

"personal Beauty": "Old Tombstones in Gloucester County," *WMQ*, 1st ser., III (Jan. 1895), 188.

"great sums": William Waller Hening, ed., *The Statutes at Large: Being a Collection of All the Laws of Virginia* (Richmond, Philadelphia, and New York, 1809–23), V, 277–284; *Journal of the Commissioners for Trade and Plantations from January 1741-2 to December 1749* (London, 1931), 163, 181, 202; H. R. McIlwaine, ed., *Journals of the House of Burgesses, 1742-1747, 1748-1749* (Richmond, 1909), 90; Parks's *Virginia Gazette*, Sept. 26, 1745; Mann Page to John Page, Aug. 3, 1779, ViWC.

Alice Page: "Old Tombstones in Gloucester County," *WMQ*, 1st ser., III (Jan. 1895), 188.

"incapable of Business": William Gooch to Board of Trade, Sept. 25, 1747, CO 5/1326, f. 276, PRO; [Note to Resignation of John Tayloe], *VMHB*, XVII (Oct. 1909), 370–372.

"detestable": Warner Lewis to Walter Jones, July 8, 1766, Edrington Family Papers, ViRHi.

40   James Patton: James Patton to John Blair, [Jan. 1753], Preston Papers, Vol. I, ff. 75–77, Draper Collection, Series QQ, WHi; Hall, ed., *Executive Journals*, 2d ed., V, 134, 172–173, 195.

41   caught fire: McIlwaine, ed., *Legislative Journals*, 2d ed., 995–996; McIlwaine, ed., *Journals of the Burgesses, 1742-1749*, 235, 246.

"vastly rich": Lawrence Washington to [?], Nov. 17, 1749, in Conway, *Barons of the Potomac*, 272–273.

"a considerable Time": William Gooch to Board of Trade, June 16, 1748, CO 5/1327, ff. 4–5, PRO; *Journal of the Commissioners for Trade and Plantations, 1742-1749*, 278, 336;

PAGE

Louis Knott Koontz, *Robert Dinwiddie: His Career in American Colonial Government and Westward Expansion* (Glendale, 1941), 157–159.

"for procuring . . . Land": Ohio Company, Minutes, Oct. 20, 1748, quoted in Alfred P. James, *The Ohio Company: Its Inner History* (Pittsburgh, 1959), 15.

42 "public" . . . "Views": Thomas Lee to Conrad Weiser, Feb. 27, June 21, 1750, PHi, copies in Lee Family Papers, ViU.

grant . . . Ohio Company: *Journal of the Commissioners for Trade and Plantations, 1742–1749*, 342, 356–357, 380; W. L. Grant and James Munro, eds., *Acts of the Privy Council of England. Colonial Series* (London, 1908–12), IV, 55–58.

"a Certain . . . Lee": Entry of May 14, 1755, *Diary of Landon Carter*, ed. Greene, I, 121.

"Mr Secretary . . . Company": Ohio Company, Minutes, June 21, 1749, in Lois Mulkearn, ed., *George Mercer Papers Relating to the Ohio Company of Virginia* (Pittsburgh, 1954), 168.

land grants: Hall, ed., *Executive Journals*, 2d ed., V, 282–283, 288, 295–297, 427; Thomas Lee to Members of the Ohio Company, June 1, 1749, in James, *Ohio Company*, 196; List of Members of the Loyal Company, Campbell-Preston-Floyd Papers, Vol. I, DLC; Williams, "Political Alignments," 332–337.

43 "a circumstantial" . . . "voluminous": Robert Beverley to John Craig, April 29, 1791, Robert Beverley Letterbook, DLC.

"so pleasing . . . Memory": Entry of May 14, 1755, *Diary of Landon Carter*, ed. Greene, I, 120.

Joshua Fry and Peter Jefferson: Hall, ed., *Executive Journals*, 2d ed., V, 310; Dumas Malone, *Jefferson and His Time* (Boston, 1948–81), I, 24–25.

"in one . . . Surveys": Hall, ed., *Executive Journals*, 2d ed., V, 297.

"use . . . fateage": Thomas Walker to William Preston, Oct. 23, 1778, Preston Papers, IV, f. 183, Draper Collection, Series QQ, WHi. See also James O. Breeden, "The Medical World of Thomas Walker," *MACH*, LII (1994), 23–37.

44 "They are . . . all": Mary Willing Byrd to Anne Willing, 1761, in Joshua Francis Fisher, *Recollections of Joshua Francis Fisher*, ed. Sophia Cadwalader (Boston, 1929), 97.

"to discover . . . Settlements": Delf Norona, ed., "Joshua Fry's Report on the Back Settlements of Virginia, [May 8, 1751]," *VMHB*, LVI (Jan. 1948), 37.

Dr. Walker's expedition: Thomas Walker, *Journal of an Exploration in the Spring of the Year 1750* (Boston, 1888); Archibald Henderson, "Dr. Thomas Walker and the Loyal Company of Virginia," American Antiquarian Society, *Proceedings*, new series, XLI (1931), 90–91; Lewis Preston Summers, *History of Southwest Virginia, 1746–1786* (Baltimore, 1966 [orig. publ. Richmond, 1903]), 48–51; William Stewart Lester, *The Transylvania Company* (Spencer, 1935), 49.

45 an executive committee: John Meriwether to James Power, July 2, 1752, Fielding Lewis to James Power, July 22, 1752, Page-Walker Manuscripts, ViU.

to James Patton: James Patton to John Blair, [Jan. 1753], Preston Papers, I, ff. 75–77, Draper Collection, Series QQ, WHi; letter of July 9, 1770, in [Samuel Wharton], [*Statement for the Petitioners in the Case of the Walpole Company Grant*] [London? 1772], appendix I. The unique copy of this pamphlet is in RPJCB.

45 "that . . . promise": John Donelson to William Preston, Oct. 1, 1778, Preston Papers, IV, f. 180, Draper Collection, Series QQ, WHi.

the Pacific Ocean: James Maury to [?], Jan. 10, 1756, in Ann Maury, *Memoirs of a Huguenot Family* (New York, 1853), 390–392.

"the chief . . . scheme": Peter Fontaine to John and Moses Fontaine, April 15, 1754, *ibid.*, 342; Henderson, "Dr. Thomas Walker," American Antiquarian Society, *Proceedings*, new series, XLI (1931), 93; [William Preston], [Affidavit], n.d., Preston Family Papers, P9267f/FA2, ViRHi; Thomas Walker to William Preston, March 23, 1778, Preston Papers, IV, f. 164, Draper Collection, Series QQ, WHi; *Journal of the House of Delegates of the Commonwealth of Virginia* (Richmond, 1804 [1805]), 94; George W. Frye, *Colonel Joshua Fry of Virginia and Some of His Descendants and Allied Families* (Cincinnati, 1966), 10. On Walker, see also Keith Ryan Nyland, "Doctor Thomas Walker: Explorer, Physician, Statesman, Surveyor and Planter of Virginia and Kentucky" (Ph.D. diss., Ohio State University, 1971), chaps. 1–3; Natalie J. Disbrow, "Thomas Walker of Albemarle," *Papers of the Albemarle County Historical Society*, I (1940–41), 5–9.

46 Mississippi River: William Byrd to Earl of Orrery, March 6, 1720, *Correspondence of the Byrds*, ed. Tinling, I, 327.

William Byrd's son: Maria Byrd to [?], Sept. 6, 1745, photostat, ViWC; William Proctor to brother, July 1739, "Letters of William Proctor, Librarian at Westover," *VMHB*, X (Jan. 1903), 300–301.

"a prodigious . . . wilderness": Andrew Burnaby, *Travels Through the Middle Settlements in North America in the Years 1759 and 1760*, ed. Rufus Rockwell Wilson, 3d ed. (New York, 1904), 39.

at Westover: Wenger, "Westover," 41, 48–49, 58, and see his chap. 5; Rasmussen, "Drafting the Plans," in Brownell *et al.*, *Making of Virginia Architecture*, 20–22; Fisher, "Fisher History," in Pecquet du Bellet, *Some Prominent Virginia Families*, II, 774; "Will of Colonel William Byrd, 3d," *VMHB*, IX (July 1901), 81–82; David Meade to Joseph Prentis, June 13, 1797, Webb Transcripts, Webb-Prentis Papers, ViU; William Wirt to Elizabeth Wirt, Nov. 8, 1803, Wirt Papers, MdBHi. On Virginia architecture and construction, see also Claude Lanciano, *"Our Most Skillful Architect": Richard Taliaferro and Associated Colonial Virginia Constructions* (Gloucester, 1981).

48 "dissatisfaction": J. F. D. Smyth, *A Tour in the United States of America* (Dublin, 1784), I, 257–258.

brothers-in-law: Robert Dinwiddie to Board of Trade, Jan. 29, 1754, *Dinwiddie Correspondence*, ed. Koontz, 445–446.

"the power of self-denial": Thomas Jefferson to John Page, May 7, 1802, *Writings of Jefferson*, ed. Ford, VIII, 135n.

"Col. Byrd . . . things": John Wayles to Farell & Jones, Aug. 17, 1769, Claim of John Tyndale Warre, T 79/9, PRO.

II: A SCHEME OF GREAT EXPECTATION

49 the Dismal Swamp: Wilmer L. Hall, ed., *Executive Journals of the Council of Colonial Virginia*, 2d ed. (Richmond, 1967), V, 423–424. On Francis Farley's partners, see Thomas M.

PAGE

Costa, "Economic Development and Political Authority: Norfolk, Virginia, Merchant-Magistrates, 1736–1800" (Ph.D. diss., College of William and Mary, 1991), esp. 95, 121, 131, 170. On Britons and eighteenth-century forests, see Simon Schama, *Landscape and Memory* (New York, 1995), chap. 3, part iii.

"Introduceing . . . Planters": William Barrell to Theodore Barrell, Feb. 2, 1769, Stephen Collins & Son Papers, DLC.

"He . . . man": William Nelson to Edward Hunt & Son, Nov. 17, 1769, William Nelson Letterbook, Vi; Samuel Martin to Baron de Botetourt, [ca. Jan. 1769], Letterbook of Samuel Martin, Add MSS 41,350, f. 83, Uk.

50 "neither . . . much": Francis Farley to Clement Tudway, Sept. 30, 1775, Tudway Papers, Somerset Record Office, Taunton.

coast of Antigua: [Jacques Nicolas Bellin], *Description géographique des isles Antilles possédées par les Anglois* (Paris, 1758), 83, 96.

"dog-drivers": Letters XX–XXIV, July 20–Nov. 9, 1787, John Luffman, *A Brief Account of the Island of Antigua*, reprinted in Vere Langford Oliver, *The History of the Island of Antigua* (London, 1894–99), I, cxxxiii–cxxxiv; Mainswete Walrond to Charles Tudway, Sept. 20, 1767, Tudway Papers, Somerset Record Office; testimony of Robert Forster, Sheila Lambert, ed., *House of Commons Sessional Papers of the Eighteenth Century* (Wilmington, 1975), LXXXII, 129–133; Edward Thompson, *Sailor's Letters* (London, 1766), II, 12–13, 18–19; Clement Caines, *Letters on the Cultivation of the Otaheite Cane* (London, 1801); Daniel Mackinnon, *A Tour Through the British West Indies in the Years 1802 and 1803*, 2d ed. (London, 1812), 57–58; J. R. Ward, *British West Indian Slavery, 1750–1834: The Process of Amelioration* (Oxford, 1988), 14–18; Ward Barrett, "Caribbean Sugar-Production Standards in the Seventeenth and Eighteenth Centuries," in John Parker, ed., *Merchants and Scholars: Essays in the History of Exploration and Trade* (Minneapolis, 1965), 147–170.

St. Johns: Janet Schaw, *Journal of a Lady of Quality*, ed. Evangeline Walker Andrews and Charles McLean Andrews (New Haven, 1922), 88, 107–108; *The Laws of the Island of Antigua* (London, 1805), I; [F. W. M. Bayley], *Four Years' Residence in the West Indies* (London, 1831), 305; entry of Jan. 11, 1784, *Seeing America and Its Great Men: The Journal and Letters of Count Francesco dal Verme, 1783–1784*, trans. and ed. Elizabeth Cometti (Charlottesville, 1969), 64; entry of Dec. 28, 1795, Francis Baily, *Journal of a Tour in the Unsettled Parts of North America in 1796 & 1797*, ed. Jack D. L. Holmes (Carbondale, 1969), 12–13; entry of May 7, 1749, Robert Poole, *The Beneficent Bee: Or, Traveller's Companion* (London, 1753), 344.

51 served without pay: Robert Holloway to Charles Tudway, Dec. 31, 1759, Francis Farley to Charles Tudway, Jan. 3, 1761, Oct. 6, 1769, Tudway Papers, Somerset Record Office.

"Every . . . Period": David Greene to Thomas Fraser, June 15, 1780, David Greene Letterbook, MiU-C.

"Lands . . . retreat": Samuel Martin to Samuel Martin, Jr., Aug. 11, 1751, Letterbook of Martin, Add MSS 41,346, f. 32, Uk. See also "Petition of Antigua Planters," Massachusetts Historical Society, *Proceedings*, LIX (1925–26), 171–176.

52 harsh drought: Samuel Davies, *Virginia's Danger and Remedy* (Williamsburg, 1756), 6; Francis Jerdone to Morgan Thomas & Co., Feb. 10, 1756, Francis Jerdone Letterbook, Jerdone Family Papers, ViW.

52 "as rich . . . Euphrates": Rebecca Johnston, ed., "William Byrd's Title Book," *VMHB*, L
(April 1942), 176; Lindley S. Butler, "Sauratown Plantation," *Journal of Rockingham
County History and Genealogy*, VIII (Dec. 1983), 84; *John Simon Farley and Elizabeth Mor-
son v. Thomas Lee Shippen and Elizabeth Carter Shippen et al.*, March 1794, in *Decisions of
Cases in Virginia by the High Court of Chancery . . . by George Wythe* (Charlottesville, 1903),
253–255; J. F. D. Smyth, *A Tour in the United States of America* (Dublin, 1784), I, 258.

"in a very" . . . "property": Francis Farley to John Simon Farley, June 11, 1777, July 13,
1778, in *Decisions by Wythe*, 255; Vere Langford Oliver, ed., *Caribbeana* (London,
1910–19), IV, 30n. On Antigua, see also David R. Harris, *Plants, Animals, and Man in the
Outer Leeward Islands, West Indies: An Ecological Study of Antigua, Barbuda, and Anguilla*
(Berkeley, 1965); Elsa V. Goveia, *Slave Society in the British Leeward Islands at the End of the
Eighteenth Century* (New Haven, 1965); Richard B. Sheridan, *Sugar and Slavery: An Economic History of the British West Indies, 1623–1775* (Baltimore, 1974); David Barry Gaspar,
Bondmen and Rebels: A Study of Master-Slave Relations in Antigua (Baltimore, 1985); David
Barry Gaspar, "Sugar Cultivation and Slave Life in Antigua before 1800," in Ira Berlin
and Philip D. Morgan, eds., *Cultivation and Culture: Labor and the Shaping of Slave Life in
the Americas* (Charlottesville, 1993), 101–123; Arthur L. Stinchcombe, *Sugar Island Slavery in the Age of Enlightenment: The Political Economy of the Caribbean World* (Princeton,
1995).

"bred . . . pocket": "Preliminary Letters," in "Dinwiddianae," Richard Beale Davis, ed.,
"The Colonial Virginia Satirist," *Transactions of the American Philosophical Society*, new se-
ries, LVII, Part I (1967), 17; [Peyton Randolph], *A Letter to a Gentleman in London, from
Virginia* (Williamsburg, 1759), 8; John Richard Alden, *Robert Dinwiddie: Servant of the
Crown* (Williamsburg, 1973), 27.

53 "land" . . . "Revenue": Robert Dinwiddie to Board of Trade, June 16, 1753, *Robert Din-
widdie Correspondence*, ed. Louis Knott Koontz (Berkeley, 1951), 298; Robert Dinwiddie to
Board of Trade, Oct. 25, 1754, *The Official Records of Robert Dinwiddie*, ed. R. A. Brock
(Richmond, 1883–84), I, 363.

"too warm . . . with": Robert Dinwiddie to Board of Trade, Dec. 29, 1753, *Dinwiddie Correspondence*, ed. Koontz, 418.

"a very" . . . "Neck": William Stith to Bishop of London, April 21, 1753, John Blair to
Bishop of London, Aug. 15, 1752, Fulham Papers, Vol. 13, "Virginia," Lambeth Palace,
London.

"some" . . . "Fee": Robert Dinwiddie to James Abercromby, Oct. 23, 1754, Robert Dinwiddie to Board of Trade, Oct. 25, 1754, *Official Records of Dinwiddie*, ed. Brock, I,
374–375, 362–363; Edmund Jenings to Richard Corbin, May 30, 1754, Edmund Jenings
Letterbook, ViRHi.

"I have . . . heart": Robert Dinwiddie to Thomas Cresap, Jan. 23, 1752, *Official Records of
Dinwiddie*, ed. Brock, I, 17–18.

"likes . . . well": Philip Ludwell Lee to John and Capel Hanbury, Aug. 1, 1753, Philip
Ludwell Lee Letterbook, Vi.

"suspected . . . lands": *State of the British and French Colonies in North America* (London,
1755), 113; Thomas Gage, Answers, "Queries of George Chalmers," Massachusetts Historical Society, *Collections*, 4th ser., IV (1858), 369.

Logg's Town: Michael N. McConnell, *A Country Between: The Upper Ohio Valley and Its Peoples, 1724–1774* (Lincoln, 1992), 95–98; Wilbur R. Jacobs, *Diplomacy and Indian Gifts: Anglo-French Rivalry along the Ohio and Northwest Frontiers, 1748–1763* (Stanford, 1950), 120–123.

"unfavourable" . . . "Company": George Washington to Earl of Loudoun, Jan. 10, 1757, *The Papers of George Washington, Colonial Series,* ed. W. W. Abbot *et al.* (Charlottesville, 1983–), IV, 79–80; James Titus, *The Old Dominion at War: Society, Politics, and Warfare in Late Colonial Virginia* (Columbia, 1991), 24–25; Hayes Baker-Crothers, *Virginia and the French and Indian War* (Chicago, 1928), 27–31; Patrice Louis-René Higonnet, "The Origins of the Seven Years' War," *JMH*, XL (March 1968), 63.

54 "go . . . them": "Preliminary Letters," in "Dinwiddianae," Davis, ed., "Colonial Virginia Satirist," *Transactions of the American Philosophical Society*, new series, LVII, Part I (1967), 17.

55 "The grants . . . dispute": Comte de Jouy to Duc de Mirepoix, Feb. 19, 1755, in Theodore Calvin Pease, ed., *Anglo-French Boundary Disputes in the West, 1749–1763* (Springfield, 1936), 134. See also T. R. Clayton, "The Duke of Newcastle, the Earl of Halifax, and the American Origins of the Seven Years' War," *HJ*, XXIV (Sept. 1981), 571–603; William J. Eccles, "Iroquois, French, British: Imperial Rivalry in the Ohio Valley," in *Pathways to the Old Northwest: An Observance of the Bicentennial of the Northwest Ordinance* (Indianapolis, 1988), 25–28; Max Savelle, *The Diplomatic History of the Canadian Boundary, 1749–1763* (New Haven, 1940), chaps. 3–4.

"rich" . . . "Acres": Robert Dinwiddie to Earl of Holdernesse, March 12, 1754, *Official Records of Dinwiddie,* ed. Brock, I, 95–96.

"general" . . . "lands": Isaac Norris to Robert Charles, April 19, 1754, quoted in William S. Sachs and Ari Hoogenboom, *The Enterprising Colonials: Society on the Eve of the Revolution* (Chicago, 1965), 148.

"universal Monarchy": H. R. McIlwaine, ed., *Journals of the House of Burgesses of Virginia, 1752–1755, 1756–1758* (Richmond, 1909), 189.

"bubbled": George Washington to Earl of Loudoun, Jan. 10, 1757, *Papers of Washington: Colonial,* ed. Abbot *et al.,* IV, 80–81.

"great ill manners": Robert Dinwiddie to James Abercromby, Oct. 23, 1754, *Official Records of Dinwiddie,* ed. Brock, I, 376.

"very disagreeable": Robert Dinwiddie to Board of Trade, Oct. 25, 1754, Robert Dinwiddie to John Pownall, March 17, 1755, *ibid.,* I, 363–364, II, 2.

56 "a very good Footing": Robert Dinwiddie to James Abercromby, Oct. 23, 1754, *ibid.,* I, 375–376.

"unjust and false": Robert Dinwiddie to Board of Trade, Oct. 25, 1754, *ibid.,* I, 363.

"said . . . A-se": Davis, ed., "Colonial Virginia Satirist," *Transactions of the American Philosophical Society,* new series, LVII, Part I (1967), 33.

"the Ingenius Franklin": Entries of [Feb.] 22–25, 1755, Thomas Walker, Diary, in Archibald Henderson, "Dr. Thomas Walker and the Loyal Company of Virginia," American Antiquarian Society, *Proceedings,* new series, XLI (1931), 122–123.

Lewis Evans: Lewis Evans, *Geographical, Historical, Political, Philosophical and Mechanical Essays* (Philadelphia, 1755), 10; Benjamin Franklin to Richard Jackson, Dec. 12, 1754, *The*

Papers of Benjamin Franklin, ed. Leonard W. Labaree *et al.* (New Haven, 1959–), V, 447–448.

56 John Hanbury: [John Shebbeare] *A Letter to the People of England* (London, 1755), 33–38; *Gentleman's Magazine*, XXV (Aug. 1755), 378, (Sept. 1755), 389; Winthrop Sargent, ed., *The History of an Expedition Against Fort Du Quesne in 1755* (Philadelphia, 1855), 107, 162; Lewis Evans, *Geographical, Historical, Political, Philosophical and Mechanical Essays. Number II* (Philadelphia, 1756), 6–7.

George Washington: George Washington to John Robinson, April 20, 1755, George Washington to Earl of Loudoun, Jan. 10, 1757, *Papers of Washington: Colonial*, ed. Abbot *et al.*, I, 255–256, IV, 89.

57 "the most . . . saw": Entry of June 13, [1755], Charlotte Brown, Journal, DLC.

"daily . . . concerned": Edward Braddock to Thomas Robinson, June 5, 1755, Amherst Papers, WO 34/73, ff. 35–37, PRO; Petition of Charles Dick and Thomas Walker, CO 5/1352, f. 44, PRO; Adam Stephen to Henry Bouquet, May 26, 1758, Bouquet Papers, Add MSS 21,643, ff. 92–93, Uk; Thomas Dunbar to Robert Napier, July 24, 1755, anonymous letter, July 25, 1755, Stanley Pargellis, ed., *Military Affairs in North America, 1748–1765: Selected Documents from the Cumberland Papers in Windsor Castle* (New York, 1936), 109, 118, 120; Robert Orme, Journal, in Sargent, ed., *History of an Expedition*, 287, 313–316; Titus, *Old Dominion at War*, 70; Douglas Edward Leach, *Roots of Conflict: British Armed Forces and Colonial Americans, 1677–1763* (Chapel Hill, 1986), 80–82.

"grave smiles": Entry of [Feb.] 25, 1755, Walker, Diary, in Henderson, "Dr. Thomas Walker," American Antiquarian Society, *Proceedings*, new series, XLI (1931), 123.

"Bragging . . . Promises": *The Expedition of Major General Braddock to Virginia* (London, 1755), 16–17, 22–23; William Sparke to [?], Nov. 22, 1755, in Sheldon S. Cohen, "Major William Sparke along the Monongahela: A New Historical Account of Braddock's Defeat," *PaH*, LXII (1995), 550; Whitfield J. Bell, Jr., and Leonard W. Labaree, "Franklin and the 'Wagon Affair,' 1755," American Philosophical Society, *Proceedings*, CI (Dec. 1957), 551–558.

"the old" . . . "Defiles": *Expedition of Major General Braddock*, 16; Richard Walsh, ed., "Braddock on July 9, 1755," *MHM*, LX (Dec. 1965), 422.

Thomas Walker: Jasper Yeates to [?], Aug. 21, 1776, *Register of Pennsylvania*, VI (Aug. 14, 1830), 104–105. See also McIlwaine, ed., *Journals of Burgesses, 1752–1758*, 328.

General Braddock: Paul E. Kopperman, *Braddock at the Monongahela* (Pittsburgh, 1977).

58 "No . . . Land": Quoted in McConnell, *A Country Between*, 119. See also Edward Braddock to Robert Hunter Morris, April 15, 1755, *Stan. V. Henkels Catalogue No. 1256* (April 1920), Item 104.

"cutting . . . families": Walsh, ed., "Braddock on July 9, 1755," *MHM*, LX (Dec. 1965), 427; Davies, *Virginia's Danger and Remedy*, 9–10; Titus, *Old Dominion at War*, 74–75.

"in droves of fifties": George Washington to John Robinson, April 24, 1756, *Papers of Washington: Colonial*, ed. Abbot *et al.*, III, 48; Matthew C. Ward, "Fighting the 'Old Women': Indian Strategy on the Virginia and Pennsylvania Frontier, 1754–1758," *VMHB*, CIII (July 1995), 297–320.

"a mere Farce": Davies, *Virginia's Danger and Remedy*, 11.

"they . . . desert": Robert Dinwiddie to George Washington, July 1, 1756, George Washington to John Robinson, Nov. 9, 1756, *Papers of Washington: Colonial*, ed. Abbot *et al.*, III, 232, IV, 11–13.

"to cause . . . Men": William Peachey to George Washington, Aug. 22, 1757, Landon Carter to George Washington, April 21, 1756, *ibid.*, IV, 382, III, 30–31.

"the most . . . measures": Richard Bland to George Washington, June 7, 1757, *ibid.*, IV, 187.

59   "good . . . Generosity": James Robertson to Earl of Morton, Dec. 19, 1758, Pargellis, ed., *Military Affairs in North America*, 431; John Richard Alden, *John Stuart and the Southern Colonial Frontier* (Ann Arbor, 1944), 47–50.

"surprised and sorry": Charles Steuart to William Bowden, Aug. 2, 1754, Charles Steuart Letterbooks, PHi; John Watts to Robert Monckton, Jan. 10, 1765, *Aspinwall Papers*, Massachusetts Historical Society, *Collections*, 4th ser., IX–X (1871), II, 548–549.

Elizabeth Carter Byrd: Maria Taylor Byrd to William Byrd, March 15, Dec. 24, 1757, [Feb. 1760?], July 13, Aug. 15, 1760, *The Correspondence of the Three William Byrds*, ed. Marion Tinling (Charlottesville, 1977), II, 623, 634, 682, 697, 701.

"in a . . . Behaviour": John Kirkpatrick to George Washington, Aug. 14, 1756, *Papers of Washington: Colonial*, ed. Abbot *et al.*, III, 352.

"your . . . love": Elizabeth Byrd to William Byrd, Aug. 16, 1757, *Correspondence of the Byrds*, ed. Tinling, II, 626.

"what . . . necessary": William Byrd, Deed of Trust, Dec. 18, 1756, in Herbert A. Elliott, "Sir Peyton Skipwith and the Byrd Land," *VMHB*, LXXX (Jan. 1972), 57–58.

"many importunate Creditors": Richard Corbin to Edmund Jenings, April 26, 1758, Richard Corbin Letterbook, ViWC; Francis Jerdone to Hugh Crawford, Dec. 28, 1756, Nov. 20, 1759, Jerdone Letterbook, ViW.

an accident: Maria Taylor Byrd to William Byrd, July 13, 18, Aug. 15, 1760, *Correspondence of the Byrds*, ed. Tinling, II, 697, 699–701.

"had . . . used": Biographical Sketch of Mary Willing Byrd, BR Box 274(57), CSmH.

"Terrible": Richard Corbin to Robert Dinwiddie, Oct. 8, 1760, Corbin Letterbook, ViWC.

60   "I have . . . durst": George Washington to Robert Dinwiddie, May 29, 1754, *Papers of Washington: Colonial*, ed. Abbot *et al.*, I, 107.

"That . . . more!": George Washington to John Robinson, Sept. 1, 1758, *ibid.*, V, 432. See also John Forbes to Henry Bouquet, Sept. 23, 1758, [Mary Carson Darlington], comp., *Fort Pitt and Letters from the Frontier* (Pittsburgh, 1892), 72–73.

"attacked" . . . "gay": John Tayloe to William Byrd, April 4, 1758, *Correspondence of the Byrds*, ed. Tinling, II, 646.

"little bastard": John Custis to William Byrd, [ca. Jan. 1725], *ibid.*, I, 351.

61   her attorney: John Mercer to Martha Custis, Jan. 4, 1758, *"Worthy Partner": The Papers of Martha Washington*, ed. Joseph E. Fields (Westport, 1994), 30.

"possibly . . . him": John Custis to Caesar Rodney, [ca. 1724], John Custis Letterbook, Custis-Lee Families Papers, DLC; *Charles Dunbar v. Daniel Parke Custis*, June 24, 1757, Add MSS 36,217, ff. 161–171, Uk; Douglas Southall Freeman, *George Washington: A Biography* (New York, 1948–57), II, 280–301; "Settlement of the Daniel Parke Custis Estate," *Papers of Washington: Colonial*, ed. Abbot *et al.*, VI, 201–313.

PAGE

61 "leave . . . Land": George Mercer to George Washington, Sept. 16, 1759, *Papers of Washington: Colonial*, ed. Abbot *et al.*, VI, 343.

"mighty" . . . "Proprietors": George Mercer to George Washington, Feb. 17, 1760, *ibid.*, 387–388.

"I . . . despised": Adam Stephen to Richard Henry Lee, Feb. 24, 1760, Lee Family Papers, ViU; Harry M. Ward, *Major General Adam Stephen and the Cause of American Liberty* (Charlottesville, 1989), 64–65.

its smallest crops: Peter V. Bergstrom, *Markets and Merchants: Economic Diversification in Colonial Virginia, 1700–1775* (New York, 1985), 136; Calvin Brewster Coulter, Jr., "The Virginia Merchant" (Ph.D. diss., Princeton University, 1944), 145.

Dr. Thomas Walker: Thomas Walker to George Washington, Aug. 14, 1758, *Papers of Washington: Colonial*, ed. Abbot *et al.*, V, 391.

"common Price": John Syme to Lidderdale, Harmer & Farell, May 8, 1757, *Jones' Exor.* v. *John Syme*, 1797, USCCVD(EC), Vi.

"all cash": Francis Jerdone to Hugh Crawford, June 10, 1758, Jerdone Letterbook, ViW.

"continually riding": John Snelson to William Montgomery & Son, June 4, 1758, Feb. 1, 1759, John Snelson Letterbook, Fredericks Hall Plantation Records, NcU.

62 1755 Twopenny Act: William Robinson to Bishop of London, Aug. 12, 1765, Fulham Papers, Lambeth Palace.

1758 Twopenny Act: Francis Fauquier to Board of Trade, Jan. 5, 1759, *The Official Papers of Francis Fauquier*, ed. George Reese (Charlottesville, 1980–83), I, 144.

"founded . . . Oppression": Petition to the King, Oct. 20, 1760, CO 5/1330, f. 52, PRO; William Nelson *et al.* to Edward Montague, Dec. 12, 1759, *VMHB*, X (April 1903), 349–350.

"they . . . fortunes": [William Burke], *An Account of the European Settlements in America* (London, 1757), II, 208.

"swallowed . . . Debt": George Washington to Robert Stewart, April 27, 1763, *Papers of Washington: Colonial*, ed. Abbot *et al.*, VII, 207; Bruce A. Ragsdale, "George Washington, the British Tobacco Trade, and Economic Opportunity in Prerevolutionary Virginia," *VMHB*, XCVII (1989), 143–149; Michael J. Rozbicki, *The Complete Colonial Gentleman: Cultural Legitimacy in Plantation America* (Charlottesville, 1998), 141–150; Robert F. Dalzell, Jr., and Lee Baldwin Dalzell, *George Washington's Mount Vernon: At Home in Revolutionary America* (New York, 1998), 53–63.

a Pennsylvania farmer: *Expedition of Major General Braddock*, 23.

"a Great . . . him": John Syme to Farell & Jones, Feb. 2, 1764, *Jones' Exor.* v. *John Syme*, 1797, USCCVD(EC), Vi; William W. Reynolds, "Merchant and Investor: Additional Chapters on the Career of Dr. Thomas Walker," *MACH*, LII (1994), 1–21; Thomson, "Merchant in Virginia," 212–213.

"the common . . . Planters": Charles Carter to Charles Goore, Aug. 10, 1763, Carter Family Letterbook, ViU.

63 "Scotch stores": Garland Anderson to Bogle & Scott, July 30, 1764, Garland Anderson Papers, ViFreJM.

marked up: "A VIRGINIAN," Rind's *Virginia Gazette* (Williamsburg), Dec. 11, 1766; William Allason to Alexander Walker, June 24, 1764, William Allason Letterbooks, Vi;

William Lee to Francis Lightfoot Lee, July 24, 1771, William Lee Letterbook, 1769–1771, duPont Library, Stratford, Virginia.

"command" . . . "Customers": William Allason to Alexander Walker, June 24, 1764, Allason Letterbooks, Vi. See also T. M. Devine, *The Tobacco Lords: A Study of the Tobacco Merchants of Glasgow and Their Trading Activities* (Edinburgh, 1975), 59–60; William R. Brock, *Scotus Americanus* (Edinburgh, 1982), chap. 3; Charles J. Farmer, *In the Absence of Towns: Settlement and Country Trade in Southside Virginia, 1730–1800* (Lanham, 1993), 174–183.

"common buckskins": Alexander Stewart, Memorial, Jan. 30, 1749, in Henry Paton, ed., *The Lyon in Mourning* (Edinburgh, 1895), II, 242.

"seated . . . Derision": Brent Tarter, ed., *The Order Book and Related Papers of the Common Hall of the Borough of Norfolk, Virginia, 1736–1798* (Richmond, 1979), 101.

"held . . . Glasgow": John Baylor to John Backhouse, July 18, 1764, John Baylor Letterbook, Vi.

Scots took care: William Lee to Landon Carter, Oct. 30, 1770, William Lee Letterbook, 1770–1771, duPont Library, Stratford.

"secrets . . . Trade": William Nelson to Edward and Samuel Athawes, Aug. 12, 1767, Nelson Letterbook, Vi.

"Engrossers": Roger Atkinson to Lionel and Samuel Lyde, July 5, 1769, Roger Atkinson Letterbook, ViU.

"the artful . . . Nation": Purdie and Dixon's *Virginia Gazette*, Nov. 25, 1773.

"unfortunate Debtors": [Randolph], *Letter to a Gentleman*, 11.

"Vassalage & Dependance": Robert Beverley to [?], n.d. [1764], Robert Beverley Letterbook, DLC.

"prudent Management": James Maury to Robert Jackson, July 17, 1762, William Earl Hutchinson, "American Families: The Maurys of Virginia," *Manuscripts*, XLII (1990), 296.

64 "maxims" . . . "future": Robert Beverley to John Bland, Nov. 16, 1761, Beverley Letterbook, DLC. On Scots, see Charles H. Haws, *Scots in the Old Dominion* (Edinburgh, 1980), chaps. 6–7; Alan L. Karras, *Sojourners in the Sun: Scottish Migrants in Jamaica and the Chesapeake, 1740–1800* (Ithaca, 1992), chap. 3; Ian Charles Cargill Graham, *Colonists from Scotland: Emigration to North America, 1707–1783* (Ithaca, 1956), 115–125; David S. Macmillan, "The 'New Men' in Action: Scottish Mercantile and Shipping Operations in the North American Colonies, 1760–1825," in David S. Macmillan, ed., *Canadian Business History: Selected Studies, 1497–1971* (Toronto, 1972), 44–103; Jacob M. Price, "The Rise of Glasgow in the Chesapeake Tobacco Trade, 1707–1775," *WMQ*, 3d ser., XI (April 1954), 179–199; Jacob M. Price and Paul G. E. Clemens, "A Revolution of Scale in Overseas Trade: British Firms in the Chesapeake Trade, 1675–1775," *JEcH*, XLVII (March 1987), 1–43. On tobacco trade and indebtedness, see also John Brewer, "Commercialization and Politics," in Neil McKendrick, John Brewer, and J. H. Plumb, *The Birth of a Consumer Society: The Commercialization of Eighteenth-Century England* (Bloomington, 1982), 210–213; Edwin J. Perkins, *The Economy of Colonial America* (New York, 1980), 30–35; Jacob M. Price, "Capital and Credit in the British-Chesapeake Trade, 1750–1775," in Virginia Bever Platt and David Curtis Skaggs, eds., *Of Mother Country and Plantations* (Bowling Green, 1971), 8–14; Jacob M. Price, *Capital and Credit in British Overseas Trade:*

PAGE

The View from the Chesapeake, 1700–1776 (Cambridge, 1980); John W. Tyler, "Foster Cunliffe and Sons: Liverpool Merchants in the Maryland Tobacco Trade, 1738–1765," *MHM*, LXXIII (Sept. 1978), 246–279; Julian Hoppit, *Risk and Failure in English Business, 1700–1800* (Cambridge, 1987), 98–103; Bruce A. Ragsdale, *A Planters' Republic: The Search for Economic Independence in Revolutionary Virginia* (Madison, 1996), chap. 1.

64 "remarkably homely": William Wirt Henry, *Patrick Henry: Life, Correspondence and Speeches* (New York, 1891), II, 128.

"seem'd . . . Husband": William Byrd, *The Writings of "Colonel William Byrd of Westover in Virginia Esqr.,"* ed. John Spencer Bassett (New York, 1901), 383. See also Eva C. Hartless, *Sarah Winston Syme Henry: Mother of Patrick Henry* (Boston, 1977).

"beginning" . . . "largely": John Syme to Lidderdale, Harmer & Farell, June 9, 1753, *Jones' Exor.* v. *John Syme*, 1797, USCCVD(EC), Vi.

"Oblig'd . . . largely": John Syme to Lidderdale, Harmer & Farell, May 27, 1754, *ibid.*

"My . . . Expensive": John Syme to Joseph Farell, June 2, 1760, *ibid.*

"extravagance . . . economy": Andrew Burnaby, *Travels Through the Middle Settlements in North America, in the Years 1759 and 1760*, 3d ed., ed. Rufus Rockwell Wilson (New York, 1904), 55, 61–62.

his mother-in-law: John Syme to Mildred Walker, June 5, 1755, Page-Walker Manuscripts, ViU.

65 "I am . . . also": John Syme to Joseph Farell, June 2, 1760, *Jones' Exor.* v. *John Syme*, 1797, USCCVD(EC), Vi.

opened a store: John Syme to Farell & Jones, May 25, 1768, *ibid.* See also *Samuel Waterman* v. *John Syme*, 1791, *John Jackson* v. *John Syme*, 1798, *Smith, Son & Russell* v. *John Syme*, 1796, *ibid.*; John Snelson to Edward Harford, Jr., June 10, 1772, Snelson Letterbook, NcU.

"Clear . . . score": John Syme to Farell & Jones, May 21, 1763, and Farell & Jones's comments on this letter, *Jones' Exor.* v. *John Syme*, 1797, USCCVD(EC), Vi.

"I . . . Vacancy": John Syme to Farell & Jones, May 25, 1768, *ibid.*

"my . . . Credit": John Syme to Farell & Jones, June 20, 1766, *ibid.*

£20,000: John Wayles to Farell & Jones, Aug. 30, 1766, John M. Hemphill, II, ed., "John Wayles Rates His Neighbours," *VMHB*, LXVI (July 1958), 304. See also Charles Steuart to William Bowden, March 4, 1762, Charles Steuart Letterbooks, PHi.

"trifling" . . . "fellow": John Wayles to Farell & Jones, March 29, 1769, Claim of John Tyndale Warre, T 79/9, PRO.

"nothing" . . . "refuse": John Syme to Farell & Jones, March 29, 1769, *Jones' Exor.* v. *John Syme*, 1797, USCCVD(EC), Vi.

avoid the sheriff: John Wayles to Farell & Jones, July 27, 1769, June 13, 1770, Claim of John Tyndale Warre, T 79/9, PRO.

66 Admiral George Anson: John Daly Burk *et al.*, *The History of Virginia* (Petersburg, 1804–16), III, 333–334; Graham Hood, *The Governor's Palace in Williamsburg: A Cultural Study* (Williamsburg, 1991), 143–144; Thomas Jefferson to L. H. Girardin, Jan. 15, 1815, *The Writings of Thomas Jefferson*, ed. Andrew A. Lipscomb and Albert Ellery Bergh (Washington, 1903), XIV, 231–232.

"no . . . happy": James Abercromby to John Blair, March 3, 1758, *The Letter Book of James Abercromby, Colonial Agent: 1751–1773*, ed. John C. Van Horne and George Reese (Richmond, 1991), 227.

Dinwiddie and the Board: *Journal of the Commissioners for Trade and Plantations from January 1754 to December 1758* (London, 1933), 386–387; Robert Dinwiddie to Richard Corbin, Nov. 1758, *Official Records of Dinwiddie*, ed. Brock, II, 723.

Fauquier and the Virginians: Francis Fauquier to Board of Trade, June 11, 28, Sept. 23, 1758, April 10, 1759, *Official Papers of Fauquier*, ed. Reese, I, 24, 43–44, 75–76, 204–205.

"The Govr . . . off": William Ramsay to George Washington, Oct. 17–19, 1758, *Papers of Washington: Colonial*, ed. Abbot *et al.*, VI, 81.

Twopenny Act: Francis Fauquier to Board of Trade, Jan. 5, 1759, *Official Papers of Fauquier*, ed. Reese, I, 144–145.

67   "it is . . . Flattery": [Randolph], *Letter to a Gentleman*, 11.

"the Darling . . . be": Francis Fauquier to Board of Trade, May 12, 1761, *Official Papers of Fauquier*, ed. Reese, II, 525.

"for by . . . carried": Robert Stewart to George Washington, March 19, 1762, *Papers of Washington: Colonial*, ed. Abbot *et al.*, VII, 121.

"designing People": James Abercromby to Richard Corbin, Jan. 1, 1760, *Letter Book of Abercromby*, ed. Van Horne and Reese, 334.

"ill" . . . "satisfaction": Committee of Correspondence to Edward Montague, June 13, 1761, *VMHB*, XI (July 1903), 25. See also Jack P. Greene, "The Attempt to Separate the Offices of Speaker and Treasurer in Virginia, 1758–1766," *ibid.*, LXXI (Jan. 1963), 11–18; Jack P. Greene, " '*Virtus et Libertas*': Political Culture, Social Change, and the Origins of the American Revolution in Virginia, 1763–1766," in Jeffrey J. Crow and Larry E. Tise, eds., *The Southern Experience in the American Revolution* (Chapel Hill, 1978), 59–62; Nellie Norkus, "Francis Fauquier, Lieutenant-Governor of Virginia, 1758–1768: A Study in Colonial Problems" (Ph.D. diss., University of Pittsburgh, 1954).

"great . . . Country": "Characters of leading Men & Descriptions of Places in Virginia," Peter Russell Papers, CaOTP. See also Robert Dinwiddie to Andrew Lewis, Oct. 1757, *Official Records of Dinwiddie*, ed. Brock, II, 711.

Thomas Johnson: H. R. McIlwaine, ed., *Journals of the House of Burgesses of Virginia, 1758–1761* (Richmond, 1908), 59, 88–90, 114. See also John Forbes to Henry Bouquet, June 2, 9, 1758, John St. Clair to Henry Bouquet, June 17, 1758, Henry Bouquet to John Forbes, Aug. 20, 1758, *The Papers of Henry Bouquet*, ed. S. K. Stevens *et al.* (Harrisburg, 1951), II, 6, 61, 110, 394; George Washington to Henry Bouquet, July 7, 1758, Thomas Walker to George Washington, July 24, Aug. 14, 1758, Charles Smith to George Washington, Aug. 17, 1758, *Papers of Washington: Colonial*, ed. Abbot *et al.*, V, 267, 324, 391–392; John Stanwix to Henry Bouquet, May 18, 1759, Bouquet Papers, Add MSS 21,638, f. 11, Uk.

68   Cherokee war: Tom Hatley, *The Dividing Paths: Cherokees and South Carolinians through the Era of Revolution* (New York, 1995), chap. 10; Gregory Evans Dowd, " 'Insidious Friends': Gift Giving and the Cherokee-British Alliance in the Seven Years' War," in Andrew R. L. Cayton and Fredrika J. Teute, eds., *Contact Points: American Frontiers from the Mohawk Valley to the Mississippi, 1750–1830* (Chapel Hill, 1998), 114–150.

69 25,000 acres: Francis Fauquier to Board of Trade, Dec. 1, 1759, *Official Papers of Fauquier,* ed. Reese, I, 276; Henry Bouquet to Thomas Cresap, Sept. 12, 1760, Bouquet Papers, Add MSS 21,653, ff. 24–25, Uk.

"well . . . Colony": Francis Fauquier to Board of Trade, Jan. 30, 1759, Board of Trade to Francis Fauquier, June 13, 1760, *Official Papers of Fauquier,* ed. Reese, I, 165, 376–377.

"no . . . procured": Henry Bouquet to Thomas Cresap, Sept. 12, 1760, Bouquet Papers, Add MSS 21,653, ff. 24–25, Uk.

"new . . . Tenure": Henry Bouquet to Thomas Gage, June 23, 1764, Bouquet Papers, Add MSS 21,637, ff. 39–40, *ibid.* See also "Hints relative to the Division & Government," [1763], Grenville Correspondence, STG Box 17(31), CSmH; Jack M. Sosin, *Whitehall and the Wilderness: The Middle West in British Colonial Policy, 1760–1775* (Lincoln, 1961), 42–46; McConnell, *A Country Between,* 168–169; Philip Lawson, *George Grenville: A Political Life* (Oxford, 1984), 185–186.

a royal proclamation: Oct. 7, 1763, Clarence S. Brigham, ed., *British Royal Proclamations Relating to America, 1603–1783,* American Antiquarian Society, *Transactions and Collections,* XII (1911), 212–218.

"a temporary . . . years": George Washington to William Crawford, Sept. 17, 1767, *Papers of Washington: Colonial,* ed. Abbot *et al.,* VIII, 28. See also Sosin, *Whitehall and the Wilderness,* 105–109; Louis DeVorsey, Jr., *The Indian Boundary in the Southern Colonies, 1763–1775* (Chapel Hill, 1966), 34–40.

"stragling Settlements": Francis Fauquier to Earl of Shelburne, Nov. 18, 1766, *Official Papers of Fauquier,* ed. Reese, III, 1394.

"Vagabonds" and "borderers": Henry Bouquet to Francis Fauquier, Feb. 8, 1762, *ibid.,* II, 677; Thomas Walpole to Earl of Hillsborough, July 16, 1770, *The Correspondence of William Nelson as Acting Governor of Virginia, 1770–1771,* ed. John C. Van Horne (Charlottesville, 1975), 22.

"very troublesome": Testimony of Mr. Hanny, Feb. 1, 1772, W. L. Grant and James Munro, eds., *Acts of the Privy Council of England. Colonial Series* (London, 1908–12), V, 207.

"extremely fine": Francis Fauquier to Earl of Shelburne, Dec. 18, 1766, *Official Papers of Fauquier,* ed. Reese, III, 1412.

"it is . . . distant": Grant and Munro, eds., *Acts of the Privy Council,* VI, 516. See also Eugene M. Del Papa, "The Royal Proclamation of 1763: Its Effect Upon Virginia Land Companies," *VMHB,* LXXXIII (Oct. 1975), 406–411.

the Mississippi Company: *Papers of Washington: Colonial,* ed. Abbot *et al.,* VII, 219–223, 242–250; Clarence E. Carter, ed., "Documents Relating to the Mississippi Land Company, 1763–1769," *AHR,* XVI (Jan. 1911), 311–319; [Samuel Wharton], [*Statement for the Petitioners in the Case of the Walpole Company Grant*] [London?, 1772], 19–20; John Armistead to John Norton & Son, Sept. 15, 1765, BR Box 18(24), CSmH; George Washington, Account with Mississippi Adventure, Ledger A, p. 169, Papers of George Washington, Series 5, Financial Records, Vol. 1, DLC; Nathaniel Whitaker to Eleazar Wheelock, March 19–22, 1766, in Leon Burr Richardson, ed., *An Indian Preacher in England* (Hanover, 1933), 114.

71 "postpond": Benjamin J. Hillman, ed., *Executive Journals of the Council of Colonial Virginia* (Richmond, 1966), VI, 257.

PAGE

Walker and the councillors: Henderson, "Dr. Thomas Walker," American Antiquarian Society, *Proceedings*, new series, XLI (1931), 101.

Walker and the Loyal Company: Statement on Behalf of Loyal Company, July 27, 1803, *The Letters and Papers of Edmund Pendleton*, ed. David John Mays (Charlottesville, 1967), II, 709; [William Preston], [Affidavit], n.d., Preston Family Papers, P9267f/FA2, ViRHi; William Nelson to Secretary of State, Oct. 18, 1770, *Correspondence of Nelson*, ed. Van Horne, 42; Lewis Preston Summers, *History of Southwest Virginia, 1746–1786* (Baltimore, 1966 [orig. publ. Richmond, 1903]), 82–83.

more than 150,000 acres: *French v. The Successors of the Loyal Company*, July 1834, 5 Leigh 663, *Reports of Cases Argued and Determined in the Court of Appeals and in the General Court of Virginia* (Charlottesville, 1903), X, 239.

"secret . . . monger": Richard Henderson to John Williams, Sept. 13, 1779, John Williams Papers, NcD.

"to the . . . Adventurer": Hillman, ed., *Executive Journals*, VI, 458.

72 Some later petitioned: Petition of Inhabitants of Washington and Montgomery Counties, [ca. May 1778?] and "Draught of Petition," Arthur Campbell Papers, KyLoF. See Thomas Walker to William Preston, May 28, 1778, Henderson, "Dr. Thomas Walker," American Antiquarian Society, *Proceedings*, new series, XLI (1931), 152.

"The Doctrs . . . broke": Robert Doack to William Preston, Oct. 28, 1772, Preston Papers, Vol. 2, f. 137, Draper Collection, Series QQ, WHi.

Norfolk: Malcolm Cameron Clark, "The Coastwise and Caribbean Trade of the Chesapeake Bay, 1696–1776" (Ph.D. diss., Georgetown University, 1970); Costa, "Economic Development"; Thomas C. Parramore, Peter C. Stewart, and Tommy L. Bogger, *Norfolk: The First Four Centuries* (Charlottesville, 1994), chap. 6.

Sparling, Jamieson, and Campbell: M. M. Schofield, "The Virginia Trade of the Firm of Sparling and Bolden, of Liverpool," *Transactions of the Historic Society of Lancashire and Cheshire*, CXVI (1965), 120; Alexander Fraser, comp., *Second Report of the Bureau of Archives for the Province of Ontario: 1904* (Toronto, 1905), 132–133, 630–633, 646; Memorandum of the Sale, Aug. 17, 1780, Norfolk County, Escheated Estates, Records, Entry 658, Auditor of Public Accounts, Vi.

"Saw . . . return": Purdie and Dixon's *Virginia Gazette*, Dec. 17, 1767.

"were . . . Builder": Hugh Edward Egerton, ed., *The Royal Commission on the Losses and Services of American Loyalists, 1783 to 1785: Being the Notes of Mr. Daniel Parker Coke, M.P.* (Oxford, 1915), 366. See also Joseph A. Goldenberg, *Shipbuilding in Colonial America* (Charlottesville, 1976), 62–65, 117–120; William M. Kelso, "Shipbuilding in Virginia, 1763–1774," Columbia Historical Society, *Records*, XLVIII (1971–72), 1–13.

73 seamen: Arthur Pierce Middleton, *Tobacco Coast: A Maritime History of Chesapeake Bay in the Colonial Era* (Newport News, 1953), 274–278; Jeremiah Morgan to Francis Fauquier, Sept. 11, 1767, *Official Papers of Fauquier*, ed. Reese, III, 1500–1502; Clark, "Coastwise and Caribbean Trade," 151.

"the Scotch" and "the Buckskin": Henry Fleming to Littledale & Co., June 7, 1773, Papers of Henry Fleming, Cumbria Record Office, Kendal.

William Aitchison and James Parker: Memorial of William Aitchison, March 18, 1784, American Loyalist Claims, AO 13/27, PRO; Egerton, ed., *Royal Commission*, 390–391;

Costa, "Economic Development," 106–107; Karras, *Sojourners,* 157–158; William Lux to Aitchison & Parker, Dec. 26, 1763, April 18, Sept. 17, 1764, William Lux Letterbook, NNHi; "Jamieson-Ellegood-Parker," *WMQ,* 1st ser., XIII (April 1905), 287–288.

employed Macknight: Thomas Macknight to John Elmsley, Nov. 1, 1791, James Parker to John Elmsley, Jan. 1, 1792, Parker Papers, Liverpool Public Library; Memorial of Thomas Macknight, American Loyalist Claims, AO 13/121–122, PRO; D. L. Corbitt, "Thomas Macknight," *NCHR,* II (Oct. 1925), 502–525; entries of May 5, Sept. 14, 1761, Pasquotank County, Granville Proprietary Land Office, Entry Books, 1751–1763, Secretary of State, Nc-Ar; Egerton, ed., *Royal Commission,* 361–368.

"a pretty little Town": Entry of Feb. 19, 1765, Journal of James Auld, William Alexander Smith Papers, Box 32, NcD. See also John W. Reps, *Tidewater Towns: City Planning in Colonial Virginia and Maryland* (Williamsburg, 1972), 213; Floyd McKnight, "The Town and City of Suffolk, 1742–1957," in Rogers Dey Whichard, *The History of Lower Tidewater Virginia* (New York, 1959), II, 157–159; entry of Sept. 13–15, 1773, "Journal of General James Whitelaw," Vermont Historical Society, *Proceedings* (1905–06), 144.

74 James Gibson: Memorial of James Gibson, American Loyalist Claims, AO 12/55 and AO 13/58, Folder G, PRO; Fraser, ed., *Second Report of the Bureau of Archives of Ontario,* 646.

cargo to Tenerife: Costa, "Economic Development," 85; Richard Corbin to Robert Tucker, Feb. 15, 1760, Richard Corbin to Capel and Osgood Hanbury, Feb. 17, 1760, Richard Corbin Letterbook, ViWC.

Tucker fell behind: Gerard R. Beekman to Archibald White, Dec. 12, 1761, *The Beekman Mercantile Papers, 1746–1799,* ed. Philip L. White (New York, 1956), I, 397.

bills of exchange: Richard Corbin to Robert Dinwiddie, June 12, 1760, Corbin Letterbook, ViWC.

"impatient": William Waller Hening, ed., *The Statutes at Large: Being a Collection of All the Laws of Virginia* (Richmond, Philadelphia, and New York, 1809–23), VII, 458–461; "The Corbin Family," *VMHB,* XXX (July 1922), 310–311.

Gawin Corbin: "Corbin Family," *VMHB,* XXX (July 1922), 312–313; John Peile, comp., *Biographical Register of Christ's College, 1505–1905* (Cambridge, 1913), II, 262.

75 *Two Sisters:* Jeremiah Banning, *Log and Will of Jeremiah Banning* (New York, 1932), unpaginated; Baynton, Wharton & Morgan to Biggen, Bacon & Co., Oct. 21, 1763, Letter Books of Baynton, Wharton & Morgan, PHarH-Ar; Oswald Tilghman, *History of Talbot County, Maryland, 1661–1861* (Baltimore, 1915), II, 358; Silvanus Grove to Samuel Galloway, Feb. 2, 1761, Galloway-Maxcy-Markoe Papers, DLC; Walter Minchinton, Celia King, and Peter Waite, eds., *Virginia Slave-Trade Statistics, 1698–1775* (Richmond, 1984), 159; James F. Searing, *West African Slavery and Atlantic Commerce: The Senegal River Valley, 1700–1860* (Cambridge, 1993), 106–109. On Banning's previous voyage, see his advertisement in *Maryland Gazette* (Annapolis), July 29, 1762, appendix.

Anthony Bacon's contracts: Charles Steuart to Anthony Bacon, Oct. 11, Nov. 10, 1757, Charles Steuart Letterbooks, PHi; Anthony Bacon to Samuel Martin, June 25, 1761, T 1/411, f. 60, PRO; Treasury Minute Books, June 19, 1759, T 29/33, p. 195, PRO; L. B. Namier, "Anthony Bacon, M.P., an Eighteenth-Century Merchant," *JEcBH,* II (Nov. 1929), 27–31.

a private gallery: George Carrington Mason, "The Colonial Churches of Spotsylvania and Caroline Counties, Virginia," *VMHB*, LVIII (Oct. 1950), 455.

76 John Thornton: Joseph Jones to James Madison, Feb. 10, 1792, *The Papers of James Madison*, ed. William T. Hutchinson, William M. E. Rachal, *et al.* (Chicago and Charlottesville, 1962–), XIV, 227; John Thornton to Robert Dinwiddie, Oct. 29, 1757, William P. Palmer *et al.*, eds., *Calendar of Virginia State Papers* (Richmond, 1875–93), I, 252–253; Hillman, ed., *Executive Journals*, VI, 74.

"the extensive . . . Ohio": Edward Athawes *et al.* to William Pitt, Feb. 6, 1759, Correspondence of the First Lord and Lady Chatham, PRO 30/8/48, f. 187, PRO.

sale of lots: William Armstrong Crozier, ed., *Spotsylvania County Records, 1721–1800* (Baltimore, 1955), 184, 190, 193, 198, 203, 208, 218, 221–222, 225–226, 255, 257; George Washington to Robert Cary & Co., March 16, 1762, *Papers of Washington: Colonial*, ed. Abbot *et al.*, VII, 119–120.

Among Bacon's customers: Account with Anthony Bacon & Compa, Financial Records, Ledger A, p. 16, Papers of George Washington, Series 5, DLC; Charles Carroll to Anthony Bacon, June 30, Aug. 20, 1758, Aug. 27, 1759, Sept. 17, 1760, Oct. 12, 1763, Oct. 2, 1764, "Letters of Charles Carroll, Barrister," *MHM*, XXXII (June 1937), 181, 185, 189–190, (Dec. 1937), 354, XXXIII (June 1938), 191, (Dec. 1938), 381, XXXIV (June 1939), 182–183; George Braxton to Anthony Bacon, Sept. 7, 1757, Frederick Horner, *The History of the Blair, Banister, and Braxton Families Before and After the Revolution* (Philadelphia, 1898), 145; *Maryland Gazette*, Sept. 6, Nov. 22, 1764.

arms and ammunition: Anthony Bacon to Principal Officers of Ordnance, May 7, Nov. 26, 1756, Feb. 28, 1757, T 1/371, 1/377, PRO; Francis Jerdone to Hugh Crawford, Dec. 28, 1756, Francis Jerdone Letterbook, ViW. See also Jenny West, *Gunpowder, Government and War in the Mid-Eighteenth Century* (Woodbridge, 1991), 143.

77 the *York*: Frank F. White, Jr., "A List of Convicts Transported to Maryland," *MHM*, XLIII (March 1948), 55–60; John M. Hemphill, II, "Freight Rates in the Maryland Tobacco Trade, 1705–1762," *ibid.*, LIV (June 1959), 178–179.

Captain Comely Coppernose: Elaine G. Breslaw, ed., *Records of the Tuesday Club of Annapolis, 1745–1756* (Urbana, 1988), 109–110, 164, 172–173; Alexander Hamilton, *The History of the Ancient and Honorable Tuesday Club*, ed. Robert Micklus (Chapel Hill, 1990), I–II; Wilson Somerville, *The Tuesday Club of Annapolis (1745–1756) as Cultural Performance* (Athens, 1997). On Thomas Bacon, see J. A. Leo Lemay, *Men of Letters in Colonial Maryland* (Knoxville, 1972), 313–342.

in Whitehaven: Jacob M. Price, *France and the Chesapeake: A History of the French Tobacco Monopoly, 1674–1791* (Ann Arbor, 1973), I, 597.

the elder William Waters: See marginal note, Oct. 21, 1757, on William Waters, Will, July 3, 1720, 205 Marlborough, 6th folio, Will-Register Books, Principal Probate Registry, London. Summarized in "Virginia Gleanings in London," *VMHB*, X (April 1903), 411–412. The powers of attorney are in American Papers, No. 34, House of Lords, London.

William Waters, the son: David Meade, "Family History," in Henry J. Peet, ed., *Chaumiere Papers, Containing Matters of Interest to the Descendants of David Meade* (Chicago,

PAGE

1883), 28; Mary E. McWilliams, "William Waters House Historical Report, 12," ViWC; Inventory and Appraisement of the Estate of William Waters, Wills and Inventories, 1760–1771, ff. 460–472, York County Records, No. 21, Yorktown, Virginia.

77 "of a . . . value": Memorial of London Merchants, [ca. June 21, 1758], *Official Papers of Fauquier*, ed. Reese, I, 38–41.

North Carolina currency: William L. Saunders *et al.*, eds., *The Colonial Records of North Carolina* (Raleigh, 1886–), VI, 16–17.

78 Earl Granville: *Ibid.*, 249–250, 307–308, 323–324, 423–424, 517, 692; Walter Clark, ed., *The State Records of North Carolina* (Winston and Goldsboro, 1895–1905), XXIII, 392–398; Memorial of Anthony Bacon, Joshua Sharpe Papers, NcU; Desmond Clarke, *Arthur Dobbs, Esquire: 1689–1765* (London, 1958), 176–177; Schaw, *Journal of a Lady*, ed. Andrews and Andrews, appendix vii; Beverley W. Bond, *The Quit-Rent System in the American Colonies* (New Haven, 1919), 76–80, 301–309; Ella Lonn, *The Colonial Agents of the Southern Colonies* (Chapel Hill, 1945), 80–83; Thornton W. Mitchell, "The Granville District and Its Land Records," *NCHR*, LXX (April 1993), 114–116.

79 Mann Page's debts: Claim of John Lloyd, Claim of John Tyndale Warre, T 79/19, 79/38, PRO.

Hanover-Town: John Pendleton Kennedy, ed., *Journals of the House of Burgesses of Virginia, 1761–1765* (Richmond, 1907), 10, 19, 22, 25, 27; Royle's *Virginia Gazette*, Nov. 4, 1763; Richard Corbin to Capel and Osgood Hanbury, Nov. 19, 1763, Corbin Letterbook, ViWC; Malcolm H. Harris, "The Port Towns of the Pamunkey," *WMQ*, 2d ser., XXIII (Oct. 1943), 511–512.

the Council and Burwell: Hillman, ed., *Executive Journals*, VI, 228–229; Francis Fauquier to Board of Trade, July 31, 1762, May 28, 1763, *Official Papers of Fauquier*, ed. Reese, II, 781–783, 957.

80 "on account . . . station": Richard Henry Lee to James Abercromby, Aug. 27, 1762, *The Letters of Richard Henry Lee*, ed. James Curtis Ballagh (New York, 1912), I, 1–2.

"dayly . . . Interests": James Abercromby to Francis Fauquier, Feb. 5, 1763, *Letter Book of Abercromby*, ed. Van Horne and Reese, 410–411.

the Board and Fauquier: Board of Trade to Francis Fauquier, March 11, 1763, Francis Fauquier to Board of Trade, July 31, 1762, May 28, 1763, *Official Papers of Fauquier*, ed. Reese, II, 929, 783, 957; Hillman, ed., *Executive Journals*, VI, 257.

81 "a scheme" . . . "certain assurances": [Samuel Johnston] to [Thomas Barker], [ca. April 1763], Hayes Collection, Johnston Family Series, Box 1, NcU.

for a grant: Hillman, ed., *Executive Journals*, VI, 257–258; Dismal Swamp Land Company Articles of Agreement, Nov. 3, 1763, *Papers of Washington: Colonial*, ed. Abbot *et al.*, VII, 271–273n.1.

82 "a low . . . Agriculture": John Harvie to Thomas Jefferson, May 15, 1798, Andrew Kidd to William Vaughan, March 3, 1805, William Short Papers, DLC.

Washington felt certain: Entry of Oct. 15, 1763, *The Diaries of George Washington*, ed. Donald Jackson and Dorothy Twohig (Charlottesville, 1976–79), I, 319–326; cash accounts, May 1763, *Papers of Washington: Colonial*, ed. Abbot *et al.*, VII, 209–212; "A survey made for the Dismal Swamp Compy," Papers of George Washington, Series 9, Box 1,

PAGE

DLC; Edmund Berkeley and Dorothy Berkeley, "Man and the Great Dismal," *Virginia Journal of Science*, XXVII (1976), 146–147.

83 "of . . . others": Articles of Agreement, *Papers of Washington: Colonial*, ed. Abbot *et al.*, VII, 273n.1.

"Gentlemen" . . . "Expectations": Francis Fauquier to Board of Trade, July 23, 1764, *Official Papers of Fauquier*, ed. Reese, III, 1132.

its first meeting: Articles of Agreement and Minutes of Meeting, Nov. 3, 1763, *Papers of Washington: Colonial*, ed. Abbot *et al.*, VII, 269–276; Miles King, Receipt, Nov. 5, 1763, Gershom Nimmo, Receipt, Nov. 5, 1763, Dismal Swamp Land Company Records, NcD.

84 Queen Elizabeth's Hospital: John Entick, *The Present State of the British Empire* (London, 1774), III, 363; C. P. Hill, *The History of Bristol Grammar School* (London, 1951), 56–59; John Latimer, *The Annals of Bristol in the Eighteenth Century* (n.p., 1893), 12, 16, 46–49, 486; William Barrett, *The History and Antiquities of the City of Bristol* (Bristol, 1789), 376–379; Roger Wilson, "Bristol's Schools," in C. M. MacInnes and W. F. Whittand, eds., *Bristol and Its Adjoining Counties* (Bristol, 1955), 313; Ronald W. Herlan, "Relief of the Poor in Bristol from Late Elizabethan Times until the Restoration Era," American Philosophical Society, *Proceedings*, CXXVI (June 1982), 218; Ivy Pinchbeck and Margaret Hewitt, *Children in English Society* (London, 1969–73), I, chap. 9; Paul Langford, *A Polite and Commercial People: England, 1727–1783* (Oxford, 1989), 128–133. On Gloucestershire weavers, see J. deL. Mann, *The Cloth Industry in the West of England from 1640 to 1880* (Oxford, 1971), esp. chap. 4.

"for my . . . Plantership": Samuel Martin to Samuel Martin, Jr., Jan. 31, 1774, Samuel Martin Letterbook, 1768–1776, Add MSS 41,348, f. 157, Uk.

"Store . . . attention": Samuel Gist to John Smith, July 21, 1767, *Jos. Smith's Admr et al. v. Gist's Exor et al.*, 1825, USCCVD(EC), Vi.

Gist and John Smith: *Jos. Smith's Admr et al. v. Gist's Exor et al.*, 1825, USCCVD(EC), Vi; William Nelson to Thomas and Rowland Hunt, July 3, 1772, William Nelson Letterbook, Vi; Claim of Samuel Gist, American Loyalist Claims, AO 13/30, T 79/39, PRO; C. G. Chamberlayne, ed., *The Vestry Book of St. Paul's Parish, Hanover County, Virginia, 1706–1786* (Richmond, 1940), 312, 339–340; Hunter's *Virginia Gazette*, May 15, 1752; Peter Wilson Coldham, *The Complete Book of Emigrants* (Baltimore, 1987–93), IV, 16; Bond, May 5, 1737, Indenture, 1737, John Shore to William Pollard, July 7, 1800, William Pollard Papers, Pollard Family Papers, ViRHi; Francis Jerdone to Morgan Thomas & Co., May 15, 1756, Jerdone Letterbook, ViW; "Massie Family," *WMQ*, 1st ser., XIII (1905), 196–199; Hening, ed., *Statutes at Large*, VII, 127–130; *Old Homes of Hanover County, Virginia* (Hanover, 1983), 17, 23–24, 64.

85 "I had . . . with it": John Snelson to Christopher Lilly, Sept. 23, 1757, John Snelson to Edward Harford, Sr., Oct. 29, 1757, Snelson Letterbook, NcU.

85 Maury trial: James Maury to John Camm, Dec. 12, 1763, in Ann Maury, *Memoirs of a Huguenot Family* (New York, 1853), 418–423; William Robinson to Bishop of London, Aug. 12, 1765, William Stevens Perry, ed., *Historical Collections Relating to the American Colonial Church* (Hartford, 1870), I, 514; Joseph Henry Smith, *Appeals to the Privy Council from the American Plantations* (New York, 1950), 607–626.

PAGE

87 "much conversation": Thomas Jefferson to William Wirt, Aug. 14, 1814, *The Writings of Thomas Jefferson*, ed. Paul Leicester Ford (New York, 1892–99), IX, 467.

Speaker Robinson and burning: Francis Fauquier to Board of Trade, June 1, 1763, Account of Treasury Notes, May 23, 1763, *Official Papers of Fauquier*, ed. Reese, II, 960–963, 971–973; Richard Henry Lee, Speech, May 1763, Lee Family Papers, ViU; Richard Corbin to Robert Cary, Aug. 8, 1763, Corbin Letterbook, ViWC; Jack M. Sosin, *Agents and Merchants: British Colonial Policy and the Origins of the American Revolution* (Lincoln, 1965), 22–29; Joseph Albert Ernst, *Money and Politics in America, 1755–1775: A Study in the Currency Act of 1764 and the Political Economy of Revolution* (Chapel Hill, 1973), 63–76.

grants: Joseph Jones and Martha Jones, Indenture, Dec. 7, 1764, John Richardson Kilby Papers, Box 43, NcD; Petition of James Murdaugh, Nov. 12, 1791, Legislative Petitions, Nansemond County, Vi; Nansemond County Land Book, 1782, Nansemond County Tax Lists, Vi; James Murdaugh, advertisement, Purdie and Dixon's *Virginia Gazette*, Jan. 13, 1771.

88 Parker, Aitchison, Macknight: James Parker to Charles Steuart, July 5, Nov. 15, 1769, Charles Steuart Papers, UkENL; Claim of Thomas Macknight, American Loyalist Claims, AO 13/121–122, PRO; Egerton, ed., *Royal Commission*, 363–365; [Samuel Johnston] to [Thomas Barker], [ca. April 1763], Hayes Collection, NcU.

89 "in the . . . line": March 26, April 16, 1763, Granville Proprietary Land Office, Entry Books, 1751–1763, Pasquotank County, Nc-Ar.

"secure" . . . "Expectation": [Samuel Johnston] to [Thomas Barker], [ca. April 1763], Hayes Collection, NcU.

Alexander Elmsly: Charles Steuart to James Parker, Feb. 6, 1770, Parker Family Papers, Liverpool Public Library; James Parker to Charles Steuart, Aug. 5–15, 1770, Steuart Papers, UkENL; Mitchell, "Granville District," *NCHR*, LXX (April 1993), 116–117.

"will . . . utility": Hening, ed., *Statutes at Large*, VIII, 18–19; H. R. McIlwaine, ed., *Legislative Journals of the Council of Colonial Virginia*, 2d ed. (Richmond, 1979), 1318–1319; Kennedy, ed., *Journals of the Burgesses, 1761–1765*, 214–219, 222.

89 Page and Burwell: Maria Beverley to Maria Carter, April 20, 1764, "Some Family Letters of the Eighteenth Century," *VMHB*, XV (April 1908), 434; Robert Burwell, Will, Jan. 10, 1777, *WMQ*, 1st ser., VII (April 1899), 311.

90 political economists: John Rutherfurd, *The Importance of the Colonies to Great Britain* (London, 1761), 5–9, 15, 29–31; Adam Anderson, *An Historical and Chronological Deduction of the Origin of Commerce* (London, 1764), I, xvi; Malachy Postlethwayt, *Britain's Commercial Interest Explained and Improved* (New York, 1968 [orig. publ. London, 1757]), 176–178; [John Mitchell], *The Present State of Great Britain and North America* (London, 1767), 143–146; Clark, ed., *State Records of North Carolina*, XXIII, 613–614.

£740,000: Peter Wyche to Charles Carter, May 30, 1761, Guard Book, Vol. 6, No. 49, Royal Society of Arts, London. Compare Rutherfurd, *Importance*, 8, 15.

£300,000: [Mitchell], *Present State*, 8–9n.

the Empress Catherine: Macmillan, " 'New Men' in Action," in Macmillan, ed., *Canadian Business History*, 83.

first lord of the Admiralty: Earl of Egmont to George Grenville, April 16, 1764, *The Grenville Papers*, ed. William James Smith (London, 1852), II, 290–291.

"of the . . . Plant": Charles Carter to Peter Wyche, [Feb. 28, 1761], Guard Book, Vol. 6, No. 47, Royal Society of Arts.

"I firmly . . . Debts": Robert Beverley to [?], [1764], Beverley Letterbook, DLC.

lapsed bounty: Charles Garth to Committee of Correspondence, Feb. 19, 1763, Charles Garth Letterbook, MiU-C; William Knox, "Reasons for granting a Bounty," William Knox Papers, MiU-C; Memorial of the Several Merchants, Nov. 30, 1763, Original Correspondence, Board of Trade, 1763–1764, CO 323/17, ff. 52–53, PRO; Extracts from a Report, Feb. 9, 1764, Liverpool Papers, Add MSS 38,337, ff. 162–173, Uk; R. C. Simmons and P. D. G. Thomas, eds., *Proceedings and Debates of the British Parliaments Respecting North America, 1754–1783* (Millwood, 1982–87), I, 517; Grant and Munro, eds., *Acts of the Privy Council*, IV, 631–636; Sosin, *Agents and Merchants*, 21–22; L. B. Namier, "Charles Garth, Agent for South Carolina," *EnHR*, LIV (Oct. 1939), 638–639; Norman Macdonald, "Hemp and Imperial Defence," *CHR*, XVII (Dec. 1936), 386–387; Herbert H. Kaplan, *Russian Overseas Commerce with Great Britain During the Reign of Catherine II* (Philadelphia, 1995), 66–72.

"I am . . . Navy": Francis Fauquier to Board of Trade, July 23, 1764, *Official Papers of Fauquier*, ed. Reese, III, 1132.

91 Bacon and contracts: Alexander Fall to Charles Jenkinson, Jan. 29, 1764, *The Jenkinson Papers, 1760–1766*, ed. Ninetta S. Jucker (London, 1949), 258–259; Lucy Sutherland, "The City of London in Eighteenth-Century Politics," in Aubrey Newman, ed., *Politics and Finance in the Eighteenth Century* (London, 1984), 43; Norman Baker, *Government and Contractors: The British Treasury and War Supplies, 1775–1783* (London, 1971).

"very extensive": Grant and Munro, eds., *Acts of the Privy Council*, IV, 551; Harold A. Innis, *The Cod Fisheries: The History of an International Economy*, rev. ed. (Toronto, 1954), 191.

Sir George Yonge: George Grenville to George Yonge, Sept. 26, 1763, George Grenville Letterbooks, ST 7, CSmH; John Bindley to Charles Jenkinson, Sept. 19, 1763, Alexander Fall to Charles Jenkinson, Jan. 29, 1764, *Jenkinson Papers*, ed. Jucker, 193–194n, 194, 259.

"he had . . . deserved": Baron Holland to George Selwyn, Aug. 4, 1765, in John Heneage Jesse, *George Selwyn and His Contemporaries* (London, 1843), I, 389; Charles Townshend to Duke of Buccleugh, Dec. 30, 1765, Charles Townshend Papers, MiU-C; Lawson, *Grenville*.

"the vulgar," "the rabble": John Wilkes to Heaton Wilkes, Sept. 3, 1760, John Wilkes to John Dell, June 22, 23, 1757, Aug. 25, 1759, Dec. 27, 1760, Jan. 1, 24, 27, 31, April 21, 1761, John Wilkes Papers, MiU-C; Alan Dell, "A Political Agent at Work in Eighteenth-Century Aylesbury," *Records of Buckinghamshire*, XXX (1988), 117–122; George Rudé, *Wilkes and Liberty: A Social Study of 1763 to 1774* (Oxford, 1962), 17–19.

seditious libel: Lawson, *Grenville*, 166–179; Peter D. G. Thomas, *John Wilkes: A Friend to Liberty* (Oxford, 1996), chaps. 1–3; John Beckett, *The Rise and Fall of the Grenvilles: The Dukes of Buckingham and Chandos, 1710 to 1921* (Manchester, 1994), 45.

92 Bacon and Grenville: George Grenville to Richard Lowndes, Jan. 21, 1764, George Grenville to Charles Lowndes, Jan. 21, 1764, George Grenville to Earl Temple, Sept. 10, 1769, ST 7 and STG Box 192(11), CSmH; Alexander Fall to Charles Jenkinson, Jan. 29, 1764, *Jenkinson Papers*, ed. Jucker, 259. See also George Grenville to James Oswald,

PAGE

March 17, 1748, in *Memorials of the Public Life and Character of the Right Hon. James Oswald* (Edinburgh, 1825), 385–388.

92 silver and gold coins: T 1/402, ff. 88–89, PRO.

"he . . . favourite": Jeremy Bentham to Richard Clark, Aug. 16, 1768, *The Correspondence of Jeremy Bentham*, ed. Timothy L. S. Sprigge (London, 1968), I, 130. See John Sainsbury, "John Wilkes, Debt, and Patriotism," *JBS*, XXXIV (April 1995), 165–195.

Wilkes's pamphlet: John Wilkes, *A Letter to the Worthy Electors of the Borough of Aylesbury* (London, 1764), 3, 10–11, 14, 16; John Wilkes to Humphrey Cotes, Jan. 20, 1764, John Wilkes Correspondence, Add MSS 30,868, f. 25, Uk.

seeking a contract: T 1/365, f. 48, PRO; John Wilkes to Heaton Wilkes, March 16, 1764, Wilkes Papers, MiU-C.

warned Grenville: Simmons and Thomas, eds., *Proceedings and Debates*, I, 508; [Anthony Bacon], *A Short Address to the Government* (London, 1775), 2–3, 6–7.

93 John Syme: John Syme to Farell & Jones, May 10, 21, Nov. 15, 1763, Feb. 2, 1764, *Jones' Exor.* v. *John Syme*, 1797, USCCVD(EC), Vi.

"miserable": Rowland Ash to Charles Tudway, July 24, 1762, May 16, July 25, 1763, Francis Farley to Charles Tudway, Nov. 3, 1762, Dec. 28, 1763, May 20, 1764, Stephen Blizard to Charles Tudway, July 16, 1763, Tudway Papers, Somerset Record Office; Samuel Martin to Samuel Martin, Jr., March 20, 1762, Martin Letterbook, Add MSS 41,347, ff. 128–129, Uk; Theodore Barrell to William Barrell, May 17, 1762, Stephen Collins & Son Papers, DLC.

"valuable property": Francis Farley to John Simon Farley, July 13, 1778, *Decisions in Chancery by Wythe*, 255.

at Louisburg: John Knox, *An Historical Journal of the Campaigns in North America*, ed. Arthur G. Doughty (Toronto, 1914), I, 112–113, 250–253n, 259n; Thomas Byam Martin, "Reminiscences and Notes," *Letters and Papers of Admiral of the Fleet Sir Thos. Byam Martin*, ed. Richard Vesey Hamilton (London, 1903), I, 95; Edward Boscawen to William Pitt, July 26, 1758, in Jeffery Amherst, *A Journal of the Landing of His Majesty's Forces on the Island of Cape-Breton, and of the Siege and Surrender of Louisbourg*, 3d ed. (Boston, [1758]), 20; entry of July 25, 1758, *The Journal of Jeffery Amherst*, ed. J. Clarence Webster (Toronto, 1931), 71; William Wood, ed., *The Logs of the Conquest of Canada* (Toronto, 1909), 65–66, 76–77, 189–190, 201; entry of July 25, 1758, "Copy of Journal Kept by—— Gordon," Nova Scotia Historical Society, *Collections*, V (1886–87), 140–141.

94 "a handsome fortune": Charles Steuart to William Aitchison and James Parker, May 4, 1764, Parker Family Papers, Liverpool Public Library.

Laforey in Virginia: John Laforey to Phillip Stephens, July 7, 1767, Adm 1/2052, PRO; Samuel Martin to Christopher Baldwin, June 22, 1765, Martin Letterbook, Add MSS 41,350, ff. 13–14, Uk; entry of April 25, 1765, "Journal of a French Traveller in the Colonies, 1765," *AHR*, XXVI (July 1921), 741–742.

Meade and Waters: Meade, "Family History," in Peet, ed., *Chaumiere Papers*, 9–29; Hugh F. Rankin, *The Theater in Colonial America* (Chapel Hill, 1965), 74, 101.

95 "inheriting . . . patrimony": Meade, "Family History," in Peet, ed., *Chaumiere Papers*, 14, 21.

Meade's debts and holdings: Claim of Wakelin Welch, T 79/3, ff. 344–346, 388–394,

PAGE

PRO; Mary Meade to St. George Tucker, June 23, 1809, Tucker-Coleman Papers, ViW; Hening, ed., *Statutes at Large*, VIII, 470–473; Deeds, June 10, July 10, 1765, Kilby Family Papers, Box 1, Vi; Nansemond County Land Book, 1782, Nansemond County Tax Lists, Vi.

96 "one . . . Country": "Characters of leading Men," Russell Papers, CaOTP.

"Dismal Adventure": Entry of April 30, 1764, Cash Account, Account with Fielding Lewis, Ledger A, p. 176, Financial Records, Papers of George Washington, Series 5, DLC.

Walker and Moore: Thomas Walker to Bernard Moore, May 27, 1764, Bernard Moore to Thomas Walker, May 28, 1764, in Philip Slaughter, *Memoir of Col. Joshua Fry* (Richmond, 1880), 63; John Baylor to John Backhouse, April 20, 1764, John Baylor Letterbook, Vi; William Allason to Alexander Walker, May 21, 1765, Allason Letterbooks, Vi.

shipment to Spain: William Lux to Robert Tucker, Sept. 27, 1764, Lux Letterbook, NNHi.

"narcotic" . . . "worst": Simon Paulli, *A Treatise on Tobacco, Tea, Coffee, and Chocolate*, trans. R. James (London, 1746), 22, 36, 118. See also James Walvin, *Fruits of Empire: Exotic Produce and British Taste, 1660–1800* (New York, 1997).

a stamp tax: Proceedings of the Virginia Committee of Correspondence, June 15, 1764, Committee of Correspondence to Edward Montague, July 28, 1764, *VMHB*, XII (July 1904), 6–13.

97 Cape Breton Island: Grant and Munro, eds., *Acts of the Privy Council*, VI, 362–364; Richard Brown, *A History of the Island of Cape Breton* (London, 1869), 354–355.

on draining: Thomas Hale, *A Compleat Body of Husbandry* (London, 1756), 105.

bills of exchange: Entries of May 4, July 28, 1764, Virginia Gazette Daybooks, ViU.

£1,794: "Account of Doct. Walker with Loyal Company," Rives Family Papers, ViU; account of the Lead Mine Company with John Robinson, William Byrd III Papers, Section 8, ViRHi; Carl Bridenbaugh, "Violence and Virtue in Virginia, 1766: or, the Importance of the Trivial," Massachusetts Historical Society, *Proceedings*, LXXVI (1964), 13.

"altogether" . . . "in": Account of Treasury Notes, Aug. 27, 1764, *Official Papers of Fauquier*, ed. Reese, III, 1143–1153.

David Campbell: John Meriditt and Fanny Meriditt, Indenture, Sept. 26, 1817, Kilby Family Papers, Box 1, Vi.

"Dismal plantation": Patent, Oct. 20, 1784, Dismal Swamp Land Company Records, NcD; Smyth, *Tour in the United States*, II, 150; Mills Riddick, Bond, Nov. 24, 1766, *Papers of Washington: Colonial*, ed. Abbot et al., VII, 476–477.

slaves: Appraisement of Dismal Swamp Slaves, July 4, 1764, *Papers of Washington: Colonial*, eds. Abbot et al., VII, 314–315; "Acct of Geo. Washington with the Dismal Swamp Comp.," Papers of George Washington, Series 9, Box 1, DLC; David Jameson to Samuel Gist, Dec. 23, 1783, Claim of Samuel Gist, American Loyalist Claims, AO 13/30, PRO. On Burwell family slaves, see Lorena S. Walsh, *From Calabar to Carter's Grove: The History of a Virginia Slave Community* (Charlottesville, 1997).

98 "set . . . work": Account with Adventurers for Draining the Dismal Swamp, Financial Records, Ledger A, p. 194, Papers of George Washington, Series 5, DLC.

thousands of . . . shingles: On colonial shingle-making, see Rob Tarule, "The Ward

PAGE

House Cedar Shingles," Essex Institute, *Historical Collections*, CXXI (April 1987), 107–115.

98 to "run about": David Jameson to Samuel Gist, Dec. 23, 1783, Claim of Samuel Gist, American Loyalist Claims, AO 13/30, PRO; entry of Dec. 15, 1764, Memoranda D. S. Company, Dismal Swamp Land Company Records, NcD.

Washington, Walker, Lewis: Stephen Wright and Ann Wright, Indenture, Dec. 7, 1764, Dismal Swamp Land Company Records, NcD; Joseph Jones and Martha Jones, Indenture, Dec. 10, 1764, James Wright, Deed, Feb. 11, 1765, Kilby Papers, Box 43, NcD; George Washington, Will, July 9, 1799, *The Writings of George Washington*, ed. John C. Fitzpatrick (Washington, 1931–40), XXXVI, 296–297; advertisement, *Virginia Gazette and General Advertiser* (Richmond), Sept. 11, 1802; Francis Walker to John Walker, Sept. 2, 1803, Washington Family Letters, ViU.

99 "that . . . Emolument": Robert Stewart to George Washington, Aug. 18, 1765, *Papers of Washington: Colonial*, ed. Abbot *et al.*, VII, 390.

wrote his will: Robert Tucker, Will and Codicil, Jan. 10–12, 1765, Norfolk County Will Book, No. 1, 1755–1772, ff. 159–166, Norfolk County Courthouse, Portsmouth, Virginia.

the depression: Ernst, *Money and Politics*, 66; Joseph Albert Ernst, "The Robinson Scandal Redivivus: Money, Debts, and Politics in Revolutionary Virginia," *VMHB*, LXXVII (April 1969), 151; Walter E. Minchinton, "The Stamp Act Crisis: Bristol and Virginia," *ibid.*, LXXIII (April 1965), 148; Richard Corbin, Memorial to the Treasury, CO 5/1330, ff. 126–127, PRO.

William Byrd: Entry of April 25, 1765, "French Traveller," *AHR*, XXVI (July 1921), 742; William Allason to Alexander Walker, June 24, 1764, Allason Letterbook, Vi; testimony of George Mercer, Feb. 12, 1766, Add MSS 33,030, f. 128, Uk.

Samuel Gist: John Snelson to Edward Harford, Jr., May 19, 1765, Snelson Letterbook, NcU.

200 percent: William Allason to Alexander Walker, June 24, 1764, Allason Letterbook, Vi.

drought: Richard Corbin to Capel and Osgood Hanbury, Aug. 1, 1765, Richard Corbin to Philip Ludwell, Aug. 2, 1765, Corbin Letterbook, ViWC; James Gibson to Neil Jamieson, June 26, 1765, Neil Jamieson Papers, DLC; James Gibson to Samuel Galloway, July 18, 1765, Galloway-Maxcy-Markoe Papers, DLC.

100 George Grenville: George Grenville to Baron de Botetourt, Nov. 3, 1765, ST 7, CSmH; Harold William Thompson, ed., *The Anecdotes and Egotisms of Henry Mackenzie, 1745–1831* (Oxford, 1927), 4; John L. Bullion, *A Great and Necessary Measure: George Grenville and the Genesis of the Stamp Act, 1763–1765* (Columbia, 1982), chaps. 2, 4; Lawson, *Grenville*, 195; Daniel A. Baugh, "Maritime Strength and Atlantic Commerce," in Lawrence Stone, ed., *An Imperial State at War: Britain from 1689 to 1815* (London, 1994), 207; Ian R. Christie, "A Vision of Empire: Thomas Whately and *The Regulations Lately Made Concerning the Colonies*," *EnHR*, CXIII (April 1998), 300–320. For a summary of American smuggling, see Thomas Gage to Earl of Shelburne, April 28, 1767, *The Correspondence of General Thomas Gage*, ed. Clarence Edwin Carter (New Haven, 1931–33), I, 135–137.

PAGE

"fondly" . . . "administer it": William Strahan to David Hall, May 10, 1766, in Robert D. Harlan, "David Hall and the Stamp Act," *Papers of the Bibliographical Society of America,* LXI (1967), 36.

"a beneficial employment": Richard Henry Lee to Printer of the *Virginia Gazette,* July 25, 1766, *Letters of Richard Henry Lee,* ed. Ballagh, I, 16.

Peter Francklyn: Peter Francklyn to Earl of Sandwich, Feb. 19, 1765, STG Box 13(8), CSmH.

chose distributors: George Grenville to Thomas Whately, April 11, 1765, ST 7, CSmH; Sosin, *Agents and Merchants,* 62.

"considerable sums": William Allason to Alexander Walker, May 21, 1765, Allason Letterbook, Vi.

unwise leniency: Richard Corbin to Philip Ludwell, Aug. 2, 1765, Corbin Letterbook, ViWC; William Allason to Alexander Walker, May 21, 1765, Allason Letterbook, Vi; Ernst, "Robinson Scandal," *VMHB,* LXXVII (April 1969), 151–152.

101 "very valuable": Henry Fitzhugh to John Stewart & Campbell, July 5, 1766, Letterbook, Henry Fitzhugh Papers, NcD.

At least £50,000: Kennedy, ed., *Journals of the Burgesses, 1761–1765,* 356–357, 359.

102 "extricate . . . Circumstances": Charles Carter to Landon Carter, May 20, 1765, Sabine Hall Papers, ViU.

"to help . . . himself": Richard Corbin to Capel and Osgood Hanbury, May 31, 1765, Richard Corbin to Philip Ludwell, Aug. 2, 1765, Corbin Letterbook, ViWC; John Syme to Farell & Jones, June 4, 1765, *Jones' Exor.* v. *John Syme,* 1797, USCCVD(EC), Vi; Ernst, "Robinson Scandal," *VMHB,* LXXVII (April 1969), 154–155.

During court days: William Allason to Alexander Walker, May 21, 1765, Allason Letterbook, Vi.

Robinson and the British Constitution: J. A. Leo Lemay, "John Mercer and the Stamp Act in Virginia, 1764–1765," *VMHB,* XCI (Jan. 1983), 21–24; Paul Carrington, Sr., to William Wirt, Oct. 3, 1815, Patrick Henry and Family Collection, DLC.

£35,000 . . . £45,000: Testimony of George Mercer, Feb. 12, 1766, Add MSS 33,030, f. 123, Uk; George Washington to Robert Cary & Co., Sept. 20, 1765, *Papers of Washington: Colonial,* ed. Abbot *et al.,* VII, 401–402.

House of Burgesses: Entries of May 30–31, 1765, "French Traveller," *AHR,* XXVI (July 1921), 745–746; Paul Carrington, Sr., to William Wirt, Oct. 3, 1815, Patrick Henry and Family Collection, DLC; Thomas Jefferson to William Wirt, Aug. 14, 1814, Aug. 5, 1815, Papers of Thomas Jefferson, DLC; William Robinson to Bishop of London, Aug. 12, 1765, Perry, ed., *Historical Collections,* I, 514–515; Francis Fauquier to Board of Trade, June 5, 1765, *Official Papers of Fauquier,* ed. Reese, III, 1250–1251.

newspapers in other colonies: Edmund S. Morgan, ed., *Prologue to Revolution: Sources and Documents on the Stamp Act Crisis, 1764–1766* (Chapel Hill, 1959), 49–50.

"exceed . . . extravagance": George Grenville to Thomas Whately, Aug. 13, 1765, ST 7, CSmH.

103 Mercer in Williamsburg: Francis Fauquier to Board of Trade, Nov. 3, 1765, *Official Papers of Fauquier,* ed. Reese, III, 1290–1295; Alfred Procter James, *George Mercer of the Ohio Company: A Study in Frustration* (Pittsburgh, 1963), 51–55. See, in general, Edmund S.

Morgan and Helen M. Morgan, *The Stamp Act Crisis: Prologue to Revolution* (Chapel Hill, 1953); Ragsdale, *A Planters' Republic*, chap. 2.

103 Richard Henry Lee: John Camm to Mrs. McClurg, July 24, 1766, *WMQ*, 1st ser., II (April 1894), 238; Oliver Perry Chitwood, *Richard Henry Lee: Statesman of the Revolution* (Morgantown, 1967), 36–38; Haws, *Scots in the Old Dominion*, 103–104.

Planters in Antigua: Letter from Antigua, Dec. 20, 1765, Historical Manuscripts Commission, *The Manuscripts of the Earl of Dartmouth* (London, 1887–96), II, 495; Selwyn H. H. Carrington, *The British West Indies During the American Revolution* (Dordrecht, 1988), 152.

"vast . . . people": Francis Fauquier to Board of Trade, Nov. 3, 1765, *Official Papers of Fauquier*, ed. Reese, III, 1291; entry of April 28, 1765, "French Traveller," *AHR*, XXVI (July 1921), 742.

Gist in Williamsburg: Entry of Sept. 27, 1765, Virginia Gazette Daybooks, ViU; Sarah Gist to Samuel Gist, Dec. 9, 1765, Claim of Samuel Gist, American Loyalist Claims, AO 13/30, PRO; Samuel Gist, Answer to Thomas R. Rootes, Oct. 29, 1805, *Jos. Smith's Admr. et al. v. Gist's Exor et al.*, 1825, USCCVD(EC), Vi.

104 his expenses: George Mercer to John Robinson, Dec. 22, 1775, T 1/445, PRO.

III: THE LAND OF CAKES

105 "safe . . . planters": John Hook to Peter Davies, Aug. 15, 1765, Letter Book of John Hook, Vi. See also James Morrison to John Hook, Feb. 9, 1783, John Hook Papers, NcD. "Land of cakes" usually refers to Scotland.

"immense" . . . "shew": Jonathan Sewall to Edward Winslow, Jan. 10, 1776, William Bell Clark *et al.*, eds., *Naval Documents of the American Revolution* (Washington, 1964–), III, 496; Thomas Heyward, Jr., to Daniel Heyward, Feb. 11, 1767, *Old Northwest Genealogical Quarterly*, VII (Oct. 1904), 259–260; entry of Jan. 14, 1779, Journal of Peter Van Schaack in Henry C. Van Schaack, *The Life of Peter Van Schaack* (New York, 1842), 135. See also William L. Sachse, *The Colonial American in Britain* (Madison, 1956), chap. 3.

"narrowly . . . Dray-horse": Entry of Sept. 18, 1766, *Narrative of American Voyages and Travels of Captain William Owen, R. N.*, ed. Victor Hugo Paltsits (New York, 1942), 6; entry of Feb. 10, 1766, Diary of Samson Occom in Leon Burr Richardson, ed., *An Indian Preacher in London* (Hanover, 1933), 83; [John] Trusler, *The London Adviser and Guide* (London, 1786), 115–116, 129–138, 146–153.

"ragged . . . Jills": Entry of July 17, 1775, *The Journal of Samuel Curwen, Loyalist*, ed. Andrew Oliver (Cambridge, 1972), I, 33; James Habersham to Joseph Habersham, May 10, 1768, *The Letters of Hon. James Habersham, 1756–1775*, Georgia Historical Society, *Collections*, VI (1904), 70.

106 "my . . . any?": Entry of Oct. 5, 1780, *Journal of Curwen*, ed. Oliver, II, 673.

"Everything . . . magnificent": Carl Philip Moritz, *Journeys of a German in England in 1782*, 2d ed., trans. and ed. Reginald Nettel (New York, 1965), 26. See also John Gray to Tobias Smollett, July 8, 1771, in [Lewis Saul Benjamin], *The Life and Letters of Tobias Smollett* (London, 1926), 248; Pierre Jean Grosley, *A Tour to London*, trans. Thomas Nugent (Dublin, 1772), I, 35–36, 47–50; Samuel Johnson to Elizabeth Johnson, Jan. 21, 1775,

Samuel Johnson to Mary Johnson, Feb. 22, 1775, *Sir Joshua's Nephew: Being Letters Written, 1769–1778, by a Young Man to His Sisters*, ed. Susan M. Radcliffe (London, 1930), 30; James H. Watmough to Anna Watmough, Feb. 5, 1787, *PMHB*, XXIX (1905), 296–306; François Auguste de Frénilly, *Recollections of Baron de Frénilly*, ed. Arthur Chuquet, trans. Frederic Lees (New York, 1909), 31; Peter Brimblecombe, *The Big Smoke: A History of Air Pollution in London Since Medieval Times* (London, 1987), chap. 4; Dan Cruickshank and Neil Burton, *Life in the Georgian City* (London, 1990), chap. 1; Jules Lubbock, *The Tyranny of Taste: The Politics of Architecture and Design in Britain, 1550–1960* (New Haven, 1995), Part I; Roy Porter, "Visitors' Visions: Travellers' Tales of Georgian London," in Chloe Chard and Helen Langdon, eds., *Transports: Travel, Pleasure, and Imaginative Geography, 1600–1830* (New Haven, 1996), 31–47.

"the tenderest affection": [Edward Pugh], *London; Being an Accurate History and Description* (London, 1805–13), III, 7.

"the most . . . London": Quoted in Nicholas Rogers, "Money, Land and Lineage: The Big Bourgeoisie of Hanoverian London," *Social History*, IV (1979), 440. See also Nicholas Rogers, *Whigs and Cities: Popular Politics in the Age of Walpole and Pitt* (Oxford, 1989), 111–112.

won other contracts: T 1/430, ff. 19–20, 1/429, ff. 422–423, PRO; W. L. Grant and James Munro, eds., *Acts of the Privy Council of England. Colonial Series* (London, 1908–12), IV, 617–618; R. C. Simmons and P. D. G. Thomas, eds., *Proceedings and Debates of the British Parliaments Respecting North America, 1754–1783* (Millwood, 1982–87), III, 181; Grey Cooper to Viscount Barrington, May 7, 1766, *An Eighteenth-Century Secretary at War: The Papers of William, Viscount Barrington*, ed. Tony Hayter (London, 1988), 347.

107 "it is . . . here": William Lee to Richard Henry Lee, March 7, 1771, William Lee Letterbook, 1769–1772, Lee Family Papers ViRHi.

108 "the most . . . saw": Entries of Feb. 24, May 8, 1767, *The Diary of Sylas Neville, 1767–1788*, ed. Basil Cozens-Hardy (London, 1950), 4, 7.

"waddle . . . duck": Samuel Martin to Samuel Martin, Jr., April 28, 1769, Samuel Martin Letterbook, Add MSS 41,348, f. 46, Uk.

"The trade . . . secret": Malachy Postlethwayt, *The Universal Dictionary of Trade and Commerce*, 4th ed. (New York, 1971 [orig. publ. London, 1774]), I, Introduction; [Daniel Defoe], *The Anatomy of Exchange-Alley: Or, A System of Stock-Jobbing*, 2d ed. (London, 1719), 42–43; E. Victor Morgan and W. A. Thomas, *The Stock Exchange: Its History and Functions*, 2d ed. (London, 1969), 67.

"a mere . . . job": John Warner to George Selwyn, May 28, 1779, John Heneage Jesse, *George Selwyn and His Contemporaries* (London, 1844), IV, 164.

109 "Room . . . Rural": Quoted in Lesley Lewis, "The Architects of the Chapel at Greenwich Hospital," *Art Bulletin*, XXIX (Dec. 1947), 265. See also Daniel Lysons, *The Environs of London*, 2d ed. (London, 1811), I, Part II, 702–703; Thomas Wright, *The History and Topography of the County of Essex* (London, 1836), II, 506–507; P. H. Reaney and Hilda E. P. Grieve, "Walthamstow," in W. R. Powell, ed., *A History of the County of Essex* (Oxford, 1973), VI, 259–260.

Merthyr Tydfil: Moelwyn I. Williams, "The Economic and Social History of Glamorgan, 1660–1760," in Glanmor Williams, ed., *Glamorgan County History: Early Modern Glamor-*

gan (Cardiff, 1974), IV, 372; Chris Evans, *"The Labyrinth of Flames": Work and Social Conflict in Early Industrial Merthyr Tydfil* (Cardiff, 1993), 11.

109 "our industrious poor": [Anthony Bacon], *A Short Address to the Government* (London, 1775), 38.

the Brownriggs: J. V. Beckett, "Dr. William Brownrigg, F. R. S.: Physician, Chemist and Country Gentleman," *Notes and Records of the Royal Society of London*, XXXI (Jan. 1977), 255–271; Richard Pococke, *The Travels Through England of Dr. Richard Pococke*, ed. James Joel Cartwright (London, 1888), I, 16–17; William Watson, "Some Account of an Oil, transmitted by Mr. George Brownrigg, of North Carolina," *Annual Register*, XIII (1770), Useful Projects, 109–111.

Charles Wood: Evans, *Labyrinth of Flames*, 58.

110 "that place . . . there": Entry of Aug. 2, 1767, *The Diary of William Thomas*, ed. R. T. W. Denning (Cardiff, 1995), 192.

"Bacon's Mineral Kingdom": Robert L. Galloway, *Annals of Coal Mining and the Coal Trade*, 1st ser. (London, 1898), 360; W. H. Chaloner, "Isaac Wilkinson, Potfounder," in L. S. Pressnell, ed., *Studies in the Industrial Revolution* (London, 1960), 23–51; Evans, *Labyrinth of Flames*, 15–16, 34–35, 147–149; Moelwyn Williams, *The Making of the South Wales Landscape* (London, 1975), 191–192; Charles Wilkins, *The History of the Iron, Steel, Tinplate, and Other Trades of Wales* (Merthyr Tydfil, 1903), 48–53, 148; Charles Wilkins, *The History of Merthyr Tydfil* (Merthyr Tydfil, 1908), 227–231; John Lloyd, *The Early History of the Old South Wales Iron Works* (London, 1906), 48–50; [John Henry Manners, Duke of Rutland], *Journal of a Tour Through North and South Wales, the Isle of Man, &c. &c.* (London, 1805), 60–74; Benjamin Heath Malkin, *The Scenery, Antiquities, and Biography of South Wales* (Wakefield, 1970 [orig. publ. London, 1804]), 164–183; Robert Erskine to Richard Atkinson, Oct. 20–24, 1770, in Albert H. Heusser, *George Washington's Map Maker: A Biography of Robert Erskine* (New Brunswick, 1966), 59.

Joseph Manesty: Joseph Manesty to Earl of Dartmouth, Jan. 8, 1766, Historical Manuscripts Commission, *The Manuscripts of the Earl of Dartmouth* (London, 1887–96), II, 32; Jack M. Sosin, *Agents and Merchants: British Colonial Policy and the Origins of the American Revolution* (Lincoln, 1965), 71.

"Reflections . . . ministry": George Grenville to Baron de Botetourt, Nov. 3, 1765, George Grenville to Mr. Sarjent, Nov. 7, 1765, George Grenville Letterbooks, ST 7, CSmH.

Charles O'Hara: *Journal of the Commissioners for Trade and Plantations from January 1764 to December 1767* (London, 1936), 295, 303, 345–346; Charles O'Hara to Board of Trade, Sept. 1, 1766, Shelburne Papers, Vol. 90, MiU-C; Eveline C. Martin, *The British West African Settlements, 1750–1821: A Study in Local Administration* (New York, 1970 [orig. publ. London, 1927]), 80–81. The correspondence concerning Bacon's conflicts with O'Hara is calendared in *List and Index Society, Volume 244: Treasury Board Papers, 1765–1770* (1991), 327–329.

"superintend": Sheila Lambert, ed., *House of Commons Sessional Papers of the Eighteenth Century* (Wilmington, 1975), LXXI, 80–81; Anthony Bacon to Charles Lowndes, Oct. 7, 1766, T 1/445, ff. 467–468, PRO.

PAGE

111 "No . . . manufactories": Gilbert Francklyn, *Observations Occasioned by the Attempts Made in England to Effect the Abolition of the Slave Trade* (London, 1789), 11; John Rule, *The Experience of Labour in Eighteenth-Century English Industry* (New York, 1981), esp. 76–85.

David Jameson: Account of Samuel Gist with David Jameson, June 1766, Claim of Samuel Gist, American Loyalist Claims, AO 13/30, PRO; David Jameson to William Nelson, Jr., Jan. 4, 1785, Dismal Swamp Land Company Records, NcD.

John and Joseph Smith: Samuel Gist, Answer to Thomas R. Rootes, Oct. 29, 1805, *Jos. Smith's Admr. et al.* v. *Gist's Exor et al.*, 1825, USCCVD(EC), Vi.

"young Ladies": Benjamin Howard to Samuel Gist, Aug. 25, 1766, Claim of Samuel Gist, American Loyalist Claims, AO 13/30, PRO.

112 "a very . . . neighbourhood": [Edward Pugh], *Walks Through London* (London, 1817), I, 12–13.

fourteen almshouses: [Pugh], *London; Being an Accurate History,* II, 212.

"whores and thieves": Walter Besant, *London in the Eighteenth Century* (London, 1902), 130–131; [Pugh], *London; Being an Accurate History,* II, 183; [Pugh], *Walks,* I, 13.

"the lame . . . maimed": Samuel Kelly, *Samuel Kelly: An Eighteenth Century Seaman,* ed. Crosbie Garstin (New York, 1925), 129.

"decayed . . . widows": Thomas Allen, *The History and Antiquities of London, Westminster, Southwark, and Parts Adjacent* (London, 1828), III, 98.

"penitent prostitutes": William Thornton, *The New, Complete, and Universal History, Description, and Survey of the Cities of London and Westminster* (London, [1784]), 429; Ivy Pinchbeck and Margaret Hewitt, *Children in English Society* (London, 1969–73), I, 119–121.

The garrets: Thomas Erskine to Alexander Gordon, June 28, [ca. 1767], in William Mure, ed., *Selections from the Family Papers Preserved at Caldwell* (Glasgow, 1854), Part II, Vol. II, 114.

"foreign" . . . "lame": William Mylne to Anne Mylne, Aug. 29–Sept. 4, 1773, in William Mylne, *Travels in the Colonies in 1773–1775,* ed. Ted Ruddock (Athens, 1993), 17.

"very elegant edifice": Thornton, *New, Complete, and Universal History,* 429, 443; Besant, *London in the Eighteenth Century,* 130–131; [Pugh], *Walks,* I, 12–13; [Pugh], *London; Being an Accurate History,* II, 183; Dorothy Stroud, *George Dance: Architect, 1741–1825* (London, 1971), 84–86; Roy Porter, "Cleaning Up the Great Wen: Public Health in Eighteenth-Century London," in W. F. Bynum and Roy Porter, eds., *Living and Dying in London* (London, 1991), 61–75; James Ayres, *Building the Georgian City* (New Haven, 1998).

Gist and Walker: Samuel Gist to Thomas Walker, March 4, 1768, Thomas Walker Papers, William Cabell Rives Papers, Box 162, DLC; entry of Oct. 7, 1767, List of Ships and Vessels Cleared Outwards in Port of York, Virginia, T 1/461, PRO; Brian L. Evans, "Ginseng: Root of Chinese-Canadian Relations," *CHR,* LXVI (March 1985), 1–26.

112 "vile" . . . "evil": Samuel Gist to John Smith, Aug. [31?], 1767, *Jos. Smith's Admr. et al.* v. *Gist's Exor et al.*, 1825, USCCVD(EC), Vi.

113 "a man . . . pay it": Samuel Gist to John Smith, Sept. 18–20, 1767, *ibid.*

"I can . . . them": Samuel Gist to John Smith, Aug. [31?], 1767, *ibid.*

a fee of two guineas: Eliot Howard, ed., *Eliot Papers: John Eliot of London, Merchant, 1735–1813* (London, 1895), 31; Warren R. Dawson, "The London Coffee-Houses and the Beginnings of Lloyd's," in *Essays by Divers Hands, Being the Transactions of the Royal Society of Literature of the United Kingdom*, 3d ser., XI (1932), 102–103; Bryant Lillywhite, *London Coffee Houses* (London, 1963), 329–334.

113 "I am . . . can be": *Report from the Select Committee Appointed to Consider . . . the State and Means of Effecting Marine Insurance in Great Britain*, 1810 (226) IV. 247, p. 67.

114 "a Man . . . America": Bourdieu, Chollet & Bourdieu to Nicholas Low, Feb. 7, 1787, Nicholas Low Papers, DLC.

"an Underwriter . . . way": Philip Eliot to John Eliot, Nov. 16, 1757, *Eliot Papers*, ed. Howard, 45.

risks: *Report on Marine Insurance*, 1810 (226) IV. 247, p. 60.

"Sea Gulls": *Ibid.*, p. 116.

"long . . . Underwriter": *Ibid.*, p. 110.

"I should . . . it": *Ibid.*, pp. 75–76.

"a merchant . . . premium": Quoted in *Annals of Lloyd's Register* ([London], 1934), 14. See also James Allan Park, *A System of the Law of Marine Insurance*, 2d ed. (London, 1790), 223–224.

115 capital of £100,000: Jeremiah Osborne to Aaron Lopez, Feb. 14, 25, 1767, Worthington Chauncey Ford, ed., *Commerce of Rhode Island, 1726–1800*, Massachusetts Historical Society, *Collections*, 7th ser., IX–X (1914–15), I, 181, 191; William Hayley to Eliza Hayley, Aug. 1, 1783, *Memoirs of the Life and Writings of William Hayley, Esq.*, ed. John Johnson (London, 1823), I, 308–309; Lewis Namier and John Brooke, *The History of Parliament: The House of Commons, 1754–1790* (New York, 1964), II, 602–603.

"intimate & close": Hayley & Hopkins to Stephen Collins, March 20, 1777, Stephen Collins & Son Papers, DLC.

"No one . . . articles": William Neate to Stephen Collins, Aug. 15, 1771, *ibid.;* Neate, Pigou & Booth to Field & Dowell, July 10, 1765, John Chaloner Collection, MiU-C.

"had the . . . House": Alexander Carlyle, *Anecdotes and Characters of the Times*, ed. James Kinsley (London, 1973), 256.

James Bourdieu: Lambert, ed., *House of Commons Sessional Papers*, XXVI, 281; Lucy S. Sutherland, *A London Merchant, 1695–1774* (London, 1962 [orig. publ. Oxford, 1933]), 71; *Journal of the Commissioners for Trade and Plantations from January 1776 to May 1782* (London, 1938), 18.

"rather . . . peremptory": Entry of Aug. 30, 1789, Gouverneur Morris, *A Diary of the French Revolution*, ed. Beatrix Cary Davenport (Boston, 1939), I, 201.

"the old . . . Respect": Isaac Low to Nicholas Low, Aug. 20, 1784, Low Papers, DLC. On Lloyd's, see also Charles Wright and C. Ernest Fayle, *A History of Lloyd's from the Founding of Lloyd's Coffee House to the Present Day* (London, 1928); G. Clayton, *British Insurance* (London, 1971), 58–59; James Oldham, *The Mansfield Manuscripts and the Growth of English Law in the Eighteenth Century* (Chapel Hill, 1992), I, 450–478; Sutherland, *London Merchant*, 54–80; Jacob M. Price, "Transaction Costs: A Note on Merchant Credit and the Organization of Private Trade," in James D. Tracy, ed., *The Political Economy of Merchant Empires* (Cambridge, 1991), 289–292; John Weskett, *A Complete Digest of the Theory, Laws, and Practice of Insurance* (Dublin, 1783), xxii–xxix.

116 "utter Ruin": Edmund S. Morgan, ed., *Prologue to Revolution: Sources and Documents on the Stamp Act Crisis, 1764–1766* (Chapel Hill, 1959), 130–131.

sent "Agents": George Grenville to Baron de Botetourt, Nov. 3, 1765, ST 7, CSmH.

"spared" . . . "instrumental": Capel and Osgood Hanbury to Charles Carter, March 27, 1766, Carter Papers, ViFreJM; Simmons and Thomas, eds., *Proceedings and Debates*, II, 195–197; Richard Champion to Caleb and John Lloyd, Feb. 15, 1766, *The American Correspondence of a Bristol Merchant, 1766–1776: Letters of Richard Champion*, ed. G. H. Guttridge (Berkeley, 1934), 11.

"insolent Rebells": Henry Cruger, Jr., to Henry Cruger, Sr., Feb. 14, 1766, Ford, ed., *Commerce of Rhode Island*, I, 139–143.

Bacon . . . also spoke: Henry Seymour Conway to the King, March 5, 1766, *The Correspondence of King George the Third*, ed. John Fortescue (London, 1927–28), I, 271.

"Act of Oppression": George Washington to Capel and Osgood Hanbury, July 25, 1767, *The Papers of George Washington, Colonial Series*, ed. W. W. Abbot *et al.* (Charlottesville, 1983–), VIII, 15.

"that unconstitutional . . . act": John Snelson to Edward Harford, Jr., May 11, 1766, John Snelson Letterbook, Fredericks Hall Plantation Records, NcU. See also Edmund S. and Helen M. Morgan, *The Stamp Act Crisis: Prologue to Revolution* (Chapel Hill, 1953), chap. 15; Sosin, *Agents and Merchants*, 71–80; P. D. G. Thomas, *British Politics and the Stamp Act Crisis* (Oxford, 1975); Paul Langford, "The Rockingham Whigs and America, 1767–1773," in Anne Whiteman *et al.*, eds., *Statesmen, Scholars, and Merchants: Essays in Eighteenth-Century History Presented to Dame Lucy Sutherland* (Oxford, 1973), 144–146.

"is now" . . . "establish'd": George Grenville to Baron Clive, July 19, 1767, ST 7, CSmH.

"do . . . future": George Grenville to R. Nugent, June 21, 1766, *The Grenville Papers*, ed. William James Smith (London, 1852–53), III, 250.

117 "exceeding" . . . "improvement": George Washington to John Lewis, April 17, 1782, *The Writings of George Washington*, ed. John C. Fitzpatrick (Washington, 1931–40), XXIV, 130–131; Marmaduke Norfleet, Deed, April 26, 1766, *Papers of Washington: Colonial*, ed. Abbot *et al.*, VII, 436–437.

bills of exchange: Robert Tucker, advertisement, Purdie and Dixon's *Virginia Gazette* (Williamsburg), Sept. 12, 1766; Judgment, May 4, 1770, *Edward and Thomas Hunt* v. *Estate of Robert Tucker*, Phillips MSS 19705, Sir Thomas Phillips Collection, DLC.

Hasenclever, Seton & Crofts: Gerhard Spieler, "Peter Hasenclever, Industrialist," New Jersey Historical Society, *Proceedings*, LIX (Oct. 1941), 231–256; Heusser, *George Washington's Map Maker*, 25–26, 103; Arthur Cecil Bining, *Pennsylvania Iron Manufacture in the Eighteenth Century* (Harrisburg, 1938), 109–110; John Watts to Robert Monckton, June 11, 1764, Nov. 11, 1766, *Aspinwall Papers*, Massachusetts Historical Society, *Collections*, 4th ser., IX–X (1871), II, 526, 593; entry of July 1, 1768, [John Lees], *Journal of J. L., of Quebec, Merchant* (Detroit, 1911), 17; Robert Erskine to Printer of *New-York Gazette*, July 10, 1773, in *New-York Gazette*, Aug. 9, 1773, reprinted in *Archives of the State of New Jersey*, 1st ser. (Paterson, 1916), XXVIII, 586–588; William Alexander *et al.* to William Franklin, July 8, 1769, *ibid.*, 247–253; Hugh Wallace to Frederick Haldimand, July 18, Nov. 7, 1770, Peter Hasenclever to Hugh Wallace, March 9, 1771, *Report on Canadian Archives: 1885* (Ottawa, 1886), 174.

117 Dismal Swamp Company: Entry of May 3, 1766, Cash Accounts, *Papers of Washington: Colonial*, ed. Abbot *et al.*, VII, 438; entries of May 3, 1766, Account with Adventurers for Draining the Dismal Swamp, Financial Records, Ledger A, Papers of George Washington, Series 5, DLC; David Jameson to Samuel Gist, Nov. 3, 1784, Claim of Samuel Gist, American Loyalist Claims, AO 13/30, PRO; Original Members, Dismal Swamp Land Company Records, NcD; Purdie's *Virginia Gazette*, May 9, 1766.

Then drought: Samuel Johnston to Thomas Barker, Aug. 20, 1766, Hayes Collection, Johnston Family Series, NcU; Benjamin Howard to Samuel Gist, Aug. 25, 1766, Claim of Samuel Gist, American Loyalist Claims, AO 13/30, PRO.

118 buy Dismal Plantation: Entry of Dec. 1766, "Acct. Go. Washington with the Disml Swamp Comp," Papers of George Washington, Series 9, Box 1A, DLC; Mills Riddick, Bond, Nov. 24, 1766, *Papers of Washington: Colonial*, ed. Abbot *et al.*, VII, 476–477; Cash Accounts, Nov. 1766, *ibid.*, 469–470; Fillmore Norfleet, *Suffolk in Virginia* (n.p., 1974), 115.

Hanover-Town: Samuel Gist to John Smith, Aug. 15, 1768, *Jos. Smith's Admr. et al.* v. *Gist's Exor et al.*, 1825, USCCVD(EC), Vi; Purdie's *Virginia Gazette*, April 25, 1766; Purdie and Dixon's *Virginia Gazette*, June 20, 1766, Oct. 15, 1767; Malcolm M. Harris, "The Port Towns of the Pamunkey," *WMQ*, 2d ser., XXIII (Oct. 1943), 511–513.

"God . . . dies": Warner Lewis to Walter Jones, July 8, 1766, Edrington Family Papers, ViRHi; Maria Beverley to Maria Carter, April 20, 1764, "Some Family Letters of the Eighteenth Century," *VMHB*, XV (April 1908), 434.

John's patrimony: Mann Page to John Page, Aug. 3, 1779, ViWC; John Page to John Norton, Oct. 11, 1771, John Page to John Hatley Norton, Feb. 27, 1790, John Norton & Son Papers, ViWC; John Page to Robert Carter, March 12, 1795, John Page Papers, NcD.

Thomas Jefferson: Thomas Jefferson to John Page, Feb. 21, 1770, *The Papers of Thomas Jefferson*, ed. Julian P. Boyd *et al.* (Princeton, 1950–), I, 35–36.

119 John Clayton: Edmund Berkeley and Dorothy Smith Berkeley, *John Clayton: Pioneer of American Botany* (Chapel Hill, 1963), 165–166; Margaret Page to John Page, Jan. 19, 1820, Page-Saunders Papers, ViW; Benjamin Smith Barton, "Memorandums of the Life and Writings of Mr. John Clayton, the Celebrated Botanist of Virginia," *Philadelphia Medical and Physical Journal*, II (1805), 141–142.

more than 15 hogsheads: John Page to John Norton, April 20, May 27, 1769, Oct. 11, 1771, John Norton & Son Papers, ViWC.

"I . . . existing": Thomas Jefferson to Albert Gallatin, Aug. 28, 1801, *The Writings of Thomas Jefferson*, ed. Paul Leicester Ford (New York, 1892–99), VIII, 85.

Peyton Randolph: Peyton Randolph to Landon Carter, May 11, 1766, ViWC; Archibald Cary to William Preston, May 14, 1766, Preston Papers, Vol. 2, ff. 95–96, Draper Collection, Series QQ, WHi.

"very considerable deficiency": Purdie and Dixon's *Virginia Gazette*, June 27, Sept. 5, 1766; Richard Bland to Richard Henry Lee, May 22, 1766, Lee Family Papers, ViU.

"Conversation . . . complaint": William Nelson to Edward and Samuel Athawes, Nov. 13, 1766, William Nelson Letterbook, Vi.

"immediately": Edmund Randolph, *History of Virginia*, ed. Arthur H. Shaffer (Charlottesville, 1970), 174.

"often" objected: Robert C. Nicholas to Richard Henry Lee, May 23, 1766, Lee Family Papers, ViU.

"arbitrary conduct": Purdie and Dixon's *Virginia Gazette*, Oct. 17, 1766.

Susanna Robinson: Joseph Albert Ernst, "The Robinson Scandal Redivivus: Money, Debts, and Politics in Revolutionary Virginia," *VMHB*, LXXVII (April 1969), 156.

120 "a considerable . . . company": Deposition of John Taylor, April 12, 1813, File 5, *Lidderdale et al.* v. *Robinson's Admrs et al.*, 1832, USCCVD(EC), Vi.

Robert Carter Nicholas: Randolph, *History of Virginia*, ed. Shaffer, 185; Purdie and Dixon's *Virginia Gazette*, June 27, 1766.

121 "that many" . . . "country": Purdie and Dixon's *Virginia Gazette*, June 27, 1766.

credit and currency: Francis Fauquier to Earl of Shelburne, Dec. 18, 1766, *The Official Papers of Francis Fauquier*, ed. George Reese (Charlottesville, 1980–83), III, 1411–1412.

"affronted": Francis Jerdone to Buchanan & Hamilton, July 14, 1750, "Letter Book of Francis Jerdone," *WMQ*, 1st ser., XI (Jan. 1903), 158.

"we could . . . Mine": Edmund Pendleton to William Preston, Feb. 6, 1768, *The Letters and Papers of Edmund Pendleton*, ed. David John Mays (Charlottesville, 1967), I, 37; Account of Lead Mine Company with John Robinson, William Byrd III Papers, Section 8, ViRHi.

"as good . . . Chiswell": Carl Bridenbaugh, "Violence and Virtue in Virginia, 1766: or, the Importance of the Trivial," Massachusetts Historical Society, *Proceedings*, LXXVI (1964), 6.

to bail: John Camm to Mrs. McClurg, July 24, 1766, *WMQ*, 1st ser., II (April 1894), 238–239; J. A. Leo Lemay, "Robert Bolling and the Bailment of Colonel Chiswell," *Early American Literature*, VI (1971), 99–142; Bridenbaugh, "Violence and Virtue," Massachusetts Historical Society, *Proceedings*, LXXVI (1964), 7–8.

"partial magistrates": John Tazewell to Thomas Burke, Sept. 28, 1766, Thomas Burke Papers, NcU.

his "connections": John Camm to Mrs. McClurg, July 24, 1766, *WMQ*, 1st ser., II (April 1894), 238–239.

"advanced . . . others": Purdie's *Virginia Gazette*, June 13, 1766.

122 no correct books: Notes on John Mercer to George Mercer, Dec. 22, 1767, Mercer Family Papers, Section 28, ViRHi.

"in great" . . . "paper": Deposition of John Taylor, April 12, 1813, *Lidderdale et al.* v. *Robinson's Admrs et al.*, 1832, USCCVD(EC), Vi; Representation of John Robinson's Administrators, Nov. 22, 1769, *Letters and Papers of Pendleton*, ed. Mays, I, 50.

"to prevent" . . . "designed": Richard Bland to Richard Henry Lee, May 22, 1766, Lee Family Papers, ViU.

"to break" . . . "trust": [Richard Bland], "A Freeholder," Purdie and Dixon's *Virginia Gazette*, Oct. 17, 1766.

"very . . . office": Richard Corbin to John Roberts, May 15, 1767, Corbin Letterbook, ViWC.

"a Scheme . . . Extent": Richard Bland to Richard Henry Lee, May 22, 1766, Lee Family Papers, ViU.

"no Influence": Robert C. Nicholas to Richard Henry Lee, May 23, 1766, *ibid.*

PAGE

122 pay their arrears: Purdie and Dixon's *Virginia Gazette*, May 23, 1766.

"can . . . excuse": *Ibid.*, Sept. 5, 1766.

123 "scurrilous": William Nelson to John Norton, Nov. 12, 1766, Nelson Letterbook, Vi.

"Error" . . . "with": William Nelson to Edward and Samuel Athawes, Nov. 13, 1766, *ibid.*

charity and circulation: Purdie and Dixon's *Virginia Gazette*, July 25, Aug. 1, 1766.

"application" . . . "resist": William Nelson to Edward and Samuel Athawes, Nov. 13, 1766, Nelson Letterbook, Vi; Purdie's *Virginia Gazette*, June 13, 1766; Representation of Administrators, Nov. 22, 1769, *Letters and Papers of Pendleton*, ed. Mays, I, 50.

"a Man . . . Disposition": Rind's *Virginia Gazette*, Aug. 8, 1766.

"shamefully bepraised": Purdie and Dixon's *Virginia Gazette*, Sept. 12, 1766.

"very great influence": *Ibid.*, Oct. 17, 1766.

"Distrust" . . . "morality": *Ibid.*, Sept. 12, 1766.

"indifferent . . . Justice": John Tazewell to Thomas Burke, Sept. 28, 1766, Thomas Burke Papers, NcU.

Robinson's debtors: For a list of the debtors, see David John Mays, *Edmund Pendleton, 1721–1803: A Biography* (Cambridge, 1952), I, appendix ii. For a list of Robinson's debts, see "A State of demands against Estate of John Robinson," *Lidderdale et al.* v. *Robinson's Admrs et al.*, 1832, USCCVD(EC), Vi.

124 "always" . . . "authors": Littleton Waller Tazewell, History of the Tazewell Family, p. 135, NcU.

"rigorous Measures": John Pendleton Kennedy, ed., *Journals of the House of Burgesses of Virginia, 1766–1769* (Richmond, 1906), 67; Representation of Administrators, Nov. 22, 1769, *Letters and Papers of Pendleton*, ed. Mays, I, 50.

"hopeless" . . . "debt": Deposition of John Taylor, April 12, 1813, *Lidderdale et al.* v. *Robinson's Admrs et al.*, 1832, USCCVD(EC), Vi; Kennedy, ed., *Journals of Burgesses, 1766–1769*, 66–67.

Dismal Swamp Company: Fielding Lewis, Receipt, April 11, 1767, *Lidderdale et al.* v. *Robinson's Admrs et al.*, 1832, USCCVD(EC), Vi.

John Chiswell: Bridenbaugh, "Violence and Virtue," Massachusetts Historical Society, *Proceedings*, LXXVI (1964), 23–24; Lemay, "Robert Bolling," *Early American Literature*, VI (1971), 111–115; Anne Y. Zimmer, *Jonathan Boucher: Loyalist in Exile* (Detroit, 1978), 62–66, 331–333. See also J. A. Leo Lemay, ed., *Robert Bolling Woos Anne Miller: Love and Courtship in Colonial Virginia, 1760* (Charlottesville, 1990).

125 Robinson's grave: Malcolm Hart Harris, *Old New Kent County* (West Point, 1977), I, 356–357.

about £4,700: William Nelson to Edward Hunt & Son, May 29, 1767, Nelson Letterbook, Vi; *Edward and Thomas Hunt* v. *Estate of Robert Tucker*, May 4, 1770, Phillips MSS 19705, Sir Thomas Phillips Collection, DLC.

"a Man . . . Reflection": William Nelson to John Norton, Sept. 12, 1766, Nelson Letterbook, Vi; Kennedy, ed., *Journal of Burgesses, 1766–1769*, 58, 63; Robert Tucker, advertisement, Purdie and Dixon's *Virginia Gazette*, Sept. 12, 1766.

"your . . . much": William Lux to Robert Tucker, Oct. 3, 1766, William Lux Letterbook, NNHi.

PAGE

126 "real" . . . "Secrecy": William Lux to Robert Tucker, Dec. 1, 1766, Jan. 13, 19, Feb. 5, 1767, *ibid.*; William Nelson to Edward Hunt & Son, May 29, 1767, Nelson Letterbook, Vi; *Edward and Thomas Hunt* v. *Estate of Robert Tucker,* May 4, 1770, Phillips MSS 19705, Sir Thomas Phillips Collection, DLC; Heusser, *George Washington's Map Maker,* 32; Alexander Mackrabie to Philip Francis, June 4, 1768, *The Francis Letters,* ed. Beata Francis and Eliza Keary (London, [1901]), I, 96.

"totally": William Nelson to Edward Hunt & Son, May 29, 1767, William Nelson to John Norton, Aug. 14, 1767, Nelson Letterbook, Vi; Charles Steuart to William Aitchison and James Parker, Oct. 15, 1767, Parker Papers, Liverpool Public Library.

"at" . . . "Appearances": William Nelson to Edward Hunt & Son, May 29, 1767, Nelson Letterbook, Vi; *Edward and Thomas Hunt* v. *Estate of Robert Tucker,* May 4, 1770, Phillips MSS 19705, Sir Thomas Phillips Collection, DLC.

written his will: William Waters, Will, Dec. 23, 1766, Wills and Inventories, 1760–1771, pp. 350–351, York County Records, No. 21, Yorktown, Virginia.

David Meade: David Meade, "Family History," in Henry J. Peet, ed., *Chaumiere Papers, Containing Matters of Interest to the Descendants of David Meade* (Chicago, 1883), 28–29.

went to probate: Inventory and Appraisement of the Estate of William Waters, Wills and Inventories, 1760–1771, pp. 460–475, York County Records.

127 was insolvent: Robert Carter Nicholas to John Norton, Oct. 3, 1768, John Norton & Son Papers, ViWC.

Tucker's obituary: Purdie and Dixon's *Virginia Gazette,* July 9, 1767.

"prepared" . . . "Purpose": William Nelson to Edward Hunt & Son, July 9, 1768, Nelson Letterbook, Vi; *Edward and Thomas Hunt* v. *Estate of Robert Tucker,* May 4, 1770, Phillips MSS 19705, Sir Thomas Phillips Collection, DLC.

"extremely weak": William Nelson to John Tucker, Feb. 20, 1768, Nelson Letterbook, Vi.

declared his love: Rind's *Virginia Gazette,* Feb. 25, 1768, reprinted in *TQHGM,* XIII (April 1932), 287. On land, see Thomas Swepson and Richard W. Byrd, Indenture, May 18, 1802, Kilby Family Papers, Box 1, Vi.

128 "buy . . . Family": William Nelson to John Norton, Aug. 27, 1768, Nelson Letterbook, Vi.

At the sale: Thomas Newton, Sr., and John Taylor, Advertisement, Purdie and Dixon's *Virginia Gazette,* Aug. 18, 1768; Letter to Mr. Rind, Sept. 20, 1768, Rind's *Virginia Gazette,* Oct. 6, 1768.

Talbot Thompson: Benjamin J. Hillman, ed., *Executive Journals of the Council of Colonial Virginia* (Richmond, 1966), VI, 320.

Tucker's land: Benjamin Waller, advertisement, Purdie and Dixon's *Virginia Gazette,* Oct. 20, 1768; Thomas Burke to Neil Jamieson, Aug. 28, 1770, Thomas Burke to Thomas Jefferson, Sept. 3, 1770, April, July 10, Aug. 19, Sept. 24, 1771, *Papers of Jefferson,* ed. Boyd *et al.,* I, 52–59, 69–70, 73–74, 81–85.

at Castle Hill: K. Edward Lay and Martha Tuzson Stockton, "Castle Hill: The Walker Family Estate," *MACH,* LII (1994), 39–63.

The Greenbrier and New rivers: William Crawford to George Washington, Sept. 29, 1767, *Papers of Washington: Colonial,* ed. Abbot *et al.,* VIII, 39.

128 "obstinate": Franklin Minor, "Memoranda of Inquiries about Dr. Thomas Walker," Virginia MSS, Vol. 13, p. 25, Draper Collection, Series ZZ, WHi; "Noland-Harrison-Powell-Gilmer: Records from Family Bible," *TQHGM*, II (Oct. 1920), 133.

casks of ginseng: Entry of Oct. 7, 1767, A List of Ships and Vessels Cleared Outwards in Port of York, Virginia, T 1/461, ff. 59–60, PRO; John Hatley Norton to John Norton, Oct. 1767, Frances Norton Mason, *John Norton & Sons: Merchants of London and Virginia* (Richmond, 1937), 33.

129 "to restore . . . Winter": Francis Farley to Charles Tudway, Oct. 24, 1767, Tudway Papers, Somerset Record Office, Taunton; "Historical and Genealogical Notes," *TQHGM*, I (July 1919), 70; John Laforey to Phillip Stephens, July 7, 1767, Adm 1/102, PRO.

Dismal Plantation: Cash Accounts, Nov. 3, 1767, *Papers of Washington: Colonial*, ed. Abbot *et al.*, VIII, 50.

"offered . . . lady": Thomas Jefferson to Robert Smith, July 1, 1805, quoted in Dumas Malone, *Jefferson and His Time* (Boston, 1948–81), I, 154.

the king's gifts: Samuel Wharton to Benjamin Franklin, Dec. 2, 1768, *The Papers of Benjamin Franklin*, ed. Leonard W. Labaree *et al.* (New Haven, 1959–), XV, 275–279.

in New York City: *Pennsylvania Gazette* (Philadelphia), Nov. 24, 1768.

130 "an absolute necessity": Andrew Lewis and Thomas Walker to William Johnson, July 29, 1768, *The Papers of Sir William Johnson*, ed. James Sullivan *et al.* (Albany, 1921–62), VI, 297.

even "disclaimed": Hillman, ed., *Executive Journals*, VI, 309.

Walker and Lewis: Andrew Lewis and Thomas Walker to Baron de Botetourt, Feb. 2, 1769, "Virginia and the Cherokees," *VMHB*, XIII (July 1905), 30–36.

House of Burgesses addressed: *Journal of the Commissioners for Trade and Plantations from January 1768 to December 1775* (London, 1937), 29–30. See also Thomas Gage to Earl of Shelburne, March 12, 1768, Clarence W. Alvord and Clarence E. Carter, eds., *Trade and Politics, 1767–1769*, Illinois State Historical Library, *Collections*, XVI (1921), 208–209.

Mississippi Company: Clarence E. Carter, ed., "Documents Relating to the Mississippi Land Company, 1763–1769," *AHR*, XVI (Jan. 1911), 318–319; John Armistead to John Norton & Son, Sept. 15, 1765, BR Box 18(24), CSmH.

William Fleming: Patrick Henry to William Fleming, June 10, 1767, Archibald Henderson, "Dr. Thomas Walker and the Loyal Company of Virginia," American Antiquarian Society, *Proceedings*, new series, XLI (1931), 141–142.

William Crawford: George Washington to William Crawford, Sept. 17, 1767, William Crawford to George Washington, Sept. 29, 1767, *Papers of Washington: Colonial*, ed. Abbot *et al.*, VIII, 26–29, 37–40.

131 at Johnson Hall: Ray A. Billington, "The Fort Stanwix Treaty of 1768," *NYH*, XXV (April 1944), 192–193; entry of May 12, 1769, *A Tour of Four Great Rivers: Being the Journal of Richard Smith*, ed. Francis W. Halsey (New York, 1906), 25.

Samuel Wharton: Jack M. Sosin, *Whitehall and the Wilderness: The Middle West in British Colonial Policy, 1760–1775* (Lincoln, 1961), 174; George E. Lewis, *The Indiana Company, 1763–1798: A Study in Eighteenth Century Frontier Land Speculation and Business Venture* (Glendale, 1941), 45–47, 63–64.

PAGE

"Necessary" . . . "Indians": William Johnson to John Blair, Sept. 25, 1768, John Blair to William Johnson, March 10, 1768, *Papers of Johnson*, ed. Sullivan *et al.*, VI, 406, 143–144; Address of Sir William Johnson, Oct. 26, 1768, E. B. O'Callaghan *et al.*, eds., *Documents Relative to the Colonial History of the State of New-York* (Albany, 1856–87), VIII, 118–119; Thomas Gage to Earl of Hillsborough, Jan. 5, 1769, May 14, Nov. 12, 1770, *The Correspondence of General Thomas Gage*, ed. Clarence Edwin Carter (New Haven, 1931–33), I, 209, 258, 282. See also Dorothy V. Jones, *License for Empire: Colonialism by Treaty in Early America* (Chicago, 1982), 83–102; Michael N. McConnell, *A Country Between: The Upper Ohio Valley and Its Peoples, 1724–1774* (Lincoln, 1992), 244–258; Eric Hinderaker, *Elusive Empires: Constructing Colonialism in the Ohio Valley, 1673–1800* (Cambridge, 1997), 161–170; William N. Fenton, *The Great Law and the Longhouse: A Political History of the Iroquois Confederacy* (Norman, 1998), 533–540.

George Mason: George Mason to Edmund Randolph, Oct. 19, 1782, *The Papers of George Mason, 1725–1792*, ed. Robert A. Rutland (Chapel Hill, 1970), II, 746–755; Deposition of [Thomas] Walker-Fragmentary Notes, in Henderson, "Dr. Thomas Walker," American Antiquarian Society, *Proceedings*, new series, XLI (1931), 147–148.

"the Rapacity . . . insatiable": John Stuart to Earl of Hillsborough, Jan. 20, 1770, David Ross to Alexander Cameron, Dec. 20, 1768, CO 5/71, ff. 52, 65–66, PRO; Thomas Gage to Earl of Hillsborough, April 1, 1769, *Correspondence of Gage*, ed. Carter, I, 221–222; John Richard Alden, *John Stuart and the Southern Colonial Frontier* (Ann Arbor, 1944), 266–281, 299; J. Russell Snapp, *John Stuart and the Struggle for Empire on the Southern Frontier* (Baton Rouge, 1996), 74–76; Louis DeVorsey, Jr., *The Indian Boundary in the Southern Colonies, 1763–1775* (Chapel Hill, 1966), 62–67; Patricia Givens Johnson, *General Andrew Lewis of Roanoke and Greenbrier* (Blacksburg, 1980), chap. 15.

131 totaling 845,000 acres: A true and full Acct of all the Orders of Council for Granting Lands, Dec. 6, 1769, CO 5/1333, ff. 54–55, PRO.

132 "I . . . Remedy": Earl of Hillsborough to Thomas Gage, June 12, 1770, *Correspondence of Gage*, ed. Carter, II, 104–105.

appointment of Botetourt: Viscount Barrington to Thomas Gage, Aug. 1, 1768, John Shy, ed., "Confronting Rebellion," in Howard H. Peckham, *Sources of American Independence* (Chicago, 1978), I, 44; Viscount Barrington to Francis Bernard, Nov. 1, 1768, *The Barrington-Bernard Correspondence*, ed. Edward Channing and Archibald Cary Coolidge (Cambridge, 1912), 175; Horace Walpole to Horace Mann, Aug. 13, 1768, *The Yale Edition of Horace Walpole's Correspondence*, ed. W. S. Lewis *et al.* (New Haven, 1937–83), XXIII, 43–44.

"writes . . . business": Simmons and Thomas, eds., *Proceedings and Debates*, III, 314.

"politest . . . manners": Ralph Bigland, *Historical, Monumental and Genealogical Collections Relative to the County of Gloucester*, ed. Brian Frith (Bristol, 1989–95), III, 1170.

"cringing . . . fawning": *A Collection of the Letters of Atticus, Lucius, Junius, and Others* (London, 1769), 45.

"If . . . iron": Horace Walpole to Henry Seymour Conway, Aug. 9, 1768, *Yale Edition of Walpole's Correspondence*, ed. Lewis *et al.*, XXXIX, 104.

132 Hillsborough and Grafton: Peter D. G. Thomas, *The Townshend Duties Crisis: The Second Phase of the American Revolution, 1767–1773* (Oxford, 1987), chap. 5.

PAGE

133 "violence & passion": William Dowdeswell to Earl of Albemarle, [Aug. 1768], Amherst Papers, U 1350, 065/46, Kent County Archives.

a "tool": *London Chronicle*, Aug. 25–26, 1768.

"answer . . . Master": Baron de Botetourt to Baron Le Despencer, May 23, 1769, "Some Letters of Sir Francis Dashwood, Baron Le Despencer, as Joint Postmaster General, 1766–1781," ed. Betty Kemp, *Bulletin of the John Rylands Library*, XXXVII (Sept. 1954), 218.

never to return: Thomas Whately to George Grenville, Aug. 4, 1768, Augustus Hervey to George Grenville, Aug. 13, 1768, *Grenville Papers*, ed. Smith, IV, 330, 341.

The Warmley Company: Bryan Little, "Norborne Berkeley: Gloucestershire Magnate," *VMHB*, LXIII (Oct. 1955), 379–409; P. K. Stembridge, *The Goldney Family: A Bristol Merchant Dynasty* (Bristol, 1998), 46–51; Armand Budington DuBois, *The English Business Company After the Bubble Act, 1720–1800* (New York, 1938), 30–34; Arthur Raistrick, *Quakers in Science and Industry* (London, 1950), 194–196; Graham Hood, *The Governor's Palace in Williamsburg: A Cultural Study* (Williamsburg, 1991), 138; Derek Jarrett, "The Myth of 'Patriotism' in Eighteenth-Century English Politics," in J. S. Bromley and E. H. Kossmann, eds., *Britain and the Netherlands, Volume V: Some Political Mythologies* (The Hague, 1975), 138; Augustus Henry Fitzroy, Duke of Grafton, *Autobiography and Political Correspondence of Augustus Henry, Third Duke of Grafton*, ed. William R. Anson (London, 1898), 184–187; Horace Walpole, *Memoirs of the Reign of King George the Third*, ed. G. F. Russell Barker (London, 1894), III, 107–108; Mary Coke, *The Letters and Journals of Lady Mary Coke* (Edinburgh, 1889), II, 332–333; Joseph Redington *et al.*, eds., *Calendar of Home Office Papers of the Reign of George III* (London, 1878–81), II, 265; *A Collection of the Letters of Atticus and Others*, 41, 45; *Junius: Including Letters by the Same Writer Under Other Signatures*, rev. ed. (London, 1850), II, 227.

"totally ruined": Horace Walpole to Henry Seymour Conway, Aug. 9, 1768, *Yale Edition of Walpole's Correspondence*, ed. Lewis *et al.*, XXXIX, 104; Walpole, *Memoirs of George the Third*, ed. Russell Barker, III, 108, 156; Little, "Norborne Berkeley," *VMHB*, LXIII (Oct. 1955), 404.

as plenipotentiary: Thomas Whately to George Grenville, Aug. 4, 1768, *Grenville Papers*, ed. Smith, IV, 331; Earl of Albemarle to Duke of Newcastle, Aug. 4, 1768, Newcastle Papers, General Correspondence, CCCV, ff. 378–379, Uk.

He arrived: Purdie and Dixon's *Virginia Gazette*, Oct. 27, 1768.

134 "basket-making": Baron de Botetourt to Baron Le Despencer, May 23, 1769, "Some Letters of Sir Francis Dashwood," ed. Kemp, *Bulletin of the John Rylands Library*, XXXVII (Sept. 1954), 218. See also [Francis Grose], *A Classical Dictionary of the Vulgar Tongue* (London, 1785), "Basket making."

Washington and Fielding Lewis: Entries of Oct. 26–28, 1768, *The Diaries of George Washington*, ed. Donald Jackson and Dorothy Twohig (Charlottesville, 1976), II, 102.

"practised . . . arts": Francis Lightfoot Lee to William Lee, March 9, 1769, Lee Family Correspondence, BR Box 4(6), CSmH.

"every . . . People": William Nelson to Arthur Lee, March 31, 1769, Lee Family Papers, ViU.

"soothing": Walpole, *Memoirs of George the Third*, ed. Russell Barker, III, 156; William Nelson to Samuel Athawes, Dec. 6, 1770, Nelson Letterbook, Vi.

by the Cherokees: Baron de Botetourt to Andrew Lewis and Thomas Walker, Dec. 20, 1768, "Virginia and the Cherokees," *VMHB*, XIII (July 1905), 28–30; Hillman, ed., *Executive Journals*, VI, 308–310; "Observations and Answers," March 5, 1771, in [Samuel Wharton], [*Statement for the Petitioners in the Case of the Walpole Company Grant*] [London?, 1772], appendix iii, 14; DeVorsey, *Indian Boundary*, 67–92; Johnson, *General Andrew Lewis*, 146–153.

James Parke Farley: Francis Farley to Charles Tudway, July 25, 1765, Tudway Papers, Somerset Record Office; Samuel Martin to Baron de Botetourt, [ca. Oct. 1768], Letterbook of Samuel Martin, Add MSS 41,350, f. 83, Uk.

135 his first grandson: John Marshall, *Royal Navy Biography* (London, 1823), I, 446.

a woman's saddle: Accot of the sales of the Furniture of John Laforey, Jan. 6, 1769, Richard Corbin Papers, ViWC.

"to stay ... order": Francis Farley to Charles Tudway, April 29, 1769, Tudway Papers, Somerset Record Office.

Land of Eden and Munford: Francis Farley to Robert Munford, Jan. 15, 1778, *Dinwiddie, Crawford & Co.* v. *Henry Skipwith and Elizabeth Hill Skipwith et al.*, 1819, USCCVD(EC), Vi.

135 Samuel Gist: On Samuel Gist and the elopement of Mary Gist and William Anderson, see Samuel Gist to John Smith, Feb. 6, July 24, Aug. 5, 1767, Jan. 9–25, Jan. 26–Feb. 12, March 4, 12, April 12, June 15–19, 1768, *Jos. Smith's Admr et al.* v. *Gist's Exor et al.*, 1825, USCCVD(EC), Vi; John Hook to Samuel Gist, Dec. 2, 1767, Letter Book of Hook, Vi; Claim of Samuel Gist, American Loyalist Claims, AO 13/30, PRO; Samuel Galloway to Silvanus Grove, Aug. 20, 1767, Samuel Galloway Letter Book, Galloway-Maxcy-Markoe Papers, DLC; Samuel Rogers to William Taylor, Feb. 2, 1779, Lovering-Taylor Family Papers, DLC; John Norton to John Hatley Norton, April 1, 1768, April 1768, William Anderson to John Norton, Sept. 20, 1771, John Norton & Son Papers, ViWC; William Anderson, Will, July 30, 1793, *VMHB*, XXXVII (Jan. 1929), 39; Account with William Anderson, Aug. 14, 1769, April 10, 1775, Garrett Minor Papers, DLC.

137 John Tabb: *Tabb's Administrators* v. *Gist*, Opinion, Dec. 9, 1802, *The Papers of John Marshall*, ed. Herbert A. Johnson *et al.* (Chapel Hill, 1974–), VI, 129–142.

DeBerdt, Burkitt & Sayre: John R. Alden, *Stephen Sayre: American Revolutionary Adventurer* (Baton Rouge, 1983), 20–24; Dennys DeBerdt to Joseph Reed, March 18, 1766, Joseph Reed to Charles Pettit, May 7, 1770, William B. Reed, *The Life of Esther DeBerdt, Afterwards Esther Reed* (Philadelphia, 1853), 77–79, Jackson & Bromfield to DeBerdt, Burkitt & Sayre, Feb. 24, 1768, in Kenneth Wiggins Porter, *The Jacksons and the Lees: Two Generations of Massachusetts Merchants, 1765–1844* (Cambridge, 1937), I, 192–194.

138 "an elegant entertainment": *London Chronicle*, Aug. 11, 1768.

"allmost kill'd me": Samuel Gist to John Smith, Jan. 26–Feb. 12, 1768, *Jos. Smith's Admr. et al.* v. *Gist's Exor et al.*, 1825, USCCVD(EC), Vi.

"best" ... "Honor": Samuel Gist to George Washington, June 17, 1769, *Papers of Washington: Colonial*, ed. Abbot *et al.*, VIII, 216. See also John Fothergill to Samuel Fothergill,

Dec. 6, 1768, *Chain of Friendship: Selected Letters of Dr. John Fothergill of London, 1735–1780*, ed. Betsy C. Corner and Christopher C. Booth (Cambridge, 1971), 292; Peter Lyons to Samuel Gist, July 4, 1768, Claim of Samuel Gist, American Loyalist Claims, AO 13/30, PRO.

138 "grave" . . . "Bankrupt": Peter Lyons to John Norton, Sept. 24, 1768, John Norton & Son Papers, ViWC.

"a set of Wilkes's": [?] Fairfax to [?], May 20, 1769, *Pickering & Chatto Ltd.*, *List Ten* (Oct. 1982), Item 15; Alexander Stephens, *Memoirs of John Horne Tooke* (New York, 1968 [orig. publ. London, 1813]), I, 178; Paul Langford, "London and the American Revolution," in John Stevenson, ed., *London in the Age of Reform* (Oxford, 1977), 56–57; Peter D. G. Thomas, *John Wilkes: A Friend to Liberty* (Oxford, 1996), chap. 10; Pauline Maier, *From Resistance to Revolution: Colonial Radicals and the Development of American Opposition to Britain, 1765–1776* (New York, 1972), chap. 6.

"some . . . drinking": Arthur Beardmore to John Wilkes, July 24, 1767, John Wilkes Correspondence, Add MSS 30,869, f. 148, Uk.

139 "another regular stock": George James Williams to George Selwyn, [March 1768], Jesse, *George Selwyn*, II, 265.

"He was . . . comedy": Nathaniel William Wraxall, *The Historical and Posthumous Memoirs of Sir Nathaniel William Wraxall, 1772–1784*, ed. Henry B. Wheatley (London, 1884), II, 48.

"abhorrence . . . government": *Annual Register*, XII (1769), 2d ed. (London, 1773), "The History of Europe," 195–196.

merchants deliver address: George Rudé, "The Anti-Wilkite Merchants of 1769," *Guildhall Miscellany*, II (Sept. 1965), 283–304; John Norton to Thomas Walker, March 8, 1769, Thomas Walker Papers, William Cabell Rives Papers, Box 162, DLC; Mrs. James Harris to James Harris, Jr., March 24, 1769, *A Series of Letters of the First Earl of Malmesbury*, ed. J. H. Harris, Earl of Malmesbury (London, 1870), I, 176–179; entry of March 22, 1769, *Journals of Charles Beatty, 1762–1769*, ed. Guy Souilliard Kent (University Park, 1962), 85; *Annual Register*, XII (1769), 84.

"I am . . . History": David Hume to Hugh Blair, March 28, 1769, David Hume to Gilbert Elliot, Oct. 16, 1769, *The Letters of David Hume*, ed. J. Y. T. Greig (Oxford, 1932), II, 197–198, 208. See also William Strahan to David Hume, April 1, 1768, John Hill Burton, ed., *Letters of Eminent Persons Addressed to David Hume* (Edinburgh, 1849), 86–90; J. G. A. Pocock, "Hume and the American Revolution: The Dying Thoughts of a North Briton," in David Fate Norton *et al.*, eds., *McGill Hume Studies* (San Diego, 1979), 325–343.

140 "absurd": [Bacon], *Short Address to the Government*, 9.

"Ministerial . . . America": Extract of a Letter from London, March 25, 1769, *Virginia Gazette*, June 22, 1769, reprinted in *Pennsylvania Gazette*, July 6, 1769.

"They" . . . "America": Roger Atkinson to Samuel Gist, July 10, 1769, Roger Atkinson Letterbook, ViU.

"meant" . . . "concern'd": Samuel Gist to John Smith, Aug. 30, 1769, *Jos. Smith's Admr. et al. v. Gist's Exor et al.*, 1825, USCCVD(EC), Vi.

Middlesex electors: George Rudé, *Wilkes and Liberty: A Social Study of 1763 to 1774* (Oxford, 1962); Lucy Sutherland, "The City of London and the Opposition to Government,

PAGE

1768–74," in Stevenson, ed., *London in the Age of Reform,* 30–54; John Brewer, *Party Ideology and Popular Politics at the Accession of George III* (Cambridge, 1976), chap. 9; Joel J. Gold, "Mr. Serjeant Glynn: Radical Politics in the Courtroom," *Harvard Library Journal,* XXIX (April 1981), 197–209; Christina Bewley and David Bewley, *Gentleman Radical: A Life of John Horne Tooke, 1736–1812* (London, 1998), 7–32; Deborah D. Rogers, *Bookseller as Rogue: John Almon and the Politics of Eighteenth-Century Publishing* (New York, 1986), chap. 2.

"A Jew . . . well' ": William Lee to Richard Henry Lee, Aug. 30, 1771, William Lee Letterbook, 1770–1771, duPont Library, Stratford, Virginia; Sir William Forbes of Pitsligo, Bart., *Memoirs of a Banking-House* (London, 1860), 25–26.

"every . . . days": Henry Laurens to James Laurens, Aug. 19, 1772, *The Papers of Henry Laurens,* ed. Philip M. Hamer *et al.* (Columbia, 1968–), VIII, 422.

141 "many thousand pounds": *Morning Chronicle* (London), July 3, 1777, reprinted in Oldham, *Mansfield Manuscripts,* I, 520n.2. See also James Peller Malcolm, *Anecdotes of the Manners and Customs of London During the Eighteenth Century* (London, 1808), 212–213; *London Chronicle,* Sept. 29, 1772; Purdie and Dixon's *Virginia Gazette,* Jan. 23, 1772; Rind's *Virginia Gazette,* May 30, 1771, April 23, 1772; *Pennsylvania Gazette,* April 9, 1772; William Strahan to David Hall, Feb. 10, 1772, "Correspondence Between William Strahan and David Hall, 1763–1777," *PMHB,* XII (1888), 241–242.

New Lloyd's: Lillywhite, *London Coffee Houses,* 395–396; Wright and Fayle, *History of Lloyd's,* 98–99; Dawson, "London Coffee-Houses," *Essays by Divers Hands,* 3d ser., XI (1932), 93–94, 103; [Pugh], *Walks,* I, 57.

"Confusion": Anthony Todd to Baron Le Despencer, March 31, 1769, "Some Letters of Sir Francis Dashwood," ed. Kemp, *Bulletin of the John Rylands Library,* XXXVII (Sept. 1954), 216–217.

"*tickets insured*": Oldham, *Mansfield Manuscripts,* I, 523–524; *London Chronicle,* Aug. 30, 1770.

"put . . . House": *Adams et al.* v. *Crouch,* in Reginald G. Marsden, ed., *Reports of Cases Determined by the High Court of Admiralty . . . 1758–1774* (London, 1885), 111.

were "put up": Duncan Campbell to Somervell & Noble & Hugh Lenox, April 30, 1773, Business Letterbook, Duncan Campbell Letterbooks, Mitchell Library, Sydney, Australia; John Norton to John Hatley Norton, July 12, 1770, John Norton & Son Papers, ViWC.

subscription books: *London Chronicle,* March 19, 21, 1772.

141 underwriters and underwriting: *Report on Marine Insurance,* 1810 (226) IV. 247, pp. 92, 63, 77.

142 "what . . . those": James Russell to Samuel Galloway, May 7, 1770, Galloway-Maxcy-Markoe Papers, DLC; Samuel Galloway to James Russell, Aug. 27, 1771, Samuel Galloway Letter Book, *ibid.*

a list of frauds: *Report on Marine Insurance,* 1810 (226) IV. 247, p. 88.

"extremely . . . health": *Public Characters of 1803–1804* (London, 1804), 388.

"Building . . . House": Wright and Fayle, *History of Lloyd's,* 110–111; Frederick Martin, *The History of Lloyd's and of Marine Insurance in Great Britain* (New York, 1971 [orig. publ. London, 1876]), 145–149.

142 to choose a committee: Wright and Fayle, *History of Lloyd's*, 112.

"If I . . . underwrite": Testimony of John Ewer, Oldham, *Mansfield Manuscripts*, I, 573.

"a contractor . . . Government": James Jenkins, *The Records and Recollections of James Jenkins*, ed. J. William Frost (New York, 1984), 457–458; John Bartlet Brebner, *The Neutral Yankees of Nova Scotia: A Marginal Colony During the Revolutionary Years* (New York, 1937), 150.

143 "broke . . . pieces": Duncan Campbell to Somervell & Noble & Hugh Lenox, Jan. 5, 1774, Campbell Letterbooks, Mitchell Library, Sydney; P. W. Matthews, *History of Barclays Bank, Limited*, ed. Anthony W. Tuke (London, 1926), 31–38.

"there . . . Country": Isaac Low to Nicholas Low, May 3, 1785, Low Papers, DLC.

May 8, 1769: Meade, "Family History," in Peet, ed., *Chaumiere Papers*, 30; John Daly Burk *et al.*, *The History of Virginia* (Petersburg, 1804–16), III, 342; Hood, *Governor's Palace*, 250–251.

"some . . . Assembly": John Page to John Norton, April 20, 1769, John Norton & Son Papers, ViWC.

"*we . . . free*": [John Dickinson and Arthur Lee], *The Farmer's and Monitor's Letters* (Williamsburg, 1769), 85.

in the same vein: William Nelson to Farell & Jones, Nov. 19, 1768, Jan. 11, 1769, Nelson Letterbook, Vi; George Washington to George Mason, April 15, 1769, *Papers of Washington: Colonial*, ed. Abbot *et al.*, VIII, 178–180.

four resolutions: William J. Van Schreeven *et al.*, eds., *Revolutionary Virginia: The Road to Independence* (Charlottesville, 1973–83), I, 70–71; Samuel Washington to William Lee, May 26, 1769, Emmet Collection, NN.

144 "completely . . . ambition": Meade, "Family History," in Peet, ed., *Chaumiere Papers*, 29–30.

"a regular Association": Van Schreeven *et al.*, eds., *Revolutionary Virginia*, I, 72–77.

"will . . . Colony": Richard Henry Lee to Arthur Lee, May 19, 1769, Shelburne Papers, Vol. 67, p. 73, MiU-C.

"seems . . . end": Baron de Botetourt to Baron Le Despencer, May 23, 1769, "Some Letters of Sir Francis Dashwood," ed. Kemp, *Bulletin of the John Rylands Library*, XXXVII (Sept. 1954), 218.

"very" . . . "Frugality": Van Schreeven *et al.*, eds., *Revolutionary Virginia*, I, 74–75.

A satirist: Purdie's *Virginia Gazette*, May 2, 1766 (supplement). The unique copy of this issue is in ViWC.

"when . . . assembly": William Allason to William Gregory, Oct. 28, 1769, Allason Letterbook, Vi; John Norton to Robert Carter Nicholas, Nov. 10, 1769, Wilson Cary Nicholas Papers, DLC; Lawrence Henry Gipson, *The British Empire Before the American Revolution* (New York, 1958–70), XI, 266; Bruce A. Ragsdale, *A Planters' Republic: The Search for Economic Independence in Revolutionary Virginia* (Madison, 1996), 85–88.

intended to repeal: Dennys DeBerdt to Caesar Rodney, May 20, 1769, "Letters of Dennys DeBerdt," Colonial Society of Massachusetts, *Transactions*, XIII (1910–11), 374.

145 "universally steady": William Lee to Richard Henry Lee, Feb. 6, 1770, BR Box 4(8), CSmH.

"to do . . . age": Baron de Botetourt to Duchess Dowager of Beaufort, Dec. 18, 1769, Botetourt Transcripts, ViWC.

PAGE

"as merchts . . . orders": William Lee to Richard Henry Lee, Feb. 6, 1770, BR Box 4(8), CSmH; William Neate to Stephen Collins, Feb. 7, 1770, Stephen Collins & Son Papers, DLC; Dennys DeBerdt to Thomas Cushing, Feb. 2, 1770, Dennys DeBerdt Letterbook, DLC; William Lee to William Fitzhugh, Jan. 19, 1770, William Lee Letterbook, 1769–1771, duPont Library, Stratford; Thomas, *Townshend Duties Crisis*, 156–158.

ship *Nancy:* Samuel Gist to Thomas Tabb & Son, Jan. 24, 1770, Mss2, G4477, a1, ViRHi; John Tabb to Samuel Gist, Jan. 6, 1770, *Samuel Gist v. John Tabb*, 1795, USCCVD(EC), Vi; *Lloyd's List*, Feb. 23, 1770; *Lloyd's Register, 1768–1771* (London, n.d.), N-55.

her happiness: William Nelson to Francis Farley, Feb. 22, 1770, Nelson Letterbook, Vi.

orders were larger: William Nelson to John Norton, July 19, 1770, *ibid.*

"large . . . Montreal": William Neate to Stephen Collins, March 26, 1770, Stephen Collins & Son Papers, DLC; William Strahan to David Hall, Aug. 24, 1770, "Correspondence Between Strahan and Hall," *PMHB*, XI (1887), 351–352; Lois Green Carr and Lorena S. Walsh, "Changing Lifestyles and Consumer Behavior in the Colonial Chesapeake," in Cary Carson *et al.*, eds., *Of Consuming Interests: The Style of Life in the Eighteenth Century* (Charlottesville, 1994), 59–166; T. H. Breen, "The Meaning of Things: Interpreting the Consumer Economy in the Eighteenth Century," in John Brewer and Roy Porter, eds., *Consumption and the World of Goods* (London, 1993), 249–260.

"merchants . . . side": Joseph Reed to Charles Pettit, May 7, 1770, Reed, *Life of Esther DeBerdt*, 149–150.

"till . . . redressed": [Arthur Lee], *The Political Detection; or, the Treachery and Tyranny of Administration* (London, 1770), 101–102.

vessels in the Thames: S. Eliot to Jonathan and John Amory, March 6, 1770, Amory Family Papers, DLC; Harry Piper to Dixon & Littledale, April 3, 1770, Harry Piper Letterbook, Douglass Family Papers, ViU; Gipson, *British Empire*, XI, 267–273.

146 "Hornsby, the Taylor": Francis Jerdone to Hugh Crawford, Aug. 21, 1753, "Letter Book of Francis Jerdone," *WMQ*, 1st ser., XI (April 1903), 239.

"acquired . . . Trade": Purdie and Dixon's *Virginia Gazette*, May 28, 1772.

Joseph Hornsby: On business activities, see *Murdock & Co. v. William Byrd's Extx.*, 1797, *Hornsby's Exors et al. v. Byrd's Exors et al.*, Nov. 1824, *Lidderdale et al. v. Robinson's Admrs.*, 1832, *Byrd v. Byrd*, 1838, USCCVD(EC), Vi; Claim of John Tyndale Warre, T 79/9, PRO; Robert Cary & Co. to William Byrd, May 13, Aug. 5, 1774, *The Correspondence of the Three William Byrds of Westover, Virginia, 1684–1776*, ed. Marion Tinling (Charlottesville, 1977), II, 789–791, 795–798.

The latest book: [John Mitchell], *The Present State of Great Britain and North America* (London, 1767), 8–9n, 143–146.

"produced but little": John Blair to Earl of Hillsborough, Sept. 20, 1768, King's 206, f. 50, Uk.

the soil of the low country: William Nelson to Samuel Athawes, July 5, 1769, Nelson Letterbook, Vi.

George Washington: Robert Stewart to George Washington, Jan. 25, 1769, *Papers of Washington: Colonial*, ed. Abbot *et al.*, VIII, 162.

147 "inexhaustible" supply: James Parker to Charles Steuart, Nov. 15, 1769, Charles Steuart Papers, UkENL.

PAGE

147 "considerably . . . deaths": David Jameson to Samuel Gist, Nov. 7, 1783, Claim of Samuel Gist, American Loyalist Claims, AO 13/30, PRO.

Venus and Jack: Purdie and Dixon's *Virginia Gazette*, Dec. 5, 1771, Feb. 18, 1773; Purdie's *Virginia Gazette*, July 10, 1778; Robert Burwell, Will, Jan. 10, 1777, "Isle of Wight County Records," *WMQ*, 1st ser., VII (April 1899), 312.

"lying out": Rind's *Virginia Gazette*, June 23, 1768; Jacob Collee to David Jameson, July 31, 1781, Dec. 26, 1784, David Jameson to John Driver, Dec. 5, 1783, David Jameson to Jacob Collee, Dec. 30, 1784, Dismal Swamp Land Company Records, NcD.

harvest, cash: Matthew Barnard to William Barrell, May 16, 1769, Stephen Collins & Son Papers, DLC.

fire swept: *Gentleman's Magazine*, XXXIX (Nov. 1769), 538–539; John Luffman, *A Brief Account of the Island of Antigua* (London, 1789), Letter V, reprinted in Vere Langford Oliver, *The History of the Island of Antigua* (London, 1894), I, cxxix; Mainswete Walrond to Charles Tudway, Aug. 25, 1769, Tudway Papers, Somerset Record Office.

148 "the ridiculous . . . making": John Page to John Norton, April 20, 1769, John Norton & Son Papers, ViWC. See also John Gilman Kolp, *Gentlemen and Freeholders: Electoral Politics in Colonial Virginia* (Baltimore, 1998), chap. 1.

"one . . . World": John Page to John Norton, May 27, 1769, John Norton & Son Papers, ViWC.

"the most . . . Rosewell": John Page to John Norton, July 31, 1771, *ibid.*

two astronomical events: Brook Hindle, *The Pursuit of Science in Revolutionary America* (Chapel Hill, 1956), 146–165, 175; David Rittenhouse to John Page, Aug. 18, 1777, *Paul C. Richards—Autographs, Catalogue 208*, Item 144.

Fielding Junior: Fielding Lewis to George Washington, Sept. 16, 1769, *Papers of Washington: Colonial*, ed. Abbot *et al.*, VIII, 245.

the "slave account": *Lewis's Executor* v. *Bacon's Legatee and Executors*, 3 Hening & Munford 100, *Reports of Cases Argued and Determined in the Supreme Court of Appeals of Virginia* (Charlottesville, 1903), III, 601.

Dr. Walker spent: Petition to the House of Delegates from Inhabitants of Washington and Montgomery Counties, Arthur Campbell Papers, C 187/22, KyLoF; *Vance* v. *Walker*, 3 Hening & Munford 288–296, *Reports of Supreme Court of Virginia*, III, 667–674.

149 "Cosmo Medici": John Thompson to Thomas Jones, July 8, 1769, Roger Jones and Family Papers, DLC; John Arthur Coke, Jr., "Lucy Gray Briggs," in Alexander Wilbourne Weddell, ed., *A Memorial Volume of Virginia Historical Portraiture, 1585–1830* (Richmond, 1930), 205; Margaretta M. Lovell, "Painters and Their Customers: Aspects of Art and Money in Eighteenth-Century America," in Carson *et al.*, eds., *Of Consuming Interests*, 284–306; T. H. Breen, "The Meaning of 'Likeness': Portrait-Painting in an Eighteenth-Century Consumer Society," in Ellen G. Miles, ed., *The Portrait in Eighteenth-Century America* (Newark, 1993), 37–60.

Parker and Macknight: James Parker to Charles Steuart, July 5, Nov. 15, 1769, Charles Steuart Papers, UkENL; Edward Egerton, ed., *The Royal Commission on the Losses and Services of American Loyalists, 1783 to 1785: Being the Notes of Mr. Daniel Parker Coke, M.P.* (Oxford, 1915), 363.

his colleagues on the Council: Hillman, ed., *Executive Journals,* 334.

150 Norfolk County: Arthur Boush, Memorandum, Aug. 7, 1770, Dismal Swamp Land Company Records, NcD.

veterans of 1754: George Washington to Baron de Botetourt, Dec. 8, 1769, George Washington, Petition to Baron de Botetourt, [ca. Dec. 15], 1769, George Washington to Charles Washington, Jan. 31, 1770, *Papers of Washington: Colonial,* ed. Abbot *et al.,* VIII, 272–279, 300–303.

"a grand . . . entertainment": Purdie and Dixon's *Virginia Gazette,* June 7, 1770.

"A meeting . . . interests": *Ibid.,* June 21, 1770.

Robert Burwell: Rind's *Virginia Gazette,* March 8, 1770; Robert Burwell to John Norton, May 9, 1770, Martha Goosley to John Norton, Sept. 1, 1770, John Norton & Son Papers, ViWC; entry of Sept. 2, 1772, *The Diary of Landon Carter of Sabine Hall, 1752–1778,* ed. Jack P. Greene (Charlottesville, 1965), II, 720. On Mildred Lightfoot, see Lyon G. Tyler, "Lightfoot Family," *WMQ,* 1st ser., III (Oct. 1894), 110.

151 the "robbery": Samuel Gist to John Smith, June 15–19, 1768, *Jos. Smith's Admr. et al.* v. *Gist's Exor et al.,* 1825, USCCVD(EC), Vi.

Higham Hill: Lewis, "Architects," *Art Bulletin,* XXIX (Dec. 1947), 265; Lysons, *Environs of London,* 2d ed., I, Part II, 702–703; Wright, *History and Topography of Essex,* II, 506–507; Reany and Grieve, "Walthamstow," in Powell, ed., *History of Essex,* VI, 260; [Pugh], *London; Being an Accurate History,* VI, 297; *The Ambulator; or, the Stranger's Companion in a Tour Round London* (London, 1774), 195.

"great" . . . "us": Anthony Bacon to J. Artiguenaret, April 18, 1761, Mercer Family Papers, ViRHi.

Church of St. Bartholomew: [Pugh], *London; Being an Accurate History,* III, 7; *Gentleman's Magazine,* XL (May 1770), 239.

Mary Bushby: Lloyd, *Early History of Iron Works,* 56–60.

cargo of the *Nancy:* Samuel Gist to Thomas Tabb & Son, Jan. 24, 1770, ViRHi; *Lloyd's List,* Jan. 12, Feb. 23, 1770.

152 "be as . . . home": Samuel Gist to John Smith, July 24, 1767, *Jos. Smith's Admr. et al.* v. *Gist's Exor et al.,* 1825, USCCVD(EC), Vi.

John Norton: John Smith to John Norton, Jan. 8, 1767, John Norton & Son Papers, ViWC.

"he will" . . . "Title": Samuel Gist to John Smith, May 20, 1767, *Jos. Smith's Admr. et al.* v. *Gist's Exor et al.,* 1825, USCCVD(EC), Vi.

"a little singular": Patrick Henry to Joseph Smith, Feb. 15, 1770, *ibid.*

"Sundry European Goods": A List of All Ships and Vessels Which Have Entered Inwards in the Port of York River, Virginia, Dec. 25, 1767–June 24, 1768, T 1/461, PRO.

a hurricane: Robert Carter Nicholas to John Norton, Sept. 16, 1769, Mason, *John Norton,* 107; *Lloyd's List,* Nov. 3, 17, 1769; Roger Atkinson to Lionel and Samuel Lyde, Oct. 26, 1769, Atkinson Letterbook, ViU; Thomas Jett to John Morton Jordan & Co., Sept. 13, 1769, "Letter Book of Thomas Jett," *WMQ,* 1st ser., XVII (July 1908), 86; Rind's *Virginia Gazette,* Sept. 14, 1769; Purdie and Dixon's *Virginia Gazette,* Sept. 14, 1769; *Maryland Gazette* (Annapolis), Sept. 14, 1769.

153 The *Fitzhugh:* Samuel Galloway to James Russell, [Jan. 1770?], Aug. 27, 1771, Samuel

Galloway and Stephen Steward to James Russell, July 20, 1770, Galloway Letterbook, Galloway-Maxcy-Markoe Papers, DLC.

153 *Fitzhugh* underwriters: James Russell to Samuel Galloway, May 7, 1770, Samuel Galloway and Stephen Steward to James Russell, July 20, 1770, Samuel Galloway to James Russell, Sept. 17, Nov. 18, 1770, Aug. 27, 1771, *ibid.* See also Nathaniel Mills to Champion, Dickason & Co., Aug. 20, 1784, "The Letter-book of Mills & Hicks," ed. Robert Earle Moody and Charles Christopher Crittenden, *NCHR*, XIV (Jan. 1937), 80–81.

154 the *Providence: Lloyd's List,* June 8, July 27, Aug. 24, 1770; *Lloyd's Register: 1768–1771,* P-400; *Maryland Gazette,* July 19, 1770. For the previous voyage of the *Providence,* see M. M. Schofield, "Lancashire Shipping in the 18th Century: The Rise of a Seafaring Family," *Transactions of the Historic Society of Lancashire and Cheshire,* CXL (1990), 8.

Phripp, Taylor & Company: Phripp, Taylor & Co. to Samuel Gist, Dec. 18, 1772, *Samuel Gist* v. *Taylor & Co.,* 1797, USCCVD(EC), Vi.

Elizabeth: Lloyd's List, Oct. 22, 1771; Samuel Gist, advertisement, Purdie and Dixon's *Virginia Gazette,* Jan. 30, 1772.

"in Advance": Samuel Gist to John Tabb, Jan. 28, Aug. 8, 1772, *Tabb's Admr.* v. *Gist et al.,* 1829, USCCVD(EC), Vi; List of Debts Contracted with Samuel Gist, Claim of Samuel Gist, T 79/31, PRO.

John Smith: John Norton to John Hatley Norton, Feb. 16, 1773, John Norton & Son Papers, ViWC; John Smith, advertisement, Purdie and Dixon's *Virginia Gazette,* Jan. 10, 1771; Edward Pleasants Valentine, comp., *The Edward Pleasants Valentine Papers* (Richmond, n.d.), IV, 2170; Commissioner's Report, June 1808, *Jos. Smith's Admr. et al.* v. *Gist's Exor et al.,* 1825, USCCVD(EC), Vi.

155 Bacon and the swamp: Charles Steuart to James Parker, Feb. 6, 1770, Parker Family Papers, Liverpool Public Library.

"advances" . . . "out": William Aitchison and James Parker to Charles Steuart, April 2, 1770, Charles Steuart Papers, UkENL.

"never would see": Viscount Barrington to Andrew Mitchell, Jan. 18, 1763, Henry Ellis, ed., *Original Letters Illustrative of English History,* 2d ser., IV (London, 1827), 459.

"superintendent of a bagnio": Quoted in George Edward Cokayne, *The Complete Peerage,* ed. Vicary Gibbs *et al.* (London, 1910–40), VI, 92n.

"He drinks . . . heated": Elizabeth Montagu to Edward Montagu, Dec. 5, 1764, *Mrs. Montagu "Queen of the Blues": Her Letters and Friendships from 1762 to 1800,* ed. Reginald Blunt (London, [1923]), I, 120.

"no" . . . "of it": Charles Steuart to William Aitchison and James Parker, June 8, Aug. 3, 1770, Parker Family Papers, Liverpool Public Library; William Senhouse to Humphrey Senhouse, May 22, 1770, in Edward Hughes, *North Country Life in the Eighteenth Century* (London, 1965), II, 252.

"a species . . . use": Testimony, June 7, 1784, Claim of Thomas Macknight, photocopies in English Records, Box ER8, Folder 20, Nc-Ar; Egerton, ed., *Royal Commission,* 363.

"Channel . . . Empire": George Washington to Thomas Johnson, July 20, 1770, *Papers of Washington: Colonial,* ed. Abbot *et al.,* VIII, 358–360.

156 Such migration: Thomas Adams to [?], July 4, 1771, in [Wharton], [*Statement for the Petitioners*], 22. See also [?] to Thomas Walpole, July 9, 1770, in *The Correspondence of William*

Nelson as Acting Governor of Virginia, 1770–1771, ed. John C. Van Horne (Charlottesville, 1975), 27.

Wharton and Walpole: Samuel Wharton to Thomas Pitt, July 3, 1770, STG Box 12(32), CSmH; Edward Montague to Committee of Correspondence, Jan. 18, Feb. 6, 1770, *VMHB*, XII (Oct. 1904), 159–165; Thomas Walpole to Earl of Hillsborough, July 16, 1770, [?] to Thomas Walpole, July 9, 1770, *Correspondence of Nelson*, ed. Van Horne, 23, 27.

"give . . . blow": George Washington to Baron de Botetourt, Oct. 5, 1770, *Papers of Washington: Colonial*, ed. Abbot *et al.*, VIII, 389.

"alarming": Thomas Walker to William Preston, May 27, 1771, Preston Papers, Vol. 2, ff. 125–126, Draper Collection, Series QQ, WHi.

George Mercer: George Mercer to George W. Fairfax, Dec. 2, 1773, in Edward D. Neill, *The Fairfaxes of England and America in the Seventeenth and Eighteenth Centuries* (Albany, 1868), 140–142; Alfred Procter James, *George Mercer of the Ohio Company: A Study in Frustration* (Pittsburgh, 1963), 62–63.

Arthur Lee: Arthur Lee to Richard Henry Lee, July 12, 1770, Lee Family Papers, ViU.

"faithless & dishonourable": George Morgan to Richard Neave, Oct. 1, 1774, Letter Books of George Morgan, PHarH-Ar.

157 "in . . . Vandals": Samuel Wharton to Joseph Galloway and Thomas Wharton, April 9, 1773, *Papers of Franklin*, ed. Labaree *et al.*, XX, 146n.

"The worst . . . undertakings": George Morgan to John Baynton, Nov. 1770, quoted in Max Savelle, *George Morgan: Colony Builder* (New York, 1932), 82.

"very" . . . "sentiment": [Wharton], [*Statement for the Petitioners*], appendix iii, pp. 19–20.

Earl of Hillsborough: Peter Marshall, "Lord Hillsborough, Samuel Wharton and the Ohio Grant, 1769–1775," *EnHR*, CCCXVII (Oct. 1965), 717–739; Sosin, *Whitehall and the Wilderness*, chaps. 7–8; Thomas, *Townshend Duties Crisis*, 66–72; B. D. Bargar, *Lord Dartmouth and the American Revolution* (Columbia, 1965), chap. 8; Gipson, *British Empire*, XI, 464–473.

"the Spirit of Association": William Nelson to John Norton, July 19, 1770, Nelson Letterbook, Vi.

"luxury and extravagance": Van Schreeven *et al.*, eds., *Revolutionary Virginia*, I, 80.

promptings from England: Baron de Botetourt to Earl of Hillsborough, June 30, 1770, Earl of Hillsborough to Baron de Botetourt, Oct. 3, 1770, K. G. Davies, ed., *Documents of the American Revolution, 1770–1783* (Shannon and Dublin, 1972–80), I, 128, 177.

the Association attracted: Van Schreeven *et al.*, eds., *Revolutionary Virginia*, I, 82–83; Thomas Jett to John Anderson, July 8, 1770, Thomas Jett Letterbook, Jerdone Family Papers, ViW; Rind's *Virginia Gazette*, Sept. 6, 1770.

called for December 14: William Nelson to Earl of Hillsborough, Dec. 19, 1770, *Correspondence of Nelson*, ed. Van Horne, 99. See also Ragsdale, *Planters' Republic*, 91–103; Thomas, *Townshend Duties Crisis*, 204–206.

death of Lord Botetourt: James Parker to Charles Steuart, Dec. 1770, Charles Steuart Papers, UkENL; William Nelson to Earl of Hillsborough, Oct. 15, 1770, *Correspondence of Nelson*, ed. Van Horne, 35.

157 burial and estate: William Nelson to Earl of Hillsborough, Oct. 15, 1770, *Correspondence*

PAGE

of Nelson, ed. Van Horne, 35; William Nelson *et al.* to Duke of Beaufort, Oct. 30, 1770, Botetourt Transcripts, ViWC; William Nelson to Samuel Athawes, Dec. 6, 1770, May 16, 1771, Nelson Letterbook, Vi; Purdie and Dixon's *Virginia Gazette*, Oct. 18, 1770; Hugh B. Grigsby to Henry S. Randall, Feb. 26, 1859, Randall-Grigsby Correspondence, CSmH.

158 "a free . . . Resignation": Hillman, ed., *Executive Journals*, VI, 367. On Blair, see Carter Braxton to William Cabell, March 10, 1768, Emmet Collection, NN; Richard Henry Lee to William Lee, Dec. 17, 1769, July 7, 1770, Lee Family Papers, Section 108, ViRHi.

"universally lamented": Purdie and Dixon's *Virginia Gazette*, Oct. 18, 1770.

"the compleatest . . . experienced": William Nelson to Samuel Athawes, Dec. 6, 1770, Nelson Letterbook, Vi.

"Wou'dbe": Robert Munford, "The Candidates," ed. Jay B. Hubbell and Douglass Adair, *WMQ*, 3d ser., V (April 1948), 231.

IV: THE LAST VOYAGE OF THE SLAVE SHIP *HOPE*

159 "French made free": Entry 2359, Register of Passes, Adm 7/96, PRO. See, for example, *London Chronicle*, Aug. 16, 1770. On the rigging of a snow, see Karl Heinz Marquardt, *Eighteenth-Century Rigs and Rigging*, 2d ed. (London, 1992), 115–116. On smuggling, see W. Rawlings to Earl of Dartmouth, Sept. 16, 1765, Historical Manuscripts Commission, *The Manuscripts of the Earl of Dartmouth* (London, 1887–96), III, 178–179; "Extracts from the Old Books of the Custom-House of Irvine," in *Topographical Account of the District of Cunningham, Ayrshire* (Glasgow, 1858), appendix, 233–234; Walter Long to Treasury Board, April 8, 1772, T 1/496/126–128, PRO, calendared in *List and Index Society, Volume 250: Treasury Board: Papers, 1771–1772* (1992); L. M. Cullen, *The Brandy Trade Under the Ancien Régime: Regional Specialisation in the Charente* (Cambridge, 1998), 19, 37–38; H. S. K. Kent, *War and Trade in Northern Seas* (Cambridge, 1973), 115; Geoffrey W. Place, *The Rise and Fall of Parkgate, Passenger Port for Ireland: 1686–1815*, Chetham Society, 3d ser., XXXIX (1994), 222–226; Cal Winslow, "Sussex Smugglers," in Douglas Hay *et al.*, *Albion's Fatal Tree: Crime and Society in Eighteenth-Century England* (New York, 1975), 125–126, 147–152; Hervey Benham, *The Smugglers' Century: The Story of Smuggling on the Essex Coast, 1730–1830* (Chelmsford, 1986), chaps. 3–4, 8, 14, 23; Robin Craig and John Whyman, "Kent and the Sea," in Alan Armstrong, ed., *The Economy of Kent* (Woodbridge, 1995), 175–181; Hervey Benham, *Once Upon a Tide* (London, 1955), chap. 14; Gebhard Windeborn, *A View of England Towards the Close of the Eighteenth Century* (Dublin, 1791), I, 153.

"African Scheme": Roger Atkinson to Samuel Gist, Jan. 10, 1771, Roger Atkinson Letterbook, ViU.

"add largely": William Nelson to Samuel Athawes, May 2, 1772, William Nelson Letterbook, Vi.

Gist offered to lend: William Nelson to Thomas and Rowland Hunt, July 3, 1772, *ibid.*

He shipped clothing: David Jameson to William Nelson, Jr., Jan. 4, 1785, Account of Dismal Swamp Company with David Jameson, Dismal Swamp Land Company Records, NcD.

PAGE

160 "it . . . fond of" and buyers: Roger Atkinson to Samuel Gist, Jan. 10, 1771, Atkinson Letterbook, Harry Piper to Dixon & Littledale, Dec. 16, 1770, Harry Piper Letterbook, Douglass Family Papers, ViU.

"what" . . . "Negroes": Oct. 10, 1770, *A Letter to an American Planter, from His Friend in London* (London, 1781), 3–4.

an annual ship: Samuel Gist to John Tabb, Jan. 28, 1772, *Tabb's Admr.* v. *Gist et al.*, 1829, USCCVD(EC), Vi. See also James A. Rawley, *The Transatlantic Slave Trade: A History* (New York, 1981), 400–404; Susan Westbury, "Slaves of Colonial Virginia: Where They Came From," *WMQ*, 3d ser., XLII (April 1985), 235–236.

the Gold Coast: Philip D. Morgan, *Slave Counterpoint: Black Culture in the Eighteenth-Century Chesapeake and Lowcountry* (Chapel Hill, 1998), 64–65; Darold D. Wax, "Preferences for Slaves in Colonial America," *JNH*, LVIII (Oct. 1973), 396; Carter Braxton to Nicholas Brown & Co., Oct. 16, 1763, Brown Family Papers, RPJCB; David Beekman to Christ[opher] and George Champlin, July 12, 1770, West Indies Collection, LU; testimony of Richard Miles, *Report of the Lords of the Committee of Council . . . Concerning the Present State of the Trade to Africa* (London, 1789), unpaginated; [John Peter Demarin], *A Treatise Upon the Trade from Great Britain to Africa* (London, 1772), appendix G, p. 42.

161 Providence: *New-Lloyd's List*, Jan. 4, Nov. 12, 1771; *Lloyd's Register: 1768–1771* (London, n.d.), P–400.

"a merchant . . . Trade": Archibald Dalziel to Andrew Dalziel, Sept. 7, 1771, Archibald Dalzel Letters, UkEU. Several years later the brothers adopted the spelling "Dalzel."

Ross & Mill: Samuel Bainbridge, Samuel Gist, John Shoolbred *et al.* to Board of Trade, [March 17, 1772], in [Demarin], *Treatise Upon the Trade*, appendix G, pp. 46–50.

The ship Peggy: *Lloyd's Register: 1768–1771*, P–495; *Lloyd's Register: 1776* (London, n.d.), P–99; Gilbert Francklyn, *Observations Occasioned by the Attempts Made in England to Effect the Abolition of the Slave Trade* (London, 1789), xv; *St. James's Chronicle* (London), May 14, 1774.

"I . . . Shoolbred": Archibald Dalziel to Andrew Dalziel, Feb. 25, 1774, Dalzel Letters, UkEU.

"the Effects . . . it": John Shoolbred to Committee of Council for Trade, Feb. 19, 1788, *Report Concerning the Trade to Africa*, Part I, Paper No. 1. See also [Edward Long], *Candid Reflections Upon the Judgement* (London, 1772), 39–40; Gilbert Ross, James Mill, John Shoolbred *et al.*, Memorial to the Lords Commissioners of Trade and Plantations, [1775?], Item 772 in K. E. Ingram, *Sources of Jamaican History, 1655–1838* (Zug, 1976), II, 820–821; B. L. Anderson, "The Lancashire Bill System and Its Liverpool Practitioners: The Case of a Slave Merchant," in W. H. Chaloner and Barrie M. Ratcliffe, eds., *Trade and Transport: Essays in Economic History in Honour of T. S. Willan* (Manchester, 1977), 59–97; Robin Blackburn, *The Making of New World Slavery: From the Baroque to the Modern, 1492–1800* (London, 1997), 395–398; David Richardson, "The British Empire and the Atlantic Slave Trade, 1660–1807," in P. J. Marshall, ed., *The Oxford History of the British Empire, Volume II: The Eighteenth Century* (Oxford, 1998), 440–464.

profits: Roger Anstey, "The Volume and Profitability of the British Slave Trade, 1761–1807," in Stanley L. Engerman and Eugene D. Genovese, eds., *Race and Slavery in the Western Hemisphere: Quantitative Studies* (Princeton, 1975), 3–31; J. E. Inikori, "Market Structure and the Profits of the British African Trade in the Late Eighteenth Century," *JEcH*, XLI (Dec. 1981), 745–766; Herbert S. Klein, "Economic Aspects of the Eighteenth-Century Atlantic Slave Trade," in James D. Tracy, ed., *The Rise of Merchant Empires: Long-Distance Trade in the Early Modern World* (Cambridge, 1990), 287–310; Blackburn, *Making of New World Slavery*, 383–390. See also David Hancock, *Citizens of the World: London Merchants and the Integration of the British Atlantic Community, 1735–1785* (Cambridge, 1995), chap. 6; Elaine Forman Crane, *A Dependent People: Newport, Rhode Island, in the Revolutionary Era* (New York, 1985), chap. 2.

162 "a man . . . service": Richard Brew to Liverpool Merchants, Oct. 1, 1771, in [Demarin], *Treatise upon the Trade*, appendix H, p. 110.

about 38,000 slaves: Kenneth Morgan, *Bristol and the Atlantic Trade in the Eighteenth Century* (Cambridge, 1993), 133.

almost 6,000: Sheila Lambert, ed., *House of Commons Sessional Papers of the Eighteenth Century* (Wilmington, 1975), XXXII, 15.

from Liverpool: James A. Rawley, "The Port of London and the Eighteenth Century Slave Trade: Historians, Sources, and a Reappraisal," *AfEcH*, IX (1980), 85–100.

"any" . . . "Guineaman": John Baker Holroyd, Earl of Sheffield, *Observations on the Project for Abolishing the Slave Trade*, 2d ed. (London, 1791), 20n; Robert Louis Stein, *The French Slave Trade in the Eighteenth Century: An Old Regime Business* (Madison, 1979), 70–71.

the *Meredith* made: Samuel Gist to John Tabb, Jan. 21, 1772, *Tabb's Admr.* v. *Gist et al.*, 1829, USCCVD(EC), Vi; entry 2096, Register of Passes, Adm 7/96, PRO; *New-Lloyd's List*, Oct. 4, 1771, Dec. 18, 1772.

"liable . . . subject": *The Case of the Mills Frigate* [London, 1765], 5; James Allan Park, *A System of the Law of Marine Insurances*, 2d ed. (London, 1790), 222–224.

163 her cargo: Marion Johnson, "The African Slave Trade and the Economy of West Africa," in Roger Anstey and P. E. H. Hair, eds., *Liverpool, the African Slave Trade, and Abolition* (Bristol, 1976), 15–19; David Richardson, "West African Consumption Patterns and Their Influence on the Eighteenth-Century English Slave Trade," in Henry A. Gemery and Jan S. Hogendorn, eds., *The Uncommon Market: Essays in the Economic History of the Atlantic Slave Trade* (New York, 1979), 303–330; Jenny West, *Gunpowder, Government and War in the Mid-Eighteenth Century* (Woodbridge, 1991), 124–127, 131–135; Anderson, "Lancashire Bill System," in Chaloner and Ratcliffe, eds., *Trade and Transport*, 64–67, 88–91; Richard Brew to [Miles Barber?], Aug. 25, 1771, [Demarin], *Treatise Upon the Trade*, appendix H, p. 104.

hired a crew: W. E. Minchinton, "The Voyage of the Snow *Africa*," *MM*, XXXVII (July 1951), 187–196; James Laroche *et al.* to David Duncombe, 1759, in C. M. MacInnes, *England and Slavery* (Bristol, 1934), 46–49; William Johnston & Co. to David Lindsay, June 10, 1754, in George C. Mason, "The African Slave Trade in Colonial Times," *American Historical Record*, I (July 1872), 340–341; testimony of Robert Norris, *Report Concerning the Trade to Africa*, Part II.

Captains met: *London Chronicle*, Sept. 25, 1770.

"a great . . . money": Samuel Gist to John Tabb, Jan. 21, 1772, *Tabb's Admr.* v. *Gist et al.*, 1829, USCCVD(EC), Vi.

The brig *Unanimity: Smith et al. Assignees of Hague* v. *DeSilva et al.*, 2 Cowper 469–472, *The English Reports* (Edinburgh, 1909), XCVIII, 1191–1192; testimony of John Shoolbred, Feb. 6, 1778, *The Parliamentary Register* (London, 1778), X, 200; Archibald Dalziel to Andrew Dalziel, Sept. 7, 1771, Dalzel Letters, UkEU; David Richardson, "Profits in the Liverpool Slave Trade: The Accounts of William Davenport, 1757, 1784," in Anstey and Hair, eds., *Liverpool*, 65.

a "Considerable" portion: Samuel Gist to John Tabb, Jan. 21, 1772, *Tabb's Admr.* v. *Gist et al.*, 1829, USCCVD(EC), Vi.

extending credit: Miles Barber to James Christie, May 14, 1762, MS tipped into Joseph Warren Keifer, *Slavery and Four Years of War* (New York, 1900), II, CSmH; R. B. Sheridan, "The Commercial and Financial Organization of the British Slave Trade, 1750–1807," *EcHR*, 2d ser., XI (Dec. 1958), 249–263; Joseph E. Inikori, "The Credit Needs of the African Trade and the Development of the Credit Economy in England," *ExEcH*, XXVII (1990), 197–231; Jacob M. Price, "Credit in the Slave Trade and Plantation Economies," in Barbara L. Solow, ed., *Slavery and the Rise of the Atlantic System* (Cambridge, 1991), 293–339; Sheffield, *Observations on the Project*, 20n.

"never" ... "push": Samuel Martin to Earl of Sandwich, Feb. 12, 1778, *The Private Papers of John, Earl of Sandwich*, ed. G. R. Barnes and J. H. Owen (n.p., 1932), I, 267–268. See also Melinda Elder, *The Slave Trade and the Economic Development of Eighteenth-Century Lancaster* (Halifax, 1992), 147–150. On high-risk slave merchants, see entry of May 23, 1774, *Radical Adventurer: The Diaries of Robert Morris, 1772–1774*, ed. J. E. Ross (Bath, 1971), 182.

Thomas Jones & Company: *Lloyd's Register: 1768–1771*, T–40.

sixteen-month voyage: David Richardson, ed., *Bristol, Africa and the Eighteenth-Century Slave Trade to America* (Bristol, 1986–96), IV, 12.

a "coast commission": James Laroche *et al.* to David Duncombe, 1759, in MacInnes, *England and Slavery*, 46–49; William Johnston & Co. to David Lindsay, June 10, 1754, in Mason, "African Slave Trade," *American Historical Record*, I (July 1872), 340–341.

"more" ... "Disposition": Testimony of Robert Norris, *Report Concerning the Trade to Africa*, Part II. Compare Norris's comments in Thomas Clarkson, *The History of the Rise, Progress, and Accomplishment of the Abolition of the African Slave-Trade* (London, 1808), I, 381.

164 Captain George Colley: Thomas Clarkson, comp., *The Substance of the Evidence of Sundry Persons on the Slave-Trade* (London, 1789), 59; Walter Minchinton, Celia King, and Peter Waite, eds., *Virginia Slave-Trade Statistics, 1698–1775* (Richmond, 1984), 161; Lambert, ed., *House of Commons Sessional Papers*, LXXXII, 29.

Captain Samuel Pemberton: Clarkson, comp., *Substance of the Evidence*, 129; entry 2116, Register of Passes, Adm 7/96, PRO; Olaudah Equiano, *The Interesting Narrative of the Life of Olaudah Equiano*, ed. Vincent Carretta (New York, 1995), 56–57; Carl B. Wadstrom, *Observations on the Slave Trade* (London, 1789), 38.

his brig *Will*: *Pennsylvania Gazette* (Philadelphia), April 13, 1774; *Daily Advertiser* (London), March 20, 1774; *Shrewsbury Chronicle*, March 5, 12, 1774; entry of June 29, 1775, *Chronicle, Annual Register*, XVIII (1775), 6th ed. (London, 1801), 134; entry 86, Register of Passes, Adm 7/98, PRO. On mortality among captains, see Stephen D. Behrendt, "The Captains in the British Slave Trade from 1785 to 1807," *Transactions of the Historic Society of Lancashire and Cheshire*, CXL (1990), 132–140. See also Peter Earle, *Sailors: English Merchant Seamen, 1650–1775* (London, 1998), chap. 10.

164 "requires . . . Harpooneers": Charles Goore to Robert Tomlinson, Jan. 26, 1775, Charles Goore Letterbook, James S. Schoff Revolutionary War Collection, MiU-C.

"Debauchery and Intoxication": Testimony of Robert Norris, *Report Concerning the Trade to Africa*, Part II.

"Beware . . . goes in": Quoted in George E. Brooks, Jr., *Yankee Traders, Old Coasters, and African Middlemen: A History of American Legitimate Trade with West Africa in the Nineteenth Century* (Boston, 1970), 13. See also Stephen D. Behrendt, "Crew Mortality in the Transatlantic Slave Trade in the Eighteenth Century," *SA*, XVIII (April 1997), 49–71, esp. 57–58.

The *Duke of Bridgewater: New-Lloyd's List*, May 28, 1771, supplement.

the *African Queen: Ibid.*, April 16, May 3, 1771.

165 the *George: Ibid.*, May 31, June 4, 1771.

the *Sam: Lloyd's List*, Jan. 10, 1772; *Daily Advertiser*, Jan. 10, 1772.

The *Loyalty: St. James's Chronicle*, May 17, 1774.

the sloop *Expedition: Lloyd's List*, April 13, Sept. 14, 1770; Edward Grace to Stevenson & Went, April 23, 1770, *Letters of a West African Trader: Edward Grace, 1767–70*, ed. T. S. Ashton (London, 1950), 38. On the *Gregson*, see also Lambert, ed., *House of Commons Sessional Papers*, LXXXII, 122–123. For another example of abandoning a foundering slave vessel, see "Extract of a letter from Philadelphia," Nov. 11, 1762, Chronicle, *Annual Register*, V (1762), 5th ed. (London, 1787), 117–118.

Gist and Tucker: William Nelson to Samuel Athawes, May 2, June 18, 1772, William Nelson to Thomas and Rowland Hunt, July 3, 1772, Nelson Letterbook, Vi.

166 Gist, *Hope*, and *Mentor*: Samuel Gist to John Tabb, Jan. 21, 28, 1772, *Tabb's Admr. v. Gist et al.*, 1829, USCCVD(EC), Vi; Susan Westbury, "Analysing a Regional Slave Trade: The West Indies and Virginia, 1698–1775," *SA*, VII (Dec. 1986), 241–256.

Vessels to the Gold Coast: John Adams, *Remarks on the Country Extending from Cape Palmas to the River Congo* (London, 1966 [orig. publ. 1823]), 223–227; Hugh Crow, *Memoirs of the Late Captain Hugh Crow of Liverpool* (London, 1830), 183–187; Selena Axelrod Winsnes, trans. and ed., *Letters on West Africa and the Slave Trade: Paul Erdmann Isert's Journey to Guinea and the Caribbean Islands in Columbia* (Oxford, 1992), 24–27, 210–211; John Matthews, *A Voyage to the River Sierra-Leone, on the Coast of Africa* (London, 1788), 33; *New-Lloyd's List*, Dec. 27, 1771, supplement; Samuel Gist to John Tabb, Nov. 2, 1772, *Tabb's Admr. v. Gist et al.*, 1829, USCCVD(EC), Vi.

Annamaboe anchorage: Lambert, ed., *House of Commons Sessional Papers*, LXVIII, 129–130; testimony of Robert Norris and Richard Miles, *Report Concerning the Trade to Africa*, Part I; Report from the Select Committee on the Settlements of Sierra Leone and Fernando Po (1830), *Irish University Press Series of British Parliamentary Papers, Slave Trade: Volume I* (Shannon, 1968), 93; John Entick, *The Present State of the British Empire* (London, 1774), IV, 510–511; David Eltis and David Richardson, "West Africa and the Transatlantic Slave Trade: New Evidence of Long-Run Trends," *SA*, XVIII (April 1997), 22–23.

Notes for Chapter IV 497

PAGE

167 "dreadfull" . . . "sharks": Charles Bell to Committee, May 12, 1762, Gilbert Petrie to Committee, Aug. 20, 1767, Company of Merchants Trading to Africa, Letterbooks, T 70/31, ff. 5, 140, PRO; [Horatio Bridge], *Journal of an African Cruiser*, ed. Nathaniel Hawthorne (New York, 1845), 137; John M'Leod, *A Voyage to Africa* (London, 1971 [orig. publ. London, 1820]), 7–9; "Remarks on Cape Coast Castle," Commonplace Book, Navigation, 1797–1817, HM 28915, CSmH.

The new white fort: A. W. Lawrence, *Trade Castles and Forts of West Africa* (Stanford, 1964), 349–355; Henry Meredith, *An Account of the Gold Coast of Africa* (London, 1967 [orig. publ. 1812]), 129–131; Lambert, ed., *House of Commons Sessional Papers*, XXXII, 29, 44; Thomas Clarkson, A Few Chosen Places for Colonization, Thomas Clarkson Papers, CN69, CSmH; Winsnes, ed., *Letters on West Africa*, 173.

a town with two districts: George Metcalf, "Gold, Assortments and the Trade Ounce: Fante Merchants and the Problem of Supply and Demand in the 1770s," *JAfH*, XXVIII (1987), 27–41; Adams, *Remarks on the Country*, 38; Thomas Thompson, *An Account of Two Missionary Voyages* (London, 1937 [orig. publ. 1758]), 49–63.

Richard Brew: Margaret Priestley, *West African Trade and Coast Society: A Family Study* (London, 1969); M. A. Priestley, "Richard Brew: An Eighteenth-Century Trader at Anomabu," *Transactions of the Historical Society of Ghana*, IV, Part I (1959), 29–46.

168 "the most . . . earth": Gilbert Petrie to Committee, Aug. 20, 1767, T 70/31, f. 141, PRO. For the diary of an African slave trader on another part of the coast, see Daryll Forde, ed., *Efik Traders of Old Calabar: Containing the Diary of Antera Duke* (London, 1968).

"our . . . ruined": David Mill to Committee, June 22, 1772, T 70/31, f. 221, PRO; Alexander Falconbridge, *An Account of the Slave Trade on the Coast of Africa* (London, 1788), 53–54; J. J. Crooks, ed., *Records Relating to the Gold Coast Settlements from 1750 to 1874* (Dublin, 1923), 37; J. K. Fynn, "Ghana-Asante (Ashanti)," in Michael Crowder, ed., *West African Resistance: The Military Response to Colonial Occupation* (New York, 1971), 24; James Sanders, "The Expansion of the Fante and the Emergence of Asante in the Eighteenth Century," *JAfH*, XX (1979), 349–364; A. Adu Boahen, "Fante Diplomacy in the Eighteenth Century," in K. Ingham, ed., "Foreign Relations of African States," *Colston Papers*, XXV (1974), 25–49.

the gold-taker: John Grossle to Committee, Sept. 8, 1769, T 70/31, f. 188, PRO; Adams, *Remarks on the Country*, 9–11; entry of May 2, 1774, [Robert Champlin], *A Rhode Island Slaver: Trade Book of the Sloop Adventure, 1773–1774*, ed. Verner W. Crane (Providence, 1922), 7; Winsnes, ed., *Letters on West Africa*, 84–87; John Kofi Fynn, ed., *Oral Traditions of Fante States* (Legon, 1974), III, 118, IV, 41.

Annamaboe slave dealers: Metcalf, "Gold, Assortments and the Trade Ounce," *JAfH*, XXVIII (1987), 30.

Philip Quaque: Philip Quaque to Samuel Johnson, Nov. 26, 1767, April 5, 1769, in Herbert Schneider and Carol Schneider, eds., *Samuel Johnson, President of King's College: His Career and Writings* (New York, 1929), I, 425, 428–430; Lambert, ed., *House of Commons Sessional Papers*, LXXXII, 40; See also Francis L. Bartels, "Philip Quaque, 1741–1816," *Transactions of the Gold Coast and Togoland Historical Society*, I, Part V (1955), 153–177; Margaret Priestley, "Philip Quaque of Cape Coast," in Philip D. Curtin, ed., *Africa Remembered: Narratives by West Africans from the Era of the Slave Trade* (Madison, 1967),

PAGE

99–139; Grace Bansa, "Quaque, P.," *Encyclopaedia Africana Dictionary of African Biography* (New York, 1977), I, 305–306.

168 Dougall, gunpowder: Bristol Port Book, April 5, 1770–July 5, 1770, ff. 17, 21, E 190/1228/2, PRO.

169 "fully . . . Fantees": Gilbert Petrie to Committee, Sept. 13, 1766, Oct. 9, 1767, T 70/31, ff. 110, 142–143, PRO; Joseph Raymond LaTorre, "Wealth Surpasses Everything: An Economic History of Asante, 1750–1874" (Ph.D. diss., University of California, Berkeley, 1978), 391, 422–424.

Gold Coast slaves: J. K. Fynn, *Asante and Its Neighbours: 1700–1807* (London, 1971), chap. 5; Johnson, "Atlantic Slave Trade," in Anstey and Hair, eds., *Liverpool*, 27–29; Kwame Y. Daaku, "Trade and Trading Patterns of the Akan in the Seventeenth and Eighteenth Centuries," in Claude Meillassoux, ed., *The Development of Indigenous Trade and Markets in West Africa* (Oxford, 1971), 170–171; Ray A. Kea, " 'I am here to plunder on the general road': Bandits and Banditry in the Pre-Nineteenth-Century Gold Coast," in Donald Crummey, ed., *Banditry, Rebellion, and Social Protest in Africa* (London, 1986), 124–125; T. C. McCaskie, *State and Society in Pre-Colonial Asante* (Cambridge, 1995), 26; John K. Thornton, "The African Background to American Colonization," in Stanley L. Engerman and Robert E. Gallman, eds., *The Cambridge Economic History of the United States: The Colonial Era* (Cambridge, 1996), 82–94; Kwasi Boaten, "Commerce in Northern Asante, 1702–1945," *Bulletin of the Ghana Geographical Association*, XIV (1969), 22–27; LaTorre, "Wealth Surpasses Everything," 421–435; Paul E. Lovejoy, *Transformations in Slavery: A History of Slavery in Africa* (Cambridge, 1983), 78–122; John Mensah Sarbah, *Fanti Customary Laws*, 3d ed. (London, 1968 [orig. pub. 1897]), 7–8, 115, 282–283. See also Clarkson, comp., *Substance of the Evidence*, 12–13, 19, 30–31, 42–43, 50–51, 62–63, 69–72; Wadstrom, *Observations*, 1–2, 17–18; Lambert, ed., *House of Commons Sessional Papers*, LXXIII, 388; Winsnes, ed., *Letters on West Africa*, 81–87, 133–134; testimony of Robert Norris, *Report Concerning the Trade to Africa*, Part I.

"The Gold . . . Languages": Testimony of Jerome Bernard Weuves, *Report Concerning the Trade to Africa*, Part I. See also Equiano, *Interesting Narrative*, ed. Carretta, 54–55; Fynn, ed., *Oral Traditions of Fante States*, I, Berase, 12–13, Ankaase, 9–10, Abirema-Agina, 9–11, II, 34–35, 50–51, 62–63, III, 13–14, 37–38, 51–52, 63–64, 87, 99, 108–109, IV, 15, 40, 63.

"they . . . power": Archibald Dalziel to Andrew Dalziel, Nov. 20, 1763, Dalzel Letters, UkEU; *Journal of the Commissioners for Trade and Plantations from January 1768 to December 1775* (London, 1937), 92, 141, 144.

ten ounces: David Mill to Committee, March 12, 1772, T 70/31, f. 215, PRO.

"the Choice . . . Trade": Thomas Westgate to Committee, April 10, 1777, T 70/32, f. 31, PRO.

169 "essential" . . . "accidentally": James Oldham, *The Mansfield Manuscripts and the Growth of English Law in the Eighteenth Century* (Chapel Hill, 1992), I, 557; Earl of Rochford to Robert Walpole, Sept. 21, 1773, Robert Walpole to Earl of Rochford, Oct. 25, 1773, Marquis de Pombal to Robert Walpole, Nov. 2, 1773, SP 89/75, ff. 116, 152, 171, PRO, calendared in *Descriptive List of the State Papers, Portugal, 1661–1780, in the Public Record Office, London* (Lisbon, 1979–83), III, 127, 129–130; José da Silva Lisboa to Domingos Vandelli, Oct. 18, 1781, in *Annais da Biblioteca Nacional do Rio de Janeiro: 1910* (Rio de

Janeiro, 1914), XXXII, 504–505; Summaries of Reports from Gov. O'Hara, July 25, 1766, Minutes of African Affairs, Shelburne Papers, Vol. 90, MiU-C; [Demarin], *Treatise Upon the Trade*, 23–24; Winsnes, ed., *Letters on West Africa*, 139. See also Joseph C. Miller, *Way of Death: Merchant Capitalism and the Angolan Slave Trade, 1730–1830* (Madison, 1988); LaTorre, "Wealth Surpasses Everything," 395, 397, 471n.227; Carlos Agostinho das Neves, *S. Tomé e Príncipe na segunda metade do séc. XVIII* (Lisbon, 1989), 100–111; Kenneth R. Maxwell, *Conflicts and Conspiracies: Brazil and Portugal, 1750–1808* (Cambridge, 1973), 214–215; Jordan Goodman, *Tobacco in History: The Culture of Dependence* (London, 1993), 162–165; Catherine Lugar, "The Portuguese Tobacco Trade and Tobacco Growers of Bahia in the Late Colonial Period," in Dauril Alden and Warren Dean, eds., *Essays Concerning the Socioeconomic History of Brazil and Portuguese India* (Gainesville, 1977), 26–69; Stuart B. Schwartz, *Sugar Plantations in the Formation of Brazilian Society: Bahia, 1550–1835* (Cambridge, 1985), 340–345; Pierre Verger, *Bahia and the West African Trade: 1549–1851* (Ibadan, 1964); A. J. R. Russell-Wood, "Ports of Colonial Brazil," in Franklin W. Knight and Peggy K. Liss, eds., *Atlantic Port Cities: Economy, Culture, and Society in the Atlantic World* (Knoxville, 1991), 196–239. On the Dutch, see also Johannes Menne Postma, *The Dutch in the Atlantic Slave Trade, 1600–1815* (Cambridge, 1990), 76–78; Harvey M. Feinberg, "Africans and Europeans in West Africa: Elminans and Dutchmen on the Gold Coast During the Eighteenth Century," *Transactions of the American Philosophical Society*, new series, LXXIX, Part 7 (1989).

170 Charles Bell and David Mill: Richard Brew to Liverpool Merchants, Oct. 15, 1770, [Demarin], *Treatise Upon the Trade*, appendix H, pp. 85–93; Benedict Der, "Edmund Burke and Africa, 1772–1792," *Transactions of the Historical Society of Ghana*, XI (1970), 12; Lambert, ed., *House of Commons Sessional Papers*, XXXII, 15–17; John Grossle to Committee, Sept. 8, 1769, T 70/31, ff. 187–188, PRO; *St. James's Chronicle*, Nov. 8, 1774; Richard Miles to John Shoolbred, April 9, 1778, in Eveline C. Martin, *The British West African Settlements: A Study in Local Administration* (New York, 1970 [orig. publ. London, 1927]), 40.

the snow *Greenwich*: David Mill to Committee, March 12, 1772, T 70/31, f. 215, PRO; Richardson, ed., *Bristol, Africa and the Slave Trade*, IV, 18.

the *Exeter*: Entry 1647, Register of Passes, Adm 7/96, PRO; *Pennsylvania Gazette*, June 25, 1772; *London Chronicle*, Aug. 8, 1772; Matthews, *Voyage to Sierra-Leone*, 3–4; Henry Laurens to John Holman, Sept. 8, 1770, *The Papers of Henry Laurens*, ed. Philip M. Hamer *et al.* (Columbia, 1968–), VII, 344–345, 344n.6.

Betty and Jenny: Daily Advertiser, Sept. 3, 1772; entry 2322, Register of Passes, Adm 7/96, PRO.

171 two slaves every three: Samuel Gist to John Tabb, Nov. 2, 1772, *Tabb's Admr. v. Gist et al.*, 1829, USCCVD(EC), Vi.

"you . . . rate": [?] to Liverpool Merchants, March 30, 1772, [Demarin], *Treatise Upon the Trade*, appendix H, pp. 122–123.

rolls of tobacco: David Mill to Committee, Nov. 19, 1770, March 12, 1772, T 70/31, ff. 202–203, 214.

John Marshall: Lambert, ed., *House of Commons Sessional Papers*, LXXIII, 383. See also Darold D. Wax, "Thomas Rogers and the Rhode Island Slave Trade," *AN*, XXXV (Oct. 1975), 289–301.

PAGE

171 The *Maesgwin:* Richardson, ed., *Bristol, Africa and the Slave Trade,* IV, 34.

172 Few slaves were brought: Samuel [Tuell] to Christopher Champlin, June 16, 1772, Worthington Chauncey Ford, ed., *Commerce of Rhode Island, 1726–1800,* Massachusetts Historical Society, *Collections,* 7th ser., IX–X (1914–15), I, 402; Crooks, ed., *Records Relating to the Gold Coast,* 37; David Mill to Committee, June 22, Dec. 12, 1772, T 70/31, ff. 220–221, 223, PRO; Margaret Priestley, "The Ashanti Question and the British: Eighteenth-Century Origins," *JAfH,* II (1961), 35–59; Sanders, "Expansion of the Fante," *JAfH,* XX (1979), 361–362; Fynn, *Asante and Its Neighbours,* 108–115.

"hideous yelling": Clarkson, comp., *Substance of the Evidence,* 20, 44–45, 75; testimony of Robert Norris, *Report Concerning the Trade to Africa,* Part II; Samuel Kelly, *Samuel Kelly: An Eighteenth Century Seaman,* ed. Crosbie Garstin (New York, 1925), 288; Equiano, *Interesting Narrative,* ed. Carretta, 56; James Irving to Mary Irving, Dec. 2, 1786, in Suzanne Schwarz, ed., *Slave Captain: The Career of James Irving in the Liverpool Slave Trade* (Wrexham, 1995), 113; Charles Garland and Herbert S. Klein, "The Allotment of Space for Slaves aboard Eighteenth-Century British Slave Ships," *WMQ,* 3d ser., XLII (April 1985), 238–248; Earle, *Sailors,* 77–78.

the *Thomas:* Purdie and Dixon's *Virginia Gazette* (Williamsburg), July 30, 1772; Richardson, ed., *Bristol, Africa and the Slave Trade,* IV, 25.

an address to the king: William J. Van Schreeven *et al.,* eds., *Revolutionary Virginia: The Road to Independence* (Charlottesville, 1973–83), I, 87; Earl of Dunmore to Earl of Hillsborough, May 1, 1772, K. G. Davies, ed., *Documents of the American Revolution, 1770–1783* (Shannon and Dublin, 1972–80), V, 94–95; Bruce A. Ragsdale, *A Planters' Republic: The Search for Economic Independence in Revolutionary Virginia* (Madison, 1996), 133–134.

Dougall and Gricewood: David Mill to Committee, June 22, 1772, T 70/31, f. 220, PRO; Samuel Gist to John Tabb, Nov. 2, 1772, *Tabb's Admr.* v. *Gist et al.,* 1829, USCCVD(EC), Vi.

173 "filled . . . Christians": Thomas Lothrop to Aaron Lopez, Dec. 11, 1774, *The Americas,* XXXV (April 1979), 574–580.

Bogle & Scott: Robert Bogle to George Bogle, Nov. 19, 1772, Bogle Papers, Mitchell Library, Glasgow; T. M. Devine, *The Tobacco Lords: A Study of the Tobacco Merchants of Glasgow* (Edinburgh, 1975), 7.

"disagreeably . . . property": Duncan Campbell to John Tayloe, June 24, 1772, Business Letterbook, Duncan Campbell Letterbooks, Mitchell Library, Sydney, Australia.

Robert Bogle, Jr.: *London Chronicle,* June 27, 1772; George F. Norton to John Hatley Norton, July 8, 1772, Frances Norton Mason, *John Norton & Sons, Merchants of London and Virginia* (Richmond, 1937), 254.

"every . . . Abyss": Robert Bogle to George Bogle, Nov. 19, 1772, Bogle Papers, Mitchell Library, Glasgow.

John Gilchrist: Rind's *Virginia Gazette,* Oct. 21, 1773.

174 close to a dead stop: Peleg Clarke to John Fletcher, July 25, Nov. 3, 1772, Samuel Tuell to Christopher Champlin, Sept. 26, 1772, in Elizabeth Donnan, ed., *Documents Illustrative of the History of the Slave Trade to America* (Washington, 1930–35), III, 259, 261, 262n; David Mill to Committee, Aug. 12, 1772, T 70/31, f. 222, PRO; Virginia Bever Platt, " 'And Don't Forget the Guinea Voyage': The Slave Trade of Aaron Lopez of Newport," *WMQ,* 3d ser., XXXII (Oct. 1975), 612–613.

PAGE

sprung a leak: David Mill to Committee, Dec. 12, 1772, T 70/31, f. 223, PRO. On leaks, see John Harland, *Seamanship in the Age of Sail* (London, 1985), 303–305.

Ilha do Príncipe: T. Boteler, "Memoir Descriptive of Prince's Island and Anno Bom," *Journal of the Royal Geographical Society*, II (1832), 274–278; Raquel Soeiro de Brito, "A Ilha do Príncipe," *Geographica*, III (April 1967), 3–17; J. K. Tuckey, *Narrative of an Expedition to Explore the River Zaire* (London, 1818), 47–54, 256–257; Gerardo A. Pery, *Geographia estatistica geral de Portugal e colonias* (Lisbon, 1875), 342–345; Clado Ribeiro de Lessa, *Crônica da uma embaixado Luso-Brasileira à Costa d'África em fins do século XVIII* (São Paulo, 1957), 140–141; das Neves, *S. Tomé e Príncipe*, 112–119, 130; Francisco Travassos Valdez, *Six Years of a Traveller's Life in Western Africa* (London, 1861), II, 8–9; "Remarks on Prince's Harbour," Commonplace Book, Navigation, HM 28915, CSmH.

175 "arbitrariedades e extorsões": R. J. da Cunha Matos, *Compêndio histórico das possessões de Portugal na África* (Rio de Janeiro, 1963), 182; Bernardo Castro de Mesquita to Martinho de Mello e Castro, April 15, 1772, in Fernando Castello-Branco, "Os Franceses e as Ilhas do Golfo da Guiné," *Arquivos de Centro Cultural Português* (Paris, 1971), III, 717–718; Samuel Swan, Memoranda of the African Trade, [ca. 1810], in Brooks, *Yankee Traders*, 339–340.

the island and slave trade: Vicente Gomes Ferreira to Martinho de Mello e Castro, March 15, 1771, in das Neves, *S. Tomé e Príncipe*, 336–341; Conde de Pavolide to Martinho de Mello e Castro, July 3, 1771, *Annais da Biblioteca Nacional do Rio de Janeiro*, XXXII, 259; Joseph Banfield, Journal, HM 57345, CSmH; Dieudonné Rinchon, *Pierre-Ignace-Liévin van Alstein: capitaine négrier* (Dakar, 1964), 264–269; Tony Hodges and Malyn Newitt, *São Tomé and Príncipe: From Plantation Colony to Micro State* (Boulder, 1988), 24–25; K. David Patterson, *The Northern Gabon Coast to 1875* (Oxford, 1975), chap. 2; Stein, *French Slave Trade*, 95–96.

the *Fancy:* Earl of Rochford to Robert Walpole, Nov. 8, 1773, April 11, 1775, Robert Walpole to Martinho de Mello e Castro, Nov. 24, 1773, May 11, 1775, SP 89/75, ff. 157, 180, 89/79, ff. 62, 156, PRO, calendared in *Descriptive List of the State Papers, Portugal*, III, 129, 131, 157, 161.

"totally irrepairable": David Mill to Committee, May 8, 1773, T 70/31, f. 231, PRO.

the *Nancy:* Letter from Barbados, June 24, 1773, *Daily Advertiser*, Aug. 5, 1773; *Lloyd's Register: 1768–1771*, N–87.

the *Hope's* surgeon: David Mill to Committee, Dec. 12, 1772, T 70/31, f. 224, PRO.

"The *Hope* . . . Africa": *Lloyd's Evening Post* (London), April 21, 1773; *Daily Advertiser*, April 21, 1773; *New-Lloyd's List*, April 20, 1773; *London Chronicle*, April 22, 1773.

Samuel Gist: Samuel Gist to John Tabb, Nov. 2, 1772, April 26, 1773, *Tabb's Admr.* v. *Gist et al.*, 1829, USCCVD(EC), Vi.

175 "Particular . . . Hope": David Mill to Committee, Sept. 12, 1773, T 70/32, f. 1, PRO.

176 *New Britannia:* Letter from Fort James, April 12, 1773, *Daily Advertiser*, Oct. 12, 1773; *Bristol Journal*, June 19, 1773; *New-Lloyd's List*, June 18, 1773; *Journals of the House of Commons: 1547–1800* ([London], 1803), XXXVII, 311–312.

number of slaves exported: Lambert, ed., *House of Commons Sessional Papers*, XXXII, 15; David Mill to Committee, July 29, 1774, T 70/32, f. 7, PRO.

"putrid" . . . "mortification": Testimony of James Chisholme, *Two Reports (One presented the 16th of October, the other on the 12th of November, 1788) from the Committee of the Honourable House of Assembly of Jamaica* (London, 1789), appendix 6, pp. 27–28; Clarkson, comp., *Substance of the Evidence*, 45–46; Sheffield, *Observations on the Project*, 2d ed., 27n; James Lind, *An Essay on the Most Effectual Means of Preserving the Health of Seamen in the Royal Navy and a Dissertation on Fevers and Infections*, 2d ed. (London, 1779), reprinted in Christopher Lloyd, ed., *The Health of Seamen* (London, 1965), 92–93; John Gabriel Stedman, *Narrative of a Five Years Expedition Against the Revolted Negroes of Surinam*, ed. Richard Price and Sally Price (Baltimore, 1988), 166–168, 174–175.

176 The *Peggy's* slaves: *New-Lloyd's List*, Jan. 18, 1774; Henry Laurens to John Lewis Gervais, March 22–April 7, 1773, Henry Laurens to Ross & Mill, July 16, 1773, *Papers of Laurens*, ed. Hamer *et al.*, VIII, 636, IX, 95.

£54: Thomas Dolbeare to Lopez & Rivera, Oct. 22, 1773, Ford, ed., *Commerce of Rhode Island*, I, 457–458. See also John Rhodes, *The Surprising Adventures and Sufferings of John Rhodes, a Seaman of Workington* (New York, 1798), 11; *St. James's Chronicle*, April 19, 1774; David Richardson, "The Costs of Survival: The Transport of Slaves in the Middle Passage and the Profitability of the 18th-Century British Slave Trade," *ExEcH*, XXIV (April 1987), 178–196.

Gist: Samuel Gist to John Tabb, Feb. 4, 1774, March 18, 1775, *Tabb's Admr. v. Gist et al.*, 1829, USCCVD(EC), Vi.

177 "if . . . halter": Elizabeth Harris to James Harris, April 6, 1773, *A Series of Letters of the First Earl of Malmesbury*, ed. J. H. Harris, Earl of Malmesbury (London, 1870), I, 271.

"Combinations" . . . "Spirit": Entry of May 19, 1778, Hester Lynch Thrale Piozzi, *Thraliana: The Diary of Mrs. Hester Lynch Thrale, 1776–1809*, ed. Katherine C. Balderston (Oxford, 1942), I, 333–335.

trading commodities: Lewis Namier and John Brooke, *The History of Parliament: The House of Commons, 1754–1790* (New York, 1964), II, 235–236; Lucy Sutherland, "Sir George Colebrooke's World Corner in Alum, 1771–1773," in Lucy Sutherland, *Politics and Finance in the Eighteenth Century*, ed. Aubrey Newman (London, 1984), esp. 450–452; *London Chronicle*, Jan. 26, 1773.

178 "very ill used": Lambert, ed., *House of Commons Sessional Papers*, LXXI, 80–84; Peter Leger and William Greenwood to John Durand, Oct. 22, Dec. 9, 1771, July 4, 1772, Peter Leger and William Greenwood to Anthony Richardson, Nov. 15, 1771, Leger & Greenwood Letterbook, MiU-C.

the East India Company: John Durand to Lords of Treasury, Feb. 21, 1771, Davies, ed., *Documents of the American Revolution*, I, 272; Bernard Pool, *Navy Board Contracts, 1660–1832: Contract Administration Under the Navy Board* (Hamden, 1966), 82–91; R. J. B. Knight, comp., *Portsmouth Dockyard Papers, 1774–1783: The American War* (Portsmouth, 1987), appendix IV.

the Kennebec River: James Bowdoin *et al.* to Lords of Treasury, Dec. 18, 1771, William Willis *et al.*, eds., *Documentary History of the State of Maine*, Maine Historical Society, *Collections*, 2d ser., I–XXIV (1869–1916), XIV, 150–151; Admiralty minutes, Oct. 27, 1768, *The Hawke Papers, a Selection: 1743–1771*, ed. Ruddock F. Mackay (Aldershot, 1990), 432.

Lumbermen: Thomas Scammell to Thomas Hutchinson, April 2, 1772, Davies, ed., *Doc-*

uments of the American Revolution, V, 58; Gordon E. Kershaw, *The Kennebeck Proprietors, 1749–1775* (Portland, 1975), 212–219.

the Court of Hustings: William Waller Hening, ed., *The Statutes at Large; Being a Collection of All the Laws of Virginia* (Richmond, Philadelphia, and New York, 1809–23), VIII, 401–402; A. G. Roeber, *Faithful Magistrates and Republican Lawyers: Creators of Virginia Legal Culture, 1680–1810* (Chapel Hill, 1981), 131–132; Calvin Brewster Coulter, Jr., "The Virginia Merchant" (Ph.D. diss., Princeton University, 1944), 239–240.

179 before the Board of Trade: *Journal of the Commissioners for Trade and Plantations, 1768–1775*, 258–259.

"Junius Americanus": Rind's *Virginia Gazette*, Oct. 17, 1771.

"a little . . . Change": William Nelson to Samuel Athawes, May 2, 1772, Nelson Letterbook, Vi.

"his character . . . one": William Lee to Richard Henry Lee, Dec. 10, 1770, William Lee Letterbook, 1769–1771, duPont Library, Stratford, Virginia.

"Ld Dunmore's Weaknesses": Entry of March 27, 1774, *Historical Memoirs from 16 March 1763 to 9 July 1776 of William Smith*, ed. William H. W. Sabine (New York, 1956), 180; Richard Bland to Thomas Adams, Aug. 1, 1771, Adams Family Papers, ViRHi; Mary Lou Lustig, *Privilege and Prerogative: New York's Provincial Elite, 1710–1776* (Madison, 1995), 158–163.

"conscious . . . do": William Nelson to Earl of Hillsborough, March 2, 1771, *The Correspondence of William Nelson as Acting Governor of Virginia, 1770–1771*, ed. John C. Van Horne (Charlottesville, 1975), 129.

180 "where . . . society": Earl of Dunmore to Earl of Hillsborough, July 2, 1771, Davies, ed., *Documents of the American Revolution*, III, 127; entry of Feb. 11, 1771, Smith, *Historical Memoirs 1763–1776*, ed. Sabine, 99.

"longer . . . Pasture": William Nelson to Rowland Hunt, May 16, 1771, Nelson Letterbook, Vi.

"I'm almost . . . him": William Aitchison to Charles Steuart, April 6, 1771, Charles Steuart Papers, UkENL.

the Dismal Swamp Company: Accounts, May 11, 1771, *The Papers of George Washington, Colonial Series*, ed. W. W. Abbot *et al.* (Charlottesville, 1983–), VIII, 454; David Jameson to Thomas Nelson, Nov. 26, 1783, and entry of May 11, 1771, Memoranda, Dismal Swamp Land Company Records, NcD.

"disposed . . . properly": William Nelson to Rowland Hunt, May 16, 1771, Nelson Letterbook, Vi.

"every . . . lost": Samuel Johnston to Thomas Barker, June 10, 1771, Hayes Collection, Johnston Family Series, NcU; Roger Atkinson to Matthew Gale, June 10, 1771, Atkinson Letterbook, ViU; Harry Piper to Dixon & Littledale, June 4, 1771, Piper Letterbook, ViU; Alexander Steuart to John Smith, June 26, 1771, Pocket Plantation Papers, ViU; Richard Bland to Thomas Adams, Aug. 1, 1771, Adams Family Papers, ViRHi; Neil Jamieson to James Glassford, May 30, 1771, Neil Jamieson Papers, DLC; Purdie and Dixon's *Virginia Gazette*, May 30, June 6, 1771; William Nelson to Earl of Hillsborough, June 14, 1771, *Correspondence of Nelson*, ed. Van Horne, 144–145.

PAGE

181 "known . . . Colony": John Pendleton Kennedy, ed., *Journals of the House of Burgesses of Virginia, 1770–1772* (Richmond, 1906), 120.

Tryon and Dunmore: Entry of July 9, 1771, Smith, *Historical Memoirs 1763–1776*, ed. Sabine, 107; Earl of Dunmore to Earl of Hillsborough, July 9, 1771, William Tryon to Earl of Hillsborough, July 9, 1771, E. B. O'Callaghan *et al.*, eds., *Documents Relative to the Colonial History of the State of New-York* (Albany, 1856–87), VIII, 278; William Tryon to [Earl of Hillsborough?], Aug. 31, 1771, *The Correspondence of William Tryon*, ed. William S. Powell (Raleigh, 1980–81), II, 831–832; Paul David Nelson, *William Tryon and the Course of Empire: A Life in British Imperial Service* (Chapel Hill, 1990), 88–91.

a marble statue: Kennedy, ed., *Journals of Burgesses, 1770–1772*, 138–140.

Lord Dunmore arrived: Purdie and Dixon's *Virginia Gazette*, Sept. 26, 1771.

100,000 acres: Earl of Dunmore to Earl of Hillsborough, March 1772, CO 5/154, ff. 35–36, PRO.

the ministry forbade: Instructions to Earl of Dunmore, Feb. 7, 1771, in Merrill Jensen, ed., *English Historical Documents, Volume IX: American Colonial Documents to 1776* (London, 1955), 206–207.

Dunmore and Nelson: Earl of Dunmore to Earl of Hillsborough, May 2, 1772, CO 5/1350, ff. 62–65, PRO; Robert Wheeler, "The County Court in Colonial Virginia," in Bruce C. Daniels, ed., *Town and County: Essays on the Structure of Local Government in the American Colonies* (Middletown, 1978), 111–133.

182 William Byrd: William Byrd to Jeffery Amherst, Dec. 31, 1771, "Some Unpublished Correspondence of William Byrd III," ed. Marion Tinling, *VMHB*, LXXXVIII (July 1980), 290.

Richard Henry Lee: Richard Henry Lee to William Lee, July 12, 1772, Lee Family Papers, Section 108, ViRHi.

a swift, abrupt reply: Earl of Hillsborough to Earl of Dunmore, July 1, 1772, CO 5/1350, ff. 72–73, PRO.

"by not . . . Reversions": Earl of Hillsborough to Frederick North, Aug. 7, 1772, *Manuscripts of the Earl of Dartmouth*, II, 86.

"very hearty": William Lee to Philip Ludwell Lee, July 12, 1770, Lee Letterbook, 1769–1771, duPont Library, Stratford.

Dartmouth and Dunmore: Earl of Dartmouth to Earl of Dunmore, Feb. 3, 1773, Earl of Dunmore to Earl of Dartmouth, Nov. 16, 1772, CO 5/1351, ff. 14–17, 1–7, PRO.

"Tory principles": John Page, Memoir, *Virginia Historical Register*, III (July 1850), 148–149.

183 "advantageous . . . family": Earl of Dunmore to Earl of Hillsborough, March 1772, CO 5/154, ff. 35–36, PRO.

the new boundary: John Richard Alden, *John Stuart and the Southern Colonial Frontier* (Ann Arbor, 1944), 282–286; Louis DeVorsey, Jr., *The Indian Boundary in the Southern Colonies, 1763–1775* (Chapel Hill, 1966), 79–92; Tom Hatley, *The Dividing Paths: Cherokees and South Carolinians Through the Era of Revolution* (New York, 1995), 211–215.

"some disturbance" . . . "Hedge": Thomas Walker to William Preston, May 27, 1771, Preston Papers, Vol. 2, ff. 125–126, Draper Collection, Series QQ, WHi.

William Crawford: Sarah S. Hughes, *Surveyors and Statesmen: Land Measuring in Colonial Virginia* ([Richmond], 1979), 102.

the Mississippi Company: Entry of Jan. 1, 1772, Account with Mississippi Adventure, Financial Records, Ledger A, p. 169, Papers of George Washington, Series 5, DLC.

"settling . . . spots": George Washington to Earl of Dunmore, June 15, 1772, *Papers of Washington: Colonial*, ed. Abbot *et al.*, IX, 55.

"People . . . Seen": William Crawford to George Washington, May 1, 1772, *ibid.*, 37.

the Loyal Company's land: Thomas Walker to William Preston, May 27, 1771, Preston Papers, Draper Collection, Series QQ, WHi.

"immediately . . . Possessions": Benjamin J. Hillman, ed., *Executive Journals of the Council of Colonial Virginia* (Richmond, 1966), VI, 458.

squatters held out: Richard Henderson to John Williams, Sept. 13, 1779, John Williams Papers, NcD; Earl of Dunmore to Earl of Dartmouth, April 2, 1774, CO 5/1352, ff. 49–51, PRO.

"they . . . doors": Alexander Cameron to John Stuart, March 19, 1771, Davies, ed., *Documents of the American Revolution*, III, 72; Thomas Gage to the Earl of Hillsborough, May 14, 1770, Oct. 7, 1772, *The Correspondence of General Thomas Gage*, ed. Clarence Edwin Carter (New Haven, 1931–33), I, 258, 336. For Shawnees' reaction, see Alexander McKee's report, June 20, 1773, in Kathrine Wagner Seineke, *The George Rogers Clark Adventure in the Illinois* (New Orleans, 1981), 136. For Creeks' reaction, see Peter Chester to Earl of Hillsborough, March 9, 1771, in Eron O. Rowland, "Peter Chester: Third Governor of the Province of British West Florida," Mississippi Historical Society, *Publications*, V (1925), 38–41.

"the established . . . settled": Earl of Dunmore to Earl of Dartmouth, Dec. 24, 1774, CO 5/1353, ff. 7–39, PRO.

184 John Stewart: *Daily Advertiser*, Feb. 21, 1772; testimony of Duncan Campbell, April 1, 1779, *Journal of the House of Commons*, XXXVII, 310–311.

Bacon's contract: John Norton to John Hatley Norton, Feb. 24, 1772, Norton Papers, ViRVal; William Lee to Francis Lightfoot Lee, March 3, 1772, Lee Family Papers, ViU; Memorial of Duncan Campbell, Feb. 24, 1772, "Transportation of Felons to the Colonies," *MHM*, XXVII (Dec. 1932), 266–267.

the contractor's vessel: Earl of Fife to George Selwyn, April 28, 1770, in John Heneage Jesse, *George Selwyn and His Contemporaries* (London, 1843), II, 389.

More than 14 percent: Testimony of Duncan Campbell, April 1, 1779, *Journal of the House of Commons*, XXXVII, 311.

contractors: A. Roger Ekirch, *Bound for America: The Transportation of British Convicts to the Colonies, 1718–1775* (Oxford, 1987), 228; Peter Wilson Coldham, *Emigrants in Chains: A Social History of Forced Emigration to the Americas, 1607–1776* (Baltimore, 1992), 67–69, 82–85; Christine Woodland, "Transportation to America," *Warwickshire History*, X (1996–97), 71–81.

Bacon and North: John Norton to John Hatley Norton, Aug. 6, 1772, March 20, 1773, Norton Papers, ViRVal; John Norton to John Hatley Norton, July 6, 1773, John Norton & Son Papers, ViWC.

"black Monday": R. Glover to Earl Temple, July 12, 1772, *The Grenville Papers*, ed. William James Smith (London, 1852–53), IV, 539–543.

185 "universal bankruptcy": *Annual Register*, XV (1772), 6th ed. (London, 1800), Chronology, 110.

"distress . . . change": Joshua Johnson to Wallace & Davidson, June 22, 1772, Wallace, Davidson & Johnson Letterbook, MdAA.

Alexander Fordyce: "An account of the examinations of Mr Alexander Fordyce," *Scots Magazine*, XXXIV (Sept. 1772), 473–480; *Harman and others, assignees of Fordyce v. Fishar*, 1 Cowper 118, *English Reports*, XCVIII, 998.

"everything is gone": William Cuninghame & Co. to James Robinson, July 1, 1772, Cuninghame of Lainshaw Muniments, GD-247, bundle P/2, SRO; William Maxwell to William Pulteney, June 18, 1772, Sir William Pulteney Collection, CSmH; [James Murray], *The Travels of the Imagination; A True Journey from Newcastle to London* (Philadelphia, 1778 [orig. publ. London, 1773]), 85.

The Bank of England: John Clapham, *The Bank of England: A History* (Cambridge, 1944), I, 247; Roger Fulford, *Glyn's, 1753–1953: Six Generations in Lombard Street* (London, 1953), 27–30; Michael C. Lovell, "The Role of the Bank of England as Lender of Last Resort in the Crises of the Eighteenth Century," *Explorations in Entrepreneurial History*, X (1957–58), 14–15.

Sir George Colebrooke: R. Glover to Earl Temple, July 12, 1772, *Grenville Papers*, ed. Smith, IV, 540; Horace Walpole, *Journal of the Reign of King George the Third*, ed. John Doran (London, 1859), I, 122; Thomas Bradshaw to Robert Murray Keith, Jan. 19, 1772 [1773], April 2, 1773, *Memoirs and Correspondence (Official and Familiar) of Sir Robert Murray Keith*, ed. Mrs. Gillespie Smyth (London, 1849), I, 364, 385–386.

"Immense . . . property": John Norton to Robert Carter Nicholas, July 9, 1772, John Norton & Son Papers, ViWC; Adam Smith, *An Inquiry into the Nature and Causes of the Wealth of Nations*, 5th ed. (Edinburgh, 1811), II, 52–65; Charles W. Munn, *The Scottish Provincial Banking Companies, 1747–1864* (Edinburgh, 1981), 29–36.

Scottish firms and others: James Robinson to William Cuninghame & Co., June 1, 1772, T. M. Devine, ed., *A Scottish Firm in Virginia, 1767–1777: W. Cuninghame & Co.* (Edinburgh, 1984), 80; Edward C. Papenfuse, *In Pursuit of Profit: The Annapolis Merchants in the Era of the American Revolution, 1763–1805* (Baltimore, 1975), 61; Jacob M. Price, "Joshua Johnson in London, 1771–1775: Credit and Commercial Organization in the British Chesapeake Trade," in Anne Whiteman *et al.*, eds., *Statesmen, Scholars and Merchants: Essays in Eighteenth-Century History Presented to Dame Lucy Sutherland* (Oxford, 1973), 163–164.

depositors' money: Julian Hoppit, *Risk and Failure in English Business, 1700–1800* (Cambridge, 1987), 136. On Colebrooke and the panic of 1772, see also Paul Langford, *A Polite and Commercial People: England, 1727–1783* (Oxford, 1989), 569–571; T. S. Ashton, *Economic Fluctuations in England, 1700–1800* (Oxford, 1959), 127–129; Richard B. Sheridan, "The British Credit Crisis of 1772 and the American Colonies," *JEcH*, XX (June 1960), 170–172; Henry Hamilton, "The Failure of the Ayr Bank, 1772," *EcHR*, 2d ser., VIII (1956), 405–417; Lucy S. Sutherland and John A. Woods, "The East India Speculations of William Burke," Leeds Philosophical and Literary Society, *Proceedings*, XI (Jan. 1966), 183–216; F. G. Hilton Price, *A Handbook of London Bankers* (London, 1891), 120–121; "Memoirs of a Late Famous Banker," *London Chronicle*, July 2, 1772; William Forbes, *Memoirs of a Banking-House* (London, 1860), 39–42.

more than £166,000: Sutherland, "Sir George Colebrooke's World Corner," in *Politics and Finance*, 451–465; Clapham, *Bank of England*, I, 243–244.

186 "Fictitious . . . notes": William Lee to Robert Carter Nicholas, Aug. 3, 1772, William Lee Letterbook, 1769–1772, Lee Family Papers, ViRHi; Samuel Johnson to John Taylor, Aug. 15, 1772, *The Letters of Samuel Johnson*, ed. Bruce Redford (Princeton, 1992–), I, 392.

"It . . . Suspicion": David Hume to Adam Smith, June 27, 1772, *The Letters of David Hume*, ed. J. Y. T. Greig (Oxford, 1932), II, 263.

"fear . . . Brother": Duncan Campbell to James Stewart, June 23, 1772, Campbell Letterbooks, Mitchell Library, Sydney.

"Continue . . . go": Samuel Gist to John Tabb, Aug. 8, 1772, *Tabb's Admr. v. Gist et al.*, 1829, Samuel Gist to Jones & Watson, Aug. 8, 1772, *Samuel Gist v. Jones & Watson*, 1806, USCCVD(EC), Vi; Joshua Johnson to John Davidson and Charles Wallace, Oct. 7, 1772, *Joshua Johnson's Letterbook*, ed. Jacob M. Price (London, 1979), 49.

buying East India Company stock: Lambert, ed., *House of Commons Sessional Papers*, XXVI, 297.

"dismall" . . . "triffle": David Ross to John Hook, Aug. 25, 1772, John Hook Papers, NcD.

more than £1,000,000: Robert Walter Coakley, "Virginia Commerce During the American Revolution" (Ph.D. diss., University of Virginia, 1949), 85; Jacob M. Price, *Capital and Credit in British Overseas Trade: The View from the Chesapeake, 1700–1776* (Cambridge, 1980), chaps. 6–7.

tobacco prices: John Norton to John Hatley Norton, Aug. 6, 1772, April 26, 1773, Norton Papers, ViRVal; Joshua Johnson to Wallace, Davidson & Johnson, May 17, 1773, Wallace, Davidson & Johnson Letterbook, MdAA; James Robinson to W. Cuninghame & Co., Dec. 19, 1772, Devine, ed., *Scottish Firm*, 100–101; Forbes, *Memoirs of a Banking-House*, 44.

Scottish storekeepers: Henry Fleming to Littledale & Co., June 7, 1773, Papers of Henry Fleming, Cumbria Record Office, Kendal; James Robinson to J. Neilson, Aug. 19, 1772, Devine, ed., *Scottish Firm*, 58–59.

187 "the Scotch . . . trade": Samuel Gist to Jones & Watson, Aug. 8, 1772, *Samuel Gist v. Jones & Watson*, 1806, USCCVD(EC), Vi.

as if stunned: Henry Fleming to Fisher & Bragg, July 31, 1773, Papers of Fleming, Cumbria Record Office; Charles J. Farmer, *In the Absence of Towns: Settlement and Country Trade in Southside Virginia, 1730–1800* (Lanham, 1993), 174–177.

Pieter Clifford & Sons: *Shrewsbury Chronicle*, Jan. 9, 1773; David Ross to John Hook, April 3, 1773, Hook Papers, NcD; Charles Wilson, *Anglo-Dutch Commerce and Finance in the Eighteenth Century* (Cambridge, 1941), 170–187, 216–223.

"It . . . Mankind": Letter from Amsterdam, Jan. 15, 1773, *Berrow's Worcester Journal*, Jan. 21, 1773.

the Royal Exchange: David Ross to John Hook, April 3, 1773, Hook Papers, NcD.

"120 . . . ruined": *Felix Farley's Bristol Journal*, Aug. 28, 1773.

bankruptcies: Hoppit, *Risk and Failure*, 132; Ashton, *Economic Fluctuations*, 129; Michael Fry, *The Dundas Despotism* (Edinburgh, 1992), 44–45.

William James: *Shrewsbury Chronicle*, Jan. 9, 1773.

PAGE

187 "little . . . Baronet": *Ibid.*, March 20, April 10, 1773.

Trustees took control: Namier and Brooke, *History of Parliament*, II, 236; Hilton Price, *London Bankers*, 42.

"a broken Heart": *Lloyd's Evening Post*, March 31, 1773.

James Russell: Papenfuse, *In the Pursuit of Profit*, 63; Jacob M. Price, "One Family's Empire: The Russell-Lee-Clerk Connection in Maryland, Britain, and India, 1707–1857," *MHM*, LXXII (1977), 186–188.

"as you . . . year": James Russell to John Galloway, April 12, 1773, Galloway-Maxcy-Markoe Papers, DLC.

188 "tis . . . Debts": Samuel Gist to John Tabb, April 17, 1773, *Tabb's Admr.* v. *Gist et al.*, 1829, USCCVD(EC), Vi.

"a new . . . Summer": *Shrewsbury Chronicle*, June 5, 1773.

The Bankrupt: Samuel Foote, *The Bankrupt: A Comedy in Three Acts* (London, 1776), 39, 45, 47. The play was submitted to the Lord Chamberlain on July 8, 1773. See Larpent Collection, LA 355, CSmH. See also Simon Trefman, *Sam. Foote, Comedian, 1720–1777* (New York, 1971), 214–215; Richard Bevis, *The Laughing Tradition: Stage Comedy in Garrick's Day* (Athens, 1980), 170–171.

Confidence and credit revived: In addition to the works cited above, see Larry Neal, *The Rise of Financial Capitalism: International Capital Markets in the Age of Reason* (Cambridge, 1990), 170–171; Edwin J. Perkins, *The Economy of Colonial America* (New York, 1980), 33; T. S. Ashton, *An Economic History of England: The 18th Century* (London, 1955), 193.

"I . . . Virginia": Henry Fleming to Fisher & Bragg, [Dec. 1773], Papers of Fleming, Cumbria Record Office.

William Nelson: William Nelson to William Lee, Aug. 1, 1772, William Nelson to Samuel Athawes, Aug. 14, 1772, Nelson Letterbook, Vi; Purdie and Dixon's *Virginia Gazette*, Nov. 19, 1772; Rind's *Virginia Gazette*, Nov. 19, 1772.

a violent gale: Letter from New York, Sept. 21, 1772, *Berrow's Worcester Journal*, Nov. 12, 1772.

189 frigate *Glasgow*: *Daily Advertiser*, Dec. 19, 1772.

"there . . . way": Benjamin Harrison to William Palfrey, Jan. 20, 1772, William Palfrey Letters, MH; Thomas Russell to Michael Harris, Aug. 4, 1772, Papers of the Principio Iron Company, Add MSS 29,600, f. 27, Uk; Neil R. Stout, *The Royal Navy in America, 1760–1775* (Annapolis, 1973), 133–134.

unusually dry weather: Charles Gordon to Clement Tudway, March 5, 1771, Francis Farley to Clement Tudway, March 5–21, Aug. 11, 1771, Tudway Papers, Somerset Record Office, Taunton.

carnivorous ants: Lowell Ragatz, *The Old Plantation System in the British West Indies* (London, [1954]), 60; E. M. Johnston, "Grenada, 1775–1779," in Peter Roebuck, ed., *Macartney of Lisanoure, 1737–1806: Essays in Biography* (Belfast, 1983), 111; Maria [Woodley] R[iddell], *Voyages to the Madeira, and Leeward Caribbean Isles* (Edinburgh, 1792), 72–73.

small ship *Tom*: *Pennsylvania Gazette*, Oct. 14, 1772; entry 1754, Register of Passes, Adm 7/96, PRO; *New-Lloyd's List*, Dec. 11, 1772.

The hurricane: *Felix Farley's Bristol Journal*, Dec. 12, 1772; De la Court Walsh to James Scott, Sept. 18, 1772, Vere Langford Oliver, ed., *Caribbeana* (London, 1910–19), II, 322;

Bartholomew James, *Journal of Rear-Admiral Bartholomew James, 1752–1828*, ed. John Knox Laughton (London, 1896), 11; Purdie and Dixon's *Virginia Gazette*, Nov. 12, 1772; *Gentleman's Magazine*, XLII (Dec. 1772), 590; William Robertson to Neil Jamieson & Co., Sept. 11, 1772, Neil Jamieson Papers, DLC; Vere Langford Oliver, *The History of the Island of Antigua* (London, 1894–99), I, cxxi; *Pennsylvania Gazette*, Oct. 14, 1772.

"was . . . dieing": James Parker to Thomas Burke, Oct. 12, 1772, Thomas Burke Papers, NcU.

He wrote his will: William Nelson, Will, Oct. 6, 1772, York County Wills and Inventories, No. 22, 1771–1783, pp. 132–136, Yorktown. Printed in *VMHB*, XXXII (April 1925), 190–192.

190 "sat . . . him": Jack P. Greene, ed., "A Mirror of Virtue for a Declining Land: John Camm's Funeral Sermon for William Nelson," in J. A. Leo Lemay, ed., *Essays in Early Virginia Literature Honoring Richard Beale Davis* (New York, 1977), 195–196.

the "great Ditch": Wills Cowper and Josiah Granbery, advertisement, Purdie and Dixon's *Virginia Gazette*, Nov. 19, 1772.

"servant . . . adventurers": Quoted in George Edward Cokayne, *The Complete Peerage*, ed. Vicary Gibbs *et al.* (London, 1910–40), VI, 93n.

"the outcasts" . . . "corruption": Josiah Martin to Earl of Dartmouth, Nov. 28, 1772, William L. Saunders *et al.*, eds., *Colonial Records of North Carolina* (Raleigh, 1886–), IX, 358–359.

Granville appointed: Earl of Dartmouth to Josiah Martin, March 3, 1773, Davies, ed., *Documents of the American Revolution*, IV, 268–269; Thornton W. Mitchell, "The Granville District and Its Land Records," *NCHR*, LXX (April 1993), 117–119.

"a shabby fellow": Thomas Nelson, Jr., to Samuel Athawes, Jan. 24, 1773, William Nelson Letterbook, Vi.

Gist's snow *Planter:* Entries of Oct. 17, 1772, Dec. 3, 1773, Lists of Ships Entered Inwards and Outwards in Upper District of James River, Oct. 1772–Jan. 1773, T 1/498, PRO; *New-Lloyd's List*, July 24, 1772; entry 191, Register of Passes, Adm 7/98, PRO; *Lloyd's Register: 1776*, P-203.

James Mercer: Purdie and Dixon's *Virginia Gazette*, Nov. 5, 1772.

"as . . . possible": Samuel Gist to Jones & Watson, Aug. 8, 1772, *Samuel Gist v. Jones & Watson*, 1806, USCCVD(EC), Vi.

191 John Smith: John Norton to John Hatley Norton, Feb. 16, 1773, John Norton & Son Papers, ViWC; Commissioner's Report, June 1808, *Gist et al., Exors of Anderson v. Henry S. Shore*, 1817, USCCVD(EC), Vi; Report of the Agent of the Board, Claim of Samuel Gist, T 79/39, ff. 245–247, List of Debts Contracted with Samuel Gist, T 79/31, PRO.

"the most . . . Colony": Purdie and Dixon's *Virginia Gazette*, Sept. 24, 1772.

Maria Byrd: William Byrd, Will, July 6, 1774, *VMHB*, IX (July 1901), 86; Robert Cary & Co. to William Byrd, Nov. 10, 1773, "Correspondence of Byrd," ed. Tinling, *VMHB*, LXXXVIII (July 1980), 290.

"uneasy" . . . James Parke Farley: Thomas Evans to Farell & Jones, Nov. 12, Dec. 6, 1771, John Wayles to Farell & Jones, Aug. 17, 1771, Feb. 24, 1772, Claim of John Tyndale Warre, T 79/9, PRO.

"equal . . . America": Purdie and Dixon's *Virginia Gazette*, Sept. 24, 1772.

Notes for Chapter IV

191 "conveniently get": John Mayo to Samuel Gist, Nov. 22, 1772, *Samuel Gist v. Mayo's Exors*, 1798, USCCVD(EC), Vi.

to sell 1,000 acres: Rind's *Virginia Gazette*, March 31, 1774.

deed of trust: *VMHB*, IX (July 1901), 82.

192 Washington and veterans: Petition, ca. Nov. 4, 1772, George Washington to Charles Mynn Thruston, March 12, 1773, *Papers of Washington: Colonial*, ed. Abbot *et al.*, IX, 118–120; entries of Oct. 24–Nov. 5, 1772, *The Diaries of George Washington*, ed. Donald Jackson and Dorothy Twohig (Charlottesville, 1976–79), III, 138–141; Hillman, ed., *Executive Journals*, VI, 513–514.

"deep affliction": Thomas Nelson, Jr., to Samuel Martin, Jan. 27, 1773, William Nelson Letterbook, Vi.

"The chief . . . Country": Peter Lyons to John Norton, Nov. 25, 1772, John Norton & Son Papers, ViWC; Purdie and Dixon's *Virginia Gazette*, Nov. 19, 1772; Rind's *Virginia Gazette*, Nov. 19, 1772.

"tread . . . steps": Greene, ed., "Mirror of Virtue," in Lemay, ed., *Essays in Early Virginia Literature*, 194–200.

"I told . . . Mistress": William Nelson to Samuel Athawes, Sept. 1, 1772, Nelson Letterbook, Vi.

"a magnificent Statue": Ralph Bigland, *Historical, Monumental and Genealogical Collections Relative to the County of Gloucester*, ed. Brian Frith (Bristol, 1989–95), III, 1170.

"America . . . continent": Rind's *Virginia Gazette*, May 13, 1773.

193 grants to Washington: Edgar B. Sims, *Making a State* (Charleston, 1956), 129–130; George Washington to Earl of Dunmore, Sept. 12, 1773, *Papers of Washington: Colonial*, ed. Abbot *et al.*, IX, 322–324; Hillman, ed., *Executive Journals*, VI, 521; Jack Sosin, *Whitehall and the Wilderness: The Middle West in British Colonial Policy, 1760–1775* (Lincoln, 1961), 226–227.

Dr. Walker and settlers: *Vance v. Walker*, 3 Hening & Munford 293, *Reports of Cases Argued and Determined in the Supreme Court of Appeals of Virginia* (Charlottesville, 1903), III, 669; Lewis Preston Summers, *Annals of Southwest Virginia, 1769–1800* (Abingdon, 1929), 624–625, 668–669.

Loyal Company surveys: Lewis Preston Summers, *History of Southwest Virginia, 1746–1786* (Baltimore, 1966 [orig. publ. Richmond, 1903]), 83.

Patrick Henry and the Council: Hillman, ed., *Executive Journals*, VI, 548–549, 551; John Blair to George Washington, Nov. 8, 1773, *Papers of Washington: Colonial*, ed. Abbot *et al.*, IX, 364–365; Archibald Henderson, "Dr. Thomas Walker and the Loyal Company of Virginia," American Antiquarian Society, *Proceedings*, new series, XLI (1931), 108–109.

194 Tea Act: Benjamin Woods Labaree, *The Boston Tea Party* (New York, 1964), chap. 4; Peter Whiteley, *Lord North: The Prime Minister Who Lost America* (London, 1996), chap. 8; W. M. Elofson, *The Rockingham Connection and the Second Founding of the Whig Party, 1768–1773* (Montreal, 1996), chap. 8; H. V. Bowen, *Revenue and Reform: The Indian Problem in British Politics, 1757–1773* (Cambridge, 1991).

"to make . . . duty": John Norton to Peyton Randolph *et al.*, July 6, 1773, William P. Palmer *et al.*, eds., *Calendar of Virginia State Papers* (Richmond, 1875–93), VIII, 24.

PAGE

"Utopian" . . . "whatever": [Anthony Bacon], *A Short Address to the Government* (London, 1775), 11–16.

"we . . . performance": Brook Watson and Robert Rashleigh to the Committee of Warehouse, July 1, 1773, in Francis S. Drake, ed., *Tea Leaves: Being a Collection of Letters and Documents* (Boston, 1884), 223; Benjamin Faneuil, Memorial, in Hugh Edward Egerton, ed., *The Royal Commission on the Losses and Services of American Loyalists, 1783 to 1785: Being the Notes of Mr. Daniel Parker Coke, M.P.* (Oxford, 1915), 234–235; Labaree, *Boston Tea Party*, 88–103.

"obvious" . . . "spirit": [Bacon], *Short Address*, 13, 15–16.

"Ld North's contractors": Earl of Pembroke to William Hamilton, May 1, 1781, Alfred Morrison, comp., *The Collection of Autograph Letters and Historical Documents Formed by Alfred Morrison, Second Series: 1882–1893. The Hamilton and Nelson Papers* (n.p., 1893), I, 70. See also J. A. Cochrane, *Dr. Johnson's Printer: The Life of William Strahan* (Cambridge, 1964), 191–193.

195 governor of New Hampshire: Benjamin Franklin to William Franklin, July 25, 1773, *The Papers of Benjamin Franklin*, ed. Leonard W. Labaree *et al.* (New Haven, 1959–), XX, 326.

a pension of £600: L. B. Namier, "Anthony Bacon, M. P., an Eighteenth-Century Merchant," *JEcBH*, II (Nov. 1929), 66–67.

"upon . . . Board": *Ibid.*, 46–47; Robert Erskine to Richard Atkinson, Oct. 20–24, 1770, in Albert H. Heusser, *George Washington's Map Maker: A Biography of Robert Erskine* (New Brunswick, 1966), 58–59; Ifor Edwards, "John Wilkinson and the Development of Gunfounding in the Late Eighteenth Century," *WHR*, XV (Dec. 1991), 524–544; James Watt to Joseph Black, March 11, 1779, *Partners in Science: Letters of James Watt and Joseph Black*, ed. Eric Robinson and Douglas McKie (Cambridge, 1970), 60. For a description of the casting of a cannon, see entry of June 6, 1774, *Radical Adventurer: The Diaries of Robert Morris, 1772–1774*, ed. J. E. Ross (Bath, 1971), 194–196.

"casting . . . way": Quoted in Edwards, "John Wilkinson," *WHR*, XV (Dec. 1991), 527.

at Broseley: Entries of Aug. 19–20, 1776, *An American Quaker in the British Isles: The Travel Journals of Jabez Maud Fisher, 1775–1779*, ed. Kenneth Morgan (Oxford, 1992), 264–267; Nikolaus Pevsner, *The Buildings of England: Shropshire* (London, 1958), 86–87, 155–157.

Merthyr Tydfil: Chris Evans, *"The Labyrinth of Flames": Work and Social Conflict in Early Industrial Merthyr Tydfil* (Cardiff, 1993), 23–29; John P. Addis, *The Crawshay Dynasty: A Study in Industrial Organisation and Development, 1765–1867* (Cardiff, 1957), 2–3; entry of Oct. 27, 1776, Arthur Young, "A Tour in Wales &c.," *Annals of Agriculture and Other Useful Arts*, VIII (1787), 48; John Lloyd, *The Early History of the Old South Wales Iron Works* (London, 1906), 48–50.

196 William Anderson: William Anderson to John Norton, Sept. 4, 1769, Jan. 11, June 20, Sept. 20, Oct. 30, Dec. 20, 1771, Feb. 7, June 17, 1772, Jan. 22, 1773, John Norton & Son Papers, ViWC.

Joseph Smith: Samuel Gist to Joseph Smith, March 20, 1770, Pleading of Thomas R. Rootes, Samuel Gist's Answer to Thomas R. Rootes, *Jos. Smith's Admr. et al.* v. *Gist's Exor et al.*, 1825, USCCVD(EC), Vi; Eugenia G. Glazebrook and Preston G. Glazebrook, comps., *Virginia Migrations: Hanover County* (Richmond, 1949), II, 29.

196 John Smith: Report of Agent, Claim of Samuel Gist, T 79/39, ff. 245–247, PRO; Commissioner's Report, June 1808, *Jos. Smith's Admr. et al.* v. *Gist's Exor et al.*, 1825, USC-CVD(EC), Vi; John Norton to John Hatley Norton, Feb. 16, 1773, John Norton & Son Papers, ViWC; John Norton to John Hatley Norton, March 23, 1773, Norton Papers, ViRVal.

197 "He . . . son": Rind's *Virginia Gazette*, Jan. 28, 1773; Purdie and Dixon's *Virginia Gazette*, Jan. 28, 1773; Mary Anderson to Thomas R. Rootes, March 27, 1800, *Thomas R. Rootes* v. *Martin Pearkes et al.*, 1817, USCCVD(EC), Vi; Schedule of Samuel Gist's Estate, Sept. 30, 1789, Claim of Samuel Gist, American Loyalist Claims, AO 13/30, PRO.

"never . . . Connexion": Samuel Gist to John Smith, June 15–19, 1768, *Jos. Smith's Admr. et al.* v. *Gist's Exor et al.*, 1825, USCCVD(EC), Vi.

"I hope . . . it": William Anderson to John Norton, Feb. 2, 1773, John Norton & Son Papers, ViWC.

to secure insurance: John Norton to John Hatley Norton, April 26, 1773, Norton Papers, ViRVal.

"Pursuant . . . Will": Purdie and Dixon's *Virginia Gazette*, Aug. 5, Oct. 14, 1773, April 21, 1774.

"I expect . . . me": William Anderson to John Norton, Nov. 28, 1773, John Norton & Son Papers, ViWC. See also Samuel Gist to Garrett Minor, March 12, 1774, Miscellaneous Manuscripts Collection, DLC.

the *Mary: Lloyd's Register: 1776*, M–185; John Tabb to Samuel Gist, June 6, 1775, *Saml. Gist* v. *Tabb*, 1795, USCCVD(EC), Vi; James Miller, Letter, Purdie's *Virginia Gazette*, May 12, 1775.

America Square: [Edward Pugh], *Walks Through London* (London, 1817), I, 12–13; [Edward Pugh], *London; Being an Accurate History and Description of the British Metropolis and Its Neighbourhood* (London, 1805–13), II, 183; Walter Besant, *London in the Eighteenth Century* (London, 1902), 130–131; Walter George Bell, *Unknown London* (London, 1951 [orig. publ. 1919]), 15, 33; Dorothy Stroud, *George Dance: Architect, 1747–1825* (London, 1971), 84–87; *The New Complete Guide to All Persons Who Have Any Trade or Concern with the City of London*, 14th ed. [London, 1774], 224. For a description of countinghouses, see Hancock, *Citizens of the World*, 90–104.

198 to hire laborers: Account with David Jameson, Dismal Swamp Land Company Records, NcD.

Norton and servants: George F. Norton to John Hatley Norton, Nov. 20, 1773, John Norton & Son Papers, ViWC; Bernard Bailyn, *Voyagers to the West: A Passage in the Peopling of America on the Eve of the Revolution* (New York, 1986), chaps. 5, 10; Ekirch, *Bound for America*, chap. 4; J. M. Bumsted, *The People's Clearance: Highland Emigration to British North America, 1770–1815* (Edinburgh, 1982), 9–18.

Gist and servants: Charles Yates to Samuel Gist, Jan. 24, 1774, Charles Yates Letterbook, ViU; Thomas Jett to Samuel Gist, March 12, 1774, Thomas Jett Letterbook, Jerdone Family Papers, ViW.

"unless . . . Contrary": Samuel Gist to John Tabb, Feb. 5, 1774, *Tabb's Admr.* v. *Gist et al.*, 1829, USCCVD(EC), Vi.

PAGE

The *Planter*'s voyage: Entries of Jan. 26–May 15, 1774, *The Journal of John Harrower*, ed. Edward Miles Riley (Williamsburg, 1963), 17–39, appendix ii; Bailyn, *Voyagers to the West*, 277; entry 1971, Register of Passes, Adm 7/98, PRO; *Daily Advertiser*, Feb. 21, 1774.

199 "in the . . . Gist": Purdie and Dixon's *Virginia Gazette*, May 5, 1774.

"Soul drivers": Entries of May 16–21, 1774, *Journal of Harrower*, ed. Riley, 39–40; Bailyn, *Voyagers to the West*, 346–348; John Tabb to Samuel Gist, March 6, 1774, *Tabb's Admr. v. Gist et al.*, 1829, USCCVD(EC), Vi.

loaded the *Planter:* James Robinson to W. Cuninghame & Co., May 28, 1774, Devine, ed., *Scottish Firm*, 141; Thomas Jett to Samuel Gist, May 6, 1774, Jett Letterbook, ViW; Thomas Shore to Samuel Gist, Aug. 21, 1774, *Saml. Gist v. Tabb*, 1795, USCCVD(EC), Vi; Rind's *Virginia Gazette*, Sept. 15, 1774.

"I yet . . . America": John Harrower to Ann Harrower, Dec. 6, 1774, *Journal of Harrower*, ed. Riley, 76.

V: THE AGE OF PAPER

200 "the natural" . . . "severity": [Anthony Bacon], *A Short Address to the Government* (London, 1775), 5, 38–39.

East India Company's tea: Benjamin Woods Labaree, *The Boston Tea Party* (New York, 1964), chap. 7; T. H. Breen, " 'Baubles of Britain': The American and Consumer Revolutions of the Eighteenth Century," *PP*, CXIX (May 1988), 97–103.

"naturally conciliating disposition": "Late Lord Guilford," *European Magazine*, XXX (Aug. 1796), 82; Peter Whiteley, *Lord North: The Prime Minister Who Lost America* (London, 1996), 15.

"to bring . . . duty": [Bacon], *Short Address*, 49.

201 "The town . . . be": R. C. Simmons and P. D. G. Thomas, eds., *Proceedings and Debates of the British Parliaments Respecting North America, 1754–1783* (White Plains, 1982–87), IV, 128; Lord North to the King, March 25, 1774, *The Correspondence of King George the Third*, ed. John Fortescue (London, 1927–28), III, 85.

"totally enslaved": *Journals of the House of Commons: 1547–1800* ([London], 1803), XXXIV, 696; John Sainsbury, *Disaffected Patriots: London Supporters of Revolutionary America, 1769–1782* (Kingston, 1987), 69–74.

"instead . . . G.B.": William Lee to Richard Henry Lee, Sept. 10, 1774, Lee Family Papers, ViU; Thomas Fisher to James Russell, Aug. 27, 1774, Russell Papers, Bundle 6, Coutts & Company, London.

"Nothing . . . Colonies": William Hoopes to James Iredell, June 21, 1774, James Iredell Papers, NcD.

"Destruction . . . War": William J. Van Schreeven *et al.*, eds., *Revolutionary Virginia: The Road to Independence* (Charlottesville, 1973–83), I, 95.

"to avoid . . . Britain": *Ibid.*, 97–98.

202 "with Horrour" . . . "Virtue": *Ibid*, 231–234.

"I . . . Sway": George Washington to Bryan Fairfax, Aug. 24, 1774, *The Papers of George Washington, Colonial Series*, ed. W. W. Abbot *et al.* (Charlottesville, 1983–), X, 155.

PAGE

203 "fixed Intention": Purdie and Dixon's *Virginia Gazette* (Williamsburg), July 8, 1774.

Anthony Bacon: [Bacon], *Short Address*, 16–17, 26.

North: *Journal of the House of Commons*, XXXIV, 696; *The Parliamentary History of England from the Earliest Period to the Year 1803* (London, 1806–20), XVII, 1315.

"unseasonable . . . remonstrances": [Bacon], *Short Address*, 39–40.

"cared . . . got?": Robert Gibbs, *A History of Aylesbury* (Chicheley, 1971 [orig. publ. Aylesbury, 1885]), 244–245, 249–250; John Entick, *The Present State of the British Empire* (London, 1774), II, 39–40; entry of Sept. 24, 1774, *The Diary and Letters of His Excellency Thomas Hutchinson*, ed. Peter Orlando Hutchinson (London, 1883), I, 249; Frank O'Gorman, *Voters, Patrons and Parties: The Unreformed Electoral System of Hanoverian England, 1734–1832* (Oxford, 1989), 28–32; Richard W. Davis, *Political Change and Continuity, 1760–1885: A Buckinghamshire Study* (Newton Abbot, 1972), 21–22, 30–31.

204 "that he . . . opponent": *Shrewsbury Chronicle*, March 20, 1773. On occasional conveyances, see Lewis Namier and John Brooke, *The History of Parliament: The House of Commons, 1754–1790* (New York, 1964), I, 30–31.

"They say . . . them": William Thomas Laprade, ed., *Parliamentary Papers of John Robinson, 1774–1784* (London, 1922), 21. See also William Strahan to David Hall, Feb. 13, 1768, "Correspondence Between William Strahan and David Hall, 1763–1777," *PMHB*, X (1886), 329.

John Aubrey: Gibbs, *History of Aylesbury*, 244; Namier and Brooke, *History of Parliament*, II, 32–33.

Lord North: Bernard Donoughue, *British Politics and the American Revolution: The Path to War, 1773–1775* (London, 1964), chap. 8.

Antigua supplies: Letter from Boston, Aug. 4, 1774, *Daily Advertiser* (London), Sept. 16, 1774; Francis Farley to Clement Tudway, Dec. 29, 1775, Tudway Papers, Somerset Record Office, Taunton.

Some planters emigrated: Simmons and Thomas, eds., *Proceedings and Debates*, IV, 14; Report of Sir Ralph Payne, 1774, CO 318/2, f. 4, PRO; D. H. Murdoch, "Land Policy in the Eighteenth-Century British Empire: The Sale of Crown Lands in the Ceded Islands, 1763–1783," *HJ*, XXVII (Sept. 1984), 549–574.

"we . . . chance": Francis Farley to Clement Tudway, Dec. 29, 1775, Tudway Papers, Somerset Record Office.

205 "much . . . writing": "Officers of Admiral Keppel's Fleet," *Correspondence of George the Third*, ed. Fortescue, IV, 226; John Charnock, *Biographia Navalis* (London, 1794–98), VI, 322; J. H. Broomfield, "The Keppel-Palliser Affair, 1778–1779," *MM*, XLVII (Aug. 1961), 195–207; Sainsbury, *Disaffected Patriots*, 146–148.

a miscarriage: Samuel Martin to George Thomas, Oct. 8, 1770, June 13, 1774, Samuel Martin to Christopher Baldwin, [ca. Nov.–Dec. 1774], Letterbook of Samuel Martin, Add MSS 41,350, ff. 142–143, 174–175, 41,351, f. 20, Uk.

entered his mare: Purdie and Dixon's *Virginia Gazette*, May 26, 1774.

Chiswell lead mine: A List of Payments Made the Treasurer, *Lidderdale et al.* v. *Robinson's Admrs. et al.*, 1832, USCCVD(EC), Vi.

James Parke Farley's debts: Claim of Dinwiddie, Crawford & Company, T 79/13, List of Debtors, p. 41, PRO; Account with Dinwiddie, Crawford & Company, *Dinwiddie, Craw-*

ford & Co. v. *Henry Skipwith and Elizabeth Hill Skipwith et al.*, 1819, USCCVD(EC), Vi; Charles Duncan to Samuel Greenhow, Oct. 20, 1804, *ibid.*; Draft of Proposed Bill, [ca. 1787], Miscellaneous Legal Materials, Box 74, Tucker-Coleman Papers, ViW.

"an advance" . . . "him": Thomas Evans to Farell & Jones, June 2, 1774, Claim of John Tyndale Warre, T 79/9, PRO; William Lee to John Tayloe, Feb. 10, 25, 1775, William Lee Letterbook, Lee Family Papers, ViRHi.

Westover: Robert Cary & Company to William Byrd, Aug. 5, 1774, *The Correspondence of the Three William Byrds of Westover, Virginia*, ed. Marion Tinling (Charlottesville, 1977), II, 798; Benjamin Waller to Monkhouse Davison and Abram Newman, May 20, Dec. 7, 1773, Dec. 24, 1774, Claim of Exors of Monkhouse Davison and Abram Newman, T 79/32, PRO; *Lloyd's Register: 1776* (London, n.d.), W–45; Purdie and Dixon's *Virginia Gazette*, Oct. 27, 1774. On Byrd's acquaintance with Gist, see William Byrd to [Thomas Willing?], April 26, 1765, *Correspondence of the Byrds*, ed. Tinling, II, 770.

"vile . . . People": Francis Farley to Clement Tudway, Dec. 29, 1775, Tudway Papers, Somerset Record Office.

206 "remain" . . . "troubles": Francis Farley to Clement Tudway, Dec. 29, 1775, Oct. 27, 1777, *ibid.*

"poor" . . . "Eden": Francis Farley to James Parke Farley, March 31, 1772, quoted in *John Simon Farley and Elizabeth Morson* v. *Thomas Lee Shippen and Elizabeth Carter Shippen et al.*, March 1794, in *Decisions of Cases in Virginia by the High Court of Chancery . . . by George Wythe* (Charlottesville, 1903), 255.

about one hundred slaves: A List of Negroes at the Land of Eden, 1773, and at Maycox, 1773, Richard Corbin Papers, ViWC; Francis Farley to Robert Munford, Jan. 15, 1778, *Dinwiddie, Crawford & Co.* v. *Henry Skipwith and Elizabeth Hill Skipwith et al.*, 1819, USC-CVD(EC), Vi.

Meade in Nansemond: David Meade to Neil Jamieson, July 1, 13, Aug. 18, 25, 1773, Neil Jamieson Papers, DLC.

He bought 600 acres: John Webb, advertisement, Purdie and Dixon's *Virginia Gazette*, Oct. 13, 1774; David Meade, "Family History," in Henry J. Peet, ed., *Chaumiere Papers, Containing Matters of Interest to the Descendants of David Meade* (Chicago, 1883), 32.

at Maycox: [Mary Virginia Terhune], *More Colonial Homesteads and Their Stories* (New York, 1899), 67; entry of April 28, 1782, François-Jean, Marquis de Chastellux, *Travels in North America in the Years 1780, 1781, and 1782*, ed. Howard C. Rice, Jr. (Chapel Hill, 1963), II, 431; entry of Feb. 26, 1782, *The Revolutionary Journal of Baron Ludwig von Closen, 1780–1783*, trans. and ed. Evelyn M. Acomb (Chapel Hill, 1958), 187; Meade, "Family History," Peet, ed., *Chaumiere Papers*, 33; John Jones Spooner, "A Topographical Description of the County of Prince George in Virginia, 1793," Massachusetts Historical Society, *Collections*, 1st ser., III (1794), 90. See also Barbara Wells Sarudy, *Gardens and Gardening in the Chesapeake, 1700–1805* (Baltimore, 1998), chap. 7; James D. Kornwolf, "The Picturesque in the American Garden and Landscape Before 1800," *Eighteenth Century Life*, new series, VIII (Jan. 1983), 93–106; Peter Martin, *The Pleasure Gardens of Virginia: From Jamestown to Jefferson* (Princeton, 1991), 103; Max F. Schulz, *Paradise Preserved: Recreations of Eden in Eighteenth- and Nineteenth-Century England* (Cambridge, 1985), 9–37; Malcolm Andrews, *The Search for the Picturesque: Landscape Aesthetics and*

Tourism in Britain, 1760–1805 (Stanford, 1989), 61–65; Keith Thomas, *Man and the Natural World: A History of Modern Sensibility* (New York, 1983), Part 5.

207 called it "Belview": Elizabeth Farley to William Byrd, June 10, July 6, Oct. 17, 1775, *Correspondence of the Byrds*, ed. Tinling, II, 807–809, 816; entry of June 29, 1775, *Records of the Moravians in North Carolina*, ed. Adelaide L. Fries *et al.* (Raleigh, 1922–69), II, 876.

"Friend & Husband": Elizabeth Farley to Thomas Taylor Byrd, June 25, 1783, Byrd Letterbook, Byrd Family Papers, ViRHi.

Saura Town: J. F. D. Smyth, *A Tour in the United States of America* (London, 1784), I, 258–259; An Account of the Property . . . on the Saura Town Plantation, Oct. 15, 1795, *Dinwiddie, Crawford & Co. v. Henry Skipwith and Elizabeth Hill Skipwith et al.*, 1819, USC-CVD(EC), Vi; Lindley S. Butler, "Sauratown Plantation," *Journal of Rockingham County History and Genealogy*, VIII (Dec. 1983), 84–85; Lindley S. Butler, *Rockingham County: A Brief History* (Raleigh, 1982), 12.

"worthy of Paris": Entry of Feb. 26, 1782, *Journal of von Closen*, ed. Acomb, 187.

"a plain . . . manners": Smyth, *Tour in the United States*, I, 250–251.

208 "Unhappy" . . . "Channel": Samuel Gist to John Tabb, Feb. 4, 1775, *Tabb's Admr. v. Gist et al.*, 1829, USCCVD(EC), Vi.

Samuel Sellick: Phripp, Taylor & Co. to Samuel Gist, March 19, 1774, *Samuel Gist v. Taylor & Co.*, 1797, *ibid.*

Lloyd's moved: Charles Wright and C. Ernest Fayle, *A History of Lloyd's from the Founding of Lloyd's Coffee House to the Present Day* (London, 1928), 113–119; Bryant Lillywhite, *London Coffee Houses* (London, 1963), 396–397; Vanessa Harding and Priscilla Metcalf, *Lloyd's at Home* (London, 1986), 90; Ann Saunders, "The Second Exchange," in Ann Saunders, ed., *The Royal Exchange* (London, 1997), chap. 14.

the subscribers' room: G. Clayton, *British Insurance* (London, 1971), 60.

209 "pestiferous" . . . "worse": John Weskett, *A Complete Digest of the Theory, Laws, and Practice of Insurance* (Dublin, 1783), xxiv; Charles Steuart to James Parker, July 6, 1792, Parker Papers, Liverpool Public Library.

The Marine Society: [Jonas Hanway], *The Bye-Laws, and Regulations of the Marine-Society* (London, 1772), 41, 34, 14, 59, 28, 16, 24; Donna T. Andrew, *Philanthropy and Police: London Charity in the Eighteenth Century* (Princeton, 1989), 109–115, 128–129; Ivy Pinchbeck and Margaret Hewitt, *Children in English Society* (London, 1969–73), I, 109–116; James Stephen Taylor, *Jonas Hanway, Founder of the Marine Society: Charity and Policy in Eighteenth-Century Britain* (London, 1985), esp. 70–74, 155–159; John H. Hutchins, *Jonas Hanway, 1712–1786* (London, 1940), chap. 4; John Noorthouck, *A New History of London* (London, 1773), 603; Henry Humpherus, *History of the Origin and Progress of the Company of Watermen and Lightermen* (London, n.d.), II, 302–303.

"as . . . subscribers": *Felix Farley's Bristol Journal*, June 4, 1774; Wright and Fayle, *History of Lloyd's*, 118.

Frederick the Great: Abraham Clibborn, Risk Book, C 107/11, PRO.

Such scenes happened often: Weskett, *Complete Digest*, lv; entry of Sept. 25, 1787, Diary of Carter Braxton, Jr., duPont Library, Stratford, Virginia; Pierre Jean Grosley, *A Tour to London*, trans. Thomas Nugent (Dublin, 1772), I, 127.

John Weskett: Weskett, *Complete Digest*, xiv, xxii–xxiii, xxix, lv.

210 "the facility . . . description": *Report from Select Committee Appointed to Consider . . . the State and Means of Effecting Marine Insurance in Great Britain*, 1810 (226) IV. 247, p. 94.

"As long . . . there": *Ibid.*, p. 86.

"calculating features": Entry of July 24, 1805, [Benjamin Silliman], *A Journal of Travels in England, Holland, and Scotland*, 2d ed. (Boston, 1812), I, 272–273; entries of Aug. 31, Sept. 13, 1799, Diary of Littleton Dennis Teackle, DLC; entries of May 10, 1781, July 30, Nov. 19, 28, 1782, *The Journal of Samuel Curwen, Loyalist*, ed. Andrew Oliver (Cambridge, 1972), II, 753, 847, 871–872, 874; N. M. Karamzin, *Letters of a Russian Traveler, 1789–1790*, trans. Florence Jonas (New York, 1957), 288–289; Warren R. Dawson, *The Treasures of Lloyd's*, 4th ed. (London, 1930), 46.

"the old" . . . "write": *Report on Marine Insurance*, 1810 (226) IV. 247, p. 86.

"had . . . you": Samuel Gist to John Mayo, July 30, 1774, *Samuel Gist* v. *Mayo's Exors*, 1798, USCCVD(EC), Vi; *New-Lloyd's List*, June 28, 1774.

that carmen working: Petition of John Hyndman & Co., Samuel Gist, and others, July 1774, Sessions Papers, SR 1774, Corporation of London Record Office; [John] Trusler, *The London Adviser and Guide* (London, 1786), 101.

"I hope . . . detain'd": Samuel Gist to John Mayo, July 30, 1774, *Samuel Gist* v. *Mayo's Exors*, 1798, USCCVD(EC), Vi; Purdie and Dixon's *Virginia Gazette*, Oct. 6, 1774; Peter Wilson Coldham, *The Complete Book of Emigrants* (Baltimore, 1987–93), IV, 225–226.

Leitch sailed: Purdie and Dixon's *Virginia Gazette*, Sept. 29, Nov. 10, 1774; Thomas Shore to Samuel Gist, Feb. 11, June 20, 1775, *Gist* v. *Tabb's Admr.*, 1795, USCCVD(EC), Vi.

211 James Barron: "A Biographical Notice of Commodore Barron," *Virginia Historical Register*, I (1848), 23–25.

"so saucy . . . do it": Henry Fleming to Fisher & Bragg, Nov. 17, 1774, Papers of Henry Fleming, Cumbria Record Office, Kendal.

the *Elizabeth:* Entry of Feb. 15, 1775, List of All Ships and Vessels Cleared Outwards, Upper District, James River, Jan. 5–April 5, 1775, T 1/512, PRO; entry of Feb. 14, 1775, James River Naval Office, Manifest Book, 1774–1775, William Bell Clark *et al.*, eds., *Naval Documents of the American Revolution* (Washington, 1964–), I, 1388; Thomas Shore to Samuel Gist, Feb. 11, 1775, *Gist* v. *Tabb's Admr.*, 1795, USCCVD(EC), Vi.

new ship *Mary: St. James's Chronicle*, Feb. 11, 16, 18, 21, 23, March 9, 1775.

buy tobacco: Samuel Gist to John Tabb, Feb. 4, April 5, 1775, *Tabb's Admr.* v. *Gist et al.*, 1829, USCCVD(EC), Vi.

the *Liberty:* Samuel Gist to John Tabb, June 28, 1775, *ibid.; Lloyd's Register: 1776*, L–124; *St. James's Chronicle*, March 18, 1775; Thomas and Rowland Hunt to Robert Carter, Feb. 24, 1775, Clark *et al.*, eds., *Naval Documents*, I, 410.

212 "if . . . Price": Samuel Gist to John Tabb, Feb. 4, 1775, *Tabb's Admr.* v. *Gist et al.*, 1829, USCCVD(EC), Vi.

a "large Fortune": Purdie and Dixon's *Virginia Gazette*, May 28, 1772.

more than £4,000: Account of the Estate of William Byrd with Mary Byrd, extx., *Murdock & Co.* v. *Wm. Byrd's Extx*, 1797, USCCVD(EC), Vi.

more than £850: Judgment on Bonds, Estate of John Robinson, *Lidderdale et al.* v. *Robinson's Admrs. et al.*, 1832, *ibid.*

Notes for Chapter v

PAGE

212 "to commence . . . Persons": Purdie and Dixon's *Virginia Gazette*, June 18, 1772, Sept. 2, 1773, Dec. 15, 1774.

"very cheap": *Ibid.*, Dec. 15, 1774.

one-half of a share: List of Partners, Dismal Swamp Land Company Records, NcD.

213 "a jolly" . . . "living": Entry of Sept. 23, 1774, "Turmoil at Pittsburgh: Diary of Augustine Prevost, 1774," ed. Nicholas B. Wainwright, *PMHB*, LXXXV (April 1961), 143.

a remonstrance: Earl of Dunmore to Earl of Dartmouth, April 2, 1774, CO 5/1352, ff. 49–51, PRO.

"Ld . . . you": Thomas Wharton to Thomas Walpole, Sept. 23, 1774, "Letters of Thomas Wharton, 1773-1783," *PMHB*, XXXII (1909), 445; deposition of William Christian, June 3, 1777, deposition of Patrick Henry, June 4, 1777, *The Papers of Thomas Jefferson*, ed. Julian P. Boyd *et al.* (Princeton, 1950–), II, 82, 69–71.

"a confederacy" . . . "inevitable": George Washington to George William Fairfax, June 10–15, 1774, *Papers of Washington: Colonial*, ed. Abbot *et al.*, X, 96–97.

"the Indians . . . friendship": Edward Johnson to William Preston, July 2, 1774, Preston Family Papers-Davie Collection, KyLoF; Alexander Hamilton to James Brown, Sr., May 18, 1774, Piscattaway Letterbooks, John Glassford & Company Papers, DLC; Richard Henry Lee to Francis Lightfoot Lee, May 21, 1775, *The Letters of Richard Henry Lee*, ed. James Curtis Ballagh (New York, 1911), I, 136–137.

214 "while . . . Indians": Earl of Dartmouth to Earl of Dunmore, Sept. 8, 1774, *Aspinwall Papers*, Massachusetts Historical Society, *Collections*, 4th ser., IX–X (1871), II, 726. On confederacy see Gregory Evans Dowd, *A Spirited Resistance: The North American Indian Struggle for Unity, 1745–1815* (Baltimore, 1992), 44–46; Woody Holton, "The Ohio Indians and the Coming of the American Revolution in Virginia," *JSH*, LX (Aug. 1994), 453–478.

"What . . . boy?": Entry of Sept. 22, 1774, "Diary of Prevost," ed. Wainwright, *PMHB*, LXXXV (April 1961), 142.

"Shocking" . . . "Indians": Earl of Dunmore to Earl of Dartmouth, Dec. 24, 1774, Reuben Gold Thwaites and Louise Phelps Kellogg, eds., *Documentary History of Dunmore's War* (Madison, 1905), 386; John Connolly, *A Narrative of the Transactions, Imprisonment, and Sufferings of John Connolly* (New York, 1889 [orig. publ. London, 1783]), 3–4; Earl P. Olmstead, *David Zeisberger: A Life Among the Indians* (Kent, 1997), chap. 18.

Shawnees withdraw: Eric Hinderaker, *Elusive Empires: Constructing Colonialism in the Ohio Valley, 1673-1800* (Cambridge, 1997), 189–195; Michael N. McConnell, *A Country Between: The Upper Ohio Valley and Its Peoples, 1724-1774* (Lincoln, 1992), 264–279; Jack M. Sosin, *Whitehall and the Wilderness: The Middle West in British Colonial Policy, 1760-1775* (Lincoln, 1961), 222–229; R. Douglas Hurt, *The Ohio Frontier: Crucible of the Old Northwest, 1720-1830* (Bloomington, 1996), 57–60; Richard White, *The Middle Ground: Indians, Empires, and Republics in the Great Lakes Region, 1650-1815* (Cambridge, 1991), 362–364; Van Schreeven *et al.*, eds., *Revolutionary Virginia*, II, 105–108.

"acted" . . . "interest": Earl of Dunmore to Earl of Dartmouth, Dec. 24, 1774, Thwaites and Kellogg, eds., *Documentary History*, 390–391.

called it Transylvania: John Richard Alden, *John Stuart and the Southern Colonial Frontier* (Ann Arbor, 1944), 290–292; deposition of Patrick Henry, June 4, 1777, *Papers of Jefferson*, ed. Boyd *et al.*, II, 70; James Hogg to Proprietors of Transylvania Company, Jan. 1776, in James Hall, *Sketches of History, Life, and Manners in the West* (Philadelphia, 1836), II, 250–254.

along the Mississippi River: Earl of Dunmore to Thomas Townshend, Aug. 24, 1782, Shelburne Papers, Vol. 67, pp. 412–415, MiU-C.

"Pretence" . . . "imprisoned": Earl of Dunmore, Proclamation, March 21, 1775, broadside reproduced in Archibald Henderson, *The Conquest of the Old Southwest* (New York, 1920), facing p. 240.

Henderson: William Stewart Lester, *The Transylvania Colony* (Spencer, 1935); Stephen Aron, *How the West Was Lost: The Transformation of Kentucky from Daniel Boone to Henry Clay* (Baltimore, 1996), 59–64.

215 Lewis's debt: Fielding Lewis to Anthony Bacon, Jan. 24, 1775, Anthony Bacon to Joseph Court, April 13, 1775, summarized in *Lewis's Executor* v. *Bacon's Legatee*, 3 Hening & Munford 92–94, *Reports of Cases Argued and Determined in the Supreme Court of Appeals of Virginia* (Charlottesville, 1903), III, 598–599.

Lewis's new house: Jane Taylor Duke, *Kenmore and the Lewises* (Garden City, 1949); Thomas Tileston Waterman, *The Mansions of Virginia, 1706–1776* (Chapel Hill, 1945), 313–326; Fielding Lewis to George Washington, April 23, 1775, *Papers of Washington: Colonial*, ed. Abbot *et al.*, X, 343.

"immediately . . . Defence": Van Schreeven *et al.*, eds., *Revolutionary Virginia*, II, 366–367.

216 "it seems . . . latter": Fielding Lewis to George Washington, April 23, 1775, *Papers of Washington: Colonial*, ed. Abbot *et al.*, X, 343.

armed men gathered: Entries of April 28, 29, 1775, *The Journal of John Harrower*, ed. Edward Miles Riley (Williamsburg, 1963), 94; Michael Wallace to Gustavus Brown Wallace, May 14, 1775, in Horace Edwin Hayden, *Virginia Genealogies: A Genealogy of the Glassell Family* (Wilkes-Barre, 1891), 705.

"that the . . . itself": Dixon and Hunter's *Virginia Gazette*, Aug. 5, 1775.

Dunmore: John E. Selby, *The Revolution in Virginia, 1775–1783* (Williamsburg, 1988), 1–6, 41–47.

"has abilities . . . in law": "Characters of leading Men & Descriptions of Places in Virginia," Peter Russell Papers, CaOTP.

217 had Dismal Plantation: John Driver to David Jameson, Jan. 15, 1790, Thomas Walker and David Jameson to John Taylor, May 17, 1777, David Jameson to John Ball, Jan. 16, 1779, Dismal Swamp Land Company Records, NcD; Purdie and Dixon's *Virginia Gazette*, March 31, 1774.

At the meeting: Entry of June 17, 1775, Memoranda Dismal Swamp Company, Thomas Walker and David Jameson to John Taylor, May 17, 1777, David Jameson to William Nelson, Jr., Oct. 25, 1784, Dismal Swamp Land Company Records, NcD; David Jameson to Samuel Gist, Nov. 7, 1783, Claim of Samuel Gist, American Loyalist Claims, AO 13/30, PRO; "Descendants of Two John Washingtons," *VMHB*, XXVI (Oct. 1918), 420.

218 "not . . . party": John Blackburn to Earl of Dartmouth, Dec. 22, 1774, quoted in Sainsbury, *Disaffected Patriots*, 75.

they do nothing: Letter from London, Jan. 6, 1775, Peter Force, ed., *American Archives* (Washington, 1837–53), 4th ser., I, 1088.

218 "a Ministerial manoeuvre": *Pennsylvania Gazette* (Philadelphia), March 9, 1775.

Gist: William Lee to Francis Lightfoot Lee, Feb. 25, 1775, William Lee to Richard Henry Lee, April 6, 1775, Lee Family Papers, ViU.

"most" . . . "Remedies": *Journal of the House of Commons*, XXXV, 71.

"committee of oblivion": Quoted in Sainsbury, *Disaffected Patriots*, 76. See also Richard Price to Josiah Quincy, Jr., [April or May 1775], *The Correspondence of Richard Price*, ed. D. O. Thomas and W. Bernard Peach (Durham, 1983–91), I, 206–207; Josiah Wedgwood to Thomas Bentley, Feb. 6, 1775, *Letters of Josiah Wedgwood*, ed. Katherine Farrer (Manchester, [1973; orig. publ. 1903]), II, 222–223.

Gist and Anderson: Claim of Samuel Gist, American Loyalist Claims, AO 13/30, PRO; William Anderson, Will, July 20, 1793, William Anderson to Samuel Gist, July 18, 1776, Indenture, Oct. 2, 1777, *Anderson's Heirs* v. *Gist's Exors et al.*, 1824, USCCVD(EC), Vi; Commissioner's Report, June 1808, *Jos. Smith's Admr. et al.* v. *Gist's Exor et al.*, 1825, *ibid.*

"must" . . . "guilt": Purdie's *Virginia Gazette*, May 5, 1775; William Reynolds to John Norton & Son, May 16, 1775, William Reynolds Letterbook, DLC. On Wilkinson, see David Syrett, "The Procurement of Shipping by the Board of Ordnance During the American War, 1775–1782," *MM*, LXXXI (Nov. 1995), 409–416; David Syrett, "The Victualling Board Charters Shipping, 1775–82," *HR*, LXVIII (June 1995), 212–224.

219 Captain Miller: Purdie's *Virginia Gazette*, May 12, 1775.

"he . . . loaded": John Tabb to Samuel Gist, June 6, 1775, *Gist* v. *Tabb, svg ptr., Hill & Co.*, 1795, USCCVD(EC), Vi.

hailed a schooner: Pinkney's *Virginia Gazette*, June 15, 1775; Richard Derby, Sr., to Daniel Hathorn, May 9, 1775, in Robert E. Peabody, *Merchant Venturers of Old Salem* (Boston, 1912), 37–38.

a plot among slaves: Letter from Norfolk, Virginia, *Felix Farley's Bristol Journal*, June 10, 1775.

"for any . . . Ex[chang]e": Samuel Gist to John Tabb, June 28, 1775, *Tabb's Admr.* v. *Gist et al.*, 1829, USCCVD(EC), Vi.

220 with 1,434 hogsheads: Jacob M. Price, ed., *Joshua Johnson's Letterbook, 1771–1774* (London, 1979), 159; Jacob M. Price and Paul G. E. Clemens, "A Revolution of Scale in Overseas Trade: British Firms in the Chesapeake Trade, 1675–1775," *JEcH*, XLVII (March 1987), 23–24; T. M. Devine, "Glasgow Merchants and the Collapse of the Tobacco Trade, 1775–1783," *SHR*, LII (April 1973), 50–63; T. M. Devine, *The Tobacco Lords: A Study of the Tobacco Merchants of Glasgow and Their Trading Activities* (Edinburgh, 1975), 119; J. F. S. Gordon, ed., *Glasghu Facies: A View of the City of Glasgow* (Glasgow, n.d.), II, 758, 1054, 1063.

he insured them: Account of Moss Armistead & Company, *Gist* v. *Tabb's Admr.*, 1795, USCCVD(EC), Vi.

Sir Robert Herries: William Lee to Edward Browne, May 20, 1775, William Lee to John Ballantine & Co., Aug. 4, 1775, William Lee Letterbook, 1774–1775, Lee Family Papers, ViRHi; William Forbes, *Memoirs of a Banking-House* (London, 1860), 45–48; Robert Cary & Co. to William Byrd, Feb. 10, 1775, "Some Unpublished Correspondence of William Byrd III," ed. Marion Tinling, *VMHB*, LXXXVIII (July 1980), 295–296; Farell & Jones to William Byrd, March 10, 1775, *Jones, svg ptr.* v. *Byrd's Extx*, 1818, USCCVD(EC), Vi.

to make small arms: William Waller Hening, ed., *The Statutes at Large: Being a Collection of All the Laws of Virginia* (Richmond, Philadelphia, and New York, 1809–23), IX, 71–73; Charles Dick to Thomas Jefferson, Jan. 23, 1781, *Papers of Jefferson*, ed. Boyd *et al.*, IV, 430–431. See, in general, Selby, *Revolution in Virginia*, chap. 3.

cleared her out of port: Entry of Aug. 14, 1775, James River Naval Office, Manifest Book, 1774–1775, Clark *et al.*, eds., *Naval Documents*, I, 1393; John Tabb to Samuel Gist, June 20, 1775, *Gist v. Tabb, svg ptr. Hill & Co.*, 1795, USCCVD(EC), Vi.

Barron quits: Biographical Notice, *Virginia Historical Register*, I (1848), 25.

221 "a fine . . . service": *Ibid.*

the *Lion* and the *Brilliant*: *Lloyd's Register: 1776*, B–315, L–155.

"his . . . abilities": Archibald Cary to Richard Henry Lee, Dec. 24, 1775, Lee Family Papers, ViU.

"We . . . Valour": Van Schreeven *et al.*, eds., *Revolutionary Virginia*, V, 277. See also William Bell Clark, *Captain Dauntless: The Story of Nicholas Biddle of the Continental Navy* (Baton Rouge, 1949), 129–130.

Lord Dunmore warned: Earl of Dunmore to Earl of Dartmouth, June 25, 1775, K. G. Davies, ed., *Documents of the American Revolution, 1770–1783* (Shannon and Dublin, 1972–80), IX, 207–208.

"to inform . . . ruin": William Byrd to Jeffery Amherst, July 30, 1775, William Byrd to Ralph Wormeley, Oct. 4, 1775, *Correspondence of the Byrds*, ed. Tinling, II, 812, 814.

"the spirit for warfare": Robert Munford to William Byrd, April 20, 1775, *ibid.*, 806.

222 "Goodness of Heart": William Byrd, Will, *VMHB*, IX (July 1901), 86.

her sister, Dorothy: Biographical Sketch of Mary Willing Byrd, BR Box 274(57), CSmH; Joshua Francis Fisher, *Recollections of Joshua Francis Fisher*, ed. Sophia Cadwalader (Boston, 1929), 72, 76–77; Burton Alva Konkle, *Thomas Willing and the First American Financial System* (Philadelphia, 1937), 23–24; Clark, *Captain Dauntless*, 38.

"Things . . . Thing": Benjamin Waller to Davison & Newman, July 5, 1775, Claim of Davison & Newman, T 79/32, PRO.

"kept" . . . "books": Answer of William Byrd Page, June 10, 1820, *James Hopkirk v. Byrd's Exors*, 1805, USCCVD(EC), Vi.

"inattention to accounts": Byrd, Will, *VMHB*, IX (July 1901), 85–86.

published an attack: Pinkney's *Virginia Gazette*, June 1, 1775.

223 "You" . . . "Foot": William Byrd to Samuel Griffin, June 7, 1775, Stephen Collins & Son Papers, DLC. See also Michael A. McDonnell, "Popular Mobilization and Political Culture in Revolutionary Virginia: The Failure of the Minutemen and the Revolution from Below," *Journal of American History*, LXXXV (Dec. 1998), 946–981.

"most . . . order": Biographical Sketch of Mary Willing Byrd, BR Box 274(57), CSmH. See also John Bartram to Peter Collinson, July 18, 1739, *The Correspondence of John Bartram, 1734–1777*, ed. Edmund Berkeley and Dorothy Smith Berkeley (Gainesville, 1992), 122.

"poets corner": Account of the Sales of the Estate of the late Honble William Byrd, *Byrd v. Byrd*, 1838, USCCVD(EC), Vi; Mary Byrd, Will, *VMHB*, VI (April 1899), 348–358.

"amenity of manners": Biographical Sketch of Mary Willing Byrd, BR Box 274(57), CSmH.

223 "the splendid . . . Westover": David Meade to Joseph Prentis, Jr., Sept. 26, 1826, Webb Transcripts, Webb-Prentis Papers, ViU.

"very" . . . "charming": Entry of Feb. 26, 1782, *Journal of von Closen*, ed. Acomb, 187; Charles Lee to William Byrd, April 17, 1776, BR Box 258(27), CSmH.

"many . . . violent": Rebecca Aitchison to James Parker, March 10, 1789, Parker Papers, Liverpool Public Library.

David Meade saw: Meade, "Family History," Peet, ed., *Chaumiere Papers*, 38.

"exposed . . . them": Thomas Taylor Byrd to Thomas Gage, July 11, 1775, Gage Papers, MiU-C.

"the brave" . . . "resolution": William Byrd to Ralph Wormeley, Oct. 4, 1775, *Correspondence of the Byrds*, ed. Tinling, II, 815–816.

224 "I flatter" . . . "purpose": William Byrd to Jeffery Amherst, July 30, 1775, *ibid.*, 812.

"a change of government": William Byrd to Ralph Wormeley, Oct. 4, 1775, *ibid.*, 814–815.

signed a proclamation: Van Schreeven *et al.*, eds., *Revolutionary Virginia*, IV, 334–335.

"Col. . . . thing": *Ibid.*, V, 386–387n; Meade, "Family History," in Peet, ed., *Chaumiere Papers*, 38; entry of Feb. 25, 1776, *The Diary of Colonel Landon Carter of Sabine Hall, 1752–1778*, ed. Jack P. Greene (Charlottesville, 1965), II, 989.

Lord Dunmore's schooners: John Johnson to [?], Nov. 16, 1775, "Intercepted Letters of Virginian Tories, 1775," *AHR*, XII (Jan. 1907), 342.

Scottish merchants: *Ibid.*; Neil Jamieson to Glassford, Gordon, Montieth & Co., Nov. 17, 1775, Papers of the Continental Congress, Microfilm Reel 65, Item 51, Vol. 1, p. 393, DNA.

"this" . . . "People": Earl of Dunmore to Earl of Dartmouth, Oct. 5, 1775, CO 5/1353, ff. 300–302, PRO.

"the elopement . . . Negroes": Dixon and Hunter's *Virginia Gazette*, Aug. 5, 1775; John Johnson to [?], Nov. 16, 1775, "Intercepted Letters," *AHR*, XII (Jan. 1907), 341.

225 at Great Bridge: Earl of Dunmore to Earl of Dartmouth, Dec. 6, 1775–Feb. 18, 1776, Davies, ed., *Documents of the American Revolution*, XII, 58–59; Earl of Dunmore to William Howe, Nov. 30, 1775, Clark *et al.*, eds., *Naval Documents*, II, 1210; Hugh Edward Egerton, ed., *The Royal Commission on the Losses and Services of American Loyalists, 1783 to 1785: Being the Notes of Mr. Daniel Parker Coke, M.P.* (Oxford, 1915), 362; John Page to Virginia Delegates to Congress, Nov. 17, 1775, Lee Family Papers, ViU.

"the language . . . President": Archibald Cary to Richard Henry Lee, Dec. 24, 1775, Lee Family Papers, ViU.

"men . . . Slaves": *Ibid.* See also Woody Holton, " 'Rebel Against Rebel': Enslaved Virginians and the Coming of the American Revolution," *VMHB*, CV (1997), 157–192; Judith Bell to Alexander Speirs, Feb. 16, 1776, quoted in William R. Brock, *Scotus Americanus* (Edinburgh, 1982), 147.

"be as . . . Country": Robert Shedden to John Shedden, Jr., Nov. 20, 1775, "Intercepted Letters," *AHR*, XII (Jan. 1907), 346.

George: "Examination of negroes George and Ned," Dec. 5, 1775, "The Letters of Col. William Woodford, Col. Robert Howe and Gen. Charles Lee to Edmund Pendleton," *Richmond College Historical Papers*, I (June 1915), 104, 111–113. For the names of many black people who joined Dunmore, see Graham Russell Hodges, ed., *The Black Loyalist Directory: African Americans in Exile After the American Revolution* (New York, 1996).

regiments: Earl of Dunmore to Earl of Dartmouth, Dec. 6, 1775–Feb. 18, 1776, Davies, ed., *Documents of the American Revolution*, XII, 59; Earl of Dunmore to William Howe, Nov. 30, 1775, Clark *et al.*, eds., *Naval Documents*, II, 1210.

226 "the Absurdity" . . . "Morass": J. D. to Earl of Dumfries, Jan. 14, 1776, CO 5/40, ff. 123–126, PRO.

HMS *Liverpool:* Earl of Dunmore to Earl of Dartmouth, Dec. 6, 1775–Feb. 18, 1776, Davies, ed., *Documents of the American Revolution*, XII, 62; H. S. Parsons, comp., "Contemporary English Accounts of the Destruction of Norfolk in 1776," *WMQ*, 2d ser., XIII (Oct. 1933), 219–224; Samuel Inglis to Robert Morris, Jan. 6, 1776, *Stan. V. Henkels Catalogue No. 1183* (Jan. 1917), Item 397.

"the people . . . them": Deposition of Robert Brett, Sept. 16, 1777, Commissioners to Examine Claims in Norfolk, Auditor of Public Accounts, Public Claims, Entry 235, General Records, Vi.

"they . . . Tory": Deposition of Samuel Willson, Sept. 17, 1777, deposition of Paul Watlington, Sept. 29, 1777, *ibid.*

Colonel Robert Howe: Robert Howe to Edmund Pendleton, Jan. 6, 1776, "Letters," *Richmond College Historical Papers*, I (June 1915), 152–153; Selby, *Revolution in Virginia*, chap. 4; Thomas C. Parramore, Peter C. Stewart, and Tommy L. Bogger, *Norfolk: The First Four Centuries* (Charlottesville, 1994), chap. 7; Charles E. Bennett and Donald R. Lennon, *A Quest for Glory: Major General Robert Howe and the American Revolution* (Chapel Hill, 1991), chap. 3.

227 "a Speculation" . . . "Chance": Testimony of James Parker, June 5, 1784, Commissioners of American Claims, copies in English Records, Box ER 8, folder 20, Nc-Ar.

Parker's property: Claim of James Parker, American Loyalist Claims, AO 13/34, PRO; Report of Commissioners to Examine Claims in Norfolk, Oct. 10, 1777, Auditor of Public Accounts, Public Claims, Entry 235, General Records, Vi; Parramore *et al.*, *Norfolk*, 97.

"most obnoxious": James Ingram to Charles Steuart, May 31, 1783, Charles Steuart Papers, UkENL; William Aitchison to James Parker, Nov. 14, 1774, Parker Papers, Liverpool Public Library.

"What . . . force": James Parker to Charles Steuart, May 6, 1775, Charles Steuart Papers, UkENL.

"did . . . hanged": Robert Shedden to John Shedden, Nov. 9, 1775, *VMHB*, XIV (Oct. 1906), 132.

worth £30,000: Josiah Martin to Lord George Germain, July 6, 1776, William L. Saunders *et al.*, eds., *Colonial Records of North Carolina* (Raleigh, 1886–), X, 655–656. Compare Egerton, ed., *Royal Commission*, 363. See also State of the Case of Mr. Thomas Macknight, Shelburne Papers, Box 87, Item 1, MiU-C; Thomas Macknight, Memorial and Petition, D. L. Corbitt, ed., "Thomas Macknight," *NCHR*, II (Oct. 1925), 509–521; Memorial of Thomas Macknight, Dartmouth Papers, Charles M. Andrews Transcripts, DLC; Claim of Thomas Macknight, T 79/21, PRO.

"I am . . . promises": James Parker to Charles Steuart, Nov. 6, 1790, Charles Steuart Papers, UkENL.

PAGE

227 "without . . . clothes": Thomas Macknight to James Macknight, Dec. 26, 1775, Clark *et al.*, eds., *Naval Documents*, III, 260–261; Thomas Macknight to Grey Cooper, Nov. 6, 1776, Corbitt, ed., "Macknight," *NCHR*, II (Oct. 1925), 506.

"Disingenuous" . . . "Liberty": Saunders *et al.*, eds., *Colonial Records of North Carolina*, IX, 1184, 1227–1228; Rob Smith to Joseph Hewes, May 23, 1775, Hayes Collection, Johnston Family Series, NcU.

"a pest of society": Quoted in Thomas Macknight to Joseph Jones, June 21, 1775, Saunders *et al.*, eds., *Colonial Records of North Carolina*, X, 34.

Aitchison's property: Memorial of William Aitchison, March 18, 1784, American Loyalist Claims, AO 13/27, PRO; Egerton, ed., *Royal Commission*, 391; Adele Hast, *Loyalism in Revolutionary Virginia: The Norfolk Area and the Eastern Shore* (Ann Arbor, 1982), 82–83.

In the fire: Certification by Earl of Dunmore, March 15, 1784, Claim of William Aitchison, American Loyalist Claims, AO 13/27, PRO.

228 "Commercial" . . . "Goods": Aitchison & Parker to Charles Steuart, May 14, 1776, James Parker to Charles Steuart, June 6, 1777, Charles Steuart Papers, UkENL; James Parker to Margaret Parker, Nov. 8, 1776, Parker Papers, Liverpool Public Library.

"he . . . Country": J. D. to Earl of Dumfries, Jan. 14, 1776, CO 5/40, ff. 123–126, PRO.

"laid . . . degree": James Parker to Margaret Parker, Nov. 8, 1776, Parker Papers, Liverpool Public Library.

death of Aitchison: Rebecca Aitchison to James Parker, July 14, 1786, *ibid.*; James Parker to Charles Steuart, June 6, 1777, Charles Steuart Papers, UkENL; Dixon and Hunter's *Virginia Gazette*, Nov. 8, 1776.

"immediately" . . . "quarters": Purdie's *Virginia Gazette*, July 19, 1776; John Page to Thomas Jefferson, July 20, 1776, *Papers of Jefferson*, ed. Boyd *et al.*, I, 469; James Cunningham's Examination, July 18, 1776, Clark *et al.*, eds., *Naval Documents*, V, 1135; Donald G. Shomette, *Shipwrecks on the Chesapeake* (Centreville, 1982), chap. 6; Selby, *Revolution in Virginia*, 104–106, 124–127.

his land and slaves: Saunders *et al.*, eds., *Colonial Records of North Carolina*, X, 529–530, 565; Walter Clark, ed., *State Records of North Carolina* (Winston and Goldsboro, 1895–1905), XXIV, 263–264.

229 "in the . . . manner": Thomas Macknight, Petition to the Treasury, Dartmouth Papers, Andrews Transcripts, DLC.

"distraction" . . . "distress": Thomas Macknight to Earl of Dartmouth, July 24, 1781, *ibid.* See decision in the case of Thomas Macknight, AO 12/103, f. 40, PRO.

Walker and Flying Crow: Reuben Gold Thwaites and Louise Phelps Kellogg, eds., *The Revolution on the Upper Ohio, 1775–1777* (Madison, 1908), 118, 107.

over the battlefield: Jasper Yeates to [?], Aug. 21, 1776, *Register of Pennsylvania*, VI (Aug. 14, 1830), 104–105.

warned western settlers: Thomas Walker *et al.* to County Lieutenants, Aug. 31, 1776, Thwaites and Kellogg, eds., *Revolution on the Upper Ohio*, 190–191.

230 "by no" . . . "Cruelty": Thomas Walker *et al.* to Committee for Indian Affairs, Sept. 25, 1776, Papers of the Continental Congress, Microfilm Reel 104, Item 78, Vol. 23, pp. 305–309, DNA.

"if you . . . fall": Thwaites and Kellogg, eds., *Revolution on the Upper Ohio*, 118.

PAGE

at Dismal Plantation: William Anderson to Samuel Gist, May 12, 1777, *Anderson's Heirs* v. *Gist's Exors et al.*, 1824, USCCVD(EC), Vi.

Scottish factors: Entry of Aug. 24, 1776, Diary of Thomas Moffat, Peter Force Collection, Series 8D, Item 106, DLC. For names of Scottish refugees, see Esther Clark Wright, *The Loyalists of New Brunswick* (Fredericton, 1955), 255–345.

"providence" . . . "me": Samuel Gist to William Anderson, May 4, 1776, *Anderson's Heirs* v. *Gist's Exors et al.*, 1824, USCCVD(EC), Vi.

Dr. Walker visited: Account with David Jameson, Dismal Swamp Land Company Records, NcD.

"have as . . . have": William Anderson to Samuel Gist, May 12, 1777, *Anderson's Heirs* v. *Gist's Exors et al.*, 1824, USCCVD(EC), Vi.

heavy rains: Entries of June 12, 13, 1777, "The Journal of Ebenezer Hazard in Virginia, 1777," ed. Fred Shelley, *VMHB*, LXII (Oct. 1954), 412–413.

231 attacks of vertigo: John Page to Thomas Jefferson, Aug. 9, 1802, Papers of Thomas Jefferson, DLC. On Virginia's government, see Selby, *Revolution in Virginia*, 116–123.

"crowded . . . House": John Page to St. George Tucker, Sept. 28, 1776, Tucker-Coleman Papers, ViW.

the lead stripped: William Harwood to John Page, Dec. 13, 1775, John Page, Memorandum, 1775, Miscellaneous Manuscripts, ViWC.

"I believe" . . . "Happiness": John Page to St. George Tucker, Sept. 28, 1776, Tucker-Coleman Papers, ViW.

232 debts in Virginia: Richard R. Beeman, *The Old Dominion and the New Nation, 1788–1801* (Lexington, 1972), 123.

Fielding Lewis: Joseph A. Goldenberg and Marion West Stoer, "The Virginia State Navy," in Ernest McNeill Eller, ed., *Chesapeake Bay in the American Revolution* (Centreville, 1981), 174–178; Shomette, *Shipwrecks*, 54–55; Robert Armistead Stewart, *The History of Virginia's Navy of the Revolution* (Richmond [1934]), 57–59; Fielding Lewis to James Hunter, July 22, 1776, Kenmore Manuscript Collection, Fredericksburg, Virginia.

"This . . . Loyd's": [William Carmichael] to Joshua Johnston [Johnson], Feb. 24, 1777, in B. F. Stevens, ed., *Facsimiles of Manuscripts in European Archives Relating to America, 1773–1783* (London, 1889–95), I, No. 39. On the *Reprisal*, see William Bell Clark, *Lambert Wickes: Sea Raider and Diplomat* (New Haven, 1932).

"The American . . . vessel": John Nicol, *The Life and Adventures of John Nicol, Mariner* (Edinburgh, 1822), 18.

nearing £600,000: Entry of June 18, 1776, *Diary and Letters of Hutchinson*, ed. Hutchinson, II, 71; William Lee to Nathan Rumsey, Sept. 3, 1776, William Lee Letterbook, 1775–1776, duPont Library, Stratford, Virginia; V. G. Lizakevich to N. I. Panin, Sept. 27, 1776, in Nikolai N. Bolkhovitinov, *Russia and the American Revolution*, trans. C. Jay Smith (Tallahassee, 1976), 205; M. Garnier to Comte de Vergennes, Oct. 18, 1776, Clark *et al.*, eds., *Naval Documents*, VII, 698; *Public Advertiser* (London), Nov. 9, 1776, reprinted *ibid.*, 734.

more than £1,800,000: *Parliamentary History of England*, XIX, 709–713; Samuel Wharton to Benjamin Franklin, Jan. 17, 1777 [1778], *The Papers of Benjamin Franklin*, ed. Leonard W. Labaree *et al.* (New Haven, 1959–), XXIII, 203. For lists of captured British vessels,

Notes for Chapter v

see Thomas Clark, *Naval History of the United States*, 2d ed. (Philadelphia, 1814), II, 161–179.

232 rose to 15 percent: William Vassall to John Wedderburn, May 21, 1777, William Vassall Letter Books, UkSh; *Parliamentary History of England*, XIX, 709; Arthur Lee to Robert Morris, Sept. 9, 1777, Clark *et al.*, eds., *Naval Documents*, IX, 636; John Bourke to Philip Francis, Oct. 29, 1776, *The Francis Letters*, ed. Beata Francis and Eliza Keary (London, [1901]), I, 273.

charged 28 percent: Roger Sherman to Jonathan Trumbull, Sr., April 17, 1777, Paul H. Smith *et al.*, eds., *Letters of Delegates to Congress: 1774–1789* (Washington, 1976–98), VI, 607; Edgar Stanton Maclay, *A History of American Privateers* (New York, 1899), xiii.

Willing & Morris: John Robinson to John Pownall, Jan. 18, 1776, Davies, ed., *Documents of the American Revolution*, X, 190.

a premium of 50 percent: Robert Morris to Silas Deane, Feb. 27, 1777, Clark *et al.*, eds., *Naval Documents*, VII, 1307.

"a considerable" . . . "Scheme": Willing, Morris & Company to William Bingham, Sept. 14, 27, Oct. 20, 1776, William Bingham Papers, DLC.

"I . . . another": Silas Deane to Elizabeth Deane, March 3, 1776, *The Deane Papers*, New-York Historical Society, *Collections*, XIX–XXIII (1886–90), I, 121.

Patrick Henry: Silas Deane to Patrick Henry, Jan. 2, 1775, *ibid.*, 35–37; James Hall, *Sketches of History, Life and Manners in the West* (Philadelphia, 1835), II, 228–233, 249–254.

233 "You . . . World": Robert Morris to Silas Deane, Aug. 11, 1776, Clark *et al.*, eds., *Naval Documents*, VI, 149.

seize Bermuda: Silas Deane to Robert Morris, April 26, 1776, *ibid.*, IV, 1277. See also Henry Wilkinson, comp., "Notes on American Privateering as Recorded in Bermuda, 1760–1781," Essex Institute, *Historical Collections*, LXXXII (April 1946), 174–178.

French aid, privateers: Earl of Rochford to Horace St. Paul, Sept. 29, 1775, Viscount Weymouth to Horace St. Paul, May 10, 1776, George G. Butler, ed., *Colonel St. Paul of Ewart, Soldier and Diplomat* (London, 1911), II, 292–293, 387–388; Silas Deane to Robert Morris, May 26, 1777, *Stan. V. Henkels Catalogue No. 1183* (Jan. 1917), Item 129; Elizabeth Miles Nuxoll, *Congress and the Munitions Merchants: The Secret Committee of Trade During the American Revolution, 1775–1777* (New York, 1985), chaps. 6–7; David Syrett, *The Royal Navy in European Waters During the American Revolutionary War* (Columbia, 1998), chap. 1; Thomas Perkins Abernethy, "Commercial Activities of Silas Deane in France," *AHR*, XXXIX (April 1934), 477–485; Thomas Perkins Abernethy, *Western Lands and the American Revolution* (New York, 1937), 181–187, 208–209; H. James Henderson, *Party Politics in the Continental Congress* (New York, 1974), 189–192; Orville T. Murphy, *Charles Gravier, Comte de Vergennes* (Albany, 1982), chap. 19; Nicholas Tracy, *Navies, Deterrence, and American Independence: Britain and Seapower in the 1760s and 1770s* (Vancouver, 1988), chap. 6; Thomas J. Schaeper, *France and America in the Revolutionary Era: The Life of Jacques-Donatien Leray de Chaumont, 1725–1803* (Providence, 1995), 208–210; Ruth Y. Johnston, "American Privateers in French Ports, 1776–1778," *PMHB*, LIII (Oct. 1929), 352–374; Alan G. Jamieson, "American Privateers in the Leeward Islands, 1776–1778," *AN*, XLIII (Jan. 1983), 20–30; Robert C. Alberts, *The Golden Voyage: The Life and Times of William Bingham, 1752–1804* (Boston, 1969), chap. 5; John D. Faibisy, "Pri-

PAGE

vateers and Prize Cases: The Impact upon Nova Scotia, 1775–83," *Prologue*, XI (1979), 185–199. On British privateers, see David J. Starkey, *British Privateering Enterprise in the Eighteenth Century* (Exeter, 1990), chap. 8.

"Roderigue" . . . 177: For the Beaumarchais–Lee correspondence, see Pierre-Augustin Caron de Beaumarchais, *For the Good of Mankind: Political Correspondence Relative to the American Revolution*, trans. Antoinette Shewmake (Lanham, 1987). See also Labaree *et al.*, eds., *Papers of Franklin*, XXIII, 425n.3; Jonathan R. Dull, *A Diplomatic History of the American Revolution* (New Haven, 1985), chap. 7; Katharine Prescott Wormeley, trans., *The Prince de Lignes: His Memoirs, and Miscellaneous Papers* (Boston, 1899), I, 291.

Anthony Bacon: Viscount Stormont to Viscount Weymouth, Nov. 6, 1776, Stevens, ed., *Facsimiles*, XIV, No. 1372. See also Lieutenant of police to Comte de Vergennes, Dec. 12, 1776, quoted in Louis de Loménie, *Beaumarchais and His Times*, trans. Henry S. Edwards (New York, 1857), 291; Edward E. Hale and Edward E. Hale, Jr., *Franklin in France* (Boston, 1888), I, 46–47n.2; Horace St. Paul to Viscount Weymouth, May 1, 1776, Butler, ed., *Colonel St. Paul*, II, 380; Prince de Masserano to Marqués de Grimaldi, July 12, 1776, Antonio Martí Alanis, ed., *Canadá en la correspondencia diplomatica de los embajadores de España en Londres, 1534–1813* (Madrid, 1980), 132–133; Buchanan Parker Thomson, *Spain: Forgotten Ally of the American Revolution* (North Quincy, 1976), 32, 36; "Information intended to be given to Ld. W[eymouth]," Sept. 4, 1776, Richard W. Van Alstyne, "Thomas Walpole's Letters to the Duke of Grafton on American Affairs," *HLQ*, XXX (Nov. 1966), 25–27; Richard W. Van Alstyne, "Great Britain, the War for Independence, and the 'Gathering Storm' in Europe, 1775–1778," *HLQ*, XXVII (Aug. 1964), 311–346.

"gaming policies": Thomas Attwood Digges to Arthur Lee, Aug. 30, 1778, *Letters of Thomas Attwood Digges*, ed. Robert H. Elias and Eugene D. Fitch (Columbia, 1982), 13–14.

234 "counter-insurance": Edward Bancroft to Thomas Walpole, n.d., Edward Bancroft to Samuel Wharton, n.d., [Joseph Wharton] to Edward Bancroft, Nov. 10, 1777, Paul Wentworth to William Eden, n.d., Stevens, ed., *Facsimiles*, III, Nos. 289, 290, 301, 324; [Edmund Jenings] to Arthur Lee, May 12, 19, 1778, Lee Family Papers, ViU; Samuel Rogers to William Taylor, March 16, 1778, Lovering-Taylor Family Papers, DLC; Arthur Lee to President of Congress, Feb. 10, 1779, in Edward D. Ingraham, ed., *Papers in Relation to the Case of Silas Deane* (Philadelphia, 1855), 158–161; Arthur Lee to Committee of Correspondence, Aug. 7, 1778, *The Revolutionary Diplomatic Correspondence of the United States*, ed. Francis Wharton (Washington, 1889), II, 680; Dull, *Diplomatic History*, 64; Samuel Flagg Bemis, "British Secret Service and the French-American Alliance," *AHR*, XXIX (April 1924), 484; Julian P. Boyd, "Silas Deane: Death by a Kindly Teacher of Treason?" *WMQ*, 3d ser., XVI (July 1959), 319–342; Donald MacDonald to nephew, [May 1778], in Richard Henry Lee, *Life of Arthur Lee* (Boston, 1829), II, 103.

"He . . . W——le": Paul Wentworth to William Eden, n.d., Stevens, ed., *Facsimiles*, III, No. 324; Lewis Einstein, *Divided Loyalties: Americans in England During the War of Independence* (Boston, 1933), 22–25.

"to make . . . accordingly": James Lovell to Samuel Adams, July 27, [1779], Smith *et al.*, eds., *Letters of Delegates*, XIII, 302; Labaree *et al.*, eds., *Papers of Franklin*, XXIII, 202n.4, XXV, 417n.5, XXVII, 229 headnote; Abernethy, *Western Lands*, 206.

234 an express messenger: *Public Characters of 1799–1800* (London, 1799), 325–326; John Cartwright, *Life and Correspondence of Major Cartwright*, ed. Frances D. Cartwright (London, 1826), I, 174–175; Van Alstyne, "Great Britain," *HLQ*, XXVII (Aug. 1964), 344; Edward Bancroft, Memorial to the Marquis of Carmarthen, Sept. 16, 1784, Bemis, "British Secret Service," *AHR*, XXIX (April 1924), 494; Pierre-Augustin Caron de Beaumarchais, Mémoire particulier pour les ministres du Roi, [Jan. 22, 1778], Gunnar and Mavis von Proschwitz, eds., *Beaumarchais et le Courier de l'Europe: Documents inédits ou peu connus* (Oxford, 1990), I, 440–446; Viscount Weymouth to Viscount Stormont, Jan. 30, Feb. 27, 1778, *British Diplomatic Instructions, 1689–1789*, ed. James Frederick Chance *et al.*, Camden Society, 3d ser., XXXII–XLIX (1922–34), VII, 175–176. See also H. M. Scott, *British Foreign Policy in the Age of the American Revolution* (Oxford, 1990), 260–261; Einstein, *Divided Loyalties*, 37–39.

Transylvania and Vandalia: Abernethy, *Western Lands*, 210–214; Boyd, "Silas Deane," *WMQ*, 3d ser., XVI (Oct. 1959), 534–535.

"Mr. . . . Life": [Silas Deane] to Edward [Bancr]oft, [Jan. 8, 1778], Stevens, ed., *Facsimiles*, V, No. 490. See also Louis W. Potts, *Arthur Lee: A Virtuous Revolutionary* (Baton Rouge, 1981), 155–163; Schaeper, *France and America*, chap. 3.

"We . . . place": Silas Deane to Barnabas Deane, May 14, 1781, Silas Deane to Simeon Deane, Sept. 29, 1780, *Deane Papers*, IV, 331, 238.

America's reunion: Benjamin Franklin to Robert R. Livingston, March 4, 1782, *The Works of Benjamin Franklin*, ed. John Bigelow (New York, 1887–88), VII, 406–407; Andrew Allen to Earl of Shelburne, Oct. 17, 1782, Silas Deane to Andrew Allen, Dec. 25, 1782, Shelburne Papers, Box 87, Items 119, 249, MiU-C; Dull, *Diplomatic History*, 116.

His will: *VMHB*, IX (July 1901), 85–88.

235 "debts of honour": Biographical Sketch of Mary Willing Byrd, BR Box 274(57), CSmH.

"her . . . Byrd": Rebecca Aitchison to James Parker, March 10, 1789, Parker Papers, Liverpool Public Library.

"heartfelt affection": Biographical Sketch of Mary Willing Byrd, BR Box 274(57), CSmH.

"my son . . . me": William Byrd, Will, *VMHB*, IX (July 1901), 87.

"civilities" . . . "spirits": Charles Lee to William Byrd, April 17, 1776, BR Box 258(27), CSmH.

"greatly" . . . "life": William Byrd, Will, *VMHB*, IX (July 1901), 85–86.

David Meade: Meade, "Family History," in Peet, ed., *Chaumiere Papers*, 36, 39.

"her great" . . . "other": Biographical Sketch of Mary Willing Byrd, BR Box 274(57), CSmH.

"extraordinary . . . grief": Nelson W. Evans and Emmons B. Stivers, *A History of Adams County, Ohio* (West Union, 1900), 530–531.

236 "too . . . her": William Byrd, Will, *VMHB*, IX (July 1901), 88.

describes Westover: Mary Willing Byrd to Anne Willing, 1761, quoted in Fisher, *Recollections*, ed. Cadwalader, 95, 97.

"great" . . . "activity": Entry of April 27, 1782, Chastellux, *Travels*, ed. Rice, II, 430.

"The Library . . . you": Mary Willing Byrd to Anne Willing, 1761, quoted in Fisher, *Recollections*, ed. Cadwalader, 95.

"Colo . . . her": Rebecca Aitchison to James Parker, March 10, 1789, Parker Papers, Liverpool Public Library.

"not . . . injured": Elizabeth Willing Powel to Martha Washington, Nov. 1787, *"Worthy Partner": The Papers of Martha Washington*, ed. Joseph E. Fields (Westport, 1994), 199.

"village of quarters": Thomas Lee Shippen to William Shippen, Dec. 30–31, 1783, Shippen Family Papers, DLC.

auctions: Account of the Sales of the Estate of the late Honble William Byrd Esqr., *Byrd v. Byrd*, 1838, Account of the estate of William Byrd with Mary Byrd, *Murdock & Co. v. William Byrd's Extx*, 1797, USCCVD(EC), Vi. The total of the first sale of slaves given in the latter account is in error. See William Nelson, Jr., to Edmund Randolph and Bushrod Washington, n.d., Byrd Family Papers, Mss2, B9966, c17, ViRHi.

"I hope . . . ever": Mary Willing Byrd to Jerman Baker, Dec. 4, 1781, Byrd Family Papers, ViRHi.

"singular intelligence": Fisher, *Recollections*, ed. Cadwalader, 102.

237 "I . . . Currency": Benjamin Waller to Davison & Newman, July 28, 1783, Claim of Exors of Monkhouse Davison and Abram Newman, T 79/32, PRO.

"the age of paper": David Jameson to David Meade, April 1784, Dismal Swamp Land Company Records, NcD.

"the very . . . LIBRARY": Dixon and Hunter's *Virginia Gazette*, March 14, 1777.

Isaac Zane, Jr.: Edwin Wolf, 2nd, "The Dispersal of the Library of William Byrd of Westover," American Antiquarian Society, *Proceedings*, LXVIII (April 1958), 19–106; Kevin J. Hayes, *The Library of William Byrd of Westover* (Madison, 1997), 95–103; entry of Dec. 3, 1773, *Jefferson's Memorandum Books*, ed. James A. Bear, Jr., and Lucia C. Stanton (Princeton, 1997), I, 327.

"neatly kept": Thomas Lee Shippen to William Shippen, Dec. 30–31, 1783, Shippen Family Papers, DLC.

"very . . . company": Entry of Feb. 26, 1782, *Journal of von Closen*, ed. Acomb, 186–187.

"smart repartee": Entry of Aug. 26, 1781, "Extracts from the Journal of Lieutenant John Bell Tilden," *PMHB*, XIX (1895), 53.

"sat . . . Beer": Rebecca Aitchison to James Parker, March 10, 1789, Parker Papers, Liverpool Public Library.

James's father's slaves: Marvin L. Michael Kay and Lorin Lee Cary, *Slavery in North Carolina, 1748–1775* (Chapel Hill, 1995), 37–38, 43.

owed £1,700: James Parke Farley to David Russell, March 14, 1775, Account of James Parke Farley, *Dinwiddie, Crawford & Co. v. Henry Skipwith and Elizabeth Hill Skipwith et al.*, 1819, USCCVD(EC), Vi; Schedule of Debts, Claim of Dinwiddie, Crawford & Co., T 79/13, PRO.

At least twenty vessels: Norfolk Customhouse Ledger, Auditor of Public Accounts, Entry 18, Solicitor General, Vi.

were glutted: John Hardin to James Hunter, Jr., Sept. 2, 1775, Hunter-Garnett Collection, ViU; Francis Farley to Clement Tudway, Oct. 23, 1775, Tudway Papers, Somerset Record Office.

238 "an obliging . . . Wife": Francis Farley to Robert Munford, Jan. 15, 1778, *Dinwiddie, Crawford & Co. v. Henry Skipwith and Elizabeth Hill Skipwith et al.*, 1819, USCCVD(EC), Vi.

"I know . . . off": Francis Farley to Clement Tudway, Dec. 29, 1775, Tudway Papers, Somerset Record Office.

238 slave uprising or a French invasion: Francis Farley to Clement Tudway, Sept. 22, 1778, *ibid.*; Samuel Martin to Christopher Baldwin, April 16, 1776, Samuel Martin Letterbook, Add MSS 41,351, f. 76, Uk; William Mathew Burt to Samuel Barrington, Sept. 22, 1778, *The Barrington Papers: Selected from the Letters and Papers of Admiral the Hon. Samuel Barrington*, ed. D. Bonner-Smith (n.p., 1937–41), II, 66.

"high Loyalists": David Greene to Thomas Fraser, Feb. 13, 1777, David Greene Letterbook, MiU-C.

selling gunpowder: James Young to Council, Aug. 14, 1775, Thomas Jarvis to James Young, Aug. 17, 1775, James Young to Thomas Jarvis, Aug. 22, 1775, James Young to Philip Stephens, Aug. 30, 1775, Clark *et al.*, eds., *Naval Documents*, I, 1148–1149, 1171, 1209, 1268.

drought settled: John Taylor to St. George Tucker, May 1, 1776, Tucker-Coleman Papers, ViW; Samuel Martin to W. Barton, May 17, 1776, Samuel Martin Letterbook, Add MSS 41,351, f. 84, Uk; Mainswete Walrond to Clement Tudway, April 18, 1776, Francis Farley to Clement Tudway, June 19, 22, July 20, 1776, Tudway Papers, Somerset Record Office; Richard B. Sheridan, *Doctors and Slaves: A Medical and Demographic History of Slavery in the British West Indies, 1680–1834* (Cambridge, 1985), 156–157.

attracted speculators: David Greene to Thomas Fraser, June 12, 1777, Greene Letterbook, MiU-C; James Young to Philip Stephens, April 7, 1776, Clark *et al.*, eds., *Naval Documents*, IV, 704–705; John Taylor to St. George Tucker, May 1, 1776, Tucker-Coleman Papers, ViW; Samuel Martin to Henry Martin, July 12, 1776, Samuel Martin Letterbook, Add MSS 41,351, f. 110, Uk; Samuel Martin, Jr., to Earl of Sandwich, April 4, 1777, *The Private Papers of John, Earl of Sandwich*, ed. G. R. Barnes and J. H. Owen (n.p., 1932–38), I, 391.

died "suddenly": Purdie's *Virginia Gazette*, May 23, 1777; Samuel Greenhow, Commissioner's Report, Oct. 1804, *Dinwiddie, Crawford & Co.* v. *Henry Skipwith and Elizabeth Hill Skipwith et al.*, 1819, USCCVD(EC), Vi.

"a Victim . . . country": Elizabeth Farley to Thomas Taylor Byrd, June 25, 1783, Byrd Family Papers, ViRHi.

Thomas Taylor Byrd: Cecil Johnson, *British West Florida, 1763–1783* (New Haven, 1943), 147; J. Leitch Wright, Jr., *Florida in the American Revolution* (Gainesville, 1975), 104 and chap. 10.

239 "a slave . . . country": Francis Farley to John Simon Farley, June 11, 1777, July 13, 1778, quoted in *Decisions in Chancery by Wythe*, 255.

"burnt" . . . "seen": William Vassall to John Wedderburn, Aug. 2, 1777, Vassall Letter Books, UkSh.

"extremely busy": Robert Martin to Clement Tudway, June 12, 1777, Tudway Papers, Somerset Record Office.

condition of slaves: Francis Farley to Clement Tudway, Oct. 27, 1777, *ibid.*; William Mathew Burt to Lord George Germain, Oct. 7, 1777, Historical Manuscripts Commission, *Report on the Manuscripts of Mrs. Stopford-Sackville* (Hereford, 1904–10), II, 272.

food for slaves: Selwyn H. H. Carrington, *The British West Indies During the American Revolution* (Dordrecht, 1988), 76–80; Richard B. Sheridan, "The Crisis of Slave Subsistence in the British West Indies During and After the American Revolution," *WMQ*, 3d ser., XXXIII (Oct. 1976), 622–624.

Farley's letter to Munford: Francis Farley to Robert Munford, Jan. 15, 1778, *Dinwiddie, Crawford & Co.* v. *Henry Skipwith and Elizabeth Hill Skipwith et al.*, 1819, USCCVD(EC), Vi. On tobacco sales, see David Greene to Lane, Son & Fraser, June 12, 1777, Greene Letterbook, MiU-C.

240 ninety-one slaves: Richard R. Beeman, "Robert Munford and the Political Culture of Frontier Virginia," *JAmS*, XII (1978), 173.

"the appearance of magnificence": Entry of May 15, 1792, "Diary of Richard N. Venable, 1791–1792," *TQHGM*, II (Oct. 1920), 138.

He had drawn: *Jamieson & Cameron, svg ptrs.* v. *Byrd, Exor of Munford*, 1798, *Johnson & Cross's Exor* v. *Byrd, Exor of Munford*, 1798, USCCVD(EC), Vi; James Robinson to William Cuninghame & Co., May 7, 1772, April 16, 1774, T. M. Devine, ed., *A Scottish Firm in Virginia, 1767–1777: W. Cuninghame and Co.* (Edinburgh, 1984), 77, 137; Otway Byrd to St. George Tucker, June 3, 1785, William Munford to St. George Tucker, Dec. 22, 1805, Tucker-Coleman Papers, ViW.

"the intemperate warmth": Robert Munford to William Byrd, April 20, 1775, *Correspondence of the Byrds*, ed. Tinling, II, 806.

"expelling . . . *Scotchmen*": James Gilchrist to James Parker, Dec. 22, 1774, "Jamieson-Ellegood-Parker," *WMQ*, 1st ser., XIII (July 1904), 69.

petitioned the House of Delegates: Peyton Skipwith *et al.* to House of Delegates, May 14, 1777, Legislative Petitions, Mecklenburg County, Vi.

"moderate" . . . "war": Robert Munford to William Byrd, April 20, 1775, *Correspondence of the Byrds*, ed. Tinling, II, 806.

The Patriots: Norman Philbrick, ed., *Trumpets Sounding: Propaganda Plays of the American Revolution* (New York, 1972), 266–337. See also Rodney M. Baine, *Robert Munford: America's First Comic Dramatist* (Athens, 1967).

241 "he was . . . aristocrat": Quoted in G. Brown Goode, *Virginia Cousins: A Study of the Ancestry and Posterity of John Goode of Whitby* (Richmond, 1887), 68. See also Dixon's *Virginia Gazette*, April 1, June 3, 1775.

"this unhappy time": Francis Farley to Robert Munford, Jan. 15, 1778, *Dinwiddie, Crawford & Co.* v. *Henry Skipwith and Elizabeth Hill Skipwith et al.*, 1819, USC-CVD(EC), Vi.

242 80 hogsheads: William Anderson to Samuel Gist, May 12, 1777, *Anderson's Heirs* v. *Gist's Exors et al.*, 1824, *ibid.*

Thomas Shore: Dixon and Hunter's *Virginia Gazette*, July 25, 1777.

plantation of Smith: *Ibid.*, July 11, 1777.

"an alien . . . country": Peter Lyons to Samuel Gist, Dec. 1, 1783, Claim of Samuel Gist, American Loyalist Claims, AO 13/30, PRO.

"to such . . . Charge": Merchants *et al.* to Viscount Weymouth, Nov. 24, 1777, Clark *et al.*, eds., *Naval Documents*, X, 1023.

"said . . . Subject": Edmund Burke to Marquis of Rockingham, Dec. 16, 1777, *The Correspondence of Edmund Burke*, ed. Thomas W. Copeland *et al.* (Cambridge and Chicago,

1958–78), IX, 417; Thomas Coutts to Earl of Stair, Dec. 10, 1777, in Ernest Hartley Coleridge, *The Life of Thomas Coutts, Banker* (London, 1920), I, 86.

242 They signed: Merchants of London to Lord George Germain, Jan. 17, 1778, Davies, ed., *Documents of the American Revolution*, XV, 30.

243 William Anderson: Peter Lyons to Samuel Gist, Dec. 1, 1783, copy of Council action, Feb. 24, 1778, Claim of Samuel Gist, American Loyalist Claims, AO 13/30, PRO.

more than $21,750: William Anderson to Samuel Gist, Feb. 1, 1783, *ibid.*

awarded him contracts: L. B. Namier, "Anthony Bacon, M.P., an Eighteenth-Century Merchant," *JEcBH*, II (Nov. 1929), 49–54; A. H. John, *The Industrial Development of South Wales, 1750–1850: An Essay* (Cardiff, 1950), 99–100; Alan Valentine, *Lord George Germain* (Oxford, 1962), 115.

Richard Crawshay: John P. Addis, *The Crawshay Dynasty: A Study in Industrial Organisation and Development, 1765–1867* (Cardiff, 1957), 3–7; G. G. L. Hayes, Introduction, in *The Letterbook of Richard Crawshay, 1788–1797*, ed. Chris Evans (Cardiff, 1990), xi.

Bacon leased: John, *Industrial Development*, 25; John Lloyd, *The Early History of the Old South Wales Iron Works* (London, 1906), 49–50.

around Merthyr Tydfil: Chris Evans, *"The Labyrinth of Flames": Work and Social Conflict in Early Industrial Merthyr Tydfil* (Cardiff, 1993), 30–34; C. W. Chalklin, *The Provincial Towns of Georgian England* (London, 1974), 44, 186; Benjamin Heath Malkin, *The Scenery, Antiquities, and Biography of South Wales* (Wakefield, 1970 [orig. publ. London, 1804]), 176–179.

244 in Cardiff: William Henry Smyth, *Nautical Observations on the Port and Maritime Vicinity of Cardiff* (Cardiff, 1840), 8; entry of July 7, 1776, *An American Quaker in the British Isles: The Travel Journal of Jabez Maud Fisher, 1775–1779*, ed. Kenneth Morgan (Oxford, 1992), 207; entry of July 31, 1777, *Journal of Curwen*, ed. Oliver, I, 388; entry of Aug. 9, 1797, [J. H. Manners, Duke of Rutland], *Journal of a Tour Through North and South Wales, the Isle of Man, &c.* (London, 1805), 77–79; William Gilpin, *Observations on the River Wye, and Several Parts of South Wales* (London, 1782), 83–84; Samuel Molyneux Lowder, *A Letter by the Rev. Mr. Lowder, to George Hardinge, Esq.* (London, 1789).

ordnance depots: Syrett, "Procurement of Shipping," *MM*, LXXXI (Nov. 1995), 409–416.

to supply coal: Namier, "Anthony Bacon," *JEcBH*, II (Nov. 1929), 61–63; Norman Baker, *Government and Contractors: The British Treasury and Supplies, 1775–1783* (London, 1971), 190–193; entry of Aug. 7, 1778, Treasury Minute Books, T 29/47, ff. 156–157, PRO.

in 1778. For 1779: *Journal of the House of Commons*, XXXVII, 224; Articles of Agreement, Nov. 13, 1778, Shelburne Papers, Vol. 139, pp. 23–27, MiU-C. See also Thomas M. Truxes, *Irish-American Trade, 1660–1783* (Cambridge, 1988), 76–78, 150–157, 186–189, 238–241.

"extremely . . . publick": Memorandum, Aug. 29, 1782, Shelburne Papers, Vol. 147, MiU-C; Contractors during the American War, PRO 30/8/344, ff. 123–125, PRO; Proposals from Anthony Bacon, T 1/389, f. 64, PRO; Edward Grace to Moses Franks, May 29, 1777, Colebrooke, Nesbitt, Colebrooke & Franks Papers, DLC; John Robinson to Comptrollers, May 9, 1777, T 27/31, pp. 570–571, PRO; Baker, *Government and Contractors*, 28–35, 46–49, 196–197; David Syrett, "Christopher Atkinson and the Victualling Board, 1775–1782," *HR*, LXIX (June 1996), 129–142.

Ordnance Board debentures: Richard Price to Earl of Shelburne, Oct. 16, 1780, George Jeffery to Richard Price, April 12, 1782, *Correspondence of Price*, ed. Thomas and Peach, II, 83–84, 120–121. See also James Pattison to Board of Ordnance, Aug. 22, 1779, *Official Letters of Major General James Pattison*, New-York Historical Society, *Collections*, VIII (1875), 103.

245 "an amazing . . . Commerce": William Lee to Richard Henry Lee, Oct. 15, 1776, Lee Family Papers, ViU; Bernard Pool, *Navy Board Contracts, 1660–1832: Contract Administration Under the Navy Board* (Hamden, 1966), Part 3.

"Once . . . nothing": [Jonathan Boucher], "Biographia Cumbria," in William Hutchinson, *The History of the County of Cumberland* (Wakefield, 1974 [orig. publ. Carlisle, 1794]), II, 87n. On Boucher, see *ibid.*, I, xix; Jonathan Boucher to John James, Oct. 23, 1776, "Letters of Jonathan Boucher," *MHM*, IX (Sept. 1914), 233; Anne Y. Zimmer, *Jonathan Boucher: Loyalist in Exile* (Detroit, 1978), 248–249.

remained loyal: Donald E. Ginter, ed., *Voting Records of the British House of Commons, 1761–1820* (London, 1995), II, 59; Sainsbury, *Disaffected Patriots*, 114–125 and appendix C.

"extraordinaries" . . . "abuses": John Hatsell, *Precedents and Proceedings in the House of Commons* (London, 1785), III, 154–155.

"The expence" . . . "money": Simmons and Thomas, eds., *Proceedings and Debates*, VI, 200–201, 22, 463; John Francis, *Chronicles and Characters of the Stock Exchange* (London, 1850), 157–160.

received complaints: Baker, *Government and Contractors*, 31–34, 108, 113–115.

"for being" . . . "society!": *The Parliamentary Register*, 1st ser. (London, 1775–80), IX, 156–157.

"We . . . Bill": John Robinson to Earl of Sandwich, May 5, 1778, *Papers of Sandwich*, ed. Barnes and Owen, II, 45.

246 £1,500 was allotted: Laprade, ed., *Parliamentary Papers of Robinson*, 58; Ian R. Christie, ed., "John Robinson's 'State' of the House of Commons, July 1780," *Camden Miscellany*, Camden Society, 4th ser., XXXIX (1990), 445.

Sir William Mayne: [Herbert Croft], *The Abbey of Kilkhampton*, 3d ed. (London, 1780), 78; Baker, *Government and Contractors*, 46; Thomas Coutts to Earl of Stair, Aug. 19, 1782, Coleridge, *Life of Coutts*, I, 149.

Robert Mayne: Namier and Brooke, *History of Parliament*, III, 124.

David Garrick: David Garrick to Grey Cooper, Jan. 29, 1776, *The Letters of David Garrick*, ed. David M. Little and George M. Kahrl (Cambridge, 1963), III, 1067–1068; *Journal of the House of Commons*, XXXV, 554, 679; George Winchester Stone, Jr., and George M. Kahrl, *David Garrick: A Critical Biography* (Carbondale, 1979), 607.

Evan Evans: Lewis Morris to Edward Richard, Aug. 5, 1758, Nov. 18, 1759, Lewis Morris to Evan Evans, Dec. 20, 1759, *Additional Letters of the Morrises of Anglesey*, ed. Hugh Owen (London, 1947–49), I, 349, II, 420, 430–431. See also Charles Wilkins, *The History of the Iron, Steel, Tinplate, and Other Trades of Wales* (Merthyr Tydfil, 1903), 59; Charles Wilkins, *History of Merthyr Tydfil* (Merthyr Tydfil, 1908), 242–243; A. O. H. Jarman, *Aneirin: Y Gododdin: Britain's Oldest Heroic Poem* (Llandysul, 1988), lxxxii–lxxxiii; Historical Manuscripts Commission, *Report on Manuscripts in the Welsh Language* (London, 1902),

II, 91; Aneirin Lewis, ed., *The Percy Letters* (Baton Rouge, 1957), xix–xxi, 18–19n.15; William Lloyd to Daines Barrington, July 16, 1774, in John Nichols, *Illustrations of the Literary History of the Eighteenth Century* (London, 1817–58), V, 600; Prys Morgan, *The Eighteenth Century Renaissance* (Llandysul, 1981), 79–80; Brinley Thomas, "A Cauldron of Rebirth: The Industrial Revolution and the Welsh Language," in Brinley Thomas, *The Industrial Revolution and the Atlantic Economy: Selected Essays* (London, 1993), 215–216.

246 "what . . . were": *Parliamentary Register,* XV, 226.

"Whatever . . . power": Samuel Rogers to William Taylor, Feb. 2, 1780, Lovering-Taylor Family Papers, DLC.

was tobacco: Neil Jamieson to Thomas Jefferson, July 12, 1784, *Papers of Jefferson,* ed. Boyd *et al.,* VII, 365–371; *New-Lloyd's List,* April 13, 1781; Benjamin Franklin to John Jay, June 25, 1780, *Papers of Franklin,* ed. Labaree *et al.,* XXXII, 592; John Robinson to Stanier Porter, Jan. 15, 1777, *Letters of Digges,* ed. Elias and Fitch, xl–xli; Caron de Beaumarchais to Comte de Sartine, Sept. 19, 1777, Beaumarchais, *For the Good of Mankind,* trans. Shewmake, 241–246; Joseph Gardoqui & Sons to Joseph Lee & Co., Aug. 31, Oct. 18, 1777, Kenneth Wiggins Porter, *The Jacksons and the Lees: Two Generations of Massachusetts Merchants, 1765–1844* (Cambridge, 1937), I, 416–417; Schaeper, *France and America,* chaps. 6–7.

247 "all . . . Risques": Robert Morris to Silas Deane, Aug. 11, 1776, Clark *et al.,* eds., *Naval Documents,* VI, 148.

fourteen ships of war: Letter from a French captain, April 14, 1778, enclosed in John Bondfield to Arthur Lee, April 25, 1778, Stevens, ed., *Facsimiles,* XXII, No. 1918.

"Tis . . . chased": Jo Vesey to Milner & Haynes, Dec. 25, 1778, Ship's Papers *Willis,* HCA 32/491, PRO; Marine Committee to Commissioners of the Navy Board, Jan. 9, 1779, *Out-Letters of the Continental Marine Committee and Board of Admiralty,* ed. Charles Oscar Paullin (New York, 1914), II, 37.

fell to one-fourth: Arthur Pierce Middleton, "Ships and Shipbuilding in the Chesapeake and Tributaries," Eller, ed., *Chesapeake Bay,* 106.

"smugglers . . . King": Testimony of Francis Moore, Charles Townshend Papers, 8/34/56, MiU-C; George Rodney and John Vaughan to Lord George Germain, June 25, 1781, Davies, ed., *Documents of the American Revolution,* XIX, 132.

248 St. Eustatius held: Robert A. Selig, "The French Capture of St. Eustatius," *JCarH,* XXVII (1993), 129–130; F. C. Van Oosten, "Some Notes Concerning the Dutch West Indies During the American Revolutionary War," *AN,* XXXVI (July 1976), 162–163; J. Franklin Jameson, "St. Eustatius in the American Revolution," *AHR,* VIII (July 1903), 700–701; Van Alstyne, "Great Britain," *HLQ,* XXVII (Aug. 1964), 318–322; Cornelius Ch. Goslinga, *The Dutch in the Caribbean and in the Guianas, 1680–1791,* ed. Maria J. L. van Yperen (Assen, 1985), 141–152; Jan Willem Schulte Nordholt, *The Dutch Republic and American Independence,* trans. Herbert H. Rowen (Chapel Hill, 1982), 37–46; Johannes Menne Postma, *The Dutch in the Atlantic Slave Trade, 1600–1815* (Cambridge, 1990), 223–224.

"Our . . . world": *Decisions in the High Court of Admiralty; During the Time of Sir George Hay and of Sir James Marriott* (London, 1801), I, 115. See also Janet Schaw, *Journal of a Lady of Quality,* ed. Evangeline Walker Andrews and Charles McLean Andrews (New

Haven, 1922), 137–138; Edmund Burke to John Noble, April 26, 1781, Maggs Bros., *Autograph Letters and Historical Documents*, No. 522 (1929), Item 696.

"a prodigious Sale": John Hatley Norton to Samuel and J. H. Delap, Dec. 9, 1778, Ship's Papers *Willis*, HCA 32/491, PRO.

"went . . . Eustatius": James Ramsay to Lord George Germain, Nov. 23, 1779, *Report on the Manuscripts of Mrs. Stopford-Sackville*, II, 279; *New-Lloyd's List*, July 30, Nov. 19, 1779; Paul Baker and William Leycester to James Dunlop, Nov. 27, 1779, Dunlop Family Papers, DLC; Robert Prescott to Lord George Germain, Nov. 20, 1779, Davies, ed., *Documents of the American Revolution*, XVI, 220.

to Martinique: Charles Greville to William Hamilton, Oct. 16, 1780, Hamilton-Greville Correspondence, CSmH. See also David H. Makinson, *Barbados: A Study of North-American–West-Indian Relations, 1739–1789* (The Hague, 1964), 101–105.

"I . . . finished": George Rodney to John Laforey, Feb. 27, 1781, in "Biographical Memoir of the Late Right Honourable George Rodney, Lord Rodney, K.B.," *Naval Chronicle*, I (1799), 385.

120 percent to 400 percent: Van Oosten, "Notes," *AN*, XXXVI (July 1976), 163; Selig, "French Capture," *JCarH*, XXVII (1993), 130–131; Ronald Hurst, *The Golden Rock: An Episode of the American War of Independence, 1775–1783* (Annapolis, 1996), 61–77. On St. Eustatius in the Seven Years' War, see Cathy Matson, *Merchants and Empire: Trading in Colonial New York* (Baltimore, 1998), 270–274.

Carter Braxton: Carter Braxton to [?], Nov. 1, 1777, HM 22612, CSmH. See also Carter Braxton to [?] Hudson, Dec. 5, 1777, *Magazine of History*, IX (March 1909), 175; Carter Braxton to Francis Lewis, July 10, 1779, in Charles Hamilton, *American Autographs* (Norman, 1983), I, 16; Alonzo Thomas Dill, *Carter Braxton, Virginia Signer: A Conservative in Revolt* (Lanham, 1983), chap. 6.

"from . . . country": William Lee to Henry Lee, June 7, 1779, *Letters of William Lee*, ed. Worthington Chauncey Ford (Brooklyn, 1891), II, 651; Robert E. Wright, "Thomas Willing (1731–1821): Philadelphia Financier and Forgotten Founding Father," *PaH*, LXIII (1996), 544–545. Compare Carter Braxton to Robert Wormeley Carter, Aug. 18, 1782, Emmet Collection, NN.

"European . . . Cost": John Hatley Norton to Samuel & J. H. Delap, Dec. 8, 1778, John Hatley Norton to J. Rocquette, T. A. Elsevier, and P. T. Rocquette, Dec. 16, 1778, Ship's Papers *Willis*, HCA 32/491, PRO.

a premium of 35 percent: John Lloyd to Ralph Izard, March 20, April 26, 1777, *Correspondence of Mr. Ralph Izard*, comp. Anne Izard Deas (New York, 1844), 260, 276–277; Daniel Crommelin & Sons to Aaron Lopez, Dec. 18, 1780, Worthington Chauncey Ford, ed., *Commerce of Rhode Island, 1726–1800*, Massachusetts Historical Society, *Collections*, 7th ser., IX–X (1914–15), II, 113.

asked 45 or 50 percent: Samuel and J. H. Delap to St. George Tucker, Aug. 15, 1778, Tucker-Coleman Papers, ViW; John Bondfield to the Commissioners, Oct. 13, 1778, Jan. 1, Feb. 2, 1779, *Papers of John Adams: The Adams Family Papers, Third Series*, ed. Robert J. Taylor *et al.* (Cambridge, 1977–), VII, 140, 329, 391; John G. Clark, *La Rochelle and the Atlantic Economy During the Eighteenth Century* (Baltimore, 1981), 193–197.

249 "that . . . States": Report of the Commissioners, March 3, 1778, Kenmore Manuscript

Collection, Fredericksburg. See also Chevalier de la Luzerne to Comte de Vergennes, Oct. 16, 1781, *Report on Canadian Archives: 1913* (Ottawa, 1914), 208 [for "five per cent" read "five hundred per cent"]; *Calendar of Historical Manuscripts Relating to the War of the Revolution* (Albany, 1868), II, 55–60.

249 *Betsey, Virginia:* Dixon and Hunter's *Virginia Gazette*, Dec. 14, 1777, April 24, 1778; Purdie's *Virginia Gazette*, Dec. 12, 1777, March 27, 1778.

"May . . . us": Samuel Davies to James Hunter, Jr., Jan. 19, 1778, Hunter-Garnett Collection, ViU.

sold for £500: Eliezer Callender, [Articles of Sale], Sept. 6, 1777, *ibid.*

"it's . . . best": Fielding Lewis to James Hunter, July 30, 1778, Kenmore Manuscript Collection, Fredericksburg.

substantial profits: William Peachey to [?], Dec. 15, 1778, Ship's Papers *Willis*, HCA 32/491, PRO; Joshua Storrs to Samuel Davies, Dec. 24, 1778, Samuel Davies to James Hunter, Jr., Feb. 15, April 23, May 19, 1779, Miscellaneous Accounts 1779, Hunter-Garnett Collection, ViU.

"would . . . Fortune": John Page to St. George Tucker, Sept. 28, 1776, Tucker-Coleman Papers, ViW.

skirting the Dismal Swamp: Entry of March 10, 1777, St. George Tucker, Journal to Charleston, *ibid.* On the Tuckers of Bermuda, see Henry C. Wilkinson, *Bermuda in the Old Empire* (Oxford, 1950).

"nearly . . . commerce": Elkanah Watson, *Men and Times of the Revolution; or, Memoirs of Elkanah Watson,* ed. Winslow C. Watson (New York, 1856), 37.

250 a 100-acre farm: Wilfred Brenton Kerr, *Bermuda and the American Revolution, 1760–1783* (Princeton, 1936), 58. On Maurice Simons, see William Pollard to B. & J. Bowers, Jan. 25, 1774, in H. Roy Merrens, ed., *The Colonial South Carolina Scene* (Columbia, 1977), 276.

South Quay: Norman C. Delaney, "The Outer Banks of North Carolina During the Revolutionary War," *NCHR*, XXXVI (Jan. 1959), 5–9; John Crump Parker, "Old South Quay in Southampton County," *VMHB*, LXXXIII (April 1975), 166–167; Petition of Inhabitants, Nov. 11, 1784, calendared in "Nansemond County Legislative Petitions," *VG*, VI (1962), 105; Thomas Pleasants to St. George Tucker, Oct. 3, 1778, Tucker-Coleman Papers, ViW.

"a bad one": Entry of Dec. 16, 1777, "Journal of Hazard," ed. Shelley, *VMHB*, LXII (Oct. 1954), 423.

The road leading: Entries of March 5–6, 1765, Journal of James Auld, William Alexander Smith Papers, Box 32, NcD.

stood South Quay: Joseph A. Goldenberg, "Virginia Ports," in Eller, ed., *Chesapeake Bay*, 321–322; John Page to Richard Henry Lee, Feb. 17, 1778, Lee Family Papers, ViU.

a cargo of salt: Josiah Jordan, Jr., to [David Ross], March 3, 1781, Revolutionary Government, Commercial Agent, General Correspondence, 1780–1782, Vi; Elbridge Gerry to Thomas Gerry, May 13, 1777, Smith *et al.*, eds., *Letters of Delegates*, VII, 72–74; Isaac J. Greenwood, ed., *The Revolutionary Services of John Greenwood* (New York, 1922), 84–85; John Bach McMaster, *The Life and Times of Stephen Girard, Mariner and Merchant* (Philadelphia, 1918), I, 28–29.

PAGE

"return'd . . . outrages": William Caswell to Thomas Burke, Sept. 4, 1781, Thomas Burke Papers, NcU; Watson, *Men and Times*, ed. Watson, 36; Thomas Newton, Jr., to Benjamin Harrison, Aug. 9, 1782, William P. Palmer *et al.*, eds., *Calendar of Virginia State Papers* (Richmond, 1875–93), III, 252; H. Murfree to Jethro Sumner, July 22, 1781, Clark, ed., *State Records of North Carolina*, XV, 560–561; Thomas C. Parramore, *Southampton County, Virginia* (Charlottesville, 1978), 38; Parramore *et al.*, *Norfolk*, 98–99; Hast, *Loyalism*, 96–120.

251 "You . . . this": John Banks to James Hunter, Jr., May 13, 1782, Hunter-Garnett Collection, ViU.

"I can . . . All)": John Cooper to James Hunter, [Jr.], Oct. 11, 1782, Hunter Family Papers, ViRHi.

"the Demon" . . . "us": John Page to Richard Henry Lee, Feb. 17, 1778, Lee Family Papers, ViU.

"the graspers" . . . "almost": Edmund Pendleton to George Washington, April 27, 1778, *The Letters and Papers of Edmund Pendleton, 1734–1803*, ed. David John Mays (Charlottesville, 1967), I, 255.

"Planters . . . monopolizers": A. Drummond to John Coles, March 13, 1780, Carter Section, Correspondence, Carter-Smith Family Papers, ViU.

"none . . . speculators": Fielding Lewis to George Washington, April 24, 1781, Papers of George Washington, DLC.

"every . . . neighbour": A. Drummond to John Coles, March 13, 1780, Carter-Smith Family Papers, ViU.

"luxury, and extravagancy": Fielding Lewis to George Washington, April 24, 1781, Papers of George Washington, DLC.

"Indolence": John Page to Richard Henry Lee, Oct. 15, 1778, Lee Family Papers, ViU.

"dissipation": George Washington to Robert Howe, Nov. 20, 1779, *The Writings of George Washington*, ed. John C. Fitzpatrick (Washington, 1931–40), XVII, 144.

goods in demand: John Holker to Jonathan Williams, Aug. 7–8, 1779, Schoff Revolutionary War Collection, MiU-C; Edward Channing, "Commerce During the Revolutionary Epoch," Massachusetts Historical Society, *Proceedings*, XLIV (Feb. 1911), 371–377.

£30,000 in Virginia currency: Edmund Pendleton to William Woodford, Nov. 1, 1779, *Letters of Pendleton*, ed. Mays, I, 303.

£240 sterling: Fielding Lewis to George Washington, April 24, 1781, Papers of George Washington, DLC.

"dirty paper": A. Drummond to John Coles, March 13, 1780, Carter-Smith Family Papers, ViU.

"no . . . leaves": Edmund Pendleton to George Washington, April 27, 1778, *Letters of Pendleton*, ed. Mays, I, 255.

7.5 percent of the value: George Washington to George William Fairfax, Feb. 27, 1785, *Papers of Washington: Confederation*, ed. Abbot *et al.*, II, 388.

"the Spirit of Traffic": John Page to Richard Henry Lee, Feb. 17, 1778, Lee Family Papers, ViU.

"the licentious . . . us": Walter Jones to Frederick Jones, Dec. 20, 1784, Roger Jones and Family Papers, DLC.

252 "probably . . . did": Carter Braxton to [?], Nov. 1, 1777, HM 22612, CSmH.

a "Dismal Crop": Langford Lovell to William Codrington, June 10, 1780, *Howard S. Mott, Inc., Catalogue 233* (1997), Item 10; *Report of the Lords of the Committee of Council . . . Concerning the Present State of the Trade to Africa* (London, 1789), Part III, A. No. 31; Henry de Ponthieu to Joseph Banks, Aug. 4, 1779, *The Banks Letters*, ed. Warren R. Dawson (London, 1958), 680.

7,600 black people: Thomas Southey, *Chronological History of the West Indies* (London, 1827), II, 459; William Mathew Burt to Lord George Germain, May 3, 1779, William Mathew Burt to Board of Trade, Sept. 26, 1779, in Lowell Joseph Ragatz, *The Fall of the Planter Class in the British Caribbean, 1763–1833* (New York, 1928), 157–158; *Report Concerning the Trade to Africa*, Part III, A. Nos. 11, 15; Mainswete Walrond to Clement Tudway, Sept. 27, 1778, Sept. 29, 1779, Francis Farley to Clement Tudway, Sept. 27, 1778, Tudway Papers, Somerset Record Office; Sheila Lambert, ed., *House of Commons Sessional Papers of the Eighteenth Century* (Wilmington, 1975), LXXII, 33, 40; James Murray to Elizabeth Murray Smyth, Nov. 14, 1779, in James Murray, *Letters from America, 1773 to 1780*, ed. Eric Robson (Manchester, 1951), 68; Sheridan, "Crisis of Slave Subsistence," *WMQ*, 3d ser., XXXIII (Oct. 1976), 624; Sheridan, *Doctors and Slaves*, 158.

"any . . . us": Francis Farley to Clement Tudway, June 10, 1778, Tudway Papers, Somerset Record Office.

wrote his will: Francis Farley, Will, March 27, 1779, *Dinwiddie, Crawford & Co. v. Henry Skipwith and Elizabeth Hill Skipwith et al.*, 1819, USCCVD(EC), Vi.

253 island of Montserrat: Alexander Willock to Clement Tudway, April 21, 1779, Mainswete Walrond to Clement Tudway, April 18, 1779, Tudway Papers, Somerset Record Office.

Admiral Augustus Keppel: Broomfield, "Keppel-Palliser Affair," *MM*, XLVII (Aug. 1961), 195–207; Syrett, *Royal Navy in European Waters*, chap. 2; Sainsbury, *Disaffected Patriots*, 146–148; N. A. M. Rodger, *The Wooden World: An Anatomy of the Georgian Navy* (London, 1986), chap. 7; Kathleen Wilson, *The Sense of the People: Politics, Culture and Imperialism in England, 1715–1785* (Cambridge, 1995), 253–260; Nicholas Rogers, *Crowds, Culture, and Politics in Georgian Britain* (Oxford, 1998), chap. 4; John Frodsham to Thomas Townshend, April 24, 1779, Sydney Papers, MiU-C. For Laforey's testimony, see *Universal Magazine*, LXIV (March 1779), 118.

"extremely happy": "Officers of Admiral Keppel's Fleet," [Nov. 1778], Earl of Sandwich to the King, Sept. 7, 1779, *Correspondence of George the Third*, ed. Fortescue, IV, 226, 429.

English Harbor: John Laforey to Charles Middleton, Aug. 8, 23, Sept. 26, Nov. 10, Dec. 25, 1780, *Letters and Papers of Charles, Lord Barham*, ed. John Knox Laughton (n.p., 1907–11), II, 84–86, 98–99, 101–104, 112–113; John Laforey to George Brydges Rodney, Feb. 23, 1782, *Letter-Books and Order-Book of George, Lord Rodney*, New-York Historical Society, *Collections*, LXV–LXVI (1932–33), I, 231–232; David Spinney, *Rodney* (London, 1969), 367–368.

254 took St. Eustatius: Kenneth Breen, "Sir George Rodney and St Eustatius in the American War: A Commercial and Naval Distraction, 1775–81," *MM*, LXXXIV (May 1998), 193–203; Hurst, *Golden Rock*; Spinney, *Rodney*, chap. 21.

Commodore Sir George Collier: George Collier to Lord George Germain, May 22, 1779, Davies, ed., *Documents of the American Revolution*, XVII, 130–131; Robert Fallaw and Marion West Stoer, "The Old Dominion Under Fire: The Chesapeake Invasions, 1779–1781," Eller, ed., *Chesapeake Bay*, 444.

other supplies: Entry of June 1, 1779, *Historical Memoirs from 26 August 1778 to 12 November 1783 of William Smith*, ed. William H. W. Sabine (New York, 1971), 111–112; John Daly Burk *et al.*, *The History of Virginia* (Petersburg, 1804–16), IV, 335.

James Parker: Parramore *et al.*, *Norfolk*, 98; Hast, *Loyalism*, 100.

"the province" . . . "cattle": George Collier to Lord George Germain, April 19, 1779, *Report on the Manuscripts of Mrs. Stopford-Sackville*, II, 126; George Collier to Henry Clinton, May 16, 1779, "Expedition to Portsmouth, Virginia, 1779," *WMQ*, 2d ser., XII (July 1932), 182; Baron Mulgrave to Earl of Sandwich, Dec. 14, 1777, *Papers of Sandwich*, ed. Barnes and Owen, I, 336–337.

a small American force: Selby, *Revolution in Virginia*, 205.

255 rich prizes: Shomette, *Shipwrecks*, 56.

surveying wharves: Return of Stores, Ships, &c., "Expedition to Portsmouth," *WMQ*, 2d ser., XII (July 1932), 183–184.

cleared £5,000: Charles Blagden to Joseph Banks, June 16, 1779, *Bulletin of the New York Public Library*, VII (Nov. 1903), 444; entry of May 19, 1779, Carson I. A. Ritchie, ed., "A New York Diary of the Revolutionary War," *New-York Historical Society Quarterly*, L (Oct. 1966), 420.

"came . . . Men": Simeon Deane to John Holker, May 26, July 16, 1779, Simeon Deane, Journal, John Holker Papers, DLC; deposition of Pierre Raphael Charlet, June 6, 1779, in R. T. Whitehurst, "A Legend of the Dismal Swamp," *VMHB*, XXXVI (April 1928), 184–186.

Deane in swamp: Simeon Deane, Journal, Holker Papers, DLC.

256 more than 3,000 barrels: Return of the Stores, May 15, [1779], in Robert Beatson, *Naval and Military Memoirs of Great Britain* (London, 1804), VI, 175–176; Shyers Singleton *et al.* to Richard Caswell, May 19, 1779, Clark, ed., *State Records of North Carolina*, XIV, 85–86, 94–95.

The fires they set: Entry of June 1, 1779, Smith, *Historical Memoirs 1778–1783*, ed. Sabine, 112; Burk *et al.*, *History of Virginia*, IV, 337; Hast, *Loyalism*, 100; Jean Blair to James Iredell, May 17, 1779, *The Papers of James Iredell*, ed. Don Higginbotham (Raleigh, 1976), II, 84.

"for . . . Negro": Entry of June 23, 1779, Account with David Jameson, Dismal Swamp Land Company Records, NcD. For the names of many black people departing with the British, see Hodges, ed., *Black Loyalist Directory*.

As the British departed: Fallaw and Stoer, "Old Dominion Under Fire," Eller, ed., *Chesapeake Bay*, 449–450.

"Speculators . . . likeness": Entry of May 29, 1779, Diary of Baylor Hill, *Virginia Colonial Abstracts*, comp. Beverley Fleet (Baltimore, 1937–61), XXXIII, 75.

257 the Indiana Company: George E. Lewis, *The Indiana Company, 1763–1798: A Study in Eighteenth Century Frontier Land Speculation and Business Venture* (Glendale, 1941), 219–222; Selby, *Revolution in Virginia*, 232.

Richard Henderson: Lester, *Transylvania*, chap. 11; Selby, *Revolution in Virginia*, 144, 158–159.

PAGE

257 "the greatest" . . . "leaders": George Dabney to Charles Dabney, July 3, 1779, Charles William Dabney Papers, NcU.

"His . . . Indiana co. &c.": Thomas Jefferson, "Notes on my title to 485 acres of land," *Papers of Jefferson*, ed. Boyd *et al.*, II, 138.

the Ohio Company: Memorial and Petition, Nov. 20, 1778, Resolutions, June 9, 1779, *The Papers of George Mason*, ed. Robert A. Rutland (Chapel Hill, 1970), I, 444–450, II, 509–512.

"mutilated . . . Peices": George Mason to Richard Henry Lee, June 4, 1779, *ibid.*, II, 507; Pamela C. Copeland and Richard K. MacMaster, *The Five George Masons: Patriots and Planters of Virginia and Maryland* (Charlottesville, 1975), 143–147.

"People . . . Land": Hugh Williamson to Thomas Ruston, Nov. 2, 1784, Smith *et al.*, eds., *Letters of Delegates*, XXII, 8; William Christian to brother, July 11, 1779, Campbell-Preston-Floyd Papers, DLC; Hinderaker, *Elusive Empires*, 204–207; Patricia Watlington, *The Partisan Spirit: Kentucky Politics, 1779–1792* (Chapel Hill, 1973), 17–18; Aron, *How the West Was Lost*, 70–73; Neal O. Hammon, "Land Acquisition on the Kentucky Frontier" and "Settlers, Land Jobbers, and Outlyers: A Quantitative Analysis of Land Acquisition on the Kentucky Frontier," *KHSR*, LXXVIII (1980), 297–321, LXXXIV (1986), 241–262; John Bradford, *The Voice of the Frontier: John Bradford's Notes on Kentucky*, ed. Thomas D. Clark (Lexington, 1993), 30–31. For purchases and grants, see Willard Rouse Jillson, *Old Kentucky Entries and Deeds* (Louisville, 1926); Willard Rouse Jillson, *The Kentucky Land Grants* (Louisville, 1925).

"I suppose . . . sum": Fielding Lewis to George Washington, April 4, 1780, Papers of George Washington, DLC. See also Mordecai Gist to Robert Munford, Oct. 24, 1780, *MHM*, IV (Dec. 1909), 371; Petition, June 1, 1782, James Rood Robertson, ed., *Petitions of the Early Inhabitants of Kentucky* (Louisville, 1914), 66–68.

258 "except . . . Swamp": Hening, ed., *Statutes at Large*, X, 38. On the legislation, see *Papers of Jefferson*, ed. Boyd *et al.*, II, 133–167.

"knowing . . . government": David Jameson to Samuel Gist, Nov. 7, 1783, Claim of Samuel Gist, American Loyalist Claims, AO 13/30, PRO.

"necessary Business": Richard Henderson to Richard Caswell, June 19, 1779, Clark, ed., *State Records of North Carolina*, XIV, 122.

"considerably . . . climacteric": Thomas Walker to Thomas Nelson, Jr., Aug. 7, 1781, Palmer *et al.*, eds., *Calendar of Virginia State Papers*, II, 299.

Loyal Company's title: Archibald Henderson, "Dr. Thomas Walker and the Loyal Company of Virginia," American Antiquarian Society, *Proceedings*, new series, XLI (1931), 113–114.

"making . . . Accurate": William Christian to brother, July 11, 1779, Campbell-Preston-Floyd Papers, DLC.

"at . . . Line": Thomas Walker to William Preston, Aug. 14, 1779, Preston Papers, Vol. 5, p. 6, Draper Collection, Series QQ, WHi.

259 329 surface miles: Entry of Aug. 26, 1779, Journal of Daniel Smith, George Rogers Clark Papers, Vol. 46, Draper Collection, Series J, WHi; Thomas Walker and Daniel Smith to House of Delegates, 1780, Hening, ed., *Statutes at Large*, IX, 562.

PAGE

Henderson sat: Richard Henderson to John Williams, Sept. 13, 1779, John Williams Papers, NcD.

"madness and rage": Richard Henderson to Richard Caswell, June 19, 1779, Clark, ed., *State Records of North Carolina*, XIV, 122.

a delegation of Cherokees: Entries of Sept. 24–27, 1779, Journal of Smith, Clark Papers, Draper Collection, Series J, WHi. See also John Page to the Delawares, Sept. 18, 1777, Reuben Gold Thwaites and Louise Phelps Kellogg, eds., *Frontier Defense on the Upper Ohio, 1777–1778* (Madison, 1912), 88–91; M. Thomas Hatley, "The Three Lives of Keowee: Loss and Recovery in Eighteenth-Century Cherokee Villages," in Peter H. Wood *et al.*, eds., *Powhatan's Mantle: Indians in the Colonial Southeast* (Lincoln, 1989), 223–248; Colin G. Calloway, *The American Revolution in Indian Country: Crisis and Diversity in Native American Communities* (Cambridge, 1995), chap. 7.

260 "in making . . . another": Arthur Campbell to Edmund Randolph, Dec. 10, 1787, Palmer *et al.*, eds., *Calendar of Virginia State Papers*, IV, 365; entries of Oct. 13–Nov. 3, 1779, Journal of Smith, Clark Papers, Draper Collection, Series J, WHi; Thomas Walker and Daniel Smith to House of Delegates, 1780, Hening, ed., *Statutes at Large*, IX, 562–563; Richard Henderson *et al.* to Richard Caswell, Nov. 17, 1779, Clark, ed., *State Records of North Carolina*, XIV, 353–355.

"The accuracy . . . gentlemen": Andrew Ellicott to James Monroe, Sept. 26, 1802, Palmer *et al.*, eds., *Calendar of Virginia State Papers*, IX, 322. See also A. W. Richeson, *English Land Measuring to 1800: Instruments and Practices* (Cambridge, 1966), chap. 6.

"this abortive undertaking": Richard Henderson *et al.* to Richard Caswell, Nov. 17, 1779, Clark, ed., *State Records of North Carolina*, XIV, 355. On Henderson, see Archibald Henderson, "Richard Henderson: The Authorship of the Cumberland Compact and the Founding of Nashville," *Tennessee Historical Magazine*, II (Sept. 1916), 155–172; entry of March 31, 1780, "John Donelson's Journal," in *Three Pioneer Tennessee Documents* (Nashville, 1964), 9; John Floyd to William Preston, Feb. 20, 1780, Louise Phelps Kellogg, ed., *Frontier Retreat on the Upper Ohio, 1779–1781* (Madison, 1917), 141–142; entry of Dec. 25, 1779, "William Fleming's Journal," Mereness, ed., *Travels in the Colonies*, 626. See also William Christian to Benjamin Harrison, Dec. 30, 1782, Executive Papers, Gov. Benjamin Harrison, Vi, and accompanying sketched map, which is reproduced in Jere L. Krakow, *Location of the Wilderness Road at Cumberland Gap National Historical Park* ([Washington], 1987), map 8; entries of Oct. 17–20, 1783, "Tours into Kentucky and the Northwest Territory: Three Journals by the Rev. James Smith of Powhatan County, Va., 1783–1795–1797," *Ohio Archaeological and Historical Publications*, XVI (1907), 356–358.

261 sounded mutinous: Entry of Nov. 22, 1779, Journal of Smith, Clark Papers, Draper Collection, Series J, WHi.

"where . . . speedily": Thomas Walker and Daniel Smith to House of Delegates, 1780, Hening, ed., *Statutes at Large*, IX, 563; Daniel Smith to William Campbell, Dec. 26, 1779, BR Box 258(54), CSmH.

"a River . . . before": Thomas Walker and Daniel Smith to House of Delegates, 1780, Hening, ed., *Statutes at Large*, IX, 563.

261 "almost . . . Capes": George Meriwether to George Rogers Clark, Jan. 24, 1780, in Ronald R. Van Stockum, "George Meriwether (1745–1782)," *FCHQ*, LXXII (Jan. 1998), 80; David Bailie Warden, "Journal of a Voyage from Annapolis to Cherbourg," *MHM*, XI (June 1916), 136; Marshall W. Butt, *Portsmouth Under Four Flags, 1752–1970* (Portsmouth, 1971), 15; Ian H. Adams, "The Complicity of Climate with the American Cause," in Owen Dudley Edwards and George Shepperson, eds., *Scotland, Europe and the American Revolution* (New York, 1977), 54–55.

"The old . . . surprizingly": Daniel Smith to William Campbell, Dec. 26, 1779, BR Box 258(54), CSmH.

remained in camp: Francis Walker to Daniel Smith, Dec. 22, 1791, Virginia MSS, Vol. 7, p. 33, Draper Collection, Series ZZ, WHi; Franklin Minor, "Memoranda of Inquiries about Dr. Thomas Walker," Franklin Minor Letters, *ibid.*, Vol. 13; entries of Jan.–Feb. 1780, Journal of Smith, Clark Papers, *ibid.*, Series J. See also entries of Jan. 2–12, 1780, "The Journal of James Nourse, Jr., 1779–1780," *FCHQ*, XLVII (July 1973), 260–262; entries of Jan. 1–Feb. 6, 1780, "William Fleming's Journal," Mereness, ed., *Travels in the Colonies*, 628–630.

262 "a tolerable" . . . "River": Thomas Walker and Daniel Smith to House of Delegates, 1780, Hening, ed., *Statutes at Large*, IX, 564; entries of Feb. 26–27, 1780, Journal of Smith, Clark Papers, Draper Collection, Series J, WHi.

had reached 36°40′: W. R. Garrett, "Northern Boundary of Tennessee," *American Historical Magazine*, VI (1901), 18–39; Samuel Cole Williams, *Tennessee During the Revolutionary War* (Nashville, 1944), chap. 14.

"fix . . . importance": Thomas Jefferson to Thomas Walker and Daniel Smith, Jan. 29, 1780, George Rogers Clark to Thomas Jefferson, Sept. 23, 1779, *Papers of Jefferson*, ed. Boyd *et al.*, III, 278, 88–89; entry of April 7, 1780, Journal of Smith, Clark Papers, Draper Collection, Series J, WHi.

263 "I . . . mine": Thomas Walker to William Preston, Feb. 21, 1781, Thomas Walker Papers, William Cabell Rives Papers, Box 162, DLC; entries of July 1780, Journal of Smith, Clark Papers, Draper Collection, Series J, WHi.

"the Sport . . . Fables": Samuel Rogers to William Taylor, March 16, 1778, Lovering-Taylor Family Papers, DLC.

The convoy: William Carmichael to John Jay, Aug. 20, 1780, *John Jay: Unpublished Papers*, ed. Richard B. Morris *et al.* (New York, 1975–80), I, 808–809; *Annual Register*, XXIV (1781), History of Europe, 2–3; Beatson, *Naval and Military Memoirs*, V, 148–154; *New-Lloyd's List*, Aug. 22, Sept. 15, 1780; Jonathan R. Dull, *The French Navy and American Independence: A Study of Arms and Diplomacy, 1774–1787* (Princeton, 1975), 193–194; Piers Mackesy, *The War for America, 1775–1783* (Cambridge, 1964), 357.

"It . . . Loyd's": Thomas Attwood Digges to John Adams, Aug. 22, 1780, *Papers of Adams*, ed. Taylor *et al.*, X, 89; Thomas Attwood Digges to Benjamin Franklin, Sept. 18, 1780, *Papers of Franklin*, ed. Labaree *et al.*, XXXIII, 301.

"many . . . Underwriters": *Report on Marine Insurance*, 1810 (226) IV. 247, pp. 43, 47, 66.

a loss of £1,500,000: Beatson, *Naval and Military Memoirs*, V, 154; C. Ernest Fayle, "Shipowning and Marine Insurance," in C. Northcote Parkinson, ed., *The Trade Winds: A Study of British Overseas Trade During the French Wars, 1793–1815* (London, 1948), 38;

Alan Cameron and Roy Farndon, *Scenes from Sea and City: Lloyd's List, 1734–1984* (London, 1984), 36; Samuel Flagg Bemis, *The Hussey-Cumberland Mission and American Independence* (Princeton, 1931), 84.

"had . . . company": James Trevenen to John Trevenen, Oct. 16, 1781, in Christopher Lloyd and R. C. Anderson, eds., *A Memoir of James Trevenen* (London, 1959), 47. See also Henry Shoolbred to John Shoolbred, July 1, 1778, *Report on Canadian Archives: 1888* (Ottawa, 1889), B 202, p. 21; George Cartwright to Joseph Banks, Sept. 14, 1778, A. M. Lysaght, *Joseph Banks in Newfoundland and Labrador, 1766* (London, 1971), 268–269.

264 losses neared £400,000: Robert R. Livingston to John Jay, Aug. 26, 1780, Smith *et al.*, eds., *Letters of Delegates*, XV, 624; *Pennsylvania Gazette* (Philadelphia), Aug. 30, 1780; *New-Lloyd's List*, Sept. 29, 1780; *Annual Register*, XXIV (1781), History of Europe, 3; Thomas Attwood Digges to Benjamin Franklin, Aug. 29, Sept. 18, 29, 1780, Thomas Ruston to Benjamin Franklin, Sept. 29, 1780, *Papers of Franklin*, ed. Labaree *et al.*, XXXIII, 236, 301, 344, 347–348. See also entry of Oct. 11, 1780, Journal of Solomon Drowne, in Maclay, *American Privateers*, 171.

provide better convoys: Memorials of Feb. 13, 1781, calendared in *Report on Canadian Archives: 1890* (Ottawa, 1891), 122.

"much" . . . "risques": Harry Clarke to R. Dunmore & Co., Feb. 17, Mar. 16, 17, Sept. 15, 1778, Cuninghame of Lainshaw Muniments, GD-247, Q/2, SRO.

the *Jamaica Pollock* and the *Friendship*: Carrington, *British West Indies*, 63–64.

"I was . . . War": John Walter to Lord Kenyon, Baron of Gredington, July 6, 1799, Historical Manuscripts Commission, *The Manuscripts of Lord Kenyon* (London, 1894), 551. See also Joshua Johnson to James Russell, Oct. 11, 1781, Russell Papers, Coutts & Co., London; Assignees of William Stead to Christopher Champlin, Aug. 9, 1780, Ford, ed., *Commerce of Rhode Island*, II, 100–101.

"Mr. Delarive": *Gentleman's Magazine*, LIII (Aug. 1783), 715.

"quitted the Coffee-house": *Report on Marine Insurance*, 1810 (226) IV. 247, p. 47.

"speculate in insurances": Johann Archenholz, *A Picture of England* (Dublin, 1791), 199–200; Pierre Nicolas Chantreau, *Voyage dans les trois royaumes d'Angleterre, d'Écosse et d'Irlande, fait en 1788 et 1789* (Paris, 1792), I, 162–163.

fluctuated around 50 percent: Samuel and J. H. Delap to St. George Tucker, Aug. 15, 1778, Tucker-Coleman Papers, ViW; Neil Jamieson to Thomas Jefferson, July 12, 1784, *Papers of Jefferson*, ed. Boyd *et al.*, VII, 368; John Rucker to Tench Coxe, May 28, 1782, Tench Coxe Papers, Series II, PHi; John Bondfield to Commissioners, Oct. 13, 1778, Jan. 1, 1779, *Papers of Adams*, ed. Taylor *et al.*, VII, 140, 329; Jacques-Donatien Leray de Chaumont to Benjamin Franklin, [before June 15, 1780], *Papers of Franklin*, ed. Labaree *et al.*, XXXII, 527.

In Spain: Joseph Gardoqui & Sons to Aaron Lopez, March 22, 1781, Ford, ed., *Commerce of Rhode Island*, II, 130.

"Merchant" . . . "Price": Lambert, ed., *House of Commons Sessional Papers*, XXXII, 130.

Of the 6,000 vessels: Wright and Fayle, *History of Lloyd's*, 156.

265 "the underwriters . . . miscarried": Samuel Martin to Earl of Sandwich, Feb. 12, 1778, *Papers of Sandwich*, ed. Barnes and Owen, I, 269; Patrick Crowhurst, *The Defence of British Trade, 1689–1815* (Folkestone, 1977), chaps. 2–3. For a journal of a convoy's voyage, see

entries of July 31–Oct. 2, 1778, Thomas Pasley, *Private Sea Journals, 1778–1782*, ed. Rodney M. S. Pasley (London, 1931), 35–50. On wages, see David J. Starkey, "War and the Market for Seafarers in Britain, 1736–1792," in Lewis R. Fischer and Helge W. Nordvik, eds., *Shipping and Trade, 1750–1950: Essays in International Maritime Economic History* (Pontefract, 1990), 33–35.

265 late vessels: Harry Clarke to R. Dunmore & Co., May 23, 1778, Cuninghame of Lainshaw Muniments, SRO; *Public Advertiser*, Aug. 20, 1776, in Clark *et al.*, eds., *Naval Documents*, VI, 556.

the ship had left convoy: *New-Lloyd's List*, Jan. 22, 1782; Samuel Martin to Earl of Sandwich, Feb. 12, 1778, *Papers of Sandwich*, ed. Barnes and Owen, I, 269; *Annual Register*, XXVI (1783), Chronicle, 198–199; Syrett, "Procurement of Shipping," *MM*, LXXXI (Nov. 1995), 410–411.

vessels retaken: Samuel Rogers to William Taylor, July 24, 1778, Lovering-Taylor Family Papers, DLC; Samuel Kelly, *Samuel Kelly: An Eighteenth Century Seaman*, ed. Crosbie Garstin (New York, 1925), 46–50, 65; Robert Stevens, *An Essay on Average and on Other Subjects Connected with the Contract of Marine Insurance*, 2d ed. (London, 1816), 182n.

"This . . . clear": *Manning* v. *Gist*, April 27, 1782, 3 Dougl. 74–75, *The English Reports* (Edinburgh, 1909), XCIX, 545–546; James Oldham, *The Mansfield Manuscripts and the Growth of English Law in the Eighteenth Century* (Chapel Hill, 1992), I, 574–576.

"this kind" . . . "profit": *Gist* v. *Mason*, Jan. 26, 1786, 1 T. R. 88–90, *English Reports*, XCIX, 987; James Allan Park, *A System of the Law of Marine Insurances*, 2d ed. (London, 1790), 243; Oldham, *Mansfield Manuscripts*, I, 608.

he had 69: An Account of the Quantities of Tobacco, July 26, 1776, An Account of the Numbers of Hhds, Feb. 12, 1782, Papers on the Tobacco Trade, Add MSS 8133B, ff. 358, 361, Uk.

266 "left . . . Brokers": Samuel Rogers to William Taylor, Feb. 2, 1779, Lovering-Taylor Family Papers, DLC; Mills & Hicks to Champion, Dickason & Co., May 27, 1782, "The Letter-book of Mills & Hicks," ed. Robert Earle Moody and Charles Christopher Crittenden, *NCHR*, XIV (Jan. 1937), 61.

French purchases and 120 shillings: Charles Goore to Mary Evans, Oct. 24, 1777, Charles Goore Letterbook, Schoff Revolutionary War Collection, MiU-C; *Parliamentary History of England*, XIX, 709; Devine, "Glasgow Merchants," *SHR*, LII (April 1973), 72–74.

Moss Armistead: Account of Moss Armistead & Co., *Gist* v. *Tabb's Admr.*, 1795, USC-CVD(EC), Vi.

Jones & Watson: Deposition of Richard Foster, May 10, 1797, Account of Jones & Watson, April 11, 1798, Samuel Gist to Jones & Watson, May 19, 1775, *Samuel Gist* v. *Jones & Watson*, 1806, *ibid*.

William Molleson: Donald MacDonald to nephew, [May 1778], in Lee, *Arthur Lee*, II, 103; Jacob M. Price, "One Family's Empire: The Russell-Lee-Clerk Connection in Maryland, Britain, and India, 1707–1857," *MHM*, LXXII (1977), 196–197.

Royal Exchange Assurance and London Assurance: Barry Supple, *The Royal Exchange Assurance: A History of British Insurance, 1720–1970* (Cambridge, 1970), 62; A. H. John, "The London Assurance Company and the Marine Insurance Market of the Eighteenth Century," *Economica*, XXV (May 1958), 130; Wright and Fayle, *History of Lloyd's*, 158; Frederick Martin, *The History of Lloyd's and of Marine Insurance in Great Britain* (New York, 1971 [orig. publ. London, 1876;]), 165.

"The distress . . . per Cent": Charles Greville to William Hamilton, May 5, 1778, Hamilton-Greville Correspondence, CSmH. On Bacon, see Gedalia Yogev, *Diamonds and Coral: Anglo-Dutch Jews and Eighteenth-Century Trade* (Leicester, 1978), 206, 310n.82.

put £100,000: Letter from London, April 2, 1784, *Virginia Gazette, or, the American Advertiser* (Richmond), Sept. 11, 1784. On investment in the funds, see David Hancock, *Citizens of the World: London Merchants and the Integration of the British Atlantic Community, 1735–1785* (Cambridge, 1995), 260–272.

267 Sir George Brydges Rodney: Thomas Jefferson to Samuel Huntington, Nov. 3, 1780, *Papers of Jefferson*, ed. Boyd *et al.*, IV, 92; Hardy Murfree to Abner Nash, Nov. 1, 1780, Clark, ed., *State Records of North Carolina*, XV, 138; Fallaw and Stoer, "Old Dominion Under Fire," Eller, ed., *Chesapeake Bay*, 453–457.

"inwardly suspected": Alexander Leslie to Francis Rawdon-Hastings, Nov. 9, 1780, Cornwallis Papers, PRO 30/11/4, ff. 78–79, PRO.

"settling Themselves": Thomas Jefferson to James Wood, Nov. 1, 1780, *Papers of Jefferson*, ed. Boyd *et al.*, IV, 87–88.

"very useful": George Gayton to George Brydges Rodney, Nov. 5, 1780, Adm 1/311, PRO.

"shy" . . . "post": George Brydges Rodney to Earl of Sandwich, Nov. 15, 1780, *Papers of Sandwich*, ed. Barnes and Owen, III, 263.

"it hurts . . . it": Alexander Leslie to Francis Rawdon-Hastings, Nov. 9, 1780, Cornwallis Papers, PRO 30/11/4, ff. 78–79, PRO.

"will . . . again": John Holloway to Curson & Gouverneur, Nov. 21, 1780, CO 5/1344, f. 371, PRO.

Black people: Hardy Murfree to Abner Nash, Nov. 1, 1780, Clark, ed., *State Records of North Carolina*, XV, 138; Robert Taylor to Neil Jamieson, April 2, 1783, Neil Jamieson Papers, DLC.

"Refugees" . . . "time": Alexander Lesie to Henry Clinton, Nov. 19, 1780, Clark, ed., *State Records of North Carolina*, XV, 300; John Saunders to John G. Simcoe, Nov. 14, 1780, Simcoe Papers, MiU-C.

"Great . . . negroes": Thomas Jefferson to Horatio Gates, Nov. 19, 1780, *Papers of Jefferson*, ed. Boyd *et al.*, IV, 127; David Jameson to James Madison, Nov. 18, 1780, *The Papers of James Madison*, ed. William T. Hutchinson and William M. E. Rachal *et al.* (Chicago and Charlottesville, 1962–), II, 187.

268 "will . . . loyalty": George Brydges Rodney to Earl of Sandwich, Nov. 15, 1780, *Papers of Sandwich*, ed. Barnes and Owen, III, 263.

"tedious and turbulent": Francis Dundas to Robert Dundas, Dec. 19, 1780, Historical Manuscripts Commission, *Report on the Laing Manuscripts* (London, 1914–25), II, 503.

James Parker after capture: Entries of Feb. 9, 24, 1781, "Alexandre Berthier's Journal of the American Campaign," trans. Marshall Morgan, *RIH*, XXIV (July 1965), 80–81; Thomas Boone to Earl Cornwallis, Aug. 13, 1782, James Parker *et al.* to Earl of Shelburne, July 6, 1782, deposition of John Cramond, Oct. 30, 1782, HO 28/2, ff. 291–292, 383–384, 395–396, PRO; James Madison *et al.* to Chevalier de la Luzerne, April 2, 1781, Smith *et al.*, eds., *Letters of Delegates*, XVII, 118, 124.

268 "intelligent . . . River": Bartholomew James, *Journal of Rear-Admiral Bartholomew James, 1752–1828*, ed. John Knox Laughton (London, 1896), 94.

"a very . . . breakfast": Entry of Jan. 4, 1781, Johann Ewald, *Diary of the American War: A Hessian Journal*, trans. Joseph P. Tustin (New Haven, 1979), 261.

Mary Byrd: Julian P. Boyd, "The Affair of Westover," *Papers of Jefferson*, ed. Boyd *et al.*, V, appendix I.

269 "to the . . . inhabitants": Benedict Arnold to Henry Clinton, Jan. 21, 1781, Davies, ed., *Documents of the American Revolution*, XX, 42.

"The whole . . . families": Ewald, *Diary*, trans. Tustin, 274.

"spreading . . . loyalists": *Ibid.*, 279. See also James Robertson to Jeffery Amherst, May 8, 1781, *The Twilight of British Rule in Revolutionary America: The New York Letter Book of General James Robertson, 1780–1783*, ed. Milton M. Klein and Ronald W. Howard (Cooperstown, 1983), 194; depositions in John Harvie Creecy, ed., *Virginia Antiquary, Volume I: Princess Anne County Loose Papers 1700–1789* (Richmond, 1954), 121–124.

About 250 black people: William Phillips to Henry Clinton, April 3, 1781, Cornwallis Papers, PRO 30/11/5, f. 161, PRO; Benedict Arnold to Henry Clinton, Feb. 13, 1781, Clark, ed., *State Records of North Carolina*, XVII, 984.

"to break . . . Carolina": William Phillips to Earl Cornwallis, April 8, 1781, Cornwallis Papers, PRO 30/11/70, ff. 1–2, PRO; Henry Clinton, Substance of Several Conversations, April 26, 1781, Shelburne Papers, Vol. 68, p. 63, MiU-C.

return to Petersburg: John Banister to Theodorick Bland, May 16, 1781, Theodorick Bland Papers, DLC; Benedict Arnold to Henry Clinton, May 12, 1781, Davies, ed., *Documents of the American Revolution*, XX, 143; William Withers to St. George Tucker, May 20, 1781, Tucker-Coleman Papers, ViW.

"much watch'd": Rebecca Aitchison to James Parker, March 10, 1789, Parker Papers, Liverpool Public Library; Arthur Lee to Theodorick Bland, March 21, 1781, in Charles Campbell, *History of the Colony and Ancient Dominion of Virginia* (Philadelphia, 1860), 711–712.

"persecutors" . . . "American?": Mary Willing Byrd to Thomas Jefferson, Feb. 23, 1781, *Papers of Jefferson*, ed. Boyd *et al.*, IV, 691; Mary Willing Byrd to Baron von Steuben, Feb. 23, 1781, *ibid.*, V, 689.

270 "if she . . . stories": Biographical Sketch of Mary Willing Byrd, BR Box 274(57), CSmH; James Hadden to Charles Mellish, May 27, 1781, Mellish of Hodstock MSS Me C 29/11, University of Nottingham.

would be compensated: Memorandum of Earl Cornwallis, n.d. [Oct. 1781?], Cornwallis Papers, PRO 30/11/74, f. 140, PRO; Earl Cornwallis to Alexander Ross, April 9, 1784, *Correspondence of Charles, First Marquis Cornwallis*, ed. Charles Ross (London, 1859), I, 173.

forty-nine slaves from Westover: Mary Byrd to Thomas Nelson, Jr., Aug. 10, 1781, Palmer *et al.*, eds., *Calendar of Virginia State Papers*, II, 312–313.

"those . . . promises": Rebecca Aitchison to James Parker, March 10, 1789, Parker Papers, Liverpool Public Library.

"extreme . . . grave": Mary Byrd to John Francis Mercer, Oct. 27, 1782, Mercer Papers, ViRHi.

"Tobacco . . . check": James Hadden to Charles Mellish, May 27, 1781, Mellish of Hodstock MSS Me C 29/11, University of Nottingham; Samuel Graham, *Memoir of General Graham*, ed. James J. Graham (Edinburgh, 1862), 36; John Banister to Robert Morris, May 15, 1781, *Stan. V. Henkels Catalogue No. 1183* (Jan. 1917), Item 218. See also William B. Willcox, *Portrait of a General: Sir Henry Clinton in the War of Independence* (New York, 1964), 385–391.

Benjamin Toler: Deposition of Benjamin Toler, March 27, 1784, Claim of Samuel Gist, American Loyalist Claims, AO 13/30, PRO.

Tarleton: Peter Lyons to Newman Brockenbrough, Sept. 20, 1784, John Cook Wyllie, ed., "A New Documentary Light on Tarleton's Raid: Letters of Newman Brockenbrough and Peter Lyons," *VMHB*, LXXIV (Oct. 1966), 457–461; Paroles, June 4, 1781, John Syme to Banastre Tarleton, June 15, 1781, Cornwallis Papers, PRO 30/11/93, ff. 12–18, PRO; Francis Kinloch to Thomas Boone, Oct. 1, 1782, "Letters of Francis Kinloch to Thomas Boone, 1782–1788," ed. Felix Gilbert, *JSH*, VIII (Feb. 1942), 92–93; Benjamin Harrison to Joseph Jones, June 8, 1781, quoted in Joseph Jones to George Washington, June 20, 1781, Smith *et al.*, eds., *Letters of Delegates*, XVII, 337; William Fleming to William Preston, June 12, 1781, Preston Papers, Defense of Southwestern Virginia, Auditor of Public Accounts, Entry 223, Vi; Malone, *Jefferson*, I, 355–358.

271 by thirty of Jefferson's slaves: Thomas Jefferson to Alexander McCaul, April 19, 1786, *Papers of Jefferson*, ed. Boyd *et al.*, IX, 389.

"all . . . enemy": Richard Henry Lee to William Lee, July 15, 1781, *Letters of Richard Henry Lee*, ed. Ballagh, II, 242.

reached the Dismal Swamp: Ewald, *Diary*, trans. Tustin, 318.

South Quay: Alexander Leslie to Earl Cornwallis, June 1781, Earl Cornwallis to Henry Clinton, July 17, 1781, Cornwallis Papers, PRO 30/11/6, f. 158, 30/11/74, ff. 43–44, PRO; Hardy Murfree to Jethro Sumner, July 22, 1781, Clark, ed., *State Records of North Carolina*, XV, 560–561; Jean Blair to James Iredell, July 21, 1781, *Papers of Iredell*, ed. Higginbotham, II, 267; Petition of Inhabitants of Nansemond County, Nov. 11, 1784, *VG*, VI (1962), 105; Parker, "Old South Quay," *VMHB*, LXXXIII (April 1975), 170.

visited Dismal Plantation: Jacob Collee to David Jameson, July 13, 1781, "Memo of Negroes &c. Feby 1783," Dismal Swamp Land Company Records, NcD; "List Losses sustain'd by the Dismal Swamp Compy," "Loss the Inhabitants of Nansemond County," Nov. 18, 1782, Losses Sustained from the British, Nansemond County, General Assembly, Office of the Speaker, Correspondence, Vi; David Jameson to Samuel Gist, Nov. 7, 1783, Claim of Samuel Gist, American Loyalist Claims, AO 13/30, PRO; Edmund Ruffin, "Observations Made During an Excursion to the Dismal Swamp," *Farmer's Register*, IV (Jan. 1, 1837), 516.

272 "if . . . with him": Thomas Nelson, Jr., to Earl Cornwallis, July 23, 1781, Earl Cornwallis to Thomas Nelson, Jr., Aug. 6, 1781, Cornwallis Papers, PRO 30/11/90, ff. 17–19, PRO; Thomas Nelson, Jr., to Eliza Fitzhugh, Aug. 17, 1781, Emmet Collection, NN.

at Portsmouth: Mathieu Dumas, *Memoirs of His Own Time* (Philadelphia, 1839), I, 54.

and their fellow merchants: Memorial of the Merchants of London, Aug. 3, 1781, Davies, ed., *Documents of the American Revolution*, XX, 214–215.

273 Brigadier General O'Hara: Charles O'Hara to Earl Cornwallis, Aug. 5, 9, 15, 17, 1781,

Cornwallis Papers, PRO 30/11/70, ff. 12, 17, 21–22, PRO; entry of July 15, 1781, Johann Ernst Prechtel, *A Hessian Officer's Diary of the American Revolution*, trans. Bruce E. Burgoyne (Bowie, 1994), 208. See also Connolly, *Narrative*, 53–54.

273 "Negro emigrants": For names of black people who may have left the Dismal Swamp Company, see Hodges, ed., *Black Loyalist Directory*, 27, 92–93, 183–184, 187, 189, 200.

the British evacuation: Benjamin Quarles, *The Negro in the American Revolution* (Chapel Hill, 1961), 167–177; James W. St. G. Walker, *The Black Loyalists: The Search for a Promised Land in Nova Scotia and Sierra Leone, 1783–1870* (New York, 1976), chap. 1; Sylvia R. Frey, *Water from the Rock: Black Resistance in a Revolutionary Age* (Princeton, 1991), chap. 6; entry of Oct. 1788, William Dyott, *Dyott's Diary: 1781–1845*, ed. Reginald W. Jeffery (London, 1907), I, 57; Wright, *Loyalists of New Brunswick*, 60.

"a change of air": Petition of Richard Brooke and James Tutt, May 13, 1784, Legislative Petitions, Fredericksburg, Vi; J. P. Custis to George Washington, July 26, 1780, "Letters from John Parke Custis to George and Martha Washington, 1778–1781," ed. Billy J. Harbin, *WMQ*, 3d ser., XLIII (April 1986), 284.

the small arms factory: Fielding Lewis to Thomas Jefferson, Feb. 2, 1780, Charles Dick to Thomas Jefferson, Jan. 23, 1781, *Papers of Jefferson*, ed. Boyd et al., III, 281, IV, 430–431; Fielding Lewis to George Brooke, Feb. 9, 1781, Palmer et al., eds., *Calendar of Virginia State Papers*, I, 502–503; Duke, *Kenmore and the Lewises*, 132–135; Kathleen Bruce, *Virginia Iron Manufacture in the Slave Era* (New York, 1931), 32–42.

274 Fielding Junior: Fielding Lewis to Fielding Lewis, Jr., May 22, 1779, Emmet Collection, NN.

George Lewis: W. Frank Craven, "George Lewis," in Richard A. Harrison, *Princetonians, 1769–1775: A Biographical Dictionary* (Princeton, 1980), 500–501.

Lewis on inflation: Fielding Lewis to George Washington, April 4, 1780, April 24, 1781, Papers of George Washington, DLC. On western land, see also Fielding Lewis to John Lewis, March 14, 1780, Kenmore Manuscript Collection, Fredericksburg.

A chicken cost: Chevalier de la Luzerne to Comte de Vergennes, Dec. 30, 1781, *Report on Canadian Archives: 1913*, 226; Benjamin Harrison to General Assembly, Dec. 3, 1782, *The Frederick S. Peck Collection of American Historical Autographs, Part Two* (March 17, 1947), Item 84; Thomas Nelson, Jr., to David Jameson, Sept. 27, 1781, *Letters of Thomas Nelson, Jr., Governor of Virginia* (Richmond, 1874), 44–45. On paper money and reaction against it, see Janet A. Riesman, "Money, Credit, and Federalist Political Economy," in Richard R. Beeman et al., eds., *Beyond Confederation: Origins of the Constitution and American National Identity* (Chapel Hill, 1987), 128–161.

"vigorously": Lloyd, *Early History of the Old South Wales Iron Works*, 11, 15.

275 "those . . . contracts": William Windham to Bartlett Gurney, March 25, 1782, *The Diary of the Right Hon. William Windham, 1784 to 1810*, ed. Cecilia Anne Baring (London, 1866), 37; Philip Ziegler, *The Sixth Great Power* (New York, 1988), 40.

Earl of Shelburne: Edmond Fitzmaurice, *Life of William, Earl of Shelburne* (London, 1876), III, 6–7; *Parliamentary Register*, XV, 226–234; John Norris, *Shelburne and Reform* (London, 1963), chaps. 7–8.

John Sawbridge: Nathaniel William Wraxall, *The Historical and the Posthumous Memoirs of Sir Nathaniel William Wraxall, 1772–1784*, ed. Henry B. Wheatley (London, 1884), III,

PAGE

244–245; Brown, Collinson & Tritton to Charles Jenkinson, Feb. 16, 1782, Historical Manuscripts Commission, *The Manuscripts of the Marquess of Abergavenny, Lord Braye, G. F. Luttrell, Esq., &c.* (London, 1887), 49. See also Philip Harling, *The Waning of "Old Corruption": The Politics of Economical Reform in Britain, 1779–1846* (Oxford, 1996), 32–42.

"they . . . absurd": Robert Gregson to Earl of Shelburne, Sept. 13, 1782, Shelburne Papers, Vol. 147, MiU-C; Baker, *Government and Contractors*, 35; Norris, *Shelburne and Reform*, 226–229.

assessments: Fielding Lewis to George Washington, April 24, 1781, Papers of George Washington, DLC.

276 "how . . . dayly": Charles Greville to William Hamilton, Dec. 3, 1775, Hamilton-Greville Correspondence, CSmH.

Nathaniel Burwell: Affidavit of Benjamin Waller, Sept. 12, 1810, Claim of John Tyndale Warre, T 79/3, ff. 407–425, PRO.

Mann Page: Mann Page to John Page, Aug. 3, 1779, ViWC; John Page to John Hatley Norton, Feb. 27, 1790, John Norton & Son Papers, ViWC; John Page to St. George Tucker, May 23, 1787, Tucker-Coleman Papers, ViW.

But John Page: John Page to St. George Tucker, March 24, 1783, Tucker-Coleman Papers, ViW; John Page to Arthur Lee, June 7, 1780, Lee Family Papers, ViU; John Page to [Theodorick Bland?], Jan. 21, 1781, Bland-Ruffin Papers, ViU; *Hanbury's Exor (Lloyd)* v. *Burwell, Page et al.*, 1803, USCCVD(EC), Vi; Jane Carson, *James Innes and His Brothers of the F. H. C.* (Williamsburg, 1965), 103–105.

"valuable . . . streets": *Virginia Gazette, or, the American Advertiser,* Nov. 2, 1782; Malcolm H. Harris, "The Port Towns of the Pamunkey," *WMQ*, 2d ser., XXIII (Oct. 1943), 512–513.

more than 2,200 acres: William Armstrong Crozier, ed., *Spotsylvania County Records, 1721–1800* (Baltimore, 1955), 356–358.

277 His will directed: Spotsylvania County Will Book E, Part I, 434–436, Vi.

talked with John Lewis: George Washington to John Lewis, April 17, 1782, *Writings of Washington*, ed. Fitzpatrick, XXIV, 129–131; George Washington to Thomas Walker, April 10, 1784, Thomas Walker to George Washington, Jan. 24, 1784, *Papers of Washington: Confederation*, ed. Abbot et al., I, 281–282, 77.

the Comte de Rochambeau: Entry of Sept. 5, 1781, [Baron de Cromot du Bourg], "Diary of a French Officer, 1781," *Magazine of American History*, IV (May 1880), 383–384; entry of Sept. 5, 1781, *Journal of von Closen*, ed. Acomb, 121–123; Count William de Deux-Ponts, *My Campaigns in America*, ed. Samuel Abbott Green (Boston, 1868), 126–127; Armand Louis de Gontaut Biron, Duc de Lauzun, *Memoirs of the Duc de Lauzun*, trans. C. K. Scott Moncrieff (New York, 1928), 204; entry of Sept. 5, 1781, Jonathan Trumbull, Jr., Minutes and Occurrences, Massachusetts Historical Society, *Proceedings*, 1st ser., XIV (1876), 332.

278 the Comte de Grasse: Thomas Graves to P. Stephens, Sept. 14, 1781, *Letters Written by Sir Samuel Hood in 1781–2–3*, ed. David Hannay (London, 1895), 40–44; captain's log, HMS *London*, Sept. 6, 1781, *British Naval Documents, 1204–1960*, ed. John B. Hattendorf et al. (Aldershot, 1993), 403–405; entries of Sept. 1–5, 1781, [Charles] L'Aîné, Ce cahier appartient à L'Aîné, pp. 63–70, HM 551, CSmH; Dull, *French Navy*, 240–248; John A. Tilley, *The British Navy and the American Revolution* (Columbia, 1987), chap. 11.

Notes for Chapter v

278 "When . . . tell": Henry Clinton to Charles Stuart, Oct. 12, 1781, in *New Records of the American Revolution* (London, 1927), 113; Willcox, *Portrait of a General*, 409–412, 423; N. A. M. Rodger, "Sea-Power and Empire, 1688–1793," in P. J. Marshall, ed., *The Oxford History of the British Empire, Volume II: The Eighteenth Century* (Oxford, 1998), 181; Daniel A. Baugh, "Why did Britain lose command of the sea during the war for America?" in Jeremy Black and Philip Woodfine, eds., *The British Navy and the Use of Naval Power in the Eighteenth Century* (Atlantic Highlands, 1989), 149–169.

British tobacco vessels: Claude C. Robin, *New Travels through North-America*, trans. Philip Freneau (Philadelphia, 1783), 53; Constance D. Sherman, trans. and ed., "Journal of the 1781, 1782, and 1783 Campaigns on the Royal Ship *Hercule*," *New-York Historical Society Quarterly*, LXI (1977), 39; Richard Oswald, Memorandum, Aug. 17, 1781, W. Stitt Robinson, Jr., ed., *Richard Oswald's Memorandum* (Charlottesville, 1953), 20–21; Egerton, ed., *Royal Commission*, 207, 257. Compare John O. Sands, *Yorktown's Captive Fleet* (Charlottesville, 1983), 181–223.

Secretary Nelson: David Ross to William Hay, Oct. 13, 1781, Commercial Agent, General Correspondence, 1780–1782, Revolutionary Government, Vi; entry of Oct. 10, 1781, "Captain James Duncan's Diary of the Siege of Yorktown," *Magazine of History*, II (Nov. 1905), 413; Chastellux, *Travels in North America*, ed. Rice, II, 385; entry of July 30, 1787, Journal of Samuel Vaughan, DLC.

279 York Town: Entry of Oct. 19, 1781, *Journal of von Closen*, ed. Acomb, 155; Robin, *New Travels*, trans. Freneau, 65; entry of Nov. 4, 1781, Journal of Enos Reeves, NcD; Graham, *Memoir of Graham*, ed. Graham, 60.

HMS *Charon*: James Thacher, *Military Journal of the American Revolution* (Hartford, 1862), 283; Shomette, *Shipwrecks*, 65–71; Sands, *Yorktown's Captive Fleet*, 187–189.

"'Tis . . . France": Samuel Pechell to Warren Hastings, Nov. 27, 1781, G. R. Gleig, *Memoirs of the Life of the Right Hon. Warren Hastings* (London, 1841), II, 350.

"Dr. Franklin . . . fools": Fitzmaurice, *Life of Shelburne*, II, 359–360.

280 would change his ministers: Sainsbury, *Disaffected Patriots*, 160–161; *Universal Magazine*, LXX (March 1782), 140; Richard Watson, *Anecdotes of the Life of Richard Watson, Bishop of Landaff*, 2d ed. (London, 1818), I, 144–145.

"He was . . . engulphed": Wraxall, *Historical and Posthumous Memoirs*, ed. Wheatley, V, 53; John Sinclair, *The Correspondence of the Right Honourable Sir John Sinclair, Bart.* (London, 1831), I, 74.

Edward Chamberlayne: Hannah More to sister, April 7, 1782, William Roberts, *Memoirs of the Life and Correspondence of Mrs. Hannah More*, 2d ed. (London, 1834), I, 245–247; *Gentleman's Magazine*, LII (April 1782), 206; William Cole to Horace Walpole, April 12, 1782, *The Yale Edition of Horace Walpole's Correspondence*, ed. W. S. Lewis *et al.* (New Haven, 1937–83), II, 310–311; Alan Valentine, *Lord North* (Norman, 1967), II, chap. 45.

Francis Homfray: Evans, *Labyrinth of Flames*, 18.

Bacon's name: Laprade, ed., *Parliamentary Papers of Robinson*, 45; Norris, *Shelburne and Reform*, 226–227. See also Ian R. Christie, *Wilkes, Wyvill and Reform* (London, 1962), chap. 4 and appendix B.

Bacon votes: Namier and Brooke, *History of Parliament*, II, 36.

and memorials: Merchants to Earl of Shelburne, Aug. 2, 1782, Merchants to Thomas Townshend, Aug. 22, Oct. 3, Nov. 28, 1782, Merchants to Charles James Fox, May 16, 1783, Davies, ed., *Documents of the American Revolution*, XIX, 315, 325, 333, 354, 395; Merchants to Earl of Shelburne, April 18, 1782, Shelburne Papers, Box 87, Item 177, MiU-C.

281 "the propriety . . . money": James Mercer to John F. Mercer, May 1, 1784, Mercer Family Papers, ViRHi.

"was . . . Virginia": William Jones to Daniel L. Hylton & Co., May 31, 1783, *Jones, svg ptr. v. Hylton & Co. et al.*, 1794, USCCVD(EC), Vi.

"The old . . . one": Brian Connell, ed., *Portrait of a Golden Age: Intimate Papers of the Second Viscount Palmerston* (Boston, 1958), 133. See also Sarah Napier to Susan O'Brien, July 9, 1782, Mary Fox-Strangways, Countess of Ilchester, and Giles Fox-Strangways (Lord Stavordale), eds., *The Life and Letters of Lady Sarah Lennox* (London, 1902), II, 19–20.

"some . . . Union": Andrew Allen to Earl of Shelburne, Oct. 17, 1782, Silas Deane to Andrew Allen, Dec. 25, 1782, Shelburne Papers, Box 87, Items 119, 249, MiU-C.

Lord Dunmore proposed: Earl of Dunmore to Thomas Townshend, Aug. 24, 1782, Sydney Papers, MiU-C. See also J. Leitch Wright, Jr., "Lord Dunmore's Loyalist Asylum in the Floridas," *Florida Historical Quarterly*, XLIX (April 1971), 370–379. On the treaty, see Richard B. Morris, *The Peacemakers: The Great Powers and American Independence* (New York, 1965); Norris, *Shelburne and Reform*, 256–270; John Cannon, *The Fox-North Coalition: Crisis of the Constitution, 1782–1784* (Cambridge, 1969), chap. 2; C. R. Ritcheson, "The Earl of Shelburne and Peace with America, 1782–1783: Vision and Reality," *International History Review*, V (Aug. 1983), 322–345; Esmond Wright, "The British Objectives, 1780–1783: 'If Not Dominion Then Trade,' " and Charles R. Ritcheson, "Britain's Peacemakers, 1782–1783: 'To an Astonishing Degree Unfit for the Task'?" in Ronald Hoffman and Peter J. Albert, eds., *Peace and the Peacemakers: The Treaty of 1783* (Charlottesville, 1986), 3–29, 70–100.

an epidemic of influenza: John Marsh, Autobiography, III, 179, CSmH; Carl Philip Moritz, *Journeys of a German in England in 1782*, 2d ed., trans. Reginald Nettel (New York, 1965), 34; Henry Mackenzie to Adam Smith, June 7, 1782, *The Correspondence of Adam Smith*, ed. Ernest Campbell Mossner and Ian Simpson Ross, 2d ed. (Oxford, 1987), 258.

Gist and Anderson: William Anderson to Samuel Gist, Feb. 1, 1783, Claim of Samuel Gist, American Loyalist Claims, AO 13/30, PRO.

282 "little . . . Collected": James Taylor to Samuel Gist, Oct. 1, 1783, *Samuel Gist v. Taylor & Co.*, 1797, USCCVD(EC), Vi.

A new law: Hening, ed., *Statutes at Large*, X, 66–71.

Mary Anderson: Petition of William Anderson and Mary Anderson, June 7, 1782, Legislative Petitions, Hanover County, Vi; Hening, ed., *Statutes at Large*, XI, 54–55.

Lyons, Andersons, Gist: Peter Lyons to Samuel Gist, Dec. 1, 1783, "A list of negroes Stock &c," Nov. 12, 1783, Claim of Samuel Gist, American Loyalist Claims, AO 13/30, PRO; William Anderson, Evidence on the Memorial of Samuel and George Martin, June 8, 1786, AO 12/56, pp. 100–102, PRO; William Anderson to Thomas Massie, May 28,

Notes for Chapter v

1783, Massie Family Papers, ViRHi; deposition of Benjamin Toler, May 7, 1807, *Anderson's Heirs* v. *Gist's Exors et al.*, 1824, USCCVD(EC), Vi; C. G. Chamberlayne, ed., *The Vestry Book of St. Paul's Parish, Hanover County, Virginia, 1707–1786* (Richmond, 1940), 535, 551, 557; Heads of Families-Virginia, 1782, in *Heads of Families at the First Census of the United States* (Baltimore, 1966), 28.

283 William Dolman: William Lee to Edward Browne, Dec. 31, 1783, William Lee to Samuel Thorp, Sept. 8, 1785, William Lee Letterbook, 1783–1787, ViRHi; Joshua Johnson to Wallace & Muir, Oct. 6, 1785, Joshua Johnson Letterbook, Peter Force Collection, Series 8D, DLC; William Armstrong Crozier, ed., *Virginia County Record Publications, New Series, I: Westmoreland County* (Baltimore, 1962 [orig. publ. 1913]), 78.

condition of the Dismal Swamp Company: David Jameson to Samuel Gist, Nov. 7, 1783, Claim of Samuel Gist, American Loyalist Claims, AO 13/30, PRO; Nansemond County Land Book, 1782, 1783, Nansemond County Land Tax Lists, Vi; Jacob Collee to David Jameson, Dec. 12, 1782, Account with David Jameson, Account with David Meade, Dismal Swamp Land Company Records, NcD.

284 "by Death" . . . "thereon": Samuel Gist to Joseph Jones & Company, Oct. 8, 1783, Joseph Jones Family Papers, NcD.

"very elegant" . . . "Horses": Peter Lyons to Samuel Gist, Dec. 1, 1783, May 10, 1784, Claim of Samuel Gist, American Loyalist Claims, AO 13/30, PRO; William Anderson, Advertisement, *Virginia Gazette, or, the American Advertiser*, March 12, 1785.

"I . . . girl": William Anderson to Thomas Massie, May 28, 1783, Massie Family Papers, ViRHi.

Anderson and Gist: William Anderson to Samuel Gist, Oct. 15, 1783, Peter Lyons to Samuel Gist, May 10, 1784, Peter Lyons, Note on Act of 1784, Claim of Samuel Gist, American Loyalist Claims, AO 13/30, PRO.

"She . . . happy": Elizabeth Farley to Thomas Taylor Byrd, June 25, 1783, Byrd Letterbook, Byrd Family Papers, ViRHi.

285 "exceed all description": Charles Stedman, *The History of the Origin, Progress, and Termination of the American War* (London, 1794), II, 346; St. George Tucker to Frances Tucker, March 2, 18, 1781, Tucker-Coleman Papers, ViW; John Buchanan, *The Road to Guilford Courthouse: The American Revolution in the Carolinas* (New York, 1997), chap. 24.

"A Letter from the Devil": Robert Munford, *A Collection of Plays and Poems by the Late Col. Robert Munford* (Petersburg, 1798), 195. See also Philip D. Morgan, *Slave Counterpoint: Black Culture in the Eighteenth-Century Chesapeake and Lowcountry* (Chapel Hill, 1998), 392–396; Philip J. Schwarz, *Twice Condemned: Slaves and the Criminal Laws of Virginia, 1705–1865* (Baton Rouge, 1988), chap. 6, esp. pp. 137–138.

a hard drinker: Baine, *Robert Munford*, 54–55.

"the estate's . . . creditors": Otway Byrd to St. George Tucker, 1786, Tucker-Coleman Papers, ViW.

"the embarrassment . . . circumstances": William Munford to St. George Tucker, June 19, 1794, Dec. 22, 1805, *ibid.*

286 "So . . . sins": Munford, "The Patriots," in Philbrick, ed., *Trumpets Sounding*, 316; Peter A. Davis, "The Plays and Playwrights," in Don B. Wilmeth and Christopher Bigsby, eds., *The Cambridge History of the American Theatre: Volume I* (Cambridge, 1998), 241; Jared

Brown, *The Theatre in America During the Revolution* (Cambridge, 1995), 19–21; Gary A. Richardson, *American Drama from the Colonial Period Through World War I: A Critical History* (New York, 1993), 43–45.

wrote a preface: Preface, Munford, *Collection of Plays and Poems*, vi.

VI: THIS ELDORADO

287 "this . . . employments": George Washington to Thomas Walker, April 10, 1784, *The Papers of George Washington, Confederation Series*, ed. W. W. Abbot *et al.* (Charlottesville, 1983–), I, 281.

"sunken . . . Country": George Washington to Patrick Henry, June 24, 1785, *ibid.*, III, 80.

to protect the company's title: David Jameson to Thomas Walker, June 22, 1783, Thomas Walker to David Jameson, June 23, 26, 1783, Dismal Swamp Land Company Records, NcD.

cutting a canal: *Journal of the House of Delegates of Virginia* [Richmond, 1783], 48.

"the Company . . . property": Thomas Walker to George Washington, Jan. 24, 1784, *Papers of Washington: Confederation*, ed. Abbot *et al.*, I, 76.

"unreservedly": Entry of Sept. 30, 1785, *The Diaries of George Washington*, ed. Donald Jackson and Dorothy Twohig (Charlottesville, 1976–79), IV, 199; John Lowry to George Washington, Aug. 2, 1785, *Papers of Washington: Confederation*, ed. Abbot *et al.*, III, 170.

an act of the General Assembly: David Jameson to Samuel Gist, Nov. 7, 1783, Claim of Samuel Gist, American Loyalist Claims, AO 13/30, PRO; David Jameson to Thomas Walker, Oct. 31, 1783, Dismal Swamp Land Company Records, NcD.

40,000 acres: Survey, Sept. 20, 1783, Dismal Swamp Land Company Records, NcD. See also plat accompanying George Washington to John Jameson, Feb. 15, 1795, Gilder Lehrman Collection, NNPM.

288 to press a claim: David Jameson to David Meade, April 1784, David Jameson to Thomas Walker, July 15, 1784, Dismal Swamp Land Company Records, NcD; Thomas Walker to George Washington, Jan. 24, 1784, *Papers of Washington: Confederation*, ed. Abbot *et al.*, I, 76–77.

"I . . . quantity": David Jameson to Samuel Gist, Dec. 23, 1783, Claim of Samuel Gist, American Loyalist Claims, AO 13/30, PRO.

"Lawyers . . . founded": Thomas Walker to David Jameson, June 23, 1783, Dismal Swamp Land Company Records, NcD.

The Supreme Court of Appeals: *Journal of the Delegates 1783*, 58–59; Archibald Henderson, "Dr. Thomas Walker and the Loyal Company of Virginia," American Antiquarian Society, *Proceedings*, new series, XLI (1931), 115.

"secret Surveys": Richard Henderson to John Williams, Sept. 13, 1779, John Williams Papers, NcD.

"a considerable" . . . "cultivation": George Washington to Patrick Henry, June 24, 1785, *Papers of Washington: Confederation*, ed. Abbot *et al.*, III, 80.

289 "no money": David Jameson to Thomas Nelson, Nov. 26, 1783, David Jameson to David Meade, April 1784, Dismal Swamp Land Company Records, NcD; David Jameson to

PAGE

Francis Walker, Nov. 2, 1791, Thomas Walker Papers, William Cabell Rives Papers, Box 162, DLC.

289 "in a . . . Bankruptcy": David Jameson to David Meade, April 1784, Dismal Swamp Land Company Records, NcD.

John Page: Advertisement, *Virginia Gazette, or, the American Advertiser* (Richmond), Sept. 21, 1782.

Thomas Newton, Jr.: David Jameson to Thomas Walker, June 22, 1783, Dismal Swamp Land Company Records, NcD; advertisement, *Virginia Gazette, or, the American Advertiser*, April 5, 1783.

Fielding Lewis, Jr.: Fielding Lewis, Jr., to George Washington, Feb. 22, 1784, George Washington to Fielding Lewis, Jr., Feb. 27, 1784, *Papers of Washington: Confederation*, ed. Abbot *et al.*, I, 145–146, 161–162.

for 4,800 acres: Willard Rouse Jillson, *Old Kentucky Entries and Deeds* (Louisville, 1926), 224.

"in . . . taste": Entry of April 9, 1773, Josiah Quincy, "Journal," Massachusetts Historical Society, *Proceedings*, 3d ser., XLIX (1915–16), 465; Marcus Whiffen, *The Eighteenth-Century Houses of Williamsburg*, rev. ed. (Williamsburg, 1984), 190–194; Mary A. Stephenson, "Peyton Randolph House Historical Report," rev. Jane Carson, ViWC.

290 Hornsby did not respond: Robert Andrews to David Jameson, Dec. 27, 1783, Dismal Swamp Land Company Records, NcD.

William Nelson, Jr.: William Nelson, Jr., to William Short, March 26, 1785, Feb. 20, 1786, William Short Papers, DLC; Thomas Jefferson to Samuel Henley, Nov. 27, 1785, *The Papers of Thomas Jefferson*, ed. Julian P. Boyd *et al.* (Princeton, 1950–), IX, 66; Wilmer L. Hall *et al.*, eds., *Journals of the Council of the State of Virginia*, 2d ed. (Richmond, 1969–82), III, 145.

"great . . . down": *New-Lloyd's List*, April 30, 1784; Robert Beverley to Samuel Gist, April 14, 1784, Robert Beverley Letterbook, DLC; Hugh James to Tench Coxe, April 20, 1784, Tench Coxe Papers, PHi.

Tom and Lewis: Jacob Collee to David Jameson, Dec. 26, 1784, David Jameson to Jacob Collee, Dec. 30, 1784, Dismal Swamp Land Company Records, NcD.

"surveyors" . . . "directions": David Jameson to Samuel Gist, Dec. 23, 1783, Claim of Samuel Gist, American Loyalist Claims, AO 13/30, PRO.

Jameson put the question: David Jameson to Samuel Gist, Dec. 23, 1783, Nov. 3, 1784, *ibid.*; David Jameson to Thomas Walker, July 15, 1784, Dismal Swamp Land Company Records, NcD.

291 "hiring" . . . "chance": David Jameson to William Nelson, Jr., Jan. 4, 1785, Dismal Swamp Land Company Records, NcD.

House of Delegates: Peter Lyons, Note on Act of October 1784, Claim of Samuel Gist, American Loyalist Claims, AO 13/30, PRO.

"Ship" . . . "confidence": *Virginia Gazette, or, the American Advertiser*, Sept. 11, 1784.

Gist testified: Testimony of Samuel Gist, June 14, 1784, Claim of Thomas Macknight, photocopy in English Records, Box ER-8, folder 20, Nc-Ar.

292 Patrick Henry wrote: Patrick Henry to Adam Stephen, June 10, 1779, in Mary Selden Kennedy, *Seldens of Virginia and Allied Families* (New York, 1911), 26–27; Patrick Henry

PAGE

to William Nelson, Jr., July 4, 1784, William Nelson Letters, ViU; William Nelson, Jr., to Patrick Henry, July 14, 1784, Patrick Henry and Family Collection, DLC; Patrick Henry to [?], May 22, 1784, in Charles Hamilton, *American Autographs* (Norman, 1983), I, 325; [John Nicholas, Jr.], "Decius," Nos. V, XII, *Virginia Independent Chronicle* (Richmond), Jan. 28, Mar. 11, 1789; Patrick Henry to George Washington, June 10, 1785, *Papers of Washington: Confederation*, ed. Abbot *et al.*, III, 48–49; Jackson T. Main, "The One Hundred," *WMQ*, 3d ser., XI (July 1954), 377; Norman K. Risjord, *Chesapeake Politics: 1781–1800* (New York, 1978), 245–247.

"a low" . . . "Canal": Andrew Kidd to William Vaughan, March 3, 1805, John Harvie to Thomas Jefferson, May 15, 1798, William Short Papers, DLC; Patrick Henry, advertisement, *Virginia Gazette and General Advertiser* (Richmond), Jan. 12, 1791.

293 to meet in Richmond: Thomas Walker, advertisement, *Virginia Gazette, or, the American Advertiser*, Oct. 2, 1784; David Jameson to Samuel Gist, Nov. 3, 1784, Claim of Samuel Gist, American Loyalist Claims, AO 13/30, PRO.

"to make . . . assembly)": David Jameson to William Nelson, Jr., Jan. 4, 1785, Dismal Swamp Land Company Records, NcD.

"the Lebanon . . . higher": Patrick Henry to George Washington, June 10, 1785, *Papers of Washington: Confederation*, ed. Abbot *et al.*, III, 48.

Hugh Williamson studied: Hugh Williamson to Thomas Ruston, Nov. 2, 1784, March 2, 1785, Hugh Williamson to Thomas Jefferson, Dec. 11, 1784, Hugh Williamson to George Washington, March 24, 1784, Paul H. Smith *et al.*, eds., *Letters of Delegates to Congress: 1774–1789* (Washington, 1976–98), XXII, 7–8, 240, 63–64, XXI, 455–457; George Washington to Hugh Williamson, March 31, 1784, *Papers of Washington: Confederation*, ed. Abbot *et al.*, I, 244–247. See also Louis W. Potts, "Hugh Williamson: The Poor Man's Franklin and the National Domain," *NCHR*, LXIV (Oct. 1987), 371–393.

"declining" . . . "ruin": George Washington to William Crawford, June 9, 1781, *The Writings of George Washington*, ed. John C. Fitzpatrick (Washington, 1931–40), XXII, 194.

showed that two-thirds: Willard F. Bliss, "The Rise of Tenancy in Virginia," *VMHB*, LVIII (Oct. 1950), 433; George Washington to Battaile Muse, Nov. 3, 1784, *Papers of Washington: Confederation*, ed. Abbot *et al.*, II, 117.

294 the Seceders: Entries of Sept. 8–Oct. 2, 1784, *Diaries of Washington*, ed. Jackson and Twohig, IV, 14–56; *Papers of Washington: Confederation*, ed. Abbot *et al.*, II, 338–356; Burton Alva Konkle, *The Life and Times of Thomas Smith, 1745–1809* (Philadelphia, 1904), 173–186; Rick Willard Sturdevant, "Quest for Eden: George Washington's Frontier Land Interests" (Ph.D. diss., University of California, Santa Barbara, 1982), 150–170.

"to take . . . Speculators": Entry of Oct. 4, 1784, *Diaries of Washington*, ed. Jackson and Twohig, IV, 57–58.

"The more" . . . "Markets": *Ibid.*, 58–68. See also Samuel Holten to Aaron Wood, Sept. 11, 1783, Smith *et al.*, eds., *Letters of Delegates*, XX, 650.

295 "much . . . flow": Thomas Jefferson to James Madison, Feb. 20, 1784, *Papers of Jefferson*, ed. Boyd *et al.*, VI, 548.

"draw" . . . "Scheme": George Washington to Jacob Read, Nov. 3, 1784, *Papers of Washington: Confederation*, ed. Abbot *et al.*, II, 121–122.

"The General . . . surmount": Entry of Nov. 16, 1785, *Quebec to Carolina in 1785–1786:*

Being the Travel Diary and Observations of Robert Hunter, Jr., A Young Merchant of London, ed. Louis B. Wright and Marion Tinling (San Marino, 1943), 193.

295 "Lurking" . . . "Villain": George Johnston to George Washington, Jan. 8, 1760, George Washington to Jonathan Boucher, May 5, 1772, *Papers of Washington: Colonial,* ed. Abbot *et al.,* VI, 382–383, IX, 40–41.

great canals of Europe: Robert Carter Nicholas to John Norton, April 7, 1772, John Norton & Son Papers, ViWC.

"Plans" . . . "Rivers": Purdie and Dixon's *Virginia Gazette* (Williamsburg), May 27, 1773. Gist and Ballendine: Samuel Gist to John Tabb, April 12–May 4, 1774, *Tabb's Admr.* v. *Gist et al.,* 1829, USCCVD(EC), Vi; List of Debts in London, No. 1, Claim of Samuel Gist, American Loyalist Claims AO 13/30, PRO; Purdie and Dixon's *Virginia Gazette,* July 7, 1774; [Fairfax Harrison], *Landmarks of Old Prince William: A Study of Origins in Northern Virginia* (Richmond, 1924), II, 540.

"fully . . . river": *Pennsylvania Gazette* (Philadelphia), Sept. 14, 1774; Pamela C. Copeland and Richard K. MacMaster, *The Five George Masons: Patriots and Planters of Virginia and Maryland* (Charlottesville, 1975), 120–121.

296 James River canal: Pinkney's *Virginia Gazette,* Oct. 26, 1775; Kathleen Bruce, *Virginia Iron Manufacture in the Slave Era* (New York, 1931), 42–50; [Harrison], *Landmarks,* II, 435–436; Copeland and MacMaster, *Five George Masons,* 202–203.

Rumsey in Richmond: James Rumsey to George Washington, March 10, 1785, *Papers of Washington: Confederation,* ed. Abbot *et al.,* II, 427; Hugh Williamson to Thomas Jefferson, Dec. 11, 1784, James Madison to Thomas Jefferson, Jan. 9, 1785, *Papers of Jefferson,* ed. Boyd *et al.,* VII, 569, 592–593; James Rumsey, *A Short Treatise on the Application of Steam* (Philadelphia, 1788), 4–5.

"next . . . impracticable": Entry of Sept. 6, 1784, *Diaries of Washington,* ed. Jackson and Twohig, IV, 9–10; George Washington to Hugh Williamson, March 15, 1785, *Papers of Washington: Confederation,* ed. Abbot *et al.,* II, 439–440.

"no doubt" . . . "navigation": Certificate, Sept. 4, 1784, *Papers of Washington: Confederation,* ed. Abbot *et al.,* II, 69.

"I . . . Unbelievers": James Rumsey to George Washington, Oct. 19, 1784, *ibid.,* 101; Alexander Fitzroy, *The Discovery, Purchase, and Settlement of the Country of Kentuckie, in North America* (London, 1786), 14–15, reprinted in Willard Rouse Jillson, *The Kentuckie Country* (Washington, 1931), 42–43.

"to . . . perfection": James Rumsey to George Washington, March 10, 1785, *Papers of Washington: Confederation,* ed. Abbot *et al.,* II, 427–428.

"the pelting" . . . "reputation": Rumsey, *Short Treatise,* 5–6; Ella May Turner, *James Rumsey: Pioneer in Steam Navigation* (Scottdale, 1930), chap. 2; Frank D. Prager, Introduction, *The Autobiography of John Fitch* (Philadelphia, 1976), 7–11; George Washington to Thomas Johnson, Nov. 22, 1787, *Papers of Washington: Confederation,* ed. Abbot *et al.,* V, 448–449.

297 "Opening . . . here": William Nelson, Jr., to William Short, Jan. 11, 1785, William Short Papers, DLC.

A visitor: Elkanah Watson, *Men and Times of the Revolution; or, Memoirs of Elkanah Watson,* ed. Winslow C. Watson (New York, 1856), 243–244.

PAGE

"proper Credentials": Entry of July 1, 1785, *Diaries of Washington*, ed. Jackson and Twohig, IV, 157–158.

"I ... circumstances": George Washington to James Rumsey, July 2, 1785, *Papers of Washington: Confederation*, ed. Abbot *et al.*, III, 99.

"upwards ... Rocks &c.": Archibald Stuart to Thomas Jefferson, Oct. 17, 1785, *Papers of Jefferson*, ed. Boyd *et al.*, VIII, 644; Turner, *James Rumsey*, chap. 3.

Canal companies: Corra Bacon-Foster, *Early Chapters in the Development of the Potomac Route to the West* (Washington, 1912); Wayland Fuller Dunaway, *History of the James River and Kanawha Company* (New York, 1922).

"the nation ... execution": Thomas Twining, *Travels in America 100 Years Ago* (New York, 1893), 77.

"this Eldorado": David Meade to Mary Grymes Randolph Meade, Oct. 20, 1796, William Bolling Papers, NcD.

"the Richest ... World": Lawrence Butler to Anna F. Cradock, Nov. 29, 1786, "Letters from Lawrence Butler," *VMHB*, XL (Oct. 1932), 362.

even more migrants: Malcolm J. Rohrbough, *The Trans-Appalachian Frontier: People, Societies, and Institutions, 1775–1850* (New York, 1978), 39; John D. Barnhart, *Valley of Democracy: The Frontier versus the Plantation in the Ohio Valley, 1775–1818* (Bloomington, 1953), 35–41.

"they ... provinces": Johann David Schoepf, *Travels in the Confederation*, trans. Alfred J. Morrison (New York, 1968 [orig. publ. Philadelphia, 1911]), II, 43.

"scarcely ... found": John Filson, *The Discovery, Settlement and Present State of Kentucke* (New York, 1962 [orig. publ. Wilmington, 1784]), 16.

"these ... patronise": John Filson to George Washington, Nov. 30, 1784, Papers of George Washington, DLC; John Filson to George Washington, Dec. 4, 1784, *Papers of Washington: Confederation*, ed. Abbot *et al.*, II, 168–169; Daniel Blake Smith, " 'This Idea in Heaven': Image and Reality on the Kentucky Frontier," in Craig Thompson Friend, ed., *The Buzzel About Kentuck: Settling the Promised Land* (Lexington, 1999), 77–98; Lester H. Cohen, "Eden's Constitution: The Paradisiacal Dream and Enlightenment Values in Late Eighteenth-Century Literature of the American Frontier," *Prospects*, III (1977), 90–91; Robert Lawson-Peebles, *Landscape and Written Expression in Revolutionary America: The World Turned Upside Down* (Cambridge, 1988), 50–51.

298 "Ask ... land": Moses Austin, "A Memorandum of M. Austin's Journey," *AHR*, V (April 1900), 525; Hazel Dicken-Garcia, *To Western Woods: The Breckinridge Family Moves to Kentucky in 1793* (Rutherford, 1991), chap. 1.

"a new ... Spontaneously": John Joyce to Robert Dickson, March 24, 1785, *VMHB*, XXIII (Oct. 1915), 413.

open to suspicion: Lowell H. Harrison, *Kentucky's Road to Statehood* (Lexington, 1992), 10–12; Patricia Watlington, *The Partisan Spirit: Kentucky Politics, 1779–1792* (Chapel Hill, 1973), 16–18; François Dupont to Etienne Clavière, Jan. 10, 1789, "A Letter from Petersburg, Virginia," ed. Charles T. Nall, *VMHB*, LXXXII (April 1974), 147.

"Here ... reputation": Caleb Wallace to James Madison, July 12, 1785, *The Papers of James Madison*, ed. William T. Hutchinson and William M. E. Rachal *et al.* (Chicago and Charlottesville, 1962–), VIII, 321.

298 Adam Smith: Adam Smith, *An Inquiry into the Nature and Causes of the Wealth of Nations,* 5th ed. (Edinburgh, 1811 [orig. publ. 1776]), I, 124–127, II, 199. Compare Etienne Clavière, Letter V, May 22, 1788, in J. P. Brissot de Warville, *New Travels in the United States of America, 1788,* trans. Mara Soceanu Vamos and Durand Echeverria (Cambridge, 1964), 47.

"opinion . . . credit": James Mercer, advertisement, *Virginia Gazette, or, the American Advertiser,* May 14, 1785.

"abused" . . . Promise' ": Thomas Ashe, *Travels in America, Performed in the Year 1806* (London, 1809), 152.

"busied . . . Lands": Stevens Thomson Mason to Leven Powell, Nov. 30, 1783, Leven Powell Papers, ViW.

Congress accepted the cession: Merrill Jensen, *The New Nation: A History of the United States During the Confederation, 1781–1789* (New York, 1965 [orig. publ. 1950]), 350–352; Peter S. Onuf, *The Origins of the Federal Republic: Jurisdictional Controversies in the United States, 1775–1787* (Philadelphia, 1983), chap. 4; John E. Selby, *The Revolution in Virginia, 1775–1783* (Williamsburg, 1988), 231–232.

299 it appointed commissioners: William Waller Hening, ed., *The Statutes at Large: Being a Collection of All the Laws of Virginia* (Richmond, Philadelphia, and New York, 1809–23), VIII, 570.

known as "Czar": Katherine Fontaine Syer, "The County of Princess Anne, 1691–1957," in Rogers Dey Whichard, *The History of Lower Tidewater Virginia* (New York, 1959), II, 79–80.

committee report: John Pendleton Kennedy, ed., *Journals of the House of Burgesses of Virginia, 1773–1776* (Richmond, 1905), 246, 270.

a bill: *Journal of the Delegates 1783,* 48, 104, 106.

"equal . . . troublesome": Hugh Williamson to George Washington, March 24, 1784, Smith *et al.,* eds., *Letters of Delegates,* XXI, 455.

feasible and desirable: George Washington to Hugh Williamson, March 31, 1784, *Papers of Washington: Confederation,* ed. Abbot *et al.,* I, 244–247.

"but . . . in it": David Jameson to Thomas Walker, July 15, 1784, Dismal Swamp Land Company Records, NcD.

declined to serve: Hall *et al.,* eds., *Journals of the Council,* III, 409, 415, 464, 515.

"that" . . . "commands": David Meade to Patrick Henry, Aug. 1785, Executive Papers, Gov. Patrick Henry, Vi.

"very cheerfully": Robert Andrews to Patrick Henry, March 9, 178[5], Patrick Henry and Family Collection, DLC. See also William P. Palmer *et al.,* eds., *Calendar of Virginia State Papers* (Richmond, 1875–93), IV, 15.

300 through the swamp: Patrick Henry to George Washington, June 10, 1785, *Papers of Washington: Confederation,* ed. Abbot *et al.,* III, 49.

"a most . . . gale": *Annual Register,* XXVIII (1786), Chronicle, 195; Donald G. Shomette, *Shipwrecks on the Chesapeake* (Centreville, 1982), 76.

"could . . . Ground": Patrick Henry to George Washington, Nov. 11, 1785, *Papers of Washington: Confederation,* ed. Abbot *et al.,* III, 353.

"the great . . . Difficulties": Robert Andrews and David Meade to Benjamin Harrison, Oct. 15, 1785, *ibid.*, 354n.2.

deferred legislation: *Journal of the House of Delegates of Virginia, [1785, October Session]* [Richmond, 1786], 38, 147–148.

"laid" . . . "trade": Petition of Walter Hopkins *et al.*, June 12, 1783, Legislative Petitions, Norfolk County, Vi.

"the canal . . . lands": William Ronald *et al.*, advertisement, *Virginia Gazette, or, the American Advertiser,* April 16, 1785; William Ronald to Patrick Henry, June 10, 1785, Palmer *et al.*, eds., *Calendar of Virginia State Papers,* IV, 33.

"I" . . . "operations": Hugh Williamson to Thomas Jefferson, Dec. 11, 1784, Thomas Jefferson to Hugh Williamson, Feb. 6, 1785, *Papers of Jefferson,* ed. Boyd *et al.*, VII, 569, 642.

"better" . . . "Scheme?": George Washington to Thomas Jefferson, Feb. 25, 1785, *Papers of Washington: Confederation,* ed. Abbot *et al.*, II, 380.

"the conveniences . . . therefrom": George Washington to James Madison, Nov. 30, 1785, *ibid.*, III, 420.

301 more than two feet: George Washington to Hugh Williamson, March 31, 1784, *ibid.*, I, 246.

surface of peat: Robert Q. Oaks, Jr., and Donald R. Whitehead, "Geologic Setting and Origin of the Dismal Swamp," in Paul W. Kirk, ed., *The Great Dismal Swamp* (Charlottesville, 1979), 4–7.

only one lock: Hugh Williamson to Thomas Jefferson, Dec. 11, 1784, *Papers of Jefferson,* ed. Boyd *et al.*, VII, 569; entry of Dec. 28, 1774, *Jefferson's Memorandum Books,* ed. James A. Bear, Jr., and Lucia C. Stanton (Princeton, 1997), I, 367.

"inconsiderable": Hugh Williamson to George Washington, March 24, 1784, Smith *et al.*, eds., *Letters of Delegates,* XXI, 457.

one lock at each end: Patrick Henry to George Washington, Nov. 11, 1785, George Washington to Patrick Henry, Nov. 30, 1785, *Papers of Washington: Confederation,* ed. Abbot *et al.*, II, 353–354, 417–418, 419n.2.

eight locks: H. M. Robinson to William Short, May 15, 1811, William Short Papers, DLC; Alexander Crosby Brown, "The Dismal Swamp Canal," *AN,* V (1945), 207, 213.

"So little . . . Morass": Report by Luke Wheeler *et al.*, [ca. 1816], Dismal Swamp Canal Company, Canal Companies, Internal Improvement Companies, Board of Public Works, Vi.

riders brought: George Weedon to John F. Mercer, March 18, 1783, Gaillard Hunt, ed., *Fragments of Revolutionary History* (Brooklyn, 1892), 123; David Buchanan to Buchanan & Hunter, March 19, 1784, *Stirling v. Hunter & Buchanan,* C 114/117, PRO.

Prices were high: Coxe & Frazier to Herries & Co., Oct. 26, 1784, Coxe & Frazier Letter Book, Tench Coxe Papers, PHi; Leighton Wood to Benjamin Harrison, May 26, 1784, Palmer *et al.*, eds., *Calendar of Virginia State Papers,* III, 589.

"every" . . . "coast": Reports from the Committee on Illicit Practices, Dec. 24, 1783, *Reports from Committees of the House of Commons . . . Not Inserted in the Journals* ([London], 1803–20), XI, 228–229, 265; entry of Nov. 10, 1783, "Extracts from the Old Books of the Custom-House of Irvine," in *Topographical Account of the District of Cunningham, Ayrshire*

(Glasgow, 1858), appendix, p. 234; William Gilpin, *Memoirs of Josias Rogers, Esq.* (London, 1808), 61–62; Joshua Johnson to Wallace & Muir, Oct. 27, 1786, Joshua Johnson Letter-book, Peter Force Collection, Series 8D, DLC; Robert Burns to James Burness, June 21, 1783, Robert Burns to John Moore, Aug. 2, 1787, *The Letters of Robert Burns*, ed. J. De-Lancey Ferguson and G. Ross Roy, 2d ed. (Oxford, 1985), I, 19, 140. Reports on smuggling in 1782 and 1783 are in the Shelburne Papers, MiU-C; some of these are printed in Arthur Lyon Cross, ed., *Eighteenth Century Documents Relating to the Royal Forests, the Sheriffs and Smuggling* (New York, 1928), 237–244, 264–267, 289–321.

301 "Strangers": Margaret Parker to James Parker, July 27, 1783, Parker Papers, Liverpool Public Library; entries of June 1–2, 1785, Diary, *The Autobiographies of Noah Webster*, ed. Richard M. Rollins (Columbia, 1989), 213, 346–347.

"modern . . . shed": James Buchanan to Neil Jamieson, Aug. 20, 1783, Neil Jamieson Papers, DLC.

302 "Verry" . . . "America": Hugh Wallace to Nicholas Low, Feb. 2, 1783, Nicholas Low Papers, DLC.

Watson, Ewer, Hake: Great Britain, Board of Trade, Committee of Council Appointed for the Consideration of All Matters Relating to Trade and Foreign Plantations, Vol. I, ff. 72–73, 136–137, DLC; Daniel Hailes to Marquess of Carmarthen, Jan. 20, 1785, Oscar Browning, ed., *Despatches from Paris*, Camden Society, 3d ser., XVI, XIX (1909–10), I, 38–39; P. K. O'Brien and S. L. Engerman, "Exports and the Growth of the British Economy from the Glorious Revolution to the Peace of Amiens," in Barbara L. Solow, ed., *Slavery and the Rise of the Atlantic System* (Cambridge, 1991), 177–209; Peter P. Hill, *French Perceptions of the Early American Republic, 1783–1792* (Philadelphia, 1988), chap. 3; T. M. Devine, *The Tobacco Lords: A Study of the Tobacco Merchants of Glasgow and Their Trading Activities, c. 1740–90* (Edinburgh, 1975), 163–165; W. A. Low, "Merchant and Planter Relations in Post-Revolutionary Virginia, 1783–1789," *VMHB*, LXI (July 1953), 308–318. See also Chevalier de la Luzerne to Marquis de Castries, Jan. 25, 1781, *Report on Canadian Archives: 1913* (Ottawa, 1914), 173–174.

Virginians' specie: Risjord, *Chesapeake Politics*, 160–176; Louis Maganzin, "Economic Depression in Maryland and Virginia, 1783–1787" (Ph.D. diss., Georgetown University, 1967), 27–36; Myra L. Rich, "Speculations on the Significance of Debt: Virginia, 1781–1789," *VMHB*, LXXVI (July 1968), 301–317; Albert Feavearyear, *The Pound Sterling: A History of English Money*, 2d ed., rev. E. Victor Morgan (Oxford, 1963), 177; Silas Deane to Thomas Munford, Jan. 15–Feb. 1784, Silas Deane Papers, DLC; James Monroe to Benjamin Harrison, March 26, 1784, Smith *et al.*, eds., *Letters of Delegates*, XXI, 460–461; Chevalier de la Luzerne to Comte de Vergennes, Nov. 25, 1781, *Report on Canadian Archives: 1913*, 217.

marked up goods: James Taylor to Samuel Gist, Oct. 1, 1783, *Samuel Gist v. Taylor & Co.*, 1797, USCCVD(EC), Vi; Francis Eppes to Thomas Jefferson, Dec. 22, 1783, *Papers of Jefferson*, ed. Boyd *et al.*, VI, 416.

"more . . . come": Duncan Hunter to Archibald Mackean, July 2, 1784, *Stirling v. Hunter & Buchanan*, C 114/117, PRO; Phineas Bond to Duke of Leeds, Aug. 15, 1789, "Letters of Phineas Bond," ed. J. Franklin Jameson, *Annual Report of the American Historical Association for the Year 1896* (Washington, 1897), I, 608–614.

PAGE

Macaulay in New York: Joseph Taylor to Samuel Rogers, Jan. 10, 1778, Joseph Taylor Letterbook, Lovering-Taylor Family Papers, DLC; Samuel Rogers to William Taylor, Feb. 24, Mar. 16–18, 1778, Family Correspondence, *ibid.*

volume of imports: Clarence L. Ver Steeg, *Robert Morris: Revolutionary Financier* (Philadelphia, 1954), 50–51, 53; Richard Buel, Jr., *Dear Liberty: Connecticut's Mobilization for the Revolutionary War* (Middletown, 1980), 260–262, 267–272; Barrent Hardwick to William Livingston, June 13, 1782, in Richard J. Koke, ed., "War, Profit, and Privateers Along the New Jersey Coast," *New-York Historical Society Quarterly*, XLI (July 1957), 331.

to get "home": Entry of March 3, 1783, "Journal of Alexander Macaulay," *WMQ*, 1st ser., XI (Jan. 1903), 189–190.

"may . . . Juncture": Alexander Macaulay to Benjamin Harrison, March 24, 1783, Executive Papers, Gov. Benjamin Harrison, Vi.

"I . . . Philosopher": Alexander Macaulay to Stephen Collins, Sept. 27, 1783, Stephen Collins & Son Papers, DLC.

settling at York Town: Alexander Macaulay to Francis Jerdone, Nov. 24, 1784, Jerdone Family Papers, ViW.

303 "a plain . . . well": Alexander Donald to Francis Jerdone, Dec. 6, 1784, Samuel Gist to Francis Jerdone, Aug. 17, 1784, *ibid.*; William Anderson to Thomas Massie, Nov. 20, 1784, Massie Family Papers, ViRHi.

"a proper" . . . "Tinsell": Patrick Parker to James Parker, Aug. 16, 1791, Parker Papers, Liverpool Public Library.

"Feathers . . . &c.": Charles Yates to James Hunter, July 13, 1786, Hunter-Garnett Collection, ViU; Maganzin, "Economic Depression," 19–25, 35–38, 93; Jensen, *New Nation*, 187.

"British . . . deceptions": *Virginia Gazette, or, the American Advertiser,* Nov. 1, 1783; Cathy D. Matson and Peter S. Onuf, *A Union of Interests: Political and Economic Thought in Revolutionary America* (Lawrence, 1990), 39.

"Extravagance . . . Europe": Archibald Stuart to Thomas Jefferson, Oct. 17, 1785, *Papers of Jefferson*, ed. Boyd *et al.*, VIII, 645; John Thurman, Jr., to William Smith, Sept. 8, 1785, "Extracts from the Letter Books of John Thurman, Junior," *Historical Magazine*, 2d ser., IV (Dec. 1868), 294–295; Charles R. Ritcheson, *Aftermath of Revolution: British Policy Toward the United States, 1783–1795* (Dallas, 1969), chap. 2.

"squanders . . . living": William Glassell to John Glassell, Dec. 24, 1786, John George Campbell, Duke of Argyll, ed., *Intimate Society Letters of the Eighteenth Century* (London, [1910]), II, 485.

London warehouses: Joshua Johnson to Wallace & Muir, Oct. 17, 1785, Joshua Johnson Letterbook, Peter Force Collection, Series 8D, DLC.

price of tobacco: Joshua Johnson to Wallace & Muir, Feb. 14, 1786, *ibid.*; Collector of Customs to Board of Commissioners, July 10, 1784, *Customs Letter-books of the Port of Liverpool, 1711–1813*, ed. Rupert C. Jarvis (Manchester, 1954), 118; Maganzin, "Economic Depression," 75.

304 flow of goods, peace: Julian Hoppit, *Risk and Failure in English Business, 1700–1800* (Cambridge, 1987), 98–99; Jonathan Jackson to Thompson & Gordon, Dec. 30, 1784, in Kenneth Wiggins Porter, *The Jacksons and the Lees: Two Generations of Massachusetts Merchants, 1765–1844* (Cambridge, 1937), I, 370.

PAGE

304 Robert Morris: Alan Schaffer, "Virginia's Critical Period," in Darrett B. Rutman, ed., *The Old Dominion: Essays for Thomas Perkins Abernethy* (Charlottesville, 1964), 158–168; Jensen, *New Nation*, 202–203; Rich, "Speculations," *VMHB*, LXXVI (July 1968), 308–309.

"I . . . Friend": Joshua Johnson to Thomas Johnson, June 5, 1787, Joshua Johnson Letterbook, Peter Force Collection, Series 8D, DLC; Joseph Fenwick to Ignatius Fenwick, May 31, 1787, "The Tobacco Trade with France: Letters of Joseph Fenwick," ed. Richard K. MacMaster, *MHM*, LX (1965), 34.

"very . . . follow": Harrison, Ansley & Co. to Stephen Collins, July 9–Aug. 9, 1784, Stephen Collins & Son Papers, DLC.

"tumbling . . . day": Joshua Johnson to Wallace & Muir, Sept. 25, 1785, Joshua Johnson Letterbook, Peter Force Collection, Series 8D, DLC; Hamilton Andrews Hill, "The Trade, Commerce, and Navigation of Boston, 1780–1800," in Justin Winsor, ed., *The Memorial History of Boston* (Boston, 1880–81), IV, 200; Johan Alstroemer to Joseph Banks, May 28, 1786, *The Banks Letters*, ed. Warren R. Dawson (London, 1958), 17.

James Dunlop: Hoppit, *Risk and Failure*, 99; Joshua Johnson to Wallace & Muir, Nov. 14, 1785, Joshua Johnson Letterbook, Peter Force Collection, Series 8D, DLC.

305 "What . . . him": Philip L. Grymes to Edmund Randolph, April 10, 1785, BR Box 6(11), CSmH.

auctioned his property: Advertisement, *Virginia Gazette, or, the American Advertiser*, March 12, 1785.

"interfering" . . . "clamour": Peter Lyons to Samuel Gist, March 4, 1786, Claim of Samuel Gist, American Loyalist Claims, AO 13/30, PRO.

Severn Eyre, Jr.: Entry of Aug. 15, 1785, Journal of Severn Eyre, ViRHi. On Nelson, see also Arthur Lee to James Monroe, Aug. 23, 1783, Smith *et al.*, eds., *Letters of Delegates*, XX, 581; Thomas Nelson, Jr., to Horatio Gates, Feb. 19, 1786, William Nelson, Jr., to [?], Jan. 7, 1790, Emmet Collection, NN.

306 "Every . . . Money": Entry of Dec. 25, 1784, *The Diary and Selected Papers of Chief Justice William Smith, 1784–1793*, ed. L. F. S. Upton (Toronto, 1963–65), I, 175. On expense and perils, see [John] Trusler, *The London Adviser and Guide* (London, 1786); George Crabbe to Edmund Burke, June 26, 1781, *Selected Letters and Journals of George Crabbe*, ed. Thomas C. Faulkner (Oxford, 1985), 8–17.

play *Douglas*: Paul Ranger, "*Terror and Pity reign in every Breast*": Gothic Drama in the London Patent Theatres, 1750–1820 (London, 1991), 112–115.

"saw . . . die": Entries of Sept. 25, Oct. 9, 1785, Journal of Severn Eyre, ViRHi; Sarah Siddons to Thomas Sedgwick Whalley, Sept. 28, 1785, *Journals and Correspondence of Thomas Sedgwick Whalley*, ed. Hill Wickham (London, 1863), I, 445.

"soul-harrowing": Anne Seward to [?], [ca. Oct. 9, 1785], quoted in Percy Fitzgerald, *The Kembles* (London, [1871]), I, 121. See also Jonathan Bate, "The Romantic Stage," in Jonathan Bate and Russell Jackson, eds., *Shakespeare: An Illustrated Stage History* (Oxford, 1996), 94–95.

"the Empress of Tragedy": William Mason to Earl Harcourt, June 2, 1786, *The Harcourt Papers*, ed. Edward William Harcourt (Oxford, [1880–1905]), VII, 118; Sarah Napier to Susan O'Brien, March 25, 1783, Mary Fox-Strangways, Countess of Ilchester, and Giles

Fox-Strangways (Lord Stavordale), eds., *The Life and Letters of Lady Sarah Lennox* (London, 1902), II, 35.

The king told her: Sarah Siddons, *The Reminiscences of Sarah Kemble Siddons, 1773–1785*, ed. William Van Lennep (Cambridge, 1942), 13.

"les grands . . . Clairon": Pierre Nicolas Chantreau, *Voyage dans les trois royaumes d'Angleterre, d'Écosse et d'Irlande, fait en 1788 et 1789* (Paris, 1792), II, 76; François, Duc de La Rochefoucauld, *Innocent Espionage: The La Rochefoucauld Brothers' Tour of England in 1785*, trans. Norman Scarfe (Woodbridge, 1995), 205.

Richard Cumberland: Richard Cumberland to Lord George Germain, Dec. 3, 1784, *The Letters of Richard Cumberland*, ed. Richard J. Dircks (New York, 1988), 240; Richard Cumberland, *Memoirs of Richard Cumberland*, ed. Henry Flanders (Philadelphia, 1856 [orig. publ. London, 1807]), 312; [John Genest], *Some Account of the English Stage from the Restoration in 1660 to 1830* (Bath, 1832), VI, 333–334.

"It . . . itself": Entry of Dec. 4, 1784, *Diary of William Smith*, ed. Upton, I, 170; entry of Dec. 11, 1784, Marc de Bombelles, *Journal de voyage en Grande Bretagne et en Irlande, 1784*, ed. Jacques Gury (Oxford, 1989), 303–304.

"a wretched" . . . "pleasure": Edward Gibbon to Dorothea Gibbon, Nov. 7, 1782, *The Letters of Edward Gibbon*, ed. J. E. Norton (New York, 1956), II, 315; Thomas Southerne, *Isabella; or, the Fatal Marriage*, adapted by David Garrick, in *The Plays of David Garrick*, ed. Harry William Pedicord and Frederick Louis Bergmann (Carbondale, 1980–82), VII, 1–50. Her mad scene: Quoted in John Alexander Kelly, *German Visitors to English Theaters in the Eighteenth Century* (Princeton, 1936), 95. See also Frederic Reynolds, *The Life and Times of Frederic Reynolds* (Philadelphia, 1826 [orig. publ. London, 1826]), I, 179; *Observations on Mrs. Siddons* (Dublin, 1784), 16–23; Linda Kelly, *The Kemble Era: John Philip Kemble, Sarah Siddons and the London Stage* (New York, 1980), 18–23; [Genest], *Some Account of the English Stage*, VI, 251–252; Paul Ranger, "I Was Present at the Representation," *Theatre Notebook*, XXXIX (1985), 18–25; Christopher Reid, "Burke's Tragic Muse: Sarah Siddons and the 'Feminization' of the *Reflections*," in Steven Blackmore, ed., *Burke and the French Revolution: Bicentennial Essays* (Athens, 1992), 1–27; Gillian Russell, "Burke's Dagger: Theatricality, Politics and Print Culture in the 1790s," *British Journal for Eighteenth-Century Studies*, XX (1997), 1–16.

307 "Five . . . stand it": Martha McTier to William Drennan, [ca. June 1785], *The Drennan Letters*, ed. D. A. Chart (Belfast, 1931), 31; entry of Oct. 21, 1782, *The Diary of Sylas Neville, 1767–1788*, ed. Basil Cozens-Hardy (London, 1950), 299; Stephen Jones, *Biographia Dramatica; or, a Companion to the Playhouse* (London, 1812), II, 334–335.

"Physicians . . . Isabella": Laetitia-Matilda Hawkins, *Memoirs, Anecdotes, Facts, and Opinions* (London, 1824), I, 136–137; Countess Spencer to Earl Harcourt, May 17, 1783, *Harcourt Papers*, ed. Harcourt, VIII, 84.

George Romney: Humphry Ward and W. Roberts, *Romney: A Biographical and Critical Essay* (London, 1904), I, 100–101, II, 142–143; William Hayley to Eliza Hayley, Jan. 1783, *Memoirs of the Life and Writings of William Hayley, Esq.*, ed. John Johnson (London, 1823), I, 288.

308 "Ascend . . . Muse": Siddons, *Reminiscences*, ed. Van Lennep, 17. Compare Robert R. Wark, *Sir Joshua Reynolds' Portrait of Mrs. Siddons as the Tragic Muse* (San Marino, 1965),

esp. 9–13; Richard Wendorf, *Sir Joshua Reynolds: The Painter in Society* (Cambridge, 1996), 153–156; Shearer West, *The Image of the Actor: Verbal and Visual Representation in the Age of Garrick and Kemble* (New York, 1991), 106–122. Edgar Wind, *Hume and the Heroic Portrait: Studies in Eighteenth-Century Imagery*, ed. Jaynie Anderson (Oxford, 1986), 42–46.

308 "most . . . pleasant": Sarah Siddons to Thomas Sedgwick Whalley, March 13, 1785, *Journals of Whalley*, ed. Wickham, I, 425; Donald J. Olsen, *Town Planning in London: The Eighteenth and Nineteenth Centuries*, 2d ed. (New Haven, 1982), chap. 4.

"forced" . . . "here": Siddons, *Reminiscences*, ed. Van Lennep, 20–21. See also Tate Wilkinson, *The Wandering Patentee; or, a History of the Yorkshire Theatres* (York, 1795), I, 253–256, III, 5–7; Sandra Richards, *The Rise of the English Actress* (New York, 1993), chap. 4; Michael R. Booth, "Sarah Siddons," in Michael R. Booth *et al.*, *Three Tragic Actresses: Siddons, Rachel, Ristori* (Cambridge, 1996), 10–65; John Brewer, *The Pleasures of the Imagination: English Culture in the Eighteenth Century* (New York, 1997), 346–348; Amanda Vickery, *The Gentleman's Daughter: Women's Lives in Georgian England* (New Haven, 1998), 231, 234; Judith Pascoe, *Romantic Theatricality: Gender, Poetry, and Spectatorship* (Ithaca, 1997), chap. 1; Pat Rogers, " 'Towering Beyond Her Sex': Stature and Sublimity in the Achievement of Sarah Siddons," in Mary Anne Schofield and Cecilia Macheski, eds., *Curtain Calls: British and American Women and the Theatre, 1660–1820* (Athens, 1991), 48–67; Leo Hughes, *The Drama's Patrons: A Study of the Eighteenth-Century London Audience* (Austin, 1971), 137–138.

"the beau" . . . "turn": Entry of March 17, 1785, "The MS Journal of Captain E. Thompson, R.N.," *Cornhill Magazine*, XVII (1867), 611. For a letter mentioning the Learned Pig and Sarah Siddons in the same paragraph, see James Thomas Flexner, *States Dyckman: American Loyalist* (Boston, 1980), 80.

arranged cards: Entry of March 10, 1785, *Diary of William Smith*, ed. Upton, I, 204–205; Peter Oliver to Elisha Hutchinson, Dec. 6, 1784, *The Diary and Letters of His Excellency Thomas Hutchinson*, ed. Peter Orlando Hutchinson (London, 1886), II, 416.

was a star: Abigail Adams [2d] to John Quincy Adams, July 4–11, 1785, *Adams Family Correspondence*, ed. L. H. Butterfield *et al.* (Cambridge, 1963–), VI, 220; Reginald Heber to Elizabeth Heber, April 9, 1785, *The Heber Letters, 1783–1832*, ed. R. H. Cholmondeley (London, 1950), 33; *New Review*, VII (April 1785), 289–290; *Gentleman's Magazine*, LV, Part 1 (June 1785), 413–414; Ricky Jay, *Learned Pigs and Fireproof Women* (New York, 1986), 9–13; Dennis Arundell, *The Story of Sadler's Wells* (New York, 1965), 37–38; Frederick Cameron Sillar and Ruth Mary Meyler, *The Symbolic Pig: An Anthology of Pigs in Literature and Art* (Edinburgh, 1961), 61–65; Joseph Strutt, *The Sports and Pastimes of the People of England*, ed. J. Charles Cox (London, [1903; orig. publ. 1801]), 183, 200, 235.

"really . . . prevented": John Tabb to Samuel Gist, Nov. 10, 1784, *Samuel Gist v. John Tabb, surviving partner of Richard Booker & Co.*, 1795, USCCVD(EC), Vi.

309 "our . . . trade": William Anderson & Co. to St. George Tucker, March 15, 1786, Tucker-Coleman Papers, ViW; William Anderson & Co. to John Cropper, March 15, 1786, John Cropper Papers, ViRHi; advertisements in *Virginia Gazette, or, the American Advertiser*, March 22, 1786, *Virginia Independent Chronicle*, Oct. 11, 1786.

Severn Eyre, Jr.: Entries of Jan. 8–Feb. 5, 1786, Journal of Eyre, ViRHi.

Venice Preserv'd: Entry of Feb. 11, 1786, *ibid.;* Act V, scene iv, ll. 27–29, Thomas Otway, *Venice Preserved,* ed. Malcolm Kelsall (Lincoln, 1969), 96; William Van Lennep *et al.,* eds., *The London Stage, 1660–1800* (Carbondale, 1965–68), V, Part II, 865–866; entry of Oct. 3, 1786, *Sophie in London, 1786: Being the Diary of Sophie v. la Roche,* trans. Clare Williams (London, 1933), 266; *Observations on Mrs. Siddons,* 1–8; Robert Bisset, *The History of the Negro Slave Trade* (London, 1805), I, 163–164; entry of Nov. 1782, Diary of John Crosier in A. F. J. Brown, *Essex People 1750–1900* (Chelmsford, 1972), 24; Thomas Davies, *Dramatic Miscellanies,* 2d ed. (London, 1785), III, 263–264; [Genest], *Some Account of the English Stage,* VI, 255–256; Aline Mackenzie Taylor, *Next to Shakespeare: Otway's Venice Preserv'd and The Orphan and Their History on the London Stage* (Durham, 1950), 187–200.

Cleone: Act III, scene ii, ll. 305–306, Robert Dodsley, *Cleone,* in *Bell's British Theatre* (London, 1791–97), V, 43; Van Lennep *et al.,* eds., *London Stage,* V, Part II, 933; James Trevenen to Elizabeth Trevenen, Dec. 4, 1786, in Christopher Lloyd and R. C. Anderson, eds., *A Memoir of James Trevenen* (London, 1959), 89; [Genest], *Some Account of the English Stage,* VI, 425; Davies, *Dramatic Miscellanies,* 2d ed., III, 264–265. See also Ranger, *Terror and Pity,* 95–98.

310 "going" . . . "hand": Joshua Johnson to Francis Charlton, Aug. 7, 1786, Joshua Johnson Letterbook, Peter Force Collection, Series 8D, DLC.

"old" . . . "up": Joshua Johnson to Wallace & Muir, June 7, 1786, *ibid.*

"lost . . . money": Joshua Johnson to Wallace & Muir, June 16, 1788, *ibid.*

"a spruce" . . . "particular": Entry of Sept. 29, 1787, Diary of Carter Braxton, Jr., duPont Library, Stratford, Virginia.

Shoolbred, Hennessy, and Saule: L. M. Cullen, *The Brandy Trade Under the Ancien Régime: Regional Specialisation in the Charente* (Cambridge, 1998), 255.

Lewis Littlepage: Lewis Littlepage to Elizabeth Lewis Littlepage, Dec. 29, 1787, in Nell Holladay Boand, *Lewis Littlepage* (Richmond, 1970), 109; Stanislas II Poniatowski to John Sinclair, Jan. 19, 1788, *The Correspondence of the Right Honourable Sir John Sinclair, Bart.* (London, 1831), I, 23.

younger Carter Braxton: Entries of Oct. 2, Nov. 6, 1787, Diary of Braxton, duPont Library, Stratford, Virginia; Anthony Amberg, *"The Gamester:* A Century of Performances," *Theatre Research International,* XV (1990), 105–125; Thomas Somerville, *My Own Life and Times, 1741–1814* (Edinburgh, 1861), 213; John Doran, *"Their Majesties' Servants,"* or *Annals of the English Stage,* 2d ed. (London, 1865), 352; Van Lennep *et al.,* eds., *London Stage,* V, Part II, 1016; Jones, *Biographia Dramatica,* II, 256–257. See also [Edward Moore], *The Gamester. A Tragedy* (London, 1753), reproduced in J. Paul Hunter, ed., *The Plays of Edward Moore* (New York, 1983).

311 a newspaper advertisement: *Virginia Gazette, or, the American Advertiser,* April 2, 1785; George Washington to Bushrod Washington, April 3, 1785, *Papers of Washington: Confederation,* ed. Abbot *et al.,* II, 474–475.

Dismal Plantation reports: John Driver to David Jameson, Aug. 26, 1786, Sept. 24, 1789, David Jameson to John Driver, Jan. 25, 1787, Dismal Swamp Land Company Records, NcD.

assembled in the Senate: Entries of May 2–3, 1785, *Diaries of Washington,* ed. Jackson and Twohig, IV, 132–134; minutes of Dismal Swamp Company meeting, May 2–3, 1785, enclosed in David Jameson to Samuel Gist, May 7, 1785, Claim of Samuel Gist, American Loyalist Claims, AO 13/30, PRO; Resolutions of the Dismal Swamp Company, May 2, 1785, *Papers of Washington: Confederation*, ed. Abbot *et al.*, II, 530–531. For "get quit of Negroes," see George Washington to Lund Washington, Aug. 15, 1778, *Writings of Washington*, ed. Fitzpatrick, XII, 328; Fritz Hirschfeld, *George Washington and Slavery: A Documentary Portrayal* (Columbia, 1997), 27–29.

312 "reclaiming," "invaluable": George Washington to Jean de Neufville, Sept. 8, 1785, *Papers of Washington: Confederation*, ed. Abbot *et al.*, III, 238–239.

"able labourers": George Washington to Robert Townsend Hooe, Feb. 21, 1786, George Washington to John Page, Oct. 3, 1785, *ibid.*, 567–568, 293–294.

313 owed more than £7,600: Wakelin Welch to James MacDonald, March 27, 1809, T 79/3, ff. 388–394, PRO; David Meade to John Driver, Aug. 9, Sept. 7, 1782, March 15, 1783, Webb-Prentis Papers, ViU.

"a good garden": John Driver, advertisement, *Virginia Gazette, or, the American Advertiser,* April 10, 1784.

being "punctuall": George Sparling to John Sparling, Aug. 20, 1783, Claim of John Sparling, William Bolden & Co., American Loyalist Claims, AO 13/33, ff. 75–76, PRO.

Suffolk: Petition of Inhabitants of Suffolk, Nov. 7, 1785, Legislative Petitions, Nansemond County, Vi; Hening, ed., *Statutes at Large*, XII, 211–212.

"pirates" . . . "store": *Virginia Gazette, or, the American Advertiser,* July 30, 1785.

"look . . . Canals": John Page to George Washington, Sept. 9, 1785, *Papers of Washington: Confederation*, ed. Abbot *et al.*, III, 241.

fortune by land speculation: Hugh Williamson to Thomas Ruston, Nov. 2, 1784, March 2, 1785, Smith *et al.*, eds., *Letters of Delegates*, XXII, 7–11, 240–241; Charles Dilly to Benjamin Rush, Feb. 1, 1786, L. H. Butterfield, "The American Interests of the Firm of E. and C. Dilly, with Their Letters to Benjamin Rush, 1770–1795," *Papers of the Bibliographical Society of America*, XLV (1951), 322.

saw Sarah Siddons: Entry of May 18, 1785, Journal of Thomas Ruston, Tench Coxe Papers, Vol. 165, PHi; Van Lennep *et al.*, eds., *London Stage*, V, Part II, 793, 798; entry of May 18, 1785, *The Diary of the Right Hon. William Windham, 1784 to 1810*, ed. Cecilia Anne Baring (London, 1866), 53.

314 George and Sarah Fairfax: George William Fairfax and Sarah Cary Fairfax to George Washington, July 2, 1785, *Papers of Washington: Confederation*, ed. Abbot *et al.*, III, 97.

gave Samuel Gist: Entry of June 17, 1785, Journal of Ruston, Tench Coxe Papers, PHi.

shingles at Dismal Plantation: David Jameson to John Driver, Jan. 25, 1787, Dismal Swamp Land Company Records, NcD.

a "beautiful bay": Advertisement, *Virginia Independent Chronicle*, March 21, 1787.

"fine . . . Horse": Advertisement, *Virginia Gazette, or, the American Advertiser,* April 16, 1785.

"Duns and Sheriffs": John Page to Thomas Jefferson, April 28, 1785, *Papers of Jefferson*, ed. Boyd *et al.*, VIII, 117.

"several young Negroes": *Virginia Gazette, or, the American Advertiser,* April 16, 1785.

take over the law practice: William Nelson, Jr., to Henry Tazewell, March 19, 1784, Tazewell Family Papers, Vi; William Nelson, Jr., to William Short, March 26, 1785,

William Short Papers, DLC; advertisements, *Virginia Gazette, or, the American Advertiser*, July 9, Aug. 27, 1785.

Nelson's clients: B. Dickson to William Nelson, Jr., April 13, 1786, Miscellaneous Letters, 516/2, NcU; Otway Byrd to St. George Tucker, Oct. 16, 1786, Tucker-Coleman Papers, ViW.

Polly Nelson died: William Nelson, Jr., to William Short, Oct. 16, 1785, Feb. 20–28, June 14, 1786, William Short Papers, DLC.

wrote his will: A copy is in the Dismal Swamp Land Company Records, NcD.

"seem'd . . . Live": Henry Tucker to St. George Tucker, April 19, June 15, 1786, Henry Tucker, Jr., to St. George Tucker, July 8, 1786, Tucker-Coleman Papers, ViW.

Page and Lee: William Lee to John Page, May 2, June 4, July 25, Aug. 13, Nov. 4, 11, Dec. 27, 1786, Feb. 20, 1787, William Lee to Samuel Thorp, Aug. 5, 19, 1786, William Lee Letterbook, 1783–1787, ViRHi; John Page to [?], May 15, 1786, Emmet Collection, NN.

315 "Every . . . standing": William Nelson, Jr., to William Short, May 4–5, 1787, William Short Papers, DLC.

"a very . . . woman": Entry of Feb. 27, 1786, *Quebec to Carolina: Diary of Hunter*, ed. Wright and Tinling, 235.

"I am . . . it": Elizabeth Farley to Thomas Taylor Byrd, June 25, 1783, Byrd Letterbook, Byrd Family Papers, ViRHi.

John Dunbar: Entry of Feb. 27, 1786, *Quebec to Carolina: Diary of Hunter*, ed. Wright and Tinling, 234–235; Joseph Hadfield, *An Englishman in America, 1785: Being the Diary of Joseph Hadfield*, ed. Douglas S. Robertson (Toronto, 1933), 2.

316 Dunbar as administrator: James Taylor to St. George Tucker, June 9, 1786, John Dunbar to St. George Tucker, Oct. 17, 1786, Aug. 19, Sept. 12, Oct. 16, 1787, draft of a bill, [ca. 1787], in St. George Tucker, Miscellaneous Legal Materials, Box 74, Tucker-Coleman Papers, ViW; *Journal of the House of Delegates of the Commonwealth of Virginia* (Richmond, 1828), [1787, October Session], 36; advertisement, *Virginia Independent Chronicle*, Aug. 16, 1786; List of Slaves sold, March 19, 1790, Account of Slaves, Oct. 15, 1790, *Dinwiddie, Crawford & Co.* v. *Henry Skipwith and Elizabeth Hill Skipwith et al.*, 1819, USCCVD(EC), Vi. Compare 1790 lists with 1773 lists, Richard Corbin Papers, ViWC.

317 "there . . . thereon": John Page to Robert Carter, Aug. 29, 1786, *Joseph Rubinfine Autographs—Historical Americana List 44*, Item 74.

Carter replied: Robert Carter to John Page, Sept. 21, 1786, Letterbook VI, Robert Carter Papers, NcD.

"equal . . . State": Advertisement, *Virginia Gazette, or, the American Advertiser*, Aug. 16, 30, Oct. 11, 1786.

"I . . . land": Patrick Henry to [?], May 22, 1784, in Hamilton, *American Autographs*, I, 325.

"as I . . . cash": Mary Willing Byrd to Patrick Henry, Nov. 22, 1786, Patrick Henry and Family Collection, DLC.

"encircled with Difficulties": Elizabeth Willing Powel to Martha Washington, Nov. 3[o], 1787, *"Worthy Partner": The Papers of Martha Washington*, ed. Joseph E. Fields (Westport, 1994), 198.

PAGE

317 "overswelling . . . swamps": John Anstey to John Forster, Feb. 22, 1787, AO 12/113, ff. 62–65, PRO.

Frances Burwell Page: John Page to St. George Tucker, June 12, 1787, Tucker-Coleman Papers, ViW; John Page to Thomas Jefferson, March 7, 1788, Anna Blair Banister to Thomas Jefferson, Feb. 19, 1787, *Papers of Jefferson*, ed. Boyd *et al.*, XII, 650, XI, 167.

advertised an auction: *Virginia Independent Chronicle*, March 21, 1787.

"I . . . Expectation": John Page to St. George Tucker, May 23, 1787, Tucker-Coleman Papers, ViW.

318 he advertised the property: *Virginia Independent Chronicle*, June 20, 1787.

Jolly Tar: John Page to Thomas Jefferson, March 7, 1788, *Papers of Jefferson*, ed. Boyd *et al.*, XII, 652; Joshua Johnson to Francis Charlton, July 8, 1787, Joshua Johnson Letterbook, Peter Force Collection, Series 8D, DLC.

Mount Vernon: George Washington to Lund Washington, May 7, 1787, *Papers of Washington: Confederation*, ed. Abbot *et al.*, V, 173.

"exceedingly anxious": George Washington to John Francis Mercer, Nov. 6, 1786, *ibid.*, IV, 336–337.

were too high: George Washington to Bushrod Washington, Dec. 3, 1787, *ibid.*, V, 473–475.

To a Frenchman: George Washington to Henry L. Charton, May 20, 1786, *ibid.*, IV, 63–66.

Pennsylvania tracts: George Washington to Thomas Smith, July 28, 1786, and advertisement, *ibid.*, 173–174, 258–259n.7.

Henry Emanuel Lutterloh: Henry Emanuel Lutterloh to George Washington, Jan. 3, June 13, 1787, George Washington to Henry Emanuel Lutterloh, April 8, 1787, *ibid.*, IV, 498–499, V, 228–229, 129–130.

"The Members . . . Part": John Page to George Washington, March 9, 1787, *ibid.*, V, 76–77.

319 "the good" . . . "fatal": Edmund Pendleton to James Madison, April 7, 1787, *Papers of Madison*, ed. Hutchinson and Rachal *et al.*, XVII, 516.

"intollerable" . . . "death": John Russell Spence to James Hunter, July 2, 1787, Hunter-Garnett Collection, ViU.

"an almost . . . loss": George Washington to Charles Lee, April 4, 1788, *Papers of Washington: Confederation*, ed. Abbot *et al.*, VI, 197–198; entry of July 31, 1787, Diary of Thomas Bolling, BR 734, CSmH.

At Dismal Plantation: John Driver to David Jameson, Oct. 1, 1787, June 2, 1788, Dismal Swamp Land Company Records, NcD; Edmund Pendleton to James Madison, Aug. 12, 1787, *Papers of Madison*, ed. Hutchinson and Rachal *et al.*, XVII, 519.

"have . . . money": George Washington to Charles Lee, April 4, 1788, *Papers of Washington: Confederation*, ed. Abbot *et al.*, VI, 198.

320 totaling 660 acres: Nicholas Long, advertisement, *Virginia Gazette, or, the American Advertiser*, July 9, 1785; Alan D. Watson, "Society and Economy in Colonial Edgecombe County," *NCHR*, L (July 1973), 239n.42.

showed more debts: List of Debts, Feb. 5, 1791, Chatham Papers, PRO 30/8/343, ff. 168–169, PRO.

Gilbert Francklyn: Sheila Lambert, ed., *House of Commons Sessional Papers of the Eighteenth Century* (Wilmington, 1975), LXXI, 80–98.

"handsome" new houses: John Lloyd, *The Early History of the Old South Wales Iron Works* (London, 1906), 74; *Kent's Directory for the Year 1785* (London, 1785), 11; John Noorthouck, *A New History of London* (London, 1773), 647–648; [Edward Pugh], *London; Being an Accurate History and Description* (London, 1805–13), IV, 87; [Edward Pugh], *Walks Through London* (London, 1817), I, 151–152; John Heneage Jesse, *London and Its Celebrities* (Boston, n.d.), II, 118.

321 signing his will: Printed in Lloyd, *Early History of Iron Works*, 52–55. On Rachel Harwood and Mary Passapae, see Oswald Tilghman, *History of Talbot County, Maryland, 1661–1861* (Baltimore, 1915), II, 490.

"Go . . . district": *Bristol Gazette*, Feb. 2, 1786, quoted in John P. Addis, *The Crawshay Dynasty: A Study in Industrial Organisation and Development, 1765–1867* (Cardiff, 1957), 15n.76.

his estate was left: Chris Evans, *"The Labyrinth of Flames": Work and Social Conflict in Early Industrial Merthyr Tydfil* (Cardiff, 1993), 17–18; Addis, *Crawshay Dynasty*, 10; G. G. L. Hayes, Introduction, *The Letterbook of Richard Crawshay, 1788–1797*, ed. Chris Evans (Cardiff, 1990), 151.

"our young Landlords": Richard Crawshay to James Cockshutt, Aug. 3, 1791, *Letterbook of Crawshay*, ed. Evans, 112.

payment of £5,000: Richard Crawshay to Winter & Kaye, Dec. 2, 1795, *Letterbook of Crawshay*, ed. Evans, 152; Addis, *Crawshay Dynasty*, 12.

"that . . . world": Entry of Aug, 8, 1797, [J. H. Manners, Duke of Rutland], *Journal of a Tour Through North and South Wales, the Isle of Man, &c. &c.* (London, 1805), 61–72; entry of May 23, 1803, M. W. Thompson, ed., *The Journeys of Sir Richard Colt Hoare* (Gloucester, 1983), 235; Charles Blagden to Joseph Banks, Aug. 24, 1791, Aug. 29, 30, Sept. 2, 1804, *Banks Letters*, ed. Dawson, 77, 95; Herbert M. Vaughan, "A Synopsis of Two Tours Made in Wales in 1775 and in 1811," *Transactions of the Honourable Society of Cymmrodorion*, XXXVIII (1927), 76–78; Frank Llewellyn-Jones, "Two Centuries of Innovation in Welsh Industry," *ibid.*, new series, III (1997), 91–92; Samuel Smiles, *Industrial Biography: Iron Workers and Tool Makers* (London, 1876), 130–131.

it had seventeen: Evans, *Labyrinth of Flames*, 20, 24–25, 28; Gwyn A. Williams, "The Merthyr of Dic Penderyn," in Glanmor Williams, ed., *Merthyr Politics: The Making of a Working-Class Tradition* (Cardiff, 1966), 9; Rick Szostak, *The Role of Transportation in the Industrial Revolution: A Comparison of England and France* (Montreal, 1991), 275n.53.

James Bacon: John Driver to David Jameson, Feb. 15, May 19, 1791, Dismal Swamp Land Company Records, NcD.

322 "generally" . . . "figure": Entry of Feb. 18, 1782, *The Revolutionary Journal of Baron Ludwig von Closen, 1780–1783*, ed. Evelyn M. Acomb (Chapel Hill, 1958), 180–181; entry of April 10–11, 1782, François-Jean, Marquis de Chastellux, *Travels in North America in the Years 1780, 1781 and 1782*, ed. Howard C. Rice, Jr. (Chapel Hill, 1963), II, 383–386.

"very anxious": Entry of Feb. 21, 1788, Diary of William Heth, DLC.

"I . . . Government": Alexander Donald to Thomas Jefferson, Nov. 12, 1787, *Papers of Jefferson*, ed. Boyd *et al.*, XII, 345.

PAGE

322 "their" . . . "war": David Humphreys to Thomas Jefferson, Nov. 29, 1788, *ibid.*, XIV, 300–301.

"it is . . . Sovereign": George Washington to John Jay, March 10, 1787, *Papers of Washington: Confederation*, ed. Abbot *et al.*, V, 80.

"impending ruin": George Washington to Thomas Jefferson, Aug. 31, 1788, *ibid.*, VI, 493.

Page and the Constitution: Archibald Stuart to James Madison, Oct. 21, 1787, Jan. 14, 1788, *Papers of Madison*, ed. Hutchinson and Rachal *et al.*, X, 202, 374; James Madison to Thomas Jefferson, April 22, 1788, John Page to Thomas Jefferson, March 7, 1788, *Papers of Jefferson*, ed. Boyd *et al.*, XIII, 98–99, XII, 650–652.

323 south of the James River: Richard R. Beeman, *The Old Dominion and the New Nation, 1788–1801* (Lexington, 1972), 50–51, 57; Risjord, *Chesapeake Politics*, 115, 325, 329–330.

"a long . . . scene": Entry of June 10, 1786, *Quebec to Carolina: Diary of Hunter*, ed. Wright and Tinling, 268.

"with . . . grace": Schoepf, *Travels*, trans. Morrison, II, 95–96.

"The whole . . . us": Archibald Stuart to John Breckinridge, June 19, 1788, Breckinridge Family Papers, DLC; Risjord, *Chesapeake Politics*, 114–116.

persisted in evasion: Rich, "Speculations," *VMHB*, LXXVI (July 1968), 314–317; Isaac Samuel Harrell, *Loyalism in Virginia: Chapters in the Economic History of the Revolution* (Durham, 1926), 140–144.

"foreigners . . . them": Merrill Jensen *et al.*, eds., *The Documentary History of the Ratification of the Constitution* (Madison, 1976–), X, 1469.

"benign . . . men": William Lee to Samuel Thorp, Nov. 29, 1792, William Lee Letterbook, 1792–1793, Lee Family Papers, ViRHi.

"indolent . . . tricksters": François Dupont to Etienne Clavière, Jan. 10, 1789, "Letter from Petersburg," ed. Nall, *VMHB*, LXXXII (April 1974), 146.

324 "I . . . State": Joshua Johnson to Wallace & Muir, Nov. 12, 1787, Joshua Johnson Letterbook, Peter Force Collection, Series 8D, DLC.

Virginians' refusal: Risjord, *Chesapeake Politics*, 116.

"The new . . . us": William Nelson, Jr., to William Short, Aug. 12, 1788, William Short Papers, DLC.

in place of Dr. Thomas Walker: John Redd, "Reminiscences of Western Virginia, 1770–1790," *VMHB*, VII (July 1899), 8; Franklin Minor, "Memoranda of Inquiries about Dr. Thomas Walker," Franklin Minor Letters, Virginia MSS, Vol. 13, Draper Collection, Series ZZ, WHi; Thomas Lewis to John Preston, Dec. 13, 1787, Preston Family Papers, ViRHi; Thomas Jefferson to John Nicholas, Sr., Jan. 20, 1790, *Papers of Jefferson*, ed. Boyd *et al.*, XVI, 115.

the Loyal Company: Thomas Walker to John Preston, Aug. 22, 1785, Preston Papers, Vol. 5, f. 20, Draper Collection, Series QQ, WHi; Francis Walker to John Preston, April 12, 1786, Preston Family Papers, ViRHi; Thomas Walker to John Breckinridge, June 27, Aug. 22, 1785, Breckinridge Family Papers, DLC; Francis Walker to Francis Preston, June 25, 1789, Sept. 2, 1790, Feb. 24, 1791, Campbell-Preston-Floyd Papers, DLC; Bill of Complaint of Successors to the Loyal Company, *TQHGM*, IV (1922), 87–95.

Landon Cabell: Entry of Dec. 17, 1785, Diary of William Cabell, in Alexander Brown, *The Cabells and Their Kin* (Richmond, 1939), 231.

325 "My son . . . it": Minor, "Memoranda of Inquiries," Virginia MSS, Vol. 13, Draper Collection, Series ZZ, WHi.

"liable to intoxication": [Francis Preston], [Draft of an answer], Preston Family Papers—Gray Collection, Folder 8, KyLoF.

"had . . . old": William Wirt to Elizabeth Wirt, April 9, 1806, William Wirt Papers, MdBHi.

"good" . . . "enjoyed": Francis Walker to Daniel Smith, Dec. 22, 1791, Virginia MSS, Vol. 7, f. 33, Draper Collection, Series ZZ, WHi.

wrote his will: Thomas Walker, Will, May 13, 1788, copies in Speed Family Papers, KyLoF, and Dismal Swamp Land Company Records, NcD.

"closely . . . accounts": Francis Walker to Francis Preston, Feb. 24, 1791, Campbell-Preston-Floyd Papers, DLC.

"drank . . . Death": Patrick Parker to James Parker, June 18, 1789, Parker Papers, Liverpool Public Library.

Elizabeth Farley Banister: Francis Walker to Francis Preston, June 25, 1789, Campbell-Preston-Floyd Papers, DLC; Maria Page to Elizabeth Farley, Dec. 26, 1787, Shippen Family Papers, DLC; Patrick Parker to James Parker, Jan. 4, 1790, Parker Papers, Liverpool Public Library.

326 his son, John: John Walker to Francis Walker, Oct. 24, 1801, John Walker Papers, ViRHi.

"an exact match": Margaret Davenport to Elizabeth Pelham, May 20, 1792, "Letters Addressed to Miss Elizabeth Pelham, William Blagrove and William Pelham," *WMQ*, 2d ser., IX (Oct. 1929), 271.

"offered love": Elizabeth Walker apparently told her husband in May 1788, when John Walker wrote a letter which Jefferson did not receive. See Thomas Jefferson to John Walker, April 13, 1803, Vi. For "offered love" and a discussion of the subject, see Dumas Malone, *Jefferson and His Time* (Boston, 1948–81), I, appendix III. See also *Papers of Jefferson*, ed. Boyd *et al.*, XVI, 157n.

Thomas Walker: Minor, "Memoranda of Inquiries" and Franklin Minor to L. C. Draper, Jan. 30, 1853, Virginia MSS, Vol. 13, Draper Collection, Series ZZ, WHi; "Inventory of the Personal Estate of Doctr. Thomas Walker," Page-Walker Manuscripts, ViU.

327 the Bank of England: Hoppit, *Risk and Failure*, 135–138; Julian Hoppit, "The Use and Abuse of Credit in Eighteenth-Century England," in Neil McKendrick and R. B. Outhwaite, eds., *Business Life and Public Policy* (Cambridge, 1986), 67–71.

the South Sea Bubble: Letter from London, *Virginia Gazette and Weekly Advertiser* (Richmond), Oct. 9, 1788.

James Russell: Jacob M. Price, "One Family's Empire: The Russell-Lee-Clerk Connection in Maryland, Britain, and India, 1707–1857," *MHM*, LXXII (1977), 207. See also John Thurman, Jr., to Sargent, Chambers & Co., June 14, 1788, "Letter Books of Thurman," *Historical Magazine*, 2d ser., IV (Dec. 1868), 297.

Parker's son, Patrick: Patrick Parker to James Parker, July 15, 1787, Aug. 26, Sept. 20, 1789, Sept. 6, Nov. 12, 1790, June 1, 1791, Parker Family Papers, Liverpool Public Library; *Riddel, Colquhoun & Co.* v. *John L. Fulwell et al.*, 1791, USCCVD(EC), Vi.

"Their . . . saw": Thomas Jefferson to John Page, May 4, 1786, *Papers of Jefferson*, ed.

Boyd *et al.*, IX, 445; Olsen, *Town Planning*, chap. 4; Andrew Byrne, *Bedford Square: An Architectural Study* (London, 1990).

328 New neighbors: *The Universal British Directory of Trade, Commerce and Manufacture* (London, [1798]), V; entry of Oct. 13, 1800, *The Diaries and Correspondence of the Right Hon. George Rose*, ed. Leveson Vernon Harcourt (London, 1860), I, 285; R. G. Thorne, *The History of Parliament: The House of Commons, 1790–1820* (London, 1986), V, 104–105; William Morice to Samuel Peters, March 24, 1790, *The Papers of Loyalist Samuel Peters*, ed. Kenneth Walter Cameron (Hartford, 1978), 76; Sarah Harriet Burney to Martha Young, June 28, 1793, *The Letters of Sarah Harriet Burney*, ed. Lorna J. Clark (Athens, 1997), 7; Horace Twiss, *The Public and Private Life of Lord Chancellor Eldon*, 2d ed. (London, 1844), I, 354; George H. Cunningham, *London* (London, 1927), 34, 268; Laurence Gomme and Philip Norman, eds., *London County Council Survey of London. Volume V: The Parish of St. Giles-in-the-Fields* (London, 1914), Part II, 150–151, 155, 185; Hubert F. Barclay and Alice Wilson-Fox, *A History of the Barclay Family* (London, 1934), III, 251–252; *Gentleman's Magazine*, LIX (Aug. 1789), 762, LX (Aug. 1790), 770; Dawson, ed., *Banks Letters*, 66–75; J. A. Fuller Maitland, ed., *Grove's Dictionary of Music and Musicians* (Philadelphia, 1926), V, 563.

"much in style": Entry of May 26, 1799, Diary of Littleton Dennis Teackle, DLC. For Gist's possessions, see his will in C 117/335, PRO. See also Dan Cruickshank and Neil Burton, *Life in the Georgian City* (London, 1990).

"The streets . . . it": Entry of Jan. 10, 1789, Diary of Carter Braxton, Jr., ViRHi; Thomas Barker to Joseph Banks, March 28, 1789, *Banks Letters*, ed. Dawson, 32.

Jerome Bernard Weuves: *Gentleman's Magazine*, LXV (June 1789), 573; testimony of Jerome Bernard Weuves, *Report of the Lords of the Committee of Council . . . Concerning the Present State of the Trade to Africa* (London, 1789), Part I.

329 go above £6: Samuel Davidson to Donald & Burton, June 30, 1789, Dunlop Family Papers, DLC.

more than £14: Rowles, Grymes & Co. to Philip L. Grymes, Feb. 3, 1790, BR Box 260(47), CSmH.

Walker's tobacco: William Anderson to Thomas Walker, Feb. 27, 1790, Thomas Walker Papers, William Cabell Rives Papers, Box 162, DLC.

"unhappy family differences": Meriwether Lewis to Lucy Marks, Oct. 16, 1791, Lewis Family Papers, Vi.

"that he . . . since": [William Jones] to Richard Hanson, Aug. 19, 1789, in W. E. Minchinton, *The Trade of Bristol in the Eighteenth Century* (Bristol, 1957), 174–175.

owed £34,000 . . . £80,000: List of Debts, Feb. 5, 1791, Chatham Papers, PRO 30/8/343, ff. 168–169, PRO; Kenneth Morgan, *Bristol and the Atlantic Trade in the Eighteenth Century* (Cambridge, 1993), 164.

"strong . . . persons": John Eardley-Wilmot, *Historical View of the Commission for Enquiring into the Losses, Services, and Claims of the American Loyalists* (Boston, 1972 [orig. publ. London, 1815]), 89–90; 29 Geo. III 1789, chap. 62, *The Statutes at Large* (Cambridge, 1762–1865), XXXVI, 687–691.

In his memorial: Memorials, July 21, Sept. 30, 1789, Claim of Samuel Gist, American Loyalist Claims, AO 13/30, PRO.

330 in a remittance: Deposition of Benjamin Toler, May 7, 1807, *Anderson's Heirs &c* v. *Gist's Exors et al.*, 1824, USCCVD(EC), Vi.

"In the . . . cold": Russell Jackson, ed., "Johanna Schopenhauer's Journal: A German View of the London Theatre Scene, 1803–5," *Theatre Notebook*, LII (1998), 151.

"convinced . . . fortnight": Sarah Siddons to Bedina Wynn, June 3, 1789, in Roger Manvell, *Sarah Siddons: Portrait of an Actress* (New York, 1971), 362.

her "nice house": Sarah Siddons to Thomas Sedgwick Whalley, Oct. 1, 1786, *Journals and Correspondence of Whalley*, ed. Wickham, I, 487.

moved in 1790: Kalman A. Burnin, ed., "The Letters of Sarah and William Siddons to Hester Lynch Piozzi in the John Rylands Library," *Bulletin of the John Rylands Library*, LII (1969), 59n.3.

Irish law student: Entry of July 8, 1804, Joseph Farington, *The Farington Diary*, ed. James Greig (London, 1923–28), II, 265; Leonard Chappelow to Hester Piozzi, June 13, 1804, *The Piozzi Letters*, ed. Edward A. Bloom and Lillian D. Bloom (Newark, 1989–93), III, 471n.2. For another episode see John Taylor, *Records of My Life* (New York, 1833), 287.

331 "He" . . . "England": Entry of Feb. 13, 1788, *The American Journals of Lt. John Enys*, ed. Elizabeth Cometti (Syracuse, 1976), 245, 249; Dennis J. Pogue, "Mount Vernon: Transformation of an Eighteenth-Century Plantation System," in Paul A. Shackel and Barbara J. Little, eds., *Historical Archaeology of the Chesapeake* (Washington, 1994), 108–110; Dennis J. Pogue, "Giant in the Earth: George Washington, Landscape Designer," in Rebecca Yamin and Karen Bescherer Metheny, eds., *Landscape Archaeology: Reading and Interpreting the American Historical Landscape* (Knoxville, 1996), 52–69; Robert F. Dalzell, Jr., and Lee Baldwin Dalzell, *George Washington's Mount Vernon: At Home in Revolutionary America* (New York, 1998), 116–119.

the stallion Magnolio: Entry of Feb. 13, 1788, *Journals of Enys*, ed. Cometti, 249; George Washington to Henry Lee, Nov. 30, 1788, *Papers of Washington: Presidential*, ed. Abbot *et al.*, I, 139 and 139–140n; entry of Dec. 9, 1788, *Diaries of Washington*, ed. Jackson and Twohig, V, 432.

332 the tracts purchased jointly: Henry Lee to George Washington, Feb. 6, 1789, *Papers of Washington: Presidential*, ed. Abbot *et al.*, I, 282.

Byrd's description: Compare "A Description of the Dismal Swamp, in Virginia," *Columbian Magazine*, III (April 1789), 234, and [William Byrd], "To the Kings most Excellent Majty," [1729], BR Box 256(29), CSmH.

"did not . . . again": John Jameson to George Washington, Jan. 30, 1795, Papers of George Washington, DLC.

William Nelson, Jr.: David Stuart to George Washington, Dec. 3, 1789, *Papers of Washington: Presidential*, ed. Abbot *et al.*, IV, 358–359; William Nelson, Jr., to William Short, Dec. 8, 1791, William Short Papers, DLC.

333 John Driver's reports: John Driver to David Jameson, June 10, 17, Sept. 5, 24, 1789, Joseph Hornsby to David Jameson, Jan. 20, 1790, Dismal Swamp Land Company Records, NcD. Major John Simon Farley: Robert Taylor to St. George Tucker, Jan. 6, 1790, Tucker-Coleman Papers, ViW; *John Simon Farley and Elizabeth Morson v. Thomas Lee Shippen and Elizabeth Carter Shippen et al.*, March 1794, in *Decisions of Cases in Virginia by the High Court of Chancery . . . by George Wythe* (Charlottesville, 1903), 253–260.

333 gave a dinner: Entry of March 4, 1790, *The Diary of William Maclay*, ed. Kenneth R. Bowling and Helen E. Veit (Baltimore, 1988), 212; Samuel Johnston to James Iredell, March 4, 1790, James Iredell Papers, NcD.

334 "having . . . them": George Washington to Warner Lewis, March 5, 1790, *Papers of Washington: Presidential*, ed. Abbot *et al.*, V, 201.

"impracticable . . . vain": Hugh Williamson to Thomas Ruston, Nov. 2, 1784, Smith *et al.*, eds., *Letters of Delegates*, XXII, 8.

for 75¢: Hugh Williamson to Thomas Ruston, March 2, 1785, *ibid.*, 240.

William Short: William Short to Peyton Short, July 28, 1800, William and Peyton Short Papers, ViW; Benjamin Harrison, Jr., to Thomas Jefferson, July 18, 1798, William Short Papers, DLC; William Short to Thomas Jefferson, Oct. 7, 1793, *Papers of Jefferson*, ed. Boyd *et al.*, XXVII, 202–204; George Green Shackelford, *Jefferson's Adoptive Son: The Life of William Short, 1759–1848* (Lexington, 1993), 15.

335 "Immense" . . . "Worth": John Harvie to Thomas Jefferson, May 15, 1798, Thomas Jefferson to William Short, April 13, 1800, William Short Papers, DLC; entry of Nov. 21, 1799, *Jefferson's Memorandum Books*, ed. Bear and Stanton, II, 1008.

"lost" . . . "jail": Benjamin Rush, *The Autobiography of Benjamin Rush*, ed. George W. Corner (Princeton, 1948), 314.

John Driver collected: John Driver to Thomas Ruston, Nov. 18, 1791 [filed as 1790], Thomas Ruston to John Driver, June 1, Nov. 2, 1794, Nov. 16, 1795, William Nivison to Thomas Ruston, Jan. 7, 1789 [1790], Ruston Papers, Tench Coxe Papers, Series II, PHi; Memorandum Book, "Virginia Suffolk Estate," Memorandum, Aug. 1, 1793, Thomas Ruston Letterbook, Coxe Papers, Vols. 179, 166, PHi; Nansemond County Land Book, 1795, Nansemond County Land Tax Lists, Vi.

"every . . . city": Rush, *Autobiography*, ed. Corner, 314.

opened his court: Edmund Randolph to George Washington, Dec. 15, 1789, *Papers of Washington: Presidential*, ed. Abbot *et al.*, IV, 415.

"extreme" . . . "citizens": G. Brown Goode, *Virginia Cousins: A Study of the Ancestry and Posterity of John Goode of Whitby* (Richmond, 1887), 56–57. See also Norma Lois Peterson, *Littleton Waller Tazewell* (Charlottesville, 1983), 3.

"the Disposition . . . Persecution": John Wickham, Jr., to Edmund Fanning, April 12, 1783, Wickham Family Papers, ViRHi. See also Dwight Holbrook, *The Wickham Claim* (Riverhead, 1986).

to study law: John Wickham, Jr., to John Wickham, Sr., March 1, 1786, Wickham Family Papers, ViRHi.

a library of law books: John Coalter to William Coalter, Feb. 30 [*sic*], 1789, Brown-Coalter-Tucker Papers, ViW.

336 "a young . . . cleaverness": John Marshall to Percival Butler, Aug. 16, 1789, *The Papers of John Marshall*, ed. Herbert A. Johnson *et al.* (Chapel Hill, 1974–), II, 36.

leader of the Richmond bar: Duke de la Rochefoucauld-Liancourt, *Travels Through the United States of America, the Country of the Iroquois, and Upper Canada, in the Years 1795, 1796, and 1797*, trans. H. Neuman (London, 1799), III, 75–76; Charles F. Hobson, *The Great Chief Justice: John Marshall and the Rule of Law* (Lawrence, 1996), 29–33.

PAGE

Richmond: Entry of Feb. 28, 1786, *Quebec to Carolina: Diary of Hunter*, ed. Wright and Tinling, 236–237; John W. Reps, *Tidewater Towns: City Planning in Colonial Virginia and Maryland* (Williamsburg, 1972), 273–275; Isaac Weld, *Travels Through the States of North America, and the Provinces of Upper and Lower Canada, During the Years 1795, 1796, and 1797*, 3d ed. (London, 1800), I, 189–191; Schoepf, *Travels*, trans. Morrison, II, 49–57.

"he ... cleaver": Charles Grymes to John Hatley Norton, Dec. 1, 1790, John Norton & Son Papers, ViWC.

British clients: William Wirt to Dabney Carr, March 25, 1803, William Wirt Letters, Vi.

"gild ... subjects": [William Wirt], *The Letters of the British Spy* (Richmond, 1803), 30–31.

"the most ... bar": William Nelson, Jr., to William Short, Sept. 30, 1806, William Short Papers, DLC.

"I ... measures": John Wickham to Henry Lee, Dec. 28, 1799, *Henry Lee* v. *Hanbury's Exors*, 1804, USCCVD(EC), Vi.

337 William Anderson: *Anderson & Co.* v. *Austin & Co.*, 1794, *ibid.*

commission of 5 percent: Dan Call to William Short, Jan. 15, 1807, William Short Papers, DLC.

charged 10 percent: John Wickham to Samuel Gist, June 16, 1803, T 79/115, pp. 308–313, PRO.

"much ... before": John Wickham, Jr., to John Wickham, Sr., Jan. 20, 1792, Wickham Family Papers, ViRHi.

"the famous lawyer": William Munford to John Coalter, Dec. 14, 1791, "Glimpses of Old College Life," *WMQ*, 1st ser., VIII (Jan. 1900), 155.

"to grow ... profitable": John Wickham, Jr., to John Wickham, Sr., Dec. 11, 1799, Wickham Family Papers, ViRHi; John J. Reardon, *Edmund Randolph: A Biography* (New York, 1974), 349.

large brick houses: Peterson, *Tazewell*, 11; Charles E. Brownell, "Laying the Groundwork," in Charles E. Brownell *et al.*, *The Making of Virginia Architecture* (Richmond, 1992), 58–59, 244–245.

"I" ... "talents": William Nelson, Jr., to William Short, Dec. 8, 1791, William Short Papers, DLC. See also Robert Douthat Meade, *Patrick Henry: Practical Revolutionary* (Philadelphia, 1969), 403–412.

338 "thought ... recovery": Edmund Pendleton to James Madison, Dec. 9, 1791, *Papers of Madison*, ed. Hutchinson and Rachal *et al.*, XVII, 552.

"to harangue ... paying": John Mason to Fulwar Skipwith, May 24, 1792, Fulwar Skipwith Papers, Causten-Pickett Papers, DLC.

"Mr. Henry ... question": [?] to [James Ritchie], June 10, 1792, in James Ritchie to William Molleson, Aug. 2–4, 1792, Melville Papers, MiU-C.

Ware v. *Hylton*: Charles F. Hobson, "The Recovery of British Debts in the Federal Circuit Court of Virginia, 1790–1797," *VMHB*, XCII (April 1984), 176–200; Emory G. Evans, "Private Indebtedness and the Revolution in Virginia, 1776 to 1796," *WMQ*, 3d ser., XXVIII (July 1971), 349–374; Herbert E. Sloan, *Principle and Interest: Thomas Jefferson and the Problem of Debt* (New York, 1995), chap. 1. Charles F. Hobson has edited the documents of *Jones* v. *Walker* and *Ware* v. *Hylton* in *Papers of Marshall*, ed. Johnson *et al.*, V,

259–329. For a summary of the arguments in *Jones* v. *Walker,* see Edmund Pendleton to James Madison, Dec. 9, 1791, *Papers of Madison,* ed. Hutchinson and Rachal *et al.,* XVII, 552–559. For William Wirt's version of a stenographic report of Patrick Henry's argument, see William Wirt, *Sketches of the Life and Character of Patrick Henry* (Philadelphia, 1817), 312–369.

338 for Samuel Gist: Gist's cases may be found under his name in USCCVD(EC), Vi.

"large sums": Examination of Samuel Gist, May 9, 1808, T 79/31, PRO.

Venice Preserv'd: Entry of Oct. 3, 1786, *Sophie in London,* trans. Williams, 266; Thomas Lee Shippen to Anne Home Livingston, Oct. 4, 1786, in Ethel Armes, ed., *Nancy Shippen Her Journal Book* (New York, 1968 [orig. publ. 1935]), 245–246; Van Lennep *et al.,* eds., *London Stage,* V, Part II, 925.

339 "I . . . grandfather": Thomas Lee Shippen to William Shippen, Sept. 24, 1790, Shippen Family Papers, DLC.

"We . . . least": Thomas Lee Shippen to William Shippen, March 3–5, 1791, *ibid.*

"the happiest" . . . "women": Thomas Lee Shippen to William Shippen, March 11, 1791, *ibid.*

"than . . . Country": M[ary Willing Byrd] to [Anne Home Livingston], n.d. [ca. 1791], *ibid.*

more than £430: Accounts of Mercers Creek Estate and Henry B. Lightfoot to [John Dunbar?], Nov. 15, 1792, *Dinwiddie, Crawford & Co.* v. *Henry Skipwith and Elizabeth Hill Skipwith et al.,* 1819, USCCVD(EC), Vi; Thomas Lee Shippen to William Shippen, Oct. 10, 1792, Shippen Family Papers, DLC.

340 for three shares: Additional Subscriptions, April 10, 1792, Dismal Swamp Canal Company Subscription Papers, Business Records, Acc. No. 22867, Vi. On Thomas Lee Shippen see also Paul C. Nagel, *The Lees of Virginia: Seven Generations of an American Family* (New York, 1990), 144–152; Randolph Shipley Klein, *Portrait of an Early American Family: The Shippens of Pennsylvania Across Five Generations* (Philadelphia, 1975), 214–219.

the Dismal Swamp canal: Walter Clark, ed., *State Records of North Carolina* (Winston and Goldsboro, 1895–1905), XXV, 83–93; Hening, ed., *Statutes at Large,* XIII, 145–146.

"the Emporium" . . . "it": Edward Jones *et al.,* Protest, Dec. 15, 1790, General Assembly, Session Records, Nov.–Dec. 1790, Box 4, Nc-Ar.

"The . . . lands": *Virginia Gazette and General Advertiser,* Jan. 12, 1791.

the roadside tract: George Washington to John Lewis, July 20, 1792, *Writings of Washington,* ed. Fitzpatrick, XXXII, 88–89; John Lewis, Deed to John Cowper, May 17, 1791, transcribed in Fillmore Norfleet Papers, Box 13, Vi; George Augustine Washington to George Washington, Dec. 7, 1790, *Papers of Washington: Presidential,* ed. Abbot *et al.,* VII, 43, 44–45n.7.

about 140 shares: Robert Andrews to David Jameson, Sept. 3, 1791, Dismal Swamp Land Company Records, NcD.

invested $12,500: *Journal of the House of Delegates of the Commonwealth of Virginia [1791, October Session]* (Richmond, 1791), 62–63.

341 Few North Carolinians: Jesse Forbes Pugh, *Three Hundred Years Along the Pasquotank: A Biographical History of Camden County* (Old Trap, 1957), 112–113.

PAGE

"very . . . children": Quoted in "Brief Life of Joseph Hornsby," KyLoF. See also William Munford to John Coalter, June 13, 1790, Brown-Coalter-Tucker Papers, ViW.

"prevented . . . leave": Thomas Newton, Jr., to David Jameson, Aug. 22, 1791, Dismal Swamp Land Company Records, NcD.

"I . . . business": Robert Andrews to David Jameson, Aug. 13, 1791, *ibid.*

"many . . . incroachments": John Driver to David Jameson, Feb. 15, 1791, Thomas Newton, Jr., to David Jameson, Aug. 22, 1791, Account with David Jameson, *ibid.*

"I . . . speedily": David Jameson to Francis Walker, Nov. 2, 1791, Thomas Walker Papers, William Cabell Rives Papers, Box 162, DLC.

paid about half: John Jameson to George Washington, Jan. 30, 1795, Papers of George Washington, DLC.

342 about $80,000: Report by President and Directors, [ca. 1816], Dismal Swamp Canal Company, Canal Companies, Internal Improvement Companies, Board of Public Works, Vi.

"in considerable forwardness": John Jones Spooner, "A Topographical Description of the County of Prince George, in Virginia, 1793," Massachusetts Historical Society, *Collections*, 1st ser., III (1794), 86.

"small . . . appearance": la Rochefoucauld-Liancourt, *Travels*, trans. Neuman, III, 30.

Laboring on the canal trench: Weld, *Travels*, I, 180–181; la Rochefoucauld-Liancourt, *Travels*, trans. Neuman, III, 13–14; Darwin H. Stapleton, ed., *The Engineering Drawings of Benjamin Henry Latrobe* (New Haven, 1980), 137–138; Brown, "Dismal Swamp Canal," *AN*, V (1945), 209; Clifford Reginald Hinshaw, Jr., "North Carolina Canals before 1860," *NCHR*, XXV (Jan. 1948), 21; Thomas C. Parramore, Peter C. Stewart, and Tommy L. Bogger, *Norfolk: The First Four Centuries* (Charlottesville, 1994), 147.

John Sparling and William Bolden: John Sparling and William Bolden to John Lawrence, Feb. 14, 1793, Letter Book of James Sparling and William Bolden, Liverpool Public Library.

"form . . . it": *Virginia Gazette and General Advertiser,* April 10, 1793.

343 for £1,000: Fielding Lewis Estate Account, Sol Feinstone Collection of the American Revolution, No. 1978, PPAmP; List of transfers, Dismal Swamp Land Company Records, NcD.

The meeting's only resolution: David Jameson, Jr., to George Washington, May 23, 1793, Papers of George Washington, DLC.

"I . . . place": Thomas Newton, Jr., to David Jameson, Jr., May 24, 1793, Dismal Swamp Land Company Records, NcD.

The canal advanced: Petition of the President and Directors of the Dismal Swamp Canal Company, Dec. 6, 1809, Legislative Petitions, Norfolk County, Vi; la Rochefoucauld-Liancourt, *Travels*, trans. Neuman, III, 14.

four assessments: George Kelly to Jacquelin Ambler, Nov. 16, 1793, Palmer *et al.*, eds., *Calendar of Virginia State Papers*, VI, 640. See also J. R. Ward, *The Finance of Canal Building in Eighteenth-Century England* (Oxford, 1974), chap. 2.

sold for $100: Elizabeth Shippen to William Shippen, April 9, 1799, Shippen Family Papers, DLC; Thomas Jefferson to William Short, April 13, 1800, William Short Papers, DLC.

PAGE

343 Margaret Lowther: John Page to Mann Page, March 12, 1790, Hunt, ed., *Fragments*, 184; entry of Aug. 26, 1789, Diary of Robert Lewis, Lewis Family Papers, ViRHi; John Page to St. George Tucker, April 18, 1790, Tucker-Coleman Papers, ViW; Thomas Jefferson to William Short, April 6, 1790, *Papers of Jefferson*, ed. Boyd *et al.*, XVI, 319.

Page's re-election: John Dawson to James Madison, Aug. 1, 1790, *Papers of Madison*, ed. Hutchinson and Rachal *et al.*, XIII, 291; John Rutledge, Jr., to William Short, Aug. 26, 1790, William Short Papers, DLC; John Page to St. George Tucker, July 4, 1790, Tucker-Coleman Papers, ViW. See also Walter Jones to Robert Carter, [Jan. 12, 1789?], Emmet Collection, NN. On Quakers, see Thomas E. Drake, *Quakers and Slavery in America* (New Haven, 1950), 102–106; Winthrop D. Jordan, *White Over Black: American Attitudes Toward the Negro, 1550–1812* (Chapel Hill, 1968), 325–327.

344 "a Democratical Member": John Page to William Blackburn, May 29, 1797, John Page Papers, NcD.

"moving" . . . "Aristocrats": John Page to St. George Tucker, June 3, 1793, Tucker-Coleman Papers, ViW; Noble E. Cunningham, Jr., ed., *Circular Letters of Congressmen to Their Constituents, 1789–1829* (Chapel Hill, 1978), I, 27–29.

Wakelin Welch: Benjamin Waller to Wakelin Welch, Oct. 1790, Jan. 1791, in Wakelin Welch to James MacDonald, March 27, 1809, T 79/3, ff. 388–394, and List of Debts, T 79/38, PRO.

"unreasonable impatient creditors": John Page to Mann Page, March 12, 1790, Hunt, ed., *Fragments*, 184; entry of Sept. 1, 1795, John Page Commonplace Book, ViRHi; John Page to Thomas Jefferson, Jan. 11, 1792, *Papers of Jefferson*, ed. Boyd *et al.*, XXIII, 36–37.

"about . . . owe": John Page to St. George Tucker, June 28, 1792, Tucker-Coleman Papers, ViW; John Page to James Brown, April 26, 1792, HM 22877, CSmH; John Page to Thomas Jefferson, Jan. 11, 1792, *Papers of Jefferson*, ed. Boyd *et al.*, XXIII, 36–37.

at 20 percent interest: John Page to [?], May 2, 1792, Paul C. Richards Collection, ViU.

"unhappy and ashamed": John Page to Thomas Jefferson, Nov. 19, 1792, *Papers of Jefferson*, ed. Boyd *et al.*, XXIV, 638–639; entry of Nov. 19, 1792, *Jefferson's Memorandum Books*, ed. Bear and Stanton, II, 883.

"justly . . . confess": John Page to [James Brown?], Sept. 8, 1792, Emmet Collection, NN.

Robert Andrews pressed: Robert Andrews to David Jameson, Aug. 13, 1791, Dismal Swamp Land Company Records, NcD.

would be "confused": Augustine Smith to Alice Page, [ca. Oct. 5, 1792], Augustine Smith Papers, ViW.

"I" . . . "Daughter": Augustine Smith to John Page, [Oct. 9, 1792], *ibid.*

345 wedding apparel: John Page to [James Brown?], Sept. 8, 1792, Emmet Collection, NN.

in secret verse: "Miss A. Page," July 1790, Augustine Smith Papers, ViWC.

"I . . . soul": Augustine Smith to William Bennet, Oct. 17, 1790, *ibid.*

"Connections . . . indigence": Augustine Smith to Alice Page, July 2, 1791, Augustine Smith Papers, ViW.

346 "Gratitude" . . . "mad": Augustine Smith to Alice Page, Aug. 29, [1791], *ibid.*

"Go Nymphs!" "To Miss A. Page on her birthday 15 Sepr 1791," Augustine Smith Papers, ViWC.

PAGE

"committed . . . him": Augustine Smith to Alice Page, [ca. Oct. 5, 1792], Augustine Smith Papers, ViW.

"my" . . . "Sacrifice": John Page to Augustine Smith, Oct. 10, 1792, *ibid.*

"the most . . . thereon": John Page to [?], May 2, 1792, Paul C. Richards Collection, ViU.

347 and in entertaining: Thomas Jefferson Page, [Autobiography], "A revolutionary family," pp. 15–18, NcD; P. Lowther to Hannah Iredell, July 11, 1800, Iredell Papers, NcD.

The Smiths settled: For possessions, see Inventory, Estate of Augustine Smith, York County Wills and Inventories, No. 23, pp. 693–697, Vi; "Smith of Gloucester, York, &c.," *VMHB*, XXIII (Jan. 1915), 89. See also Jan Lewis, *The Pursuit of Happiness: Family and Values in Jefferson's Virginia* (Cambridge, 1983), chap. 5.

one of his quarter-shares: List of transfers, Dismal Swamp Land Company Records, NcD; John Page to Robert Carter, March 12, 1795, John Page Papers, NcD; John Page to George Washington, Oct. 14, 1795, Gratz Collection, PHi.

advertised other land: John Page to St. George Tucker, June 27, 1793, Tucker-Coleman Papers, ViW; *Virginia Gazette and General Advertiser,* April 10, July 24, Aug. 21, 1793.

"extreme . . . health": Charles Grymes to John Hatley Norton, Oct. 19, 1793, John Norton & Son Papers, ViWC.

slaves and livestock: Gloucester County Personal Property Taxes, Vi; Estimate of Assets, John Page Commonplace Book, ViRHi.

"Slippery" . . . "Sweated": Patrick Parker to James Parker, Jan. 4, 1790, Parker Papers, Liverpool Public Library.

ship *Powhatan:* Nathaniel Anderson, advertisement, *Virginia Gazette and General Advertiser,* Nov. 9, 1791, March 14, 1792.

348 Naval Office clerks: William Graves to Edmund Randolph, May 8, 1787, Josiah Parker to Beverley Randolph, June 20, 1787, entry of Sept. 4, 1787, Journal of Bolling Stark, Palmer *et al.*, eds., *Calendar of Virginia State Papers,* IV, 282, 298, 384; Médéric-Louis-Elie Moreau de Saint-Méry, *Moreau de Saint Méry's American Journey,* trans. Kenneth Roberts and Anna M. Roberts (Garden City, 1947), 51.

wheat and flour speculators: Patrick Parker to James Parker, Jan. 4, 1790, Parker Papers, Liverpool Public Library.

for about $8,000: la Rochefoucauld-Liancourt, *Travels,* trans. Neuman, III, 25.

borough of Norfolk: Entry of Feb. 28, 1788, *Journals of Enys,* ed. Cometti, 265–266; [George Tucker], *Letters from Virginia* (Baltimore, 1816), 19; Charles William Janson, *The Stranger in America, 1793–1806,* ed. Carl S. Driver (New York, 1935), 333; Thomas Fairfax, *Journey from Virginia to Salem, Massachusetts, 1799* (London, 1936), 4–5; Harry Toulmin, *The Western Country in 1793: Reports on Kentucky and Virginia,* ed. Marion Tinling and Godfrey Davies (San Marino, 1948), 14, 24–26; John Joyce to Robert Dickson, March 24, 1785, *VMHB,* XXIII (Oct. 1915), 407–408; Moreau de Saint-Méry, *American Journey,* trans. Roberts and Roberts, 46–47; la Rochefoucauld-Liancourt, *Travels,* trans. Neuman, III, 7–12; Weld, *Travels,* I, 174; Francis Baily, *Journal of a Tour in Unsettled Parts of North America in 1796 & 1797,* ed. Jack D. L. Holmes (Carbondale, 1969), 21–22.

"There . . . market": James Fisher to Israel Whelen, Nov. 4, 1792, Israel Whelen Papers, MiU-C.

PAGE

348 "this place . . . advantages": Thomas Newton, Jr., to George Washington, June 9, 1795, Papers of George Washington, DLC.

rumors of insurrections: See letters to and from Henry Lee, May 1792, in Executive Letterbooks, Nos. 9–10, Vi, and in Palmer *et al.*, eds., *Calendar of Virginia State Papers*, V, 540–542, 547, 551–552, 555; *Virginia Herald and Fredericksburg Advertiser*, May 24, 1792; Henry Lee to [?], May 17, 1792, PHi; Philip J. Schwarz, *Twice Condemned: Slaves and the Criminal Laws of Virginia, 1705–1865* (Baton Rouge, 1988), 323; Jordan, *White Over Black*, 391–392.

349 "Liberty" . . . "Blood": George Weare Braikenridge to Francis Jerdone, Aug. 13, 1792, Jerdone Family Papers, ViW. See also Judith Jennings, *The Business of Abolishing the British Slave Trade, 1783–1807* (London, 1997), chap. 5; Gretchen Gerzina, *Black London: Life before Emancipation* (New Brunswick, 1995), chap. 6; James Walvin, *England, Slaves and Freedom, 1776–1838* (Jackson, 1986), chap. 5.

passed new laws: Tommy L. Bogger, "Slave Resistance in Virginia During the Haitian Revolution, 1791–1804," *HIJES*, V (April 1978), 87.

from Cap Français: Carolyn E. Fick, *The Making of Haiti: The Saint Domingue Revolution from Below* (Knoxville, 1990), 158–159; John D. Garrigus, " 'Sons of the Same Father': Gender, Race, and Citizenship in French Saint-Domingue, 1760–1792," in Christine Adams *et al.*, eds., *Visions and Revisions of Eighteenth-Century France* (University Park, 1997), 137–153; Frances Sergeant Childs, *French Refugee Life in the United States, 1790–1800* (Baltimore, 1940), 12–16; Althéa de Puech Parham, trans., *My Odyssey: Experiences of a Young Refugee from Two Revolutions* (Baton Rouge, 1959), 89–96. See also Sara Shannon, *"The Horrible Combats"* ([Minneapolis], 1992).

"too many negroes": Thomas Newton, Jr., to Henry Lee, July 9, 1793, Palmer *et al.*, eds., *Calendar of Virginia State Papers*, VI, 443.

350 Those who had brought slaves: Bogger, "Slave Resistance," *HIJES*, V (April 1978), 89; Parramore *et al.*, *Norfolk*, 102–105, 113; Moreau de Saint-Méry, *American Journey*, trans. Roberts and Roberts, 50–51, 61. See also Christopher Phillips, *Freedom's Port: The African American Community of Baltimore, 1790–1860* (Urbana, 1997), 70–73.

reports of plots: Palmer *et al.*, eds., *Calendar of Virginia State Papers*, VI, 453, 470, 475, 488, 490, 494, 504, 523–524, 547, 571–572; Bogger, "Slave Resistance," *HIJES*, V (April 1978), 90–91.

"a design . . . Domingo": Henry Lee to Speaker, Oct. 21, 1793, Executive Letterbooks, Vi.

the Norfolk militia: Moreau de Saint-Méry, *American Journey*, trans. Roberts and Roberts, 57–58.

"French" . . . "other": Thomas Newton, Jr., to James Wood, April 28, 1795, Palmer *et al.*, eds., *Calendar of Virginia State Papers*, VII, 475.

"with" . . . "important": *Virginia Herald and Fredericksburg Advertiser*, Nov. 3, 1795; Thomas Jefferson to William Moultrie, Dec. 23, 1793, *Papers of Jefferson*, ed. Boyd *et al.*, XXVII, 614. See also James Sidbury, "Saint Domingue in Virginia: Ideology, Local Meanings, and Resistance to Slavery, 1790–1800," *JSH*, LXIII (Aug. 1997), 531–552; James Sidbury, *Ploughshares into Swords: Race, Rebellion, and Identity in Gabriel's Virginia, 1730–1810* (Cambridge, 1997), 39–48.

351 "had . . . disposal": [Wilson Cary Nicholas], "Lee vs Nicholas," Wilson Cary Nicholas Papers, Box 3, DLC; Paul Demund Evans, *The Holland Land Company* (Buffalo, 1924), 13–33; William Chazanof, *Joseph Ellicott and the Holland Land Company* (Syracuse, 1970), chap. 1. On Cazenove, see also Lucy S. Sutherland and John A. Woods, "The East India Speculations of William Burke," Leeds Philosophical and Literary Society, *Proceedings*, XI (Jan. 1966), 200–201.

"in fertility" . . . "worth": Memorandum for Governor Henry Lee, Feb. 18, 1793, *Writings of Washington*, ed. Fitzpatrick, XXXII, 349–351.

seemed "timid": George Washington to Robert Morris, May 26, 1794, *ibid.*, 381.

his "manufacturing town": Henry Lee to Bryan Fairfax, March 6, 1793, Henry Lee Papers, ViRHi.

"the best . . . affliction": Henry Lee to George Washington, April 23, 1793, Papers of George Washington, DLC; Arthur Campbell to Isaac Shelby, July 27, 1792, Shelby Family Papers, DLC.

"I will . . . you": Henry Lee to Armistead Burwell, April 20, 1793, Burwell Family Papers, Subseries 1:1, Box 1, NcU.

Maria Farley: [Samuel] Storrow to sister, Sept. 6–10, 1821, Lee Family Papers, duPont Library, Stratford, Virginia. Storrow was the husband of Maria Farley's oldest daughter. See also Ethel Armes, *Stratford Hall: The Great House of the Lees* (Richmond, 1936), 274–275; Anna Mary Wells, *Dear Preceptor: The Life and Times of Thomas Wentworth Higginson* (Boston, 1963), 24–43.

352 "I . . . possible": Henry Lee to Alexander Hamilton, May 6, 1793, *The Papers of Alexander Hamilton*, ed. Harold C. Syrett *et al.* (New York, 1961–87), XIV, 416.

"we . . . Wife": Charles Carter to Henry Lee, May 20, 1793, Henry Lee Papers, Vi.

Washington turned: George Washington to Robert Morris, May 26, 1794, Land Memorandum, May 25, 1794, *Writings of Washington*, ed. Fitzpatrick, XXXIII, 381, 377–380.

"can . . . hope": Henry Lee to [Robert Morris?], 1794, *Goodspeed's Autographs, Catalogue 496* (1961), Item 373. See also Robert Morris to Henry Lee, Dec. 30, 1794, Robert Morris Letterbooks, DLC.

bought Belvidere: Edward L. Ryan, "Note on 'Belvidere,' " *VMHB*, XXXIX (April 1931), 142–143.

353 "there are . . . sum": Henry Lee to Patrick Henry, Feb. 4, 1795, HM 19957, CSmH.

in Crosby Square: W. Lowndes, *The London Directory for the Year 1790* [London, 1790], 15; W. Lowndes, *The London Directory for the Year 1791* [London, 1791], 13; Lucy Paradise to Thomas Jefferson, March 1, 1791, *Papers of Jefferson*, ed. Boyd *et al.*, XIX, 354; George Walter Thornbury, *Old and New London* (London, [1873–85?]), II, 155–158; J. Saunders, "Crosby Place," in Charles Knight, ed., *London* (London, 1841–44), I, 317–322; K. I. Garrett, "Maria Hackett, Crosby Hall and Gresham College," *Guildhall Studies in London History*, III (Oct. 1977), 42–43.

he had representatives: *Virginia Gazette and General Advertiser*, Nov. 9, 1791, Jan. 9, 1793.

"The premiums . . . free of": Turnbull Forbes & Company to Nicholas Low, Sept. 7, 1792, Nicholas Low Papers, DLC.

War suddenly brought: Nathaniel Cutting to Thomas Lee Shippen, June 8, 1793, Shippen Family Papers, DLC; *The Annual Biography and Obituary*, VII (London, 1824), 277;

George Gairdner to Francis Jerdone, May 8, 1793, Jerdone Family Papers, ViW; S. R. Cope, "Bird, Savage & Bird of London: Merchants and Bankers, 1782 to 1803," *Guildhall Studies in London History*, IV (April 1981), 202–204; John Bruce to Viscount Melville, Oct. 15, 1794, *Maggs Bros. Bibliotheca Americana, Part VII, No. 502* (1928), Item 5945; William Robertson to John Askin, April 10, 1793, June 24, 1794, *The John Askin Papers*, ed. Milo M. Quaife (Detroit, 1928–31), I, 471, 507–508.

353 A crisis of credit: Henry B. Lightfoot to Thomas Lee Shippen, June 15, 1793, Nathaniel Cutting to Thomas Lee Shippen, June 8, 1793, Shippen Family Papers, DLC; Hoppit, *Risk and Failure*, 122–127; John Ehrman, *The Younger Pitt: The Reluctant Transition* (Stanford, 1988), 385–387; Lucyle Werkmeister, *A Newspaper History of England, 1792–1793* (Lincoln, 1967), 391–392; Feavearyear, *Pound Sterling*, rev. Morgan, 177–178.

354 "the great . . . Underwriters": *Report from Select Committee Appointed to Consider . . . the State and Means of Effecting Marine Insurance in Great Britain*, 1810 (226) IV. 247, p. 69.

in Exchequer bills: Ehrman, *Younger Pitt: Reluctant Transition*, 385–387; Hoppit, *Risk and Failure*, 138–139.

the New Concern: Complaint and Answer, and Accounts of Henry S. Shore, *Gist et al., Exors of Anderson* v. *Henry S. Shore*, 1817, USCCVD(EC), Vi; deposition of Thomas Noyes, Oct. 24, 1823, C 117/335, XC1244, PRO.

wrote his will: William Anderson, Will, July 20, 1793, *Anderson's Heirs &c* v. *Gist's Exors et al.*, 1824, USCCVD(EC), Vi. See also *VMHB*, XXXVII (Jan. 1929), 39–41.

355 "to run . . . &ca": Benjamin Day to John Hatley Norton, Jan. 24, 1794, John Norton & Son Papers, ViWC. On the *Powhatan*, see advertisement, *Virginia Herald and Fredericksburg Advertiser*, Nov. 21, 1793.

"the monied" . . . "by": Nathaniel Cutting to Thomas Lee Shippen, June 8, 1793, Shippen Family Papers, DLC.

"they . . . Lands": Enoch Edwards to Tench Coxe, Aug. 17, 1793, Tench Coxe Papers, Series II, PHi. See also L. S. Pressnell, "The Rate of Interest in the Eighteenth Century," in L. S. Pressnell, ed., *Studies in the Industrial Revolution* (London, 1960), 178–214.

worth £80,000,000: Entry of Feb. 1, 1795, *Farington Diary*, ed. Greig, I, 90.

cautious chartered companies: A. H. John, "The London Assurance Company and the Marine Insurance Market of the Eighteenth Century," *Economica*, XXV (May 1958), 130; Barry Supple, *The Royal Exchange Assurance: A History of British Insurance, 1720–1970* (Cambridge, 1970), 53, 61–62; Frederick Martin, *The History of Lloyd's and of Marine Insurance in Great Britain* (New York, 1971 [orig. publ. London, 1876]), 229.

"Lloyd's . . . itself": *Public Characters of 1803–1804* (London, 1804), 389.

Joseph Jones: Samuel Gist to Joseph Jones, March 31, 1794, Joseph Jones to Thomas Shore, Dec. 30, 1798, Joseph Jones Family Papers, NcD; *Samuel Gist* v. *Jones & Atkinson, surviving partners*, 1798, USCCVD(EC), Vi.

"The Piece . . . Audience": Entry of Feb. 4, 1792, Gouverneur Morris, *A Diary of the French Revolution*, ed. Beatrix Cary Davenport (Boston, 1939), II, 361; Kelly, *German Visitors*, 125.

warned Robert Morris: Barbara Ann Chernow, *Robert Morris: Land Speculator, 1790–1801* (New York, 1978), 87.

PAGE

356 "that the . . . day": Entry of March 21, 1786, Frederick Haldimand, "Private Diary of Gen. Haldimand," *Report on Canadian Archives: 1889* (Ottawa, 1890), 157.

proceedings for divorce: A. C. E. Greenleaf to Sylvanus Bourne, March 24, 1797, North American Land Company Papers, ViU. See also James Greenleaf to Noah Webster, Jan. 19, 1788, Aug. 18, 1789, in Emily Ellsworth Fowler Ford, *Notes on the Life of Noah Webster,* ed. Emily Ellsworth Ford Skeel (New York, 1912), I, 188, 205; P. J. Van Winter, *Het aandeel van den Amsterdamschen handel aan den opbouw van het Amerikaansche Gemeenebest* (The Hague, 1927), I, 209n.2.

"tempted" him: Robert Morris to George Washington, Sept. 21, 1795, Papers of George Washington, DLC.

357 "Washington . . . come!": Robert Morris to John Nicholson, Sept. 2, 1793, quoted in Robert D. Arbuckle, *Pennsylvania Speculator and Patriot: The Entrepreneurial John Nicholson, 1757–1800* (University Park, 1975), 115.

"with uncommon difficulty": John Steele to Joseph Winston, July 20, 1790, Ernest Haywood Papers, NcU.

358 "the Grand" . . . "pounds": Samuel Davidson to Thomas Shore, April 12, 1791, Letterbook, Samuel Davidson Papers, DLC.

"the pleasure . . . world": Christopher Gore to Tobias Lear, Dec. 28, 1791, Tobias Lear Papers, DLC.

"in a stagnant state": George Washington to Daniel Carroll, Jan. 7, 1795, *Writings of Washington,* ed. Fitzpatrick, XXXIV, 80.

"promise" . . . "acquisition": George Washington to Commissioners, Aug. 20, 1793, *ibid.,* XXXIII, 57–58.

359 Morris and Lee: Robert Morris to James Marshall, Sept. 17, 1796, Robert Morris to Henry Lee, Sept. 30, 1796, Robert Morris Letterbooks, DLC; Henry Lee to George Washington, Sept. 28, 1798, Feb. 28, 1799, Papers of George Washington, DLC; la Rochefoucauld-Liancourt, *Travels,* trans. Neuman, III, 624–625; entry of Oct. 5, 1796, Baily, *Journal,* ed. Holmes, 40.

the Federal City: Entry of Oct. 5, 1796, Baily, *Journal,* ed. Holmes, 38–39; Weld, *Travels,* I, 86–87; entry of April 27, 1796, Twining, *Travels,* 100–103; entry of April 3, 1797, Louis-Philippe, Duc d'Orléans, *Diary of My Travels in America,* trans. Stephen Becker (New York, 1977), 21–27.

"The value . . . sterling": David John Jeremy, ed., *Henry Wansey and His American Journal* (Philadelphia, 1970), 135.

"were . . . States": Entry of Oct. 5, 1796, Baily, *Journal,* ed. Holmes, 39.

"in case . . . *blanche*": James Greenleaf to Sylvanus Bourne, June 25, 1794, Sylvanus Bourne Papers, DLC. Compare Tobias Lear to James Greenleaf, May 10, 1794, Emmet Collection, NN.

William Duer: Robert F. Jones, *"The King of the Alley": William Duer, Politician, Entrepreneur, and Speculator, 1768–1799* (Philadelphia, 1992), 201, 206.

"commercial Speculation": Turnbull Forbes & Co. to Nicholas Low, June 25, 1794, Nicholas Low Papers, DLC.

"immense profit": George Washington to Daniel Carroll, Jan. 7, 1795, *Writings of Washington,* ed. Fitzpatrick, XXXIV, 79–80.

360 Daniel Carroll: Daniel Carroll to George Washington, Jan. 13, 1794 [1795], Papers of George Washington, DLC. See also Nathaniel W. Appleton to Noah Webster, Nov. 23, 1793, July 26, 1794, in Ford, *Notes on the Life of Webster*, ed. Skeel, I, 376, 384–385.

"a man . . . understanding": David Stuart to George Washington, Feb. 25, 1796, Papers of George Washington, DLC.

"Betsey . . . Husband": *Ibid.*

"I . . . myself": Robert Morris to Thomas Law, Dec. 11, 1796, Morris Letterbooks, DLC.

"he . . . speculation": la Rochefoucauld-Liancourt, *Travels*, trans. Neuman, III, 661–662; Duc de la Rochefoucauld-Liancourt to Thomas Law, Aug. 26, 1797, Emmet Collection, NN; "An Account of the City of Washington. Drawn Up by a Foreigner, in 1803," reprinted in Eugene L. Schwaab, ed., *Travels in the Old South* (Lexington, 1973), I, 47; entry of July 10, 1820, William Faux, "Memorable Days in America: Being a Journal of a Tour to the United States," in Reuben Gold Thwaites, ed., *Early Western Travels, 1748–1846* (Cleveland, 1904–07), XII, 112–113. On the founding and early years of the District of Columbia, see Kenneth R. Bowling, *The Creation of Washington, D.C.: The Idea and Location of the American Capital* (Fairfax, 1991); Bob Arnebeck, *Through a Fiery Trial: Building Washington, 1790–1800* (Lanham, 1991); Stanley Elkins and Eric McKitrick, *The Age of Federalism* (New York, 1993), chap. 4; Sloan, *Principle and Interest*, chap. 4; Allen C. Clark, *Greenleaf and Law in the Federal City* (Washington, 1901); Arbuckle, *Pennsylvania Speculator and Patriot*, chap. 8; Chernow, *Robert Morris*; George Alfred Townsend, "Thomas Law, Washington's First Rich Man," Columbia Historical Society of Washington, D.C., *Records*, IV (1901), 222–245.

Charles William Janson: Janson, *Stranger*, ed. Driver, xxiv, 333–335, 210, 270, 269. See also Charles Albert, Chevalier de Pontgibaud, Comte de Moré, *A French Volunteer of the War of Independence*, trans. Robert B. Douglas, 2d ed. (Paris, 1898), 129–132.

361 George Washington had lost: George Washington to Tobias Lear, May 6, 1794, George Washington to Edmund Randolph, April 12, 1795, George Washington to Alexander Spotswood, Nov. 23, 1794, *Writings of Washington*, ed. Fitzpatrick, XXXIII, 358, XXXIV, 174, 47–48.

"perfectly . . . spirits": David Humphreys to Tobias Lear, March 9, 1795, Tobias Lear Papers, DLC.

"get" . . . "Company": John Jameson to George Washington, Jan. 30, 1795, Papers of George Washington, DLC.

"Having . . . advance": George Washington to John Jameson, Feb. 15, 1795, *Writings of Washington*, ed. Fitzpatrick, XXXIV, 112–114.

362 United States Circuit Court: Henry Lee to Patrick Henry, April 22, 1795, Patrick Henry and Family Collection, DLC.

"I . . . dry": Hugh Williamson to James Wilson, June 29, 1795, Gratz Collection, PHi.

in the Green Sea: Charles Page Smith, *James Wilson, Founding Father: 1742–1798* (Chapel Hill, 1956), 374–378; Henry Lee to Patrick Henry, April 22, 1795, Patrick Henry and Family Collection, DLC; Patrick Henry to James Wilson, Sept. 18, 1795, Emmet Collection, NN.

the Belvidere estate: Ryan, "Belvidere," *VMHB*, XXXIX (April 1931), 143.

the "highest price": George Washington to Thomas Newton, Jr., Sept. 23, 1795, George Washington to John Page, Sept. 23, 1795, *Writings of Washington*, ed. Fitzpatrick, XXXIV, 313–314.

more than £1,000: Thomas Newton, Jr., to George Washington, Sept. 30, 1795, Papers of George Washington, DLC; John Page to George Washington, Oct. 14, 1795, Gratz Collection, PHi.

"the land" . . . "activity": Isaac Sexton to Thomas Newton, Jr., Sept. 30, 1795, Papers of George Washington, DLC.

363 "wished" . . . "quantity": John Driver to David Jameson, July 11, 1791, Dismal Swamp Land Company Records, NcD.

"that . . . Swamp": Deposition of Peter Culpeper, Nov. 15, 1809, *Etting & wife* v. *Wilson et al.* and *Mordecai* v. *Wilson et al.*, BR Box 211, Deposition of Peter Culpeper, Oct. 17, 1810, Virginia Courts—County Courts—Norfolk County, BR Box 222(21), CSmH.

John Cowper surveyed: William Nelson, Jr., to John Brown, Oct. 8, 1800, Dismal Swamp Land Company Records, NcD.

"that . . . Sexton": Thomas Shepherd to Thomas Swepson, June 30, 1800, *ibid.*

"the injury" . . . "interests": Entry of July 19, 1796, *The Virginia Journals of Benjamin Henry Latrobe, 1795–1798*, ed. Edward C. Carter II *et al.* (New Haven, 1977), I, 167.

"rather . . . productive": George Washington to John Page, Sept. 23, 1795, *Writings of Washington*, ed. Fitzpatrick, XXXIV, 314.

sale to Lee: Entry of July 19, 1796, *Journals of Latrobe*, ed. Carter *et al.*, I, 167; Henry Lee to George Washington, Nov. 7, 1795, Papers of George Washington, DLC; Henry Lee, Schedule of Assets, quoted in John James Chew to William Selden, Aug. 8, 1835, BR Box 5, CSmH; George Washington to Members of the Dismal Swamp Company, Nov. 16, 1795, *Writings of Washington*, ed. Fitzpatrick, XXXIV, 363.

364 Weston Alcock: Minor, "Memorandum of Inquiries," Virginia MSS, Vol. 13, Draper Collection, Series ZZ, WHi; Goode, *Virginia Ancestors*, 215; Parole of Officers, Dec. 13, 1777, E. B. O'Callaghan, ed., *Orderly Book of Lieut. Gen. John Burgoyne* (Albany, 1860), 178.

he was "right": James Madison to Thomas Jefferson, April 12, 1793, *Papers of Madison*, ed. Hutchinson and Rachal *et al.*, XV, 7.

Francis Walker drunk: "Bonds returned to Francis Walker by Francis Preston, Nov. 8, 1793," Campbell-Preston-Floyd Papers, Vol. 3, DLC; [Francis Preston], [Draft of an answer], Preston Family Papers—Gray Collection, KyLoF.

"extensive" . . . "palate": William Wirt to Elizabeth Wirt, April 9, 1806, Wirt Papers, MdBHi.

"was . . . Roanoke": Brown, *Cabells*, 204.

"the speculating" . . . "liberty": Cunningham, ed., *Circular Letters*, I, 39–43.

"lacked" . . . "descendants": Franklin Minor to L. C. Draper, Jan. 30, 1853, Virginia MSS, Vol. 13, Draper Collection, Series ZZ, WHi.

365 "indefatigable" . . . "grog": Thomas Jefferson to James Madison, Feb. 5, Mar. 5, 1795, *The Republic of Letters: The Correspondence Between Thomas Jefferson and James Madison, 1776–1826*, ed. James Morton Smith (New York, 1995), II, 871, 875. See also Daniel P. Jordan, *Political Leadership in Jefferson's Virginia* (Charlottesville, 1983), chaps. 5–7.

365 "great . . . care": John Cook Wyllie, ed., "New Documentary Light on Tarleton's Raid: Letters of Newman Brockenbrough and Peter Lyons," *VMHB*, LXXIV (Oct. 1966), 461n; Minor, "Memoranda of Inquiries," Virginia MSS, Vol. 13, Draper Collection, Series ZZ, WHi.

to be £1,000: Thomas Lee Shippen to William Shippen, Oct. 10, 1792, Shippen Family Papers, DLC.

litigation: *John Simon Farley and Elizabeth Morson* v. *Thomas Lee Shippen and Elizabeth Carter Shippen et al.*, March 1794, *Decisions in Chancery by Wythe*, 253–260.

Williamsburg: William Nelson, Jr., to William Short, Oct. 16, 1785, William Short Papers, DLC; entry of July 28, 1787, Journal of Samuel Vaughan, DLC; entry of Feb. 26, 1786, *Quebec to Carolina: Diary of Hunter*, ed. Wright and Tinling, 233; [Tucker], *Letters from Virginia*, 121–123; la Rochefoucauld-Liancourt, *Travels*, trans. Neuman, III, 46–52; entry of April 5, 1796, *Journals of Latrobe*, ed. Carter *et al.*, I, 87; [St. George Tucker], *A Letter, to the Rev. Jedediah Morse, A.M.* (Richmond, 1795), 13–15n; J. Prentis to Benjamin Harrison, Dec. 1782, Executive Papers, Gov. Benjamin Harrison, Vi; Weld, *Travels*, I, 61, 167–169; William Winterbotham, *An Historical, Geographical, Commercial, and Philosophical View of the American United States*, 2d ed. (London, 1799), III, 100; [William Wirt], Memoirs of Patrick Henry, Patrick Henry and Family Papers, DLC; Schoepf, *Travels*, trans. Morrison, II, 78–81; Jedediah Morse to Ezra Stiles, Dec. 30, 1786–Jan. 1, 1787, *Letters and Papers of Ezra Stiles*, ed. Isabel M. Calder (New Haven, 1933), 69.

John Dunbar: George Izard to John Wickham, Jan. 12, 1807, Amount of Annual Expences for Mercer's Creek Estate, Payments Made to John Dunbar, Nov. 15, 1795, *Dinwiddie, Crawford & Co.* v. *Henry Skipwith and Elizabeth Hill Skipwith et al.*, 1819, USCCVD(EC), Vi; Answer of George Tucker to a Bill of Complaints, April 16, 1823, Davidson County—Estates Records, Henry, Patrick and Francis and Simon Farley, 1803–1822, Nc-Ar; Richard Corbin to Thomas Lee Shippen, July 20, 1795, Shippen Family Papers, DLC.

367 His decision awarded: *John Simon Farley and Elizabeth Morson* v. *Thomas Lee Shippen and Elizabeth Carter Shippen et al.*, March 1794, *Decisions in Chancery by Wythe*, 253–260.

"a Hermitess" . . . "Letter": Maria Corbin to Richard Corbin, Nov. 3, Dec. 3, 1794, n.d. [Nov. 1794], Corbin Family Papers, Vi.

at Laneville plantation: Malcolm Hart Harris, *Old New Kent County* (West Point, 1977), I, 340–341.

368 he wrote his will: Thomas Lee Shippen, Will, March 4, 1795, Shippen Family Papers, DLC.

"what . . . present": Richard Corbin to Thomas Lee Shippen, June 26, 1795, *ibid.*

"be . . . friends": Elizabeth Dunbar to Thomas Lee Shippen and Elizabeth Shippen, Sept. 26, 1796, *ibid.*

"finely situated": Julian Ursyn Niemcewicz, *Under Their Vine and Fig Tree: Travels Through America in 1797–1799, 1805*, trans. Metchie J. E. Budka (Elizabeth, 1965), 289–290; George Tucker to St. George Tucker, Aug. 12, 1797, Tucker-Coleman Papers, ViW.

compromised: Answer of George Tucker, April 26, 1823, Davidson County—Estates Records, Henry, Patrick and Francis and Simon Farley, 1803–1822, Nc-Ar.

369 $2 per acre: William Armstrong Crozier, ed., *Spotsylvania County Records, 1721–1800* (Baltimore, 1955), 485–486. For "Sama" read "Saura."

"more . . . tranquillity": William Nelson, Jr., to William Short, Dec. 8, 1791, William Short Papers, DLC; Charles T. Cullen, "St. George Tucker and Law in Virginia, 1772–1804" (Ph.D. diss., University of Virginia, 1971), 113–117, 122.

a deed of trust: Charles Grymes to John Hatley Norton, Oct. 19, 1793, John Norton & Son Papers, ViWC; John Page Commonplace Book, ViRHi. See also Philip D. Morgan, *Slave Counterpoint: Black Culture in the Eighteenth-Century Chesapeake and Lowcountry* (Chapel Hill, 1998), 512–515.

500 acres around it: John Page to Robert Carter, March 12, 1795, John Page Papers, NcD.

He resigned: John Page to Robert Brooke, July 3, 1795, Palmer *et al.*, eds., *Calendar of Virginia State Papers*, VIII, 271.

promised a creditor: John Page to St. George Tucker, Dec. 3, 1795, Tucker-Coleman Papers, ViW.

Abby Nelson: [Memorandum of] A[nn] W[illing] Byrd, May 5, 1796, Byrd Family Papers, ViRHi.

370 A "feeling letter": William Nelson, Jr., to St. George Tucker, Jan. 5, 1796, Tucker-Coleman Papers, ViW.

John Tabb: Gist's suits, 1795, are in USCCVD(EC), Vi. For "derangement," see *Papers of Marshall*, ed. Johnson *et al.*, VI, 129.

gold watch for $60: John Page Commonplace Book, ViRHi.

"John . . . out": John Page, Memoir, *Virginia Historical Register*, III (July 1850), 150.

"No . . . Canal": John Page to George Washington, Oct. 14, 1795, Gratz Collection, PHi.

the way to succeed: Advertisement, *Virginia Gazette and General Advertiser*, Sept. 28, 1796.

"by which . . . purpose": David Meade to John Driver, Oct. 28, 1794, Webb-Prentis Papers, Box 38, ViU.

371 "there . . . care": David Meade to Anne Randolph, Oct. 20, 1796, William Bolling Papers, NcD.

1,000 acres in Frederick County: Ferdinand-M. Bayard, *Travels of a Frenchman in Maryland and Virginia*, trans. Ben C. McCary (Ann Arbor, 1950), 68–70, 81–82; David Lynn Holmes, Jr., "William Meade and the Church of Virginia, 1789–1829" (Ph.D. diss., Princeton University, 1971), 48–50.

ate rice: Account of David Meade, June 2, 1795, Dismal Swamp Land Company Records, NcD.

Meade and Waller: David Meade to Wakelin Welch, Dec. 9, 1797, List of Debts, Affidavit of Benjamin Waller, Sept. 12, 1810, T 79/3, ff. 344–345, 346, 407–425, PRO; Joseph Prentis to St. George Tucker, June 23, 1809, Tucker-Coleman Papers, ViW.

Benjamin Grymes: Richard Kidder Meade to St. George Tucker, Jan. 16, 1796, Tucker-Coleman Papers, ViW; "Grymes of Brandon," *VMHB*, XXVIII (April 1920), 187–188, (July 1920), 284; Crozier, ed., *Spotsylvania Records*, 211.

Justice James Wilson: George Keith Taylor to James Wilson, Jan. 30, 1796, quoted in Smith, *James Wilson*, 377–378, where "Taylor" is erroneously spelled "Saylor"; George

Keith Taylor to Henry Lee, [1798], Ethel Armes Collection of Lee Family Papers, DLC; Thomas Swepson and Richard W. Byrd, Indenture, May 18, 1802, Kilby Family Papers, Box 1, Vi; David Meade to Joseph Prentis, June 13, 1797, Webb-Prentis Papers, ViU.

372 "in . . . China": David Meade to John Driver, Aug. 14, 1796, Webb-Prentis Papers, ViU. "purchase . . . capitals": Smith, *Wealth of Nations*, 5th ed., II, 199. See also Peter McNamara, *Political Economy and Statemanship: Smith, Hamilton, and the Foundation of the Commercial Republic* (DeKalb, 1998), 129–133.

"a genteel" . . . "best": Thomas Blount to John Gray Blount, Jan. 11, 1794, *The John Gray Blount Papers*, ed. Alice Barnwell Keith *et al.* (Raleigh, 1952–82), II, 342–343.

373 "I wish" . . . "Secret": John Hall to John Gray Blount, June 5, 26, 1794, *ibid.*, 402, 412.

"good" . . . "Carolina": John Gray Blount to John Nicholson, Aug. 18, 1794, quoted in Arbuckle, *Pennsylvania Speculator and Patriot*, 181.

"you . . . Land": John Hall to John Gray Blount, June 26, 1794, *Blount Papers*, ed. Keith *et al.*, II, 412.

"that fully . . . Acre": Thomas Blount to John Gray Blount, Feb. 19, 1795, *ibid.*, 495–496; Robert Morris to John Nicholson, Nov. 27, 1798, *Stan. V. Henkels Catalogue No. 1194* (June 1917), Item 640.

an "amazing quantity": Samuel Yorke to Hore Browse Trist, Oct. 25, 1796, Nicholas P. Trist Papers, NcU; William H. Masterson, *William Blount* (Baton Rouge, 1954), 299–301.

"positive" . . . "civil": Entries of Aug. 6, 30, 1789, Morris, *Diary of the French Revolution*, ed. Davenport, I, 179, 201.

intercepted his mail: Interceptions, Vol. 35, Shelburne Papers, MiU-C; Edmund Burke to James Bourdieu, Dec. 2, 1781, *The Correspondence of Edmund Burke*, ed. Thomas W. Copeland *et al.* (Cambridge and Chicago, 1958–78), IV, 383.

374 "he seems . . . Canaan": Bourdieu, Chollet & Bourdieu to Nicholas Low, Jan. 5, 1785, Nicholas Low Papers, DLC.

"the Name . . . Community": Entry of Aug. 6, 1789, Morris, *Diary of the French Revolution*, ed. Davenport, I, 179–180.

"While . . . place it": Bourdieu, Chollet & Bourdieu to Duc de Talleyrand-Périgord, Aug. 6, 1794, *Talleyrand in America as a Financial Promoter, 1794–96: Unpublished Letters and Memoirs*, trans. Hans Huth and Wilma J. Pugh (Washington, 1942), 66–68.

"at a" . . . "gambler": Thomas Law to James Greenleaf, Jan. 8, 1795, in Clark, *Greenleaf and Law*, 101; Robert Morris to James Greenleaf, Jan. 6, 1795, Morris Letterbooks, DLC.

"a very . . . home": Rebecca Aitchison to James Parker, March 10, 1789, Parker Papers, Liverpool Public Library.

"a purchaser . . . there": Thomas Cooper, *Some Information Respecting America* (London, 1794), 25. See also "Some Particulars Relative to . . . Kentucky," reprinted in Schwaab, ed., *Travels in the Old South*, I, 58.

to scrutinize closely: Robert Morris to Charles W. Byrd, Feb. 10, Nov. 11, 1795, Morris Letterbooks, DLC.

"hundreds" . . . "Honey": Austin, "Memorandum," *AHR*, V (April 1900), 525–526.

"two" . . . "Land": Elijah Poage to Archibald Woods, June 23, 1790, Archibald Woods Papers, ViW.

PAGE

"the speculating" . . . "doubtful": John Breckinridge to James Greenleaf, Aug. 1, 1805, North American Land Company Papers, ViU.

375 the North American Land Company: Robert Morris to Bird, Savage & Bird, March 20, 1795, Robert Morris to William Temple Franklin, April 22, 1795, Morris Letterbooks, DLC; *Plan of Association of the North American Land Company* (Philadelphia, 1795); Norman B. Wilkinson, *Land Policy and Speculation in Pennsylvania, 1779–1800* (New York, 1979), 185–207; Arbuckle, *Pennsylvania Speculator and Patriot*, chap. 10.

archvillain: Durand Echeverria, *Mirage in the West: A History of the French Image of American Society to 1815* (Princeton, 1957), 209–210; Jean Antoine Joseph Fauchet to Committee on Public Safety, May 4, 1995, Frederick Jackson Turner, ed., *Correspondence of the French Ministers to the United States, 1791–1797* (Washington, 1904), 679–680.

"TIM. BROADBACK": *Virginia Gazette and General Advertiser,* April 15, 1795; Weld, *Travels,* I, 403–404.

"the best . . . America": Robert Morris to Bird, Savage & Bird, March 20, 1795, Morris Letterbooks, DLC.

"the uncultivated . . . world": Robert Morris to Amyand & Osborne, May 7, 1795, *ibid.*

a pamphlet: (London, 1796), 34–37.

376 "daily falling due": Robert Morris to Benjamin Harrison, Jr., July 1, 1795, Morris Letterbooks, DLC.

Morris and Lee: Henry Lee, Schedule, quoted in John James Chew to William Selden, Aug. 8, 1835, BR Box 5, CSmH; Henry Lee to George Washington, Feb. 28, 1799, Papers of George Washington, DLC. See also Barbara A. Chernow, "Robert Morris: Genesee Land Speculator," *NYH,* LVIII (April 1977), 202–219.

"The Lands . . . certain": Robert Morris to William Temple Franklin, Nov. 14, 1795, Morris Letterbooks, DLC.

377 a packet of papers: Robert Morris and John Nicholson to James Marshall, Oct. 16, 1795, Robert Morris Collection, CSmH; Robert Morris to James Marshall, Oct. 17, 1795, Morris Letterbooks, DLC. On Morris's operations, see also Chernow, *Robert Morris,* chap. 5.

"Let . . . land": Harry Toulmin to James Leigh, May 19, 1794, in Toulmin, *Western Country,* ed. Tinling and Davies, 136.

VII: TERRAPHOBIA

378 large bills of exchange: See the suits against Macaulay, 1795–1799, USCCVD(EC), Vi.

"suffered greatly": Alexander Macaulay to Francis Jerdone, May 23, 1795, Jerdone Family Papers, ViW.

"his own use": Dismal Swamp Company's Pleading in Chancery, Legal Papers of Dismal Swamp Company, Jerdone Family Papers, Box 12, ViW.

"Self . . . $8040.34": *Dismal Swamp Land Company* v. *Alexander Macaulay,* Anderson-Macaulay Legal Papers, BR Box 50(1d), CSmH.

Macaulay's troubles: Alexander Macaulay to Francis Jerdone, May 23, 1795, William Douglass to Francis Jerdone, Jan. 4, 1796, Jerdone Family Papers, ViW; *Virginia Herald and Fredericksburg Advertiser,* Aug. 21, 1795.

PAGE

378 "an intelligent . . . gentleman": Entry of June 12, 1797, *The Virginia Journals of Benjamin Henry Latrobe, 1795–1798*, ed. Edward C. Carter II *et al.* (New Haven, 1977), I, 238.

379 the company and Shepherd: "Agreement dated 1 Jan '96," Dismal Swamp Land Company Records, NcD.

"hold possession": Thomas Shepherd to John Jameson, Nov. 28, 1798, Swamp Account for 1795 & 1796, Dec. 31, 1796, *ibid.*

and about forty slaves: David Meade to Anne Randolph, June 6–7, 1796, William Bolling Papers, NcD.

380 to Lexington: Entry of Dec. 17, 1795, Thomas Chapman, "Journal of a Journey Through the United States, 1795–6," *Historical Magazine*, 2d ser., V (June 1869), 363; Bernard Mayo, "Lexington: Frontier Metropolis," in Eric F. Goldman, ed., *Historiography and Urbanization: Essays in American History in Honor of W. Still Holt* (Baltimore, 1941), 21–42; Lee Shai Weissbach, "The Peopling of Lexington: Growth and Mobility in a Frontier Town," *KHSR*, LXXXI (1983), 115–133.

fixed there for life: Robert Morris to Charles W. Byrd, Aug. 29, 1796, Robert Morris Letterbooks, DLC.

"Mr. West . . . acquaintance": David Meade to John Driver, Aug. 14, 1796, Webb-Prentis Papers, Box 38, ViU.

Chaumière des Prairies: Horace Holley to Mary Holley, May 27, 1818, Horace Holley Papers, MiU-C; Charles Caldwell, *A Discourse on the Genius and Character of the Rev. Horace Holley* (Boston, 1828), 153–154; Mayo, "Lexington," in Goldman, ed., *Historiography and Urbanization*, 23–24; [Mary Virginia Terhune], *More Colonial Homesteads and Their Stories* (New York, 1899), chap. 3; Mary Cronan Oppel, "Paradise Lost: The Story of Chaumiere des Prairies," *FCHQ*, LVI (April 1982), 201–210; James D. Kornwolf, "David Meade II: Pioneer of 'Le jardin anglais' in the United States, 1774–1829," *Journal of Garden History*, XVI (1996), 254–274. See also Craig Thompson Friend, " 'Work & Be Rich': Economy and Culture on the Bluegrass Farms," in Craig Thompson Friend, ed., *The Buzzel about Kentuck: Settling the Promised Land* (Lexington, 1999), 125–151.

381 "adds . . . family": David Meade to Anne Randolph, June 1797, William Bolling Papers, NcD.

Richard Hanson: *Jones's Exors* v. *David Meade*, Nov. 1797, USCCVD(EC), Vi; extracts of Richard Hanson's letters, Dec. 15, 1797, T 79/9, PRO; entries of July 13–14, 1798, Rough Minutes, No. 2, Records of Commissioners on the Sixth Article of British Treaty, CSmH.

"extreamly" . . . "persecution": David Meade to Wakelin Welch, Dec. 9, 1797, T 79/3, ff. 344–345, PRO.

"the fabled . . . revived": David Meade to Anne Randolph, Sept. 1, 1796, William Bolling Papers, NcD.

"I . . . Virginia": David Meade to Thomas Swepson, Sept. 13, 1797, Webb-Prentis Papers, ViU.

Hornsby's property: See James City County Tax Lists, Vi, and *WMQ*, 1st ser., XXIII (Oct. 1914), 136. See also Dixon and Hunter's *Virginia Gazette* (Williamsburg), April 24, 1778.

Byrd's old debt: *Hornsby's Exors et al.* v. *Byrd's Exors et al.*, Nov. 1824, USCCVD(EC), Vi.

his slave James: Advertisement, *Virginia Gazette and General Advertiser* (Richmond), June 26, 1798.

382 irritated David Meade: David Meade to Joseph Prentis, June 13, July 29, 1797, Webb-Prentis Papers, ViU.

the Reverend John Bracken: "Original Partners in Dl. Swamp Co.," Dismal Swamp Land Company Records, NcD.

"Mr. Hornsby . . . Negroes": David Meade to Joseph Prentis, Nov. 25, 1797, Webb-Prentis Papers, ViU.

Hornsby's routine: See his Diary, KyLoF, and his Will, March 6, 1799, Shelby County, Will Book B, 1804–1811, pp. 199–203, microfilm at KyU.

He found few buyers: Robert Morris to Thomas Morris, July 12, 1796, Robert Morris Collection, CSmH.

"compleatly . . . securities &c.": John Johnston to Nicholas Low, July 12, 1798, Nicholas Low Papers, DLC. See also Robert Ernst, "Nicholas Low: Merchant and Speculator in Post-Revolutionary New York," *NYH*, LXXV (Oct. 1994), 357–372.

"that . . . terra-phobia": "A Farmer" to *Wilkes-Barré Gazette*, Oct. 25, 1796, quoted in Isaac Weld, Jr., *Travels Through the States of North America, and the Provinces of Upper and Lower Canada, During the Years 1795, 1796, and 1797*, 3d ed. (London, 1800), II, 337.

383 "that . . . money": Samuel A. Law to Ephraim Kirby, June 23, 1795, Kirby Papers, NcD. See also William Beckford to James Wadsworth, Sept. 7, 1798, in [Lewis Saul Benjamin], *The Life and Letters of William Beckford of Fonthill* (London, 1910), 252–255.

"The North . . . in": Robert Morris to James Marshall, March 25, 1796, Morris Letterbooks, DLC.

obtaining Dutch loans: Robert Morris to Sylvanus Bourne, Jan. 5, 1796, Sylvanus Bourne Papers, DLC.

384 "the real . . . Land": Advertisement, Feb. 1, 1796, *The Writings of George Washington*, ed. John C. Fitzpatrick (Washington, 1931–40), XXXIV, 441.

"land . . . disgrace": George Washington to Joseph Fay, Feb. 19, 1797, *ibid.*, XXXV, 393.

away from Mount Vernon: Weld, *Travels*, I, 94; entry of July 19, 1796, *Journals of Latrobe*, ed. Carter *et al.*, I, 163; Horace Holley to Mary Holley, April 15, 1818, Holley Papers, MiU-C.

"Agricultural" . . . "ruin": George Washington to Oliver Wolcott, May 15, 1797, George Washington to George Washington Parke Custis, April 3, 1797, *The Papers of George Washington, Retirement Series*, ed. W. W. Abbot *et al.* (Charlottesville, 1983–), I, 142, 70.

"could . . . cash": George Washington to Henry Lee, Sept. 8, 1797, *ibid.*, 341–342.

Franklin, the Directory: William Temple Franklin to James Monroe, Sept. 12, 1796, HM 22855, CSmH. See also Claude-Anne Lopez and Eugenia W. Herbert, *The Private Franklin: The Man and His Family* (New York, 1975), 308–309.

385 Charles Willing Byrd: Robert Morris to Charles W. Byrd, May 9, 19, Aug. 29, Dec. 6, 1796, Morris Letterbooks, DLC.

on James Marshall: Robert Morris to James Marshall, Sept. 16, 1796, *ibid.*

a valuation of 17¢: Bob Arnebeck, *Through a Fiery Trial: Building Washington, 1790–1800* (Lanham, 1991), 392; Samuel Yorke to Hore Browse Trist, Oct. 25, 1796, Nicholas P. Trist Papers, NcU.

sold forty shares: Robert Morris to James Marshall, Feb. 10, 1797, Morris Letterbooks, DLC.

385 "Blanks" . . . "amphitheatre": Robert Morris to John Nicholson, Nov. 22, 1796, *ibid.*

"I . . . end": Samuel Myers to Moses Myers, Dec. 22, 1796, Samuel Myers Letterbook, BR 122, CSmH.

Ruston and Wilson: Benjamin Rush, *The Autobiography of Benjamin Rush*, ed. George W. Corner (Princeton, 1948), 236–237; Benjamin Rush to Samuel Bayard, Sept. 22, 1796, *Letters of Benjamin Rush*, ed. L. H. Butterfield (Princeton, 1951), II, 781; Edward Burd to Jasper Yeates, Aug. 4, 1796, *The Burd Papers*, ed. Lewis Burd Walker (n.p., 1899), 191–192; W. Barry Grove to Henry W. Harrington, Feb. 26, 1797, Henry William Harrington Papers, NcU.

"no . . . Speculating": Entry of Nov. 22, 1796, Diary of Thomas Bolling, CSmH.

traded for 12¢: Rush, *Autobiography*, ed. Corner, 236–237.

"I consider . . . them": Robert Morris to John Nicholson, Jan. 18, 1797, Morris Letterbooks, DLC.

386 "The money . . . dissolved": Robert Morris to John Nicholson, Jan. 6, Feb. 1, 1797, Robert Morris Collection, CSmH.

notes at 10¢: Robert D. Arbuckle, *Pennsylvania Speculator and Patriot: The Entrepreneurial John Nicholson, 1757–1800* (University Park, 1975), 191.

sell the land back to Lee: Robert Morris to James Greenleaf, Feb. 16, Mar. 8, 1797, Morris Letterbooks, DLC.

"take . . . *destruction*": James Greenleaf to Henry Pratt *et al.*, April 13, 1797, North American Land Company Papers, ViU.

"My . . . means": Robert Morris to Reed & Forde, Aug. 3, 1797, Morris Letterbooks, DLC; Thomas Peter to George Washington, March 29, 1797, Papers of George Washington, DLC; Robert Morris to John Nicholson, Dec. 18, 1797, *Magazine of American History*, XXVI (July 1891), 71–72; Robert Morris to John Nicholson, Jan. 18, 1798, *Stan. V. Henkels Catalogue No. 1189* (April 1917), Item 37.

Morris and Lee: Robert Morris to Henry Lee, July 28, Sept. 18, 1797, Morris Letterbooks, DLC.

The Wheel of Fortune: Tucker-Coleman Papers, ViW.

387 the Chestnut Street Theatre: Arthur Hobson Quinn, "The Theatre and the Drama in Old Philadelphia," *Transactions of the American Philosophical Society*, new series, XLIII, Part 1 (1953), 313–317; Gresdna Ann Doty, *The Career of Mrs. Anne Brunton Merry in the American Theatre* (Baton Rouge, 1971); John Bernard, *Retrospections of America, 1797–1811*, ed. Mrs. William Bayle Bernard (New York, 1887), 69, 261; Frances Norton Mason, *My Dearest Polly: Letters of Chief Justice John Marshall to His Wife* (Richmond, 1961), 77–78; Glenn Hughes, *A History of the American Theatre, 1700–1950* (New York, 1951), 80; Arthur Hornblow, *A History of the Theatre in America* (Philadelphia, 1919), I, 221; Simon Williams, "The Actors," and Mary C. Anderson, "Scenography, Stagecraft, and Architecture in the American Theatre," in Don B. Wilmeth and Christopher Bigsby, eds., *The Cambridge History of the American Theatre: Volume I* (Cambridge, 1998), 306, 392–393.

"suffering" . . . "Stage": John Page to St. George Tucker, July 18, 1797, Tucker-Coleman Papers, ViW.

PAGE

"Scene . . . Friar": [Robert Merry], "The Tuscan Tournament," Act I, scene ii, Robert Merry Papers, DLC; entry of Nov. 10, 1797, *Diary of William Dunlap*, New-York Historical Society, *Collections*, LXII–LXIV (1929–31), I, 169; Thomas Clark Pollock, *The Philadelphia Theatre in the Eighteenth Century* (Philadelphia, 1933), 331; M. Ray Adams, "Robert Merry and the American Theatre," *Theatre Survey*, VI (May 1965), 1–11.

"property . . . confidence": Robert Morris to Henry Lee, Dec. 14, 1797, Morris Letterbooks, DLC.

Justice James Wilson: Charles Page Smith, *James Wilson, Founding Father: 1742–1798* (Chapel Hill, 1956), 384–386; George Keith Taylor to Henry Lee, [1798], Ethel Armes Collection of Lee Family Papers, DLC.

388 "a negotiable note": Henry Lee to George Washington, Aug. 27, 1797, *Papers of Washington: Retirement*, ed. Abbot *et al.*, I, 320.

"Let . . . accustomed": George Washington to Henry Lee, Jan. 25, 1798, *ibid.*, II, 46.

Simms's notes: George Washington to Jesse Simms, April 22, 1799, *Writings of Washington*, ed. Fitzpatrick, XXXVII, 186.

the Saura Town property: William Armstrong Crozier, ed., *Spotsylvania County Records, 1721–1800* (Baltimore, 1955), 485–486; Account of William Sisson, Corbin Family Ledger, Vi; George Tucker to St. George Tucker, Sept. 30, 1803, Tucker-Coleman Papers, ViW.

to Patrick Henry: Henry Lee to Patrick Henry, Jan. 30, 1798, Patrick Henry and Family Collection, DLC; Patrick Henry, Will, Codicil, Feb. 12, 1799, in George Morgan, *The True Patrick Henry* (Philadelphia, 1907), 457–459.

"The Punishment . . . tormentingly": Robert Morris to John Nicholson, Feb. 8, 1798, Ferdinand J. Dreer, ed., *A Catalogue of the Collection of Autographs Formed by Ferdinand Julius Dreer* (Philadelphia, 1890), I, 455; Robert Morris to John Nicholson, Feb. 5, 1798, *Stan. V. Henkels Catalogue No. 924* (Jan. 1905), Item 81.

"a remarkable" . . . "spiritless": Abigail Adams to Mary Cranch, Feb. 21, 1798, *New Letters of Abigail Adams, 1788–1801*, ed. Stewart Mitchell (Westport, 1973 [orig. publ. Boston, 1947]), 134–135.

the Prune Street prison: William B. Wood, *Personal Recollections of the Stage* (Philadelphia, 1855), 38–39; Samuel Breck, *Recollections of Samuel Breck*, ed. H. E. Scudder (Philadelphia, 1877), 204. On Morris, see Barbara Ann Chernow, *Robert Morris: Land Speculator, 1790–1801* (New York, 1978); Arbuckle, *Pennsylvania Speculator and Patriot*, chaps. 10–11; Norman B. Wilkinson, *Land Policy and Speculation in Pennsylvania, 1779–1800* (New York, 1979); Arnebeck, *Through a Fiery Trial*.

389 "I confess . . . here": Robert Morris to John Nicholson, April 22, 1799, *Historical Manuscripts in the Public Library of the City of Boston, Number Four* (Boston, 1903), 171.

James Wilson: Smith, *James Wilson*, 386–388.

"I" . . . "demand": Henry Lee to George Washington, Aug. 26, Sept. 28, 1798, Papers of George Washington, DLC.

"You" . . . "solution": George Washington to Henry Lee, Sept. 29, 1798, *Writings of Washington*, ed. Fitzpatrick, XXXVI, 472–473.

Bushrod Washington: George Washington to Bushrod Washington, Dec. 31, 1798, *ibid.*, XXXVII, 81.

389 left Patrick Henry: John Minor to Henry Lee, March 17, 1811, John Minor Letterbook, ViRHi; Henry Lee to Patrick Henry, [Feb. 1, 1799], Patrick Henry and Family Collection, DLC; Patrick Henry, Will, Codicil, Feb. 12, 1799, in Morgan, *True Patrick Henry*, 457–459; Lindley S. Butler, "Sauratown Plantation," *Journal of Rockingham County History and Genealogy*, VIII (Dec. 1983), 85.

"all" . . . "tranquility": Henry Lee to George Washington, May 22, 1799, Papers of George Washington, DLC.

390 "Gist . . . furnished": "List of Creditors of Genl Thos Nelson," BR Box 11 (1c), CSmH.

his ship *Ceres:* Advertisement, *Virginia Herald and Fredericksburg Advertiser*, Aug. 21, 1795.

"Crusty & harsh": Nathaniel Anderson to Thomas Massie, Feb. 27, 1795, Massie Family Papers, ViRHi.

"in . . . Health": William Anderson, Will, Codicil, Sept. 15, 1795, *Anderson's Heirs v. Gist's Exors et al.*, 1824, USCCVD(EC), Vi; *Gentleman's Magazine*, LXVI (Jan. 1796), 83.

Thomas R. Rootes: Pleading of Thomas R. Rootes, and William Anderson to Thomas Reade Rootes, Aug. 18, 1794, *Jos. Smith's Admr. et al. v. Gist's Exor et al.*, 1825, USCCVD(EC), Vi.

391 "the chief . . . acting": Notes for defendant's counsel, *Gist's Reprs v. Anderson et al.*, Wickham Family Papers, ViRHi.

sent almost £1,500: George Syme to Thomas Macdonald, Oct. 16, 1807, T 79/31, PRO; Ralph Wormeley to George Syme, Oct. 10, 1796, Ralph Wormeley to Samuel Gist, July 18, 1797, Ralph Wormeley Letterbook, ViU; Nathaniel Anderson to Thomas Massie, Nov. 1, 1797, Massie Family Papers, ViRHi; Power of Attorney, Feb. 21, 1798, *Thomas Callis v. Gist, Fowke et al.*, 1805, Pleading and Answer, *Gist et al., Exors of Anderson v. Henry S. Shore*, 1817, USCCVD(EC), Vi; Power of Attorney, calendared in *VMHB*, XLII (Oct. 1934), 357; Deposition of Thomas Noyes, Oct. 4, 1823, *Josiah Gist et al. v. William Fowke et al.*, C 117/335, XC 1244, PRO.

John Lyons: John Lyons to Edward Hill and John O'Mealy, Nov. 12, 1797, *Samuel Gist v. Hill & O'Mealy*, 1797, USCCVD(EC), Vi.

"though . . . fortune": Adam Smith, *An Inquiry into the Nature and Causes of the Wealth of Nations*, 5th ed. (Edinburgh, 1811), I, 147.

in northern Gloucestershire: The first account of George Hillhouse, *Josiah Gist et al. v. William Fowke et al.*, C 117/335, XC 1244, PRO; Benjamin Pitts Capper, *A Topographical Dictionary of the United Kingdom* (London, 1808), "Wormington"; Stephen R. Glynne, *Gloucestershire Church Notes*, ed. W. P. W. Phillimore and J. Melland Hall (London, 1902), 112–113; David Verey, *The Buildings of England: Gloucestershire, Volume II: The Vale and the Forest of Dean*, 2d ed. (London, 1976), 412–413; John Bateman, *The Great Landowners of Great Britain and Ireland*, 4th ed. (Leicester, 1971 [orig. publ. London, 1883]), 184; C. R. Elrington and Kathleen Morgan, "Alderton with Dixton," in C. R. Elrington, ed., *A History of the County of Gloucester* (London, 1965), VI, 189–192. On merchants' becoming landed gentlemen, see David Hancock, *Citizens of the World: London Merchants and the Integration of the British Atlantic Community, 1735–1785* (Cambridge, 1995), Part III; James Raven, *Judging New Wealth: Popular Publishing and Response to Commerce in England, 1750–1800* (Oxford, 1992), chap. 10.

"Sacred . . . Years": Ralph Bigland, *Historical, Monumental and Genealogical Collections Relative to the County of Gloucester*, ed. Brian Frith (Bristol, 1989–95), IV, 1517.

392 "retain . . . made": Deposition of Thomas Noyes, Oct. 4, 1823, deposition of Timothy Chisman, July 21, 1820, *Josiah Gist et al.* v. *William Fowke et al.*, C 117/335/1245 and XC1244, PRO.

Anderson's brothers and sisters: Notes for defendant's counsel, *Gist's Reprs* v. *Anderson et al.*, Wickham Family Papers, ViRHi.

a list of 545 debts: Records of Commissioners on the Sixth Article of British Treaty, Register, Vol. 2, p. 140, CSmH; List of the Agents and Collectors of S. Gist in Virginia, List of Debts No. 1, T 79/31, List of Claims, T 79/123, pp. 141–142, PRO.

Teackle: Entry of May 26, 1799, Diary of Littleton Dennis Teackle, DLC.

Hardwick in Oxfordshire: For these transactions, see the documents in C 117/335, PRO. See also Janet Cooper, "Banbury Hundred," in Alan Crossley, ed., *A History of the County of Oxford* (Oxford, 1972), X, 44–57.

393 a "full meeting": *Virginia Gazette and General Advertiser*, Sept. 28, 1796.

only the managers: Extracts from Minutes, Nov. 18, 1796, Anderson-Macaulay Legal Papers, BR Box 50 (1b), CSmH.

more than $8,000: *Dismal Swamp Land Company* v. *Alexander Macaulay*, BR Box 50 (1d), CSmH.

Latrobe and the Dismal Swamp: *Journals of Latrobe*, ed. Carter *et al.*, I, 167–169, 229–235, 239, II, 341, 364; B. Henry Latrobe to Thomas Swepson, June 21, 1797, Dismal Swamp Land Company Records, NcD.

394 "Doghole" . . . "wrongly": B. Henry Latrobe to Henry Banks, Nov. 28, 1797, *The Correspondence and Miscellaneous Papers of Benjamin Henry Latrobe*, ed. John C. Van Horne and Lee W. Formwalt *et al.* (New Haven, 1984–88), I, 64.

Macaulay had other things: Alexander Macaulay, Deed of Trust, Nov. 15, 1797, and Pleading, *Dismal Swamp Land Company* v. *Alexander Macaulay*, Legal Papers of Dismal Swamp Company, Jerdone Family Papers, Box 12, ViW.

395 *An Apology*: Talbot Hamlin, *Benjamin Henry Latrobe* (New York, 1955), 87–89; *Journals of Latrobe*, ed. Carter *et al.*, I, 274, II, 333–346, 350–356, 373–374; Forrest McDonald, *Alexander Hamilton: A Biography* (New York, 1979), 334–336.

company's title not good: Thomas Shepherd to John Jameson, Sept. 14, Nov. 23, 1798, Dismal Swamp Land Company Records, NcD.

"bid" . . . "life": Thomas Shepherd to William Nelson and John Jameson, Aug. 17, 1798, Thomas Shepherd to John Jameson, Sept. 14, 1798, *ibid.*

"Every . . . Earth": Thomas Shepherd to Alexander Macaulay, May 15, 1798, *ibid.*

long had been ill: George Braikenridge to Francis Jerdone, March 15, 1799, Jerdone Family Papers, ViW.

396 His trustees: Corbin Griffin to Francis Jerdone, Aug. 23, 1798, *ibid.*

the estate auction: Elizabeth Macaulay to Francis Jerdone, May 6, 1799, *ibid.*

his two quarter-shares: Extracts from Minutes, Dec. 22, 1798, Anderson-Macaulay Legal Papers, BR Box 50 (1b), CSmH; Charles Young to Thomas Swepson, Sept. 5, 1799, Dismal Swamp Land Company Records, NcD.

396 "excellent pine": Thomas Swepson to John Brown, Aug. 31, 1798, Dismal Swamp Land
Company Records, NcD; Extracts from Minutes, Jan. 18, 1809, BR Box 50 (1b), CSmH;
Nansemond County Land Book, 1799, Nansemond County Land Tax Lists, Vi.

397 "a very" . . . "incendiaries": Thomas Shepherd to John Brown, Jan. 13, April 11, Aug. 17,
1799, John Brown to Thomas Swepson, May 6, 1799, Dismal Swamp Land Company
Records, NcD; B. Henry Latrobe to Luke Wheeler, Dec. 16, 1803, *Correspondence of Latrobe*, ed. Van Horne and Formwalt *et al.*, I, 394.

from Edward Rushton: Edward Rushton, *Expostulatory Letter to George Washington, of
Mount Vernon, in Virginia, on His Continuing to Be a Proprietor of Slaves* (Liverpool, 1797),
9–11, 13–14, 23–24, 3; Fritz Hirschfeld, *George Washington and Slavery: A Documentary
Portrayal* (Columbia, 1997), 192.

398 "To sell" . . . "afloat": George Washington to Robert Lewis, Aug. 18, 1799, *Writings of
Washington*, ed. Fitzpatrick, XXXVII, 338–339.

"A mind . . . composure": George Washington to Jonathan Trumbull, Aug. 30, 1799,
ibid., 349–350.

wrote a new will: *Ibid.*, 275–303; Eugene E. Prussing, *The Estate of George Washington, Deceased* (Boston, 1927); Brenda E. Stevenson, *Life in Black and White: Family and Community
in the Slave South* (New York, 1996), 209–212; Robert F. Dalzell, Jr., and Lee Baldwin
Dalzell, *George Washington's Mount Vernon: At Home in Revolutionary America* (New York,
1998), 129–149, 212–217.

399 "5$ is . . . land": "Estimate of Property belonging to the Estate of Genl. Geo. Washington
unsold by the Executors," Washington Family Letters, ViU.

Walter Jones: Walter Jones to Thomas Jefferson, Nov. 25, 1813, Papers of Thomas Jefferson, DLC.

"He" . . . "projects": Thomas Jefferson to Walter Jones, Jan. 2, 1814, *The Writings of
Thomas Jefferson*, ed. Paul Leicester Ford (New York, 1892–99), IX, 448–449.

emancipation remained rare: Winthrop D. Jordan, *White Over Black: American Attitudes
Toward the Negro, 1550–1812* (Chapel Hill, 1968), 347, 353; Tommy L. Bogger, "Slave Resistance in Virginia during the Haitian Revolution, 1791–1804," *HIJES*, V (April 1978), 86.

"endeavour" . . . "unavoidable": St. George Tucker to Jeremy Belknap, June 29, 1795, *The
Belknap Papers*, Massachusetts Historical Society, *Collections*, 5th ser., II–III (1877), II, 406.

his proposal: St. George Tucker, *A Dissertation on Slavery; with a Proposal for the Gradual
Abolition of It in the State of Virginia* (Philadelphia, 1796); St. George Tucker to Jeremy
Belknap, Nov. 27, 1795, *Belknap Papers*, II, 418–422; Jordan, *White Over Black*, 558–560;
Douglas Egerton, *Gabriel's Rebellion: The Virginia Slave Conspiracies of 1800 and 1802*
(Chapel Hill, 1993), 13–15.

400 "The calamities . . . stand": St. George Tucker to Jeremy Belknap, June 29, 1795, *Belknap
Papers*, II, 406.

"the smallest . . . argument": St. George Tucker to Jeremy Belknap, Aug. 13, 1797, *ibid.*,
427–428; *Journal of the House of Delegates of the Commonwealth of Virginia; 1796* (Richmond, 1796), 52; Ludwell Lee to St. George Tucker, Dec. 5, 1796, *Virginia Silhouettes:
Contemporary Letters Concerning Negro Slavery in the State of Virginia*, comp. Mary Haldane
Coleman (Richmond, 1934), 4–5; Thomas Jefferson to St. George Tucker, Aug. 28, 1797,
Writings of Jefferson, ed. Ford, VII, 167–168.

PAGE

A petition: Remonstrance and Petition of the Free Inhabitants of Mecklenburg County, Legislative Petitions, Mecklenburg County, Vi.

401 Prosser's slave Gabriel: James Sidbury, *Ploughshares into Swords: Race, Rebellion, and Identity in Gabriel's Virginia* (Cambridge, 1997); Egerton, *Gabriel's Rebellion;* Tommy L. Bogger, *Free Blacks in Norfolk, Virginia: 1790–1860* (Charlottesville, 1997), 26–27; Philip J. Schwarz, "The Transportation of Slaves from Virginia, 1801–1865," *SA,* VII (Dec. 1986), 220–223; Jordan, *White Over Black,* 393–394.

"we . . . property": Gervas Storrs and Joseph Selden, Communications made . . . by Solomon, Sept. 15, 1800, William P. Palmer *et al.,* eds., *Calendar of Virginia State Papers* (Richmond, 1875–93), IX, 147.

"The conspiracy . . . thoughts": Letter from Richmond, Sept. 20, 1800, *Felix Farley's Bristol Journal,* Nov. 29, 1800.

"Is . . . people?": Chapman Johnson to David Watson, Jan. 24, 1802, *VMHB,* XXIX (July 1921), 280. See also Alexander McCaine to Robert Roberts, Sept. 29, 1802, *Calendar of the Ezekiel Cooper Collection of Early American Methodist Manuscripts, Garrett Biblical Institute, Evanston, Illinois* (Chicago, 1941), 27–28; entry of Jan. 13, 1805, "Diary of Hon. Jonathan Mason," Massachusetts Historical Society, *Proceedings,* 2d ser., II (March 1885), 19.

"for his" . . . "other": William Wirt to Dabney Carr, Dec. 30, 1827, William Wirt Letters, Vi; Joseph C. Robert, "William Wirt, Virginian," *VMHB,* LXXX (Oct. 1972), 398.

Bushrod Washington: B. Henry Latrobe to Thomas Jefferson, Sept. 22, 1798, *Correspondence of Latrobe,* ed. Van Horne and Formwalt *et al.,* I, 96.

John Page: John Page to Henry Tazewell, [1798], Tazewell Family Papers, Vi; Henry Tazewell to John Page, June 28, 1798, ViRHi; John Page to St. George Tucker, Feb. 25, 1801, Tucker-Coleman Papers, ViW; John Page to Thomas Jefferson, June 21, 1798, Papers of Thomas Jefferson, DLC; James Roger Sharp, *American Politics in the Early Republic: The New Nation in Crisis* (New Haven, 1993), 192–193. See also John Marshall, *An Autobiographical Sketch by John Marshall,* ed. John Stokes Adams (Ann Arbor, 1937), 14–27.

402 the Buchanan Spring Barbecue Club: George Wythe Munford, *The Two Parsons* (Richmond, 1884), 327–328.

William Nelson, Jr.: William Wirt to Elizabeth Wirt, Oct. 13, 1804, and Obituary for William Nelson, Jr., in Unpublished Literary Works, William Wirt Papers, MdBHi.

403 "The Americans . . . drink": "A Journal of the Cruise of the Fleet of His Most Christian Majesty, under the Command of the Count De Grasse-Tilly, in 1781 and 1782," in [John Dawson Gilmary Shea], ed., *The Operations of the French Fleet under the Count De Grasse in 1781–2* (New York, 1864), 87.

"The Republican . . . Governments": John Page to Thomas Jefferson, April 19, 1802, Papers of Thomas Jefferson, DLC.

in the governor's house: John Page to St. George Tucker, May 21, 1804, Tucker-Coleman Papers, ViW.

"for . . . discarded": William Wirt to Ninian Edwards, Dec. 16, 1802, in Ninian W. Edwards, *History of Illinois, from 1778 to 1833; and Life and Times of Ninian Edwards* (Springfield, 1870), 407.

"a hearty . . . fellow": William Wirt to Peachy Gilmer, Aug. 9, 1802, Letterbook, Wirt Papers, MdBHi; Robert, "William Wirt," *VMHB,* LXXX (Oct. 1972), 402–403.

403 "gay and extravagant": Chapman Johnson to David Watson, Dec. 19, 1799, *VMHB*, XXIX (July 1921), 266; William T. Barry to brother, Jan. 30, 1804, "Letters of William Barry," *WMQ*, 1st ser., XIII (Oct. 1904), 109–110.

"Williamsburg . . . days": [St. George Tucker], *A Letter, to the Rev. Jedediah Morse, A. M.* (Richmond, 1795), 15n.

Statue of Lord Botetourt: Henry St. George Tucker to St. George Tucker, Aug. 8, 1801, Tucker-Coleman Papers, ViW; Henry Howe, *Historical Collections of Virginia* (Charleston, 1856), 326; [George Tucker], *Letters from Virginia* (Baltimore, 1816), 124–125.

404 "Goddess of Dullness": [Tucker], *Letters from Virginia*, 122. See also Weld, *Travels*, I, 61, 166–169; William Hodgson to Samuel Thorp, Oct. 4, 1803, William Hodgson Letterbook, Vi; William Prentis to Joseph Prentis, July 26, 1801, Webb-Prentis Papers, ViU.

"Williams[bur]g . . . Rouge": Evelina Skipwith to St. George Tucker, May 15, 1811, Tucker-Coleman Papers, ViW.

moving to Kentucky: William Wirt to Dabney Carr, March 28, June 6, 1803, Wirt Papers, MdBHi; William Wirt to Dabney Carr, Jan. 16, 1804, Wirt Letters, Vi; William Wirt to Ninian Edwards, March 2, 1803, Sept. 17, 1805, William Wirt to Benjamin Edwards, March 17, 1805, Jan. 10, 1806, in Edwards, *History of Illinois*, 409–410, 413, 420, 457, 465.

"through . . . Norfolk": William Wirt to Benjamin Edwards, March 17, 1805, Jan. 10, 1806, in Edwards, *History of Illinois*, 456, 417–418; William Wirt to Dabney Carr, June 6, 1803, Wirt Papers, MdBHi; Norma Lois Peterson, *Littleton Waller Tazewell* (Charlottesville, 1983), 27.

405 "on Law . . . general": William Nelson, Jr., to St. George Tucker, Sept. 11, 1804, Tucker-Coleman Papers, ViW; William Nelson, Jr., to William Short, Aug. 16, 1804, William Short Papers, DLC.

"that many" . . . "damages": Agreement, July 22, 1803, Kilby Family Papers, Vi.

a British spy: A modern edition is William Wirt, *The Letters of the British Spy* (Chapel Hill, 1970).

"was exceedingly angry": William Wirt to Dabney Carr, Dec. 30, 1827, Wirt Letters, Vi.

"lives" . . . "*cash*": William Wirt to Ninian Edwards, Sept. 17, 1805, in Edwards, *History of Illinois*, 415. On Wirt's book, see also Richard Beale Davis, *Francis Walker Gilmer: Life and Learning in Jefferson's Virginia* (Richmond, 1939), 270–271, and Davis's introduction to the 1970 edition of *The Letters of the British Spy*, vii–xxii.

406 "every . . . cases": William Wirt to Benjamin Edwards, Jan. 10, 1806, in Edwards, *History of Illinois*, 417.

a fee of $100: Martha Turberville to Gawin Corbin Turberville, Feb. 27, 1806, Papers of Cazenove G. Lee, Jr., DeWint-M.

"a most . . . library": William Wirt to Benjamin Edwards, Jan. 10, 1806, in Edwards, *History of Illinois*, 417.

"All . . . dainties": George Tucker to St. George Tucker, Jan. 19, 1806, Tucker-Coleman Papers, ViW.

the plantation Tuckahoe: Horace Holley to Mary Holley, April 17, 1818, Holley Papers, MiU-C.

PAGE

"manners . . . societies": Thomas Moore, *Epistles, Odes, and Other Poems* (London, 1806), 151n.

wrote periodically to Gist: A file of copies of these letters is among the papers of *Anderson's Heirs &c v. Gist's Exors et al.*, 1824, USCCVD(EC), Vi.

more than \$7,500: John Wickham to Samuel Gist, June 16, 1803, T 79/115, pp. 308–313, Samuel Gist to Thomas Macdonald, Henry Pye Rich, and John Guillemard, Oct. 5, 1803, T 79/31, PRO; *Samuel Gist v. Samuel Shepard and Philip N. Nicholas*, May 31, 1803, Escheated Estates, Records, Proceedings, Entry 658, Auditor of Public Accounts, Vi.

filed a memorial: T 79/31, PRO.

"assiduity and intelligence": *The Parliamentary Debates from the Year 1803 to the Present Time* (London, 1812–20), XXVI, 1211.

rejected almost 80 percent: Bradford Perkins, *The First Rapprochement: England and the United States, 1795–1805* (Philadelphia, 1955), 138–143; American Loyalists' Petition, Jan. 22, 1812, *Parliamentary Debates*, XXI, 281–286.

William Waller Hening: Reports, Aug. 22, 1801, T 79/73, f. 306, Reports on the claims of Samuel Gist, T 79/90, pp. 153–154, T 79/92, pp. 83–84, T 79/94, pp. 64–65, PRO.

407 "very" . . . "were": Mary Pearkes to Thomas Massie, June 17, 1805, Massie Family Papers, ViRHi.

Leighton Wood, Jr.: Samuel Gist to Thomas Macdonald *et al.*, June 18, 1806, T 79/31, PRO. On Wood's earlier services, see Leighton Wood to St. George Tucker, Sept. 7, 1787, Tucker-Coleman Papers, ViW.

"time" . . . "come": Samuel Gist to Thomas Macdonald *et al.*, Dec. 31, 1806, April 23, 1808, T 79/31, PRO.

to testify: T 79/31, PRO.

Gist and the commissioners: Samuel Gist to Thomas Macdonald *et al.*, May 16, July 6, 18, 21, 1808, *ibid.*

409 a report from their agent: Report, Oct. 21, 1808, T 79/39, ff. 245–247, PRO.

"it would . . . you": Samuel Gist to Thomas Macdonald and John Guillemard, July 31, 1810, T 79/31, PRO. Henry Pye Rich died on July 18, 1809. See John Preston Neale and John Le Keux, *Views of the Most Interesting Collegiate and Parochial Churches in Great Britain* (London, 1824), I, St. Albans, Hertfordshire, 8.

the commission awarded: Katharine A. Kellock, "London Merchants and the Pre-1776 American Debts," *Guildhall Studies in London History*, I (Oct. 1974), 125.

Mary Byrd Farley: Robert Colin McLean, *George Tucker: Moral Philosopher and Man of Letters* (Chapel Hill, 1961), 9; George Tucker to St. George Tucker, May 8, 1797, Tucker-Coleman Papers, ViW; Thomas Lee Shippen to Alice Lee Shippen, April 20, 1797, Shippen Family Papers, DLC.

had begun a suit: Salisbury District Superior Court, Equity Minute Docket, 1788–1798, p. 177, DSCR.207.314.3, Nc-Ar. See also James Taylor, Affidavit, Sept. 28, 1797, and Summons to George Tucker and Mary Tucker, Sept. 19, 1796, in Rowan County, Estates Records—Farley, Francis, 1796, Nc-Ar.

supervise a division: A copy of the report on division of the Saura Town tract, Feb. 2, 1798, is in the Richard Corbin Papers, ViWC.

409 The Corbins: Accounts of William Shermer and William Sisson, Corbin Family Ledger, Vi.

a deed of trust: March 27, 1799, in Davidson County, Estates Records—Henry, Patrick, and Francis and Simon Farley, 1803–1822, Nc-Ar.

410 Henry Benskin Lightfoot: Henry Benskin Lightfoot to George Tucker, July 21–24, Nov. 27, 1799, *Dinwiddie, Crawford & Co.* v. *Henry Skipwith and Elizabeth Hill Skipwith et al.*, 1819, USCCVD(EC), Vi.

"I . . . ever": George Tucker to St. George Tucker, Oct. 23, 1799, Tucker-Coleman Papers, ViW.

for £20,000: John Browne Cutting to Richard Corbin, Oct. 25, 1800, Corbin Papers, ViWC; Account of Henry B. Lightfoot, Corbin Family Ledger, Vi.

"fair" . . . "sobriety": George Tucker to St. George Tucker, Feb. 24, 1801, Tucker-Coleman Papers, ViW.

for £500 currency: McLean, *George Tucker*, 15; Commissioner's Report, Oct. 1804, *Dinwiddie, Crawford & Co.* v. *Henry Skipwith and Elizabeth Hill Skipwith et al.*, 1819, USCCVD(EC), Vi.

"a numerous" . . . "resort": Joshua Francis Fisher, *Recollections of Joshua Francis Fisher*, ed. Sophia Cadwalader (Boston, 1929), 271–273.

411 using "flirtations": Entry of Oct. 2, 1815, *The Diary of Harriet Manigault, 1813–1816*, ed. Virginia Armentrout and James S. Armentrout, Jr. (Rockland, 1976), 118.

"fine . . . manners": Fisher, *Recollections*, ed. Cadwalader, 271–273.

forcing Izard to choose: George Izard, "Memoirs of General George Izard, 1825," ed. Charlton de Saussure, Jr., *SCHM*, LXXVIII (Jan. 1977), 47–50; entry of June 23, 1802, *Philadelphia Merchant: The Diary of Thomas P. Cope, 1800–1851*, ed. Eliza Cope Harrison (South Bend, 1978), 127.

"which . . . June": Izard, "Memoirs," ed. de Saussure, *SCHM*, LXXVIII (Jan. 1977), 54.

"that . . . husband": Entry of Dec. 7, 1804, "Diary of Mason," Massachusetts Historical Society, *Proceedings*, 2d ser., II (March 1885), 13; Fisher, *Recollections*, ed. Cadwalader, 271.

at Farley: Julian Ursyn Niemcewicz, *Under Their Vine and Fig Tree: Travels Through America in 1797–1799, 1805*, trans. Metchie J. E. Budka (Elizabeth, 1965), 289–290. See also Manigault, *Diary*, ed. Armentrout and Armentrout.

Henry in his will: Morgan, *True Patrick Henry*, 457–459.

"I think . . . law": July 27, 1801, Note by Dorothea Henry on Henry Lee to Dorothea Henry, Oct. 16, [1800?], *Stan. V. Henkels Catalogue No. 1021* (Dec. 1910), Item 377.

412 "concluded . . . him!": Judge Spencer Roane's Memorandum, in Morgan, *True Patrick Henry*, 452–453.

413 "The Question . . . Reimbursement?": George Izard to John Wickham, Jan. 12, 1807, *Dinwiddie, Crawford & Co.* v. *Henry Skipwith and Elizabeth Hill Skipwith et al.*, 1819, USCCVD(EC), Vi.

the Virginia Resolution: *Journal of the House of Delegates of the Commonwealth of Virginia [1799, December Session]* (Richmond, 1799 [1800]), 72. For an earlier vote, see *Journal of the House of Delegates of the Commonwealth of Virginia [1798, December Session]* (Richmond, 1798 [1799]), 33.

"the patrons . . . quarter": James Madison to Thomas Jefferson, April 27, 1800, *The Republic of Letters: The Correspondence Between Thomas Jefferson and James Madison, 1776–1826*, ed. James Morton Smith (New York, 1995), II, 1134.

"A . . . Walker": John Brown's marginal note on William Nelson, Jr., to John Brown, Oct. 9, 1800, Dismal Swamp Land Company Records, NcD.

a new board of managers: Minutes, Jan. 9, 1801, *ibid.*

"extensive . . . reflection": [William Wirt], "Obituary of Mrs. Jane B. Walker," Literary Papers, Wirt Papers, MdBHi.

414 "the affairs . . . loosely": James Henderson to Benjamin Oliver, Jr., May 25, 1809, BR Box 52(14), CSmH.

the Dismal Swamp canal: Report of Presidents and Directors, in Thomas Newton, Jr., to John Page, Nov. 16, 1804, Executive Papers, Gov. John Page, Vi.

Francis Walker's death: William Wirt to Elizabeth Wirt, April 5, 9, 1806, Wirt Papers, MdBHi.

brought severe drought: Thomas Jefferson to James Madison, Aug. 25, 1805, *Republic of Letters*, ed. Smith, III, 1381.

"the great . . . 1806": *Norfolk Gazette and Publick Ledger*, May 5, 1806; Charles William Janson, *The Stranger in America, 1793–1806*, ed. Carl S. Driver (New York, 1935), 339; William Wirt to Benjamin Edwards, May 6, 1806, Wirt Papers, MdBHi; Ebenezer Pettigrew to James Iredell, Jr., April 18, 1806, *The Pettigrew Papers*, ed. Sarah McCulloh Lemmon (Raleigh, 1971–), I, 384–385; Edmund Ruffin, "Observations Made during an Excursion to the Dismal Swamp," *Farmer's Register*, IV (Jan. 1, 1837), 519–520.

415 rain began to fall: William Wirt to Elizabeth Wirt, May 15, 1806, Wirt Papers, MdBHi.

"I . . . Rosewell": Mary Willing Byrd to Abigail De Hart Mayo, Jan. 5, 1806, ViRHi.

"Poor . . . support": Lelia Tucker to Frances Coalter, [Jan. 1806], Brown-Coalter-Tucker Papers, ViW.

$500 in a year: Margaret Page to St. George Tucker, Oct. 16, 1809, Tucker-Coleman Papers, ViW.

a strong Christian faith: John Page to St. George Tucker, June 29, 1806, *ibid.* On Wythe, see Julian P. Boyd, *The Murder of George Wythe* (Philadelphia, 1949); Imogene E. Brown, *American Aristides: A Biography of George Wythe* (Rutherford, 1981), chap. 16; Munford, *Two Parsons*, chap. 28.

416 "Rosewell . . . it!": John Page to Thomas Jefferson, Sept. 13–17, 1808, Papers of Thomas Jefferson, DLC.

"I" . . . "unhappy": *Ibid.*; Margaret Page to St. George Tucker, May 30, 1808, Tucker-Coleman Papers, ViW.

Page's memories: John Page, Memoir, *Virginia Historical Register*, III (July 1850), 142–151. On Sir Gregory Page, Bart., see George Edward Cokayne, ed., *Complete Baronetage* (Exeter, 1900–06), V, 24, 77–78. On John Page's career, see T. B. McCord, Jr., "John Page of Rosewell: Reason, Religion, and Republican Government from the Perspective of a Virginia Planter, 1743–1808" (Ph.D. diss., American University, 1990).

417 "To clear . . . Object": Margaret Page to St. George Tucker, Jan. 8, 1809, Tucker-Coleman Papers, ViW.

417 "I know . . . Future": Margaret Page to St. George Tucker, March 22, 1817, *ibid.*

the big brick mansion: Bennie Brown, Jr., "Rosewell: An Architectural Study of an Eighteenth Century Virginia Plantation" (M.A. thesis, University of Georgia, 1973), 11–13.

"two" . . . "have": Robert Morris to Henry Lee, Aug. 27, 1801, ViRHi.

418 "You . . . granted": John Wickham to Henry Lee, Dec. 28, 1799, *Henry Lee* v. *Hanbury's Exor,* 1804, USCCVD(EC), Vi.

"he . . . insolvent": Jonas Clapham to John Lloyd, July 19, 1804, T 79/38, PRO.

"the situation . . . land": Alexander Moore to Henry Lee, March 14, 1798, Charles Campbell Papers, ViW.

"as all . . . so": Charles Blackburn to William A. Washington, April 30, 1805, Tracy W. McGregor Collection, ViU.

from William Hodgson: William Hodgson to Richard Bland Lee, May 7, 1805, Hodgson Letterbook, Vi.

"I . . . Fairfax": Nathaniel Pendleton to George Deneale, July 18, 1805, George Deneale Papers, ViRHi.

"I . . . jail": Henry Lee to James Breckinridge, March 4, 1809, James Breckinridge Papers, *ibid.*

was willing to return: Bushrod Washington and Lawrence Lewis to William A. Washington, May 13, 1809, Washington Family Collection, Box 3, DLC.

"right . . . interest": Prussing, *Estate of George Washington,* 282.

"the Body . . . Lee": Thomas Hicks, Receipt, May 13, 1809, *N. Pendleton* v. *Henry Lee,* 1811, USCCVD(EC), Vi.

419 "prison bounds": Peter J. Coleman, *Debtors and Creditors in America: Insolvency, Imprisonment for Debt, and Bankruptcy, 1607–1900* (Madison, 1974), 203–205.

"The fame . . . desolate": George Washington Parke Custis, *Recollections and Private Memoirs of Washington,* ed. Benson J. Lossing (New York, 1860), 363.

a list of his holdings: Henry Lee's Schedule quoted in John James Chew to William Selden, Aug. 8, 1835, BR Box 5, CSmH.

Thomas Newton, Jr.: Thomas Newton, Jr., to James Monroe, Sept. 27, 1802, Executive Papers, Gov. James Monroe, Vi; Thomas Newton, Jr., to John Page, Sept. 27, 1804, Palmer *et al.,* eds., *Calendar of Virginia State Papers,* IX, 418. See also Report of the Dismal Swamp Canal Company, in Thomas Newton, Jr., to John Page, Nov. 16, 1804, Executive Papers, Gov. John Page, Vi.

Workers in the swamp: Ruffin, "Observations," *Farmer's Register,* IV (Jan. 1, 1837), 518; Frederick Law Olmsted, *A Journey in the Seaboard Slave States* (New York, 1856), 151–156; Jack Temple Kirby, *Poquosin: A Study of Rural Landscape and Society* (Chapel Hill, 1995), 154–161. Compare William Dusinberre, *Them Dark Days: Slavery in the American Rice Swamps* (New York, 1996).

420 "The Negroes . . . sold": Summary of minutes, Dismal Swamp Land Company Records, NcD.

they made 1,285,900: James Henderson to Benjamin Oliver, Jr., May 25, 1809, BR Box 52(14), CSmH.

"it is" . . . "valuable": A copy of Nelson's will is in the Dismal Swamp Land Company Records, NcD.

PAGE

"should . . . refusal": Charles C. Page to James Henderson, March 7, 1813, *ibid.*

Nelson, Jr., almost missed: St. George Tucker to Joseph C. Cabell, March 13, 1810, Bryan Family Papers, ViU; William Nelson, Jr., to St. George Tucker, April 12, 1810, Tucker-Coleman Papers, ViW.

"direct" . . . "indecision": James Henderson to Benjamin Oliver, Jr., May 25, 1809, June 18, 1811, BR Box 52(14), CSmH.

421 paid steady dividends: Estate of George Washington, Executors' Accounts, Washington Family Collection, DLC.

"The handsome . . . committed": Bushrod Washington to James Henderson, Feb. 20, 1811, Bushrod Washington Papers, NcD. See also Minutes of Meeting, May 2, 1811, Anderson-Macaulay Legal Papers, BR Box 50, CSmH; Thomas Swepson to Benjamin Oliver, Jr., March 26, 1811, Benjamin Brand Papers, ViRHi.

"Among . . . Interest" and report: James Henderson to Benjamin Oliver, Jr., June 18, 1811, BR Box 52(14), CSmH.

"Our . . . getting": Robert Douthat to Bushrod Washington, Aug. 13, 1824, Washington Family Letters, ViU.

death of Nelson: Lelia Tucker to William Short, April 13, 1813, William Short Papers, DLC; St. George Tucker to Joseph C. Cabell, Feb. 8, Mar. 13, 1813, Bryan Family Papers, ViU.

obituary: March 23, 1813.

Anne Byrd: Biographical Sketch of Mary Willing Byrd, BR Box 274(57), CSmH.

"the deepest dejection": William Wirt to Elizabeth Wirt, Nov. 4, 1813, Wirt Papers, MdBHi.

422 "poor . . . beggars!": William Wirt to Elizabeth Wirt, Nov. 18, 1813, *ibid.*

"if 100 . . . bubble": William Wirt to Dabney Carr, Jan. 15, 1814, Wirt Letters, Vi.

the first vessel: Alexander Crosby Brown, "The Dismal Swamp Canal," *AN*, V (1945), 212–215.

"chain-gangs" . . . "devil": Louise E. Catlin, "A Day in the Great Dismal Swamp," *Magazine of History*, II (Nov. 1905), 341, 343. See also Richard Blow to Samuel Proctor, Jan. 21, 1806, Richard Blow Letterbook, ViRHi; Fillmore Norfleet, *Suffolk in Virginia* (n.p., 1974), 117.

423 "brought . . . unsuspected": Ruffin, "Observations," *Farmer's Register*, IV (Jan. 1, 1837), 517–518; Joseph Martin, *A New and Comprehensive Gazetteer of Virginia, and the District of Columbia* (Charlottesville, 1835), 41, 237–238.

Dismal Plantation lay unused: Lease, Oct. 11, 1813, Dismal Swamp Land Company Records, NcD.

for the Dismal Swamp Land Company: *Journal of the House of Delegates of the Commonwealth of Virginia (1814, October Session)* (Richmond, [1814]), 104, 108, 120, 124, 129.

an average annual dividend: Estate of George Washington, Executors' Accounts, Washington Family Collection, DLC; Fielding Lewis Accounts, Douthat Family Papers, ViRHi.

Lake Drummond Hotel: Jesse F. Pugh and Frank T. Williams, *The Hotel in the Great Dismal Swamp* (Old Trap, 1964), 14–21.

424 the dividend in 1810: John Bracken to Thomas Jefferson, Aug. 13, 1811, in "Charles

Bellini, First Professor of Modern Languages in an American College," *WMQ*, 2d ser., V (Jan. 1925), 16.

424 "sought . . . property": *Gentleman's Magazine*, LXXXV, Part I (Feb. 1815), 182.

Josiah Sellick: William Matthews, *Matthews's New Bristol Directory, for the Year 1793–4* (Bristol, [1793]), 73.

425 Gist bequeathed: For Gist's will and for the disposition of Gist's estate, see the documents in C 117/335, PRO. For the codicils, see the copy of Gist's will in Hanover County Legislative Petitions, 1815, Vi. On the East India Company, see also Huw V. Bowen, "The East India Company and Military Recruitment in Britain, 1763–1771," reprinted in Pierre Emmer and Femme Gaastra, eds., *The Organization of Interoceanic Expansion, 1450–1800* (Aldershot, 1996), chap. 16; P. J. Marshall, *East Indian Fortunes: The British in Bengal in the Eighteenth Century* (Oxford, 1976), chap. 1. For Josiah Sellick's change of name, see W. P. W. Phillimore and Edward Alexander Fry, comps., *An Index to Changes of Name Under Authority of Act of Parliament or Royal Licence* (London, 1905), 128.

at Queen Elizabeth's Hospital: John Latimer, *The Annals of Bristol in the Nineteenth Century* (Bristol, 1887), 61–62; F. H. Towill, "Bristol Charities, Past and Present," in C. M. MacInnes and W. F. Whittand, eds., *Bristol and Its Adjoining Counties* (Bristol, 1955), 299.

426 received £500 per year: Petition by Martin Pearkes, Mary Pearkes, William Fowke, and Elizabeth Fowke, Hanover County Legislative Petitions, 1815, Vi.

427 after 1806 Virginia law: Benjamin Joseph Klebaner, "American Manumission Laws and the Responsibility for Supporting Slaves," *VMHB*, LXIII (Oct. 1955), 448–449; Robert McColley, *Slavery and Jeffersonian Virginia*, 2d ed. (Urbana, 1973), chap. 7.

freeing slaves: Chap. CXXIX, *Acts Passed at a General Assembly of the Commonwealth of Virginia [1815–1816]* (Richmond, 1816), 240–243.

These three quarter-shares: Account of William F. Wickham with the Estate of Samuel Gist, Wickham Family Papers, ViRHi.

more than $17,000: *Anderson's Heirs &c* v. *Gist's Exor et al.*, 1824, *Jos. Smith's Admr. et al.* v. *Gist's Exor et al.*, 1825, USCCVD(EC), Vi. For other documents on this litigation, see Wickham Family Papers and John Minor to Dabney Minor, March 6, 1811, John Minor Letterbook, ViRHi.

Gist's freed former slaves: Michael Trotti, "Freedom and Enslaved Soil: A Case Study of Manumission, Migration, and Land," *VMHB*, CIV (1996), 455–480. See also William Buckner McGroarty, "Exploration in Mass Emancipation," *WMQ*, 2d ser., XXI (July 1941), 208–226.

428 visited the church: Glynne, *Gloucestershire Church Notes*, ed. Phillimore and Hall, 112–113; Verey, *Buildings of England: Gloucestershire, II*, 2d ed., 412–413.

"Sacred . . . Years": Bigland, *Historical Collections of Gloucester*, ed. Frith, IV, 1517–1518.

arms of the House of Gist: F. Were, "Heraldry," Bristol and Gloucestershire Archaeological Society, *Transactions*, XXV (1902), 208, XXVIII (1905), 264, 396–397. See also *Return of Owners of Land, 1873* (London, 1875), I, Gloucester, 19, II, Oxford, 9; G. E. Mingay, *English Landed Society in the Eighteenth Century* (London, 1963); Nicholas Rogers, "Money, Land and Lineage: The Big Bourgeoisie of Hanoverian London," *Social History*, IV (1979), 437–454; Roy Porter, *English Society in the Eighteenth Century* (Har-

PAGE

mondsworth, 1982), 72–93; F. M. L. Thompson, "Life After Death: How Successful Nineteenth-Century Businessmen Disposed of Their Fortunes," *EcHR*, 2d ser., XLIII (Feb. 1990), 40–61; Hancock, *Citizens of the World.*

"whose" . . . "Philadelphia": David Meade to Anne Randolph, [1800], William Bolling Papers, NcD; Robert Morris to [?], July 20, 1798, *Stan. V. Henkels Catalogue No. 1042* (Nov. 1911), Item 251; Charles Willing Byrd to Timothy Pickering, Mar. 30, 1800, Clarence Edwin Carter *et al.*, eds., *The Territorial Papers of the United States* (Washington, 1934–75), III, 81.

Arthur St. Clair: Charles Willing Byrd to Thomas Jefferson, May 27, Oct. 15, 1802, Carter *et al.*, eds., *Territorial Papers*, III, 226–227, 251–253; Charles Willing Byrd to Nathaniel Massie, Sept. 24, Nov. 26, 1800, May 20, 1802, in David Meade Massie, *Nathaniel Massie: A Pioneer of Ohio* (Cincinnati, 1896), 163–165, 205–206; Jonathan J. Bean, "Marketing 'the great American commodity': Nathaniel Massie and Land Speculation on the Ohio Frontier, 1783–1813," *Ohio History*, CIII (1994), 164–165; Donald J. Ratcliffe, *Party Spirit in a Frontier Republic: Democratic Politics in Ohio, 1793–1821* (Columbus, 1998), 39–43.

429 Byrd and family: Stephen J. Stein, ed., *Letters from a Young Shaker: William S. Byrd at Pleasant Hill* (Lexington, 1985), 1–46; Nelson W. Evans, "Charles Willing Byrd," *Old Northwest Genealogical Quarterly*, XI (Jan. 1908), 1–8; Nelson W. Evans and Emmons B. Stivers, *A History of Adams County, Ohio* (West Union, 1900), 526–532; W. H. Burtner, "Charles Willing Byrd," *Ohio Archaeological and Historical Publications*, XLI (1925), 237–240.

at Chaumière des Prairies: Henry J. Peet, ed., *Chaumiere Papers, Containing Matters of Interest to the Descendants of David Meade* (Chicago, 1883), 53–57; Horace Holley to Mary Holley, May 27, 1818, Holley Papers, MiU-C; [Terhune], *More Colonial Homesteads*, 77–78; Oppel, "Paradise Lost," *FCHQ*, LVI (April 1982), 206; Kornwolf, "David Meade," *Journal of Garden History*, XVI (1996), 254–274. Compare the description of Sturton Park in entry of April 20, 1779, Journal of Peter Van Schaack, in Henry C. Van Schaack, *The Life of Peter Van Schaack* (New York, 1842), 139–141.

"the son" . . . "County": David Meade to Joseph Prentis, Jr., Sept. 26, 1826, Webb-Prentis Papers, ViU; Stephen J. Stein, "The Conversion of Charles Willing Byrd to Shakerism," *FCHQ*, LVI (Oct. 1982), 395–414. See also Powel T. Byrd to Evelyn T. Byrd, June 14, 1830, R. Baylor Hickman Collection, KyLoF; Peet, ed., *Chaumiere Papers*, 79.

"my dismal . . . been": William S. Byrd to Charles Willing Byrd, June 22, 1826, and William S. Byrd, Will, Nov. 4, 1828, *Letters from a Young Shaker*, ed. Stein, 51–52, 125–126. On Pleasant Hill, see also Earl Gregg Swem, ed., *Letters on the Condition of Kentucky in 1825* (New York, 1916), 56–67; Clay Lancaster, *Antebellum Architecture of Kentucky* (Lexington, 1991), 88–99.

430 moved to Richmond: Anya Jabour, *Marriage in the Early Republic: Elizabeth and William Wirt and the Companionate Ideal* (Baltimore, 1998), chaps. 1–3.

"in 1762 . . . later": Thomas Jefferson, Memorandum, in Thomas Jefferson to William Wirt, April 12, 1812, *Writings of Jefferson*, ed. Ford, IX, 339; William Wirt, *Sketches of the Life and Character of Patrick Henry* (Philadelphia, 1817), xi–xii; William Wirt to Peachey Gilmer, n.d. [1806?], Wirt Papers, MdBHi.

430 "business . . . truth": William Wirt to Dabney Carr, Aug. 20, 1815, Wirt Letters, Vi.

"these crude sketches": Wirt, *Henry*, xiv.

"a discourse . . . morals": William Wirt to Thomas Jefferson, Jan. 18, 1810, Papers of Thomas Jefferson, DLC.

"you . . . etc.": William Wirt to Ninian Edwards, Nov. 26, 1808, Edwards, *History of Illinois*, 436.

"Were . . . pigmies": [William Wirt *et al.*], *The Old Bachelor* (Richmond, 1814), 138, 141–142.

431 In Williamsburg: Wirt, *Henry*, 39.

"in easy . . . colony": *Ibid.*, 1.

"It . . . proceeded": William Wirt to Francis Gilmer, Letter I, n.d., William Wirt and Elizabeth Washington (Gamble) Wirt Papers, NcD.

was Thomas Jefferson: Thomas Jefferson to William Wirt, Aug. 5, 1815, *Writings of Jefferson*, ed. Ford, IX, 473–474.

"the descendants . . . aristocracy": William Wirt to Thomas Jefferson, Oct. 23, 1816, Papers of Thomas Jefferson, DLC.

"the old . . . principles": Jefferson, Memorandum, *Writings of Jefferson*, ed. Ford, IX, 340–341. See also Jack P. Greene, "Society, Ideology, and Politics: An Analysis of the Political Culture of Mid-Eighteenth-Century Virginia," in Richard M. Jellison, ed., *Society, Freedom, and Conscience: The American Revolution in Virginia, Massachusetts, and New York* (New York, 1976), 14–76; Thad W. Tate, "The Coming of the Revolution in Virginia: Britain's Challenge to Virginia's Ruling Class, 1763–1776," *WMQ*, 3d ser., XIX (July 1962), 323–343.

"the spirit" . . . "birth": Thomas Jefferson to William Wirt, Aug. 14, 1814, Papers of Thomas Jefferson, DLC.

"genuine" . . . "Aristocrat": Francis Lightfoot Lee to Ludwell Lee, Nov. 23, 1796, The Rosenbach Company, *The History of America in Documents: Part Two* (Philadelphia, 1950), Item 227. For Jefferson on aristocracy, see Thomas Jefferson to John Adams, Oct. 28, 1813, Lester J. Cappon, ed., *The Adams-Jefferson Letters* (Chapel Hill, 1959), II, 387–392. Spencer Roane: Roane, Memorandum, in Morgan, *True Patrick Henry*, 442, 450, 452–453. See also Spencer Roane to Philip Aylett, June 26, 1788, Emmet Collection, NN.

432 "aberrations" . . . "imitation": William Wirt to Thomas Jefferson, Oct. 23, 1816, Papers of Thomas Jefferson, DLC. On Wirt's book, see also Maxwell Bloomfield, *American Lawyers in a Changing Society, 1776–1876* (Cambridge, 1976), 173–176; Robert P. Sutton, "Nostalgia, Pessimism, and Malaise: The Doomed Aristocrat in Late-Jeffersonian Virginia," *VMHB*, LXXVI (Jan. 1968), 41–55; William R. Taylor, *Cavalier and Yankee: The Old South and American National Character* (New York, 1969 [orig. publ. 1961]), 78–89.

"it is . . . work": Notes of Mr. Jefferson's Conversation 1824 at Monticello, 1825, *The Papers of Daniel Webster: Correspondence*, ed. Charles M. Wiltse *et al.* (Hanover, 1974–86), I, 373.

"I have . . . fustian": John Randolph of Roanoke to Francis Scott Key, Feb. 9, 1818, in Hugh A. Garland, *The Life of John Randolph of Roanoke* (New York, 1851), II, 96.

Spencer Roane: Spencer Roane to William Wirt, 1816, Wirt Papers, NcU.

PAGE

The public attention: John P. Kennedy, *Memoirs of the Life of William Wirt*, rev. ed. (Philadelphia, 1856), II, chap. 2.

"Who" . . . "friend": St. George Tucker to William Wirt, April 14, 1813, Wirt Papers, MdBHi.

433 Gothic novels: Ian Duncan, *Modern Romance and Transformations of the Novel: The Gothic, Scott, Dickens* (Cambridge, 1992), chap. 1; Paul Ranger, *"Terror and Pity reign in every Breast"*: *Gothic Drama in the London Patent Theatres, 1750–1820* (London, 1991).

"on . . . grave": William Byrd, Will, July 6, 1774, *VMHB*, IX (July 1901), 88.

"there . . . meditate": Curtis Carroll Davis, *The King's Chevalier: A Biography of Lewis Littlepage* (Indianapolis, 1961), 21. See also Constance Cary Harrison, "Colonel William Byrd of Westover, Virginia," *Century Magazine*, XLII (June 1891), 171.

434 "I have . . . Spy": William Wirt to Elizabeth Wirt, Nov. 8, 1803, Wirt Papers, MdBHi. See also [Samuel Jackson] Pratt, *Gleanings in England* (London, 1801), I, 251–255.

ACKNOWLEDGMENTS

I owe many debts of gratitude to those who helped me with this book. I can acknowledge these obligations, though I remain in debt.

I thank the archivists of the libraries mentioned in the Notes, both for their assistance and for permission to quote from manuscripts in their keeping. I am especially grateful to George Stevenson of the North Carolina Archives and to Susan Berg and her colleagues in the Colonial Williamsburg Foundation Library.

For the privilege of time spent at the Henry E. Huntington Library I thank Robert C. Ritchie, and I salute all the Huntington regulars, whose names and kindnesses have grown too numerous to list.

Louisiana State University generously supported my research and writing.

I have had the benefit of readings and suggestions by James Boyden, William J. Cooper, Jr., Michael Edwards, Gaines Foster, John Kushma, Burl Noggle, Lewis P. Simpson, Frank S. Smith, Victor Stater, Thad Tate, and Paul Zall. Jill Ker Conway gave me a piece of valuable advice not long after I started work.

Early in my research, Dan Frost helped me gather material. I owe many thanks to Peggy Seale, who went through these pages repeatedly. My colleague Stanley Hilton helped me read documents and scholarship published in Portuguese. David Barry Gaspar shared valuable sources with me.

To no one do I owe more gratitude than to Paul Paskoff in his capacities as friend, chief, and historian.

Jane Garrett, exemplary editor, befriended the project from the start.

I dedicate this book to a company which has paid incalculably large dividends since I first invested in it, buying a ticket to *A Midsummer Night's Dream* in 1955.

INDEX

Owing to limitations of space, not all names in the text are in the index.

PERMISSIONS ACKNOWLEDGMENTS

Special thanks go to the following for permission to reprint material from their collections:

Department of Manuscripts, The British Library, London; William L. Clements Library, Ann Arbor, Michigan; Special Collections, Colonial Williamsburg Foundation Library, Williamsburg, Virginia; Archive Service, Cumbria Record Office, Kendal; Rare Book, Manuscript, and Special Collections Library, Duke University, Durham, North Carolina; Jesse Ball duPont Memorial Library, Stratford, Virginia; Special Collections, Edinburgh University Library, Edinburgh; The Filson Club Historical Society, Louisville, Kentucky; Henry E. Huntington Library, San Marino, California; Liverpool Record Office, Liverpool Central Library, Liverpool; Maryland Historical Society Library, Baltimore; James Monroe Museum and Memorial Library, Fredericksburg, Virginia; Mitchell Library, State Library of New South Wales, Sydney; New-York Historical Society, New York, New York; Southern Historical Collection, University of North Carolina, Chapel Hill; Department of Manuscripts & Special Collections, Hallward Library, University of Nottingham, Nottingham; Public Record Office, Kew; Manuscripts Division, National Library of Scotland, Edinburgh; Scottish Record Office, The National Archives of Scotland, Edinburgh; Special Collections Centre, Toronto Reference Library, Toronto, Ontario; Virginia Historical Society, Richmond; Special Collections, Alderman Library, University of Virginia, Charlottesville; Manuscripts and Rare Book Department, Earl Gregg Swem Library, College of William and Mary, Williamsburg, Virginia; State Historical Society of Wisconsin, Madison.

A NOTE ABOUT THE AUTHOR

Charles Royster was born in Nashville, Tennessee, in 1944. He was educated at the University of California, Berkeley. Since 1981 he has taught at Louisiana State University, where he is Boyd Professor of History. This is his fourth book. He divides his time between Baton Rouge, Louisiana, and Little River, California.

A NOTE ON THE TYPE

This book was set in Janson, a typeface long thought to have been made by the Dutch-man Anton Janson, who was a practicing typefounder in Leipzig during the years 1668–1687. However, it has been conclusively demonstrated that these types are actually the work of Nicholas Kis (1650–1702), a Hungarian, who most probably learned his trade from the master Dutch typefounder Dirk Voskens. The type is an excellent example of the influential and sturdy Dutch types that prevailed in England up to the time William Caslon (1692–1766) developed his own incomparable designs from them.

Composed by North Market Street Graphics, Lancaster, Pennsylvania
Printed and bound by Quebecor Martinsburg, Martinsburg, West Virginia
Designed by Soonyoung Kwon